ZIMBABWE
THE POLITICAL ECONOMY OF TRANSITION 1980-1986

Edited by IBBO MANDAZA

CODESRIA BOOK SERIES

ZIMBABWE: The Political Economy of Transition 1980-1986

© CODESRIA

ISBN 0 906968 10 0 (paperback)
     0 906968 11 9 (hardback)

First published in October 1986 by CODESRIA,
B. P. 3304, Dakar, Senegal

Typeset by Grassroots, London NW6 6PS
Printed in England by Whitstable Litho, Kent

HC
910
.Z3198
1986

CONTENTS

Maps
Abbreviations
Notes on Contributors
Acknowledgements
Foreword

Introduction: The Political Economy of Transition   1
by Ibbo Mandaza

POLITICS
1. The State and Politics in the Post-White Settler Colonial Situation   21
   Ibbo Mandaza

2. The General Elections: 1979-1985   75
   Masipula Sithole

THE ECONOMY
3. The Economy: Issues, Problems and Prospects   99
   Xavier M. Kadhani

4. Foreign Capital   123
   Theresa Chimombe

5. Problems of Industrialisation Structural and Policy Issue   141
   Daniel B. Ndlela

THE AGRARIAN QUESTION
6. The Land Question   165
   Sam Moyo

7. Continuity and Change in Agricultural Policy   203
   Clever Mumbengegwi

8. The Political Economy of Hunger   223
   Thomas D. Shopo

THE LABOUR MOVEMENT
9. State, Capital and Trade Unions   243
   Lloyd M. Sachikonye

10. Human Resources Development and the Problem of Labour Utilisation   275
    Brian Raftopoulos

SOCIAL DEVELOPMENT
11. Education and the Challenge of Independence   319
    Rungano Zvobgo

12. Progress and Problems in the Health Care Delivery System   355
    Samuel T. Agere

13. The Women Issue   377
    Joyce L. Kazembe

Bibliography
Index

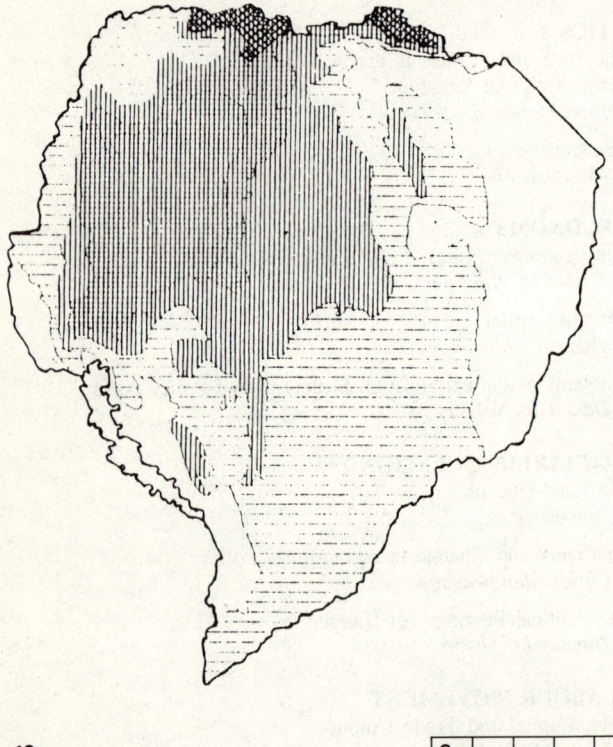

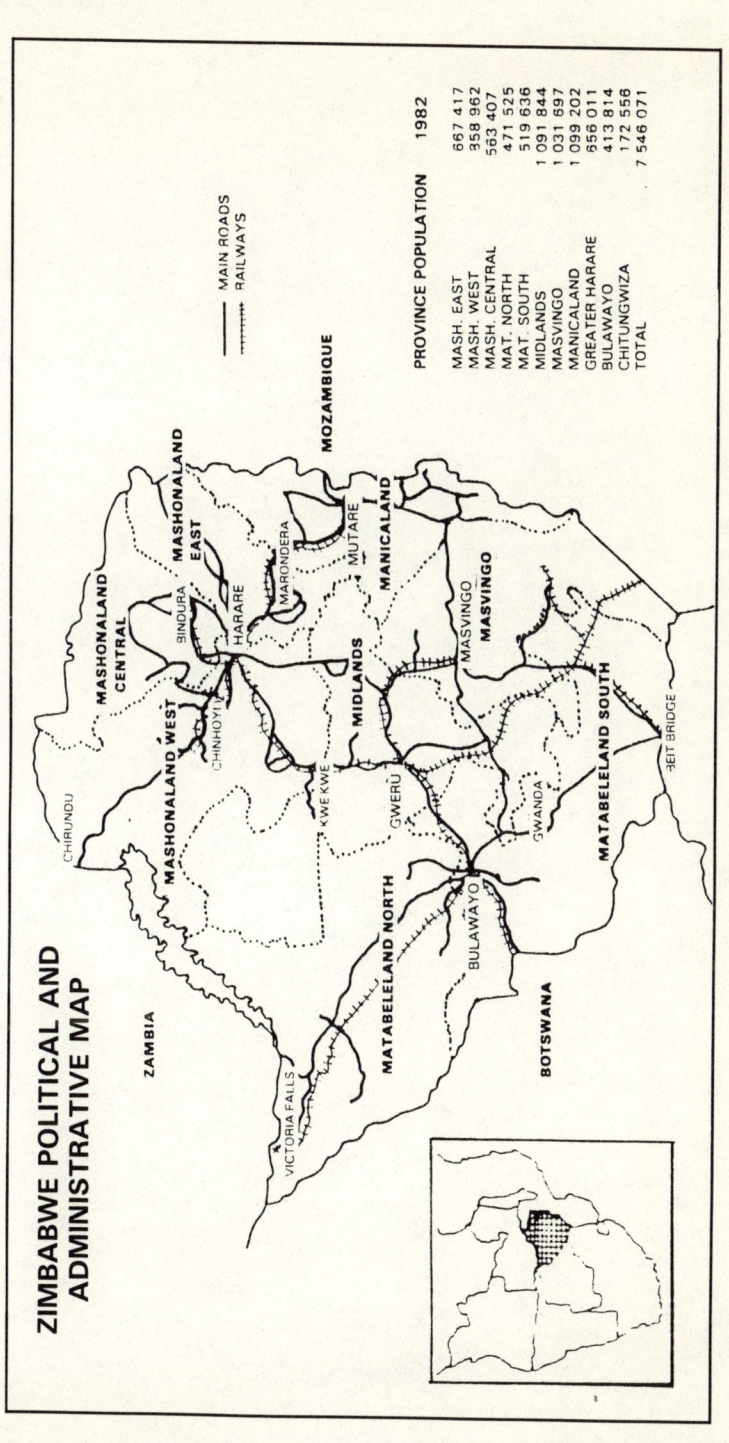

ABBREVIATIONS

ADB	African Development Bank
AFC	Agricultural Finance Corporation
AMA	Agricultural Marketing Authority
ANC	African National Congress of Southern Rhodesia
APA	African Purchase Areas
ARDA	Agricultural and Rural Development Authority
ATUC	African Trade Union Congress
BSAC	British South Africa Company
CA	Communal Area
CAZ	Conservative Alliance of South Africa
CFU	Commercial Farmers' Union
CIP	Commodity Import Programme
CNC	Chief Native Commissioner
CODESRIA	Council for the Development of Economic and Social Research in Africa
CSO	Central Statistical Office
FAO	Food and Agricultural Organization
FRELIMO	Front for the Liberation of Mozambique
FYDP	Five Year Development Plan
GFCF	Gross Fixed Capital Formation
GDP	Gross Domestic Product
GMB	Grain Marketing Board
GNP	Gross National Product
IBRD	International Bank for Reconstruction and Development (World Bank)
ICU	Industrial and Commercial Workers' Union
ILO	International Labour Organization
IMF	International Monetary Fund
IZG	Independent Zimbabwe Group
LDC	Less Developed Country
LPA	Lagos Plan of Action
LRA	Labour Relations Act
LSCF	Large Scale Commercial Farming Sector
MMCZ	Mineral Marketing Corporation of Zimbabwe
NC	Native Commissioner
NDP	National Democratic Party
NIBMAR	No Independence Before African Majority Rule
NMS	National Manpower Survey
PF	Patriotic Front
PF-ZAPU	Patriotic Front—Zimbabwe African People's Union
PSIP	Public Sector Investment Programme
PTA	Preferential Trade Area
RALSC	Rhodesian Native Labour Supply Commission
RF	Rhodesian Front
RNFU	Rhodesia National Farmers Union
RNLB	Rhodesia Native Labour Bureau
SADCC	Southern African Development Coordination Conference
SSCF	Small Scale Commercial Farming Sector
TNDP	Transitional National Development Plan
UANC	United African National Council
UDI	Unilateral Declaration of Independence
UN	United Nations

UNICEF	United Nations Children's Fund
UNIDO	United Nations Industrial Development Organization
USAID	United States Agency for International Development
VTC	Vocational Training Centre
WB	World Bank
WHO	World Health Organization
ZANLA	Zimbabwe African National Liberation Army
ZANU	Zimbabwe African National Union
ZANU-PF	Zimbabwe African National Union—Patriotic Front
ZAPU	Zimbabwe African People's Union
ZCTU	Zimbabwe Congress of Trade Unions
ZIMCORD	Zimbabwe Conference on Reconstruction and Development
ZINTEC	Zimbabwe Integrated Teacher Education Course
ZIPA	Zimbabwe People's Army
ZISCO	Zimbabwe Iron and Steel Corporation
ZMDC	Zimbabwe Mining Development Corporation
ZNA	Zimbabwe National Army

Notes on Contributors

Ibbo Mandaza was born in May 1948 at Mushangwe Village, Seki Communal Area, Marondera (near Harare). He began his university education at the local University where he graduated with a BA degree in 1970. After completing a BSc Special Honours in 1972, he began research in an MPhil in 1973. In August of the same year, he was expelled from the University for political activity. In 1974, he left the country to continue his research at York University, England, which he completed by obtaining a PhD in Political Economy. The thesis is to be published soon as *Race, Colour and Class in Southern Africa: Malawi, Zambia and Zimbabwe, 1900-1980*, forthcoming 1987.

Between 1977-80, he lectured at the Universities of Botswana and Dar es Salaam, as well as engaging in active political work for the National Liberation Movement. In 1980, he worked in the Election Directorate of ZANU (PF), and after the victory of ZANU (PF) became a founder member of the Ministry of Manpower Planning and Development. As Deputy Secretary of the Ministry, he was appointed Directory of the National Manpower Survey and was instrumental in the establishment of the Zimbabwe Institute of Development Studies (ZIDS). In 1982 he became the Permanent Secretary of the Ministry, until his promotion to Public Service Commissioner in 1983.

He is a member of a number of Pan African organisations: notably, Vice-President of the African Association of Political Science (AAPS); and Chairman of the Governing Board of the Eastern and Southern African Management Institute (ESAMI). He has published widely on Zimbabwe and Southern Africa.

Xavier Kadhani was born in Mhondoro, near Chegutu, in 1951. He studied Economics at the University of Zimbabwe and the University of York, England. He holds a Masters in Development Studies from the University of Sussex, and is a Fellow of the Economic Development Institute of the World Bank.

He lectured in Economics at the University of Zimbabwe, 1979-1981. He served as a member of the Presidential Commission of Inquiry on Incomes, Prices and Conditions of Services, 1980-1981. Member of the 1983 University of Zimbabwe Triennial Review Committee. Member of the Zimbabwe Economics Society Executive Committee, 1979-1984. Sits on Boards of Directors of a number of Zimbabwean corporations. Director for Zimbabwe on the Board of the Trade and Development Bank of the Eastern and Southern Africa Preferential Trade Area.

1981-1982, Under Secretary (Economic and Fiscal Policy), Ministry of Finance, Economic Planning and Development. From mid-1985, Senior Executive Officer, Zimbabwe Development Bank.

Masipula Sithole was born on 23 August 1946, in Shabani (now Zvishavane) near Gweru. He went to primary school at Mount Selinda Mission, near Mutare, and completed his secondary schooling at Fletcher High School, near Gweru. In 1970 he graduated with a BA degree in Political Science from Muskingum College Ohio, in the USA By 1974 he had completed an MA and PhD political science, from the University of Cincinnati. He has taught at Universities in the USA and is currently Dean of the Faculty of Social Studies at the University of Zimbabwe.

He has written widely on ethnicity and among notable publications in his

Struggle-within-the-struggle, Salisbury, 1979. He is currently Treasurer of the Zimbabwe Chapter of the World University Services (WUS).

Theresa Chimombe was born on 1 December 1959 in Kwekwe (near Gweru); she completed her primary schooling at Mpumelelo Primary School (near Masvingo) and her secondary education at Mpopoma and Mzilikazi Secondary Schools in Bulawayo. In 1981 she graduated with a BSc (Economics) from the University of Zimbabwe, and in 1983 completed an MPhil (Economics) from the same university.

She is currently a lecturer in the Department of Economics at the University of Zimbabwe, and engaged in ongoing research on transnational corporations.

Daniel Doda Ndlela was born in 1942 at Matopo Mission south of Bulawayo where he began his education up to secondary school. Thereafter educated at Karl Marx Higher Institute of Economics, Sofia, Bulgaria. He completed his PhD in Economics at the University of Lund In Sweden. He is currently Lecturer in Economics at the University of Zimbabwe, though he spent almost one year in the Ministry of Economic Planning and Development (1981-82).

His main field of work is in economic planning and industrial economics. He has published widely in the areas of planning, manufacturing sector, science and technology.

Samson Moyo was born on 23 September 1954 in Harare, and grew up in South-Western Zimbabwe, Midlands and Harare. He did his Secondary Education at Bernard Mizeki College in Marondera and his first degree in Sierra Leone combining Education and Geography. His postgraduate studies were carried out in Canada specialising in Economic and Rural Geography.

He lectured in Nigeria for 3 years, and is currently a Senior Research Fellow at the Zimbabwe Institute of Development Studies.

Published papers including: *Landuse and Agricultural Productivity in Zimbabwe, The Roots of Hunger in Zimbabwe, The Impact of Foreign Aid on Agricultural Policy in Zimbabwe, Vulnerable Labour Segments in Zimbabwe*. Currently researching agricultural cooperatives; labour use and valuation in Zimbabwe.

Clever Mumbengegwi was born in September 1952 in Chibi, near Masvingo. He completed his secondary education at Tegwani Secondary School before proceeding to Monash University in Melbourne, Australia. He completed two degrees in Economics, BEcon (Hons) and Master of Economics. He returned to Zimbabwe in 1980 and worked as an Economist in the Ministry of Economic Planning and Development for 2 years before joining the University of Zimbabwe in 1982 as a Lecturer in Economics.

His main fields of interest are agricultural policy and economics of agricultural cooperative development.

He has published mainly on cooperatives in Zimbabwe.

Thomas D. Shopo was born in Harare, on 21 June 1952. He was educated at Mutanda Primary School, Mutare, Chipembere School Highfields, Saint Augustine's School Penhalonga, Saint John's Avondale, Harare, Ardbennie Primary School and Morgan High School in Harare.

He received his university education at the University of Zimbabwe and the

London School of Economics and Political Science. He is a former lecturer in Economic History at the University of Zimbabwe. He has also worked as a Senior Research Officer in the National Manpower Survey, and in the Parliamentary Research Unit.

He is currently a Senior Research Fellow at the Zimbabwe Institute of Development Studies. His main research interests are on the historical problems of science and technology in Africa since World War II.

Lloyd M. Sachikonye was born in March 1954 in Bonda Mission near Nyanga in Eastern Zimbabwe. He carried out his primary and secondary schooling at Bonda and Sadziva respectively. Obtained BA and MSc degrees in Political Science at Ahmandu Bello University, Nigeria where he taught in the Department of Political Science from 1979 to 1981. Served in the Ministry of Foreign Affairs, Zimbabwe before joining the Zimbabwe Institute of Development Studies as Senior Research Officer in 1983.

He is an Executive Member of the Zimbabwe Chapter of the African Association of Political Science (AAPS). His review articles have been published in the *Nigerian Journal of Political Science*, *Political Science Journal* (Ahmandu Bello University), *Africa Development* and *West Africa*.

His current research interests include the development of trade unions in Zimbabwe and the the role of state and mulitinationals in agribusiness. He is currently researching on a doctoral thesis on the *State and Agribusiness in Zimbabwe* at the University of Leeds.

Brian Raftopoulos was born on 26 August 1954. He attended his primary schooling at Moffat Primary and Hartmann House, and completed his secondary schooling in 1973. In 1974 he left the country and began a Certificate of Education at All Saints College, London, which he completed in 1977. The following year he completed a BEd (Hons) with the University of London. In 1980 he completed an MA (Area Studies) at the School of Oriental and African Studies. In the same year he returned to Zimbabwe and took up a Research Officer post in the Ministry of Manpower Planning and Development.

He is currently Director of Research and Planning in the Ministry of Labour, Manpower Planning and Social Welfare, and his current field of research concerns problems of the labour movement, labour organisation and labour utilisation.

Rungano Zvobgo was born in Masvingo on 27 December 1949. He was educated at Chikore and Tegwani High Schools and obtained his first Bachelors (Honours) degree in 1974 and Masters degree in English in 1976 from St. Stephens College (University of Delhi). Thereafter, he obtained the Master of Philosophy degree in Education from the Jawaharlal Nehru University in New Delhi in 1977. He proceeded to Edinburgh University in Scotland where he obtained a Doctoral degree in Education in 1980.

Since his return to Zimbabwe in 1981, he has been extensively involved in Teacher Education first as Lecturer at Gweru Teachers' College and thereafter as Principal Lecturer in charge of the Zimbabwe Integrated National Teacher Education Course (ZINTEC) in the Midlands Province. He has been Vice Principal of Mkoba Teachers College in Gweru since 1982. He has recently published a book entitled: *Transforming Education—The Zimbabwean Experience*, College Press, Harare, 1985.

Samuel Agere was born in Rusape (near Mutare) in 1940. In 1966 he obtained a Diploma in Social Work form the Upperhelmer College of Social Work in Zambia, and in 1970 graduated with a BSc in Sociology and Social Work from the University of Zambia. In 1973 he completed an MSc (Econ) degree in Applied Social Studies from University College Cardiff in South Wales, UK. He graduated with a Masters degree in Social Work from Washington University, in 1978, and then went on to obtain a PhD in Social Development Studies from St. Louis University in the USA. From 1981-85 he held the post of Deputy Secretary in the Ministry of Community Development and Women's Affairs, and at present he is Permanent Secretary in the Ministry of Youth, Sport and Culture. His publications include: *Health care delivery system in the US—Lessons for Africa*; and *The promotion of self-reliance and self-help organizations in community development in Zimbabwe: a conceptual framework.*

Joyce Laetitia Kazembe (nee Chindove) was born in 1949 in Bulawayo where she began her schooling. She completed her Primary Schooling in Masvingo before proceeding to Monte Casino Girls Secondary School in North Eastern Zimbabwe. She died her 'A' level at Goromonzi Secondary School, after which she taught for more than ten years before enrolling at the University of Zimbabwe for a BAdmin degree (1981-1983). Her degree results were so good that she was offered a Research Fellowship in the Centre for Applied Social Science, University of Zimbabwe, where she has been since January 1984.

She is currently engaged in Research on Fundamental Rights and Personal Law; and is registered for an MPhil research degree on 'Children's Rights in Zimbabwe'. Her main publications are in the field of human rights with particular reference to women and children.

ACKNOWLEDGEMENTS

This book was intended to honour Zimbabwe's fifth anniversary of independence. That project never got off the ground and died altogether because of the difficulty in finding a publisher that could assist and allow us the degree of independence that we envisaged. We are therefore grateful to the Council for the Development of Economic and Social Research in Africa (CODESRIA) for according us, in October 1985, both the facilities and independence which made this book a reality. Under its programme of encouraging indigenous research and publications projects in Africa, CODESRIA funded the entire production and publication of the book. (This is not the first time that CODESRIA has come to assist Zimbabwe; notably, it assisted in the establishment of the Zimbabwe Institute of Development Studies). We are immensely grateful to CODESRIA and hope that this book will recover through its sales the resources that will in turn sponsor other national working groups in other parts of Africa.

Zimbabwe is so rich in intellectual and analytic skills in the field of social science research that it is inherently difficult to decide on the best line-up for the writing of a book such as this. No doubt there will be other individuals and groups in Zimbabwe that will produce books on this complex subject of the post-colonial situation. Our intention in this venture, however, was to put together a team of researchers who were already familiar with the subjects that they were to write about. Also, we sought persons who shared broadly a similar framework and perspective of analysis, which would render the book as coherent and cohesive in its main theme as was possible under the circumstances. We are particularly glad that the book has also emerged as the work of a *nationally* representative group of Zimbabwean authors.

Given the exigencies of time and the size of a group some of whose members were not always within the reach (as some were sometimes outside the country) of the editor, the task of co-ordinating the project and editing proved extremely difficult. Besides all of us are otherwise in full-time employment, so that the pace of the project depended on how much free time was available to write, in addition to our many other responsibilities. This meant that the project has taken much longer to complete than we originally envisaged: it began officially in December 1985 and ended in August 1986. A record time by any standards within which to complete a book of this size and with all the related demands on time and resources!

Deserving of speical gratitude, therefore, are our wives, husbands, families and friends, for their immense patience, understanding and encouragement in an exercise that often took us away from them for many a night and weekend. We remember with sincere appreciation and gratitude those of our initial team who, due mainly to pressure of work and related problems, were not able to be with us in the completion of the project: Sam Geza, Joseph Made, Peter Dzvimbo and Solomon Nkiwane. This made it necessary to include towards the end of the project three new members, all of whom have done well to complete within the scheduled time the chapters on agriculture, hunger and education.

Each author will have his or her own debts of gratitude for assistance received during the preparation of their chapters. But we acknowledged with thanks the help we received from the numerous persons that have come to be acquainted with this book in one way or another: the various typists and proof-readers; and those like Thandika Mkandawire and Bernard Magubane for their comments on one or the other aspect of the product that is now before the reader. A special thanks for such good service to Esi Honono and her staff at the library of the Zimbabwe Institute of Development Studies. Sincere gratitude also to Gloria Jinadu for the use of the word-processor; to Diane Mandaza for collecting and proof-reading the word-processed work; Godfrey Chanetsa for helping us get the manuscript to the typesetter; Ruhi Hamid for advising us on the cover design, and Dunstan Chan for organising the typesetting.

The editor must be held responsible for the organisation and presentation of the final product that is now this book. But all the authors were independent and free in the presentations that constitute their respective chapter for this book.

This is a book by Zimbabweans for Zimbabweans. It is not intended to be exhaustive in its purview and survey of the Zimbabwean postcolonial situation. We offer no answers; there are no easy answers in a subject so complex as the field of socio-economic and political analysis. Ours is only an attempt to contribute to a debate that has already begun concerning the nature of the historical reality that most Zimbabweans are so keen to have transformed.

Harare, Zimbabwe *Ibbo Mandaza*
August 1986 *Editor*

FOREWORD

This book is one in a series of works by national research working groups operating under the aegis of CODESRIA in a number of African countries. The groups, autonomously run by the researchers themselves, were established for various reasons. First, there was the growing demand by African scholars to be on the forefront of studies of their respective countries and thus break the stronghold on the analysis of African reality by researchers elsewhere. If Africa was to develop, it was incumbent upon African scholars that a large part of our understanding of our societies should be generated from within Africa.

There is no continent in which the presence of expatriate scientists is as pronounced as in Africa. It is thus still regarded as quite legitimate to write on African countries without any reference to local scholarship or, where the work of local researchers is used, without proper attribution of one's findings to these sources, especially if they are in the form of some obscure mimeographed publication. How often have African scholars complained of outright plagiarism of their work by visiting scholars who claim that their work came from primary sources? One of the most humiliating experiences of African scholars is witnessing intellectual 'debates' on their countries in which nationals are only marginally engaged, if at all. Anthologies of works on African countries are published consisting entirely of studies by non-nationals. One response to this challenge (or effrontery) is the provision of publication outlets for African scholars.

A third reason is the need for teaching material in the universities. As is now well-known, the transnational houses dominating book publication and distribution in Africa are pulling out of the tertiary school level books and confining themselves to the more lucrative primary and secondary school texts. Furthermore, there is a growing demand by students for locally produced reading material, not out of some perverse nationalist sentiment, but out of genuine intellectual curiosity for an authentically African interpretation of our reality.

Finally, there are numerous manuscripts in African universities and research institutes desperately seeking publication outlets. Here African scholars have to contend with two formidable forces—commercial attitudes about what books are saleable and the publication policies of research and teaching establishments outside Africa.

This book by Zimbabwean researchers is part of CODESRIA's contribution to the formidable task of extending Africa's sovereignty in the realm of scientific mastery of the continent's reality and destiny. Many more publications by national working groups are forthcoming. When we initially sent out information about CODESRIA's plan to assist national working groups, we imagined we would work with a maximum of four in any given year. The response to our offer has been simply overwhelming, reflecting the changed socio-political atmoshpere and intellectual responses to current societal crises. In less than a year twenty such groups have sought CODESRIA'S assistance. Our financial resources are limited. However, no effort will be spared to ensure that all properly constituted and well thought-out research and publication projects receive adequate support.

We hope that the political climate in Africa will permit the wide local dissemination of these series.

Thandika Mkandawire
Acting Executive Secretary,
Council for the Development of
Economic and Social Research in
Africa (CODESRIA)

August 1986

INTRODUCTION:
The Political Economy of Transition

Ibbo Mandaza

'Our problem is to see who is capable of taking control of the state apparatus when the colonial power is destroyed...the peasants cannot read or write...The working class hardly exists as a defined class...There is no *economically viable* bourgeoisie because imperialism prevented it being created. What there is is a stratum of people in the service of imperialism who have already learned how to manipulate the apparatus of the state— the African petty bourgeoisie: this is the only stratum capable of controlling or even utilizing the instruments which the colonial state used against our people. So we come to the conclusion that in colonial conditions it is the petty bourgeoisie which is the inheritor of state power (though I wish we could be wrong). The moment national liberation comes and the petty bourgeoisie takes power we enter, or rather return to history, and thus the internal contradictions break out again.

When this happens, and particularly as things are now, there will be powerful external contradictions conditioning the internal situation and not just internal contradictions as before. What attitude can the petty bourgeoisie adopt? Obviously people on the left will call for the revolution; the right will call for the 'non-revolution', i.e. a capitalist road or something like that. The petty bourgeoisie can either ally itself with imperialism and the reactionary strata in its own country to try and preserve itself as a petty bourgeoisie or ally itself with the workers and peasants, who must themselves take power or control to make the revolution. We must be very clear exactly what we are asking the petty bourgeoisie to do. Are we asking it to commit suicide? Because if there is a revolution, then the petty bourgeoisie will have to abandon power to the workers and the peasants and cease to exist qua petty bourgeoisie. For a revolution to take place depends on the nature of the party (and its size), the character of the struggle which led up to liberation, whether there was an armed struggle, what the nature of this armed struggle was and how it developed and of course, on the nature of the state.'

Amilcar Cabral, Brief Analysis of the Social Structure in Guinea, *Revolution in Guinea: An African People's Struggle*[1]

This book focuses on the post-colonial state in Zimbabwe. This is a situation which must be understood in the context of a society just emerging from white settler colonial rule, which the first chapter of this book characterises as the *post-white settler colonial state*. This is the thrust that pervades the entire study. The main objective of the first chapter is to throw into sharp focus the historical background and the main elements of this post-white settler colonial state. The latter is best comprehended through a brief analysis of the history of white settler colonialism; the imperatives of imperialism in Zimbabwe as part of the Southern Africa sub-region; and the nature of the national liberation struggle, against imperialism and white settler colonialism, and in pursuit of national independence and democracy.

The first section of chapter one is therefore quite appropriately entitled 'The Road to Lancaster House'. The Lancaster House Agreement (1979) in essential respects reflects a compromise in the balance of forces that characterises Zimbabwe after almost ten years of armed struggle. Zimbabwe emerged out of the condition of colonial domination into national independence, reflecting the compromise of class forces. The Agreement constituted a landmark in the history of Zimbabwe's transition from colonialism to political independence. As a compromise, it has pervaded the process and structures through which the new state has sought both to consolidate national independence and provide a basis for genuine economic and social development. The Lancaster House Agreement provides therefore the historically based framework and parameters for political, economic and social action in the period following the attainment of national independence. That is, on the one hand, the Lancaster House Conference was called because the guerrilla war had produced a strategic stalemate and had shifted the balance of forces against white settlerdom and the imperialist interest, in favour of the liberation movement.

Yet the conduct of the Conference itself, the various concessions that the guerrilla representatives had to make, and the outcome which is the basis of the Agreement itself: all tended to reflect a result less than that which might have been expected of a national liberation movement had it won an outright victory on the battlefield.

The second section of chapter one deals with the main elements of the Lancaster House Agreement itself. But it does so against the vantage of a historical background that exposes the high level of duplicity on the part of the British imperialists and their attempt to entrench the interests of their kith and kin in the new Zimbabwe. It is now known that the British imperialists were party to the Unilateral Declaration of Independence (UDI).[2]

The aim of the British was that any 'settlement' would have to take into account the white settler factor. The British government found itself at Lancaster in a fairly strong position, especially when it came to dealing with an African nationalist leadership which, given the vagaries of the Zimbabwean liberation struggle, tended to welcome and accept Britain's role as the decolonising power.

The joint British-United States strategy at the talks was to assign the white settler factor an importance not quite commensurate with the normal decolonisation situations in which it should have been regarded as a declining factor. Imperialist policy in Southern Africa has, in effect, fed the false confidence and arrogance of white settler colonialism. In turn, this tended to intimidate the African nationalists and their supporters of the frontline states into a compromise with imperialism itself. In 1979, the white settler colonial state was in an untenable position; and yet Smith had sufficiently divided the nationalists to create an internal settlement which, in turn, became a factor at Lancaster. The frontline states had been a vital rear base for the guerrilla forces but, by 1979, Zambia and Mozambique had taken such a hammering at the feet of a dying horse that they were now more inclined to pressurise the Patriotic Front (ZANU and ZAPU) into an agreement that would bring some kind of peace for the sub-region and political independence to Zimbabwe.

In the final analysis, the Lancaster House Conference provided imperialism with the opportunity to be an 'umpire' in a 'match' in which it had a vested interest. That is, imperialism tried to resolve the problem it had created in its own favour.

The historical conjuncture in which the Lancaster House Agreement was concluded explains the emergent economic, political and social structures that characterise the post-colonial Zimbabwe. To some, the character of the new state appears to be a little more than the conventional neo-colonialism. However, the peculiarity of the new state lies as much in the relative strength of the former white settler colonial state and the high level of support it received from Britain, as in the relative weakness of a national liberation movement that had not yet developed the military, political and ideological capacity to be the kind of revolutionary movement that would dismantle the white settler colonial state and transform the socio-economic structure after independence.

In Zimbabwe today, we have a post-white settler colonial situation in which the former white settlers find themselves with such political and economic guarantees as would be the envy of any former colonisers in any decolonisation process. Equally important, however, is that this situation in itself provides a framework for the development and expression of the class forces among the African people themselves, particularly the African petit bourgeoisie which has a vested interest in the post-white settler colonial state. This is the subject of the third section of chapter one:

> *The post-white settler colonial state* becomes the agency through which international finance capital seeks to maintain Zimbabwe under imperialist hegemony.

The various chapters of the book hinge around this theme that receives elaboration under Part One, which is entitled 'Politics.' But the authors do so on a sectoral basis designed to highlight the key aspects of Zimbabwean society—Part Two: the Economy; Part Three: the Agrarian Question; Part Four: the Labour Question; and Part Five: Social Development. The book is not intended to be exhaustive; nor can it be a final statement on a subject that is bound to provoke more and more discussion. One of its main intentions is to try to dispel the corpus of myths about Zimbabwe's contemporary development, hopefully clearing the way, so to speak, for deeper and more incisive analysis in the future.

The Theory of the Logic of Protracted Struggle: Myth or Reality?
The analysis of the historical factors and processes leading to national independence constitutes a necessary precondition for understanding the present and future developments of any post-colonial society. In the Southern African situation, however, even this task is often clouded and obstructed by the mythology that has developed around the issue of the *armed struggle*. In his 'Foreword' to Gérard Chaliand's book, *Revolution in the Third World*,[3] Immanuel Wallerstein reminds us of the political function of 'revolutionary myths':

> It does not take long to realize that the major function myths play is to mobilize people, by their promise and their optimism... Myths are an essential element in the organising process, and in sustaining the troops during the long political struggle...Myths then are necessary.

The danger arises, however, when this mythology is in turn imbibed by the analyst, academically refined, and then re-imposed on to the characterisation of social and political processes in a given society. The danger is compounded if the analyst is largely removed from the dynamics of those processes; and more so if, in a particular historical conjuncture, the objects of the analysis are themselves either unable to expose these new myths or find it convenient to integrate the latter into their own mythology about their struggles.

The radicals of North America and Western Europe have contributed significantly through their writings to mobilising support for the struggles of the African people. At times, this has required the need to project a level of mythology about these struggles, partly in an attempt to answer the very negative propaganda of the enemies of the African people, and partly in the hope that the mythology itself might indeed become reality.

Indeed the impact of 'revolutionary mythology' on the struggle of the African peoples cannot be underestimated. The first section of chapter one seeks to show the relationship between the struggles of South East Asia (China and Vietnam) and Latin America (Cuba) and those of Southern Africa; and how a Marxist-Leninist tradition began to develop in Zimbabwe in the context of the liberation struggles in the 1970s. The contribution of African radicals to the development of a 'revolutionary mythology' cannot be underestimated. For it was mainly the radical intellectuals who articulated and wrote the radical speeches and publications that increasingly projected the liberation movements as revolutionary and Marxist-Leninist. Whatever disparity there was—and there was—between this conception of the struggle by a few radicals on the one hand,

and that of the reality of the mass of the people on the other, was lost as part of the overall revolutionary mythology that had to sustain and defend the struggle against its many enemies.

The difficulty arises in the post-independence situation, particularly in the attempt to explain why things are what they are. The analyst has, if the challenge is accepted, to dispel the mythology as a precondition for real analysis. This point is pertinent when one considers the analyses of the Mozambique situation in particular;[4] but also those of Zimbabwe are informative in this regard.[5] The problem arises essentially in the kind of conclusions. about the aims and objectives of the struggle, that flow out of the 'revolutionary mythology' of such radical analysts, of whom John Saul is a leading figure.

No individual writer has done so much to mobilise support throughout North America (and even throughout the world) for the liberation struggles of Southern Africa; and yet his writings have, by the same token, constituted a romantic rendition on the liberation struggles that are, in reality, much more complex in their historical origins and development. Sadly, too, it has created a precedent, and indeed even the belief on the part of many in North America and Western Europe—that only the *'gurus'* of the 'African Studies' industries of the northern hemisphere can with authority write on the situation in Southern Africa.[6] As the 'Foreword' to our book has stated, this is one of the 'most humiliating experiences of African scholars'; but the effect of this radical paternalism of the northern hemisphere has been to hamper discussion on the crucial issues of the situation in our sub-region. For, even our universities in Africa have tended to accept these writings as the final authority on African political experiences.

For a long time now, it has also meant that 'revolutionary mythology' would be maintained at the expense of those who have a more direct interest in the furtherance of the revolution. Many an African scholar and political activist has had to imbibe and mimic these academic trends of the 'Radical Northern Hemispherena',[7] not only to gain legitimacy but even to survive in the form of research fellowships and access to publication.

It is a trend—indeed an 'effrontery' as Mkandawire calls it in the 'Foreword'—that must be challenged by concerned African scholars in the course of fulfilling the major objective of explaining the political and socio-economic reality that we seek to transform through the agency of the African revolution.

More than a decade since it was adopted by North American and Western European radicals, the theory of the 'logic of protracted struggle'[8] has done more to confuse than enlighten us on the problems of national liberation in Africa. The theory became almost a mechanistic view that the dynamics of the armed struggle against an intransigent and formidable enemy would develop *logically* a revolutionary capacity for national liberation and thereby advance almost immediately towards socialism. As such, the national liberation struggle was a struggle against both imperialism and reactionary forces within. It would, in the words of John Saul, cleanse the national movement of 'those not prepared to make the transition to revolutionary practice'.[9] The 'logic of protracted struggle' would transcend 'elitism' and 'it was moving beyond the economic self-interest and Africanized exploitative practices'[10] of bad nationalists.

Saul has dichotomised the history of decolonisation[11] between, on the one hand, 'false decolonization' which is an outcome of the conventional transfer of power from the European colonisers to African governments north of the Zambezi and, on the other hand, 'genuine independence' as emanating from such a protracted armed struggle as was waged in Angola, Mozambique and Zimbabwe. The two variants produce their respective leaders in the decolonisation process: a 'reactionary nationalism' which leads to neo-colonialism and a 'revolutionary nationalism' whose aim is the establishment of socialism under the revolutionary democratic alliance dominated by the proletariat and peasantry. According to Saul, therefore, the protracted struggle would in Mozambique pre-empt 'false decolonization which emerged in much of the rest of Africa'[12] and thereby the 'knot of neo-colonialism was being untied at an early moment in Mozambique'.[13]

Euphoric and, perhaps, even surprised at their discovery that Africans could in fact struggle and win national independence, these scholars overlooked the complexity of both the struggle itself and the Southern African situation. Rather than re-examine those historical, socio-economic and strategic factors—indeed rather than try to understand the nature of both imperialism and the class forces that emerge as a result of its impact in Southern Africa—they are now more inclined to attribute all that has gone wrong to the African petit bourgeoisie, without, however, identifying and analysing the conditions which influence the action of this class.

Thus, Machel, who in 1975 was viewed as a revolutionary leader of a socialist state, in 1984 became a sellout leader of a country going capitalist! Similar analyses will no doubt greet the Zimbabwean situation, if they have not already done so!

It is not difficult to see why writers like John Saul cannot easily acknowledge the great disparity between *their* conception of the liberation struggle in Mozambique and the reality of the post-colonial situation in that country. For how easily can one argue against his own self-made 'revolutionary mythology'? The words of a senior Mozambican leader whom John Saul quotes might be more applicable to himself: 'Lies have short legs, they do not walk far'.[14] In his latest book John Saul appears to acknowledge that radicals have sometimes created such myths:

> Those sympathetic to socialism have probably done themselves and the revolutions they support a singular disservice when they have presented the processes involved in an unproblematic manner. As the rosy picture we have been tempted to paint—of Russia, of China, of Cuba, of Vietnam, of Tanzania, and the like—has proven to be a much more shaded one in reality, it

has become apparent that a naive perspective virtually guarantees eventual disillusionment.[15]

Jacques Depelchin has warned against 'methodologically unsound and unscientific' modes of analysis of the African situation. His brief critique[16] of the works of John Saul,[17] Joe Hanlon[18] and Horace Campbell,[19] is really an account on the writings of people who are largely detached from political practice. But it is also a call for those of us who are not so divorced from the experience of the struggle to transcend 'revolutionary mythology' through a careful analysis of the concrete situation in our countries.

This is how Depelchin poses the problem:

> ...Horace Campbell tried to answer...by asserting that FRELIMO was in the process of becoming the opposite of what it had promised to be during the armed struggle and the first years following independence. Campbell's article while it may satisfy those who are constantly on the lookout for revolutionary Meccas contains two major flaws: at a subjective level they express a disappointment which comes from having accepted, uncritically, not only the history, but also the problematization of FRELIMO's account of the armed struggle. Yet, after having accepted that version, Campbell proceeds to provide a condemnation, not on the basis of that history, but on the basis of an ideal version of what revolutions ought to be. Drawing examples from other countries that may have gone further than Mozambique in advancing socialism does not make his points more valid. They merely contribute to emphasizing the methodological problem that does exist in trying to study the history of the revolutionary process initiated by FRELIMO in terms of other struggles.
>
> The greatest respect one could pay to FRELIMO would be by analysing its struggles as objectively as available evidence will permit it. Sympathy pushed to the extreme will ultimately result in a falsification of a history which, more than ever before, needs to be studied, analysed, discussed so as to learn from it. Analytically, there is something methodologically unsound and unscientific when a Marxist problematic is vigorously applied to dissect Mozambican colonial society, and when this same problematic is used with mittens in order to confront the post-independent period. Yet, this is precisely one of the tendencies of most writings on post-colonial Mozambique.[20]

Imperialist Hegemony, African Nationalism and Neo-Colonialism

The point surely is how best to analyse and comprehend the specificities of the political and ideological terrain on which the armed struggle unfolds. The history of Africa in general and Southern Africa in particular has been all about struggle for freedom and self-determination, regardless whether this was through armed struggle or peaceful means.

It is therefore both cynical and tending towards ideological self-indulgence that anyone should draw a dichotomy between the violent and non-violent courses to national independence, a dichotomy between so-called 'false decolonisation' and 'genuine independence.' It is an attempt to indict the struggle of a whole continent; it is not only paternalist but also reflects a gross misunderstanding of Africa's history and its domination by imperialism.

Ideological self-indulgence can cause the analyst and political activist to overlook the currency of African nationalism as both an inspiration for social and political action in the struggle for African liberation and an impediment, on the part of its adherents, to the understanding of imperialism and the latter's neo-colonial strategies. African nationalism has its roots in the century-old ideology of white supremacy, the indignities of slavery and colonialist oppression and exploitation; and it continues to survive in the apparent coincidence between the dominance of the northern hemisphere and the deprivation of the dark races, in the division of the world into whites and blacks; in the survial of racism as an ideology. To ignore the importance of African nationalism in any analysie of the African situation renders the analysis incomplete. But to dismiss it as reactionary and inconsequential is to overlook the bloody struggles that have been fought in pursuit of African liberation; and it is an indictment of the hundreds of thousands of African heroes and heroines that have so far perished in the pursuit of this objective.

African nationalism is the indipensable force in the movement for national liberation; and yet it is also the basis for the neo-colonialism by which the masses are betrayed. The apparent irony in this historical process should not however lead us into the kind of analyses that dismiss nationalist movements as merely movements of the African petit bourgeoisis and not those of the masses. The epigram (at the head of this Introduction) from Amilcar Cabral is as good an explanation as any for this apparent historical irony. The point, however, is that African nationalism—and the African petit bougeoisie—remains at the centre of Africa's quest for total liberation, for the re-assertion of African dignity, for Africa's return to history.

The fact of apartheid South Africa remains a symbol of Africa's unique historical experience as a continent—and its diaspora—which has had to endure overall oppression and exploitation almost on the basis of colour. It is this unique historical experience that is Africa's basis for 'African unity', a rallying call that remains unique to Africa (as a continent) alone. By its very strength and dominance, African nationalist ideology will tend to disguise the class structure of African societies, to hide the reality of the class struggle and even thereby to reinforce neo-colonialism. But these are all issues to be examined and confronted in analyses of African societies; we cannot resolve them by running away from them.

Kwame Nkrumah's adage about the primacy (before all else, including the economic) of the political kingdom emphasises the importance and significance of political independence for any society. But it also highlights the historical conjuncture in which imperialist hegemony is a serious factor in the determination of the course to be taken in the post-independence phase. Nyerere, like Nkrumah, soon discovered that:

> The reality of neo-colonialism quickly becomes obvious to a new African Government which tries to act in economic matters and in the interest of national development and for the betterment of its own masses. For such a Government immediately discovers that it inherited the power to make laws, to direct the civil service, to treat with foreign Governments and so on but it did not inherit effective power over economic developments in its own country. Indeed it often discovers that there is no such thing as a national economy. Neo-colonialism is real.[21]

This book is an attempt to explain this reality, *i.e. we account for why things are what they are, rather than what they ought to be.* It seeks to show that imperialism is neither a bogey nor a convenient peg on which to hang Africa's ills.

In recent years there has developed in the North American and Western European academic world another variant of the radical tradition, namely that mode of analysis that is cynical of attempts by African radicals to analyse the African situation in terms of an emphasis on the dominant role of imperialism. Unlike the romantic though supportive variant that we have just described, this tradition is couched in scepticism about revolutionary processes. Gavin Kitching[22] represents this cynical tradition. He is impressed by the apparent non-changeability and stability of the world capitalist system; and by the 'fact that all of the various socialist experiments and regimes in black Africa to date have at best had ambiguous results for the welfare of the peasants and workers who live under them, and at worst have been an unambiguous disaster'.[23] Ignorant of the African situation, Gavin Kitching now assigns blame to the African radicals. For him, 'imperialism' and 'dependency' are no longer factors to contend with. The African revolution must wait for the arrival of a 'sophisticated socialist working class in Africa'[24] before African radicals can with justification comment on the African condition:

> In general, or at least until quite recently, dependency theory in Africa was advocated by men and women who were socialists, radicals, or revolutionaries (at least in self-image) of one form or another. That is to say, it was advocated by people who were dedicated to struggle against imperialism, against inequality and poverty, for 'real' independence and socialism. And yet it was premised upon a vision of 'the enemy', of imperialism, of multinational capital, which endowed 'it' with apparently all-conquering power, total clarity and unanimity of purpose, and almost omnipotent causal potency. Now logically a commitment to such a conception of the enemy, of the opposing forces, should be productive of simple fatalism and hopelessness. After all if imperialism really is like that, the only thing to do is give up,

'lie back and enjoy it,' throw down one's puny arms and bow to superior force, insight and power.[25]

The various chapters of this book are in their respective ways adequate testimony to the reality of imperialism and dependency. Chapter one in general seeks to highlight imperialist objectives with regard to Zimbabwe in particular and Southern Africa in general. As we have pointed out elsewhere,[26] imperialist policy today still reflects in its global expression the main features as outlined in V. I. Lenin's theory of Imperialism: The Highest Stage of Capitalism.[27] For the purposes of our analysis it is appropriate to restate them:

(a) the gap in economic development between the industrialised Western (and European-settled) countries and those restricted to primary production. The gap is widening under continued imperialist domination.
(b) the export of capital from the more developed countries to the less.
(c) the division, especially in the late nineteenth century, of territories throughout the world by the more developed nations as part of the rivalry and competition for strategic and economic advantages. This competition for colonies led to two world wars.
(d) the further concentration and centralisation of capital and the integration of the world capitalist economy into the structures of the giant US-based multinational corporations or integrated monopolistic enterprises. These multinational corporations not only accelerate technological change but also control trade, prices and profits.
(e) the decline in the period since the Russian Revolution of 1917 of national rivalries among the leading capitalist countries as an international ruling class is consolidated and constituted on the basis of ownership control of the multinational corporations: and as the world capital market is internationalised by the World Bank and other agencies of the international ruling class.
(f) the evolution of global imperialist foreign policy which corresponds to the global interests and perspectives of the multinational corporations.
(g) the intensification of these tendencies (outlined in d,e,f, above) arising from the threat of world socialism to the world capitalist system.

It is important to emphasise in this respect the particularities of the imperialist interest in Africa, an interest that is as old as Europe's contact with Africa and has assumed a special significance ever since the balkanisation of the continent at the Congress of Berlin of 1884/1885.

Reagan's recent pronouncement[28] on the South African situation is yet another reaffirmation of the US imperial claim on Africa and its resources. The belief that not only Southern Africa but Africa as a whole is a US sphere of influence is imperial arrogance of the first order. The architect of current US Africa policy, Chester Crocker, has given a new definition of US objectives in Africa. Addressing a State Department Foreign Policy Conference in Washington on 2 June 1981, he stated:

> The Reagan administration recognizes that Africa is a region of growing importance to US global objectives—economic, political, strategic, human and so forth. We cannot afford to neglect a region where our interests are so clearly growing and I would simply refer here in passing to the obvious facts of our long history of involvement with Africa: to the many links of culture and blood that tie an important portion of our own citizenry to Africa; to our growing import-dependence on fuel and non-fuel minerals produced in Africa; to Africa's growing place as a focus of world politics and its growing role as an actor in world politics.[29]

Accordingly, the intention is to 'support regional security in Africa' and to

> cooperate with our allies and friends in Africa to deter aggression and subversion by our global adversary. We intend to assure the US and our allies fair commercial access to essential fuel and non-fuel minerals and other raw materials produced in Africa, and at the same time to promote the growing engagement of the American economy and the American private sector in Africa's growing economy.[30]

So-called 'constructive engagement' is based on these imperial assumptions. In US neo-globalism the South African white minority regime and white settlers are the key both to the stability of Southern Africa and to the perpetuation of imperial interests.

The factors—i.e. 'economic, political, strategic, human and so forth'—which led to the colonisation of Africa are sadly still relevant a century afterwards. The point is that no country in the world—least of all the small countries—can afford to be oblivious to the reality of imperialism as a threat to world peace. It continues to wrangle even with those of our world that have undergone socialist revolutions; and threatens to undermine the political independence of those small countries that seek to de-link from the capitalist world system and its related imperialist hegemony. It is impossible to explain Africa's current condition without acknowledging imperialism as the basic cause. As Nyerere stated in a recent speech:

> The evidence is all around us. The gap between African poverty and the wealth of the developed nations gets larger. African nations get further into debt and have less and less ability even to sustain such economic progress as they had earlier made. Then, when the natural disasters of drought or flood strike, or when indebtedness becomes extreme, the quid pro quo for temporary relief is liable to be 'facilities' for military or communication units of a Great Power, or the forced adoption of their

economic policies. And if an African nation is not sufficiently cooperative, then the lessons of Angola and of Libya are there to see—to say nothing of the more subtle and camouflaged interventions in our political systems which are frequent.[30]

Elsewhere,[31] we have described and analysed imperialist policy in Southern Africa. Chapter one of this book helps to highlight its dimensions in the Zimbabwean situation: the reality of economic imperialism; political blackmail; the threats of economic blockades and manipulation of 'aid' administration by the US and its allies; the heavy hand of international financial institutions (the World Bank and the International Monetary Fund); in addition to the threat of open aggression and intervention by South Africa.

Dependency therefore is an integral feature of imperialist hegemony: during the colonial situation it is complete and influences and prescribes the broad parameters of the economic and social action of the post-colonial state itself. The emergence of the African petit bourgeoisie is an important aspect of this colonial situation; and determines also the conditions under which this leading class may pursue or sell out the revolution. The apparent 'sell-out' is therefore a reflection of the overall dominance of imperialist hegemony at a particular stage in the development of the society; a reflection of the weakness of nationalist movements in this imperialist epoch, the inability to dismantle the state and change the socio-economic structures after independence. This does not mean that imperialism thereby imposes a permanent solution in its favour nor does it thereby also subsume all internal contradictions and antagonisms. On the contrary, these societies continue to be characterised by sharp internal conflicts, by and in antagonism to imperialism itself. Imperialism is incapable of resolving the contradictions that it has created. Only the labouring people can resolve that contradiction: *A Luta Continua* is more than just a symbolic rendition about a struggle that must continue until genuine liberation.

The Political Economy of Transition

The job of the analyst is not only to identify oneself with this process but also to search for ways to analyse the ongoing struggles. Accordingly, the focus of this book is on the relationship between the imperialist and white settler colonial legacy on the one hand, and the pattern of political and socio-economic development in the post-independence era on the other. To what extent and with what consequences does the white settler colonial experience itself—and the gamut of political, economic, social, cultural and ideological manifestations and structures that it inherited—constitute a series of structural limitations to the momentum and ambitions of the new post-colonial situation? Given the nature and history of the national liberation movement, its class and ideological content, how is the new state in Zimbabwe to be characterised—in terms of new alliances and stances, and in the light of the current configuration of forces at the regional and global levels? And, therefore, what have been the achievements and pitfalls? And, on the basis of such analysis, what of the future?

This study is the reflection of a national commitment of a group of Zimbabweans who think broadly alike, the evidence of a commitment to the continuing struggle against the forces that made the attainment of national independence so bloody and protracted; and in whose eventual defeat the people of Zimbabwe will find genuine (economic and political) independence and peace. It is a rejection of analyses and assumptions based either on wishful or otherwise misreading of the historical process or ideological self-indulgence. Ours is an attempt to explain why things are what they are; and how, on the basis of the current configuration of social, regional and global forces, those interested may begin to organise and plan for the way forward.

The book provides a broad framework within which to understand post-independence Zimbabwe. In particular it outlines and analyses the main elements of the post-white settler colonial state in the context of the overall role of imperialist hegemony in Zimbabwe in particular and Southern Africa in general. The discussion flows out of the Leninist conception of the state as a specially organized and coercive force, 'a machine for holding in obedience to one class other, subordinated classes'.[32] Also politically and ideologically, the state seeks to disorganise and demobilise the exploited classes as much through the threat of repression as through the granting of limited actual or expected benefits and promoting and sustaining ideological illusions. The discussion also takes into account the current debate among African and Third World scholars on the nature of the post-colonial state; the debate emphasises:

> the historical specificity of post-colonial societies, a specificity which arises from structural changes brought about by the colonial experience and alignment of classes and by the superstructure of political and administrative insitutions which were established in that context, and secondly from radical re-aligments of class forces which have been brought about in the post-colonial situation'.[33]

The post-white settler colonial state reveals essential structural similarities with those of other post-colonial states. This is particularly so with regard to the dominant role of international finance capital in these states.

> The post-colonial state may foster or frustrate its national bourgeoisie or its landed classes or both, but short of a revolution which puts the direct producers into power it cannot escape its servitude to the metropolitan bourgeoisie.[34]

In the post-colonial situation, the state plays an important and somewhat new role of concealing for a time the full and direct impact of international finance capital as it continues to exploit the human and material resources in this neo-colonial situation. In general, therefore, this state seeks to reconcile on the one hand the pursuit of the developmentalist objectives of independence, in response to the popular aspirations and expectations of the masses; and, on the other, the sheer weight—economic and political—of the imperialist forces of international finance capital:

> herein lies the contradictory character of the post-colonial state. It is at the best of times a state split in two—a schizophrenic state, a state torn apart between on the one hand the democratic forces of the people, and on the other hand the imperialist forces of the international financial oligarchy. This split is in evidence right through all the institutions of the state—the army, the police, the court system, the parliament and even the government itself (including the cabinet), and we might add, even the political parties. Indeed, even individual political leaders sometimes display schizophrenic tendencies when they feel impelled on the one hand to respond to the democratic demands of the people, and on the other hand feel the pressure of international capital on them which impels them to suppress those very demands they would want to respond to but cannot.[35]

Initially, therefore, the post-colonial state might be able to conceal the ongoing exploitative role of international capital through the political and ideological paraphernalia that accompany the arrival of national independence. In the African situation, in particular, nothing is more enthralling and lulling to the masses—and to the African petit bourgeoisie itself—than the arrival of black majority rule, especially when, in the mind of the average person, this event immediately offers the promise of total (political and economic) liberation. Gradually, however, the post-colonial state, and particularly that component of it that comprises the African petit bourgeoisie, begins to develop an ideological superstructure within which to explain the ever-growing disparity between these popular demands and the economic and social realities of the neo-colonial situation.

It might at first try to enhance, through both ideological expressions and social development programmes (e.g. education reform, democratisation of the employment system, etc.), the myth of equality of opportunity and mobility in a capitalist society; make available and distribute resources in such a way as to mobilise and maintain 'national' support for the governing class; or develop a populist ideology that is imbued 'with a harmonistic dream' of a society in which the interests of the African petit bourgeoisie 'might be reconciled with the interests of all other non-capitalist classes and the more enlightened sectors of the metropolitan bourgeoisie'.[36] As Mkandawire observes:

> The ruling class must harp more on the myth of a homogeneous nationalist cause and movement to conceal the profound division engendered by the adopted model of accumulation which has denuded the historical social alliance that sustained the independence struggle.[37]

However, like all states, the post-colonial state in the final analysis depends on the repressive apparatus which it invariably expands and strengthens. It will use this, if necessary, as an effective threat against any action by the exploited and disgruntled masses that may unduly undermine the neo-colonial *status quo* of which the post-colonial state itself is an expression.

> The metropolitan bourgeoisie needs activist states on the periphery, states that are strong enough to suppress, by whatever means, growing social contradictions and states that can make foreign investments profitable and profits secure despite various unfavourable circumstances within the national and world economy.[38]

The *post-white settler colonial state* acquires a special meaning in the context of the foregoing, precisely because of the historical legacy of white settler colonialism; the inherited economic and social structures that are associated with it; and its persistent and pervasive role within both the state itself and the society at large, as a viable conduit through which the imperialist forces of international finance capital can compromise and control the new state. But it is a state which, in the circumstances of post-independence Zimbabwe, provides a framework within which the leading sections of the African petit bourgeoisie can also find fulfilment of their class aspirations as they enter the arena that was hitherto restricted and confined largely to the white classes.

The white presence itself continues to obstruct and forestall the development of an African national bourgeoisie. But the post-white settler colonial situation offers bright prospects for at least a significant section of the African petit bourgeoisie; and in turn the new excitement also fosters a spate of ideological illusions as even the workers and peasants begin to believe that they can graduate to the petit bourgeois class and beyond. Thus, to some extent, rather than become an entirely negative feature of the post-independence situation, the white presence can at times be used by the ruling African petit bourgeoisie as an excuse to explain the delay in the fulfilment of the popular demands of the mass of the people; while this in turn only intimidates and softens both the white petit bourgeoisie and white bourgeoisie (and the international bourgeoisie) into making more and more economic and social concessions to an African petit bourgeoisie with which it develops in time an (class) alliance *vis-à-vis* the popular masses.

All these aspects of the post-white settler colonial state determine and influence the arena of domestic and external policies. This highlights the fact that imperialist forces have a particular interest in Zimbabwe, partly because of the nature of the colonial history of the country itself and partly because Zimbabwe is regarded as quite pivotal within the overall strategic and economic considerations of imperialist policy in Southern Africa.[39]

The Struggle Continues

The post-white settler colonial state is inherently unable to fulfil the popular demands of the masses. Masipula Sithole's chapter on the 'The

General Elections' shows that ZANU (PF) was able to retain the support of the peasants and workers in the 1985 general election because of the overall impact of the democratisation process that came with independence: the dawn of peace in a country that had been torn by war; the 'mushrooming of roads, clinics, and wells' around the country; and the institution of minimum wage laws that created a favourable contrast with conditions that prevailed during the colonial days. Part five of the book is an elaboration of the government's attempt to maintain the mass orientation carried over from the liberation struggle, as Rungano Zvobgo and Sam Agere have sought to show in their respective chapters on education and health. Brian Raftopoulos reveals, in great detail, the advances made in the field of human resources development; as does Joyce Kazembe in her outline of the 'women issue'. But much remains to be done with regard to the latter and the government's progressive policy on human resources is already meeting strong resistance from capital. The arena of 'social development' is one in which post-independence governments at first find themselves with both the momentum and leverage to pursue progressive policies. The provision of educational, health and social security facilities become the most visible of the 'fruits' that political independence brings with it. Deprivation and inequalities in these very fields were also the burning questions during the struggle for national independence. In this regard, social development programmes became not only imperative for a government that is so conscious of its mass base but also relatively easier to implement than it is to attend to economic transformative issues in a country in which the economy is virtually foreign-dominated. Sooner or later, however, the economic reality re-asserts its dominance, compelled to do so as social development programmes begin to cut into the profits of capital.

At the end of the day, therefore, the new state had gradually become an apparent mediator between capital and labour, between the aspirations of the people for the 'fruits of independence' and the role of international capital in its quest for more profit. The overall dominance of capital in the economy of the country is adequately described by the three authors—Xavier Kadhani, Theresa Chimombe and Daniel Ndlela—who have provided us with a broad outline of the problem. Each has respectively tried to show the relationship between this dominance and policy implications for the political economy of transition, particularly the immense constraints imposed upon a government that is keen to satisfy popular demands. Likewise, Sam Moyo has produced a chapter that throws into sharp focus the 'land question': a question that remains largely unsolved in spite of the government's attempt to do so through the establishment of a resettlement programme. More than that, Sam Moyo shows how the 'question' is compounded by the development of a black agrarian bourgeoisie, the pervasive capitalist policies on land utilisation and the new class formation that is developing in the countryside. As Clever Mumbengegwi takes up the theme, he raises issues connected with the so-called 'agricultural success story' of Zimbabwe. For, in the long run, the question is simply this: success for whom and at whose expense?

Thus there has been more continuity than change in agricultural policy. Until the eradication of this 'colonial inheritance' in agricultural and food policy, argues Thomas Shopo, hunger will remain a feature amongst the 'born free'.

All this may give the impression that capitalism and capitalist ideology reign supreme in the continuity that is implicit in the post-white settler colonial situation. For even the working class—the motive force of change and development—appears as yet unable to organise and challenge a system antithetical to its interests. In an outline of the 'labour movement', Lloyd Sachikonye traces the historical (and colonial) origins of the weakness of the trade unions in Zimbabwe. He endorses the view of Perry Anderson that trade unions

> do not challenge the existence of classes but merely express it: thus trade unions can never be vehicles of advance towards socialism in themselves (because) by their nature they are tied to capitalism. They can bargain with society, but not transform it.

Yet his own outline of the spate of labour unrest in the period since independence is concrete evidence of both the increasing sharpening of contradictions in Zimbabwean society and the high potential that out of it *must* develop a working class organisational and ideological capacity with which to confront capital. The struggle is bound to be a long one but it has already started; nay, it is inherent in the very structures and in the very 'monster' that has been in the making ever since colonialism (and capitalism) established itself in Zimbabwe.

There is an attempt to analyse the class structure of post-independence Zimbabwe, indicating wherever possible the economic interests of the respective classes, and assessing the level of consciousness and commitment of the various sections of the African petit bourgeoisie. In the analysis of the post-white settler colonial state, an attempt is made to distinguish, albeit broadly, between radical and reactionary nationalists with regard to the responses to both the white settler backlash and imperialist ploys. Because of the principal contradiction between imperialism and the mass of the people, the national question remains a central issue in any country such as Zimbabwe; and the characterisation of the class struggle in such societies will have to be undertaken within the context of the national question. This is particularly so because of the over-arch of imperialist hegemony which also affects the relationship between the state and social classes; and defines broadly, within a given historical epoch and for a given society or region, the parameters of political, economic and social action.

However, it behoves progressive intellectuals and political activists to identify, within the broad framework of the principal contradictions in our society, the possibilities for the development of a progressive development policy. The latter must seek to break (to 'de-link' as Samir Amin suggests[40]) with the structures of dependence and must rely on effective planning. It is a difficult and long-drawn task but one that has to be attempted, beginning with a clear perception of the causes of underdevelopment. As Samir Amin suggests in his repudiation of a unilinear view of society, socialism has to be planned for,[41] rather than developing countries having to wait, as Kitching suggests, for the arrival of fully-fledged capitalism and its 'sophisticated working class'.[42] Accordingly a start can be made:

> The perception of underdevelopment naturally shapes the strategies for its transcendence. At one level, there must be a development policy, which must be based, on another level, on a social structure capable of sustaining it. The policy must aim at achieving three objectives. First it must create a homogeneous national economy, progressively transferring the working population from low productivity, mainly agricultural, sectors into the high productivity sectors.
>
> Second, it must aim at the overall cohesion missing from the underdeveloped economy by deliberately creating integrated industrial groups made up of complementary activities. Third, it must aim at imparting to the economy its own 'dynamism', freeing it from dependence on the outside economy. On the technical level this strategy demands, according to Amin, the use of modern techniques for the immediate improvement of productivity and of the condition of the masses. This, he maintains, necessarily goes with the spread of 'specific forms of democracy' at every stage and at every level, village, region and state, making real development at once 'national socialist, and popular democratic.' The strategy also demands autonomous scientific and technological research in the Third World, an undertaking that precludes the imitation of the technology of developed countries and entails the use of rather elementary levels of technology. These objectives depend on effective planning for their realization, and effective planning itself depends on a break with the World market. 'The failure of planning in the Third World ..... is essentially due to (the) refusal to break with the World market.'[43]

This raises the question about the need to develop not only appropriate planning skills in the state sector but also the correct orientation—and political will—to plan for socialism.

But this ties up with the need to assess the political and ideological capacity for Zimbabwe to recover from the dominance of these imperialist forces. The book's conclusion is that both the nature of the colonial experience and the exigencies of the Southern African situation have contributed towards the development of an imperialist hegemony that has, over time, influenced both the formation and the conduct of classes among the African people. This has influenced the ideological outlook of a society which remains essentially capitalist.

It will be some time before the party that was so important during the liberation struggle can be transformed into one that can mobilise the people towards not only the long-term goal of socialism but also the urgent one of confronting the imperialist forces of international finance capital. These problems should be understood sympathetically in the light of a historical conjuncture within which these forces are still so dominant; and in the hope that the struggle in South Africa will soon throw up new opportunities for the struggle against neo-colonialism. As this book illustrates, Zimbabwe is pregnant with hope and potential.

REFERENCES

1. Selected texts by Cabral, Amilcar, Stage 1, London, 1969, pp. 56-57.
2. See, for example, Verrier, Anthony, *The Road to Zimbabwe, 1890-1980* Jonathan Cape, London, 1986; and Granada Television Series: on 'End of Empire: Rhodesia', London, 1985.
3. Penguin Books, Harmondsworth, 1978.
4. See, in particular Saul, John S. (ed), *A Difficult Road: The Transition to Socialism in Mozambique,* Monthly Review Press, New York, 1985; and also his earlier article, FRELIMO and the Mozambique Revolution, in Arrighi, Giovanni and Saul, John S. (eds), *Essays on the Political Economy of Africa,* Monthly Review Press, London, 1973, pp. 378-405.
5. Saul, John S., Zimbabwe: The Next Round. *Monthly Review,* Vol. 32 No. 4, September 1980, pp. 1-43; and Astrow, Andre, *Zimbabwe: A Revolution That Lost Its Way,* Zed Press, London, 1983.
6. Note, for example, *Monthly Review* (Vol. 37, No. 11, April 1986): not a single black South African in an issue that dealt with 'South Africa in struggle'.
7. Following on another (British) variant of it, 'Radical Africana' or *The Review of African Political Economy,* which has also assigned itself the honour of being the authority on African affairs.
8. See, for example, Saul, John S., *op. cit.,* 1973.
9. Saul, John S., *op. cit.,* 1985, p. 54.
10. *Ibid.,* p. 56.
11. This is the major thrust of his theory of the struggle in Southern Africa; but his latest work on Mozambique lays particularly emphasis on these dichotomies.
12. Saul, John, *op. cit.,* 1985, p. 51.
13. *Ibid.,* p. 53.
14. *Ibid.,* p. 13.
15. *Ibid.*
16. Depelchin, Jacques, From Lumumba to Mandela: Peoples' Struggles to Own their History, in Mandaza, Ibbo (ed), *Conflict in Southern Africa,* to be published in *Contemporary Marxism,* October 1986.
17. *Op. cit.,* 1985.
18. Hanlon, J., *Mozambique, Revolution Under Fire,* Zed Press, London, 1984.
19. Nkomati, Before and After, *The Journal of African Marxists,* 6, October 1984.
20. Depelchin, Jacques, *op. cit.*
21. Cited in Jonah, Kwesi, Imperialism, The State and the Indigenization of the Ghanian Economy, 1957-84, *Africa Development,* Vol. X,

No. 3, 1985, p. 64.
22. *Politics, Method and Evidence in the 'Kenya Debate' in Bernstein, Henry and Campbell, Bonnie K. (eds), Contradictions of Accumulation in Africa: Studies in Economy and State*, Sage Publications, London, 1985, pp. 115-152.
23. Kitching, Gavin, *op. cit.*, pp. 144-145.
24. *Ibid.*, p. 148.
25. *Ibid.*, pp. 143-144.
26. Mandaza, Ibbo, Southern Africa: US Policy and the Struggle for National Independence, in Magubane, Bernard and Mandaza, Ibbo (eds) *Whither South Africa?* (Papers Presented at a Seminar of the African Association of Political Science (AAPS) Southern Africa Region's Conference on *Whither South Africa?* Harare, March 1986), to be published Africa World Press, 1986. See also Mandaza, Ibbo, Conflict in Southern Africa, in Mandaza, Ibbo (ed), *Conflict in Southern Africa, Contemporary Marxism,* October 1986.
27. Progress Publishers, Moscow.
28. Reagan outlines Peace Plan for South Africa, USIS Special Report, 22 July 1986.
29. Cited in Mandaza, Ibbo, Southern Africa: US Policy, *op. cit.*
30. Speech by Dr. Julius K. Nyerere at University of Zimbabwe, Harare, 7 June 1986.
31. See note 26 above.
32. Lenin, V.I., *The State: A Lecture Delivered at the Sverdlov University, July 11, 1919,* Foreign Languages Press, Peking, 1973, p. 14.
33. Alavi, Hamza, The State in Post-Colonial Societies: Pakistan and Bangladesh, in *New Left Review,* 74, (July-August 1972), pp. 59-81.
34. Von Freyhold, Michaela, The Post-Colonial State and its Tanzanian Version: Contribution to a Debate, in Othman, Haroub, *The State in Tanzania: Who controls it and whose interest does it serve?*, Dar es Salaam University Press, Dar es Salaam, 1980, p. 88.
35. Tandon, Yash, The Post-Colonial State, *Social Change and Development,* No. 8, 1984, pp. 2-4.
36. Von Freyhold, Michaela, *op. cit.*, p. 100.
37. Mkandawire, Thandika, State Policy Responses to Economic Crisis in Africa, *Eastern Africa Social Science Research Review,* Vol. 1, No. 2, June 1985, pp. 31-51.
38. Von Freyhold, Michaela, *op. cit.*, p. 87.
39. Ibbo, Mandaza, Southern Africa: US Policy *op. cit.*
40. See Folson, Kweku G., Samir Amin as a Neo-Marxist, *Africa Development,* Vol. X, No. 3, 1985, pp. 112-135.
41. *Ibid.*
42. See note 24 above.
43. Folson, Kweku G., *op. cit.*, pp. 122-123.

1. THE STATE IN POST-WHITE SETTLER COLONIAL SITUATION
Ibbo Mandaza

Historical Background: the Road to Lancaster House

The history of white settler colonialism is now so well documented that it leaves us to make only a summary of its main elements, keeping in mind the need to emphasise the historical and economic linkage between this social formation and its source, imperialism. For, in examining the nature of imperialist domination in Southern Africa, it is important to underline the relationship between it and the development in the sub-region—particularly in Namibia, South Africa and Zimbabwe—of the historical phenomenon of white settler colonialism. In turn, this might be described as a particular expression of imperialist domination or as colonialism *par excellence*.[1]

The main distinguishing features—as compared, for example, with colonialism elsewhere in Africa—may be briefly divided into three broad categories. First, the historical development of the Southern African sub-region as we know it today, in the definition of which South Africa in particular became and has remained the fulcrum, will be examined. It is on this basis that imperialist operations in this part of the world have been largely centred. The origins of this sub-regional configuration are to be found in European expansion from the fifteenth century onwards, as this southern part of the earth became a vital strategic centre on the route to India and to the rest of the Asian and Far Eastern subcontinents. Accordingly, Southern Africa in general, and South Africa in particular, featured prominently in this and other respects throughout the three successive stages of capitalist imperialism—mercantile imperialism, free trade imperialism and modern monopoly imperialism. All these cover the modern history of Southern Africa, from 1652—when the first Europeans arrived at the Cape—to the present.

The era of modern monopoly imperialism coincided with the discovery in the late nineteenth century of such vital minerals as gold and diamonds. These discoveries would partly influence the pace of developments in South Africa itself and throughout the Southern African sub-region. It was this era that saw the partitioning of Africa at the Berlin Conference of 1884/85; and prompted Cecil John Rhodes and his fellow-imperialists to begin to plot the 'Cape to Cairo' road as part and parcel of the British colonisation process in Southern Africa and beyond. Significantly, it was along this road, and in the quest for minerals, land and labour, that Zimbabwe would be colonised into Southern Rhodesia in 1890.

The rest is well known and may be summarised as follows.

(a) The character of the colonisation process, in the circumstances of the determined and aggressive group of colonialists against African resistance, was bloody, rapid and almost total in its impact on the entire colony.

b) White settler colonialism pre-empted the development of an African bourgeoisie of any significance, and determined that even the African petit bourgeoisie would be weak. It consisted mainly of the educated elements. White settler colonialism disorganised and rendered incoherent the African wage-earning class, and caused the most serious impoverishment and proletarianisation of the peasantry. White settler colonialism was almost complete in its domination: political, economic, social and cultural.

(c) A formidable white settler state arose, partly as a result of the large concentration of white settlers who were keen to safeguard and maintain their economic, political, and social privileges against the growing demands of the African people, and partly as an outcome of the overt and covert support that it continued to receive from Britain and, in late years, directly from South Africa. Through the racial ideology of white supremacy, the white settler colonial state successfully mobilised all the whites—the bourgeoisie, the petit bourgeoisie, the working class and the so-called 'poor whites'—behind it; and all whites in general assisted in the fulfilment of the functions of the white settler colonial state.

(d) The nature and complexity of the colonial situation gave rise to new class forces within the colonised society; and, because of the dominance of the capitalist mode of production in such a society, a capitalist ideological framework developed which pervaded the entire fabric of colonial society, through the economic, political and social structures that emerged in the process of colonisation. More specifically, liberalism (as part of the capitalist ideology) was imparted into the colonised through the colonialist educational system, the Christian religion and various other forms of the cultural and ideological expression of colonial life. Furthermore, liberalism tended to become a counterpoint to white settler colonialism and its brand of racism, and created thereby a false dichotomy, in the minds of the colonised, between white settlers on the one hand and on the other the British Colonial Office, which was regarded as the 'protector' of African interests when in fact it was in collusion with white settler colonialism.[2]

(e) It is in this context that African nationalism arises, both as opposition to a colonialism that frustrates the class aspirations of the colonised in this new situation's and as an expression of liberal ideology that is itself part of the capitalist ideology and therefore facilitates the hegemonisation of the African classes under capitalism. The point is that African nationalism *competes* with white settlerism for political and economic power but does not necessarily challenge the unequal and exploitative structures of that capitalist society. Thus even the colonised would find themselves, in different ways and in a variety of situations, having to aid the colonial system, though colonialism was inherently contradictory to their well-being.

(f) Given the capitalist nature of the socio-economic terrain in which it develops, African nationalism is, contrary to its declared aim of *nation-building* and *national unity*, potentially given to divisiveness and rivalry, particularly within the ranks of the African petit bourgeoisie. Factions and fractions within the colonised classes have their origins in the nature of colonialism itself, particularly its differential impact and the resultant uneven and unequal development of capitalism in the country. But African nationalism itself is an expression of class interests, only appearing to conceal the aspirations of the various fraction and factions within the African petit bourgeois class. Initially, the African petit bourgeoisie competes with the white settlers for political and economic power; later, in the post-colonial stage, the competition and rivalry afflicts the African petit bourgeoisie itself, as each faction and fraction makes its bid for the 'fruits of independence', for 'development' of its area, for power and influence—but all, invariably, in the name of 'tribe', 'region', colour, ethnic grouping or other 'historical' claim. But since the 'fruits of independence'—and economic capacity of a neo-colony—are inherently limited and distorted, factionalism and rivalry among the African petit bourgeoisie can become so serious as to threaten not only *national unity* but even the post-colonial state. A major preoccupation of the leadership becomes that of trying to reunite and unite all these groups of the African petit bourgeoisie around the post-colonial state as further reinforcement against the threat of the oppressed and exploited classes.

The important point to emphasise here is that of the relation and balance of forces between a white settler colonialism which is strong and supported by imperialism on the one hand and, on the other, the nature of the African resistance that grows only slowly and, because of the immense strength of the joint forces of white settler colonialism and imperialism, does not fully develop into the kind of force that will in the end dismantle the white settler colonial state and immediately begin to establish new socio-economic structures. It is an African nationalist movement that develops against the background of British paternalism and liberalism, for a long time able neither to recognise the umbilical relationship between imperialism and white settler colonialism nor to develop a political and ideological framework within which to forestall neo-colonialism.

Even the struggle for national independence was under the cloud of imperialist hegemony, reinforced in the belief—and practice—of the African nationalists that imperialism could be an arbitrator in a racial conflict. It was a situation that for a time allowed the white settlers and their imperialist supporters to be disdainful of African resistance; a disdain expressed at first in the belief that a 'settlement' could be obtained on white settler terms; and later in the quest for a compromise within which the interests of the whites could be accommodated and guaranteed by imperialism.

This is the broad outline of the long road to the Lancaster House Agreement of 1979. But it may be useful to reveal the full extent of British complicity in the UDI affair, if only to underline the element of continuity in a policy that has always regarded Zimbabwe as Britain's special area of influence. This is followed by a brief analysis of the armed struggle in the context of African nationalism.

Imperialist Objectives and UDI

The demise of colonialism—including white settler colonialism—may have been accepted as a fact by the British government ever since Prime Minister Harold MacMillan's 'winds of change' speech of 3 February 1960. But the apparent failure to conclude a decolonisation programme in Zimbabwe at a time, the 1960s, when most African countries had undergone this as a matter of course suggests, perhaps, that the British regarded Southern Rhodesia as some kind of exception to this trend. Others might argue that, in the face of an intransigent white settler colonial state that was in turn backed by a powerful South Africa, there was nothing that Britain could do in either forestalling UDI or suppressing it in the interests and pursuit of black majority rule in Zimbabwe. There was also the 'kith and kin' consideration which, according to many, will have constituted an important restraint to any British government intent on military intervention following UDI in 1965. Yet all these arguments are not exclusive of, nor contradictory to, the belief later to be enshrined in US policy documents that the white factor was an indispensable and integral component of any political settlement in Zimbabwe. For the US, certainly, its policy in Southern Africa was based on the premise that:

> The whites are here to stay (in Southern Africa) and the only way that constructive change can come about is through them. There is no hope for the blacks to gain the political rights they seek through violence, which only leads to chaos and increased opportunities for the communists. We can, by selective relaxation of our stance toward the white regimes, encourage some modification of their current racial and colonial policies and through more substantial economic assistance to the black states (a total of about $5 million annually in technical assistance to the black states) help to draw the two groups together and exert some influence on both for peaceful change.
>
> Our tangible interests form a basis for our contacts in the region, and these can be maintained at an acceptable political cost.[3]

With but a few modifications forced by the advance of the national liberation struggle in Southern Africa, there would be an interesting correlation between this policy statement in 1969 and the Lancaster House Agreement in 1979. It might at one level perhaps reveal the coincidence of views on the sub-region between the British and US imperialists in later years or reflect, as we shall see shortly, the US dominance in the resolution of the Zimbabwe problem itself. But in the 1960s the British policy on Zimbabwe would appear retrospectively to have been tantamount to an acceptance that Rhodesia was a white man's country. For, even before UDI, and notably since Southern Rhodesia was accorded 'self-governing' status in 1923, the British tended to endorse the belief that Southern Rhodesia was to be a dominion, like Canada or Australia.

The experience of the abortive Federation of Rhodesia and Nyasaland might have forced upon them the realisation that majority rule was inevitable, even in Southern Africa. Hence their own policy of *No Independence Before Majority Rule* (NIBMAR), a policy which nevertheless appeared no more than political rhetoric as the British still hoped that Southern Rhodesia might still have a political future quite different from that which Zambia and Malawi would attain in 1964. To quote Commonwealth Relations Secretary Duncan Sandys, speaking in the House of Commons on 15 November 1963, just as the Federation of Rhodesia and Nyasaland was about to be dissolved:

> Southern Rhodesia, we must remember, has for over forty years enjoyed complete internal self-government. Up to the creation of the Federation she was responsible for her own defence and was represented by a High Commissioner in London. I hope that those outside who always tell us we ought to interfere and do this or that in Southern Rhodesia will realise there is not a single official or soldier in Southern Rhodesia responsible to the British Government. We have long ago accepted the principle that Parliament at Westminister does not legislate for Southern Rhodesia except at its request.[4]

As has now been adequately documented,[5] UDI would come in the strength of such thinly veiled imperial assurances. Besides, thanks partly to British connivance in the dissolution of the Federation in 1963, Southern Rhodesia found itself stronger economically and militarily than Northern Rhodesia and Nyasaland—Zambia and Malawi respectively. The federal period had been largely to the economic advantage of Southern Rhodesia; and as an important rear base for the Zimbabwean nationalists in later years, Zambia was to find herself particularly vulnerable to the Smith regime, economically and militarily. For Britain's division of the Federation's military spoils—particularly the air force—also left Southern Rhodesia with the resources that contributed significantly to the further development of a powerful military, police, state security and public service infrastructure. This was mobilised under the white settler ideology into a formidable defence of the white settler colonial state, frustrating the efforts of the African nationalists throughout most of the 1960s and even in the period leading to the Lancaster House Conference. It would in the late 1970s even threaten the frontline states that were the rear bases of the Zimbabwe liberation movement. The Rhodesia Security Forces, (RSF)—notably the Rhodesia Air Force, which succeeded the Royal Rhodesia Air Force—had developed and grown out of the strong links with Britain in the period up to UDI. The white settler colonial state would find unflinching support from the South African state throughout the UDI period and the Rhodesians were able to obtain much of their arms through 'an international network of arms merchants and sanctions busters.'[6]

It was naive, therefore, to expect that Britain in particular would intervene to crush the UDI rebellion. On the contrary, a recent account[7] of this period reveals that Britain encouraged the act of UDI, that the British government did not seriously consider the question of suppressing the rebellion and that even if they had, the kith and kin factor would have made it difficult to sell to the British public the idea of a military intervention against forces which were mostly white; that the British government knew, at UDI, that oil refinery capacity at Beira had been increased as part of the plan to subvert sanctions and that as long as there were to be no sanctions against South Africa itself, the British call for sanctions was a mere face-saving act;[8] and that the British government increasingly hoped that UDI would in time become a *fait accompli*. There were even plans for the British government to intervene in the interests of the white settlers should the African response to UDI pose a security threat.

> The British Chiefs of Staff forwarded a Joint Planning Staff appreciation to the Cabinet on the eve of Federation's break-up ...which, in circumlocutory language, argued that although contingency plans for assisting in the restoration of order in Southern Rhodesia *at the request of a Government in Salisbury* should be revised, no plan would be prepared for the deterrence or containment of a unilateral declaration of independence. Doubtless, the Chiefs were influenced by Butler's [British Secretary of State for Central Africa] 'secret and personal message' to Field (the Rhodesia Front Prime Minister who was succeeded by Ian Smith) of 20 April 1963 (the substance of which would have been conveyed to Lord Mountbatten as Chief of the Defence Staff) which [stated]: 'In my letter of 9 April, I affirmed the Government's acceptance in principle that Southern Rhodesia will proceed through the normal processes to independence'. So far as military appreciations were concerned, it was the fact, not the nature of independence or the means by which it was achieved which mattered (original emphasis).[9]

In retrospect, therefore, UDI was not such a rebellion after all. Ian Smith would conclude his UDI speech with the words 'God Save the Queen'.[10] It was a British-Rhodesian conspiracy against the African people, particularly at a time when, due to the influence of the imperialist ideology of decolonisation, the African nationalist leadership regarded the British government as one to be trusted in the policy of 'paramountcy of African interests' *vis-à-vis* those of the white settlers. On the contrary:

> Butler, in effect, not only ditched Britain's chances of honouring its obligations regarding paramountcy; in handing over the

RRAF to Field and his successors, he also provided the Rhodesian Security Forces with their most valuable asset (mobility) for fighting the liberation war. One of Butler's advisers subsequently remarked: 'The Royal Rhodesia Air Force was seen as a white bastion on the Zambezi rather than the Limpopo.' Eventually, however, it was from South of the Limpopo that the rebel Rhodesia Air Force was to draw its strength, indeed its very means of existence.[11]

Of course, Britain might have considered at the dissolution of the Federation the possibility of conceding black majority rule, but on condition that the new black government would safeguard the overall strategic and economic interests of Britain and her allies, certainly not excluding strong constitutional (and other) guarantees for the whites.

In fact, this had been the purpose of the 1961 constitutional provisions, the *Tiger* and *Fearless* proposals of December 1966 and October 1968 respectively; and both the Pearce proposals of 1972 and even the Lancaster House proposals of 1979, all of which were intended as a 'whitewash' of black majority rule. But some analysts[12] have argued that, from the British point of view, there was neither a nationalist movement nor a leader to whom they would entrust such responsibilities in the 1960s. There was even the fear that the rivalry between ZAPU and ZANU might, in the event of majority rule, flare up into the kind of chaos that would not only jeopardise these economic and strategic interests but also endanger the security of the white population.

The point, therefore, was not so much about the availability of a good and strong African nationalist leadership to whom to hand over political independence: Malawi, Zambia and other former colonies had been accorded self-determination with far fewer credentials than the Zimbabwean nationalists had in the 1960s. It was more that the British still believed that the white settlers could pull off a white dominion and, given the abject dependence of the African nationalists on a British initiative to bring about black majority rule, they were then quite confident that there would be no real challenge to the white settler colonial state.

In fact, it is fair to conclude that were it not for the international uproar at the time, Britain might have treated UDI as a *fait accompli*. If this is so, then *all* the various attempts at a constitutional settlement of the Zimbabwe problem should be viewed as either, at worst, a British face-saving response to such international pressure as was vociferous against UDI: or, at best, a desire by the British and the US to find, particularly as the guerrilla war developed, a compromise that would safeguard both imperialist interests and the security of whites. At any rate, the British position—both towards and in the aftermath of UDI—only strengthened the white resolve in Rhodesia. So confident and arrogant was Ian Smith that he would declare, following the abortive *Fearless* talks in October 1968:

> There will be no majority rule in my life-time—or in my children's.[13]

Thus, in his view, the new Rhodesia constitution of 1969 was a 'world beater'; it 'sounded the death knell of the notion of majority rule' and 'would entrench government in the hands of civilised Rhodesians for all time'.[14] When the Pearce Commission of 1972 had revealed that 'African apathy' to UDI was only apparent and even when, in the late 1970s, it was evident that black majority rule was in sight, Smith would state in March 1976, following the breakdown of his talks with Joshua Nkomo:

> But I don't believe in majority rule, black majority rule, ever in Rhodesia, not in a thousand years.[15]

It is true that the nature of the white settler ideology gave rise to an acute sense of white solidarity among all the white classes in Rhodesia, developed in the conviction that white power was not only right and defensible but also therefore representative of, if not synonymous with, all the positive features of 'Western Christian Civilisation' in Africa. But imperialist policy also helped to reinforce these views and further enhanced this sense of false confidence. Doubtless the demise of the Smith regime was delayed by the extent to which the Zimbabwean question became, particularly in the period following the collapse of Portuguese colonialism in Mozambique and Angola, increasingly entwined with US (and British) policy in South Africa in particular and Southern Africa in general. As will be illustrated shortly in the next section of this chapter, these policy considerations would colour the Lancaster House Agreement and ensure that Ian Smith and his henchmen would have another lease of life in an independent Zimbabwe.

The Armed Struggle

The period leading to the Lancaster House Conference represented an important turning-point in the history of Southern Africa. The Portuguese coup of 25 May 1974 is therefore viewed as synonymous with the first visible signs of the demise of white settler colonialism in Southern Africa. Yet only those blind to the laws of historical development could have failed to recognise that white settler colonialism had begun to die right at its very inception in the nature of the antagonistic contradiction between the coloniser and the colonised. The demise of the Portugese empire was only one result of the process of resolving that contradiction. Through the armed struggle, Africans in Southern Africa would prove false the imperialist and white settlers' dream, shattering thereby the liberal view that conflict in Southern Africa could be resolved peacefully.

It is, perhaps, premature for a comprehensive analysis of the Zimbabwean liberation struggle, a history that should lay bare the class composition of the liberation movement and reveal the nature of its ideological and political development. There is, of course, general agreement on how the struggle for Zimbabwe developed, from the inception of white settler colonialism to the attainment of national independence: the primary resistance of the 1890s; the pressure group lobbies in the 1920s and 1930s;

the early but not fully-fledged nationalist expressions of the 1940s; the 'partnership' (with white liberals) politics of the 1950s (and for some Africans, even into the 1960s and 1970s, as they joined such liberal-type white settler political parties as the United Federal Party, Central Africa Party, Centre Party, Rhodesia Party etc.); conventional nationalism that began with the African National Congress (1957-1959), the National Democratic Party (1960-1961), the earlier (before the ZANU break-way) Zimbabwe African People's Union (1961-1962), and ZAPU and ZANU from 1963 onwards; and then, within the history of the latter movements, the first stage of revolutionary nationalism, beginning with ZANU's decision, in 1963, on a policy of 'confrontation'[16] and continuing into the 1970s when ZANLA and ZIPRA broadly represented the most militant expressions of the two movements that would lead Zimbabwe to national independence.

Initially reformist in character, the nationalist movement developed a radical nationalism that sought to overthrow white settler colonialism and thereby win national independence. It was a process through which many a moderate and reformist nationalist would fall by the wayside, ensuring that only those leaders who had remained true to this radical nationalism would emerge the winners with independence in 1980. It was this militancy, this belief that only through armed struggle could independence be won, that mobilised the Zimbabwean masses into the motive force of the struggle itself. In turn, it was the certainty of the demise of the colonial system that gave momentum to the struggle: the visible testimony of an African people now armed with the latest weaponry and for the first time maintaining an offensive against an enemy that had hitherto appeared invincible; the complete loss of faith in the colonial system (of limited material benefits) as thousands of youngsters fled into ranks of the liberation forces; the relentless determination of the latter to continue the struggle, even at a time when a large section of the leadership were keen to settle for compromises following the detente exercise of the mid-1970s; and the virtual 'people's war' as the relationship between the guerrillas and the mass of the peasantry was almost synonymous with that of 'fish in water'.

Yet there is no historical evidence to suggest, as others have been keen to extrapolate from this momentous process of the liberation struggle, that this armed struggle encompassed within it even the idea of a socialist revolution. It is true that it had by the late 1970s transcended in some respects the earlier strategy and tactics of the 1960s which saw violence as merely the means to pressure Britain into an intervention that would bring independence sooner rather than later. But the armed struggle was, at best, viewed as a means to dismantle the white settler colonial system and replace it with an African government and, at worst, as a pronounced way of pressurising the imperialists into convening a conference that would bring about an African government in Zimbabwe. National independence was the central goal; the methods whereby to attain it were, of course, important but could be either justified or condemned in the light of whether or not this central goal was attained. It is significant, therefore, that the editors (or publishers) of *Our War of Liberation*[17] should have used this lead quotation from Robert Gabriel Mugabe as a correct reflection of the main objective of the national liberation struggle:

> The first object of our armed struggle is the attainment of total and unfettered independence so we can rule ourselves as we deem fit and develop our country in the general interests of the masses. This means we completely reject and would never entertain any mission whatsoever which seeks to preserve the interests or privileges of a minority as this vitiates the principle of total independence and derogates upon the sovereignty of the people of Zimbabwe.[18]

To suggest, however, that the armed struggle had a socialist thrust as its inspiration would be to overlook not only the serious ideological deficiencies of the nationalist movement but also its limited military and political capacity when it came to dealing with the full weight of joint white settler and imperialist intrigue at the Lancaster House Conference.

For a socialist thrust would have required a clearly articulated ideology that would fully explain the historical reality of imperialism; reveal the class structure of the liberation movement; and constitute the basis for a vanguard party that would in turn inform, teach, guide and translate the political gains of national independence into an onward movement towards socialist construction. It would have required not only an acceptance that the masses—the peasants and workers—are the basis for such momentous processes of transformation, but also seeking to conscientise and mobilise them towards the socialist goal.

This may smack of a degree of historical determinism and voluntarism and yet it is difficult to understand how, in the context of the historical evidence before us, it should have been expected that an essentially nationalist movement could have developed a revolutionary capacity that would overthrow both white settlerism and imperialist hegemony.

On the contrary the national movement of Zimbabwe reflects, in its development and expression, the features of a society paternalised by Western imperialism and therefore disinclined towards socialism. Thus one of the founders of modern Zimbabwean nationalism wrote:

> Africa as a whole seems well fortified against communism since both the European powers and the African people have been conditioned against it. Africa as a whole has been predominantly westernized economically, politically, socially, ideologically, and educationally. Practically all highly educated Africans have been Western-educated. The Russianization of Africa is a possibility immediate or remote, but not a fact, whereas the Westernization of Africa is an accomplished fact that has historical roots. Even at present thousands of African students being educated overseas are in British, West European, and American colleges. Millions of Africans speak English, French, Portuguese, and Spanish, but we have not met one who speaks

> Russian. What we are trying to say here is that there is already a common ground between the West and Africa, and this common ground is based on practical interests, and this is why we believe that if the African people ceased to be treated like strangers in the land of their birth, a genuine understanding between black and white would develop and this in turn would strengthen the anti-communist forces.[19]

Ndabaningi Sithole's words in 1959 might today be rejected as being the less important in his treatise. But in essence, these views were shared by the average member of the African petit bourgeoisie throughout the period of the armed struggle; and continue to pervade the society in this post-white settler colonial phase. Even among the guerrillas themselves, there is evidence less of Marxist ideological fervour than of adherence to traditional and supernatural beliefs.[20] Thus, the forerunners and symbols—e.g. *Mbuya* Nehanda, *Sekuru* Kaguvi, Chaminuka, etc.—of the Zimbabwean struggle against white settler colonialism became, in ZANU, the virtual spiritual inspiration (nay even a deity) towards bravery and relentless determination in the minds and hearts of guerrillas.

Similarly in ZAPU, the feudal legacy of a Ndebele kingdom, intense loyalty to the symbol (Joshua Nkomo) of that heritage, and even the (conscious and subconscious) myth of cultural and ethnic superiority over other African groups: all played a much more important role than ideological commitment to Marxism in the development of the struggle.

The fact that many of the ZAPU cadres would be trained in socialist countries had little impact on this trend; nor is there evidence of a systematic correlation within the entire Zimbabwean national liberation movement between such exposure to socialist society and a commensurate theory and practice of socialist revolution. In the end, the latter was of less importance than the military technology and skills that Zimbabweans would learn from our allies of the socialist bloc.

Within the perspective of a romantic perception of revolutionary nationalism,[21] there had been the view that the Zimbabwe People's Army (ZIPA) reflected and represented the arrival of that phase of the liberation struggle that would lead Zimbabwe simultaneously to national independence and socialist revolution. Formed in late 1975 at the instigation of the frontline states (namely Nyerere and Machel), ZIPA was led by a War Council consisting of nine members each from ZANU and ZAPU. In that lay the hope that the Zimbabwean national liberation movement had now shed and transcended the worst of its defects: factionalism and regionalism, reformist and opportunist politics of the conventional nationalist leadership. ZIPA had been formed against the background of notable successes in the revolutionary struggle of the peoples of the Third World, particularly that of Vietnam in South East Asia and of the former Portuguese colonies in Africa. Around these experiences had developed the idea of the protracted struggle as it was first experienced in South East Asia, with the thoughts of Mao Tse Tung and Ho Chi Minh providing a ready testimony to the infallibility of this theory and practice of revolution.

The Zimbabwean national movement was gradually exposed to these developments; and the intellectuals and academicians—not to exclude even the military strategists—sought to translate them into the Zimbabwean experience. There developed almost a new paradigm in Zimbabwean liberation politics, the articulation of an anti-imperialist ideology, populist media that daily churned out the new message of revolution through the *Zimbabwe News* of ZANU and *Zimbabwe Review* of ZAPU and through the radio, on Radio Maputo, Radio Zambia and Radio Tanzania. Indeed Marxism-Leninism had, in the course of the struggle, become known in the Zimbabwean situation, even if it would be some time before it would sink its roots in the society.

Both this new trend and the writings of romantic (but radical) analysts within the developed countries of Europe and North America helped to develop a mythology about the Zimbabwean liberation struggle, a mythology which was useful in mobilising support for the struggle at home and abroad, but which nevertheless pitched the aims and objectives of the armed struggle over and above those of attaining national independence.

It is, perhaps, too early to undertake a comprehensive analysis of the short-lived history of ZIPA. But it was short-lived against the main current of African nationalist politics; and there is no evidence to suggest that it had itself fully transcended the mainstream of conventional African nationalism, nor evidence of a clearly defined agenda for the transformation of Zimbabwean society towards socialism. ZIPA had hoped to transcend the established nationalist leadership which it viewed as 'opportunists and the defenders of monopoly capitalism',[22] and some of its membership showed a determination to resist the neo-colonial objectives of the Anglo-American proposals that came with the Geneva Conference of 1976. But it was precisely on the basis of this position that ZIPA ran foul of both the established nationalist leadership and the frontline states. It appeared inconceivable in those days—as it does now—that a guerrilla force could act independently of the nationalist leadership,[23] and even doubtful that it could have the political legitimacy—especially within Zimbabwe itself—with which to supplant the authority of that established nationalist leadership. Even before ZIPA saw its final demise in 1977, the ZAPU component of it had already broken off, following ZANLA-ZIPRA clashes in the camps in Tanzania.

The clashes had been sparked by differences in military tactics and strategy between ZIPRA and ZANLA; but also over the question of what attitude ZIPA should adopt towards the established leadership.

> Mangena (of ZAPU) explained that whereas his contingent in ZIPA had always remained loyal to ZAPU and its leadership, there were ex-ZANLA guerrillas who saw ZIPA as an independent military and political force.[24]

It should be recalled, however, that ZIPA had been created by the frontline states as a military force that would make good the losses suffered through the impact of the *detente* exercise of 1974-1975; and thereby ensure that a negotiated settlement—which they saw as inevitable—would find the Zimbabwe nationalist movement in a better stead than that in which it found itself in 1975. But they had never intended that ZIPA should necessarily overtake the established African nationalists, less still develop a stance that appeared to challenge the formula of a negotiated settlement, especially when the latter offered as good prospects as any for majority rule. Both within the African nationalist leadership of Zimbabwe and within the governments of the frontline states and the Organisation of African Unity (OAU), armed struggle was viewed primarily as a means of putting pressure on the white settlers and imperialism to negotiate. Guerrillas would be the main force in this process but they would fight under party leadership. With the demise of ZIPA, therefore, the frontline states formed, on 9 October 1978, the Patriotic Front (of ZANU and ZAPU) in another bid to create a united force that would minimise any imperialist or white settlerist attempts to divided the nationalist movement as it pushed towards final victory.

Of course, all this reveals and exposes the weakness of the Zimbabwean national liberation movement on the eve of the Lancaster House Agreement; a political, ideological and military weakness only disguised by the fact that white settlerism and imperialism decided to negotiate before any further strengthening and radicalisation of the liberation struggle. It was a weakness which allowed for the paternalism of the frontline states; and would also determine the character of both the Lancaster House Agreement itself and the parameters of political, economic and social action in the period following the attainment of national independence in April 1980. Besides, the Lancaster House Conference would be convened at a time when the Patriotic Front had not only scored significant victories on the battlefield but also mobilised moral, diplomatic and humanitarian support for their cause throughout the world, and in thereby isolating the white settler regime and its 'internal settlement' projected the Patriotic Front as the legitimate force representing the masses of Zimbabwe. Efforts were already underway to institutionalise and transform the guerrilla movement in to a 'respectable and responsible'[25] government-to-be:

> Rejecting the claim made by RF Minister van der Byl that majority rule would amount to unconditional surrender and produce a Marxist-backed state, Senator George McGovern said 'if the Russians come out against small pox, that's no reason we have to be for small pox in order to show that we are patriotic Americans'. Such pragmatic support for majority rule was the first step necessary for creating an 'orderly transition' to African rule[26]

The Lancaster House Agreement
Viewed retrospectively in terms of previous attempts at a settlement of the Zimbabwe problem, there was nothing essentially new in the Lancaster

House Conference proposals. As has already been outlined elsewhere,[27] Britain's objective was to resolve the problem through constitutional arrangements designed to strike a compromise between white settler colonialists and African nationalists. This conformed to both British and US imperialist interests and remained a constant feature in the policy on Zimbabwe, from the first London 'Constitutional Conference on Southern Rhodesia' in 1961 to the London 'Constitutional Conference on Rhodesia' in 1979. Thus this decolonisation strategy involved a significant departure from the conventional neo-colonialist one that involved the handover of political power to an African nationalist leadership, with few or no political guarantees for the former white settler elements. The 'constitutional safeguards' for the white settler element in Zimbabwe were to be an integral factor in all the attempts at a settlement of the Zimbabwe problem.

African nationalists would, throughout the UDI period, draw much comfort from the British commitment to NIBMAR. For them, it was almost a guarantee that the British would not 'sell out' the black majority to the white minority. Yet these principles said more about the priority that Britain placed on the white minority, a sad reflection on the weakness of the African nationalists *vis-à-vis* the strength of the white settler element. The 'six principles' which the British coined in 1966 typify the evolutionary perspective that guided the British attitude to African political development. The six principles argued for:

1. Unimpeded progress to majority rule to be maintained and guaranteed.
2. Guarantees against retrogressive amendment of the constitution.
3. Immediate improvement in the political status of the Africans.
4. Progress towards ending racial discrimination.
5. Any basis proposed for independence must be acceptable to the people of Rhodesia as a whole.
6. Regardless of race, no oppression of the majority by the minority or of the minority by the majority.[28]

As we would point out, even before the Lancaster House Conference of 1979, the 'constitutional safeguards' for the white settlers were synonymous with a neo-colonial plan for Zimbabwe:

(a) the retention of white settler economic power as a safeguard for the continued efficient exploitation of material and human resources;
(b) consequently, retention of such military (i.e. a significant component of the white settler army and police and administrative, technical and managerial staff) machinery as would inspire the 'confidence' and 'maintain the high standards' of both the white settler element itself and the imperialist world as a whole.[29]

Some African nationalists almost reached a deal based on this formula.

For example, during his abortive negotiations with Ian Smith in December 1975 to February 1976, Joshua Nkomo

> had proposed a transitional period of two or three years, during which a 'government of National Unity' would prepare for elections. Black voters would elect the majority of MPs, but with an entrenched bloc of white seats, and other guarantees. When this failed, Nkomo made a last offer—one that only Smith could refuse. The formula called for political control by Africans within a twelve month transitional period but with 36 black and 36 white voting contituencies, plus a further 72 seats to be contested on a qualified voting franchise such that 50 would be in black hands. The intransigence of the RF which was still thinking in terms of majority rule within about 15 years, forced Nkomo to temporarily abandon his efforts...[30]

The Kissinger proposals (or the Anglo-American proposals), which became the subject of the Geneva Conference of 1976, suggested a structure for a transitional government: a Council of State with a white chairman and comprising as many whites as blacks; and a Council of Ministers with a black Prime Minister and a majority of black ministers. But the whites would retain control of 'law and order'; sanctions were to be lifted and a huge Zimbabwe Development Fund (ZDF) was to be established by the British and US governments.[31] It has been argued that the Geneva Conference foundered on the question of elections, Robert Mugabe (and ZANU) arguing that there should be no need for elections as part of the independence process 'because power should automatically pass to the national liberation forces'; and Joshua Nkomo (and ZAPU) agreeing to the idea of elections.[32]

Equally true, however, was that the Ian Smith regime had not as yet seen the need for compromise. If anything, the regime viewed the Anglo-American proposals as a time-buying opportunity, one that would place them 'in a better position to fight the war than at present.'[33] With minor modifications, the Anglo-American proposals would constitute the framework for the British-US imperialist initiative: from the US-British diplomatic offensive of September 1977, to the Malta talks of January 1978, the Anglo-American meeting with the Patriotic Front in Dar es Salaam in April 1978 and finally the Lancaster House Conference in September 1979. The major objectives remained the same: a transitional government (under a British 'resident commissioner') that would ensure the development of a stable govenment while real power would continue to be held in the hands of the whites. Thus, for example, the Anglo-American proposals of September 1977 sought to ensure that African politicians were to be 'tried out' while whites controlled state power. The proposals also included a Bill of Rights and sought to reinforce and maintain the socio-economic *status quo* in post-independence Zimbabwe:

> Protection from deprivation of property: this will confer protection from expropriation of property except on specified

grounds of public interest and even then only on condition that there is prompt payment of adequate compensation... and that the compensation may be remitted abroad within a reasonable period.[34]

The Malta talks of January 1978 included the idea of 'free elections' under 'impartial supervision'; and an advisory Governing Council that would include the British High Commissioner, a UN representative and two members each from the RF, UANC, ZANU (Sithole), ZAPU and ZANU.[35] Refusing to be in a minority of four to eight overall or four to six against the parties of the internal settlement talks, the Patriotic Front insisted that it should constitute the bulk of the security forces during the transition period.[36] Britain and the US refused[37] to concede on an issue which as, will be seen in the Lancaster House Agreement, would be so vital in the kind of post-colonial situation that imperialism was designing for Zimbabwe.

In Dar es Salaam in April 1978, the Patriotic Front agreed to the principles of according full executive authority for defence and for law and order to the British Resident Commissioner, and to a UN 'peacekeeping force' to ensure 'free and fair elections'. There remained disagreements as to the details and mechanics of the transition period.[38] In any case the basis for a settlement that would emerge at Lancaster was now on the table. A number of events between 1978 and 1980 would make this outcome appear inevitable. We must consider all these forces in the context of the relation of forces during this period; i.e. there were the interests of imperialism, of white settlers, of the national liberation movement and of the frontline states.

By 1978, the war had so escalated that Smith found himself increasingly compelled to find refuge in the Anglo-American initiatives and their proposals. The idea of a transitional government attracted him as a basis for buying time. But he would seek to forestall a Patriotic Front government by making a deal with the internal African leaders. The latter had, in turn, so isolated themselves from the guerrillas that they had no choice but to accept Smith's offer of an 'internal settlement' on 3 March 1978, in the vain hope that they could thereby inherit full power from Smith and prevent the Patriotic Front from ever winning power. The 'internal settlement' failed also because it did not have the support of the mass of the people of Zimbabwe. It would be denied full international recognition, as long as the Patriotic Front remained united in their claim to be the legitimate representatives of the Zimbabwe masses, and as long as they showed the capacity to maintain the war initiative. The 'internal settlement' leaders were doomed.

Yet, in retrospect, the Patriotic Front was shaken by both the occasion of the 'internal settlement' (and the establishment of its Zimbabwe-Rhodesia), and at the threat that Britain and the US might recognise such a settlement as constituting the fulfilment of the much-desired compromise between whites and blacks. Writing at the time, *The Economist* of Britain in a commentary (of 26 May 1979) entitled, 'Towards Recognition', noted:

Rhodesia-Zimbabwe's new constitution, it is true, is a zebra-like curiosity, with wide stripes of continuing white influence superimposed, for a time, on the principle of black majority rule. But it has always been the aim of British policy (and of American policy too, since the Americans have had one) to bring Rhodesia to independence in a way that keeps a place for the white community. This requires a transition that will reassure white as well as black.[39]

These manoeuvres threatened the unity of the Patriotic Front, especially when in August 1978 Nkomo began 'clandestine'[40] negotiations with Smith, raising thereby the suspicion that ZAPU might join the 'internal settlement' and leave ZANU isolated. There is no doubt that the imperialists sought to encourage a split in the Patriotic Front: it would weaken the guerrilla war and render more feasible the kind of compromise they envisaged.

The survival of PF unity certainly forestalled an earlier, if not more blatant, compromise than the one that emerged at Lancaster. These events had, nevertheless, revealed the PF's vulnerability to imperialist pressure: Britain and the US would hereafter seek to play on ZANU-ZAPU differences in the pursuit of a compromise. The continuation of the guerrilla war would, of course, ensure that the PF remained a major and indispensable factor in the months leading to Lancaster. But both the delicate nature of ZANU-ZAPU relations and the possibility that the imperialists might recognise the internal settlement were bound to leave the Patriotic Front itself quite apprehensive and particularly keen for a settlement within which it could be quickly acknowledged as the main force in Zimbabwe politics.

The internal settlement elections of April 1979 were by any description quite farcical and in retrospect bound to be inconsequential in the power equation that evolved in 1980. But at the time, the event alone sent shivers through Patriotic Front ranks and made the idea of the Lancaster House Conference not unacceptable. The role of the frontline states was quite crucial in the inauguration of the Lancaster House conference. Because of the Rhodesian cross-border raids, the war had from 1977 onwards been extended to the frontline states of Zambia, Mozambique and Botswana. In particular, the economies of Zambia and Mozambique were seriously disrupted and their political stability equally threatened. The frontline states were therefore as much in need of a settlement as the very forces that were directly involved in Zimbabwe.

The Presidents of the Frontline states were more eager than ever to see Britain assume her 'colonial responsibilities'. As late as January 1979, Nyerere was still urging Britian to intervene militarily, supposedly for peace-keeping purposes. Tremendous pressure was, therefore, put on the PF leaders to compromise. Machel in particular, played a key role, forcing ZANU to accept Carrington's terms. By late 1979, faced with growing internal political problems and repeated attacks on Mozambique by the

(Rhodesian) security forces, Machel was determined to help put an end to the war.[41]

In general, however, all forces and parties involved in the Zimbabwe debacle were sorely in need of a settlement: the Smith-Muzorewa group, because they could not stop a war that might soon engulf them; South Africa, because it could not continue to support the Rhodesian war indefinitely and therefore welcomed a chance that might just legitimise the internal settlement and thereby hopefully also buy time for apartheid; the Patriotic Front, because, as has already been explained, it had not as yet completely won the war against the Smith-Muzorewa regime and therefore needed at least this opportunity to isolate the latter and emerge as the legitimate African nationalist leadership in the Zimbabwe situation; and the imperialists (Britain and its ally, the US), because this offered the most favourable opportunity to get all concerned to accept a compromise the elements of which had, since the genesis of the Anglo-American proposals in 1976, been on the table.

In fact, it would be quite ahistorical to attribute blame to anyone for the reality of the Lancaster House Conference. No doubt, many an African nationalist felt uncomfortable about both the course and outcome of the conference; and Robert Mugabe himself would express disquiet and anxiety at the dangers inherent in the entire affair:

> Yes, even as I signed the document I was not a happy man at all. I felt we had been cheated to some extent...that we had agreed to a deal which would to some extent rob us of the victory that we had hoped to have achieved in the field.[42]

But so opportune for the imperialist strategy was the Lancaster House Conference that none of the actors and forces dared let it fail. Even before the conference resumed in September, it was clear to the PF leaders and their entourage in London that this was the final chance. It was a point of no return.

> Tongogara also wanted to conclude a settlement. 'We just have to have a settlement. We can't go back empty-handed...The nationalist leadership was determined to come to terms with British imperialism. Obviously, it sought to secure the best deal possible, which meant reducing concessions to a minimum, but under pressure from imperialism and the Frontline states, it was only a question of time before a compromise agreement would be reached.[43]

The Lancaster House Agreement constituted a substantial setback for the Patriotic Front, at least in terms of the broad objectives that the national liberation movement had set for itself in the course of the armed struggle.

First, the white settler colonial state was not to be dismantled. On the contrary, this was to remain largely intact. The cease-fire agreement would ensure that the guerrillas would not pose a threat: accordingly the PF's 35,000 guerrillas were to be isolated in assembly points scattered around the country. A British governor would represent the return of British rule for a brief period, to ensure that a suitable and acceptable black goverment came to power. In turn, the British governor would make sure that the state machinery—the army, the police, the prisons, the public service, the air force, the judiciary, etc.—remained in white hands throughout the transition period. Britain was back in control of its colony, backed by a white settler colonial state apparatus, and with the help of a Commonwealth force of 1,200 men and about 500 British policement. To add insult to injury, the future government of Zimbabwe would have to guarantee the pensions of Rhodesian civil servants and to guarantee citizenship to all white residents.

Second, the PF was now deprived of the possibility of winning undiluted and total political power, as would be expected in a decolonisation process. The whites would retain 20 reserved seats in a parliament with 100 seats: a notable victory for a group (of less than 250,000) that had, for ninety years denied the African population (about 7 million in 1980) access to political power.

Third, the socio-economic structures would remain intact: the Bill of Rights ensured this with the (Lancaster House) constitution's section on 'Freedom from Deprivation of Property'. There was to be a ten-year guarantee on the inviolability of private property. But of particular significance—and this is elaborated in the chapter on the 'land question' in this book—was that the land issue remained unresolved. It ran counter to ZANU's revolutionary programme of agrarian reform.

> The extent of the compromise by the PF leaders can be measured by those sections of the Constitution referring to the crucial land question. As one authority on land points out, the cost of buying the estimated 40-60% of European land not being fully utilized would be so high that even if a new government of Zimbabwe were committed to implementing a comprehensive land resettlement programme *under the constitution it would find it well nigh impossible to carry it out* (original emphasis).[44]

The promise of massive aid from Britain and the US became an additional factor in ensuring not only that the Lancaster House Agreement itself would seek to entrench capitalism in Zimbabwe but also that the country should remain firmly in the Western sphere of influence.

The almost abject weakness of the PF *vis-à-vis* these imperialist manoeuvres can be discerned from the extent to which their objections to most of these proposals fell on deaf ears.[45] The PF was inherently vulnerable to the ceasefire and electoral arrangements; and more specifically, the two attempts on Robert Mugabe's life on 6 and 10 February 1980 were just the more serious illustrations[46] of the physical danger that faced those who had played key parts in the struggle for liberation. To make matters worse, the assembly places to which the guerrillas were to be confined were themselves part of a South African plan[47] that had been developed together with the Rhodesian Central Intelligence Organisation (CIO) and military intelligence. The PF's suggestion that a UN (or Commonwealth) force of 10,000 military personnel should supervise the cease-fire[48] may have been based on the realisation of their vulnerability during this period.

This request was turned down by the British, in favour of a more modest number of 500 British policemen and the Commonwealth Monitoring Force. The PF would have to rely for its safety and survival on the Zimbabwean masses.

The Lancaster House Agreement also included in its package the question of a general election that all parties were free to contest. The emissaries and delegates who came from inside Zimbabwe to the conference assured the PF leadership that there was a good chance that it would win such elections, though the ZANU members were wont to emphasise that such a victory was certain if ZANU stood alone, without its PF partner ZAPU. Not only Bishop Abel Muzorewa himself but also the British and the South Africans believed the UANC would win. Allaying Smith's fears that the outcome of the Lancaster House conference might be tantamount to a PF—in particular a ZANU—victory, Carrington explained that the very purpose of the conference had been to prevent such an outcome.[49] A recent account of this period confirmed this:

> The Lancaster House Conference had certainly not gone quite as planned in London, Salisbury and Pretoria, above all in the establishment of the CMF (Commonwealth Monitoring Force). But the very intensity of effort by Carrington personally and the Foreign Office collectively to hobble the PF proved beyond reasonable doubt that full support from the British Government would be given to white interests, and would continue throughout a two-month election campaign in which 'no holds barred' might serve as a slogan for all parties. Carrington's 'first-class solution' of a second electoral victory for Muzorewa would lead to a situation in which the country's affairs remained firmly in white hands, even if black gloves were worn as a gesture to the new constitution...Mugabe's determination to dissolve the PF despite—or because of—Nkomo's vehement objections... also encouraged many whites in the hope that Muzorewa's South African-financed UANC would come home a clear winner.[50]

Both the British and South Africans continued, until the eve of the election results, to believe that the UANC would win; and that if it did not win a majority, there was a chance of a coalition—that might involve ZAPU—against ZANU. They hoped that ZANU would not win such a majority as to render all other parties small minorities. It was expected that the whites would naturally support such a coalition.

The optimistic expectations that the respective groups had about the elections were certainly a factor in facilitating and expenditing the Lancaster House Agreement. To some extent, this tended to allay anxiety among the respective groups about the full import of the agreement itself. At best, the PF hoped that their success in the elections would settle at least some of the more unacceptable aspects of the agreement. The major concern of all concerned was less about the nature of the agreement they had just signed than about who would win political power at the general election.

The hopes and expectations of returning home and winning the elections created its own momentum among all concerned. This meant that all would try to work towards a successful conclusion of the Lancaster House Agreement. No doubt, prior knowledge that the Patriotic Front—and in particular ZANU (PF)—would win the elections might have led to more organised attempts, by an alliance of British, South African and white Rhodesian forces, to prevent such an outcome. Similarly, it would have been foolish for the Patriotic Front—and ZANU (PF) in particular—to sit back and accept a victory by groups that least deserved it in terms of the war effort. As it was, the result of the general election was a clear reflection of both the relation of forces and the popularity (or the lack of it) of the respective parties: ZANU (PF) won a majority with 57 seats (62.992% of the poll); ZAPU 20 seats (24.113%); and Muzorewa's UANC 3 seats (8.227). The other parties won nothing; while Smith's Rhodesia Front took all 20 white seats. An estimated 93.6% of those Africans eligible to vote did so.

The Post-White Settler Colonial State

Some analysts and political activists in Zimbabwe hoped that the election results of 4 March 1980 (the date on which the results were announced) might constitute a basis for ZANU (PF) and its allies to make good the losses suffered through the Lancaster House Agreement. For both the results of the elections and the mass response to ZANU (PF) shook the country on that Tuesday morning.

It threw fear into the hearts of ZANU (PF)'s enemies at home and abroad, both black and white. Indeed any hope that General Walls had for a coup against a ZANU (PF) government-to-be quickly disappeared in the face of a mass response that symbolised both victory and the determination to defend it.

For years immersed in self-deception and false propaganda, most whites could not believe the outcome, let alone accept that they could live under 'terrorists'. For them, it was the end of the world, it was a state of shock:

> Tuesday, 4 March, marks the nadir of white morale. It is the Day of Despair. Many women snatch their children out of school. A woman working in the recently reopened British Airways office in Baker Avenue says she will leave Rhodesia, after twenty-five years. There is panic. A leading accountant is immediately inundated not only by phone calls but by desperate clients hurling themselves into his office. 'I felt like a doctor.' A woman in her 40s heading a leading nursing agency calls in to describe Mugabe as a Marxist in sheep's clothing—but she will never go to socialist Britain. A wealthy farmer from Marandellas wants to know how he can buy silver bars to

smuggle out of the country. 'I can't live under Communism,' he says.

The telephones of estate agents ring continuously while orders pile up on the desks of the removal firms. At Fox and Carney half a dozen houses are put up for sale within forty-five minutes; nothing like it since Angola 'fell'.

The whites wheel out their toys; heavy guns, troop carriers, armoured vehicles. At street intersections and junctions on the outskirts of Salisbury, the soldiery stages a pantomime display of final resolve. Housewives and secretaries bring cups of tea to the statuesque warriors of the RLI, guardians of our shopping precincts.[51]

Mugabe's reconciliatory speech on the evening of 4 March helped to allay white fears and perhaps even forestalled whatever punitive action the imperialists—and South Africa in particular—might have wished to consider in support of any white settler faction with the courage to challenge the new government.

'We will ensure', Mugabe told the nation, 'that there is a place for eveyone in this country. We want to ensure a sense of security for both the winners and the losers.' There would be no sweeping nationalization; the pensions and jobs of civil servants were guaranteed; farmers would keep their farms; Zimbabwe would be non-aligned. 'Let us forgive and forget. Let us join hands in a new amity.'[52]

Mugabe's reconciliatory speech should be understood in the context of the forces and circumstances surrounding the Lancaster House Agreement. Mugabe would have to begin the delicate task of state-building—and nation-building—in an atmosphere of intense suspicion and even hostility on the part of those he had defeated at home; against the background of overt and covert threats of military, political, and economic destabilisation from South Africa; and with the pervasive threat of economic and political blackmail by the imperialist powers that had been the undertakers of the Lancaster House Agreement but were now seeking to keep the new state in line. The policy of reconciliation and national unity became almost necessary and even inevitable in these difficult circumstances, if only to avert any opportunities for enemies (within and without) to lure this and that faction to the detriment of national security. There was an urgent need for ZANU (PF) to eliminate any dangers that might threaten the country—and therefore the need to heal the divisions between ZANU (PF) and ZAPU on the one hand whilst on the other appeasing the white settlers.

The first cabinet reflected this objective, particularly in the inclusion of two whites (one of them from the RF) and five from ZAPU in a cabinet of 24. Both the size and composition of the cabinet was no doubt also partly an attempt to project and develop this national outlook. But the choice of the two whites was also significant in that it not only appeased the white settlers but also reassured capitalists at home and abroad: RF member David Smith became Minister of Commerce and Industry; Denis Norman, President of the Commercial Farmers' Union, accepted the Agriculture portfolio. In keeping with the objectives of national unity and national security during these delicate days, South Africa was to to be kept as far as possible at bay by giving it no excuse (e.g. the establishment of guerrilla bases for the South African liberation movements) to attack Zimbabwe.

The pervasive nature of imperialist hegemony—over the state, classes and social formation of the society—is an important aspect in any characterisation of the post-colonial situation. But the peculiar role and dominance of the white settler factor in the society in general, and in the economy in particular, assigns a special character to a situation such as that of post-independent Zimbabwe. Hence the concept of the post-white settler colonial state.

The main problem arose from the fact that Zimbabwe intherited the key elements of the white settler colonial apparatus. As has been outlined in the previous section, this was precisely the intention of the Lancaster House Agreement: to provide for the continuity of the state as a guarantee for 'stability', the 'maintenance of high standards' and the survival and maintenance of the economic (capitalist) *status quo*. The reality of the white settler colonial state was brought home to the African nationalists during the ceasefire and election processes, in which the Rhodesian state was dominant. This fact was reaffirmed with the birth of a new government that had to depend on the goodwill of elements of the old in its attempt to build new structures. The problem of reconciling the old and new into the new state would persist throughout the period which this book covers. Only time, and the vantage of a deeper—if only because retrospective—analysis, will reveal the extent to which the inherited state structures would in turn influence the nature and character of the new state in Zimbabwe.

Within this overall situation, the most difficult and pressing problem was, of course, that of the army and air force. The major objective of the government was to unify the three formerly separate and even antagonistic armies: ZANLA, ZIPRA and the Rhodesian army. So threatening was the white settler colonial army that the new govenment found it more than prudent to incorporate the former Rhodesian Army Commander General Walls into the new military hierarchy in the period immediately following the elections in 1980. This facilitated the demobilisation of the more unacceptable elements of the Rhodesian army: mainly the Selous Scouts, the Grey Scouts and the Rhodesia Light Infantry. But this did not completely immobilise General Walls himself, as is evidenced by the government's decision to sack him subsequently. There was also the problem of the delicate relations that existed between ZANLA and ZIPRA, posing a grave challenge to the government's objective of developing an integrated and united army—the Zimbabwe National Army—out of the three formerly separate armies. Following the open rift between ZANU (PF) and ZAPU in February 1982, about 3,000 former ZIPRA guerrillas deserted from the National Army with their weapons, forming a large resource base for the dissident problem that was to afflict Western Zimbabwe in subsequent years.

In general, however, the integration of the armed forces was a major success, considering the hard road that had to be traversed towards this goal. By the end of 1980 most of the Rhodesian elements had voluntarily left the army, police and air force. This was part of the white exodus that left Zimbabwe with a white population of under 170,000, a decline on the pre-independence figure of about 250,000. But this was an element particularly antagonistic to black rule; and as evidenced in their attempt in 1982 to undermine and destroy the air force, which they saw as theirs, and therefore prevent blacks from inheriting it, some of these elements had also been particularly dangerous.

It was left largely to the British Military Advisory Training Team (BMATT) to train the former guerrillas into a regular army. Six years ago, one analyst, imbued obviously by a somewhat romantic conception of the armed struggle, had pointed at the long-term danger of transforming a classic (and politicised) guerrilla army into a regular army:

> It also has been argued that ZANLA, in consequence of... practice inside the country, had become the source of much of the pressure towards radicalization of the parent movement, ZANU, over the years. Does the possibility arise that in order to placate a settler army a people's army will have had to be demobilized? And what kind of standing army will emerge from the ministrations of a General Walls and of 'British military instructors'? Time alone will tell.[53]

The point is that the former ZANLA now constitutes the bulk of the Zimbabwe National Army. The fact the such a radical and politicised guerrilla army could, with relative ease, be transformed into a regular and largely depoliticised army perhaps goes to show that such analysts as have been cited above tended to exaggerate the radicalism of the guerrilla army. As has already been pointed out in the first section of this chapter, the radicalism of the guerrillas was related to the desire to attain national independence through the armed struggle. But if as a regular army the same people now appear depoliticised, there is no reason to expect that they will not again respond appropriately if and when national security and national independence are seen to be in jeopardy. At any rate, the evidence so far suggests that the former guerrillas see no contradiction between their former and present roles, even though it may be true that the level of British involvement in training the army is yet another of the many attempts 'to lock the new government's various compromises firmly into place'.[54]

This danger was no less prevalent in the other sections of the state apparatus, particularly the public service (including the police, state security, prisons and judiciary). The rapid rate of Africanisation in the public sector might easily conceal the extent to which the old and new were to be welded and moulded into a public service that had more to do with preservation of the *status quo* than with challenging it. Even in the period just before Lancaster, there would be warnings from the white leadership against meddling with the public service and the judiciary:

> Any drastic changes in the public service would undermine white confidence. Farmers and businessmen need a sound civil service infrastructure. Your security forces would wither away. Go and ask... one of the strongest nationalist... go and ask... what happened in Zambia and Mozambique after the whites left.[55]

The letter and spirit of the Lancaster House Agreement would reaffirm this. Besides, it was a subject about which the African nationalists were anxious in their pre-independence manpower plans. It fell within the larger concern about skills shortages in the event of what was expected to be a massive exodus of white skills. As the Patriotic Front's Zimbabwe Manpower Survey of 1979 was to illustrate, this concern was based on three assumptions: the dominance of white skills in all sectors of the economy; the dearth of skills among the African population; and the fear of expatriatism which has become a scourge in most of the African states.[56]

The Zimbabwe National Manpower Survey (NMS) (1981) would help to expose the fallacy of these assumptions, establishing at least a basic quantitative and qualitative bench mark against which to gauge the manpower requirements of the country. As is also elaborated in chapter ten of this book, the NMS also helped to blow the myth—perpetrated by both the legacy of white settler colonialism and its white settler ideology—of the indispensability of white skills in Zimbabwe. In the context of the period leading to independence in 1980, however, the manpower question loomed large. It was quite a central factor in the Lancaster House deliberations—generally in the context of the white settler factor and its exaggerated role in a future Zimbabwe but, more specifically, in relation to the public service and related structures of the state apparatus.

In reality, the new government of 1980 found itself having to rely on a public service that was almost entirely white in composition. There was at the time of independence a total of 10,570 established posts in the public service. Only 3,368 (31.86%) of these were black, though none of the latter was of a rank above that of a Senior Administrative Officer (equivalent to the junior echelon of the administrative cadreship). The new African ministers invariably found themselves having to:

> rely on white secretaries (with intimate experience in the initial development of repressive weapons for use *against* many of these same ministers and their African constituency). Today, these secretaries play an absolutely key role in both policy formulation and in overseeing the execution of policy. Some continuities in top personnel are stunning. Despite the fact that from February 1980 to January 1983 the number of white officers in the civil service dropped from 7,202 to 4,495, and the number of non-white officers increased from 3,368 to 17,693... the location of whites with experience in repressive governance in key posi-

tions in contemporary apparatuses may well have an impact on the kinds of decisions that are made...[57]

The author of the above statement may have overstated his case in trying to highlight the specific 'repressive apparatuses' that Zimbabwe inherited from Rhodesia. But in focusing on the question of the 'continuity of personnel' in this respect he has lost sight of the essential nature of the state as a coercive machinery, seeking to maintain law and order within a given historical, socio-economic and political framework. Continuity in the structures and personnel might just be one feature of the continuity of the state, from the white settler colonial situation to the post-independence era. But it has more to say about the nature of the state itself than about the race or character of its personnel. Black personnel operated in these state structures as competently as their white counterparts, and in the interests of both the colonial and the post-colonial state. The issue here is that the state in the post-independence era continued to reflect white settler colonial interests. The dominance of white personnel in key state apparatus—but including the parastatals and the University of Zimbabwe—is only one factor illustrating this.

For the post-white settler colonial state would continue to serve the interests of the former white settlers—and of all other people with similar class and economic interests—provided that there was no fundamental dislocation in those state structures that ensured continuity in social and economic life. This continuity could be maintained even under a different set of personnel; and for that matter, even black personnel might reinforce this continuity, in the interests of capital, of the former white settlers and of the African petit bourgeoisie.

In short, international capital and the former white settlers might even find more security for their class and socio-economic interests in this post-independence situation. They were prevented from expecting this outcome because of the combined weight of the racial ideology of white supremacy and the fear—and indeed normal (even from the racial point of view) expectation—that the African leadership might, after independence, implement that (socialist) revolutionary programme.

Besides there was a belief, current among both white settlers and their imperialist allies, that a black government was synonymous with a general breakdown of services, rampant mismanagement and untold corruption and nepotism. This conception of the post-colonial situation in Africa was, of course, also coloured by the racial ideology of white supremacy.

It expressed itself particularly as part of a white settler ideology that viewed the black as naturally given to dishonesty and an incapacity to manage. But it appeared to gain credence in the exaggeration, because of the influence of this ideology, of the negative features of the post-colonial experience in Africa. As has already been mentioned with regard to the Lancaster House Agreement, this was a factor which pervaded any consideration about the role of the whites in a future Zimbabwe.

Even the African nationalist petit bourgeoisie was not entirely untainted by the imperialist and white settler ideology, at least to the extent that some of them doubted their own capacity to rule efficiently without the assistance of the whites. Among them were many who had lived in black Africa and had developed a negative view of the post-colonial experience. Failing to understand fully the dynamics of this experience, they tended to attribute all these negative features to the flight of white skills. It is a sad reflection of the subconscious or inverted racism of some elements of the African petit bourgeoisie. But this was related also to an ideological predisposition which viewed socialism as unattainable in Zimbabwe; and felt that an attempt to introduce it might result in the havoc, hunger and decline that now afflict those societies—e.g. Tanzania and Mozambique—that are perceived as pursuing a 'socialist' path.

But all this contributed, on the part of the reactionary petit bourgeoisie, to an avid and blind commitment to the concepts of 'efficiency,' 'stability' and 'maintenance of high standards', etc.—all of which coincided with both white settler and imperialist ideology.

In practice, the latter expressed itself, as we have seen, in the various pre-emptive and entrenched safeguards for the socio-economic *status quo*. The new post-white settler colonial state would be imbued by all these and similiar considerations about the need to safeguard and preserve the economic order in the transition from Rhodesia to Zimbabwe and beyond.

Racial ideology and fear characterised the Lancaster House Agreement, leading to various pre-emptive and entrenced safeguards for the economic *status quo*. Thus, the presence and political and economic role of the whites would be a further guarantee of continuity, 'stability', the 'maintenance of high standards', 'expertise', 'experience', 'good government' and 'development'. The 'indispensability' of the white factor was viewed as synonymous with and integral to all these euphemisms for neo-colonialism. It was the goose that lay the golden eggs; it had to be preserved, pampered and, as far as possible, left alone, undisturbed in its historical god-given role!

The discussion brings us to that of the relationship between the white settler factor and international capitalism. There has been much theoretical debate about this, particularly the view that the white settler colonial bourgeoisie was so 'national' in character that it could, by implication, mobilise the entire white settler community in opposition to international capitalism.[58] Suffice it to state that history has since shown how *unnational* the white settler colonial factor was bound to be: it would be 'national' only as long as its claim for a 'white Rhodesia' remained sustained and unchallenged; faced with the reality of the African nationalist bid for national independence, it could survive politically only at the hands of its source, British imperialism, and, in economic terms, as part of international capital.

Similiarly, we should dispel those romantic notions about the 'revolutionary potential' of the white working class in Southern Africa. The most ready victims of the white settler ideology and the related negative propaganda about black rule, the white workers constituted the majority of those whites who fled Zimbabwe just before and after independence. The white exodus was at the rate of 1,500 per month; and between independence and October 1981, 32,000 had departed.

> Clearly, material factors played a part; the rapid integration of the schools and health services; a harsh budget; higher minimum wages for all categories of workers, including domestic servants; a freeze on salaries over Z$20,000; tighter exchange control regulations; long queues outside petrol stations, particularly in Salisbury; a shortage of butter and cheese. Yet the material standard of living of the whites remained exceptionally high; nor was their style of life substantially threatened. The crucial factor were cultural and psychological. White artisans and engineers departed because they could not stomach a black government led by 'terrorists' against whom they had fought a bitter, and ultimately humiliating, war. The rapid Africanization of the army, the police and the civil service symbolized the substantive shift in racial power and status which the internal settlement had been designed to stall... young men with skills soon recognized that they held their jobs on sufferance; scanning an uncertain future, they took the gap.[59]

Therefore, quite contrary to those analyses which envisaged a unity between white and black workers in the struggle against capital in Southern Africa, there was even greater antipathy, with the white workers retreating from any situation—such as national independence—which might undermine their historical privileges. But as the NMS revealed in 1982, the increase of African industrial skills also meant the gradual mobility of most of those white skilled workers that remained in Zimbabwe after independence.

They moved from the 'dirty jobs' of the industrial sphere to more protected skilled functions, including the managerial, executive and administrative occupations. Indeed, independence constituted a new political and psychological reality for the white community: a reality highlighted in such visible forms as the pulling down of the statues of Cecil John Rhodes; a new stance in the media which now sought to project the new political order, while vilifying the white settler colonial system of the immediate past; a National Manpower Survey that was viewed by many—both black and white—as the agency for rectifying the economic inequalities of the past; the growing militancy of the workers and peasants as they expected more immediate material benefits out of the independence situation; and even what appeared, at least from the various speeches by the party leadership, to be the possibility of a socialist programme.

But, as we shall see shortly, such was the nature of the transition that all the white classes soon discovered that their fears were largely groundless. It is, however, true that the white workers were the hardest-hit, psychologically and economically, by the trauma of black rule, particularly now that many of those who remained would, in the long run, be exposed to the full impact of black competition.[60] Those of them who retreated to South Africa faced again the danger of being drafted into the South African Defence Forces, to defend a system that would inevitably go down like the one they had, in vain, just defended.

All this facilitates our attempt to answer the question about the post-white settler colonial state: who controls it and whose interests does it serve? It should appear obvious now, at least from the thrust of the argument in this chapter, that the white settler factor only facilitates—a crucial and peculiar facilitator at that—the overall dominance of international capital. The white settler factor serves an important role in confronting and compromising the revolutionary demands of the African people; and it becomes a viable force during that phase of the post-white settler colonial situation, a phase which, if we accept that the white settler factor will inevitably decline in the Zimbabwean social formation, is a transitional one. Thereafter, the African petit bourgeoisie gradually moves into the centre-stage of post-colonial politics, sometimes even in a compradorial relationship with international capital.

As we have seen from the Lancaster House Agreement, the transitional phase is, therefore, an important one as far as imperialism (and international capital) is concerned. Its value to the white settler factor is unquestionable. But is has also turned out to be immensely useful to a significant section of the African petit bourgeoisie; including even those elements of it who had either actively collaborated with the white settler colonial regime or feared that the arrival of national independence might threaten their existence and class aspirations:

(a) the governing class: i.e. the ministers, permanent secretaries and other senior personnel and directors of the administrative apparatus, the general managers of the large parastatals (not excluding the university and other higher institutions of learning and training), the heads of the appointed party bureaucracy at the different levels, the heads of repressive apparatuses—the army, air force, police, prisons and state security;
(b) the comprador elements for whom Zimbabwe's political independence has meant an increase in both their numbers and scope with regard to their link with international capital: as either the general managers and chief executives of the major multinational corporations, or mere business 'front men' and 'public relations' trouble-shooters in the intermediary role between these large corporations and elements of the state apparatus;
(c) the (more lucky) emergent business people—the middle level merchants, transport operators and land owners—for whom national independence has meant an increase in opportunities and access to capital accumulation;
(d) all other sections of the African petit bourgeoisie who, through either the fact of national independence or the accompanying democratisation (and *Africanisation*) of the society, find themselves in better employment, with a higher standard of living and, as is the case with students and trainee professionals, are generally in a potentially better position to partake of the 'fruits of independence'.

The post-white settler colonial state became, therefore, the agency through which international capital hoped to maintain Zimbabwe under imperialist hegemony. But, unlike the white settler colonial state, which depended primarily on coercion and repression to control and exploit the wage-earners and peasants, the post-white settler colonial state had to develop a new ideology with which to contain popular demands for economic and social change in the period after independence. Like all other post-colonial states, it is caught in a 'serious contradiction within itself'.[61] On the one hand it has to seek to complete the mandate and momentum of the armed struggle, beyond political independence; in particular, to begin to resolve the land question, which is a burning one for the peasants, and to attend to the equally popular demands of the working people for more jobs, more pay and better conditions of service. All this was, of course, compounded by the fact that the peasants and workers attributed the land hunger, the exploitation and the inequalities in general to the white settlers, a great number of whom were still in the country, and in the same positions of economic and social privilege as they had been before independence. It is true that national independence is a great achievement for all the classes among the African people: it ushers in democracy, a sense of security and real peace; and raises new hopes for a qualitative change in the lives of people the majority of whom had been dehumanised by the weight of colonial oppression and exploitation. Yet, the mass of these people expected that national independence would totally liberate them from oppression and exploitation: the end of white rule, the end of racism, the end of yesterday! The African nationalist struggle had mobilised the masses precisely on the basis of these promises. But independence would fulfil the promise only for a few more of the African petit bourgeoisie, leaving the mass of the people only with promises which, even with the best will on the part of the leadership, could not be fulfilled under this economic order.

On the contrary, the post-white settler colonial state was inherently unable to fulfil these popular demands. At the end of the day, the new state had become an apparent mediator between capital and labour, between the aspirations of the mass of the people for the 'future of independence' and the role of international capital in its quest for more profit. With time, however, this state would become weighted in favour of the latter, inclined—as is discussed in Parts Two, Three and Four of this book—towards controlling these popular demands, if only to appease capital in the name of 'stability', peace and security.

The State and Politics

For the post-white settler colonial state is more than just a neo-colonial state. It is born fettered and historically constrained by the midwife of imperialism; and in growing, it has to contend with the former white settlers who, by their economic, social and political existence, also influence the nature and direction of the state, in league with imperialism and international finance capital. There is also the threat of a South African state on which the new Zimbabwean state finds itself economically dependent mainly for transport and trade links; but also one that could, either on its own initiative or as part of the imperialist strategy in the Southern African sub-region, quite easily inflict terror on the new state. All these factors have to be considered also in relation to the role of the African petit bourgeoisie which, as has already been indicated, had developed a vested interest in this new set of affairs. Both the imperatives of this transitional phase that we have just described, and the class interests of the African petit bourgeoisie, would gradually undermine the mass political mobilisation and momentum that might have at least tempered this trend. Indeed, it became increasingly imperative, as an act of survival for the new state, to put a rein on its mass base. In turn, this began the process of demobilising a mass political base through which political independence had been won and without which no petit bourgeoisie, no matter how progressive its leadership, could effectively either contain imperialist and former white settler machinations or wage the struggle for genuine economic and social progress.

In general, therefore, *change* in the economic sphere meant essentially the gradual *embourgeoisement* of the African petit bourgeoisie, as the latter found their class aspirations fulfilled, albeit with such limitations as this post-white settler colonial situation prescribed more for the mass of the people than for this class itself.

It was expected that there would be conflict between the African petit bourgeoisie and the former white settlers. But, as the African petit bourgeoisie began gradually to find access to the same economic and social status as their white counterparts so, too, did it become increasingly unable to respond effectively to the aspirations of the workers and peasants. The leadership would find it increasingly difficult to confront the former white settlers, let alone international capital.

There was more than a symbolic commitment to the capitalist order as the members of the African petit bourgeoisie variously bought houses, farms, businesses, etc; political principles and ideological commitment appeared mortgaged on the altar of private property!

There had never been a clearly articulated ideology in the Zimbabwean national liberation movement. But whatever there was of a commitment to socialist transformation became increasingly isolated as the rhetoric of a few committed leaders in a society whose appetite was so much whetted for capitalist development. The increased access to the markets for the peasantry, the increase in minimum wages for the workers, the very sense and feel of a new democratisation process—all helped to reinforce rather than weaken this thrust.

As a concept, 'development' became confused between, on the one hand, the tendency to translate it in terms of making capitalism accessible to the masses; and, on the other, the social democratic view of 'bridging the gap' between the rich and the poor. Therein lay the hope for the transformation of the capitalist system and for the transition to socialism; while at the same time foreign aid was viewed as an important component in that 'development' strategy. If it was impossible now to institute a development process from a mass base, it was necessary to institute a framework for the very difficult exercise of ensuring an equitable distribution of very scarce development resources. This became the major focus of the provincial administration policy that was inaugurated by the government in 1984.[62]

The party lost the momentum that it had developed in the period leading to independence—a momentum that had been based more on the popular mass response to the struggle for national independence than on an organised party structure throughout the country. The latter task became the major objective in the period leading to the next general election in 1985. But the political and ideological content did not change; the declared goal of socialist construction could not be translated into the organisational political framework of the party without creating a fundamental contradiction with the post-white settler colonial state. With time, therefore, the party became an agency for the leadership to try and explain the 'slowness of change', to plead for patience, to highlight the achievement of the post-independence period in contrast to the deprivation of the colonial past, to listen to general as well as parochial complaints, to promise change, to emphasise the goal of national unity, and so on and so forth.

Ideologically, the party became immobile, divested of innovativeness by the apparent supremacy of the affairs of the state and the economy. It was caught in the same trap as that in which other parties in the post-colonial situation had found themselves once the excitement of independence had waned. The level of depoliticisation began to show in the reports that people were now being forced (by youths) to attend party meetings which, in the words of the ZANU (PF) Secretary for Administration and Acting Secretary of the Commissariat for Culture, Maurice Nyagumbo, were 'only sloganeering and singing party songs'.[63] He added:

> Such people are destroying the party and not building it. People are not interested in chanting slogans and singing party songs when there is nothing big that is to be said. Such acts are unbecoming to the party and the Government. We can send them [youths] to jail for that. It is not difficult to do... On complaints that senior [officials] in both the public and private sector were reluctant to attend party meetings, he said they might be busy with other issues but urged the people to persuade them (officials) to attend progressive meetings.[64]

Not suprisingly in these circumstances, the major ideological controversy centred on the Leadership Code, a code of conduct for party and government leaders, introduced in 1985 at the Second National Congress of ZANU (PF). Herein was another attempt to introduce socialism from the top so that a moral, incorruptible and non-capitalist oriented leadership might ward off criticisms in the rank and file, and reinforce an ideological framework which sought to legitimise the current state of affairs. Conversely, a greedy leadership might just expose the entire system, create cracks in the party and undermine the state. Maurice Nyagumbo again:

> We are meeting difficulties in implementing the Leadership Code because leaders have acquired property and do not seem prepared to part with it... we should call an emergency congress and tell the people that we are unable to fulfil one of our important resolutions... mainly that of scientific socialism, because the leaders acquired property... appear to have adopted capitalism, become property owners and appear to be deceiving our people.[65]

Unlike other leaders who continued to acquire such properties as farms and hotels, Cde Nyagumbo sold his own farm in accordance with the party's decision adopted at Chimoio (in Mozambique) in 1977 that 'Socialism would be scientifically based on the principles of Marxism-Leninism'.[66]

From a strictly scientific socialist perspective, it was more than ambitious to expect socialists within a capitalist framework. The demands that were being made on the leadership in terms of the Leadership Code remained essentially on the moralistic level and excluded, at least by implication, all those who were not leaders in the party. There was, therefore, no real structural challenge to the capitalist system as a whole. All the same, it is a reflection of the ideological outlook of the society that adherence to the Leadership Code itself on the part of an individual leader (particularly the Prime Minister himself) has enhanced the latter's standing in the eyes of the mass of the people. Indeed, a brief survey of the post-colonial experience in Africa would confirm the extent to which an exemplary leader—particularly the leader of a country—confers a degree of legitimacy and stability on a society that would otherwise have been exposed as having failed in its attempt to reconcile the dominance of international capital (and with it the compradorial national leadership) and the popular demands of the masses.

There has developed in Zimbabwe a significant leftist intellectual and political tradition, as can be discerned partly in the reference to Marxism-Leninism within the party and state sectors, and partly in social science activities[67] in the society at large. It is true that, at the level of the party and government, such declared commitment to Marxism-Leninism appears to be no more than mere rhetoric and even unrealistic against the economic, political and ideological terrain that we have tried to paint in this chapter. But it is nevertheless a positive development in a society whose history so far would have otherwise—if compared to other post-colonial situations in Africa—not only militated against but also actively suppressed such a development.

It is a reflection of the (modest) intervention of the Marxist-Leninist ideology, particularly during the course of the struggle; of a genuine concern, on the part of the progressive leadership of the party and government, with the need to advance the revolution; of the potential for a radical intellectual and political tradition in the society; and of evidence that the left has at least some room for political expression in a society that is currently so dominated by bourgeois ideology and culture. But, as is the case in other societies like Zimbabwe, the overall dominance of capitalism and its (bourgeois) ideology gives rise to an ultra-leftist counterpoise. The latter increasingly reflects extreme impatience and irritation at both the 'slow pace of change' and the arrogance of the rightist tendencies in the society. Not surprisingly, ultra-leftism becomes the stance not only of the intellectuals and academicians, who are largely outside the state sector, but also of elements that belong to such opposition parties as ZAPU. Ultra-leftism has, as always, a basis in the absence—particularly in the post-colonial situation, which emphasises the conventional role of a mass party—of an organisational and political link between radical intellectuals and the submerged classes.

In turn, the failure—and indeed even the state's role in ensuring such a failure—to develop such an organisational capacity inevitably gives rise to ultra-leftist adventurism, leftist factionalism and, ultimately, to the danger of reducing even the left tradition itself to ridicule (and possibly suppression) by the rightists in the society. The left in Zimbabwe is at this crossroads, dependent on the overall socio-economic and political development in society as to which way it develops.[68]

The major preoccupation in the arena of politics in this post-independence situation has been, quite characteristically, that of the pursuit of national unity. In turn, the focus on national unity not only is a reflection of the post-colonial situation in Africa but also de-emphasises, within this kind of society, the aspect of class and class struggle. These become quite secondary, and are viewed as secondary, to the aim of uniting all classes around the party and state. Characteristically, therefore, *national unity* becomes an imperative in a country that has undergone unequal and uneven capitalist development and is therefore faced with the usual threats of 'tribal', 'regional' and factional expressions, particularly at the level of the leadership.

This is particularly imperative in a society, in which these tendencies were, in the past, fanned and promoted by the 'divide and rule' politics of the colonial era; and in a society in which even the history of the armed struggle itself did, to some extent, compound 'regional' and 'tribal' conflicts (as is illustrated, for example, by the ZANU-ZAPU conflict).

As has been explained in the first section of this chapter, since the 'fruits of independence' are inherently limited and distorted within the neo-colonial situation, factionalism and rivalry among the petit bourgeoisie can become so serious as to threaten not only national unity but also the state itself. Accordingly, the first six years of independence may be described as largely a successful movement towards national unity, expressed firstly through the ZANU (PF)'s Second National Congress of 1985 and secondly in the current ZANU (PF)-ZAPU unity talks.[69] Prime Minister Robert Mugabe has himself been the central figure in this process. He has become a symbol of reconciliation and national unity; indeed it is difficult to envisage, in the current stage of the country's development, that any other national leader could have attained what he has during these very difficult years. Nor is it easy to imagine that any group or fraction of the petit bourgeoisie would have done more or better in the circumstances of the post-white settler colonial situation.

There is a need to consider briefly two other questions with regard to the issue of the state in the post-colonial situation. Both relate to whether or not this type of state does, in the final analysis, have any level of independence of action, whether it has a choice with regard to matters of policy and development strategy. The attempt to answer these questions falls within the wider discussion about who controls the state and whose interests it serves.

The first concerns the role of international capital in the context of imperialist hegemony and how, in this phase of the post-white settler colonial situation, it seeks to shape and control the domestic and external policies of the state. The second is related to the first, in that it raises the issue of the nature and role of factions within and among the dominant/governing classes in the post-colonial state.

For, if such factions are an important and fundamental factor in the conduct and operations of the state, then there is a need to reconsider the conception of the post-colonial state as merely a reflection of the dominance of international financial capital in this historical contjuncture. As has already been indicated in the brief survey of politics in the post-independence period, this conception of fractions exposes as nonsense recent writings that conceive of the 'Zimbabwean State' as being split between 'technocratic' and 'populist' factions.[70] Our analysis shows that such writings are, at best, based on a gross misunderstanding—and even crass ignorance—of both the Zimbabwean situation and the theory of the state.

There is nothing unusual about the existence of conflicts between different factions within the governing class, 'differences being a reflection of uneven development of the economy, different relations of the fractions to the domestic and external economy and differences in the economic bases or positions of these factions'.[71] Initially, there was conflict between the African nationalist petit bourgeoisie and the former white settlers. As has already been outlined, the conflict was primarily about the control of the state apparatus as well as about the conduct and direction of state policy following the ZANU (PF) victory in 1980.

The former white settlers feared that the state might be subverted against their interests, with the African petit bourgeoisie seeking to oust from the state that component of it that the Lancaster House Agreement intended as a guarantee of both continuity and the maintenance of the economic and social status of the whites in Zimbabwe. Reference has already been made to the efforts by the dominant sections of the white community to resist black majority rule even when it had already arrived. In fact many whites remain to this day quite unreconciled to the reality of independence under a black government. As has already been mentioned, many left the country, some to Europe, the United States or Australia, but most to South Africa, 'a country that seemed to embody the political ideals of white dominance that vanished here suddenly in 1980'.[72]

But some would decide to stay and make Zimbabwe their home; and, for a variety of reasons, others had no choice but to try and make the best of a new world in which they had less hope than apprehension. These could find refuge and relief in the government's policy of reconciliation, a policy which sought to embrace anyone who was willing to be liberal enough.

In turn, this policy contributed to some extent to the balkanisation of the Rhodesia Front in the years following the attainment of national independence. The following account captures the contradictions that lay beneath the surface among white settlers who supported Smith:

> The knives were out. Bill Irvine, a dire and diehard Rhodesian Fronter since 1965, who had held important portfolios under Smith, dripped malice through cold eyes and a mouth joined to his jaw by lines so bleakly Presbyterian that one would not have been surprised to find a tawse in his Scottish-born hand. 'It's all very well for P.K. van der Byl to abuse the blacks, he's got money down in the Cape. I want to stay in this country.' A prosperous farm and industrial consultant, Irvine accused former Rhodesian military leaders of having betrayed the cause by whoring and drinking in Salisbury instead of getting out into the bush. Irvine showed me a carbon copy of a letter he had sent to Smith shortly before his defection; it read less like the message of an old colleague than an invoice from an undertaker to a dead man. 'We never saw our future', Irvine told me, 'in white domination. Not in the long term, anyway.'[73]

The whites would continue to play a key role in the state; restraining, cajoling, threatening, appeasing, warning, barking—depending on the circumstances and on how best they could get their view across to their African nationalist counterparts. Those directly involved in the state structures would also seek to create new alliances with factions within the African petit bourgeoisie, with a view either to projecting a particular line of policy or to isolating, victimising or smearing those they viewed as radical.

The objective was to ensure that no faction among the African petit bourgeoisie developed the strength and confidence to pursue policies that might upset the economic and social *status quo*. The white lobby was particularly concentrated in parliament which, in turn, appeared to make news only when contentious issues were being debated. But it expressed itself also in such newspapers as the *Financial Gazette* which tended to represent also the interests of (big) capital.

For, as in the case of the white settler colonial situation before it, and indeeed in any capitalist society, the state would be used by the governing classes as the means for access to power, privilege and wealth accumulation. The African petit bourgeoisie in post-colonial Zimbabwe behaved no differently. But, as can be expected in such situations, the quest for power and wealth expressed itself sometimes in open corruption and nepotism. The long years of colonial domination and deprivation, not to mention imprisonment and the hard days of the struggle, became almost the licence—albeit for only a few among the many who might claim such a licence—to accumulate quickly; and the state (and the power and influence associated with it) appeared the most viable agency for such accumulation in an economy so dominated by foreign capital and by the former white settlers.

This was particularly so in a country wherein the peculiarity of the white settler colonial experience had, to a large extent, precluded the development of an African bourgeoisie. It would be expected, therefore, that the remaining white settler factor would challenge and impede the ascendancy of the African petit bourgeoisie into a bourgeoisie just as keen to break and transcend these obstacles.

In the final analysis, the various facets of what might be broadly described as the white lobby contributed significantly towards the restraint of the African petit bourgeoisie, particularly since the key leaders of the government were also persons keen to keep the society clean. It helped publicise the affairs of the state in a country wherein 'democracy' had hitherto been confined to white settler society. Initially, such negative publicity tended to develop among the public the belief that those in the state and politics were merely out for self-aggrandisement and wealth accumulation.

Not surprisingly, therefore, many among those of the petit bourgeoisie not directly involved in the affairs of the state found their views also in the voice of the white lobby, especially when it was more politically feasible for white politicians to be critical about a black government. In turn, the presence of such public opinion as developed in the context of a new democratic tradition would act as effective brakes against excesses by the ruling African petit bourgeoisie.

It is true that there were occasional cases of gross mismanagement and isolated cases of corruption but even those most critical of the new government would admit that, despite the many problems that it had to encounter, the new state had done well to maintain 'high standards' and 'efficiency'. At any rate, there was no 'breakdown of services' nor did corruption and maladministration even threaten to become the order of the day. To some extent, therefore, the former white settlers had succeeded in moulding the kind of a state in which they would continue to have a stake, both in terms of the personnel within the state apparatus and, more importantly, with regard to the direction of policy, which remained broadly within the capitalist framework. Their power in the private sector would remain unassailable, reducing the threats to their position of the National Manpower Survey to mere whimpers (by the African petit bourgeoisie) for Africanisation and 'black advancement' in this sector.[74] The fears that the social status of whites would be undermined were therefore groundless; and even those who had retreated to South Africa realised this as they drifted back, fearful now of the demise of apartheid as they were of the downfall of Rhodesia. One returning white Zimbabwean puts it thus:

A lot of people had that feeling of fate about this country... But a lot of people are surprised. I think they've managed to maintain most of the standards—medically, educationally, the police... I didn't think of England as my country. I came back two years ago... I will say there are a lot of things wrong with this country... but by God, that Mugabe has run a pretty good show... We have a house, a swimming pool, a tennis court, three servants. We live very well. Someone is cooking dinner tonight. Someone is watering the garden tomorrow. Someone is looking after the tennis court. And they don't bother us and we were on the other side of the fence. We're not living in Rhodesia. We're living in Zimbabwe.[75]

There was, therefore, understandable surprise and even disappointment among the Africans when, in the 1985 elections, the white electorate revealed that they were still in support of Ian Smith and his vision of the survival and maintenance of a white bloc in Zimbabwean society. Many observers had naively believed that the government's policy of reconciliation would cause the majority of the whites to desert Ian Smith and his Conservative Alliance of Zimbabwe (formerly Rhodesia Front) and vote for the Independent Zimbabwe Group (IZG). The latter was a loose alliance of whites some of whom had broken away from Ian Smith but all of whom hoped to create a new white lobby that would seek an alliance with the ruling African petit bourgeoisie and international capital. There were even suggestions that representatives of international capital, anxious to consolidate its position within this post-colonial white settler state, had encouraged the formation of IZG around an alliance between the more liberal whites and the African petit bourgeoisie. At any rate, the latter supported the IZG, hoping that a defeat of Ian Smith (and his CAZ) would put paid to white sectional interests, i.e. do away with the 20 reserved seats for whites and build on the dream of a 'multi-racial' and 'non-racial' Zimbabwe.

Besides, these expectations reflected on the African nationalist ideology as an offshoot of liberal ideology, opposed to racism of any kind and emphasising individual—rather than minority group—rights, 'equality' and 'non-racialism'. For the chief animating principle of African nationalist political life is a desire to convince the colonialists, former colonialists and whites in general of its commitment to non-racialism, justice, equality, democracy, etc., i.e. criteria by which post-colonial governments will be judged by the metropolitan power—which, in fact, is the audience to which African nationalist appeals are mainly intended.[76]

As it turned out, Ian Smith's Conservative Alliance of Zimbabwe (CAZ) won 15 of the 20 white roll seats, with four to the IZG and one to an Independent, Chris Andersen. There was general disappointment in nationalist and liberal white circles; it was expressed in the moans and mourning of the media, as illustrated by this editorial entitled 'Whites Showed PM their True Colours':[77]

The Prime Minister yesterday, in his first official reaction to last Thursday's shock election victory for Mr. Ian Smith... left nobody in any doubt the poll result had taken him by surprise. If Cde Mugabe feels bitter and disappointed because of the obvious slap in his face nobody in their right senses least of all the white population of Zimbabwe, can blame him.

The Prime Minister has had his now famous hand of reconciliation extended to his former oppressors for the past five years now, a gesture which, it now appears, has not been appreciated by those who should have gripped that hand firmly, the whites who elected to stay on in Zimbabwe after independence.

Up to 1980 white Rhodesians were fearful that given the nature of the confrontation between Ian Smith's illegal regime and the forces fighting for the liberation of Zimbabwe there would be massive recrimination against them after independence. Cde Mugabe surprised not only the whites of Zimbabwe, but the rest of the world as well by his conciliatory stance once he came to power. What appears to have not been registered in the minds of those people who gave Ian Smith his massive victory last week is the fact that the ZANU (PF) leader even risked losing the support of his followers with his talk of reconciliation...The majority of the white electorate have clearly shown that they are not capable of changing, that they have not reconciled themselves to the new order now prevailing in Zimbabwe. The only positive aspect of (the white) election is that the whites of Zimbabwe have at least shown all concerned their true colours.

Yet on the basis of an analysis of the history and nature of white settler colonialism, of the Lancaster House Agreement itself and of the character and attitudes of the majority of whites in the period since independence, the outcome of the white elections should have been no surprise. The short-lived columnist—'The Scrutator'—of *The Herald* wrote:[78]

It was either sheer misplaced goodwill, self-deception or both, that black Zimbabweans should have expected so much from a group of people who only yesterday we had to force to the Conference table. They could neither change their attitudes, repent for the past, nor accept the hand of reconciliation, because the conditions under which the Lancaster constitution was signed accorded the white fact the impression that the latter would remain a permanent feature in this country. This invariably fed the racist arrogance among the 'Rhodies': the belief that their kith and kin in Britain (and South Africa) would ensure their survival: the myth that their 'skills', 'expertise', etc. would for all time be indispensible to this country. Call it whatever you wish—racism, paternalism, arrogance—these are the essential features of an ideological superstructure that settler colonialism threw up in this country...White arrogance found resource as much in the myth of their own superiority as in the coincidence of economic interests between imperialism and Ian Smith's. The latter remains—consciously or sub-consciously—an important buffer to any attempt that the new Zimbabwe can attempt on the economic front... if international capital (and big capital in this country) did strive, in the formation and encouragements of such independents as the IZG, to create a new alliance between the less rabid of the former white settlers and the new black petty bourgeoisie. Many of the African petty bourgeoisie were prepared to buy that option; and hence the immense disappointment at the outcome of the white elections...In short, race and colour remain so dominant a force among the majority of our white brothers and sisters that it almost undermines a neo-colonial strategy that would bring more blacks into the sphere of the petit bourgeois and bourgeois classes...the white settler deceit has until now hid behind the aspirations of the black petit bourgeoisie in post-independence Zimbabwe. For, are we not all hoping for—or already within—the socio-economic structures that have for decades defined the white settler arena of privilege?.

It was the white liberals themselves who led the outcry against the results of the white election, keen to show, through a statistical juggling of the voting figures, that it was really not the majority of whites that had voted for CAZ; that those who voted for the latter belonged to the mad (and ungrateful) fringe; that there was generally goodwill among the whites, all of whom had already accepted the government's hand of reconciliation; and that the racial clause (which allowed for a separate white voters' roll) should be scrapped forthwith.

The media responded by flooding their columns with these letters of repentance;[79] and in the end all this tended to reinforce the government's commitment to non-racialism. Even the CAZ appeared embarrassed by the entire episode; and soon one of its senators would complain that people were not paying enough attention to the national anthem, *'Ishe Komborera Afrika'!* The confluence was developing; and perhaps the slow but certain discovery was being made by the whites that they had nothing to fear out of black majority rule after all. They could have a few more blacks joining their ranks in the bourgeoisie without however losing anything they possessed, economically and socially. The General Manager of the Zimbabwe Stock Exchange, W.A.F. Burdett-Coutts, expressed the new mood in his speech of 19 June 1986:

> Recent Company Reports have not only shown improved earnings but chairmen's comments have in the main shown greater confidence than last year. I do believe that it is a credit to our government under the leadership of our Prime Minister, Cde Robert Mugabe, that after six years of independence, the economy of this country should be in such relatively good shape, that the stock exchange, although still smaller than I would like, is now soundly based and structured and that black and white are working harmoniously together, for the future advancement of Zimbabwe. It demonstrates that, despite the rhetoric, the

policies followed by our government have been mainly pragmatic. The increased agricultural production in the communal lands is particularly noteworthy.

The process of identifying fractions and factions within the post-white settler colonial state may, in time, prove useful as a means of ascertaining how the more progressive among them might, in the future, possibly link up with the mass base within a revolutionary framework of change and transformation of the existing socio-economic order. However, six years after independence, it would be naive to attribute the major thrust of state policy to any fraction other than the totality of forces that established the broad parameters of political and socio-economic action in the post-white settler colonial situation.

It is true that certain sections of the African petit bourgeoisie were as fearful and apprehensive as the white settlers and international capital about what a ZANU (PF) government might do in the period following the elections of 1980. After all, many of these people had been active and ready participants in the internal settlement.

Together with the latter, many others had looked forward to the day when black majority rule would come with the guarantee that Zimbabwe would remain in the Western camp. Once in the state structures or any position of influence within the society at large, these elements would seek to lock the new government's compromises, emanating from Lancaster, firmly into place.

But from what has already been outlined in this chapter it is difficult to identify a faction or fraction within the petit bourgeoisie that, in any significant way, challenges the major thrust of the post-white settler colonial state.

The State and Foreign Powers[80]

The bases of Zimbabwe's current economic dilemma find full expression in the Lancaster House Agreement; and in the consequent contradiction between what is viewed as the imperative to maintain white and international confidence in the economy on the one hand and satisfing the expectations and aspirations of the mass of the people on the other hand. This is reflected quite clearly in the first economic policy document, *Growth with Equity*.[81] In such post-colonial situations, economic policies are likely to reflect these contradictions and constraints. The *Three Year Transitional National Development Plan*[82] and the *Five Year Plan*[83] in turn express and reveal the nature of the post-white settler colonial state. The contradictions are complicated rather than resolved by the belief that capitalism, whether as inherited or through foreign aid, can be mobilised towards the fulfilment of the popular demands of the masses.

In the final analysis, the government finds itself increasingly having to follow the broad guidelines of international finance capital, even when those directly responsible for economic policy may want to think that these policies are 'home-grown', independent of external influence. Such was the controversy when the government announced the 1983 austerity measures designed to improve the economy. Were these home-grown or a reflection of the influence of international finance capital? Thandika Mkandawire[84] argues:

> Whatever is the true story, we shall give the government of Zimbabwe the benefit of doubt and simply assume that the austerity programme is indeed 'home grown'. We note, in passing, however, that the controversy does illustrate the problems of reconciling the exigencies of capitalist accumulation and the quest for political legitimacy. Having decided that accumulation in Zimbabwe would need a large dose of private capital—local and foreign—the state had to enjoy the 'confidence' of capital and the IMF stamp of approval which is often considered crucial. This in turn, demanded a set of policy measures that would tilt the scales in favour of capital and against the popular classes so central in the struggle for independence and the political legitimacy of the state.[85]

Controversy will, for the foreseeable future, linger on as to the possible reasons why foreign aid became an important—if not central—component of state policies in the period since the attainment of national independence. There can be no doubt that there was much international goodwill towards a new nation that had been the victim of a long war and therefore required massive reconstruction in the economic sphere. Equally, however, such aid and assistance as did come were not entirely politically disinterested and therefore tended to be premised on the need to develop a 'stable' Zimbabwe. It was a continuation of a theme already established at Lancaster. In turn, it was predictable that the government would be 'too anxious to establish its credentials with the financial world'.[86]

Indeed, it is of little consequence now to consider what might have been the alternative economic policy were it not for the various 'wrong-headed' and 'high risk' policies that government introduced in the months following independence, in the hope of liberalising the economy and thereby attracting foreign investment.[87] Nor is it important now to consider what might have been the alternative scenario had the new state adopted a cautious approach towards foreign capital, relying mainly on the available local resources in a development programme. The latter would have been much slower in its implementation but dependent largely on people who, just emerging from the huge sacrifices of war, would have been quite patient and motivated towards such a self-reliant programme. The point, however, is that international finance capital has, since the Lancaster House Agreement, been the major factor in the character of the internal and external policies of the state in Zimbabwe. The role of the former settlers is important only in as far as it tends to coincide with and reinforce the overall interests of international finance capital and those of imperialism. The African petit bourgeoisie remains quite weak and is forced, in the interests of both its class and the need to maintain the state, to make compromises with both the former white settlers and international finance capital; not to mention the fact that there would be a significant and influential section within the African petit bourgeois class that would rather see Zimbabwe's destiny continue in the sphere of the West than move towards socialism.

Likewise, both the dominance of international finance capital and the imperatives of imperialist policy in Southern Africa tend to define the broad parameters of state action on the external front. Obviously there is a close correlation between domestic and external policies within any state. But it is in the field of foreign policy that the government is most keen to project the impression of independence of action, even though it should be obvious that *international relations* by definition prescribe and proscribe the limits of that 'independent' action on the part of the individual state. Such a conception of international relations raises the question of the hierarchy in global politics, with the major powers not only defining the arena of international politics but also controlling it; and the small states, in their 'foreign policies', merely reflecting or at best just responding or singing to the music of these giants. At times, small states will have to behave accordingly if they are to survive and not fall victim to the revengeful wrath of big powers. In any event, dependent states will in turn tend to exhibit external policies that are a reflection of that condition of dependence.

With regard to Zimbabwe, for example, both Britain and the US have tended to adopt pre-emptive and aggressive postures, all designed to ensure that the new state does not unlock itself from the grip that imperialism sought to reaffirm in the Lancaster House Agreement. The role of the former white settlers has therefore a direct bearing in the field of external relations. This is illustrated in the attempt of the white leadership to highlight the role (and threat) of South Africa as an additional buffer to pre-empt any action by the African petit bourgeoisie that might undermine white confidence. This stance is quite integral to that which views white interests as dependent on the prevailing influence of the West in Zimbabwe. Not surprisingly, therefore, the British and the US would, from time to time, utilise key white politicians within Zimbabwean society in the pursuit of their neo-colonial policies. It is true that the whites—particularly the chiefs of industry and commerce as represented by the Confederation of Zimbabwe Industries (CZI) and the Zimbabwe National Chambers of Commerce (ZNCC) respectively—obviously favoured a pragmatic policy towards South Africa, and would therefore be generally opposed to sanctions against that country. Such a position was greatly reinforced by the attitude of the US and Britain. In the end, whatever decision the Zimbabwean state would take with regard to the question of sanctions, for example, would depend to a large extent on how far it could take the private sector with it; and on how far the governing class was agreed on the wisdom of such a decision. But, as has been pointed out elsewhere,[88] the issue of sanctions against South Africa rests more on the role of the Western countries than on that of the African states.

No doubt some of the white leaders will have tried to project the view that the white presence in Zimbabwe is a guarantee that South Africa will not harm Zimbabwe. As a columnist of *The Herald* wrote in reply to some of the white leaders during the 1985 election campaign:

> It was offensive (for the white leaders like Ian Smith of CAZ and Bill Irvine of IZG) to claim that post-independence Zimbabwe is living off the fat of UDI; and that for the last five years the (white) parliamentarians—jointly or individually—have been the custodians of good government and financial management...
>
> Lastly, it was rather unfortunate that Mr. Irvine's interview should have been screened on the very day the South African Army invaded another Frontline State, Botswana. For, Mr. Irvine had the temerity to tell us that South Africa would not invade or destabilize Zimbabwe.
>
> My question is: What to do the likes of Mr. Smith or Mr. Irvine know that we do not know? Is this another attempt to hold Zimbabwe to ransom, implying that unless the 'white community's' interests are sustained and maintained, South Africa will be a threat to Zimbabwe?[89]

Whether or not the government of Zimbabwe considered this in terms of a conscious policy is difficult to determine, but there would appear to be some relationship between the presence of a sizeable number of whites in Zimbabwe and the limited (in comparison, for example, to those suffered by Mozambique and Angola) physical and economic attacks that Zimbabwe has had to endure at the hands of South Africa in the period since independence. But this would not, in itself, explain the more fundamental reason which accounts in part for the white presence in Zimbabwe: namely that Zimbabwe has threatened neither South Africa itself, the former white settlers nor the strategic and economic interests of imperialism. Any South African attack on Zimbabwe will therefore be viewed as uncalled for and unreasonable, subject to the strongest condemnation by both Britain and the US. Such was the case when South Africa attacked Zimbabwe on 19 May 1986. It is interesting that similar attacks on Angola and Mozambique have not always met with the same kind of disapproval on the part of the US, Britain and other Western countries.

There is therefore the implied threat that Zimbabwe might find herself in similar circumstances if she does not 'behave' herself. Thus good behaviour requires that Zimbabwe condemn 'terrorism' (and, with regard to South Africa, that it not offer rear base support to the freedom fighters); pursue a pragmatic course; shun Marxist ideology and keep the socialist bloc at arm's length; and in general not fundamentally run counter to the broad objectives of imperialist policy in Southern Africa. Mr. David Charles Miller, the US Ambassador, on 25 January 1985, expressed the theme of US policy towards Zimbabwe. (It should be noted from this statement that the US expected African countries to be 'non-aligned' to the socialist bloc and, therefore, by implication, aligned to the US itself.)

For those of us who are optimists and who believe that constructive engagement will work, we see a number of exciting and positive changes in Southern Africa which are only halfway to fruition. These would include the return of Mozambique to a truly non-aligned status—and hopefully domestic tranquility; a dialogue with the Angolan Government which however difficult is much improved over our position of no dialogue a few years ago; and a great deal of what is required to implement Resolution 435 is in place. The final elusive steps remain precisely that—elusive...

All of this has important bearing on Zimbabwe. If the mainly liberal community in the United States succeeds in crippling foreign policy objectives of drawing South Africans into the world, I am confident that the conservative community will see to it that aid and diplomatic outreach to Marxist governments in Southern Africa will be adversely affected. If the policy of constructive engagement comes unraveled, I am confident that it will mean not only less engagement with South Africa, but also with Zimbabwe, Mozambique and our budding relationship (sic) Angola.

While bilateral relations between the United States and Zimbabwe are in an acceptable state today, they could easily become the victim of a domestic political fight in the United States with the Prime Minister's occasional Marxist speeches being used as the rationale for reducing our presence here. Rarely have your personal interests been so directly at stake in our legislative process. If we in effect withdraw from South Africa and they retreat down a conservative road, while at the same time we withdraw support for Zimbabwe and Mozambique—and possibly Angola—my guess is that the region has the possibility of taking a large and distinct step backward.[90]

It is difficult to believe that the US would ever consider withdrawing from Southern Africa, let alone Zimbabwe. The threat is therefore perhaps based on the confidence that imperialist policy in the sub-region—and in Zimbabwe—has been so largely successful that even the African governments would find a US withdrawal very much to the detriment of the security and prosperity of their countries. As has been outlined elsewhere,[91] the frontline and SADCC states themselves tend to give credence to this position. In terms of their reliance on the imperialist powers to pressure South Africa, and in the light of a SADCC that is dependent for its existence and operations largely on the Western countries, the African states of Southern Africa have tended to act within the ambit of imperialist policy (and hegemony) in Southern Africa.

They will invariably complain about aspects of US policy— particularly with regard to South Africa. But, as a US diplomat explained, 'No one is saying to us, get out of the region...No one has told us to pack our bags and go...They want the US to be constructively engaged in Southern Africa'.[92]

It is, accordingly, a curious aspect of this situation that it is precisely on this basis that the frontline and SADCC states have been able to mobilise Western support for the cause of African political liberation and thereby enhance the process of isolating South Africa internationally.

Furthermore, the Zimbabwean experience so far would suggest that it is the kind of model that the Western countries would like to project in terms of an overall Southern Africa of tomorrow. But it is also a model that provides a lynchpin for the maintenance of imperialist interests in the sub-region. It is, therefore, appropriate to quote at length the 'Zimbabwe Testimony'[93] given by the US Deputy Assistant Secretary of State for African Affairs, Frank Wisner. Addressing the Sub-Committee on Africa of the Foreign Affairs Committee of the House of Representatives on 24 May 1984, he said:

> In the four years of its independence, Zimbabwe has captured the interest of many Americans. It is only right that it should. Zimbabwe's coming to independence—via the 1979 negotiations at Lancaster House between the British Government and the Zimbabwean parties—was a triumph of diplomacy and one in which the US played an important supporting role. We have watched Zimbabwe emerge from a bloody civil war and begin the construction of a new nation, committed to national reconciliation, non-racialism, democratic procedures, the rule of law, social justice, and economic development. There have been no war crime trials. Instead, opposition parties have taken seats in Parliament, from which they freely criticized the government of Prime Minister Mugabe. Zimbabwe inherited a reasonably strong economy, with an active private sector. While buffeted heavily by world recession, transportation difficulties, drought, *and a certain amount of Socialist rhetoric*, it has been managed by the new leadership with a respect of market principles and international economic realities and in cooperation with international economic institutions...Flatly stated, Zimbabwe is critical to our policy in Southern Africa...(my emphasis)

Zimbabwe, quite obviously, is a model to the region and the world 'about the prospects of lasting negotiated settlements' and 'of reconciliation among the region's strife-torn peoples'; and the Zimbabwean economy was evidence of the successful 'mix' between a vibrant private sector (of commercial agriculture, privately-owned business, communal farms, state-provided infrastructure) and a 'commitment to public welfare'. In turn, both as a model and as an engine of development, the Zimbabwean economy could, with the support of the US and other Western countries, 'grow, and stimulate growth elsewhere in the region'.

The 'Zimbabwe Testimony' concluded with an outline of five regional policy objectives, designed to consolidate the US policy in the sub-region, with particular regard to Zimbabwe' and to ensure that Zimbabwe itself remains firmly in line:

> First, we want to see Zimbabwe succeed...Second, we want to see Zimbabwe continue to enjoy the benefits of an economic infrastructure and potential that would be the envy of any other developing country, and turn that economy to the task of stimulating growth elsewhere in the region. The United States has contributed generously to Zimbabwe's reconstruction and development—in fact, the US is Zimbabwe's largest aid donor, bar none—and we are committed to helping Zimbabwe avoid the economic tarpits into which some of its less fortunate neighbours have fallen. Zimbabwe will recover from present economic adversity if it maintains social and economic policies, works closely with the IMF during this time of adjustment, offers incentives to the private sector, provides a favourable climate for foreign investment, and manages its budget prudently. Third, *we want to see Zimbabwe complete the transition from liberation movement to responsible government...* Fourth, we have engaged the Zimbabweans as a partner in the work of bringing about peaceful change in the region... its pragmatic policy toward South Africa and its influence among the Frontline states makes Zimbabwe a crucial element in our search for regional stability—Fifth, we want to develop a more mature relationship with Zimbabwe in international affairs... *We have a lot at stake at Zimbabwe's success...*(my emphasis)

Against this very favourable assessment, it would have been expected that the US might have dismissed as minor issues the differences with Zimbabwe on the latter's decision to abstain on the resolution condemning the Soviet downing of the Korean airliner, and for co-sponsoring a resolution condemning the US action in Grenada. On the contrary, the US cut aid to Zimbabwe as punishment for these actions; a threat to be repeated in July 1986, following the Zimbabwean foreign minister's condemnation of the US position on South Africa. As Prime Minister Mugabe retorted in response to these threats:

> There have been these threats and I understand some aid which was due to be signed has not been signed for. This is the behaviour of a country which in one vein would want us to believe that it does not ever want to impose sanctions (against South Africa) and in another it is imposing sanctions against us for saying it refused to impose sanctions against South Africa. I find that quite ironical, but what I find quite objectionable is the fact that the United States, of all countries, tends to use its aid as a weapon to coerce or impel countries which are the beneficiaries to toe a certain political line, even contrary to their own political and ideological persuasion. Perhaps, it is their tradition but of course such aid comes to us generously, if the donor decides to withdraw we still say thank you for what you gave

us in the past. But, let it be known that when we fought for our independence and sovereignty, we never meant to sell it at all and so what I give you for the future is independent Zimbabwe with resources and determined population to exploit those resources and become their own masters and not beggars and beneficiaries.[94]

Yet the US did not cut the aid completely nor did it do anything to contradict the main import of the 'Zimbabwe Testimony' cited above. Some might dismiss these threats as a mere token, the bullying tactics of a superpower, designed more to flaunt Reaganism than a trend towards disengagement. More seriously, however, it could be indicative of a lingering nervousness on the part of the imperialist centre, the fear that this Zimbabwe might still break out of the Lancaster cage and revert to the revolutionary course that it *appeared* so far to have rejected. If so, then these threats should be taken seriously, indicating the US resolve not only to keep Zimbabwe in line but even to resort to more drastic action should Zimbabwe decide to 'break away' altogether. But only if Zimbabwe should decide—nay, should develop and show a capacity—to chart such a course.

A closer analysis of British policy towards Zimbabwe in the years since Lancaster reveals an acute suspicion that the country might just 'degenerate' into the kind of anarchy that Lancaster was designed to avoid. It is, as yet, not possible for us to determine precisely whether the British Foreign Office policy on Zimbabwe is as sensational in its assessment as some of the British media; or that it relies more on a careful and concrete analysis that would show that Zimbabwe has, in the words of Lord Soames on his last visit to the country in 1986, confounded the prophets of doom. There is also evidence to suggest that the Foreign Office is kept appraised of the Zimbabwe situation by a team that includes notable liberal academicians who are viewed as 'experts' on Zimbabwe and are themselves concerned about maintaining Zimbabwe within the tradition of 'Western democracy'.

At any rate, the occasional benedictions by such people as Lord Soames would tend to confirm the view in British official circles that Zimbabwe is firmly following the letter and spirit of the Lancaster House Agreement. In the words of another observer of the Zimbabwean situation:

> That document remains largely intact. Following independence a new dynamic has evolved in Zimbabwe in which the government has sought to demonstrate adherence to the Lancaster House agreement as a means of maintaining the support of the economically critical domestic white community and of those Western governments and international agencies that have supplied high levels of financial assistance.[95]

Conclusion

Such entrenched clauses as relate to safeguards for the whites have largely served their purpose in the course of this transitional period. Not only do they fall away in 1987, but also a large section of the white population now realises that to retain them would tend to expose and undermine their economic and social comforts. Black majority rule *à la Lancaster* has done more to enhance white security and confidence within the post-white settler colonial situation than white settler colonial rule itself. Unless there is a spillover from the South African conflagration, it is likely that political developments in Zimbabwe will gradually move away from the black-white dichotomy, towards an overall class confrontation between the haves and have-nots. The whites will, of course, be caught up in such a situation but they have to rely, as they have slowly grown to realise, on the political ingenuity of their black counterparts, the African petit bourgeoisie. The new ideology of this class has contributed greatly to the postponement of the expression of the class struggle; and the weight and influence of imperialist hegemony will continue for the foreseeable future to convey the impression of 'stability' and 'prosperity'.

But the cracks are beginning to show as the contradiction between the imperatives of imperialist hegemony and the popular demands of the masses is played out. There is evidence that the progressive section of the African petit bourgeoisie may, one day, realise the futility of trying to balance such an antagonistic contradiction; and that, impelled by the march of the class struggle, and growing consciousness of the working people, it may find itself again at the head of a struggle that will be both anti-imperialist and anti-capitalist. The unfolding South African situation is, of course, a key factor in all this. For, even if South African liberation should finally come through a negotiated settlement, the stalling of a revolutionary process will be even more temporary than in the Zimbabwean situation.

And then it is bound to have such repercussions on the entire region that imperialism will find itself in deep waters. In addition to these problems it will be faced, at home and in other parts of the Third World, with growing unemployment and economic crises; and the inexorable and inevitable rising tide of the resistance of the oppressed and exploited peoples of the world.

REFERENCES

1. Mandaza, Ibbo, Conflict in Southern Africa, *Eastern Africa Social Science Research Review*, Vol. 1, No. 2, June 1985, pp. 53-72, also Mandaza, Ibbo (ed), *Conflict in Southern Africa*, in *Contemporary Marxism*, October 1986.
2. On these and other aspects of the African nationalist ideology and its relationship to liberalism, see Mandaza, Ibbo, White Settler Ideology, African Nationalism and the 'Colour' Question in Southern Africa, 1900-1976, unpublished D. Phil. Thesis, Department of Politics, University of York, England. Soon to be published under the title *Race, Colour*

and Class in Southern Africa: Malawi, Zambia and Zimbabwe, forthcoming, 1987.
3. *The Kissinger Study of Southern Africa* (with an Introduction by Barry Cohen and Mohamed A. El-Khawas), Spokesman Books, London, 1975, p. 66.
4. Verrier, Anthony, *The Road to Zimbabwe, 1890-1980*, Jonathan Cape, London, 1986, p. 133.
5. *Ibid.*
6. *Ibid.*, p. 152.
7. *Ibid.*
8. *Ibid.*, p. 156.
9. *Ibid.*, p. 154.
10. *Ibid.*, p. 156.
11. *Ibid.*, p. 154.
12. *Ibid.*, p. 152.
13. *Ibid.*, p. 160.
14. Meredith, Martin, *The Past is Another Country: Rhodesia: UDI to Zimbabwe*, Pan Books, London, 1979, p. 62.
15. Caute, David, *Under the Skin: The Death of White Rhodesia*, Penguin Books, Harmondsworth, 1983, pp. 91-92.
16. For an outline of the history of ZANU—especially its beginnings— see *Zimbabwe African National Union Central Committee Report*, presented by the President of ZANU, Cde R.G. Mugabe, to the Second Congress of the Party, Harare, 8 August 1984.
17. Mugabe, Robert Gabriel, *Our War of Liberation: Speeches, Articles, Interviews, 1976-1979* (with an Introduction by N.M. Shamuyarira and C.M.B. Utete), Mambo Press, 1983.
18. *Ibid.*: a lead quotation on the back cover of the book.
19. Sithole, Ndabaningi, *African Nationalism*, Cape Town, 1959, pp. 144-145.
20. See for example Lan, David, *Guns and Rain: Guerrillas and Spirit Mediums in Zimbabwe*, James Currey, London, 1985.
21. See the Introduction to this book, particularly the reference to Saul J., Transforming the Struggle in Zimbabwe, *Southern Africa*, January-February 1977, Vol. 10, No. 1, pp. 12-27; and Andre Astrow's comment on this in *Zimbabwe: A Revolution That Lost Its Way*, Zed Press, London, 1983, p. 122, note 109:

> Certain left-wing supporters of the Zimbabwe liberation struggle also believed that ZIPA represented a clear break from the petit bourgeois factionalism of ZAPU and ZANU. An underestimation of the political struggle required for creating a real socialist movement was usually predominant in such cases. A notable example is J. Saul...

It is interesting to note, however, that, despite such a profound observation about the nature of the African nationalist movement, Astrow's general theme (in the book) tends to lean towards a romantic, if not ultra-leftist and Trotskyist, conception of the struggle.

22. A ZIPA leader cited in Astrow, Andre, *op. cit.*, p. 105.
23. Thus Robert Gabriel Mugabe would emphasise this point during the Geneva Conference of 1976:

> ZIPA being an entity, a military organ which has autonomy, does not come into it at all. ZIPA, which is synonomous now with ZANLA, is a ZANU wing so it must be under the ZANU leadership' (Astrow, Andre *op. cit.*, p. 106.)

24. Astrow, Andre, *op. cit.*, p. 99.
25. As will be seen from p. 67, US Deputy Assistant Secretary of State Frank Wisner's 'Zimbabwe Testimony' would use precisely these words.
26. Astrow, Andre, *op. cit.*, p. 100.
27. Mandaza, Ibbo, Imperialism, the Frontline States and the Zimbabwe Problem *UTAFITI* (Journal of the Faculty of Arts and Social Sciences, University of Dar es Salaam), Vol. V, No. 1, 1980, pp. 129-163.
28. *Ibid.*, p. 163, n. 56.
29. *Ibid.*, p. 148. I wrote the paper just before the Lancaster House Conference began in September 1979, expecting that the conference would be doomed to failure, given what appeared to be the irreconcilable contradictions between imperialism and the liberation movement. Like many others, I had underestimated the nature of the relation and balance of forces that would give birth to independent Zimbabwe in 1980.
30. Astrow, Andre, *op. cit.*, p. 97.
31. *Ibid.*, p. 101.
32. *Ibid.*, p. 105.
33. *Ibid.*, p. 101.
34. *Ibid.*, p. 111.
35. *Ibid.*, p. 131.
36. *Ibid.*
37. *Ibid.*
38. *Ibid.*, p. 132.
39. Cited in Mandaza, Ibbo, Imperialism, the Frontline States and the Zimbabwe Problem, *op. cit.*, p. 163, n. 58.
40. Astrow, Andre, *op. cit.*, p. 132.
41. *Ibid.*, p. 154. At the crucial stage of the conference, when Mugabe and ZANU had decided that they would rather return to the battlefield than make a deal than was so unfavourable to them, the British would pressurise Machel into pressurising ZANU. The British warned Machel that the success of the conference was the last chance to end a war that had so adversely affected his country. Accordingly, Machel issued 'fresh instructions' that 'we the Mozambique Government did not feel that there were any issues at stake... which would justify the breaking of the Conference,' and, therefore, the PF had 'to take the plunge' or else 'things were not going to be as they had been before' (Fernando Honwana, President Machel's personal assistant, on Granada Television, *End of Empire: Rhodesia*, London, 1985).
42. Granada Television, *End of Empire: Rhodesia*.
43. Astrow, Andre, *op. cit.*, p. 155.

44. *Ibid.*
45. For a good account of the conference see Verrier, Anthony, *op. cit.* See also Davidow, Jeffrey, *A Peace in Southern Africa: The Lancaster House Conference on Rhodesia, 1979*, Westview Press, Boulder and London, 1984.
46. For other references to this see, for example, Verrier, Anthony, *op. cit.*, p. 291.
47. Verrier, Anthony, *op. cit.*, p. 256.
48. *Ibid.*, p. 260.
49. Granada Television, *End of Empire: Rhodesia.*
50. Verrier, Anthony, *op. cit.*, pp. 277-278.
51. Caute, David, *op. cit.*, pp. 425-426.
52. *Ibid.*, p. 427.
53. Saul, John S. Zimbabwe: The Next Round, *Monthly Review*, Vol. 32, No. 4, September 1980, p. 14.
54. *Ibid.*, p. 15.
55. Caute, David, *op. cit.*, p. 329.
56. Mandaza, Ibbo, The National Manpower Survey in the Context of the Political Economy of Zimbabwe, Director's Introduction to the *National Manpower Survey, NMS*, Ministry of Manpower Planning and Development of Zimbabwe, Harare, 1983, p. 21.
57. Weitzer, Ronald, Continuities in the Politics of State Security in Zimbabwe, in Schatzberg Michael G. (ed), *The Political Economy of Zimbabwe*, Praeger, 1984, pp. 84-85.
58. See, for example, Arrighi, Giovanni, The Political Economy of Rhodesia, in Arrighi, Giovanni and Saul, John S. (eds), *Essays on the Political Economy of Africa*, Monthly Review Press, London, 1973, pp. 336-377.
59. Caute, David, *op. cit.*, p. 439.
60. Even up to now, white workers remain largely protected by the system of racial discrimination—now mainly more subtle than blatant—in a private sector which has so far successfully resisted pressures to Africanise.
61. Tandon, Yash, The Post-Colonial State, *Social Change and Development*, No. 8, 1984. See also his monograph, *The People Versus the IMF: The Struggle of the Poor in Zimbabwe.*
62. See the Prime Minister's *Statement of Policy and a Directive on Provincial Councils and Administration in Zimbabwe*, Harare, 27 February 1984.
63. *The Herald*, 21 July 1986.
64. *Ibid.*
65. *The Herald*, 5 June 1986. Nyagumbo added: 'At independence, I personally did not know that the Party had adopted scientific socialism as its official ideology and so I bought a farm in Headlands.'
66. Cde Nyagumbo concluded: 'I sold the farm, not to anyone else but to the Government, to ensure that the farm would not be sold to any of my relatives.'
67. For example, there are monthly meetings held respectively by the

African Association of Political Science (AAPS), Zimbabwe National Chapter and the Zimbabwe Economic Society (ZES). Both bodies seek to encourage intellectual discussion on issues—political and economic mainly—pertinent to society.

68. There are also reports about the rise of spiritual revivalism in Zimbabwe, a feature, it is claimed by some observers, now prevalent among a significant section of the students at the University of Zimbabwe.

69. 'There was thunderous applause at State House (in Bulawayo) on Wednesday night when the Prime Minister, Cde Mugabe, said time had come for ZANU (PF) and ZAPU to conclude the unity talks completely, satisfactorily and effectively' (*The Herald*, 25 July 1986). 'The leader of ZAPU Dr. Joshua Nkomo has pledged to unite the people of Zimbabwe before he dies because God would not accept him in Heaven if he does not.' (*The Herald*, 28 July 1986).

70. Such is the facile analysis of Ronald T. Libby, Development Strategies and Political Divisions within the Zimbabwean State, in Schatzberg, Michael, *op. cit.*, pp. 144-163.

71. Mkandawire, Thandika, *op. cit.*, p. 33.

72. 'Whites who Left Zimbabwe, Fearful of Future, Drift Back' *(New York Times*, 18 May 1986).

73. Caute, David, *op. cit.*, p. 441.

74. By the way, there were also reports that there were elements within the University of Zimbabwe intent on sabotaging the new campaign for black advancement. There was fear among some of the university staff that the new government might radically transform the University, especially since there were some among the staff who had collaborated with the Smith (and Muzorewa) regime. The democratisation process within the education sphere had resulted in a sudden and historic rise in the number of black students who enrolled in the university, threatening, in the eyes of the conservative elements in the university, the so-called 'high standards' that had in the past kept out—and failed—many an African student. Amidst allegations and fears that the high failure rate at the university (in 1980 and 1981) was abnormal and artificial, the new Vice-Chancellor, Professor W.J. Kamba, set up a Committee of Inquiry to investigate the entire affair. The Report did confirm to some extent these fears; indicating thereby that it had been quite a characteristic feature of the University of Rhodesia that some white lecturers regarded blacks as intellectually less capable than their white counterparts. (In one of the interviews, the inquiry was confronted by a white professor who believed blacks could not think three-dimensionally.)

Accordingly, assessment of black students would have been adversely affected from time to time, depending on the individual lecturers and/or departments of the University. Many black students who had been either refused admission or failed in the university of Rhodesia would later emerge in other Universities of the world as strong graduates and professionals. (I was an 'observer' on the Committee of Inquiry, as a representative of the government.) (See *Report of the Principal's Committee of Inquiry into the Failure Rate*, University of Zimbabwe, Harare,

June 1982).
75. *New York Times*, 18 May 1986.
76. For an elaboration of this account of the African nationalist ideology, see Mandaza, Ibbo, White Settler Ideology, African Nationalism... , *op. cit.*
77. *The Chronicle*, 1 July 1985.
78. *The Herald*, 6 July 1985.
79. 'Hundreds of Letters Flood *The Herald*' (*The Herald*, 6 August 1985).
80. For an elaboration of this, see Mandaza, Ibbo, *The State and Foreign Powers: The Case of Zimbabwe*, CODESRIA publication, forthcoming, 1986.
81. Government Printers, Harare, February 1981.
82. Government Printers, Harare, November 1982.
83. Government Printers, Harare, April 1986.
84. Home-Grown (?) Austerity Measures: The Case of Zimbabwe, *Africa Development*, Vol X, No. 1/2, 1985, pp. 236-263.
85. *Ibid.*, p. 237.
86. *Ibid.*, p. 259.
87. *Ibid.*
88. Mandaza, Ibbo, Perspectives of Economic Cooperation and Autonomous Development in Southern Africa, paper prepared for the United Nations University's Project on *African Regional Perspectives*, Dakar, 1986.
89. The Scrutator in *The Herald*, 22 June 1985.
90. Text of an address to the National Forum, at the Park Lane Hotel, Harare.
91. Mandaza, Ibbo, Southern Africa: US Policy and the Struggle for National Independence, *op. cit.*
92. *Ibid.*
93. 'Wisner: Zimbabwe Testimony', USIS, SR 51/5/29/84. Unless otherwise stated, the following references are from this document.
94. *Hansard*, Vol. 13, No. 11, 16 July 1986.
95. Davidow, Jeffrey, *op. cit.*, p. 94.

2. THE GENERAL ELECTIONS 1979-1985
Masipula Sithole

Introduction

Although Zimbabwe was first organised as a colonial state called Southern Rhodesia in 1890, general elections are a new development and experience for this country's nearly eight million African majority. Until 1979, white settlers ruled the country without the consent of the African majority, who were denied all civil and political rights. Africans were excluded from the political process by denying them the franchise. As such, white rule was an imposed dictatorship of the few over the many, an oligarchy based on colour.

African agitation for majority rule started in the late 1950s with the organisation of the African National Congress (ANC) of Southern Rhodesia. Banned in 1959, the ANC was succeeded by the National Democratic Party (NDP) in 1960. After the ban on the NDP, the Zimbabwe African People's Union (ZAPU) was formed in 1961 but also banned in the same year. The Zimbabwe African National Union (ZANU) was founded in 1963, following major differences in the nationalist movement concerning the handling and direction of that movement. As happened to its predecessors, ZANU, too, was banned in 1964. From 1965 until the signing of the Lancaster Constitution in 1979, both ZAPU and ZANU operated from bases in exile. But 1971 saw the formation of the African National Council, later the United African National Council (UANC), which flourished throughout the 1970s.

There were a number of short-lived factions in exile in the 1970s, and similarly, inside the country, there were some factions formed during the period leading towards the elections held in 1979 and 1980. For a brief period (1976-79), ZAPU and ZANU formed a loose coalition called the Patriotic Front (PF) which lasted until the eve of the 1980 independence election. Throughout the 1970s the three major parties were ZANU, ZAPU and the UANC, although there were nine parties contesting the 1980 independence election. In the 1980s, only ZANU and ZAPU emerged as the major parties following the electoral defeat and complete eclipse of the other parties.

Following many years of bitter struggle, the white settlers conceded to African demands for majority rule and one-man, one-vote at the Lancaster House Agreement on Zimbabwe. But even before the majority rule election of 1980, the African majority had taken part, in 1979, in general elections based to some extent on this principle of universal adult suffrage. This election excluded the guerrilla movement in an attempt to legitimise the Zimbabwe-Rhodesia government of Bishop Muzorewa and Ian Smith. This chapter outlines and discusses three such elections: (1) the 'internal settlement' election of 1979, (2) the independence election of 1980, and (3) Zimbabwe's first post-independence election of 1985. These elections together constitute, in fact, Zimbabwe's experience with electoral politics. The latter two, in particular, are illustrative of democratic government since periodic general elections are the epitome of the democratic process.

Internal Settlement Election: 1979

The first one-man, one-vote election in this country was held during the period of Zimbabwe-Rhodesia in 1979.[1] It was held amidst both local and international controversy as to its authenticity. This stemmed from the questionable legitimacy of the so-called 'internal settlement' that authored it.

Following the failure of the 1979 Geneva Conference on Rhodesia, and under increasing pressure from nationalist guerrillas, Ian Smith identified those nationalist factions which had lost favour with either the frontline states or the guerrilla forces and enticed them into a political deal in the hope that this would undercut the Patriotic Front alliance of Robert Mugabe and Joshua Nkomo, then based in exile, while at the same time keeping the political outcome securely under the control of whites.[2] This led to the 'internal settlement talks' culminating in the 'March 3rd Agreement' of 1978 between Bishop Muzorewa's UANC, Ndabaningi Sithole's faction of ZANU, and Chief Chirau's Zimbabwe United People's Organisation (NUPO), on the one hand, and Ian Smith's Rhodesia Front (RF), on the other.[3]

We do not intend here to get into a detailed critique of the 'internal settlement'. We only wish to outline its salient features, on the basis of which the white Rhodesians conceded superficial majority rule, and on the basis of which the Patriotic Front boycotted the subsequent election of April 1979. However, we detail somewhat the election arrangements and procedures for this election because similar arrangements were to be repeated for the next general elections in 1980, and many features were again repeated for the 1985 elections. Further, although the 'March 3rd Agreement' did not transfer substantive power—the army, police, economy and civil service—the 1979 elections on which they were based was the first time that a substantive section of the African majority took part in an electoral process.

Let us begin with the constitution of Zimbabwe-Rhodesia. After tedious and often frivolous deliberations, a constitution was agreed upon between the internal black and white leaders. On 20 January 1979 this constitution was put to a referendum of white electors, who voted for it overwhelmingly. There was a referendum to ascertain African opinion on the same constitution.

The provisions of the Zimbabwe-Rhodesia constitution, as they relate to an elected legislature, are a follows. The Legislature consisted of a President and a Parliament, comprising a House of Assembly and a Senate. The President, who acted on the advice of the Prime Minister and Executive Council, was appointed by an electoral college consisting of all the senators and all members of the House of Assembly. The Senate consisted of 30 members, of whom 10 were blacks elected by 72 black members of the House of Assembly, 10 were whites elected by 28 white members of the House of Assembly, and 10 were African chiefs elected by the Council of Chiefs. Of the latter, five were from Mashonaland and five from Matebeleland, a sort of 'ethnic balance' to be repeated in the Lancaster House constitution.

The House of Assembly consisted of 100 members. Seventy-two were blacks elected by voters on the common roll. However, for the first Parliament, these members were to be elected on a party-list system and not on a constituency basis. Twenty seats were for whites elected on a preferential voting system by voters enrolled on the white roll for 20 constituencies. An additional eight white members were elected by the 92 members of the House of Assembly, from 16 white candidates who were to be nominated by the 28 white members of the previous House of Assembly. For the purposes of the first election, the 16 candidates were nominated by the 50 white members of the previous House of Assembly. At the end of 10 years or after the second Parliament, whichever would have been the later, a commission was to be established to review the question of retaining the 28 white seats. It was made deliberately complex.

All male and female citizens of 18 years of more, whether black, or white, 'coloured' or Asian, were eligible to be enrolled on the common voters' roll. In addition, all whites who had attained the age of 18 or more were eligible to be enrolled on the white voters' roll. For the first election those entitled to vote were all persons over 18 who were either citizens or had been permanently resident in Zimbabwe-Rhodesia for a continuous period of two years before the election. Provision was also made in the constitution for the first government elected to be a government of national unity, on the basis that each party with five seats or more in the House of Assembly would be represented in the cabinet in proportion to the number of seats won.

An important feature of the 1979 elections was the establishment of an Electoral Supervisory Commission charged with ensuring that the elections were free and fair. This feature was repeated in the 1980 election and again in the 1985 election. Persons wishing to complain either about election irregularities or about related matters were asked in press notices to inform the commission accordingly.

The 72 blacks who contested the common roll elections were elected on a party-list system under which voters indicated their choice of political party rather than candidate. Each competing party received a number of seats, calculated on the proportion of votes cast for that party in relation to the total votes cast in the election. The country was divided into eight electoral districts to encourage parties to nominate candidates representative of each district. In turn, each district was allocated a number of seats based on the estimated number of voters in that district. A party had to obtain at least 10% of the votes cast in any election district for it to be eligible to have seats allocated to it in that district.

Parties were represented on ballot papers by name and by an election symbol distinctive of each party. Common roll voters had to indicate the party of their choice by a cross or other satisfactory mark in the square next to the relevant party name and symbol. Prior to the elections, the government instituted a widespread information programme to encourage people to vote, and to explain both the election process and eligibility of voters. A popular advertisement on radio, television and newspapers stated: 'We are all going to vote! That is what the people want!' A difference between the white roll elections and the common roll elections was that the white representatives were elected on a constituency basis and by preferential voting.

There were elaborate procedures for this 'one-man, one-vote' election. These procedures were followed during the subsequent two elections in 1980 and 1985. Hundreds of polling stations (including mobile ones) were established in urban and rural locations to provide as wide a spread of polling locations as possible. Polling officers were required, if in doubt, to check eligibility to vote by conducting a check of age and residential qualifications.

Polling officers were also required to check that a person had not voted previously. Each voter had to dip his fingers in a colourless liquid containing a dye visible only under ultra-violet light and which stayed on a person's fingers for a week or more. Before voting, a person had to place both hands in a black scanning box containing an ultra-violet light to check whether he or she had voted before. If not, the voter was given a numbered ballot paper, stamped on the back with the stamp of that particular polling station and directed to a polling booth. If a voter was unsure as to what to do, polling officials would explain the ballot paper and how a vote should be indicated.

Once a voter had marked the paper, he/she was required to fold it so that his/her mark could not be seen, but in doing so also ensuring that the polling station stamp on the reverse was visible to the polling official at the ballot box. The voter would then place his/her ballot in the box. Representatives of the competing political parties, international observers and the press were able to enter polling stations at any time and scrutinise the voting process. They were also empowered to be present at the sealing and re-opening of ballot boxes, and to affix their own seals if they so desired. Full ballot boxes, and at the end of the election period all ballot boxes, were returned to regional counting centres in each of the eight electoral districts. It was an elaborate process.

The total figure for the 1979 common roll poll was 1,852,772 out of an estimated voting population of 2.9 million. Thus, 64.45% of potential voters cast their vote. The total national strength of each party taking part in the 1979 elections is shown in Table 1.

Although there was disruptive pressure from the Patriotic Front guerrillas, these elections were pronounced to have been 'substantially free and fair' by both the Electoral Supervisory Commission and several international 'observer' groups. All contesting parties except ZANU (Sithole) concurred with this assessment. On losing to Muzorewa's UANC, ZANU (Sithole) alleged 'gross irregularities' in the conduct of the elections. Accordingly, it lodged a petition with the Executive Council calling for an 'independent' commission of inquiry. The irregularities that were alleged included:

> ...breaches of laws and regulations governing the elections, people having voted before the official start of the elections, people having voted more than once, busing people to vote, certain candidates invoking spirit mediums, undue influence on people to vote or not to vote for certain parties, intimidation by auxiliary forces, election officials directing some voters whom to vote for, employers ordering voters to vote for certain political parties, and prisoners being selected for release on condition that they vote for a particular party.[4]

The Executive Council rejected the petition on the grounds that machinery already existed (the Electoral Supervisory Commission) for the investigation of complaints about the election. Anyone dissatisfied with its verdict could go to the High Court.

TABLE 1.
ZIMBABWE-RHODESIA:
RESULTS FOR THE 1979 ELECTION

Party	Valid Votes	% of Valid Votes	Seats Won
UANC (Muzorewa)	1,212,639	67.27	51
ZANU (Sithole)	262,928	14.59	12
UNFP (Ndiweni)	194,446	10.79	9
ZUPO (Chirau)	114,570	6.35	-
NDU (Chiota)	1,870	1.00	-
Total	1,786,453	100.00	72

Spoilt papers: 66,319 or 3.55% of total votes cast.
Total poll: 1,852,772

The 12 ZANU (Sithole) members initially boycotted Parliament but later took up their seats when it had become apparent that nobody in the system really believed their story. Also, it had become clear that if they remained outside parliament, they would be excluded from the Zimbabwe-Rhodesia delegation to the impending all-party conference in London. For his part, Muzorewa formed a government which failed to gain international recognition and which, contrary to local expectations, attracted intensification of guerrilla pressure until he and his internal colleagues were summoned to London by Mrs. Thatcher's government to discuss a new constitution with the leaders of the Patriotic Front late in 1979.

The principal issue in the 1979 election was the seven years' guerrilla war which was going from bad to worse, with life becoming, in the Hobbesian formulation, 'solitary, nasty, brutish, and short'. Muzorewa, by far the most popular of internal leaders, believed he could stop the war once he was in power. He believed that, since most guerrillas from 1974 onwards were recruited under the guise of the UANC, they would be loyal to his government. Moreover, the whites, comfortable in the former's piety, also calculated that they could stop the war and retain control of (state) power. Sithole, for his part, believed that since he was father to the armed struggle he could command it to stop. He believed that everybody, particularly the masses, in the equation could see the 'self-evident' logic. But time would tell and reveal that the masses had already another father in Robert Gabriel Mugabe. Thus, as we shall see, in 1980 when they shifted their support from Muzorewa, it was not to Sithole but to Mugabe.

That Ndiweni won any seat at all, let alone nine seats, came as a big surprise for a party formed only a few months before the election. Largely believed to be a creation of Ian Smith, the United National Federal Party (UNFP) never made the war an issue. It articulated federation and ethnicity:

> The United National Federal Party solidly advocates a federal system of government in the country. We are strongly opposed to a military system advocated by other parties because such a system falls short of satisfying the political aspirations of the diverse people constituting our nation...all future governments must be equally shared between the two major communities of this country in order to avert civil war. My party will fight domination of any kind.[5]

Interestingly, the other parties never raised the unitary or federal state issue. Ndiweni simply raised and cashed in on it. Cleverly, the UNFP used a cow (incidentally, perhaps, also Nkomo's totem) as its election symbol. For this reason it has been suggested that many peasants in Matebeleland believed Nkomo had given his blessings to the UNFP.[6] Sithole's ZANU faction polled overwhelmingly in the Chipinge region, stronghold of the Ndau ethnic group to which he is affiliated. For this reason a good number in this group believed Sithole's allegations about 'gross irregularities' in the elections.[7]

With the exception of Patriotic Front guerrilla activities and the activities of auxiliary forces (army support units), as well as the presence of armed forces in some parts of the rural areas, inter-party violence was negligible in the 1979 elections. There were, however, isolated incidents of intimidation by party youths, particularly during the eve of star rallies. Complaints about intimidation were usually expressed by the weaker party, in this case ZANU (Sithole), levelling such allegations against the UANC. As we shall see, this pattern was to be repeated in subsequent elections.

Finally, the elaborate and meticulous election arrangements and procedures were meant to convince the suspicious international community that the results were a true reflection of the wishes of the African people, and that Africans were in favour of the 1979 Zimbabwe-Rhodesia constitution. More than anything else, however, voter turnout was crucial to the Zimbabwe-Rhodesia authorities. This would be their loudest statement to both the international community and to the Patriotic Front that the internal settlement had the support of the African people. As such, the international community would be under a moral obligation to recognise a government that resulted from these elections. The 64.45% voter turnout which they finally registered gave the victors in the internal settlement some comfort, though very short-lived.

The Muzorewa government did not last long for a number of reasons. First, it expressed internal problems soon after the election. The UANC Vice-President, James Chikerema, and nine other MPs pulled out of the party to form their own party amidst recriminations. Furthermore, for a while ZANU's (Sithole's) twelve MPs, as we have seen, boycotted parliament, alleging electoral fraud. Second, amidst these internal quarrels, the international community withheld recognition, including the more critical support of the British and American governments which the internal settlement had counted on. Third, and perhaps more importantly, the armed struggle further intensified notwithstanding Muzorewa's electoral claims that he would be able to stop it once in power.

Thus, by the end of 1979, the British government summoned Muzorewa's government and the Patriotic Front leaders Joshua Nkomo and Robert Mugabe to lead delegations to London for an all-party conference which produced a new constitution for an independent Zimbabwe. The Muzorewa government was forced to resign and an interim administration put in place. Led by British Governor Lord Soames, its immediate task was to conduct new general elections that would decide who among the nationalists would govern during the first five years of independent Zimbabwe. It is to these elections we now turn.

Independence Election: 1980
Zimbabwe government and politics operate within the framework of the 1979 Lancaster House constitution. It is not the place here to detail the provisions of this constitution or the transitional arrangements leading to the 1980 election; its governmental and electoral provisions were much the same as those stipulated in the Zimbabwe-Rhodesia constitution already discussed. I wish, however, to single out some important exceptions and innovations.

Although the House of Assembly still consisted of 100 members, 80 rather than 72 were to be elected by Africans on the common roll, and the white seats were brought down from 28 to 20. While the Zimbabwe-Rhodesia constitution had specifically required the formation of a government of national unity by proportional representation in cabinet, the Lancaster constitution was silent on this issue. Cabinet selection was now entirely the prerogative of the prime minister. The only requirement, as in the previous constitution, was that he should select his cabinet from either the House of Assembly or the Senate.

A critically important innovation of the Lancaster talks was the question of nationalist guerrillas. What would happen to them during the transitional period? During the Zimbabwe-Rhodesia period, the guerrillas were required to 'surrender' to the Rhodesian Army, but now they would go into assembly points where they would remain with their arms throughout the course of the election. From their number, and from the former Rhodesian Army, a new Zimbabwe National Army (ZNA) would be created with the help of British military experts.

Another innovation of the Lancaster House constitutional talks, and which pertained specifically to the question of transfer of power and to elections, was the provision of a British governor. He was charged with the responsibility of administering the country during the transition period, supervising the conduct of the elections and asking the leader of the winning party to form a government. In Zimbabwe-Rhodesia these procedures were the responsibility of Ian Smith's Rhodesia Front government machinery.

The most significant innovation in the Lancaster constitution, however, was the provision of a subsection (2) of section 75 of Chapter VII which stated:

> The President may give general directions of policy to the Public Service Commission with the object of achieving a suitable representation of the various elements of the population in the Public Service and the Prison Service.[8]

Popularly known as the 'Presidential Directive', this claim allowed for the appointment of personnel and lateral entry into any section of the Public Service if the president (on the advice of the prime minister) deemed it necessary in order to redress past imbalances. This advice was particularly important since key Public Service posts had, hitherto, been stacked with the 'old-order' types whom it would take decades to replace on the basis of the normal course of experience. 'Presidential Directives' have been utilised to full effect since independence in 1980. Ibbo Mandaza, a Commissioner in the Public Service, observed:

> Were it not for the Presidential Directive, and the fact that qualified Zimbabweans returned home in their numbers at independence, there would have been little change in the structure and direction of this important component of the State machinery.[9]

Such a provision was absent in the Zimbabwe-Rhodesia constitution, rendering it unacceptable to the generality of the African intelligentsia, the direct beneficiaries of such a provision. The civil service is the mainstay of any government on a day-to-day basis. In fact, it is the government in the real sense that it runs government, that is to say, implements policy. But during Muzorewa's government, all of the top and most of the middle civil servants were white and there was no provision either to remove them or to bring in blacks. It is for this reason that many believed Muzorewa was in fact prime minister of a white government, even though he was elected by blacks.

Among the more significant features of previous constitutions that were retained in the 1979 Zimbabwe (Lancaster) constitution were the Senate and Presidency. This meant that Zimbabwe would have a two-tier legislature and a basically ceremonial president, much like the British monarchy. Like the House of Lords in relation to the Commons, the Zimbabwe Senate was essentially a vetting, if not a rubber-stamp, body on legislation passed by the House of Assembly. Significant in the composition of the Senate was the retention in the constitution of a Ndebele-Shona representation on the basis of party. It is equally significant that none of the nationalists at the Lancaster talks commented on the merits or demerits of this party mechanism or structure. Once presented, it was accepted, taken for granted as it were, as if by conditioned habit.

A total of nine political parties contested in the independence elections held over a period of three days, 27-29 March 1980. However, only three parties, ZANU (PF), PF (ZAPU) and the UANC won any seats. ZANU (PF), by far the dominant party, won 57 of the 80 common roll seats, and 63% of the popular vote. Coming second, PF (ZAPU) won 20 seats, and 24% of the popular vote. The UANC came last with three seats and only 8% of the popular vote. The other six parties which lost completely together got 5% of the popular vote. The total valid votes cast were 2,649,529. Spoilt papers were 52,746, or 2% of the votes cast which totalled 2,702,275. Table 2 shows the results of the 1980 common roll elections.

TABLE 2
ZIMBABWE: 1980 ELECTION RESULTS

Party	Valid Votes Cast	% of Valid Votes	Seats Won
ZANU-PF (Mugabe)	1,668,992	62.99	57
PF-ZAPU (Nkomo)	638,879	24.11	20
UANC (Muzorewa)	219,307	8.28	3
ZANU (Sithole)	53,343	2.01	-
ZDP (Chikerema)	28,181	1.06	-
NFZ (Mandaza)	18,794	.71	-
NDU (Chiota)	15,056	.57	-
UNFP (Ndiweni)	5,796	.22	-
UPAM	1,181	.05	-
Total	2,649,529	100.00	80

Spoilt papers: 52,746 (1.99% of votes cast) Total poll: 2,702,275.

The twenty white roll seats were all captured by Ian Smith's Rhodesia Front in a poll held two weeks before the common roll poll. The RF ran unopposed in 14 of the 20 white constituencies, and swept the six contested constituencies. Significant in the 1980 white poll was the continued popularity of the Rhodesia Front, even when their 1962 white supremacy agenda had collapsed following a bitter and costly war.

Several factors explain the overwhelming victory of Mugabe's party in the 1980 elections. First and foremost, the preponderant majority of the people of Zimbabwe, tired of the seven years' war which Muzorewa was not able to stop, now believed Mugabe and his ZANU (PF) would stop it. Moreover, it had become clear to most people that ZANU (PF) was in control of the ZANLA guerrillas whose presence was felt in over two-thirds of the country, mostly in the Shona-speaking regions. The people were left without any doubt that peace meant a ZANU (PF) victory.[10]

Second and significantly, Mugabe as a personality appeared not only the most straightforward of all leaders in the Zimbabwe nationalist movement, but also the most unpopular with Ian Smith's Rhodesia Front in particular, and with South Africa and the West in general. This endeared him to the African people, particularly among the Shona, whether peasant, proletarian or bourgeois. Moreover, Mugabe portrayed a humble yet stern and disciplined demeanour. He looked more honest, and was very articulate. For a people let down several times by this and that leader, Mugabe was what they were waiting for in the election of 1980, someone without a smear. This did not significantly change in the election of 1985.

Third, the internal settlement leaders, notably Muzorewa and Sithole, who might have put up a serious challenge to Mugabe in the Shona-speaking regions, had already been discredited by the failure of the 'internal settlement' itself. Moreover, Muzorewa's flamboyant and colourful campaign (openly using aircraft presumably donated for the purpose by South Africa) cost him whatever political integrity he had retained since the 'internal settlement'.[11]

Finally, the real opponent for ZANU (PF) in 1980, as was to be the case also in 1985, was Joshua Nkomo's PF (ZAPU). Once ethnicity became in the 1970s a political issue in the nationalist movement, ZAPU became a minority party, a position that is likely to be maintained for the foreseeable future. Ever since the 1970s, ZAPU has retained loyalty mainly in Matebeleland, as ZANU (PF) has done in the Shona-speaking areas. ZANU (PF) is likely to maintain its position as a majority party for the foreseeable future. More than that, ZANU (PF) is likely to remain in power for a long time, with or without a one-party state. The 20 seats won by PF (ZAPU) were mainly in Matebeleland North, Matebeleland South and the Midlands, where the Ndebele presence is fairly significant.[12]

There were allegations and counter-allegations of violent intimidation by all political parties, particularly among the major ones: ZANU (PF), PF (ZAPU), UANC and ZANU (Sithole), with the latter three complaining that they could not campaign in any of the rural areas formerly controlled by ZANLA guerrillas. ZANU (PF)'s complaints were mainly directed at Lord Soames who was accused of bias against ZANU (PF) in favour of the UANC, in particular, and the other parties generally.[13] Moreover, there were several attempts on Mugabe's life during the 1980 campaign.[14] On the complaint that other parties could not campaign in former ZANLA areas, the ZANU (PF) attitude was: 'Why should any party go where it is not wanted? Why should any party wish to go and reap where it did not sow?'[15] Certainly ZANU (PF) was not about to give safe passage to rival parties into its areas of dominance. In a contest one does not play on the side of the opponent. In the big cities, there were numerous clashes between rival parties. A number of fatalities were reported during the election campaign.

Nothwithstanding the accusations and counter-accusations of imtimidation and violence, the elections were pronounced by both Governor Soames and the international observers to be a fair reflection of the people's wishes.[16] Even if the other parties had been given 'safe passage' into former ZANLA areas or the others into former ZIPRA areas, it is quite unlikely that the results would have been otherwise. The campaign of 1980 did not start in February of that year, but several years back through guerrilla warfare and mass politicisation. In an informed analysis of the 1980 election, Martyn Gregory is correct when he writes:

> What can be said with confidence is that those who assumed a volatile electorate and ignored evidence of underlying patterns of support for the guerrillas forged during the war, tended to overemphasise the importance of the election campaign as an influence on voters' loyalty... Mugabe's victory can only be satisfactorily understood in the context of over two decades of organised African resistance to white rule and, specifically, in terms of the seven-year armed struggle.[17]

The same can be said for areas like Matebeleland where PF (ZAPU) was dominant over a long period of time. As such, election manifestos meant little compared to traditional loyalties.[18] Moreover, the fact that areas of dominance fell along ethnic lines was not an accident and certainly not a factor to be ambivalent about as Gregory infers when he says: 'The crude nature of the electoral data makes it impossible to prove or disprove theories that "tribal" identifications decisively influenced the outcome.'[19]

But this is precisely what happened. It was no accident that ZIPRA guerrillas found it easier to enter and operate from the west and north-west part of the country, i.e. Matebeleland. Similarly, it was easier for ZANLA to enter and operate in the Shona-speaking areas. Moreover, by the end of the war, ZANLA had penetrated deep into a traditionally ZAPU area in Matebeleland South around Gwanda where, for about three years, they engaged in *pungwes* (marathon night meetings for mobilisation and politicisation). However, when elections came, Matebeleland South preferred PF (ZAPU) candidates without exception.[20] What had happened to the three years of *pungwes?* This phenomenon was to be repeated even more vividly in the election of 1985 to which we turn.

The Election of 1985

Zimbabwe's first, and perhaps most important, experiment with elections as the democratic means of deciding who shall govern was the general election held on 1-4 July 1985. This election is significant in many respects.

First, it was the first general election Zimbabwe has held as an independent sovereign state, the 1980 election having been held under British supervision. Second, with the exception of some parts of Matebeleland, the 1985 election, unlike the earlier ones, was largely held in an atmosphere of peace; as such, it was not a single issue election. Third, like the 1979 and 1980 elections, the 1985 election was held in a multi-party context; some six black political parties contested the election, notwithstanding suggestions by the ruling party for a one-party state. Fourth, while the two previous common roll elections were based on the party-list electoral system, the election of 1985 was conducted on a single constituency basis. Finally, although the white electorate held a separate election (as they had done in 1979 and 1980), there was a significant development in white politics in the 1985 election. White unity and fifteen years of Rhodesia Front hegemony in the white community had ended. For the first time in a long while two white factions (both with a Rhodesia Front background) contested the white roll elections in 1985.

In 1980, ZANU (PF) had its first experience in running an election campaign; then it was a party out of government. In 1985 it had two onerous responsibilities. As the party in government, it was responsible for the administration and conduct of the general election, as well as for its own campaign for re-election in a contest in which five other parties also sought office (although with varying degrees of vigour and appetite). This dual responsibility placed ZANU (PF) both at an advantage and disadvantage. For the first task it had gained enormous experience from years of mobilisation during the liberation struggle as well as from the actual election campaign of 1980. For the second task, that of administering a national election, ZANU (PF) had very little prior experience. It had to take the blame for anything wrong about the elections. Moreover, while the black population had prior experience with the party-list system of election (1979 and 1980), they had not experienced a constituency-based election. The need for prior administrative experience in conducting elections was manifest throughout the exercise. It was a learning experience.

In a candid report to the Chairman of the Election Supervisory Commission on the conduct of the 1980 General Election, the Registrar-General accepts, 'at the outset that preparation for the elections was an onerous and difficult exercise', and that, 'Being the first post Independence general election, some inherent problems were inevitable'. The registration of voters was 'bedeviled from the start'. There were 'security problems to be overcome as access to some parts of the county was difficult due to the dissident factor'. Moreover, the call for the registration of voters was 'not readily accepted by the community for various reasons'. There were those who now 'believed the country was already a one party state' and therefore saw no need to register as voters.[21] Others, particularly among minority parties, were 'suspicious' about the whole exercise, believing that voter registration officers, deployed at various centres throughout the country, were nothing but 'agents for the ruling party'. Moreover, another 'setback' was the 'shortage of supplies and transport' to speed up the National Registration. The National Registration exercise was a necessary initial procedure since people could not register as voters without identity cards (or pink forms indicating that such a card was being processed).

Preparations for the 1985 general election started with the convening of the first Delimitation Commission on 8 June 1981 as required by the Zimbabwe constitution. The commission drew eight provisional common roll constituencies to facilitate voter registration. Further, the Delimitation Commission was responsible for defining constituency boundaries and estimating the number of eligible voters in each of the constituencies. The commission published its provisional report in November 1981, thus enabling voter registration to start. The second Delimitation Commission (as required by the constitution) was appointed in November, 1984 to divide Zimbabwe into eighty common roll and twenty white roll constituencies in terms of section 60 of the Zimbabwe constitution. However, the commission could not start its work until the voter registration exercise ended on 15 February 1985. Final delimitation could not be carried out until the total voters registered on the common roll and on the white roll were known. The required figures were available from the Registrar-General in March 1985.

Voter registration commenced in May 1982. The initial response was very poor. By October, or six months after the exercise started, only about 367,000 voters or about 13% of the estimated eligible electorate of 2,982,000 had registered. There was no sign of the trend picking up momentum. By mid-April 1983, 869,199 people were on the common roll register, a figure which the Registrar-General found to be 'well below a million voters and yet the target figure was 3 million voters by 31 October 1983 to enable the second Delimation Commission to convene in November 1983,' The Registrar-General was not flattered by this shocking state of affairs. As such:

> After a close analysis of the position so far, it was decided to change the approach. A new approach became the only alternative to speed up the exercise. A 'go-to-the-people' voters' registration scheme was introduced. Under the scheme the registration officers were to go and register voters at their places of employment or where population concentrations could be found.[22]

Then, mobile units were dispatched all over the place and they registered '600 voters within a matter of hours instead of 10 voters per day', as had been the case with static units. By September 1983, a period of only four months, the number of registered voters had risen from the April figure of 869,199 to 1,488,832. However, because of time already lost, this figure was still far below the target figure of close to 3 million by 31 October 1983, a month away. As such, the registration period was extended to 31 October 1984, and by the end of that month the total figure had risen to 2,139,730. However, another extension for a further period up to 31 January 1985 was granted, and in January-February a supplementary voters' registration was introduced as the last resort to capture voters. This enabled many aliens to register to vote. Thus, by the time the election took place in July 1984, some 2,972,146 voters had been registered.

The delay and extensions of voters' registration inevitably affected the other aspects of the election preparations such as the second Delimitation Commission, which could not start its work until the final voters' roll was published. This, in turn, affected the timing of the actual election. Originally scheduled for March, the election, for these reasons, was postponed to July. Scheduled to take place over only two days (1-2 July), this period was actually doubled during polling, ending on 4 July. This was due to inadequate preparations and other logistical problems that had not been anticipated.

As in the 1979 and 1980 elections, there was an Election Directorate appointed by the Prime Minister 'to oversee the voters registration exercise...', and to 'propose legislation on matters relating to elections and to assist the Registrar-General in the holding and conducting of the general election, etc.'. This was appointed in November 1984. Also the constitution provided for the appointment of an Electoral Supervisory Commission. Its functions were to 'supervise the registration of voters and the conduct of the election of members of the Senate and the House of Assembly...' The Supervisory Commission was appointed in June 1984.

Given their duties, perhaps both the Election Directorate and the Electoral Supervisory Commission should have been appointed much earlier to oversee the Registrar-General's efforts. Moreover, voter registration commenced in 1982. But as it happened both bodies were appointed in November 1984, four months before the election, which was then scheduled for March 1985. Furthermore, the Registrar-General lost a lot of time, over a year—May 1982 to April 1983—before he realised he had to 'go-to-the-people'. Under normal circumstances people do not go around looking for voter registration offices. Unless non-voting is met with sanctions, voting facilities will have to be brought nearer the people as much as possible.

Much as in the previous two elections, the Registrar-General's office issued a lot of literature explaining the election, its importance to the citizen, its secrecy, and voting procedures. The names and symbols of all contesting parties were displayed openly at public places on huge posters. The three main languages—English, Shona, and Ndebele—were used on radio, television, and in print in the election-education programme and activities of the government. Once the parties began campaigning, they augmented the government effort in voter registration and education. Towards polling day, everybody's efforts, with or without design, worked towards a huge voter turnout recorded as 2,893,285 out of a potential of 2,972,146.

We have left out a lot of detail concerning the problems encountered in administering and conducting this election, and these were enormous, including, for example, the blocking and coding of constituencies, the impact of the new legal age of majority, inadequate computer facilities and personnel to staff and service them, multiple registrations by fraudulent or anxious potential voters, problems of voter confirmation slips and so on. The effort by the Registrar-General and his team, as well as by those commissions such as the Election Directorate and the Electoral Supervisory Commission appointed to assist the Registrar-General, was enormous. They were often on the receiving end of criticism. It was a first experience to gain experience, and the cost to the state was put at some $9,587,050.[23]

The actual conduct of the election on 1-4 July was beyond reproach. Everything possible was done to ensure voter secrecy. Assistance was given to those with any form of disability: the old, the crippled, the illiterate, and the like. The presence at every polling station of good-mannered officials with identity tags pinned on their jackets ready to assist at any time was reassuring. The visibility of uniformed police officials gave the whole atmosphere the assurance of law and order. And, for their part, the voters were civil and exemplary. Rather than shouting party slogans at each other, or wearing tee-shirts in the queues, rival voters took turns behind each other in more civil attire, with the more humorous among them saying loudly, 'My vote is my secret', an adaptation of the government's poster which read: 'Your vote is your secret'. For four full days the people quietly cast their secret ballots to choose representatives of their choice. Even in dissident-affected parts of Matebeleland, relative quiet reigned as the people chose their representatives in the privacy of the secret ballot. According to the Registrar-General, the success and orderly conduct during the polling days was attributable to the 'prohibition of certain activities, including the wearing of Party uniforms, the banning of canvassing and political activities within 100 metres of the polling stations'.[24]

ZANU (PF) came on top with another victory. It picked up seven more seats, bringing the 57 won in 1980 to 64. It took all the seats in Mashonaland Central, East, and West as well as in the Midlands where in 1980 PF (ZAPU) had managed to win four out of the twelve seats. In Manicaland, ZANU (PF) won all but one seat in the Chipinge constituency, stronghold of Sithole's faction of ZANU which won the one seat. PF (ZAPU), defeated in all other six of the eight provinces, swept all 15 seats in Matebeleland North and South, defeating two incumbent Ministers in Mugabe's cabinet. Table 3 presents the results of the 1985 common roll elections.

To everyone's surprise, the white roll elections were won by Ian Smith's Conservative Alliance of Zimbabwe (CAZ), taking 15 seats out of the 20 white seats. The CAZ was opposed by the Independent Zimbabwe Group (IZG), a splinter group from Smith's former Rhodesia Front. Although this group won only four seats, they had posed the most serious challenge to Smith's leadership of the white community in a long time. They were more conciliatory toward the new socio-political order under black rule than CAZ, although one had really to read between the lines to see any difference. The difference seemed to be that of temperament only.

TABLE 3
ZIMBABWE: COMMON ROLL ELECTION RESULTS, 1985

Party	Valid Votes	% of Valid Votes	Seats Won
ZANU (PF)	2,233,320	77.190	64*
PF (ZAPU)	558,771	19.313	15
ZANU (Sithole)	36,054	1.246	1
UANG	64,764	2.238	-
NDU	295	0.010	-
NFZ	81	0.003	-
Total	2,893,285	100.00	80

Spoilt papers: 78,861
Total votes 2,972,146

Source: Adapted from Appendix B of Registrar-General's *1985 General Election Report*, Harare, 13 September 1985.

*This figure was initially reported as 63 because of the death of a ZANU (PF) candidate, Robson Manyika, in the Kariba Constituency. A by-election later was conceded to a ZANU (PF) candidate.

For instance, both CAZ and IZG were opposed to the introduction of the one-party state, and favoured a free market economy, as well as a pragmatic foreign policy, particularly in relation to South Africa. These were the three policy issues with which the white electorate was very much concerned. There were no differences either on concerns with education, health and security matters. What IZG could finally come up with was simply that Smith was 'too confrontational', which Smith publicly denied, saying he was prepared and wanted to work closely and constructively with the government, and then conveniently called his opponents and former supporters 'opportunists'. Table 4 shows the white roll election results.

TABLE 4
ZIMBABWE: WHITE ROLL ELECTION RESULTS, 1985

Party	Valid Votes	% of Valid Votes	Seats Won
CAZ	18,731	55.025	15
IZG	13,513	39.696	4
Independent	1,486	4.365	1
PF (ZAPU)	311	.914	-
Total	34,041	100.00	20

Spoilt papers: 1,721
Total votes 35,753

Source: Adapted from Appendix 'A' of Registrar-General's 1985 General Election Report (Harare, 13 September 1985).

Most likely the strong vote for CAZ came from the geriatric group. The CAZ leader, Ian Smith, himself was now 66 years old. Moreover, this group, now retired or about to retire, had all the time to indulge in nostalgia for the good old days. Moreover, given that the 1985 election was the last to be held on a separate roll, it was unlikely that the geriatric vote would rebel against a man they grew up and rebelled with against the British in 1965. Many had voted for Smith all their lives, and not voting for him now in what many believed was the very last election would be a betrayal of past loyalty. The story of an elderly white lady in the city of Mutare typifies what is being argued here. In a telephone interview with the author, during the election, she spoke on and on in answer to the simple question: *Which Party are you going to vote for: IZG, CAZ, or Independent?*

> Now you see it's hard. You say you are from the University doing some research. I don't want to get into trouble you see. You are not CIO I hope... but it did not matter. I am old and retired you see... I lost my husband... Yes I am going to vote. Some Europeans say we should vote for the other party, what do you call it... the Independent Group. I guess it's the party they will vote for. But I have always voted for Mr. Ian Smith. He is a nice chap you know... He has been my leader all my life... He tried his best. God knows he tried... I know he is now finished. There is little he can do about the communists when Britain and America have let him down... Don't get me wrong. I like Mugabe. He speaks well. I suppose the African people like to have their own Smith... You know what I mean? Anyway, it's the last time the Europeans are going to vote, I don't think we should forsake good old Smithy. At my age it's the last time I am voting anyway. I rather vote for one I have always voted for.[25]

When Ian Smith appeared on Mike Munyati's election programme 'Face to Face' on 25 June 1985, he was alert, cool, composed, informed and unrepentant. He still believed everyone was wrong and he was right. Whites who saw him handle questions thus had either to vote for him yet again, or not vote at all.

The elections were pronounced 'free and fair' by all international observers who came in their private capacities. Independent groups within Zimbabwe itself passed similar judgements of approval, although Nkomo did express disappointment with the results.[26] The Electoral Supervisory Commission was pleased with the conduct of the election. Its chairman, Professor Walker J. Kamba, also Vice-Chancellor of the University of Zimbabwe, commented:

> We were satisfied, beyond doubt, that the elections were conducted fairly at every stage of the process. My Commission visited many places in the country observing the election preparations, during the polling period, and the counting of votes. We

were satisfied that the officials acted and behaved with probity and impartiality. I have no doubt that the electorate expressed its choice at the polls freely. In every area, and in every constituency, people voted for the party or candidate of their choice.[27]

The irony of the 1985 election, however, was the almost unbelievable reaction of many ZANU (PF) supporters, mainly among women and the youth in the urban areas. A few days after the news of the victory, they went on a rampage, beating up and evicting members of minority parties from their houses. Whole families and their belongings were thrown out on the streets during the cold July weather, and several people were killed in this post-election violence.

Further, there were very strong, if unfamiliar, anti-Nkomo manifestations in several urban communities by some party officials and enthusiasts. At several places mock funerals were held with people carrying 'coffins' of Nkomo and ZAPU for burial. At one such mock funeral in Kadoma, a live bull (the ZAPU election symbol) was actually axed to death in front of a huge crowd to symbolise the death of ZAPU. Although other minority parties were also the object of similar ridicule, the anti-ZAPU manifestations were many and more pronounced.

ZANU (PF)'s victory is fairly simple to explain; moreover, many of the factors attendant on the overwhelming victory of 1980 had not changed in 1985. Although the war of liberation was now a thing of the past, ZANU (PF)'s claim to be the continuing benefactor was still very vivid. Moreover, PF (ZAPU), as the chief opponent again in 1985, was perceived by many traditional ZANU (PF) supporters as not only a 'bad loser' in 1980 but also as having therefore started another and unnecessary war. Of all the parties in the contest, only ZANU (PF) was seen to be seasoned enough to deal with PF (ZAPU) in this regard.

As in 1980, ZANU (PF) again appeared the most reliable group to maintain genuine independence, no matter what the difficulties. The feeling seems to run like this: 'If it is difficult for ZANU (PF) and Mugabe, anyone else will certainly fail'. Moreover, Ian Smith's CAZ victory did not pass unnoticed by many Africans. Coming only a few days before the common roll poll, it made handy political capital for those who would hazard the investment. Mugabe was quick and uncompromising in his reaction to the CAZ victory. The sins of CAZ were visited on all descendants of the white man:

> The vote cast by the majority of the white electorate has shown us that the trust we placed in whites and our belief that they were getting reconciled to the new political order was a trust and belief that was not deserved... [Whites] have spilled the blood of thousands of our people... The vote has proved that they have not repented in any way.[28]

Again Mugabe became the celebrity of an African electorate, which was well aware of the unrepentant attitudes and behaviour of whites who still were in the commanding heights of the economy. He certainly came out the most vigilant of the contenders. While mistrust still exists between black and white, the African electorate will prefer a leadership that projects itself as aware of the white man's machinations. Mugabe has consistently projected this image, during and after the liberation struggle.

Another reason for the ZANU (PF) victory will have to be its ideological orientation and performance over the past five years. While the bourgeois and petit bourgeois may question the validity and wisdom of socialism on the grounds of poor performance elsewhere in Africa, the common people of Zimbabwe have, thus far, felt overall satisfaction that they are better off today than they were five years ago. This attitude is expressed much more in rural than in urban areas. Zimbabwe, like many other African states, is still predominantly peasant, and a party that keeps this peasant majority pleased and satisfied should be expected to be retained in power. Moreover, the urban worker, for one reason or another, has also maintained trust in ZANU (PF). Minimum wage laws and worker protection from unscrupulous employers have been attributed to the ZANU (PF) government. It is questionable, however, whether popular satisfaction has been due to a socialist ideology or to able governance. For Zimbabwe's economy was predominantly in the private sector during the first five years of independence.

ZANU (PF)'s performance over a trying first five years has not been mediocre by any objective standards. The management of the economy and the welfare of the people during three years of drought and world recession was appreciated by many, including those not inclined to vote for ZANU (PF) under any circumstances. The mushrooming of roads, schools, clinics, and wells around the country were political assets to a party unashamed of reciting its successes and promising more in the next five years. Futhermore, ZANU (PF) could claim it brought peace to most parts of the country. Where there was no peace, as in some parts of Matebeleland, the obvious suggestion was that it was because of ZAPU 'malcontents' and not ZANU (PF)'s fault.

Thus, as an incumbent party, ZANU (PF) did not do badly. It had a lot to show for the first five years, while the opposition could only promise to do better, a promise the incumbent ZANU (PF) could also make. Herbert Ushewokunze (candidate, Chinamora constituency and also Director of the 1985 ZANU (PF) election campaign) could not have stated his case any better when he persuaded Borrowdale domestic workers (used to carrying letters of reference) to vote for him and his party because it had experience. 'Who would you employ', he asked, 'one with letters of reference or one without'? The audience replied: 'One with reference', to which he asked: 'Why then, ZANU (PF) has letters of reference showing five years experience. We now know the job. Muzorewa's reference shows he only worked six months in 1979 and was fired. Nkomo has never worked before...'[29] Like most ZANU (PF) candidates who won, Ushewokunze won his constituency with an overwhelming margin, 96% to 4%. However, ZAPU victors in Matebeleland had similar huge margins.

There is, however, the Chipinge constituency where the ZANU (PF) candidate lost to the ZANU (Sithole) candidate. Did he not have also a 'letter of reference?' He did, but as we all know, not all letters of reference are favourable. All evidence in the Chipinge constituency points to the fact that the incumbent could have done with the services of a public relations expert, notwithstanding the fact that Chipinge is Ndabaningi Sithole's home area.

Another, and extremely important, factor in the ZANU (PF) victory, which also derives from the vantage point of incumbency, was superior organisation and effective use of the state machinery to advantage. ZANU (PF)'s 1985 campaign started from the victory of 1980. The party embarked on a programme of reorganisation and restructuring at cell, branch, district and provincial levels culminating in the Party's Second National Congress of 8-13 August 1984. In fact, by the time of the Congress, only ZANU (PF) had an organisational infrastructure in most parts of the country, with those of the other parties either destroyed or waiting to resurface during the election campaign in 1985. When 1985 came, the weight of ZANU (PF) had become so heavy that none could resurface. Very early in the first five years, the ZANU (PF) government took decisive steps to monopolise the news media: radio, television, and the newspapers. When the opposition lamented the obvious media bias, it bordered on the academic. The ideas of the first five years had become those of the ruling party, a trend likely to continue for the next five years and beyond. Important to note here is not the fact of state control of the media but the fact of its effective use to advantage.

Finally, and critically important, is the role of ethnicity in the 1985 election. The voting patterns revealed an even stronger manifestation of Ndebele-Shona ethnicity than in 1980. The question of class was quite secondary, if at all significant. Joshua Nkomo's party won all seats in Matebeleland. Similarly, ZANU (PF)'s victory in the Shona-speaking areas was overwhelming. This is not to deny that Mugabe himself inclined towards the peasants and workers.

Summary and Conclusions

In conclusion, there are a number of observations to be made on the Zimbabwe electoral process, deriving from the foregoing evidence. The list can be long but I cite and comment on only three observations.

First, all three elections experienced varying degrees of inter-party violence. This suggests intolerance in our political culture—perhaps a culture acquired from the circumstances of settler authoritarian rule as well as from the need for conformity and commandist approaches in the exigencies of prosecuting the liberation struggle. Intolerance of political differences saps a society's vibrancy, verve and dynamism. It produces an unhappy family. Moreover, inter-party intolerance leads to intra-party intolerance. As such, intolerance destroys democracy within the party and within society. Coffins and mock funerals should not be viewed lightly because today we put a member of the 'other' party in a mock coffin for a mock funeral; tomorrow a real funeral might be for a party colleague who holds different views but which are equally genuine and patriotic.

Second, there was a very strong 'bad-loser' and 'ill-will' tendency in all three elections. Sithole in 1979 lost and complained of 'gross irregularities' and boycotted Muzorewa's government of national unity. In 1980 Nkomo turned down Mugabe's offer to him of the presidency. Subsequently, hundreds of former ZIPRA fighters and ZAPU supporters took to the bush, resulting in the current conflict in Matebeleland that began some three years before the 1985 general election. The government reasserted its authority, albeit at times heavy-handedly. Thus, part of the country has been bleeding even after thirty thousand had already died during the liberation struggle. Yet the Zimbabwe constitution adopted by both ZANU (PF) and ZAPU at Lancaster is clear that every five years elections should be held to give the electorate an opportunity to change, modify, or return governments. Unless we, as a people, can learn to respect our constitution and the legal rules of seeking and losing power, independence will not have been well worth fighting for, and the thirty thousand will have died in vain. It is worth mentioning here that those who adopted constitutions and constitutional governments before us had realised that other forms of acquiring and managing power led to self-perpetuating chaos and misery. We are no wiser.

Third, politicised ethnicity is pervasive in the Zimbabwe polity and it would be a crime against scholarship not to investigate this phenomenon for the benefit of government policy and the management of ethnically based conflict such as exists in Matebeleland. It is unscientific to wish conflict were class-based because it is not. Until class begins to express itself as the more basic and conscious factor in the political perceptions of the Ndebele and Shona, or Karanga and Zezuru, and so forth, we are obligated to tackle the problem from the angle of current perceptions. There is no choice for our parties, governments, and scholars but to examine and deal with the problem in the form in which it presents itself.

Thus, the people of Matebeleland, regardless of class background, have twice (in the 1980 and 1985 elections) said they prefer to be represented by ZAPU in both parliament and government. That sentiment ought to be respected. But if this outcome is perceived as militating against the overall goal of national unity, then it would be better to examine the basis for healing a national rift that expresses itself in ethnic terms. The wishes of the people must be seen to be respected; in that way the people respect rather than fear those who govern.

Similarly, supporters of ZAPU ought to respect the wishes of the majority which currently prefers ZANU (PF) to rule. Even if this preference of the people is maintained indefinitely, ZAPU supporters, indeed the Ndebele, ought to respect that. It is wrong to resist, by any means at all, a government that derives its legality constitutionally from the people. Any attempt to alter the wishes of the people by force of arms, if allowed to succeed, sets a very dangerous precedent. Already a child has asked: 'Baba, does it mean that if one loses an election he becomes a dissident and takes up arms against the state?' Therefore, the government has a responsibility far beyond ZANU (PF) to see to it that this precedent is not set.

REFERENCES

1. For about a year (March 1979 to February 1980) Zimbabwe was known as 'Zimbabwe-Rhodesia', a frivolous compromise name agreed to between the RF government which preferred the name Rhodesia, and the internally-based nationalist leaders who preferred the name Zimbabwe.
2. It was at the Geneva Conference that Smith noticed the extent and magnitude of the factionalisation in the nationalist movement and the forces behind this and decided to exploit the situation.
3. The 'March 3rd Agreement' is the subject of a publication by Ndabaningi Sithole, *In Defence of the March 3rd Agreement* (Graham Publishing Co., Salisbury 1979). It is articulate but unconvincing.
4. *Report of the Australian Parliamentary Observer Group On The Zimbabwe-Rhodesia Common Roll Elections*, May 1979, pp. 26-27.
5. *The Herald*, 5 April 1979. Also in Sithole, M., 'Ethnicity and Factionalism in Zimbabwe Nationalist Politics 1957-79', *Ethnic and Racial Studies*, Vol. 3, No. 1, 1980, p. 33.
6. This is one instance where choice of party symbol may have been politically fruitful. Nkomo, however, never endorsed the 1979 election in general, nor the UNFP in particular.
7. This also happened in 1980 in rural areas in Matebeleland where peasants, unaware of the length and breadth of Zimbabwe, found it difficult to believe that Nkomo could have lost when they all voted for him.
8. *The Constitution of the Republic of Zimbabwe*, Chapter VII, section 75, subsection (2). Also there is a detailed discussion of the actual impact of the 'Presidential Directive' in a paper, 'The Zimbabwe Public Service', by Ibbo Mandaza of the Zimbabwe Public Service Commission, presented at the United Nations Inter-Regional Seminar on Reforming Civil Service Systems for Development, Beijing, China, 14-24 August 1985. See in particular pp. 8-9 and 23-26.
9. *Ibid.*, p. 24. Mandaza observes that in 1980 there were 10,570 established officers in the Public Service. Of these only 3,368 or 31.86% were black. By July 1981, the number of black officers had increased to 62.5%.
10. Moreover, some ZANU (PF) activists during the election campaign did not hide from the people their intentions to 'return to the bush' if they voted for the wrong party. An unsuccessful ZANU (PF) candidate for Matebeleland South, Enos Nkala, now Minister of Home Affairs, was suspended from campaigning by Lord Soames for suggesting ZANU (PF) would go back to wage more war if it lost the election. See *The Herald*, 11 February 1980, p. 1.
11. One such colourful spectacle was aircraft flying all over the place playing African music and shouting UANC slogans in mid-air!
12. PF (ZAPU) won four of the 12 Midlands seats. The rest went to ZANU (PF).
13. Every other party seemed to gang up against ZANU (PF). Some were even speculating on a factional arithmetic which would deprive ZANU

(PF) of victory. See Gregory, Martin, Zimbabwe 1980: Politicisation Through Armed Struggle and Electoral Mobilization, *Journal of Commonwealth and Comparative Politics*, Vol. XIX, No. 1, March 1981, p. 68 where he quotes some estimates of the Rhodesian Ministry of Home Affairs as 'Muzorewa 34 seats, Mugabe 26, and Nkomo 20'.

14. One of these incidents took place in the province of Masvingo when Mugabe was on a campaign tour of the area. See *The Herald,* 10 February 1980.

15. Edison Zvobgo, Director of the 1980 ZANU (PF) campaign, was fond of making such comments at meetings with the Election Directorate where officials of other parties lodged complaints.

16. *The Herald,* 5 March 1980.

17. Gregory, Martin, *op. cit.*, p. 67.

18. *Ibid.*

19. *Ibid.*, p. 68

20. For a more modest attempt to explain electoral behaviour in Matebeleland North and South, see J.M. Mpofu's paper, 'The February 1980 Zimbabwe Elections: The Matebeleland North and South Provinces', Zimbabwe Conference, Leeds University, June 1980. See also Mpofu *et al*, in *Review of African Political Economy,* No. 18, 1981, pp. 44-88.

21. See the Registrar-General's *1985 General Election Report* (Harare), 13 September 1985, p. 1.

22. *Ibid.*, p. 6.

23. *Ibid.*, p. 7.

24. *Ibid.*, p. 22.

25. This comment was made during a pre-poll confidential telephone interview conducted by the author in the city of Mutare on 24 June 1984.

26. In an interview following the announcement of the results, Nkomo said that, 'ZANU (PF) rule over the last five years has divided the country into tribal and racial groups. This is a tragedy that has never happened before' (*The Sunday Mail*, 7 July 1985). This, however, does not deny that the elections themselves were free and fair.

27. Interview by author on 4 November 1985.

28. See *The Herald,* 1 July 1985. Also editorial comment in the same issue.

29. Cited from a campaign speech in Borrowdale televised on ZBC.

30. See commentary on constituency in *The Herald*.

3. THE ECONOMY: ISSUES, PROBLEMS AND PROSPECTS

Xavier M. Kadhani

Introduction

The international political isolation caused by the unilateral declaration of independence (UDI) by white settlers in 1965 ended with the establishment of majority rule in 1980. Of similar significance in economic terms was the reinstatement of Zimbabwe's open access to world trade, finance and capital markets, thus ending 16 years of involuntary autarky. Combined with expectations of significant external capital inflows engendered by ZIMCORD,[1] these events tended to influence much of the optimistic perception of Zimbabwe's prospects, at least in the early years of independence.

During the period 1980-1985, macroeconomic policy concerns were very much centred on the twin objectives of *growth* and *equity*, which served as the two key formal pillars of the economic policy (as distinct from the *management*) framework. 'Transformation' over the period gradually established a presence in the policy lexicon as a third broad objective. However, the notion did not receive a clear enough definition to assume operational meaning separate and distinct from the production and consumption changes that might flow from the pursuit of efficient resource deployment (growth), and an acceptable distribution of the costs and benefits of development (equity).

Five years is too brief a period upon which to attempt definitive descriptions of underlying processes, particularly so in economic history; and even more so in the case of a socio-economy enmeshed in multi-level transitions such as Zimbabwe has been, and still is. But Zimbabwean history does not begin with 1980. The fabric of the economy, the systems of management and direction, and the forces and interests surrounding its historical performance all need to be adequately appreciated, as they supply the substance of the reality upon which in 1980 Zimbabweans set out to write their national history, beginning, as regards economic development, with the Transitional National Development Plan.

The *Five Year Development Plan* (FYDP) adopted in 1986 as the Zimbabwe government's official framework for managing socio-economic development over the period 1986 to 1990 begins with a succinct assessment of the gains and setbacks registered in the first five years of independence[2].

The *Transitional National Development Plan* (TNDP) which covered the period 1982 to 1985 had embodied a range of goals aimed at completing the programme of post-war reconstruction, generating sufficient growth to facilitate a rapid restoration of income levels—particularly at the lower end—and redressing the social imbalances that had characterised the pre-independence political order.[3]

As a transitional instrument towards a more comprehensively structured framework, the TNDP deliberately cast national development priorities in a short-term perspective. Specifically, the central macroeconomic plan goals encompassed GDP growth of 8% per year, with production of goods rising faster than that of services, and a 3% annual growth in wage employment.

This growth performance was to be underwritten by raising Gross Fixed Capital Formation (GFCF) from the 19% of GDP achieved in 1981/82 to 23% in 1984/85, and domestic savings from 11% of GDP in 1981/82 to 17% by 1984/85. Further, the TNDP envisaged an increase in the GDP shares of imports and exports to 26 and 23% respectively over the Plan period. In addition, 37.5% of GFCF was expected to be funded from net external resource inflows in the form of loans, grants and direct investment.

Actual performance, the FYDP notes, was significantly below plan targets. Overall GDP registered a negative growth in 1982 and 1983 (-2%;-3%) with a slight 1.3% recovery in 1984, and its distribution showed a pattern quite the opposite of the intended growth structure, with production in the non-material sectors (mostly government related) growing at 4.2% per year, and material production registering only 1.4%: in both cases still falling far short of the 8% overall target. Employment generation was equally poor, with significant job losses being suffered (except in the social sectors) in spite of administrative interventions aimed at stabilisation.

In terms of TNDP sector-specific targets, and because of its central role as an index of movement towards the creation of the material conditions for growth with equity, the FYDP makes particular reference to the very limited progress made in the land asset redistribution programme, noting that 'the programme of land reform and redistribution which was one of the cornerstones of the TNDP fell far short of resettling the 162,000 families, in that only one-fifth of the target was achieved'. Against this, however, although the result contributed towards the violation of the targeted relative shares, social services development—particularly in respect of health, education and skill formation—registered significant quantitative gains.

Overall, how does one explain this very wide divergence between plan and performance, and what is its significance? The FYDP identifies three explanatory factors. First there was drought, which over most of the TNDP period generated various negative influences on the economy. In turn, these affected production, demand and domestic resource availability, and therefore ultimately capacity to stay within planned development programmes. The economic environmental factors resulting from drought had not been incorporated in the construction of the plan, and since actual programmes had to address reality, departure from the planned path became unavoidable.

The second major reason for divergence cited in the FYDP was the adverse impact arising from the world recession, which would have affected such key plan variables as the availability of foreign resources expected to be generated to sustain the plan (37.5% of GCFC), and the extent of Zimbabwe's own earned import capacity from domestic exports (23% of GDP). The FYDP, however, does not, beyond noting the extensive external technological dependence of production (and consumption) of the economy, in fact elaborate on how the world recession of the early 1980s exactly inhibited plan implementation.

The third factor identified in the FYDP as a major reason for poor growth performance in both output and employment over the TNDP period was a progressive deterioration in investment activity:

> Investment declined significantly over the three year plan period. By 1985, the volume of investment in fixed assets was one fifth below its 1982 level, and the share of productive sectors in total investment fell below 40.0% (p. 5).

We have dwelt at some length on the official record of the TNDP era primarily because the TNDP did represent the first (and for that reason perhaps the closest to the pre-1980 'party spirit') expression of the reading by ZANU as a party in government of what the people of Zimbabwe expected from the dismantling of the Rhodesian order. The TNDP translated the expectation as rapid economic (therefore income) growth, increase in formal sector jobs, and access to educational opportunities, to health services and to more and better land.

In *political economy* terms, therefore, successful implementation of the TNDP would have served as a key index of the extent to which the state and its machinery were beginning to serve as vehicles for articulating and managing the transition from the settler-colonial society and economy towards an order that, to some degree, accommodated the social and political objectives which guided the struggle for independence.

In *historical* terms, however, the official record of the first post-independence five years as reflected in the FYDP review outlined above would seem inadequate and incomplete in three important respects. First, the record lacks an interpretation, beyond the mere citing of the investment effect upon growth, of the constraints upon the TNDP implementation arising from the basic structural and functional relationship of the economy to external (viz. South African and OECD) systems. These constraints, as the 1982-85 experience demonstrated, specifically mean that, unless through some means or other import levels are sustained at a steady level, production generally, and investment in particular, becomes highly susceptible to violent fluctuations.

Secondly, the absence in the TNDP of a mechanism for creating access to resources for the implementation of the plan in all its components receives mention again only by inference from the insufficiency of realised investment levels to generate movement towards plan objectives. But this immediately begs the third question (of significance not only to the TNDP but also to all future plans), namely to what extent it is meaningful to 'plan' an economy over which ownership and control of the productive assets reside in private hands, and foreign private hands in large measure at that. To the extent that the FYDP sets 'the establishment of a broadly-based planning machinery' and 'the creation of a national economy' as key objectives of the 1986-90 plan period, the beginnings of a resolution of this essentially ideological problem will clearly make a significant difference in establishing the plan as an instrument of change.

Because these have tended, in the hands of critics from various points of view,[4] to serve to discredit the concept of planning itself, and also to reduce the credibility of the national plan as a basis for viable national programmes, these gaps in the matching of plans as expressions of development objectives to the means for supporting their implementation require that we briefly comment on the planning process in Zimbabwe, and on the influences that have shaped it. This we shall do at appropriate stages in what follows.

In view of some of the conclusions drawn in later sections, and especially so with regard to prospective issues in the years immediately ahead, it is appropriate that the Zimbabwean experience of the 1980s be related to contemporary continental African developmental concerns, in at least two respects.

Barely a fortnight after formal accession to independent status, Zimbabwe participated in April 1980 in the adoption by OAU Heads of State of the *Lagos Plan of Action* (LPA),[5] which was an African initiative aimed at addressing the problems of economic decline and critical structural disequilibria that had come to afflict most countries on the continent. Among its six guiding principles, the LPA called for drastic departures from past socio-economic structures and patterns, and for the adoption of well-articulated policies of internalisation of the development process.

Meeting in Addis Ababa five years later in April 1985 in a UNECA Conference, African ministers expressed distress at the little progress made in this regard:

> National development plans as well as annual budgets have, in most countries, tended to perpetuate and even accentuate the dependency of our economies through, *inter alia* (i) over-reliance on foreign resources (financial and human) leading in many cases to the distruption of national priorities to comply with those of donor countries and institutions; (ii) misallocation of domestic resources with reduced shares for such high priority areas as agriculture, manpower and industry and massive expenditure on foreign consumer goods and non-productive investment projects.[6]

Partly 'responding' to the lPA, but also arising from the momentum of empirical research that increasingly and clearly demonstrated that African economic decline and dislocation in reaction to the world recession was reaching politically unsustainable proportions, a number of extra-continent 'initiatives' began to emerge. The most notable of these were the World Bank's 'Agenda for Action'[7] and the United States government's special action programme for Africa.

Two features of these initiatives are noteworthy with respect to the Zimbabwean context. First, they were all informed by the conclusions of the plethora of studies which coincidentally surfaced at this time. The studies located the root cause of the 'African malaise' in government-induced limitations on the functioning of market forces in the regulation of the economies (which, it was argued, led to inefficient resource allocation, distortion of incentives, and hence low growth). This was exacerbated by what the World Bank referred to as 'overextended public sectors'[8] which not only operated inefficiently and wastefully but also, it was argued, pre-empted resources from the rest of the economy. From these premises, the now familiar conclusion was easy to draw, namely that the necessary adjustment and recovery plans for African economies must aim at expanding the range of play of market forces, and denationalising ownership and control.

Secondly, in contradistinction to the de-emphasis on externally sourced programme funding that the LPA sought to promote, these initiatives placed mobilisation of foreign resources at the centre of recovery plans for the African continent. Married to this attempt to plug Africa's 'resource gap', however, and referred to—if at all—only in very muted terms,[9] was an acknowledgment of the fact that in the 1980s, in spite of its dire poverty and debilitating balance of payments squeeze, the African continent was in net terms paying into the international trade and finance system more than it was drawing out. Thus the problem was fundamentally not one of resource availability to Africa but of resource flows between Africa and the international financial centres. We shall return, in later pages, to an examination of the variations of these themes in the Zimbabwean context.

The next section sketches a backdrop to the 1980 independence watershed, tracing the way that structural, institutional and policy issues were integrated in that era, and identifying highlights of that integration process throughout the UDI period. The third section traces, again in largely qualitative fashion, the fusion of the same three elements in the immediate post-independence period, placing particular emphasis on a delineation of the crises characteristic to the economy that began to crystallise during this phase. An outline of the main features of the economy at the inception of the first Five Year Development Plan in 1986 is presented in the fourth section, together with a brief identification of the major issues that are likely to occupy centre-stage in the formulation and implementation of economic policy in the period ahead. We conclude in the fifth section with a tentative statement of prospects on the development and resolution of the issues identified in the fourth section.

Background to Independence

The termination of the federation arrangement in 1963 gave significant impetus to the process of economic restructuring and the strengthening of an inward-looking strategy in pre-independence Zimbabwe. One of the consequences of political uncertainty in the period leading to the break-up of the Federation had been a rapid contraction in economic activity, which was reflected in the emergence of idle industrial capacity as access to the regional markets began to shrink. Economic sanctions, which were the consequence of UDI, enforced autarky on an economy which was already experiencing difficulties in the utilisation of capacities built up over a decade to service a much larger market. At the macroeconomic management level, the loss of access to federal surpluses (both revenue and foreign exchange) caused by the Malawian and Zambian divorces further emphasised the necessity of a government lead in readjusting macro-balances to sustainable limits.

Partly as a consequence of the dismembering of the Federation, but immediately legitimised by the imposition of sanctions, an outstanding feature of the 16 years of UDI became the forcefulness and coherence of state intervention in the economy.[10] This consisted of carefully chosen and systematically targeted instruments, ranged, however, in support of an essentially privately controlled economy, in which the major economic interests exhibited little disconsonance with the nature, objectives and methods of the state. State intervention in this era closely approximated in form and content the two conditions of essentiality identified by S. de Brunoff in the relationship between 'public' and 'private' in a so-called mixed economy. As such the management of the two key areas of *money* and *labour power* are central in expressing the real concern of macroeconomic policy. This concern, de Brunhoff observes, is that of maintaining a certain state capacity for economic management destined to meet needs of capital which capital itself cannot meet directly.[11]

The nature of the state in this era is discussed in detail in chapter one. Here it is sufficient to note that the intervention was primarily prompted by the systemic need, given the structure of production and consumption, to keep a tight rein on fiscal and external account balances, and to maintain stability in the labour market (hence the centrality of the industrial relations legislation and the network of institutions created in support thereof). Politically also, market forces had to be carefully attenuated in order to protect the high income levels and standard of living of the local white 'tribe' on which the regimes largely depended for legitimacy and, technical and administrative skills, as well as military muscle.

In growth terms, the economy passed through two distinct swings: an expansionary phase in 1965-72, and contraction over 1973-79. Through both phases the directional influence of the state was sufficiently decisive to ensure internal economic stability.[12] This was achieved in spite of adverse international market forces to which the economy remained vulnerable even with formal isolation, and in spite of lack of open access to sources of financial support for adjustment. Indeed the observation has been made that political isolation made it possible for the Rhodesians to institute and—within the terms of an *apartheid* framework—

successfully run an IMF-type stabilisation programme over much of the UDI period without a direct association with the IMF.

The initial economic costs of sanctions was fairly comfortably borne as a result of the 1965-72 boom. This enabled a rapid restructuring of the economy at the sectoral level, producing an average annual GDP rate of growth of 6%—considerably higher in fact than that attained over much of the Federation period.

Economic sanctions gave rise to certain situation-specific constraints. In the external sector imported input costs escalated by up to 20 % because of the necessity to pay premia. Conversely, export earnings losses of similar size were incurred due to discounting and middlemen costs. And as already noted, access to financial markets, at a time when petrodollars were being freely recycled to virtually all other oil-import dependent economies, was severely restricted. These constraints combined to elevate concern with the maintenance of balance on the external account to a central and pivotal role in the management of the economy. In broad outline, the overriding objective of economic policy became the maintenance of capability to finance the current account deficit on the balance of payments. This had to be achieved by a combination of trade surplus and strict enforcement of restrictions on factor payments and other external remittances.

This general orientation had three major consequences worth noting. First, among its many paradoxes, UDI had the effect of *widening* the economy's access to investible financial surpluses, primarily in the shape of the large blocked balances which would otherwise have been remitted abroad. In the circumstances foreign firms were, for all intents and purposes, now compelled to redirect the surpluses towards reinvestment or at any rate retain them within the overall domestic system. Secondly, while this temporary domestication of surpluses made possible investment in product diversification, the process also led to an acceleration of tendencies towards monopolies, and to a deepening of the extent of foreign capital in most key sectors of the economy.[13]

The third effect occurred at the institutional level. The siege outlook initially spawned by sanctions, and subsequently intensified by the outbreak of war, facilitated the emergence of the Treasury (in conjunction with the Reserve Bank) as the central locus of influence and authority in the running of the economy. Within the government, Treasury views on the structuring and implementation of fiscal policy, as well as on the management of the foreign exchange budget, became largely unassailable; and the private sector accepted the directional role of these government organs with hardly any demur.

The enhanced influence of the Treasury and the Reserve Bank became evident in the tight control that was exercised over the use of foreign exchange and the level of the budget deficit, as well as in the deliberate direction of resources towards the productive sectors, particularly those designated to spearhead diversifiction and the development of greater import substitution capability (metal and engineering products; enhanced mineral beneficiation; agro-industrial linkages; de-emphasis on tobacco and expansion of the other agricultural exports).

The deliberately engineered 1965-72 boom, however, led to the overheating of the economy, reflecting in large part the persistence of high import-intensity in production (particularly in respect of investment activity). In turn, this led to an unsustainable widening of the current account deficit. Combined with the effects of the 1973 oil price shock (in the circumstances of sanctions with accentuated intensity), this led to the rapid institution of radically restrictionist policies of the classical IMF short-run stabilisation variety. Thereafter, a tight reign was consistently maintained on the Current Account Deficit until 1979.

The results were quite typical of what has been the common experience in other developing countries where stabilisation programmes have been executed with a single-minded focus on short-run considerations: external balance was restored, but the economy stagnated and indeed a prolonged recession set in; GDP per head declined in each year up to 1979; capacity utilisation fell from the peak of 98% in 1974 to a low of 75% by 1978; and employment growth, specifically amongst the blacks, turned negative, all with far-reaching distributional implications. From a capital accumulation point of view, the steady erosion of profits as a percentage of GDP (see Table 1) and the decline in average returns to capital that characterised this period, began to add influence in turning the tide towards the search for greater stability in the political environment as a precondition for a relaxation of the austerity regime.

TABLE 1
DISTRIBUTION OF NOMINAL GROSS DOMESTIC INCOME, 1974-83 (%)

	1974	1975	1976	1977	1978	1979	1980	1981	1982	1983
Wages and Salaries	50.5	55.2	55.9	60.3	61.5	60.0	73.9	59.9	60.7	59.7
Rent	3.4	3.2	3.1	3.3	2.9	2.4	2.4	1.3	1.5	1.4
Gross Operating Profit	46.2	41.6	40.9	36.4	35.7	38.6	39.4	38.3	37.8	38.9

Source: CSO, *Quarterly Digest of Statistics*, September 1985.

The major economic lessons of UDI can be quickly summarised. At the level of technical and structural parameters, the overall production performance of the economy continued to exhibit very rapid responses to the international environment, in spite of the clarity in the articulation of instruments of domestic control that was evident throughout the period. The programmes of import substitution and economic diversification that were pursued on the basis of hostage capital, initially through force of circumstance but subsequently as deliberate policy programmes, quickly ran into two problems. One was the structure and size of the local market, which reflected the limitations imposed by the central socio-political objectives of the system. The other was the scope for growth, given ultimately by the economy's capacity to finance imported inputs. The latter, however, emerged as the major constraint, in the end overriding all other macro-management concerns. Added to the escalation of military pressure and the intensification of South African and American pressure on the Smith regime to move towards a political settlement, this factor was not insignificant in the mobilisation of political support for the reversal of UDI.

1980-84 : The First Five Years

The economic machinery outlined above had, after independence in 1980, to be driven with the purpose of servicing the political objectives of a government significantly quite different in orientation, a government, moreover, which was required to respond to aspirations of a much expanded range of constituencies.

While the political and economic goals of the post-independence order were implicitly different from those pursued by previous regimes, the process of specifying and articulating them in a coherent format that would inform direct concrete economic management concerns in the immediate post-independence period was slow and drawn-out. It took an entire year before the basic economic policy statement, 'Growth with Equity', could be published, and another 18 months to the surfacing of the TNDP. Read together, these two documents contain the essence of post-1980 economic development objectives and broad socio-political concerns.

In brief, these were, as already noted, the restoration of per capita consumption levels among the black population, which had been severely eroded since 1974; the implementation of a programme of rapidly expanding access to basic social services, especially in education and health; the restoration of peasant agricultural production through the introduction and expansion of input and extension support systems, and the expansion of access to more and better quality land; and the generation of wage employment to match the growth of population.

Actual economic performance between 1980 and 1984 can be traced through two phases. The period up to 1982 witnessed a massive upswing, supported by a combination of (largely transient) factors such as:

(a) a once-off terms-of-trade 'gain' with the lifting of sanctions;
(b) renewed access to sources of borrowed external finance, with lenders showing exceptional readiness to take up the 'slack' created by the forced abstention of the UDI years;[14]
(c) a significant capacity underutilisation of 25%, which could be reactivated with pretty quick results in production;
(d) exceptionally good rains in the 1980 and 1981 seasons, which impacted favourably on agricultural production.

As a result, GDP grew at phenomenal rates of 11% and 15% in 1980 and 1981. Gross investment in capital stock rose steadily as a percentage of GDP, from 13.7 (1979), to 14.8 (1980), 15.5 (1981) and 17.5 (1982). Capacity utilisation followed the same trend, rising from 76%

(1979), to 83% (1980), 95% (1981) and dipping to 91% in 1982.

Lower scale incomes, wages and salaries rose sharply, both through deliberate statutory adjustments, expanded employment access through the elimination of the more obvious forms of racial discrimination, and high producer prices for farmers. Gains, though small, were also registered in employment, which grew by about 3% in 1980, 2.8% in 1981 and about 1% in 1982.

At the level of macroeconomic direction, the 1980-82 boom was, in addition to being made technically possible by the combination of capacity factors noted above, *permitted* in financing terms, by the relaxation of both budgetary and external account controls over much of that period, in sharp contrast to the tight reins exercised in the 1973-79 period. The relaxation is evidenced by the movement of:

(a) the Balance of Payments current account from a surplus of $2.5m. in 1978 to deficits of $74m. in 1979, $157m. in 1980, $439m. in 1981 and $533m. by 1982;
(b) the current account and overall budget deficit which followed a similar trend.

It is also worth noting that for three reasons, the relaxations of controls in the early post-independence period went beyond a simple reflation of the economy through the rapid expansion of imports. The relaxations reflected first a significantly reduced cohesion, relative to the pre-1980 era, in the macro-management strategies of this period. Secondly, there was great diversity in the concerns and orientations that expressed themselves through the various levels of policy implementation. And thirdly, immense pressures were generated as a result of the reversal of UDI to liberalise (especially) exchange controls. The gates for *outflows* were also opened considerably wider. Thus, net factor payments and remittances abroad rose from $14m. in 1979 to $72m. in 1980, $123m. in 1981 and $206m. in 1982, the increases incorporating higher emigrant and pension remittances, and payments of interest, profits and dividends. Pension remittances, it must be emphasised, were a legal constriction embodied in the provisions of the Lancaster House constitution. As such, they represented a first, and legally inescapable, charge on national resources.

Purely on the basis of the large disequilibria that emerged in external account and fiscal balances, clearly the 1980-82 boom could not be sustained. The constraints of capacity ceilings and, as the subsequent experience dramatically showed, weather shocks added impetus to the downswing that followed from the middle of 1982 to 1984.

The recession reflected itself in a 2% real GDP decline in 1982, followed by a fall of 3.5% in 1983, and a slight positive recovery in 1984. Employment followed a similar trend, declines going to as much as 2.5% by 1983, which in reality meant a much higher net joblessness level given the population growth rate of around 3.5%.

The economic crisis of 1982-84 was expressed through production bottlenecks, job losses, sharp reductions in government revenue resources

TABLE 2
BALANCE OF PAYMENTS, 1977-9183 (Z$m Currrent Prices)

	1977	1978	1979	1980	1981	1982	1983
EXPORTS	+624.1	+687.1	+816.3	+1,062.1	+1,125.5	+169.3	+1,300
Visible	520.2	579.2	667.5	813.7	925.6	857.7	1,025
Gold	45.7	46.1	66.6115.2	76.3	140.5	100	
Invisible	58.1	61,882.2	133.2	133.6	171.1	175	
IMPORTS	-558.6	-594.0	-775.8	-1,106.0	-1,419.1	-1,434.2	-1,475
Visible	421.7	443.1	594.9	860.5	1,059.4	1,114.3	1,130
Invisible	136.9	150.9	180.9	245.5	359.7	319.9	345
Net factor payments	-64.7	-76.1	-76.3	-72.4	-122.7	-206.4	-285
Net transfers & remittances	-9.6	-12.0	-38.0	-40.4	-23.0	-62.3	-75
Deficit (A)	8.8	(25.2)	73.9	156.7	439.2	532.8	535
Gold-Stock change	-8.5	+5.8	+14.3	+29.7	+41.7	-17.7	-88
Deficit (B)	17.3	(31.0)	59.6	127.0	397.5	550.5	446

Sources: CSO—Digest of Statistics, various
Reserve Bank of Zimbabwe—Quarterly Economic & Statistical Review, various.

and a rapid escalation in pressure on the current account of the balance of payments—reflected in severe inability to sustain imports of essential inputs. Its roots can be traced to a combination of structural (mainly the import-dependent nature of the production systems), exogenous (drought, transport logistics, and the recession in world commodity markets), and conjunctural (chiefly the macroeconomic management institutions, systems and procedures) factors. These factors combined to generate a pattern of resource allocation and absorption that ultimately bore little resemblance to the objectives of the TNDP. Indeed the plan had, as early as 1982, ceased to serve as a significant reference point (for both government and non-government sectors), excepting in the case of social programmes, which were kept on the planned course more by virtue of the political momentum they generated than as components of a consistent development framework.

In the event, the crisis was resolved by abandoning the pursuit of both growth and (to the extent that the TNDP had programmed movement towards income redistribution by widening involvement in production through formal employment in industry and access to assets in agriculture) equity. With the suspension of plan programmes, the crisis was reduced to a *financial management level*, at which resolution could be more easily secured through budget squeezes (1982, 1983, 1984) to restore fiscal balance, and import-cutting combined with suspension of most factor income remittances (March 1984) to restore external balance.

Introducing the budget for the fiscal year 1981/82 in Parliament, the Minister of Finance raised a cautionary note against the 'tyranny of the plan', i.e. the dangers of rigidity in managing the economy that might arise if plan targets and programmes were pursued without adequate regard to prevailing conditions and realities at specific stages in the plan period.

The specific conditions of the TNDP years differed substantially in a number of key respects from the environmental assumptions around which the major objectives of the plan had been built. Correctly perceived, however, 'planning' is not an event that occurs at discrete intervals in the history of an economy; less still, as fears of tyranny might suggest, a simple documentation of decisions that determine in advance of time and in an immutable sense the direction of development and the distribution of resources. At the most general level, planning is a process that, with varying degrees of elaboration, and to varying degrees of formality, must necessarily remain continuous, adjusting general guidelines to incorporate changes in political objectives, and refining targets to reflect possibilities, opportunities and constraints which emerge with time. In this sense, 'planning' of course goes on all the time, in all economies. One can only meaningfully distinguish between 'good' and 'bad' planning on the basis of the efficiency with which plans integrate national appreciation of environmental factors into objectives, and in turn articulate programmes for managing those environmental factors.[15]

In the context of our analysis of post-1980 Zimbabwe, these rather elementary remarks are made necessary by the obvious question that is begged by the observation made above: that the resolution of the 1982-84 crisis was effected through the implicit abandonment of the TNDP as the framework for guiding national economic policy and management. What, without the plan, became the reference?

The simple answer is that the annual government budget became not only the central, and independent, instrument for resource mobilisation and distribution but also the major mechanism for the structuring of economic and financial policy. Because of this, economic management took an essentially short-run, fiscal and external balance stabilisation orientation. The budget, unlike the TNDP, programmed purely public sector activities, and in that sense can be said to have contained an operationalisaion of the TNDP reduced to the government sector, narrowly defined.

It has been suggested that the austerity programmes pursued during 1982-84 have not only been shaped by the direct and indirect external pressures exerted upon the government by external authorities and multilateral institutions (through the conditionalities contained in the post-war reconstruction and balance of payments support programmes) and by the South African government (through actual or threatened interference with the movement of Zimbabwe's external trade via Mozambican or South African ports). There has also, it is contended, been a coincidence of views on basic economic policy between the Zimbabwean authorities and economic interests seeking to maintain undisturbed the structure of the economy inherited at independence.[16]

An assessment of the significance of these views is clearly necessary, for two reasons. First, the assessment would serve as a synthesis of the basic economy policy issues generated in the management of the economy in the post-1980 period. Secondly, an appreciation of these issues will serve as a basis on which the prospects for the years ahead can be presented.

1986: Main Features and Major Issues

In a recent paper on the Jamaican experience with managing crisis and planning economic development, Omar Davies[17] observes that Jamaica's 1978-83 Five Year Development Plan, published in 1978, was never used in directing policies at any subsequent stage. The reason, Davies observes, was that the government of Jamaica had, in 1978, secured from the IMF an Extended Fund Facility, which 'provided the guidelines for all socio-economic decision-making'. Not only did policy determination revolve around IMF conditionality, but also the skill-and time-intensive servicing of Fund programmes pre-empted attention from all other planning requirements. In assessing the impact of the IMF programmes on Jamaica, Davies comments:

> Although the Government was actually bound by the conditions attached to agreements for only a half of the four year period 1977-1980, the fact is that *every action of significance it took over the period was influenced by the anticipated reactions of*

the IMF or the perceived impact which it could have on the conditions of the Agreement in force. Within such a framework, Government actions were guided by what would seem to be the most relevant section of the current Agreement. As such, *the idea of long-term economic planning became more and more remote* as senior State technicians were fully occupied in either implementing and monitoring the current programme or involved in negotiating a future agreement (emphasis added).

Zimbabwe became a member of the IMF in 1980, and exercised the usual virtually automatic right to a drawdown in the low conditionality first credit tranche. The resources were used to support the increased import allocations arising, as we saw earlier, from the partial relaxations of controls in the early years, which was a significant factor in the rapid GDP growth experienced in 1980 and 1981.

By 1982, significant internal and external economic imbalances began to show, threatening to escalate pressure for a tightening of import controls and also to generate rapid deficit-induced inflation. On the domestic front, rapid increases had taken place in government expenditures, especially on recurrent items, without corresponding increases in revenues, so that the overall budget deficit moved from 7.7% of GDP in 1981/82 to 10.7% in 1982/3.

As regards the external sector, the growth that was permitted in imports in the period 1979-81, without a matching improvement in export earnings, led to an increase in the current account deficit from 6% of GDP in 1980 to 11% by the end of 1981. Net foreign assets declined from $178m. at the end of 1980 to *negative* levels by 1982. The debt service ratio stood at an estimated 30% by 1983, a 300% increase in 3 years from the 1980 levels.

In respect of domestic policy government moved rapidly—prompted in part by the wave of industrial unrest that occurred in 1980—to institute statutory minimum wage guidelines applicable to all sectors and to expand popular access to education and health services. Another significant income support measure took the form of consumer subsidies, which rose rapidly from the pre-1980 levels as a result both of increased access to subsidised consumer goods and of the removal of indirect taxes on some major basic commodities. The expansion of social services also had significant beneficial effects on employment creation in the public sector. Defence consolidation assumed priority of place in expenditure programmes, to address the problems of integrating armies, demobilisation, post-war reorientation, as well as the issue of South African-sponsored destabilisation activities.

The net result of the expansionary programmes of 1980-82 was that a significant financing gap emerged in the balance of payments, which the government sought to meet by soliciting IMF support. While the details of the 18-month stand-by facility in the upper credit tranche that was negotiated in early 1983 cannot be appropriately discussed here it is relevant to outline the basic objectives of the programme.

The fundamental thrust of the understanding reached with the IMF, as in all Fund programmes, was the restoration of financial balances on government and external accounts. Regarding the former, the Fund would normally require a reduction of the total government expenditure and net lending levels. While for performance measurement purposes the size of the deficit would supply the benchmark, the essential features of this condition take the form of curtailment of development programmes (unless these are externally funded), reduction of subsidies and curtailment of growth in social service development.

In the case of the external sector, emphasis normally rests on downward currency realignments to strengthen financial incentives to produce for export, and general domestic demand compression, on the argument first that resources can then be diverted to exports, and second that reduced domestic inflation and production costs again enhance export sector performance.

How does one assess the impact of the various external influences, summarised in the shape of the standard IMF position outlined above, on what actually happened in Zimbabwe in 1980-84? It seems to me that the answer to this question must be supplied at two levels. First, at the purely technical, it must be established whether, and how efficiently, the fiscal and external balance objectives sought through the programmes were in fact attained.

The Zimbabwean experience is mixed. While the 1983 stand-by arrangements were suspended in early 1984 because of Zimbabwe's failure to perform in respect of credit targets, the expenditure restraint measures inspired by the IMF relationship have evidently consistently informed the budgeting process, the management of the exchange rate and incomes policy from 1982 onwards. Apart from the retention of domestic price and foreign exchange controls, the range of administrative interventions in the economy has generally tended to improve incentive systems, rather than have the reverse impact that the standard IMF approaches would suggest. Producer price effects on agricultural performance, devaluation impacts on mining output and the subsidy effect on manufactured export growth are all cases in point.

Generally, while at the time of the cancellation of the standby in 1984 the economy appeared to have been struck by a mild form of the Jamaican syndrome (Seaga's 'Grow what you eat' vs. Manley's 'Eat what you grow'[18], the maintenance of a supportive level of domestic demand, and the decisive exercise of administrative controls in March 1984 to curb the outflow of foreign exchange surpluses (both outside the spirit of the IMF programmes) have been largely effective in arresting further economic retrenchment, and indeed returning the economy to a positive growth path.

At the technical level, there is not a limitless range of instruments that national authorities can select from in managing economies; and the room for originality in approach is very narrow. Incentives have to be provided to generate production whether for home consumption or for export markets. And overall expenditure programmes have to be tailored broadly to match resource availability. That the measures employed in Zimbabwe to resolve the problems of imbalance happen broadly to fit the types normally crudely prescribed by the IMF elsewhere; and that the timing of policy positions of the Zimbabwe government tended to leave Fund programmers rather short on what exactly to suggest as conditionalities, does *not* make the prescriptions *per se* inappropriate for the circumstances. Which is not to suggest that agreement was thereby easily reached. But that is the *technical* level. As several analysts have clearly demonstrated, there is also always a fundamentally ideological dimension to Fund programming which it would be naive in the extreme to ignore.

> IMF programmes are very evidently based on the ideology that the price mechanism and the market system are intrinsically superior to planning and physical controls in the allocation of resources, and hence in dealing with the problems of development....IMF-type programmes are not ideologically neutral. Their logic is evidently to support the socio-economic groups which control capital, property and finance, and which are therefore in a position to take advantage of the 'market'.[19]

This basic orientation in IMF standby arrangements, if not carefully assessed, can lead to far-reaching limitations upon a government's room for manoeuvre, particularly in situations requiring intervention of state power to promote a long-term development strategy. First, as we have seen, Fund programmes are essentially short-run, stabilisation focussed, whereas the major problems of development are long-term, structural in nature. Secondly, Fund programmes are highly demanding upon the time and skill of personnel in institutions that perform critical economic management roles. Consequently the construction and maintenance of Fund arrangements denude governments of (usually critically short) planning capacity, the result being that often, outside of the work performed around Fund programmes, no other coherent frameworks are generated. Hence plans are jettisoned in favour of budgets, which supply the vehicle for implementing Fund programme-based solutions. Thirdly, in effect, Fund programmes are constructed to limit command over resources by the public sector and, by corollary, enhance the role of private capital. The IMF:

> systematically bases its prescriptions on market ideology giving the preponderant role to local private enterprise and transnational investment. It envisages the state in a restrained and subsidiary role, promoting the free play of national and international market forces. The principle of state participation and intervention, involving a significant presence of public enterprises, is anathema to it.[20]

These effects have not been insignificant in the context of 1980-85 Zimbabwe. Because of budget restraints, the capital development programmes in the public sector hardly grew, with the proportionate role of government in the economy showing remarkable stagnation, in some areas of significance being reduced well below levels attained pre-1980 (see Tables 3 and 4).

TABLE 3
GDP BY KIND OF ACTIVITY AND OWNERSHIP AT CURRENT PRICES (Z$m)

Industry	1974 Public	1974 Private	1974 Total	1979 Public	1979 Private	1979 Total	1983 Public	1983 Private	1983 Total
Agriculture	5	310	315	8	317	325	24	568	592
Mining and Quarrying	-	136	136	-	226	226	3	281	284
Manufacturing	17	404	421	36	587	623	109	1275	1384
Electricity and Water	42	-	42	71	-	71	134	-	134
Construction	18	64	82	36	56	92	55	139	194
Finance and Insurance	12	61	73	30	93	123	53	221	274
Real Estate	-	46	46	-	44	44	-	59	59
Distribution	24	234	258	18	407	425	13	724	737
Transport & Com.	105	33	138	130	58	188	192	172	364
Public Adminstration	109	-	109	269	-	269	375	-	375
Education	33	22	55	62	36	98	275	68	343
Health	17	16	33	33	27	60	64	45	109
Domestic Services	-	40	40	-	53	53	-	89	89
Other Services	17	68	85	28	108	136	54	262	316
Inputed Bank charges (−)	11	31	42	32	49	82	53	120	173
GDP	388	1430	1791	689	1963	2651	1298	3783	5081
Percentage Shares	21.7	78.3		26	74		25.5	74.5	

Source: CSO—National Income and Expenditure Report, October 1985.

TABLE 4
GENERAL GOVERNMENT OUTLAYS BY TYPE, 1974-1983 ($m)

	CURRENT DISBURSEMENTS	%	CAPITAL OUTLAY	%	TOTAL OUTLAY
1974	349	78.8	94	21.2	443
1975	370	75.8	118	24.2	458
1976	474	81.0	111	19	585
1977	595	85.2	103	14.8	698
1978	722	87	108	13	830
1979	788	87.7	111	12.3	899
1980	1,014	89	124	10.9	1,138
1981	1,145	87.6	162	12.4	1,307
1982	1,574	84.4	290	15.6	1,864
1983	1,739	85.1	305	15	2,044

To the extent that the development programmes of the years ahead, in the terms of the 1986-90 Five Year Development Plan, turn around the expansion of the public sector and the creation of a 'national' economy, the extent to which these influences are appreciated and concretely addressed will clearly affect prospects. To those we turn briefly in the next section.

Prospects

The 1986-1990 Five Year Development Plan has, as major economic objectives, an average annual GDP rate of growth of 5.1%, and the creation of 28,000 jobs a year. The resource programme to support movement towards these objectives is a $7.13 billion cumulative investment plan, to be funded 60:40 from domestic and foreign sources, with the domestic component split 18:72 as between the public and the local private sector respectively.

With population growing at over 3% per year, clearly the targeted income growth rate is necessary to maintain standards of living and to support some improvement. More immediately, however, employment generation has obviously become an issue requiring urgent solution. Seen against the current annual addition to the labour market of upwards of 70,000 school leavers alone, the target of 28,000 appears woefully low. Thus we have the dreadful spectacle, unfolding throughout the plan period, of something akin to traffic on a six-lane highway converging upon a two-lane bridge.

The achievement of even these modest targets much depends upon the successful mobilisation, and appropriate deployment, of the necessary resources. The planned 60:40 contributions to GCFC by domestic and external sources implies an extremely high rate and mobilisation of domestic savings. The absolute amounts would nonetheless not seem to lie beyond conceivable levels, provided expenditure programmes—particularly in the public sectors—are restructured quickly enough away from current patterns,[21] and provided positive growth is sustained in the productive sectors.

TABLE 5
PLANNED FINANCING OF GROSS FIXED CAPITAL FORMATION, 1986-1990 (Z$m 1985 Prices)

		CUMULATIVE TOTAL	PERCENTAGE SHARE
Gross Fixed Capital Formation		7,126	100
Financing:		7,126	100
Public Sector		1,208	1,208	17
Government	700		
Parastatals	508		
Private Sector		3,066	3,066	43
Households	600		
Corporate	2,466		
Total Domestic		4,274	60
Foreign Investment		200	3
Foreign Borrowing		2,152	2,152	30
Government	1,060		
Parastatals	792		
Private Sector	300		
Grants		500	7
Total Foreign		2,852	40

Source: Five Year Development Plan, 1986—1990

The anticipated level of participation of both foreign sources and the domestic private sector does, however, raise a critical issue to do with the central theme of the FYDP, viz. the creation of a 'national economy'. While the concrete programmes to underpin this thrust still require specification, it is perhaps at this stage enough, in order to highlight the problematic, to sketch a taxonomy of meanings that the theme might assume. There are three levels in the matrix.

First, there is clearly the matter of the dominance of foreign control and ownership over productive assets and in key institutions, which have been recognised as limited the scope for growth, structural change and development [22]. Secondly, 'domestication' along the foreign-private to local-private vector raises the question of racial balance in ownership and control of production, which poses its own difficulties even in the present circumstances, and which it is not possible for the government to overlook.

Thirdly, outside the public domain, there is clearly not—even if the racial balance issue were to be discounted—anything like the kind of resources, financial and managerial, to support a process of transfer of ownership from foreign hands on any meaningful scale. This inevitably places the state at the centre of any 'nationalisation' programme, a position that would be consonant with the analysis of the FYDP, wherein the combination of a dominant role of private capital in the economy with a limited involvement of the state in productive spheres is singled out as a major factor in explaining the lacklustre investment performance of the post-1980 period.

This position, however, raises a very wide range of doubts about the robustness of the financing plan outlined above, as it rests on the assumption that the nature of incentives necessary to lend the plan credibility, both within the Zimbabwean private sector and the external sources of finance, will be in place over the currency of the FYDP.

Since growth depends largely upon investment, and investment is critically driven by decisions made on the basis of control over investible surpluses, our conclusion would be that the projected performance in respect of income and employment growth may have to be traded off, to some degree, against the execution of a determined programme of domestication of ownership and control in the economy.[23]

Beyond these questions of broad direction and control, enhancement of prospects for overall growth and for the deepening of integration within the national economy over the decade ahead still requires that policies and strategies be put in place to address a number of specific sectoral and subsectoral problems.

Agricultural development strategy in the post-1980 period has revolved around the two concerns of *securing food supplies*, while at the same time *maintaining high production levels*, especially of exportable commodities. Further development of the sector clearly requires that policy focus be retained on these objectives, but also that the questions of efficiency in land use and equity in land distribution, which remain unresolved, be handled much more directly and concretely than hitherto. The experience of the past five years, together with the results of recent research into these issues, clearly show that these important policy concerns with maintenance of good production performance and improvement of growth prospects in the agricultural sector will, contrary to conventional wisdom, be positively assisted if programmes of reallocating currently underutilised and unused land assets to willing and able or potential farmers are vigorously executed.

The rural resettlement programme must be given focus, greater impetus and more resources. Many concerns of a crucial nature at the national level hang on its success, or can be deliberately made to revolve around it. Food production and export crop output have already been noted. Employment generation—at all segments of the labour spectrum, including the young and the college bibliocrats—will significantly depend on new breakthroughs on land holdings and land use. The problem of rural-urban drift, which becomes increasingly explicit with each passing year, is capable of lasting solution only with the creation of viable income opportunities in the countryside. This, in turn, must inevitably also centre around policies, patterns and practices of land asset access and usage.

In the manufacturing sector, growth and further development will very much depend on the maintenance of high capacity utilisation levels and on enhanced investment activity within the economy generally. These conditions in turn require that demand, in both the home and external markets, be sustained at appropriate levels, and that input and technology supplies be secured at supportive magnitudes. The current delicate position of the sector in these respects means that good performance in the years ahead will very much be influenced by the degree to which sectoral development programmes support a sustained retooling of existing manufacturing capacity, an expansion of the existing market base beyond the present domestic confines and a deepening of intersectoral linkages, particularly in the metal, chemical and energy-related fields.

Other sectoral issues relate to the management of regional economic and trade integration programmes, in which Zimbabwe can play a significant catalytic role to its advantage as well as that of its partners; and to the optimal management of external borrowing capacity to maximise resource availability for development and restructuring programmes.

At the regional level, the successful completion of the Southern African Development Coordination Conference infrastructural rehabilitation programmes, in particular those relating to surface transport and harbours, would spell two immediate advantages. First, it would be possible to reduce reliance on the longer South African routes, procurement costs for imports would be greatly reduced, and export competitiveness would be enhanced. Secondly, the strengthening of supply lines connecting Zimbabwe with its partners within SADCC, and more broadly within the Preferential Trade Area (of East, Central and Southern Africa), would significantly improve the prospects of meaningful commercial exchange, thus providing a necessary, currently missing, but by no means in itself sufficient, link in the regional programmes of economic integration.

SADCC: DIRECTION OF TRADE, 1982
(Percentage Distribution)

	Exports To: SADCC	PTA.nes*	RSA	Imports From: SADCC	PTA.nes	RSA
Angola	0.1	-	-	0.8	0.0	-
Botswana	11.9	0.1	11.3	6.3	0.1	85.1
Lesotho	0.1	0.0	41.3	0.1	0.0	97.1
Malawi	9.7	1.1	5.7	9.6	0.4	34.0
Mozambique	11.6	7.8	1.8	3.0	0.2	8.1
Swaziland	2.7	1.1	36.9	0.7	0.1	82.9
Tanzania	0.8	2.9	-	4.2	1.8	-
Zambia	3.5	0.2	0.3	6.3	0.4	14.5
Zimbabwe	11.5	0.7	17.1	7.6	0.0	22.1
SADCC Total:%	5.0	0.9	7.0	4.4	0.3	30.2
SADCC Total:US$m	276	47	382	316	24	2161

*PTA. nes = SADCC PTA countries, including Madagascar & the Seychelles.
Source: SADCC, SADCC Intra-Regional Trade Study, January 1986.

But success in reorienting Zimbabwean commercial links away from the 'traditional' links with Europe and South Africa does not only depend on the availability and reliability of physical communication links. For PTA trade in particular, the tariff preference advantages could remain largely nominal for Zimbabwe if the foreign ownership aspects surrounding the Rules of Origin are applied with any significant degree of firmness within the zone. This in itself serves to reinforce the long-term significance of one of the central objectives in the FYDP, viz. the creation of a 'national economy' in Zimbabwe.

REFERENCES

1. The *Zimbabwe Conference on Reconstruction and Development* (ZIMCORD), held in Harare in 1981, through which close on $1.3 billion was secured in pledges towards post-war rehabilitation and development programmes.
2. *Zimbabwe: First Five-Year National Development Plan: 1986-1990*, Vol. 1, April 1986.
3. *Zimbabwe: Transitional National Development Plan, 1982/83-1984/85*, Vol. 1, November 1982.
4. An excellent critique of the planning process in Zimbabwe is Wittich, G., Why Development is Needed and a Suggestion on How it could be Improved, Conference Paper No. 30, Department of Economics, University of Zimbabwe, September 1980 (hereafter 'UZ 1985 Conference').
5. *The Lagos Plan of Action and the Final Act of Lagos*.
6. Recommendations of the ECA Conference of Ministers concerning the economic issues on the Draft Agenda (of the 21st OAU Summit), United Nations, E/ECA/CMII/Rev 1: Addis Ababa, 25-29 April 1985.
7. World Bank *Accelerated Development in Sub-Saharan Africa: An Agenda for Action*, August 1981; *Sub-Saharan Africa: Progress Report on Development and Programmes*, 1983.
8. *Ibid*.
9. The embarrassment of a situation where Africa, in spite of its celebrated dire straits, increasingly pays out in debt service more than it receives by way of fresh capital inflows is now extended, on a continent-wide basis, to include both the World Bank and the IMF repayment obligations.

For a succinct general discussion of the issues of debt overhang, see World Bank Staff Paper, 'Achievement of Sustained Growth in Middle Income Countries Encountering Debt Servicing Difficulties...', April 1986. More specifically on Africa, the World Bank has recently (see *Financing Adjustment with Growth in Sub-Saharan Africa, 1986-1990*, February 1986) been exceptionally forceful in appealing for a reversal of the resource drain:

> Additional resources will be needed to pay for imports during 1986-1990 and to cover debt service payments, so they must be in quick-disbursing form. The correct pattern of assistance will vary from case to case... But one general rule should be

observed: *no donor country should be a net recipient of resource flows from any African country undertaking credible economic reforms* (emphasis in original).

10. See, for example, papers by Lawrence Harris and by Colin Stoneman and Rob Davies in *Zimbabwe's Inheritance*, Stoneman, C. (ed), Macmillan, 1981.

11. De Brunhoff, S., *The State, Capital and Economic Policy*, Press, 1978.

12. 'Stability' here, and elsewhere in this chapter, connotes broad balance in macroeconomic accounts, and does *not* at all imply either the absence of systemic political discord, or political acceptance of results attained.

13. See Stoneman, C., Foreign Capital in Zimbabwe, in *Zimbabwe: Towards a New Order*, Vol. 1, United Nations, 1980.

14. The general approach in 1980 in both government and the multilateral institutions was that Zimbabwe was 'under-borrowed'. While it is true that by any standard the 1980 debt service ratio of around 10% was exceptionally low, the subsequent indiscriminate use of this capacity without due regard to either the structure of the debt or the use to which the resources were put became largely responsible for the strain that was placed on foreign exchange resource availability by 1983.

15. Ultimately, the issue reduces to one of the *quality* of planning, and the *status* of the plan. The issue can become a problem in situations, such as in Zimbabwe, where the tradition and the legal status of the budget will tend to generate 'answers' ahead of and more coherently than, the fledgling planning process. See Wittich, *op.cit.*

16. The most forceful expression of this view is in Mkandawire, T., Home-made (?) Austerity Measures: The Case of Zimbabwe, mimeograph, 1984. C. Stoneman's conclusions (Strategy or Ideology: The World Bank/IMF Approach to Development, UZ 1985 Conference, Paper 10) are much more cautious, but in my view still tenuous.

17. Davies, Omar, Crisis Management and Economic Planning, The Jamaican Experience 1972-1985, UZ 1985 Conference, Paper No. 17.

18. Marton, Andrew, The Bungled Experiment, *Institutional Investor*, March 1986.

19. Girvan, Norman, Swallowing the IMF Medicine in the Seventies, *Development Dialogue*, 2, 1980.

20. *Ibid.*

21. In respect of the central government budget, for example, this requires a reversal of the position of net dis-saver that the Government sector has exhibited in every year from 1980.

22. In *Zimbabwe: Towards a New Order* (*op. cit.*), Stoneman quotes Vornschier, Chase-Dunn & Rubinson's conclusions from 'Cross-national evidence of the effects of foreign investment and aid on economic growth and inequality':

> ...foreign investment tends to produce uneven growth across economic sectors. Such uneven development may be one mechanism by which foreign investment leads to increasing

income inequality, early monopolisation and structural unemployment, thus favouring early saturation of effective demand and lowering the rate of capital formation... And since capital formation is a major cause of increasing growth, this reduction in capital formation is another mechanism by which foreign investment reduces growth. Finally ... one of the ways in which foreign investment reduces growth is by reducing State power, and hence the ability of the State to undertake a policy of growth, independent of the class interests created by foreign capital.

23. The remarks of the Chief Executive of ZNCC in 1979 may assume prophetic significance:

Whichever government gets in is going to find that they have inherited a very sophisticated and diverse economy. They will find a momentum that will be difficult to divert in terms of imposing completely radical policies (quoted in Stoneman, *op.cit.*)

4. FOREIGN CAPITAL
Theresa Chimombe

Introduction

For most developing countries (LDCs) development features as the primary goal of the national plans. Under the difficult circumstances of inadequate resources (especially capital and expertise), they are driven to obtain foreign capital, whether from the Western or Eastern bloc countries. Evidence, however, suggests that most of the capital comes from the former bloc, and very often with disastrous consequences for the development efforts of the least developed countries. There exists, therefore, a growing paradox between the heavy dependency on foreign capital by LDCs and the negative impact of such capital on actual development. Furthermore, despite a wide realisation of these negative effects, more and more LDCs make a concerted effort to attract foreign capital, on whatever terms it is offered. Looking at the African countries in particular, it is interesting to note the contradiction between the widely acclaimed goals of 'self-reliance' on the one hand, and the highly dependent development which is fostered by foreign capital on the other hand.

The dilemma for these countries is threefold. Firstly, LDCs have limited capital resources but they do have relatively rich natural resources. For Africa, due to many years of colonisation, these resources were extracted in order to build up the economies of the now developed countries. Local expertise was neither mobilised nor encouraged, and consequently there is an acute manpower problem. Hence, the shortage of capital has led many LDCs to seek it from elsewhere. Given that the LDCs are, by and large, poor countries, this assistance was seen as obtainable only from the developed world. Now this constitutes the second dilemma. This outward-looking and dependent approach militated against any efforts to formulate viable, locally-based and self-reliant development strategies. The latter alternative was definitely costly and did call for extensive sacrifices, which these countries were not prepared to make. Despite attainment of political independence, they in fact chose to leave the colonial structures intact so as to continue to obtain help from the former colonial masters. And given that the colonial powers were eager to pursue their imperialistic ambitions in the neo-colonial era, the dominant attitude with regard to foreign capital in LDCs provided a very good avenue for the penetration of imperialism.

The third dilemma is that those who can provide the capital (mainly the Western capitalist nations) only do so on their own terms in order to serve their political, economic, and social interests. Consequently, very little gain accrues to the developing country.

In the case of the newly-independent Zimbabwe, there have been some interesting developments with regards to foreign capital. Despite the stated objective of building a socialist economy based on the scientific principles of Marxism-Leninism, the government found it necessary to invite foreign capital to assist in the development process.

Thus, foreign capital has continued to feature in Zimbabwe's post-independence development strategy. Figures on development assistance funds received from 1980 to 1985 show that a total of US$2.61 billion was committed to Zimbabwe (commitment refers to a firm pledge or a signed agreement whilst disbursement refers to an actual expenditure). Of this, about US$1.68 billion was actually disbursed. Table 1, however, shows the problem that disbursements in each year were below the pledges and this presented problems in project implementation.

TABLE 1

Total Annual Commitments US$ (millions)		Total Annual Disbursements US$ (millions)
1980	292	121
1981	585	266
1982	498	297
1983	611	277
1984	285	372
1985	339	347
Total	2,610	1,680

Source: *Status Report on External Development Assistance to Zimbabwe, 1980-1985*, June 1986. The Status Report further notes that about 43% of the US$2.61 billion committed over the period were grants. 55% of all aid received from bilateral resources has been in grant form. 46% of the US$1.68 billion came as untied assistance, 40% was tied (CIPs).

Although smaller than had been expected, funds raised at the Zimbabwe Conference on Reconstruction and Development (ZIMCORD) and from direct private foreign investment further added to the already high level of foreign capital in the economy. In addition, Zimbabwe became a member of the International Monetary Fund, and received some funds for balance of payments adjustment. It also became a member of the World Bank whereby it could obtain loans for infrastructural development. This trend has very significant implications in terms of its impact on development in general and in attaining the specific objective laid out in the plan in particular.

Much has been written about the pros and cons of foreign aid and private foreign investment in the development process. Popular arguments to support foreign capital regard it as a necessary or useful injection into a foreign-exchange/manpower/technology/capital-deficient country and that, therefore, it constitutes a positive aspect in the development and growth process. Transnational corporations (TNCs) are seen as important partners in development. But very often such arguments ignore important facts in evaluating the impact of such capital in development. TNCs must be seen as a type of monopolistic organisation of all the various stages of economic activity on an international scale. They regard the capitalist part of the world as a single area for the accumulation and investment of capital, and an enormous source of capital. Profit is their driving motive. Unless the host country is prepared to offer the 'acceptable' rate of return or other attractive incentives (e.g. long tax holidays, low taxation, easy terms of profits repatriation, etc.) they will not venture into production. A number of studies have also pointed out that superior management and information systems assist the companies to continue siphoning out profits through transfer pricing, fees for management and consultancies, trade names and the supply and servicing of machinery and equipment. In this case, very little benefit accrues to the host.

Zimbabwe's colonial experience with foreign capital provides evidence of the predominantly negative impact of such capital. Foreign capital was part and parcel of the forces of plunder which visited the country in 1890. The period 1890-1923 has been described by some as an era of 'company government in which foreign finance and investment was the *fons et origo* of economic development during that period'.[1] The British South African Company became the administrative power in the land, although the British Colonial Office intervened from time to time. The company eventually spread its activities into agriculture, mining and manufacturing.

More foreign capital flowed in from South Africa and Britain and it got heavily involved in the extractive and export-oriented sectors. It collaborated with the state in repressing the indigenous black population. The Land Tenure Acts, the low wages policies and the poor working conditions of black labour worked against the indigenous population. The benefits of foreign investment accrued to the international capitalist class, the minority national capitalist class, the minority national bourgeoisie and the white working class.

Foreign companies also ventured into banking, with the formation of Standard Bank (1892) at the personal request of Cecil John Rhodes; Barclay's (1895); Grindlays (1953); and finally Rhobank (now Zimbank) in 1951.

The post-war period brought more foreign companies. According to D.G. Clarke, in the first decade of the century Foote Minerals and Union Carbide (both of American origin) began mining chrome. Lonrho also started operations in ranching and mining. Liebigs ventured into large-scale ranching enterprises. Turner and Newall moved into asbestos mining. A number of South African companies spread their activities in the country through their subsidiaries.[2] In short, this was a period when foreign capital established itself firmly in the economy. The state provided the necessary support such as low wages policy and the provision of transport infrastructure. Over the colonial period, foreign capital increased its hold on the economy and despite sanctions during UDI there was evidence that its interests had strengthened. With headquarters in South Africa, it worked closely with local white settler minority interests. Estimates show that in 1978-79, total private capital stock approximated Z$2,713 million and Z$3,610 million compared with Z$88 million in the 1935-39 period (at 1980 prices).[3] Another comprehensive study[4] emphasised that the economy of Zimbabwe was one of the most heavily dependent on external capital in black Africa as evidenced by the following statistics:

(a) about $3.3 billion or 70% of the capital stock of the country was under foreign control (mainly British and South African);
(b) foreign investment during 15 years of sanctions grew by about $1 billion, roughly 300%;
(c) it is also estimated that British capital rose from $200 million during UDI while South African capital increased from $215 million to $967 million;
(d) at least 130 British and 43 South African companies provided most of the foreign interest in Zimbabwe;
(e) foreign-owned mining operation account for more than 90% of production and employ more than 80% of the miners. Those operations are led by South Africa's Anglo-American, Messina Transvaal, Britain's Lonrho and Rio Tinto and Falcon Mines and America's Union Carbide.

The aim of this chapter is fourfold. Firstly, it assesses the objective reasons for the inflows in the light of stated development objectives. Secondly, it examines the trend in the flow of foreign capital into the economy, its origins and impact in the various sectors in which it became involved. It also seeks to explain why, despite concerted government effort (alongside key private sector organisations) to attract foreign investment, the result had been mixed.

Thirdly, it discusses the terms and conditions under which such capital came in. An assessment of the foreign investment code is therefore central in this respect. Fourthly, the chapter purports to assess the implications of foreign capital for achieving greater economic independence, growth and development, meeting manpower and technology needs; and finally, in maintaining balance in key macro-economic variables such as the balance of payments, employment and monetary stability.

It must be mentioned, however, that a complete evaluation of the impact of foreign capital five years after independence is greatly constrained by the limited availability of crucial data, especially on direct private sources, and also the mere fact that some projects started long after the pledges had been made and are still in their infancy stage.

Government Economic Policy and Foreign Capital After Independence

Government economic policy after independence has strongly welcomed foreign investment—whether public or private—in the interests of 'pragmatism'. The government made concerted effort to 'sell' Zimbabwe to predominantly Western capital. The result has been a poor and slower response than expected. The crucial question about this policy is whether it was justified or not. Whilst Clarke's study on foreign companies in Zimbabwe is a comprehensive description of the structure of TNCs, not much analysis has been made to assess the real net benefit which the country derives from foreign capital, whether in terms of employment, appropriate technology, manpower training, government revenue, reinvestment of profits, backward and forward linkages etc. There is also a contradiction that, in policy statements, the government is critical of the operations of foreign capital in the past. Yet at the same time it makes a concerted effort to attract foreign capital, as reflected in the foreign investment code.

The *Growth With Equity Policy Statement* and the *Three Year Transitional National Development Plan* (TNDP) clearly state the government's economic policy objectives. The establishment of a socialist and egalitarian society remains as the prime objective, so that more equitable income and wealth distribution accompanies economic growth. Foreign capital must also be considered within such a framework in order to assess its potential contribution to such a goal.

In the plan document, government realises the already high degree of foreign investment concentration especially in mining, manufacturing and commerce. Given the high level of foreign capital, government policy stated that:

> Government is anxious to reduce the degree of foreign control by increasing state participation in the economy, and establishing new socio-economic institutions run and controlled by the people.[5]

The Prime Minister made the position of the government clear when he said:

> While the inherited economy, with its institutions and infrastructure, has in the past served a minority it would be simplistic and naive to suggest that therefore it be destroyed in order to a make a fresh start. The challenge lies in building upon and developing on what was inherited, modifying, expanding and, where necessary, radically changing structures and institutions in order to maximize benefits from economic growth, and to develop Zimbabwe as a whole.[6]

These policy statements seem to indicate a definite concern about the dominance of foreign capital in the country. The government recognises the exploitative nature of this capital and it endeavours to redress these effects. However, its approach to dealing with foreign capital is a very cautious one, as reflected in the Prime Minister's statement. Consequently, there has not been a radical attitude to foreign capital. In fact, the predominant stance seems to be conservative.

The government also makes provision for attracting domestic and foreign investment and emphasises the need to create a favourable investment climate. However, it cautions that:

> Government maintains that the existence of such a climate need not and should not compromise the overriding need to ensure maximum net benefits of such investment to the Zimbabwean economy. In addition, it requires that the creation and maintenance of such a climate can and should be consistent with the aspiration of creating an egalitarian, socialist and democratic society.[7]

Details of the government's foreign investment policy are most clearly laid out in the investment code. During the process of continued efforts by the government to attract foreign capital, interested foreign businessmen and organisations began to pressurise the government to formulate a code of conduct in order to show in more precise form the prospects for profitability and security of property that investment in Zimbabwe would offer. That the code was primarily a product of direct international and, to some extent, local private sector pressure minimised any independence and careful formulation of policy by planners. The code became another means or part of the strategy to obtain much-desired foreign capital. Consequently, its provisions were geared to achieve this specific goal by addressing itself to the pertinent issues of profit repatriation and security of property.

The code makes it clear that the government encourages and welcomes investment, from both foreign and local private sources. It recognises the need for the private sector and emphasises that it must be of a type which is:

> ...also conscious of the state of Zimbabwe and its people, to promotion of production, employment, development, training and the adequate supply at reasonable prices of the goods and services needed and for export.[8]

The confidence and hope in the role of the private sector in fulfilling the socialist objectives of government prevails in other key government policy documents such as the Growth with Equity Statement (GWE) and the *Three Year Transitional National Development Plan (TNDP)*. Such government confidence in the private sector was unfounded and rather over-ambitious. The code states the government's investment priorities as laid down in paragraph 2:2.[9]

Foreign investment will be welcome in the following areas:

(i) new enterprises in rural areas where socio-economic benefits may be expected to occur;
(ii) new enterprises, particularly those requiring specific technology available to the foreign investor, which will make an additional net contribution to the economy, including the training of Zimbabweans;
(iii) new enterprises on a joint-venture basis, where the investor

specifically wishes to have either an immediate domestic or a state equity participation and which will make an additional net contribution to the economy,

(iv) existing enterprises where an injection of additional foreign capital or technology will mean an increase in productivity and improvement in the end product. As a general rule, subject to review and modification in appropriate cases, the absolute amount of existing domestic participation in domestic enterprises should not be diluted, in future, by sale to foreign interests; nor should an existing domestic control level of equity holding be allowed to pass to foreign investors. But there is no objection to new foreign investment being introduced into existing enterprises for expansion or to improve efficiency, technology etc.;

(v) undertakings in which more intensive use of local raw materials and processed inputs is promoted;

(iv) areas in which labour-intensive technology and, in addition, technology that is appropriate and easily adaptable is promoted;

(vi) activities in which generation of exports within a reasonable period is possible.

The policy also includes the participation of government on a joint-venture basis in key sectors affecting strategic facilities or basic infrastructural development.

The provisions are very general to start with and foreign investors would like to see more detailed and specific statements. However, to the extent that these guidelines would be strictly followed by policy-makers, they represent an important step in the area of regulating the levels and areas of operation of foreign capital. Some developments after independence, unfortunately, cast some doubts on this. For instance, clause 2.2 (iv) was clearly negated in the case of the Cairns-Dalgety deal and others where locally-owned companies went into liquidation and were acquired by foreign interests (see p. 136).

In addition, the question of joint ventures as laid out in 2.2 (iii) in itself may be of little significance. Joint ventures have been encouraged in order to encourage state and/or local equity participation. The experience of other countries with TNCs shows that joint ventures are usually organised on a parity basis and a TNC does not hold a major part of the share capital. For that reason, the TNC then adopts various supplementary methods of control in order to ensure that, even though it does not own a majority of shares, it is in charge and can subordinate the joint venture to its own global strategy. The whole mechanism of control over joint ventures is based on the fact that many countries badly need financial and material resources, the latest technology and the management of production. This kind of policy forms the natural expression of a completely new type of colonialism.

Foreign companies also try to reduce the benefits of a joint venture. They often manage to retain for themselves the right to decide such key questions as the area of operations for the new enterprise and the sale of part of its assets; they also manage to place various of their own representatives on the board of directors of the joint enterprises. In addition, the lack of skills and training which characterises local/government managers adds other advantages to the corporation. TNCs can also reserve for themselves the post of managing director for production and technical matters. Of the three top managers responsible for the operational running of Merck, Sharp and Dohme of India (a joint company of the United States pharmaceutical company, Merck), the managing director was an Indian, the head of marketing an Australian, while the production department was headed by an American. Yet another favourite device is the dilution of shares where, although the TNC holds a minority share, the majority shares are spread across very small shareholders who take no direct part in running the company. Astapovich quotes the example that about half the shares in joint ventures with the participation of Merck, Union Carbide and Pfizer in India, and Kaiser in Brazil, were distributed in this manner and yet the United States corporations retained managerial control. Consequently, in some countries, governments are going into joint ventures with TNCs not on the basis of common ownership but on restrictive contracts and agreements, e.g. that a TNC provides the technical services needed for a project but without participation in the ownership of the project. And as developing countries adopt a tougher stance on foreign capital, joint ventures will assume greater importance by the giant corporations to obtain maximum benefits.

On legal provisions, the Zimbabwean guidelines assure foreign investors about the security of their investment to the extent allowed for by the constitution. This requires that reasonable notice of intention to acquire property shall be given to the owner; that nationalisation can only be undertaken in the interests of defence, public safety or public order; and that compensation shall be paid. This whole clause in the document makes it absolutely clear that there is room for private property being nationalised and foreign investors cannot accept this. In fact, during the period 1981 to 1983, there was much 'lobbying' or pressure from American businessmen for government to sign the OPIC (Overseas Private Investment Corporation (US) Agreement). OPIC provides political risk insurance programmes to cover expropriation, the suspension of income and dividend remittances and war/riot damage. It also provides loans or loan guarantees to help US investors captialise investment projects, with preference being given to small-scale projects. The government must be applauded for its refusal to yield to the pressures which would have led it to sign the agreement and one hopes this stance will be maintained. As the Finance and Development Minister himself observed:

> We have seen that nearly all African countries have signed OPIC, but not a penny has come in, and we are asking why. It appears that the agreement in fact allowed more money to go out of a country than into it.[10]

Another aspect that investors have found most unattractive are the foreign exchange controls, despite the fact that the code provides for the repatriation of 50% of after-tax profits and the payment of any excess dividends into a local blocked account of the foreign shareholder. In the interests of balance of payment stability, this guideline is subject to revision. Exchange control rules also allow for the repatriation of proceeds from disinvestment, albeit over a period of two years.

Whether these conditions were adhered to in every agreement can only be assessed by a closer review of negotiations which went on at the ZIMCORD, the IMF and with private investors.

Zimbabwe Conference on Reconstruction and Development (ZIMCORD)

The exact origin of ZIMCORD seems unclear—whether it was initiated by the government or by the United States or by Britain at Lancaster House. However, it is quite clear that the concept was not new. The Marshall Plan of Action for the reconstruction of post-war Europe resembled ZIMCORD in its objectives and strategies. The objectives of ZIMCORD were:

> to mobilise the support of the international community to assist the government and people of Zimbabwe with financial and technical resources for land resettlement and rural agricultural development conceived within the framework of rural development.[11]

The Zimbabwe Conference on Reconstruction and Development (ZIMCORD), held in March 1981, involved about 45 countries or organisations which pledged approximately $1.2 billion. There were 26 delegates from 45 countries, 15 UN agencies, and 10 other international agencies including OPEC and the EEC. Participants came mainly from the Western capitalist countries. China and Yugoslavia were the only ones from the socialist bloc (see Table 2).

The significance of ZIMCORD was that it was to contribute about one-third of the financial requirements of the TNDP. The TNDP was to be funded by ZIMCORD and domestic sources. $6,094 million was required to finance the plan. Foreign capital inflows were expected to contribute $2,279 million (37% of GFCF) and of this, the largest proportion of these funds were earmarked for the Public Sector Investment Programme (PSIP).

The World Bank (IBRD) was the biggest donor (new pledges made totalled Z$287.5 million). Its funds were advanced for the typical IBRD-funded projects, i.e. infrastructural development. These included some of the following:

> transport rehabilitation;
> imports of vehicles and spare parts (US$42 million);
> the Power Projects at Hwange (US$105 million);
> manufacturing industry import and export programme (US$50.6 million);
> railway development project (US$43 million);

small-scale enterprise project assistance (US$ million);
rural afforestation (US$7.3 million);
petroleum fuels (US$12 million).

The big contributors at ZIMCORD were the EEC members and the Commission of the European Community, which together contributed about 40% of the total pledges. The absolute figures given by the EEC members are shown on Table 1. The United Kingdom was the biggest donor in the EEC (Z$177 million).

The African Development Bank gave loans with a rural bias — Z$158 million for rural development: Z$31 million was given to the Agricultural Financial Corporation, which since independence has drastically increased its assistance to communal/peasant farmers. The grace period for the ADB loans is five years and they can be repaid in twenty years; interest of 9.86% per annum is charged.

The biggest bilateral aid is from the United States and is largely tied to, and under, the Commodity Import Programme (CIP). Accordingly, Zimbabwe obtained loans to buy essential imports of equipment, machinery, spares parts and raw materials from the United States. USAID pledged Z$201 million and this included Z$37.6 million for the CIP.

Britain's funds were for resettlement purposes. They were to promote Model A Schemes based on individual ownership of land. The government wanted the development of co-operatives (Model B) and state farms (Model C), but funds for these later models have not been forthcoming. British aid also came in very slowly, consequently the resettlement programme has been very slow such than only about one-fifth of the intended families were resettled by 1983. *Zimbabwe's experience with British aid constitutes one of the most glaring examples of how aid is not really 'aid' but a kind of weapon used by the donors to promote their own interests.* It may, in fact, have been naive on the government's part to expect Britain to give money which was to be used for land redistribution when, for all these years, Britain had stood for white interests. The Lancaster House agreement was adequate testimony to this. Another lesson for Zimbabwe was that 'aid' could not be depended on since its availability rests on the interests of the donor.

Almost every donor required that between 10% and 30% of aid be used in the procurement of goods and services from the donor country. By 31 December 1982, the Treasury had disbursed some of the ZIMCORD funds thus:

Lands, Resettlement/Rural Development	16,041,617.31
District Development Fund (DDF)	21,455,096.00
Department of Social Services	17,535,512.57
Ministry of Health	1,189,100.00
Works	2,713,119.00
Education and Culture	1,326,288.41
Division of District Administration	17,160,000.00

Of these allocations, the District Development Fund put $8,388,085.00

towards building roads and bridges; Social Services put $13,802,169.36 for the provision of food; and the District Administration channelled $17 million for construction of Council Schools.

The report also shows the ZIMCORD funds allocated to the Public Sector Investment Programme (PSIP).

Ministry	PSIP Commitment ($ m)	Interest ($ m)
Transport	72.30	5.0
PTC	9.75	-
Education	143.30	-
Water Development	9.50	5.0
Agriculture	18.00	7.0
Lands	48.50	26.4
Housing	12.90	1.0

Source: Status Report on External Development Assistance to Zimbabwe, 1980-1985, June 1986.

Table 3 provides a summary of the major sectors which have been the main recipients of external assistance, and the % assistance received.

The allocation of funds was heavily biased towards agriculture and infrastructural support. Since 1982, industry has received less assistance. However, more specific sectoral information is required to make a conclusive statement.

The success of ZIMCORD cannot be measured in terms of how faithfully the donors have met their pledges but by the extent to which funds have helped in achieving development, especially in the rural areas, and also at what social costs. A major drawback of the programme was that, whilst donors pledged funds at the conference, the rate at which these were paid has been slow and coming in the form of trickles; it became difficult to plan and implement projects efficiently. The failure or limited success of the resettlement programme has been due to such factors. And interestingly, the programme has failed to carry out a major land reform to redress the highly skewed distribution of land in the rural areas.

Some of the projects have also left question marks, particularly in the context of regional integration. Zimbabwe could obtain cheaper hydroelectric power from Cabora Bassa and thus promote the objectives of SADCC regional integration. Yet it went ahead to secure the loan from the World Bank for the Hwange Power Project.

A significant achevement has been in the provision of dams, boreholes and wells, all of which have improved the living standards of the rural population. But for the bulk of the projects an evaluation may be premature as some of them only got on their feet a year or two after the conference and financial constraints slackened their pace of development.

TABLE 2
AID COMMITMENTS TO ZIMBABWE
1981

Donor	Gross Total US$000's	Former Pledges Z$000's	New Pledges Z$000's	Gross Total Z$000's
African Devel. Bank	69,000	-	43,131	43,131
Australia	23,300	7,650	6,955	14,604
Badea	50,000	-	31,250	31,250
Belgium	12,800	-	8,000	8,000
Canada	53,300	5,556	27,778	33,334
China	28,000	17,500	2,500	20,000
Commonwealth	7,180	1,565	2,926	4,492
Denmark	20,000	9,622	2,830	12,452
Egypt	2,000	-	1,250	1,250
E.E.C.	192,000	12,139	107,862	120,000
Finland	8,270	2,667	2,500	5,167
France	114,300	35,715	35,715	71,430
Germany	100,000	30,714	31,607	62,321
Ghana	100	-	63	63
Holy See	20,000	8,125	4,375	12,500
Iraq	3,000	1,875	-	1,875
Ireland	70	45	-	45
Italy	37,000	11,250	11,875	23,125
Japan	4,900	1,960	15,040	17,000
Jersey	120	-	75	75
Kuwait	52,000	-	32,500	32,500
Luxemburg	3,000	5	1,875	1,880
Netherlands	26,000	6,126	10,107	16,233
New Zealand	280	-	174	174
Nigeria	20,000	12,440	-	12,440
Norway	18,000	1,250	10,000	11,250
OPEC Fund	10,000	-	6,250	7,250
Suadi Arabia	5,000	3,125	-	3,125
Sierra Leone	90	-	56	56
Sweden	87,000	9,933	44,478	54,411
Switzerland	26,000	903	15,367	16,270
United Kingdom	283,000	140,454	36,577	177,031
United Nations	42,250	11,250	15,156	26,406
United States	276,210	32,008	140,625	172,633
World Bank	460,000	-	287,500	287,500
Yugoslavia	4,500	938	1,875	2,813
	2,058,670	364,815	921,852	1,286,666

Source: ZIMCORD

TABLE 3
PERCENTAGE OF EXTERNAL ASSISTANCE RECEIVED BY MANOR SECTORS

(Summary of the major Sectors which have been the main receipients of external assistance and the proportion of assistance received)

Year	Sector	%
1980	Emergency Aid (including food)	43%
	Agriculture, Forestry, Fisheries	28%
	Education	24%
	Others	5%
1981	Industry	21%
	Agriculture, Forestry, Fisheries	18%
	Mining	15%
	Education	12%
	Transport and Communications	11%
	CIPs and Balance of Payments Support	11%
	Others	12%
1982	Transport and Communications	24%
	BOP Support and CIPs	23%
	Education	13%
	Agriculture, Forestry, Fisheries	9%
	Industry	8%
	Others	23%
1983	CIPs and BOP Support	26%
	Tansport and Communications	21%
	Industry	14%
	Agriculture, Forestry, Fisheries	9%
	Education	10%
	Others	20%
1984	CIPs and BOP Support	25%
	Transport and Communications	12%
	Industry	12%
	Agriculture, Forestry, Fisheries	11%
	Education	11%
	Others	29%
1984	CIPs and BOP Support	26%
	Agriculture, Forestry, Fisheries	13%
	Transport and Communications	12%
	Education	10%
	Industry	8%
	Others	31%

Source: Status Report on External Development Assistance to Zimbabwe, 1980-1985, June 1986.

Direct Private Foreign Investment Inflows

Although the period after independence witnessed a slow growth in direct private foreign investment inflows, it seems that the bulk of this came from the United States and Britain, and the Federal Republic of Germany.

Towards the end of 1980, an American MNC, Columbus McKinnon, declared its intentions to expand its operations in Zimbabwe and make the country the centre for exports to East, Central and Southern Africa. Another American Company, Heinz, a giant food corporation, took over Olivine industries and bought a controlling share of 51% whilst the government held the rest. The agreement, negotiations for which took about nine months, involved about Z$23 million and was quoted to be Heinz's largest investment in Africa and the country's biggest foreign investment since independence. American banks also took the opportunity: Citibank (which has recently decided to move to Botswana) and the Bank of Boston opened offices in Harare. Several United States firms have sought joint ventures in manufacturing, agriculture and consumer goods industries but the outcome of those efforts is not apparent.

British capital also poured in. The United Kingdom-based company, Dalgety, acquired a 30% equity in Cairns Holdings. Cairns Holdings then lost its locally-owned status and management status when it went into partnership with Dalgety whereby three million dollars would be injected into the companies. The effect was to dilute local equity participation in favour of Dalgety. According to the former Minister of Industry and Technology, Cde Simba Makoni, the deal was in breach of three basic national economic policies.

Firstly, the partnership led to a substantial dilution of local equity control transforming a wholly locally-owned, viable and profitable enterprise into a one-third externally-controlled one, with the external partner becoming the single largest shareholder.

Secondly, the deal did not yield immediate inflows of foreign financial or capital resources to the country or company.

Finally, the investment input from the foreign partner was not directed at the establishment of additional or completely new productive capacity.

The Cairns-Dalgety deal clearly proves Astapovich's point about how TNCs can develop and utilise new techniques and ensure that they effectively have a controlling share in a joint venture situation.

Another development with regards to British capital involved the sale of two Zimbabwean subsidiaries, Wallace Laboratories (Pvt) Ltd and Ferndale (Pvt) Ltd by international brewers Arthur Guinness and Sons plc, to a London-based group, ITM International. Thus it was a transfer from one set of foreign hands to another.

This also happened in the case of the Norwegian fertiliser giant Norsk Hydro which took over all shares previously held by United Kingdom-based Fisons in Zimbabwe Fertiliser Company Ltd (ZFC) and Sable Chemical Industries.

A British firm, Dashwood Finance Company Ltd., was to invest US$300 million in Zimbabwe for the first stage of the Chisumbanje sugar ethanol project.

Aberfoyle Holdings, a British and local firm (Masimba Export and Import Company) went into a joint venture to establish a 12,000 hectare palm oil plantation at Rutenga. This would cost about US$50 million and employ 10,000 people and establish 4,000 smallholders. Benefits exist, especially for detergent firms, but not for the people around the place, who may be worse off in terms of switching from food production to cash crop production.

Another British company, Cliff Oil, announced plans to start extracting gold ore from a new mine at Filabusi, which involved about 10,500 fine ounces of gold worth around $4 million, so this is a small venture.

A few West German firms have also invested in the country. By the end of 1981, 12 West German firms had opened offices in Zimbabwe and three were apparently engaged in joint ventures. Siemens and the Industrial Development Corporation of Zimbabwe became partners in a joint venture know as Electro Technologies Corporation (Pvt) Ltd. Siemens' global turnover approximates US$10 billion and it employs 344,000 in 129 countries.

One or two Japanese firms have since joined the investment fever. A joint venture was established between Sanyo and Marubeni (Japan) and Zimbabwe Electronics Corporation.

Some of the investments are certainly of doubtful and questionable value in terms of our development priorities. An example is Europe's largest exporter of chewing gum, Dandy Chewing Gum Limited of Denmark, which became the first Scandinavian company to embark on a joint venture in Zimbabwe. The chewing gum project was approved on grounds of its export potential. It would also employ 100 people.

It must also be noted that the period 1980 to 1985 was characterised by some disinvestment of capital. However, very little capital was withdrawn (roughly $20 million). Some of the companies closed down and went either to South Africa or Botswana, where profits were greater. Their reasons for closing down included high production costs (due to the government's minimum wage legislation), low profit margins due to high costs and price controls and also the 'uncertain future for business in a Socialist State'. This trend resulted in an increase in unemployment levels. It also illustrated the mistake which the government had made by assuming that the private sector would assist in the socialist development of the economy, and at the expense of their profits. More important, such disinvestment reflects the undependable nature of foreign capital in the face of economic crises. When economic conditions turn adverse, they seek more favourable situations where business prospects are high. Despite the government's pleas for these companies to stay, they left the country. The redundancies, unemployment and gloom which resulted from the closure of these companies may in fact have pressurised the government to relax its policies on minimum wage legislation and price controls—a position of forced compromise.

Another lesson which should have been learnt was the danger of heavy reliance on foreign capital. When it left the country, there was a crisis because little effort had been made to encourage and establish locally-based enterprises to carry on the work of the foreign enterprises.

Zimbabwe and the International Monetary Fund

Foreign capital also manifested itself through the International Monetary Fund when Zimbabwe became a member after independence. The government resorted to the IMF to get assistance for a balance of payments adjustment. The deficit on current account had risen from $156.7 million in 1980 to $532.9 million in 1982, when negotiations with the IMF started. According to the IMF analysis, the deficit was due to excessive government expenditure. From the point of view of the government, the expenditure was justified since it was on essential items such as defence, education and health. It therefore recommended short-term demand management which included the removal of subsidies on maize, bread and milk; and reduction in a civil service employment programme by $200 million. It also had to freeze civil service employment. In December of the same year, it devalued the Z$ by 17% and the exchange rate was allowed to drift until the effective devaluation was nearly 40%.[12]

In March 1983, the IMF announced that it was giving a loan of $375 million to Zimbabwe. Of this, $59 million was made available immediately, and the rest ($316) was a 'stand-by credit' whose disbursement was determined by Zimbabwe's fulfilment of the performance criteria. Developments in the later part of 1983 revealed some problems. The mini-budget deficit had in fact increased, contrary to the IMF stipulations. In addition, Zimbabwe refused to take sides in the UN Security Council on the issue of the downing of the South Korean airliner by the Soviet Union and also condemned the US invasion of Grenada. In order to obtain the funds, the government had to start negotiations again with the IMF.

Conclusion

An interesting feature of the post-independence era was the concerted effort made by the government to attract foreign investment from multilateral, bilateral and private sources. However, the response was not as expected because investors still regarded Zimbabwe as risky and also felt that returns to capital were not high enough. The bulk of the capital came in through ZIMCORD, whose participants mainly came from the developed Western capitalist nations. Private investment also came in from this source, but there was a very insignificant inflow. Reasons included the restrictive foreign exchange controls, minimum wage policy, price controls and the government's proclaimed socialist objectives. The country has also suffered a very negative international press coverage over the security situation, particularly in Matebeleland, and this could have affected investment.

The formulation of the foreign investment code to a large extent was due to the pressures of foreign investors. Despite the government's effort to offer some incentives in the code, foreign investors felt that the terms were not very attractive and, in some ways, that the code was rather narrow or generalised and therefore they wished to see a more elaborate code. Consequently, the government is in the process of making a new and more detailed code. Given the poor investment received, and the government's desire to attract more investment, the new code could make more concessions and so offer better 'terms' to meet the demands of foreign capital. The areas most likely to be revised are the repatriation of profits and dividends, taxes, wage and price policies. This kind of policy, once implemented, would benefit foreign capital but greatly reduce any benefits to the country.

Zimbabwe's experience with foreign capital after independence clearly shows the true colours of foreign capital—the drive for profit as the primary motive as against a desire to develop and serve the country. Against this background, there are two choices for policy-makers. One is to go ahead and draft a more 'acceptable' and 'appropriate' code to attract investors but, in so doing, sacrifice the development aspirations of the country. The other is to maintain the existing code and monitor any foreign capital to ensure that it meets the objectives of the plan. If no significant levels of capital are attracted, there will be need for an alternative strategy on a national scale. This strategy should examine ways of mobilising local resources. It has become clear that any development strategy which depends on foreign capital for its implementation, under the existing economic, ideological and political considerations, has a doubtful chance of success. In fact, that capital in the final analysis serves to maintain the *status quo*. No significant structural changes have been achieved in any of the crucial sectors such as agriculture, mining and manufacturing. Foreign capital has been involved in the non-productive sphere such as infrastructural, long-term development projects which are not immediately or directly productive. Foreign debt-servicing costs have consequently increased.

There was a fundamental contradiction in government policy on foreign capital and the costs of this are reflected in the failure to attract capital. On the one hand the government outlines a most convincing economic policy to be based on Marxist-Leninist principles and at the same time expects Western capitalist countries to assist it in that line. Yet it would be obviously against the interest of foreign capital to assist Zimbabwe on its socialist path. Foreign capital could have very easily been received if Zimbabwe had not proclaimed socialist goals.

After such a bitter war of liberation, it is inconceivable that Zimbabwe would opt for a non-socialist path of development—which would clearly negate the gains of the masses. But Zimbabwe's approach to its socialist development is contradictory. Instead of carrying out fundamental reforms in the inherited economy (such as land reform), the short-cut to development was to get aid. The result has been dismal. Thus, the ambiguous stance on foreign capital can hardly be of any benefit to the country although it has been justified on the grounds of pragmatism.

REFERENCES

1. Clarke, D.G., *Foreign Companies and International Investment in Zimbabwe*, Mambo Press, Gweru, 1980, p. 16.
2. *Ibid.*, p. 20
3. *Economic Symposium Papers on TNCs*, September 1980.
4. Clarke, D.G., *op. cit.*
5. TNDP, Vol. 1, paragraph 3.1.
6. TNDP, Vol. 1, paragraph 1.6, p. 1.
7. *Foreign Investment: Policy Guidelines and Procedures*, September 1982.
8. *Ibid.*, paragraph 1.
9. *Ibid.*, paragraph 2.2.
10. *The Herald.*
11. Zimbabwe Conference on Reconstruction and Development Document 1981.
12. Information on the Zimbabwe government's deal with the IMF is very scanty. Main sources of data in this section include *The Herald*, March 1983, *Africa Confidential*, 1983 issues and *Reserve Bank Quarterly Economic and Statistical Review*, 1983.

5. PROBLEMS OF INDUSTRIALISATION: STRUCTURAL AND POLICY ISSUES

Daniel B. Ndlela

Introduction

Most often, industrialisation is defined as consisting of divisions 1 to 5 of the International Standard Industrial Classification (ISIC), namely: mining and quarrying (division one), manufacturing (divisions two and three), construction (division four) and electricity, gas, water and sanitary services (division five). Using this criterion, R.B. Sutcliffe first assigned any country with about 25% of its gross domestic product (GDP) arising from the industrial sector as industrialised'.[1] Sutcliffe, however, does not regard this criterion as sufficient as it would easily admit as industrialised countries with large foreign-owned mining sectors that dominate the economy; for example, Zambia. A further criterion of industrialisation which more clearly points to structural changes in the economy rather than a change in one variable assigns about 60% of output of the total industrial sector as originating from manufacturing (ISIC divisions two and three). Even this classification still needs the additional criterion that a certain proportion—say 10%—of the population should be employed in the industrial sector. This composite definition for categorising industrialisation refers both to a proportion of the national product and to a proportion of the labour force engaged in industry.

Though these criteria are by no means satisfactory ones in describing the properties of industrialisation, they go a long way towards ascertaining a statistical level of industrialisation that a given country will have attained. Table 1 shows that the manufacturing sector contributes by far the largest part of industrial activity in Zimbabwe's economy. When this criterion is applied, between 1979 and 1982 the manufacturing sector's share in total industrial activity averaged about 72%. This might indicate that Zimbabwe is industrialised. But when the criterion of the share of labour force involved in total industry is employed, Zimbabwe is found not to be industrialised at all. Between 1979 and 1982 industrial employment was only about 4% of the country's population. The latter is a definite indicator of a historically skewed distribution of economic activity. However, at the same time, it is an indicator of a challenging situation where Zimbabwe finds itself at a crossroads, with immense opportunities for industrialising through the use of a fairly well integrated existing industrial base.

The problem connected with the definition might not be that important in itself. This is particularly the case if the definitional issues seem to override the more important aspects of the essence and role to be played by the industrial sector in the national reproduction process. However, for purposes of national economic management, planning and co-ordination, it is important that the statistical definition and carving out of the sectoral structure of the economy be understood. This is still an unresolved problem in Zimbabwean official statistics since the national economic statistical definition of the Central Statistical Office (CSO) is still far from being accurate. Products made in the manufacturing sector are classified by the CSO according to the 33-subsector index of production. This excludes the products made in the informal sector. In fact, classified manufacturers are registered companies that submit returns to the CSO. The requirement for this is a minimum initial capital outlay of Z$30,000.

This means that small formal and informal manufacturing activities are excluded from the definition. It is clear then from this approach that policy recommendations for small-scale manufacturing should be based on the official statistics available. There are other *ad hoc* definitional mishaps. For example, official statistics exclude from the definition of manufacturing 'Establishments operating on a mining site as refiners/smelters of non-ferrous or precious metals...'[2] On the other hand, excluded from the definition of mining activity are mines and quarries operated by manufacturers as a source of their raw materials, such as limestone mines operated by cement manufacturers. These form part of the manufacturing sector.[3]

The manufacturing sector is the leading sector in terms of its contribution to GDP, averaging about 25% in the decade up to 1981. The second largest contributor to GDP is agriculture, which is also an important source of raw material inputs for the manufacturing sector. The manufacturing sector has on average contributed 32% of the material production over the period 1980-84. The material sphere of production is a wider concept than the United Nations ISIC's definition of industrialisation used above. It is defined to include agriculture, restaurants and hotels and transport and communications.

Since the manufacturing sector is the nerve centre of the industrial base, this paper will focus on those subsectors of the manufacturing sector that are decisive in influencing the pace and structural features of the development of the economy. In presenting empirical analytical data of selected key subsectors of the manufacturing sector the key question to be asked is what constraints face the growth and structural transformation of industrialisation in Zimbabwe. The issues concerning the resources endowment structure, skill formation and technology will not be treated separately from the fundamental issue of the dominance of international capital. Zimbabwe's industrial strategy will inevitably have to address the question of the transformation of an industrial sector that is historically linked with international capital with the goal of a national industrial economy. Because of its strategic role in the provision of inputs to the metal goods subsectors, the mining sector is also discussed in view of its links with the industrialisation process.

Finally, the role of the state and industrial policy in the post-independence period is discussed with a view to examining the main trends, constraints on structural change and opportunities facing the industrialisation of Zimbabwe within the existing national, regional and international situation.

The Bases, Structure and Role of the Manufacturing Sector

The development of the present structure of Zimbabwe's manufacturing industry dates back to the 1950s when the Federation of Rhodesia and Nyasaland provided a captive market for Southern Rhodesian industry. However, more significantly, a deepening in import-substitution industrialisation and diversification in production took place in the post-Unilateral Declaration of Independence (UDI) period. Between 1966 and 1974 the manufacturing sector registered an average annual growth rate of 9%. Between 1966 and 1974 the light industry branches of foodstuffs, drinks and tobacco, textile and wood products had average annual growth rates of 7.1%, 6.1%, 10.8% and 6.4% respectively. The heavy industrial branches of chemicals and petroleum products, non-metallic mineral products, metals and metal products and transport equipment grew on the average by 9.4%, 13.4%, 13.2% and 5% respectively.[4] This suggests that a high level of capital formation took place during this period and that there was also an intensification of import substitution industrialisation in the production of capital and intermediate goods.

In fact the most favourable trend in economy was the high proportion of investment devoted to basic metal products and an increase in efficiency achieved by the remaining portions of the manufacturing sector. But after the decline in the economic activity from 1974 the average growth rates never picked up to the 1966-74 level.

During the 1974-80 period the combined average annual growth rates of foodstuffs, drinks, textile and wood products was only 2.8% compared to 7.6% in the previous period. The combined average annual growth rates of chemicals, non-metallic mineral products, metals and transport equipment was 3.1% compared with 7.25% in the 1966-74 period. The decline in economic activity affecting the manufacturing sector has been attributed to the intensification of the liberation war and severe foreign exchange shortages that characterised the late 1970s.

Following Zimbabwe's independence, and the end of the war, increasing domestic demand and expanded foreign exchange allocations provided renewed momentum for growth. The volume index of the manufacturing sector output rose by 15% in 1980 and increased by almost 10% in 1981.

However, by 1982 the immediate upward adjustment spurt that fuelled this growth had suddenly come to an end. A number of factors adversely affecting the sector and its performance had clearly taken shape. Manufacturing output declined by nearly 3% during the first ten months of 1982 compared to the same period in 1981 and indications are that this trend continued and even accelerated during the course of 1983 and

1984.

Zimbabwe inherited a fairly sophisticated and broad-based manufacturing sector. But this sector is beset with structural problems on both the supply and the demand side. Zimbabwe's manufacturing sector, especially its production of a wide range of consumer goods, has a high import content in the form of intermediate goods which are assembled locally. The transformation of such a dependent production system will definitely need clearly articulated policies on structural change of the manufacturing sector. Perhaps the major question of the post-independence period may well be how far does the state intervene or stay out of productive activity. If the state is to intervene, then it will be important to consider the forms that such intervention should take. The present institutional mechanism of state intervention, the Industrial Development Corporation (IDC), will need to be transformed in order to address the demands of investment policies and procedures that are meant to reduce dependence on international capital.

In 1982/83 there were 1,344 separate manufacturing units and only 7.8% of these were responsible for 41% of total net output: these employed 750 persons and above. About 52% produced 8% of the total net output and employed 50 persons or less. There is, therefore, heavy concentration of production in the hands of a few firms.

Much of the sector is resource-based, with two main industrial groupings: metals and metal products on one hand, and foodstuffs, drink and tobacco on the other. Together these contribute about 46% of the industrial value added and provide about 48% of employment in the sector. The metals and metal products sector has the largest number of units, is responsible for the largest contribution to net and gross output, is the largest earner of foreign exchange, employs the greatest number of people and has the highest value of capital employed. Using the above indicators but with the exception of that of foreign exchange (and here it is third after textiles), foodstuffs come second. Foodstuffs, drink and tobacco, textiles and chemical and petroleum products have net and gross output which is proportionately higher than the number of units. This would probably mean that the subsectors are dominated by a few very large firms.

In the period 1980-84, the average employment in the manufacturing sector was 170,600 a year, which was 16.1% of the total formal employment. But as shown above, total industrial employment was only around 4% of the country's population. Manufacturing employment was second to agriculture with a figure of 284,920 and was 27.6% of total formal employment. According to the National Manpower Survey (NMS) the manufacturing sector employs only 4% of all professionals, 13% of skilled workers and 26% of semi-skilled workers.[5]

The sector is also a major source of government revenue through direct and indirect tax receipts. Direct taxes come in the form of company taxes, taxes paid by unincorporated enterprises and income taxes from employees of manufacturing. Indirect taxes are in the form of sales taxes and excise duties paid by manufacturing employees from purchasing using their disposable income and customs duty on products imported for manufacturing purposes.

In a separate study of the metals and metal products subsector, out of a sample of 144 firms it was found that graduate engineers were only 5% of the composite number of graduate engineers, technicians and skilled personnel, the latter category including fitters, turners and other journeymen. The skilled and technician categories were 65% and 30% respectively.[6] Given the paucity of the sector's absorption of the higher professional personnel, the manufacturing sector as a whole is at a disadvantage as far as the stability of the skilled and professional labour force is concerned.

Wages in manufacturing are relatively higher and the sector's total wage bill is higher than the economy-wide average. This is because the lower-paid employees in manufacturing receive higher incomes and the sector pays higher wages to proportionately larger groups than the national average.

Labour productivity as measured by value added per employee is higher than the national average. However, here, the sector is fourth after finance and insurance, distribution, and electricity and water.

In terms of exports, manufacturing industry contributed 52% of export earnings in 1980-83. The sector is, however, a major user of foreign exchange through the import of raw materials, plant and equipment and spares as well as fuel energy supplies. This is typical of the import substitution industrialisation (ISI) which grows up under protection and subsequently with characteristics of inefficiency and high import content in productive activities.

The current debate on whether or not the manufacturing sector is a net user of foreign exchange can easily be misplaced in terms of policy analysis and formulation. In so far as the sector is characterised by a high import content in terms of its heavy dependence on intermediate goods, there is clearly the need to make more use of domestic material and human resources in order to enhance domestic value added and improve the sector's earnings or savings of foreign exchange. This, however, does not mean that the use of foreign exchange should be understood in terms of drawing a balance sheet of only its use or earning capacity by the manufacturing sector. Even if the sector happens to be a net user of foreign exchange, it contributes in a crucial sense to the viability of those sectors that directly earn the country much-needed foreign exchange. The efficiency of the agricultural sector, the mining sector, the transport sector and so on all depend on the support these sectors receive from the manufacturing sector through the provision of both direct inputs and other services.

Role of the Mining and Capital Goods Sectors in the Industrialisation Process

Zimbabwe's geological structure contains a great variety of minerals. The country is at present mining over 40 different minerals and metals, the more important being gold, asbestos, nickel, copper, coal and chrome ore. These are followed by iron ore, lithium and tin, silver and cobalt by-products.

Between 1973 and 1980 mineral production increased from the amount of Z$135.9 million to Z$414.8 million which was a rise of 205% over the period (cf. Table 1). Thereafter mineral production began to decline from Z$414.8 million to Z$393.5 million in 1981 which was 2.6% lower than the 1981 output. Of the 1982 output gold was valued at Z$122.7 million, asbestos Z$76.6 million, nickel Z$49.7 million, coal Z$35.8 million and copper at Z$26.8 million.

In the ten-year period up to 1982 Zimbabwe's value of mineral output averaged about 10.5% of the GDP. Mining and quarrying contributed 8.8% of the GDP in 1979 but fell to 5.4% in 1982 while mineral exports contributed 40% of total exports. The mining sector directly employed an average of 6% of total employment. Between 1972 and 1982 the mining sector employed an average of 62,233 workers per year. In 1982 the mining sector employed a little over 67,200 workers. The breakdown in employment was as follows: gold—39.93%, asbestos—15.5%, chrome ore—11.71%, coal—7.99%, copper—6.78% and nickel—7.27%. Other minerals acount for the remaining 10.88% of employment in the sector.[7]

The mining industry is largely in the hands of the TNCs, the most important being the Anglo American Corporation (South African) in nickel and ferrochrome; Union Carbide (USA) in ferrochrome; Rio Tinto Zinc (UK) in gold; Lonhro (UK) in gold and copper; and Turner and Newall (USA) in asbestos. The post-independence era has seen an increase in state participation in the mining sector. In coal mining the state has the largest shareholding though Anglo American Corporation still provides management services. The state owns the iron and steel industry (ZISCO) and tin mining (Kamativi). In 1984 a newly-formed state enterprise, the Zimbabwe Mining Development Corporation (ZMDC), bought out the mining interests of Messina (South Africa) which gave it control over most of Zimbabwe's copper production. Also, through the Mineral Marketing Corporation of Zimbabwe (MMCZ), the state handles all mineral and metal trade with the exception of gold, which is bought by the Reserve Bank of Zimbabwe.

As in the case of the manufacturing sector, sanctions also had a profound effect on the mode of development by way of self-sufficiency in a number of products. The shortage of foreign exchange, the impact of sanctions and the land-locked position of the country all led to a downstream development of the mining industry in order to increase value and decrease weight and volume. Most of the major metals are reduced in their pure form, including copper cathodes, nickel cathodes, ferrochrome and pure tin and steel. There is also the mining of several minerals on a small scale as inputs to the local industry. Examples are: pyrites for sulphur and bauxite for aluminium sulphate.

In 1979, nearly 88% of the total value of mining output was exported. Such concentration of the country's mining output on the export market exposes the country to the uncertainties of the world market. This is compounded by the fact that Zimbabwe still exports most of her mineral products in raw and semi-processed form. Some minerals are exported annually in crude form. For example between 1978 and 1981, an annual average of 243,000 tonnes of asbestos was exported in crude form. During the same period, an average of 16,000 tonnes of lithium was also exported in crude form. Other minerals exported as ores included crude magnesite, tungsten ores and concentrates and tantalum ores. Thus, in part, the nature of the problem is the disarticulation between the mining sector and the manufacturing sector. The reversal of this situation would lead to a number of favourable developments. First, a reduction of dependency of mineral exports on external markets. Second, the mineral products will increase foreign exchange earnings in that the value of minerals rises substantially through successive stages of processing and refining. Third, though the smelting processes are themselves highly capital-intensive, they facilitate the establishment of labour-intensive backward and forward linkage activities. Fourth, there is an addition to national value added in the strategy that seeks to link mineral processing with further stages of manufacturing capital goods.

Thus, while the argument for domestic further-stage processing of minerals prior to their being exported is welcome, it is even more desirable that in certain lines of production local minerals are used for the different needs of the domestic metallurgical and engineering industries. This division of labour within the national framework offers benefits that would otherwise be denied to a mineral-exporting country if all its mineral products were exported.

The argument for establishing facilities for domestic processing of minerals to a further stage may be complicated by the fact that, on one hand, the value of minerals rises substantially through successive processing and refining, but, on the other hand, very large investments are commonly required for the establishment of economically efficient processing facilities. In the case of Zimbabwe the problem may be further complicated by the fact that most of the processing projects are owned by transnational corporations (Anglo American, Lonrho, Rio Tinto, Turner and Newall and Union Carbide). Secondly, the long-term nature of investments in mineral processing makes the rate of discount an important variable in the choice of such projects. Thirdly, the profitability of processing activities is often crucially dependent on subsidiary activities utilising the by-products of mineral processing.

Bearing in mind that there are large differences between the prices of the raw materials and those of the refined metals, it is in the interest of Zimbabwe to process most of her minerals to an optimum level that satisfies the domestic, regional and international markets.[8]

In Zimbabwe full domestic processing of minerals is limited to clays, gravel, phosphate and limestone. Processing is advanced to the stage of refined metals in the case of the exported products such as chromite, copper, nickel and tin, gold and iron ore (cf. Table 2). Thus, iron ore is exported at four stages of processing, as pig iron, ingots and billets, iron and steel bar, rod and sections and as wire. Because the country benefits relatively little when it exports this mineral in crude form, exports of pig iron (the lowest stage in the processing of ore) are becoming less and less important when compared to the exports of ingots and billets and rolled iron and steel bars, rod and sections.

Iron and steel manufacturing occupies a key role in terms of transforming the mining sector into an integrated industrial sector. ZISCO, the country's only iron and steel plant, is the nation's largest investment project in the manufacturing sector, employing approximately 5,000 workers. Of its present output of about 705,000 tonnes per year, 75% of the output is exported in various forms. The remaining 25% of ZISCO's output is consumed by the local metal industries manufacturing machinery, intermediate goods and other forms of equipment.

The next important mineral product mined and processed in Zimbabwe is chrome ore. The main user for chromium ores is the production of ferro-alloys which supply chromium for the manufacturers of chromium alloy steels and stainless steels. A small amount of chromium ores is also used for the production of refactories and for the manufacture of chromium chemicals.[9] Of the total of 541,800 tonnes of chromium ore produced in Zimbabwe in 1979, approximately 94% was converted into ferrochromium alloys (a product of chrome ore and steel) and only 5% exported as ores.[10]

Thus a very high proportion of the chromium ore produced in Zimbabwe is processed into ferrochrome silicon and some low carbon ferrochrome. At this point in time it may still be safe to work on the assumption that, since the high carbon ferrochrome commands higher prices and a distinct market advantage, the world market for the product is increasingly going to depend on the Zimbabwean product. South Africa is the other main producer of chromium but it has low-grade ores although at present it has lower mining costs than those of Zimbabwe. The two large producers of ferrochromium ore in Zimbabwe are Rhodal, owned by Anglo American Corporation, and Rhonet, belonging to Union Carbide. Both firms have fairly similar outputs and have a combined total output of approximately 235,000 tonnes per annum.

The other refined minerals in Zimbabwe include nickel metal, copper metal and tin metal. The nickel processing industry in Zimbabwe was established from scratch during the post-1965 period, i.e. during the UDI years. In 1980 nickel processing was valued at Z$52.7 million. Zimbabwe's production, from both the Bindura Nickel Mine Company (owned by Anglo American Corporation) and the Eiffel Flats (owned by Rio Tinto) refineries ranks quite high in quality terms.[11]

The Zimbabwean nickel processing industry produces 99.9% pure nickel. This is the best in the world and has proved a fine protective cushion in times of sanctions and poor world nickel markets. The nickel price will follow demand for stainless steel, which consumes nearly half the world's nickel product.

The smelting of copper concentrates from Mhangura, Norah and Shackleton mines is done by MTD's smelter at Alaska. There are at present two electrolytic copper refineries in addition to one fire refinery in the country. Approximately 20% of copper is a by-product of nickel and gold mining while a large proportion of the electrolytically refined copper is used in the local copper processing industry. Between 1973 and 1982 the value of processed copper in Zimbabwe averaged Z$24.5 million annually.

Finally Zimbabwe's only mineral fuel, i.e. coal, is processed to produce coke, which is largely used as an input in the local industries. However, coke is playing an important role as an export product; the volume exported has increased from 110,528 tonnes in 1978 to 128,221 tonnes in 1982. The processing of coal into coke is undertaken both at the Hwange Collieries and by ZISCO at Redcliffe which produces sufficient coke in the domestic and other markets.

Zimbabwe, like other developing countries, would get greater benefits from her mineral wealth if emphasis could be put on integrating the mineral industry with the rest of the economy. This would mean that, besides the strategy of processing and refining crude minerals, the country would develop the manufacture of a wide range of capital goods, including machinery and equipment and intermediate goods using inputs from the mining sector. As shown above, a downstream development of the mining industry was necessary for import substitution for the metal inputs for industry as a whole. The development of capital goods provides on the upstream side a variety of inputs to the sectoral structure of the economy, including the mining industry, that are manufactured locally.

It is also clear from the analysis above that the rationale for processing most of the mineral products in Zimbabwe was to achieve a stage sufficient to increase the value of the processed product to a point that significantly reduced the unit cost of transport. This is particularly the case since Zimbabwe is a land-locked country with no easy routes to the sea.

While the mining sector provides downstream development of metal inputs used in the capital goods sector, the latter is the upstream source of a wide variety of inputs to the sectoral structure of the economy. Thus, for instance, Zimbabwe's capital goods sector manufactures a wide variety of machinery and equipment for the mining sector, including switch gear, conveyor idlers, ventilation ducting, mine cars, hydraulic equipment, ball mills, rail and rolling stock. A discussion of the wide variety of products manufactured in the capital goods sector for the other sectors of the economy follows below.

The ownership structure of a large sample of firms in the capital goods sector shows that out of a sample of 144 large, medium and small firms, 62.5% were locally owned, 28.5% foreign-owned, 6% joint ventures between local private and foreign private capital, and only 3% joint ventures between government and foreign private capital.[12] The largest firms in terms of employment, average turnover and fixed assets are joint ventures between government and private, followed by joint ventures between local private and foreign private capital, and then foreign-owned firms. Local firms are generally small and mostly engaged in subcontracting activities and rarely engaged in the final product outfit like agricultural implements and machinery. The latter seems to be a domain of foreign-owned firms. Since the joint ventures between government and private capital are mostly concentrated in the largest firms, it shows a peculiar case in the Zimbabwean situation where large firms with large overheads are relatively inefficient.[13]

As the hub of the engineering industry, capital goods provides a base for self-sustaining industrialisation, and provides opportunities for training and development of skills, especially engineering and technical skills. It contributes immensely to the training of people in technical and managerial skills, in creating production and design capabilities, and improving organisational methods of production.

The engineering core industries for the manufacture of capital goods service both industry and other priority sectors, e.g. agriculture, construction, transport, mining and energy and telecommunications. They are required for the production, *inter alia*, of building and construction materials, agricultural tools, spare parts, implements and machinery, and other products which are essential for the development of a diverse mixed and complex production covering a wide range of sectors in the economic system. It can be argued that the capital goods sector is important in determining the viability of the economic system as a whole, technological change and absorption and displacement of labour. An economy or region without well-developed metal products, machinery and subsidiary industries cannot produce enough capital goods and thus invest a high proportion of its income, however high its potential saving propensity may be. Such an accumulation path is not only meant for closed economies as is often cited in the literature.[14] Open and trading economies have been shown to be vulnerable to the adverse terms of trade resulting from their lack of capacities in the production of capital goods and the associated deficiencies of shortage of skilled manpower, externalities and facilities of learning processes.

What use can be made of the economic surplus depends on the material structure of the productive system. Even if savings in developing countries are improved to quite substantial levels, there is still the structural inability to convert these savings or economic surplus into investment. This situation results in the usual phenomena of 'conspicuous' consumption, hoarding, capital flights, and so on. Thus, the existence of a capital goods sector is crucial for those physical technical aspects that cannot be replaced by purely financial aspects of savings and investment. If this sector is to be understood as a necessary though not sufficient condition for autonomous industrialisation, it should be considered a political issue of the highest order, involving a strategy of 'selective de-linking' and the time horizon over which technological autonomy can be achieved.

Basic support facilities such as foundries, heat treatment, forging and machine tool shops will be needed for the production of components, spare parts and other products required for the manufacture of capital goods. Zimbabwe's capital goods sector provides 'backward integration' for ZISCOSTEEL feedstock as these units use blooms, billets, bars, rods and coils. The metal products, machinery and equipment—other than the electrical subsector—is the largest subsector in the metals and metal products group with gross output in 1982 representing 47% of the group's total output, 54% of total net output, 48% of wages and salaries and 51% of employment. Company activity in this subsector includes the heavy engineering firms involved in the design and production of machinery, equipment and spares for other industries. There is also a great deal of general jobbing and maintenance activity. Examples of machinery production, machine tools and equipment in Zimbabwe include the production of agricultural machinery, construction machinery, mining and other areas of activity.

Agricultural implements production includes a wide variety of products including tractor-drawn implements for the large-scale commercial farming sector, irrigation equipment, agricultural boilers for tobacco farmers, coffee processing machines, tobacco curing equipment and implements for the small-scale peasant sector. Zimbabwean firms have built up a reputation of original design in the production of agricultural implements and equipment that is suitable to local conditions. Firms in this group have been exporting to neighbouring countries. Most of the steel used in the production of agricultural implements is locally produced. Imported sheet steels are used for the manufacture of specialised parts of implements but this represents a small proportion of the implements both by mass and value.

The electrical machinery and equipment and communications equipment subsectors' production includes electrical machinery, industrial electrical goods including geysers, cookers and stoves, communications equipment, and electric cables and wire which come under capital and intermediate goods.

In 1982 the motor vehicle (including reconditioning) subsector accounted for 78% of both total gross output and employment of the transport equipment group. Its major commodity outputs were motor vehicle bodies (61%), trailers for trucks and other vehicles (15%), motor spares and accessories (10%), metal products, machinery and spares (6%), assembled motor vehicles (5.5%) and caravans (2%). The main activity of the subsector is motor vehicle bodies, which has a high local content.

The most expensive inputs going into the subsector are motor spares and accessories — including completely-knocked-down (CKD) kits, which were 38% of the subsector's total inputs in 1982. CKD kits do not come under capital goods. For local content to be increased further, continuous policy assessment could be maintained to assess those elements of input components for every model that is manufactured or assembled locally in order to improve on the local content. What is probably of greater importance, however, is to consider reducing the range of models assembled so as to be able to standardise on spare parts, maintenance equipment and skills. There can be no doubt that the present wide proliferation of the number of tractor and private fleet vehicle models militates seriously against increasing local content.

Other major inputs used in the subsector—e.g. iron and steel products (19%) and industrial rubber products (9%)—will in turn increase their local content as their scale of operations increases in response to increases in the demand for their products.

The other vehicle and equipment subsector includes the manufacture of railway equipment and other transport equipment, especially heavy equipment and machinery coming under capital goods. Whilst the subsector's growth rate was more or less on par with that of other sectors in the 1967-74 period, it was one of the worst hit by the intensification of the liberation war and sanctions in the post-1974 period.

The manufacture of railway rolling stock represents a significant and important substitution in the production of capital goods. Only in the last five years Zimbabwe Engineering Company (ZECO), a firm in this group, undertook the refurbishment of approximately 80 steam locomotives. This was necessary to cushion the National Railways of Zimbabwe against massive increases in the prices of diesel oil until the electrification project of the railways is completed. Morewear Industries is also involved in the manufacture of freight-type rolling stock. Another company that has made an important contribution to the railway rolling stock is F. Issels Limited, who manufacture bogies and cast steel railway wheels. This facility is unique in Africa outside South Africa.

The Chemicals, Foodstuffs and Textile Sectors

The chemical and petroleum, foodstuffs and textiles products group occupies an important place in Zimbabwe's industrialisation. This is not so much because of its output shares in the total manufacturing sector, but more significantly because of its strategic role in providing what can be termed central links in the economic structure.

The growth of Zimbabwe's modern industry requires chemicals in one form or another in almost the entire spectrum of the manufacturing sector. This is because 'most basic chemicals are converted in subsequent processing into materials, synthetic products both structural and non-structural, which are thereafter converted into consumable products in the "down-stream" processing industries.'[15] The economic development of Zimbabwe will crucially depend on the use of chemically-derived synthetics.

In the Zimbabwean case, however, the growth of the chemical industry is constrained by the underdevelopment of the basic chemicals which in turn inhibits the growth of other industrial branches of production. For instance, though Zimbabwe's plastic industry is one of the most buoyant subsectors in the manufacturing sector, at present there is no production of plastic resins of either the thermoplastic or thermosetting varieties. Before a solution to this problem is found, the country will continue the present import of PVC resin which alone amounts to $5-$6 million per annum. There is also at present a major project to manufacture a woven plastic grain bag. In 1985, imported grain bags (between 19 and 21 million) used for handling and for stockpiling maize were estimated to cost approximately $26 million. The chemical products subsectors are:

(a) fertilisers, insecticides and pesticides;
(b) paint, varnishes and filling material;
(c) soaps, detergents, toilet preparations;
(d) matches, ink, candles, glue, polishes and other chemical products;
(e) rubber products;
(f) plastic products.

As shown in Table 3, the chemical group occupies third place in net output ranking of the manufacturing sector. In 1982 the group accounted for 13% of gross manufacturing output (12.6% of net output) and 7% of the manufacturing sector's employment. Products turned out in this sector are fertilisers, pesticides and insecticides, plastics, synthetic rubbers and fibres and heavy chemicals, e.g. detergents. In terms of sub-sectoral shares the fertiliser group is the leading subsector followed by detergents, rubber, plastics, basic chemicals, matches, etc. and paints in descending order.

This largest subsector in 1982 contributed 33% of total gross output of the chemical industry. This subsector comprises the manufacture of ammonium nitrate fertiliser from ammonia and nitric acid, and phosphate fertiliser from phosphate rock, pyrites and sulphuric acid.

Four firms formulate and manufacture various types of crop chemicals, which represents an oligopolistic structure of production. Also manufactured is copper oxychloride, a technical pesticide used for treating tobacco, coffee and tea. The only major pesticides not produced in the country are ethylene dibromide and methyl bromide. A strategy in the area of the production of fertilisers has to be worked out, particularly concerning the production of ammonia. In 1982 Sable Chemicals Ltd imported approximately $9.3 million of anhydrous ammonia for the production of ammonium nitrate. Efficiency in the production or application of ammonium [16] is an essential part of the strategy of industrialising in this branch of production.

In 1982 the soap, detergents, toilet preparation and pharmaceuticals subsector contributed 24.5% to gross output of the chemicals group. The products turned out here are soaps, detergents and cleaners (35%), vegetable oil and margarine (20%), medicinal and pharmaceuticals (19.8%) and toiletries. The subsector's products include: basic industrial chemicals except fertiliser e.g. sulphuric acid, phosphoric acid and aluminium sulphate; products of petroleum refineries such as lubricating oils; and coal and petroleum products.

Another important sector is that of rubber products, which in 1982 contributed 16.7% to the chemicals' net output. The main products are tyres and retreads, industrial rubber products, tubes, gaskets, conveyor belts, hoses and tiles. The main inputs, i.e. rubber, synthetic resins, man-made fibres and chemical products, are imported.

The plastic products subsector is highly diversified. The main product in this is plastic containers. Other products are various types of plastic products, asphalt bitumen and tar. The paints and varnishes subsector is the smallest subsector in the chemical industry; it represents only 5.6% of the output of the industry in 1982.

The rubber products are central links for the national and regional road transport and the tractor population in the region. Zimbabwe also has immense possibilities for both further import substitution and production for exports in the region in the area of chemicals, including medicinal pharmaceuticals.

The chemicals group provides important links with the rest of the industrial subsectors and other sectors in the economy. For example, the single largest input for the agricultural sector is fertiliser, whose value was 14% of agricultural output in 1983. However, the import bill for fertiliser products of around $25 million in 1982 undermines this important domestic linkage. This provides a case for serious consideration of measures for further import substitution of fertiliser production and also in the area of pesticides.

The foodstuffs and textile subsectors occupy an important place in the manufacturing sector in terms of the provision of the nutritional and clothing requirements of the population. The balance in the relationship between the agricultural sector and processing of foodstuffs and clothing provides the basis for stable prices, stability in income elasticities of demand and overall control of inflation in the economy. The foodstuffs products group comes second only to the metal product group in net output terms, employment absorption and wages and salaries. In 1982 the group contributed 26% to gross manufacturing output and 7.8% to net output.

The foodstuffs subsector has the following subgroups:

(a) slaughtering and processing of meat;
(b) canning and preserving of fruit and vegetables;
(c) grain mill products and animal feeds;
(d) bakery products;
(e) chocolate and sugar confectionery;
(f) dairy and other food products.

In 1982, the slaughtering and meat processing subgroup accounted for 27% of gross output and 22% of employment in the foodstuffs subsector. Its major products are beef and pork. The other products are poultry, beef, lamb and mutton. The Cold Storage Commission — a parastatal—is the largest operator in the slaughtering of beef, accounting for 86% of cattle slaughtering and 25% of all frozen and chilled meat in the domestic market in 1983.

The textile group includes cotton ginning and textile manufactures, knitted products, rope and cordage and other textile products. In 1982 gross total output totalled about $448 million (around $179 million net) or 14.7% of the gross output of manufacturing (14% of net). The average number employed totalled 37,319 or 21.2% of employment in manufacturing.

Textiles employ relatively more labour than their proportionate share of either gross or net output. This would suggest that these sectors are relatively labour-intensive, a factor confirmed by their lower share of capital stock.

The textiles have a relatively low score of new output as a percentage of gross output, indicating a relatively high contribution of value added.

The cotton ginning and other textile subsectors comprise cotton ginning, weaving, finishing textiles and carpets and other textile products, i.e. firms 'making up' from textile materials. The Cotton Marketing Board dominates or has a near-monopoly of cotton ginning. Together, in 1982 these components had a gross output of $265 million or 8.7% of manufacturing and around 7% of net output and a total employment of 16,479 or 9% of total manufacturing employment.

The most immediate problem facing cotton production is that ginning capacity is increasingly inadequate for the expanding seed cotton crop produced in Zimbabwe. For example, a surplus of more than 10,000 tonnes of seed cotton could not be ginned in time in the 1984 season and such delays are detrimental to the quality of the product. About 80% of cotton lint produced in Zimbabwe is exported while the textile manufacturers absorb 20% for both the local and export markets. It would appear that Zimbabwe has a comparative advantage in the manufacture of textiles. Export earnings of this subsector increased from $7.9 million in 1982 to $14.6 million in 1983 (84%) and then reached a record level of just over $24 million in the first nine months of 1984.

Zimbabwe's textile subsector is mainly dependent on local raw material inputs. In 1984 local input totalled $65.4 million or 69.4% of total inputs while imported inputs made up the remaining 30.6%. An important raw material input that can be reduced over time depending on changing tastes in fibres and yarn. It has been suggested that cotton textile manufacturing based on locally produced lint is more efficient than manufacture of polyester fabric based on imported polymers.

The Role of the State and Policy Issues for Industrialisation
According to the neo-classical economic analysis, the principal social process through which development is achieved is the extension and development of market relations. The prescriptive approach of the neo-classical theory abstracts the economic from the social and political dimension in its analysis. The tendency is to abstract from the social determination of the technical coefficients or any parameters governing the behaviour relationships in production and consumption. This view is contested in Gershenkron's thesis that successful late development is characterised by a pervasive involvement of an interventionist state.[17] Thus the state has become a major agent of social transformation in both capitalist and socialist contexts. In the West the rise of the welfare state and the Keynesian 'managerial' state took this form and in socialist countries planned industrialisation is tantamount to direct state involvement. In most developing countries the state, however, has met with counter-trends, viz. pervasive corruption, ineffectiveness and distorted impact of the plans, widespread authoritarianism or political instability. These adverse factors have undermined the simpler statist conceptions of the development process.

More recently, the debate on the problematic nature of the development state had turned the focus to the social basis of the state, its institutional form, modes of operation and the development impact.[18] This debate seeks to clarify thinking about the economic role of the state and practical ways of how it should get involved in the development process. The matter of development is not reduced to mere planning or intervention by the state or mere ideological aura. Gordon White argues that the strength of the development state depends on (i) its social nature; (ii) the state's politico-administrative capacity; and (iii) the specific mode of involvement.[19]

As empirical evidence presented above shows, the historical success of Zimbabwe's industrialisation during the colonial period conditioned a development pattern that is today posing the very constraints of Zimbabwe's post-independence industrialisation. The dominance of international capital, dependence on imported inputs and technologies and a very close link of the development of local industry to international capital characterise Zimbabwe's industrialisation.

Historically, positive aspects of growth manifested themselves, when the early phase of the UDI period provided favourable conditions for an inward-looking industrial policy. Manufacturing grew significantly during the period when international sanctions provided a strong impetus for a deepening of import substitution and diversification of production. It can be argued that sanctions acted like a policy of protection. Combined with export promotion, these were institutional conditions for industrialisation policy during the UDI years. This unusual combination of protection and simultaneous export expansion stems from two sources: the need to maintain the high level of consumption of luxury goods of the privileged minority; and state intervention to perpetuate both the export bias of the economy and close links with South Africa.

In Zimbabwe's *Transitional National Development Plan* (TNDP) 1982/83-1984/85, a general framework of objectives pertaining to expansion of the manufacturing sector is laid out. The TNDP set out to expand the linkages within and between the manufacturing sector and other sectors in the economy; the promotion of import substitution policies wherever possible; the decentralisation of industries; the promotion of labour-intensive industries; the increase in local participation; and the promotion of energy efficiency. These general objectives on the macroeconomic level were, however, not translated into specific subsectoral programmes either in scope or in a time perspective.

The *First Five-Year National Development Plan* 1986-1990 goes further and spells out the government's intention 'to control industries which are deemed strategic to socio-economic development'.[20] It intends that structural transformation will be achieved through expanding the intermediate, capital goods and chemical goods sectors using the nation's available resource endowments and technical skills. The major challenge before the policy makers and planners will, therefore, be finding the adequate means and instruments for implementing these set goals of the five-year plan period.

In the quest for shaping a national industrial strategy the major question is what are the class forces and social interests behind the development of industrialisation in post-independence Zimbabwe? In an attempt to answer this question, it is important to examine the role of the state and that of capital in consciously shaping the system of material incentives that will affect the development of the industrial sector of the economy.

A clear industrialisation strategy has, however, not yet emerged in the Zimbabwean context for various reasons. At independence, the composition of those forces which were favourable to industrialisation were at best a mixed bag. At the level of the state one was not clear on this, thereby making it difficult not to confuse proclaimed goals with the actual impact. In Zimbabwe the proclaimed 'planned' goals remained at the general level. Gordon White observed, 'If we know on whose behalf a given state is acting, we have a more substantive idea of its effectiveness.'[21] At least in respect of industrialisation this has not been clearly sorted out in the Zimbabwean situation. The necessary biases or policy options on whether to emphasise accumulation by local-based capital, or by the state in the industrialisation process *vis-à-vis* foreign direct investments remains a stalemate. It is obvious that the solution of this problem will give direction to the development of the ownership relations in Zimbabwe's industry. The complexity of industrialisation in Zimbabwe demands that the state be involved in processes of industrial investment, production and so on.

The co-ordinative capacity of the state still leaves much to be desired. This is particularly the case in defining and disseminating an ideology of industrialising and industrial programmes, and successfully co-ordinating and implementing them.

This has the implication that both on a time sequence and an intra-regional perspective the development of the industrial structure of the economy is determined by the tasks themselves as they arise, and not by the long-term task of development in which certain subsectors of the manufacturing sector are planned to play the leading role in shaping the economic structure. Assuming that Zimbabwe's internal class forces behind industrialisation are sorted out with the state playing the leading role, and that the priorities of industrial development are set out, the country's optimal industrial strategy will depend on the nature of plans and the planning system of industrialisation. Planning issues will deal with co-ordination problems among government ministries, the question of the state's involvement in production, the development of employment and skills, planning as a programme approach at the subsectoral level, etc.

Although representing a specific sector approach, industrial plans are not independent, self-contained plans but are part and parcel of the national plan. Both in the short and medium term, sectors act in close relationship with one another as suppliers and consumers; and at the same time compete for certain scarce resources (e.g. skilled manpower, investments and imports). The development of manpower, research and development (R & D), investment and market research are necessarily long-term and specific sector-oriented.

Industrialisation is understood as a complex task that requires co-ordination with the whole economy. Therefore, an analysis of specific sector approach is helpful in making decisions on concrete problems in different industries. This approach has the further advantages of determining whether or not the trends which have become recognisable in the subsector will prove to be lasting, whether there are possibilities of change in these trends. The sectoral approach also helps in determining to what extent long-term or short-term aspects of planning are in conflict and the possible and essentially diverging alternative development strategies that could benefit specific sectors considered separately. The sectoral approach to planning provides the central planning authorities with information on the potential of each sector as well as the demand put forward by the development of other sectors of the national economy.

The prioritisation of selected subsectors important for growth is not necessarily an end in itself but is meant to create favourable conditions for technical progress and production of 'appropriate' products.

The harmonisation of plans is meant to overcome the disproportions in the sectoral structure of the economy, especially in the existing scientific and technological base of production, the structure of indigenous capacities in the fields of training and R & D. As shown above, Zimbabwe already has fairly diversified intermediate and capital goods sectors which form the basis for the 'deepening' of the technological infrastructure.

The present state of the art of innovation processes suggests a number of constraints, particularly in the field of research which is exacerbated by the distributional structure of professional personnel. In order to build on the already-acquired learning experience represented by the country's human capital resource, there is a need to undertake more training of scientific and technological workers. Innovation processes have, therefore, to be managed and planned from research, investment and production to marketing and utilisation of production processes and new product varieties. The main thrust of planning technological progress is oriented towards introducing new products and methods, and improvement of the quality of the products and technological level of production. Again success in the area of technology will depend on the extent of the state's role in the key subsectors influencing technological development, the capital goods sector, the chemical industry group, foodstuffs and textiles. Such measures as the development of state-sponsored technologies through the establishment of a R & D infrastructure, policy on the number and brands of products and training of science and technology personnel are essential for the success of various segments of the manufacturing sector, particularly the capital goods sector.

An important aspect of Zimbabwe's industrialisation is the potential development of regional co-operation within the Southern African Development Coordination Conference (SADCC) and the Preferential Trade Area of Eastern, Central and Southern Africa (PTA). The regional strategy is important both for the procurement of inputs for Zimbabwe's manufacturing sector and for providing the export market.

Though Zimbabwe's manufacturing output is mainly geared to the domestic market, manufactured exports for the region have always played an important part. Thus, for example, in 1981, Zimbabwe's exports of capital goods represented 11.5% of her total exports of manufactured products to the region. From a regional point of view, it is possible that Zimbabwe could specialise in the production of capital goods including machinery and transport equipment. This point was emphasised in 1984 by SADCC with specific reference to machine tools, irrigation pumps, mining equipment and railway wagons and rolling stock.

Conclusions

The basic strategy of the development of Zimbabwe's industrialisation, while being clearly pointed out in major government policy documents—such as the *Transitional National Development Plan* and the *First Five-Year National Development Plan*—has not yet clearly emerged. As shown in this article, the success of a national industrial strategy will depend on the nature of the class forces and social interests behind the development of industrialisation in Zimbabwe.

An identification of the constraints that lie behind further growth of the industrial sector must necessarily look at the question of who owns the manufacturing sector enterprises and other elements of the country's industrial sector, particularly the mining sector. A consensus has already emerged on the need for more government involvement in direct productive activities and particularly in new areas of strategic importance in terms of influencing the direction of the sectoral structure of the economy. But this approach can only be realised through planning the manufacturing sector in response to demands on its inputs in other sectors of the economy.

Depending on how the major questions of the ownership relations are solved in the medium-term period, Zimbabwe's industrialisation strategy will inevitably be emphasising the roles of the capital goods sectors and that of the chemical industry. The importance of these sectors lies in their provision of more intensive use of local raw material resources, and domestic skills required by the entire manufacturing sector and other sectors of the economy. It is believed that emphasis on these subsectors will enhance the utilisation of those natural resources under exploitation, available resources, production capacities, and available manpower, and lessen dependence on imported raw material inputs, intermediate goods and technologies.

TABLE 1
ZIMBABWE'S INDUSTRIAL STRUCTURE

YEAR	G.D.P.	MINNING & QUARRYING Gross	Net	Employed	MANUFACTURING Gross	Net	Employed	ELECTRICITY & WATER Gross	Net	Employed	CONSTRUCTION Gross	Net	Employed
1975	1,902,000	216,390	136,211	57,811	1,234,441	506,950	152,181	95,934	53,893	5,992	244,604	109,497	59,320
1976	2,064,000	264,411	161,673	58,859	1,269,535	518,538	146,629	108,285	60,798	5,734	218,952	109,902	51,621
1977	2,069,000	280,420	163,823	56,676	1,290,351	515,770	141,233	120,331	69,157	5,459	209,183	101,690	47,942
1978	2,168,000	289,913	168,698	53,948	1,389,504	584,421	137,814	131,472	68,795	5,425	188,543	92,903	41,201
1979	2,546,000	341,298	214,552	55,447	1,682,570	704,224	147,423	147,292	76,550	5,276	220,567	102,752	39,482
1980	3,206,000	452,581	298,148	61,129	2,180,941	920,674	160,748	168,731	82,384	5,499	271,265	128,555	41,274
1981	3,995,000	441,804	274,786	60,913	2,721,504	1,163,749	172,942	191,782	89,923	5,705	364,173	173,751	46,781
1982	4,465,000	435,951	246,167	57,316	3,049,005	1,248,914	176,223	217,893	100,613	5,330	448,558	218,783	46,907

Source: Census of Production 1982/83, Mining, Manufacturing, Construction, Electricity and Water Supply., CSO, Tables 2 & 12

TABLE 2
ZIMBABWE'S MAIN MINERALS IN $'000

Year	Gold	Asbestos	Nickel	Copper	Coal	Chrome	Iron Ore	Other	Total
1973	19,013	26,044	18,339	39,869	10,275	10,196	1,326	10,753	135,966
1974	29,829	32,375	20,456	45,796	10,359	9,647	1,271	14,920	165,154
1975	31,956	41,701	19,616	24,686	13,677	22,056	3,033	16,115	177,838
1976	30,116	61,077	35,227	29,457	23,297	26,859	5,829	18,796	230,477
1977	37,214	67,032	42,826	21,964	21,051	19,917	6,833	20,649	237,489
1978	51,855	67,007	39,456	23,044	23,708	13,452	7,851	25,823	252,196
1979	80,912	65,964	45,077	35,149	25,843	16,139	7,397	38,430	314,801
1980	144,875	70,201	55,571	35,390	28,001	18,447	14,815	47,460	414,760
1981	117,390	91,277	51,733	27,900	29,649	20,405	14,841	40,518	393,524
1982	122,733	76,634	49,753	26,839	35,834	19,873	13,949	26,919	383,044

Source: Monthly Digest of Statistics, March 1983, Central Statistical Office, Harare

TABLE 3
RANKING OF SUBSECTORS OVER TIME AS INDICATED BY PERCENTAGE OF TOTAL MANUFACTURING WITH REGARD TO NET OUTPUT AND EMPLOYMENT

Year	Metal Products O	E	Food-stuffs O	E	Chemical Products O	E	Beverages Tobacco O	E	Clothing & Footwear O	E	Textile & Cotton O	E	Paper, Print, & Publish O	E	Wood & Furniture O	E	Non-Metallic Minerals O	E	Transport Equipment O	E
1960	1	1	2	2	4	9	3	3	9	4	8	7	7	10	10	6	6	8	5	5
1965	1	1	2	2	4	8	3	4	7	3	8	5	6	9	9	6	10	10	5	7
1970	1	1	2	2	2	7	4	6	5	3	6	4	7	9	9	5	8	8	1	10
1975	1	1	2	2	3	6	4	5	5	3	6	4	7	9	10	7	8	8	9	10
1980	1	1	2	2	3	7	5	6	6	3	4	4	7	8	8	5	9	9	10	10

Source: Calculated from the Census of Production in C. Brecker, mimeo 'The Clothing & Footwear Subsector in Zimbabwe'. Project for Industrialisation Course 1985.

REFERENCES

1. Sutcliffe, R.B., *Industry and Underdevelopment: Development Economic Series*, edited by Arthur Hazlewood, Addison-Wesley Publishing, Harare, 1971, p. 17.
2. *Study of the Manufacturing Sector in Zimbabwe*, Technical Report, Vol. II, Main Report, DP/ZIM/84/018, UNIDO, 12 September 1985.
3. *Census of Production*, 1982/83, COS, Harare, 1985, p. 2.
4. Ndlela, D.B., Sectoral Analysis of Zimbabwe Economic Development with Implications for Foreign Trade and Foreign Exchange, *Zimbabwe Journal Of Economics*, Vol. 1, No. 1, July 1984.
5. *National Manpower Survey 1981 Vol. 1*, Ministry of Manpower and Development, Causeway, Harare, Table 2.2.
6. For details see Ndlela et al, A Study of the Transfer of Technology in Zimbabwe's Metals and Metal Goods Sector, presented to the *East African Technology Policy Study Workshop*, Lusaka, Zambia, 14-18 October 1985.
7. Ndlela, D.B., Generation of Change in Zimbabwe's Mining Sector, paper presented at the Arne Ryde Symposium, *The Primary Sector in Economic Development*, University of Lund, Sweden, 29-30 August 1983.
8. For example between 1967 and 1972 the price of refined copper in Zimbabwe was US$1.154, while the price of copper wire in France was US$1.762. See Hamid, G.M., *Preliminary Notes On The Lagos Plan Of Action And The Development of Mineral Industries In Africa*, paper presented at the Conference of Directors of Social Science Research Institutes and Policy Makers on the Third UN Development Decade, the Monrovia Strategy and the Lagos Plan of Action, 2-4 March 1982, Addis Ababa.
9. In 1976 approximately 70% of the US chromium requirement was used in the steel industry, approximately 18% in the chemical industries and 13% in the refractory industries. National Material Advisory Board, *Contingency plans for chromium utilisation*, National Research Council, National Academy of Sciences, Washington D.C., 1978.
10. *Ibid.*
11. Clutten, J.M., *The Nickel Resource in Zimbabwe*, paper presented at the Zimbabwe Economic Conference, Mining Section, September 1980, Salisbury.
12. See Ndlela et al, Table 3.1.1.
13. The joint ventures between government and private capital after independence mostly came about as a result of these firms going bankrupt. Almost invariably these were amongst the largest firms in the country, including F. Issels and Sons, and Aluminium Industries.
14. Earlier theoretical models of capital goods, originating in the Soviet Union and later on applied in the case of India, had stressed that this was possible in the condition of a closed economy. Thus in the original Draft Recommendation during the elaboration of the Second Five Year Plan of India, Professor P.C. Mahalanobis proposed that a quarter of all investments were to be in industry, and of this some two-thirds in

the capital goods sector. Dobb, M., *An Essay on Economic Growth and Planning*, Routledge and Kegan Paul, London, 1960.
15. Sadcheva, S.S., Review of Chemical Industry in Zimbabwe, United Nations Consultant, United Nations Financing System, New York, August 1983.
16. *Study of the Manufacturing Sector in Zimbabwe, op. cit.*, p. 226.
17. Gershenkron, *Economic Backwardness in Historical Perspective*, CUP, 1966.
18. White, G., Developmental States and Socialist Industrialisation in Third World, *Journal of Development Studies*, Vol. 21, No. 1, October 1984.
19. *Ibid.*
20. *First Five Year National Development Plan 1986-1990*, Vol. 1, April 1986, Harare, p. 30.
21. White, G., *op. cit.*

6. THE LAND QUESTION
Sam Moyo

Introduction

The unfolding of events in Zimbabwe's last six years—beginning with the Lancaster House negotiations and Agreement, the government policy of reconciliation, the articulation of development policy[1] and plans,[2] the manner and progress of development policy implementation and the development programmes outcomes, especially those related to the 'peasant' sector (or communal lands)—today present the 'land question' in Zimbabwe in an interestingly different light from that espoused during the liberation war.

Before independence the 'land question' was not clearly articulated by the liberation movement. However, it was determined in its objective to expropriate alienated land for the benefit of the hitherto marginalised peasantry, and to develop the land and production through socialist forms of organisation and social relations of production. Since independence, however, these objectives have been more cautiously stated and slowly or 'pragmatically' implemented, resulting in a much more complex configuration of issues, realities and determinations of the 'land question', which require careful consideration in order fully to comprehend the position of the state on the one hand, and that of the peasantry on the other hand.

On its part the state is today still grappling with quite fundamental issues concerning the 'land question'; such as, 'The Land Acquisition Bill', 'The Cooperatives Act', The Communal Lands Development Plan and Agrarian Reform policy (using in some cases the 'expert' advice of foreign consultants). These ongoing exercises will continue to clarify the 'land question' as it is seen by the state and possibly resolve a range of contradictions that have unfolded in the years following independence.

What seems clear, given the interest of the 'West' in the resolution of Zimbabwe's 'land question', is that there is growing international consensus and local acceptance that there may really be no 'land question' worth talking about in 1986, given Zimbabwe's star agricultural performance. It is now common internationally to acclaim Zimbabwe as a unique 'success' story in comparison to other African countries, because of increasing aggregate output of agricultural products, especially food products which are locally consumed. The fact that Zimbabwe has been able to export grains and meat (besides the traditional cash crops of tobacco, cotton, tea, etc.), during normal years, and was able to maintain a measure of food self-sufficiency, on the aggregate, during the three years of drought, has reinforced this placard of 'success'. It is because of this that Zimbabwe appears to have assumed a major role in SADCC's food security programmes.

This issue of 'success' is relevant to the 'land question' when we consider specifically the role of the peasantry attributed to this performance and the assumed benefits derived in Communal Areas. The following quote subtly demonstrates the manner in which the 'land question' is wished away:

> But miracle really isn't the right word. The success of farmer Makuyana and thousands like her is the result of a conscious government policy and a lot of hard work. Since independence in 1980 the government of Prime Minister Robert Mugabe has *vigorously promoted agricultural production, particularly among the country's peasant farmers*. While many African countries were making headlines with tragic stories of famine and starvation, Zimbabwe's farmers brought 925,000 tons of corn to market last year, almost enough to feed the entire country despite three consecutive years of drought. *What's more, small-scale or peasant farmers like Makuyana marketed 378,000 tons of corn, or over 40% of the crop and over four times their pre-independence record of 80,000 tons.*[3]

Although this type of eulogy on the 'land question' has gained much currency, on close scrutiny estimates suggest that less than 20% of the peasantry have directly gained from these developments. It will be useful, therefore, carefully to examine the full pattern of agrarian change and its effects in order to understand the unfolding 'land question'.

In pursuing such analyses, however, it is necessary to look at the 'land question' in its broader context, given that the economy is largely agricultural, with the major industrial activities linked to servicing and processing for the agricultural sector, which also employs the largest proportion of workers (see chapter three). The importance of this sector in ensuring cheap food and wage goods to industry and mining, and in the earning of foreign exchange places the 'land question' in a pivotal position in the whole debate on 'national transformation'.

Moreover, the state machinery associated with this sector (government ministries, departments, and parastatals) is one of the largest which suggests a mammoth task of transformation of institutions and bureaucratic apparatuses required to deal with the 'land question'. The co-ordination, specific policy objectives, interpretation of overall government policy and its implementation by these multifarious agriculture-related state organs is in itself a critical determining factor in the configuration of the 'land question'. We may ask, for example, what are the rational and institutional procedures which have led to:

> This careful balance of support for the white commercial farmers

who still produce much of the country's output, while beginning to nurture the peasant farmers, is what produced Zimbabwe's miracle.[4]

It is this 'balancing' that needs to be identified in order to grasp the 'land question' in Zimbabwe. Some of the more specific questions this chapter will address include:

1) To what extent has land deprivation (quantitative and qualitative) been alleviated since independence?
2) What forms of state participation in food and raw-materials production have been adopted, and what national objectives does this fulfil?
3) What state support has so far been directed at the poorest rural peoples and what are the achievements?
4) What forms of social organisation and relations of production have been promoted in the attempts to resolve the 'land question'?
5) What is the efficacy of the current rural development strategies in ensuring the stable and viable long-term material and social development of the majority of the peasantry and urban workers?

The theme of the chapter will be to outline the land question and the debates surrounding it, to point out how and to what extent the question has been resolved, through an analysis of the role of the peasantry since 1980; and finally to assess changes in the agrarian structure, outlining the results and effects of various agrarian reforms. The more specific agricultural policy changes will be addressed in the chapter that follows this one. We begin first with a brief historical contextualisation of the 'land question'.

Zimbabwe's Land Question in Perspective

It is not the objective of this chapter to give any detailed historical account of the origins of the land question, in particular the nature and processes of land alienation that have occurred in Zimbabwe since the early colonial wars. (There are numerous accounts of these historical processes included in the bibliography.)

What is crucial here is that extensive land alienation took place, with the settlers occupying the larger and more fertile tracts (see Maps 2 and 3), while the peasantry were forced into the more marginal lands which, under a growing population, could not sustain their farming systems, and thus led to further land deterioration. The Land Apportionment Act (1930) and other policies (see chapter seven) largely put a seal on the development of production among the peasantry, which had no access to the inputs necessary for technologically advanced and productive farming. In this situation, and through various extra-economic coercive colonial practices, the labour reserves emerged; feeding the developing mining, commercial farming and industrial activities, dominated by foreign capital. Population movements were also controlled to maintain the labour reserves through a variety of measures, including the Natives Urban Areas Accommodation and Registration Act (1946), Vagrancy Acts, etc.

The extent of land alienation (quantitative and qualitative) over time may readily be discerned in Tables 1 and 2.

TABLE 1
LAND DISTRIBUTION WITHIN AGRO-ECOLOGICAL REGIONS UNDER THE LAND TENURE ACT

```
|                1965                                                      |
| Tribal Trust Land   | A  | National    | European Area                   |
|                     | P  | & Unre-     |                                 |
|                     | A  | served      |                                 |
|                1961                                                      |
| Native Reserves | SNA | NPA | Nat-     | European Area                   |
|                 |     |     | ional    |                                 |
|                 |     |     | Land     |                                 |
|                1931                                                      |
| Native          | NPA | Forest and   | European Area                    |
| Reserves        |     | Unassigned   |                                  |
|                1925                                                      |
| Native          | Crown Land-Unassigned | European Area                 |
| Reserves        |                       |                               |
|                1911                                                      |
| Native          | Held by B.S.A. Company       | European Land          |
| Reserve         |                              |                        |
| 0   10   20   30   40   50   60   70   80   90   100                     |
|              PERCENTAGE OF TOTAL LAND                                    |
```

Source: Kay, G. (1970)

TABLE 2
PRINCIPAL LAND CATEGORIES UNDER THE LAND TENURE ACT (1969)

Land Category	Area (hectacres)	% of Total
European Land		
General Farming Land	15,337,096	39.4
Other Land—parks, forests etc.	2,768,020	7.1
	18,145.116	46.5
African Land		
TTL (Communal Land)	16,291,670	41.7
APL (SSCF)	1,415,921	3.6
Other Land—parks, forests etc.	494,617	1.3
	18,202.084	46.6
National Land	2,727,617	6.9
Total Zimbabwe	39,074,817	100.0

On the other hand the settler state developed a machinery to provide systematic technical, financial, marketing and infrastructural support to the large-scale white farmers, who over the decades were to achieve advanced levels of productivity and the major contributions to the GDP and export earnings (see also chapter seven).

It is because these levels of productivity, achieved by white farmers through state support, were counterpoised to a declining growth in the reserves 'land degradation', due to the marginality of the land, that there emerged a dual agricultural set-up in Zimbawe. As a result of this dualistic production system, a sharp historical polarisation in the conception of the land-use capabilities of white farmers on the one hand, in comparison to the peasantry on the other, became part of the folkore of Rhodesia: the 'Africans did not understand land husbandry and inherently could not achieve levels of productivity equitable to the whites, nor were they motivated (given their limited income and needs targets) to achieve these'! This mythology persisted right into the 1980s, even among black officials.

In spite of this mythology, the various settler regimes—realising the rapidly deteriorating environment in the reserves and the unviability of these reserves, especially for the reproduction of the cheap labour required in the 'modern' enclaves—attempted to 'develop' the rural Africans through various strategies, given the optimism over an imminent industrialisation process expected to take place in the 1950s.[5]

The main attempts were:
(a) to develop a yeoman class of successful ('master') farmers, who were to be granted larger portions of land (between 30 and 300 acres) in the newly created African Purchase Areas (APAs). Indeed such a class of 'large' peasants developed; they are today called the Small Scale Commercial Farmers (SSCF);
(b) other peasants (mainly 'squatters') were resettled after the Land Apportionment Act (1930) around 1948, to relieve pressure from APAs, thus adding more land to the reserves. Approximately 113,000 were resettled between 1936 and 1960 in this exercise;
(c) the Land Husbandry Act (1951), intended to control the land-use practices and ownership tenure norms, with the hope that the landless would be employed by the expected industrialisation, was also implemented. The changes in land ownership between the state, APAs and white farmers over time during these programmes are clear in Table 1.

As can be seen, the idea of resettlement *per se* is not new, although it then, as now, emphasisd the numbers of hectares and people to be juggled and not the qualitative development of the peasantry. In fact the two decades following the 1950s were to see a decline in African output, in spite of these resettlement programmes.

The disastrous and direct effects of the colonial regime's sharply exploitative agrarian policy became unbearable from the 1960s, throughout the liberation war period, and up until independence. According to Shopo, for example;

> Population pressure and widespread land degradation became major problems in the communal areas. Estimates indicate that over the period 1961 to 1977, the number of communal area cultivators increased by 88% from 349,000 to 675,000. The total area under cultivation increased by 91% from 1.15 to 2.2 million hectares at the expense of grazing land. Cattle numbers increased by 70% from 2 million to 3.4 million, resulting in overstocking of the reduced grazing area. However, the breakdown in disease control during the liberation war resulted in the loss of at least 1 million cattle in communal lands. Although the cattle population fell, the number of cultivators increased resulting in draught-power problems, which led to delayed crop establishment by the majority of households.[6]

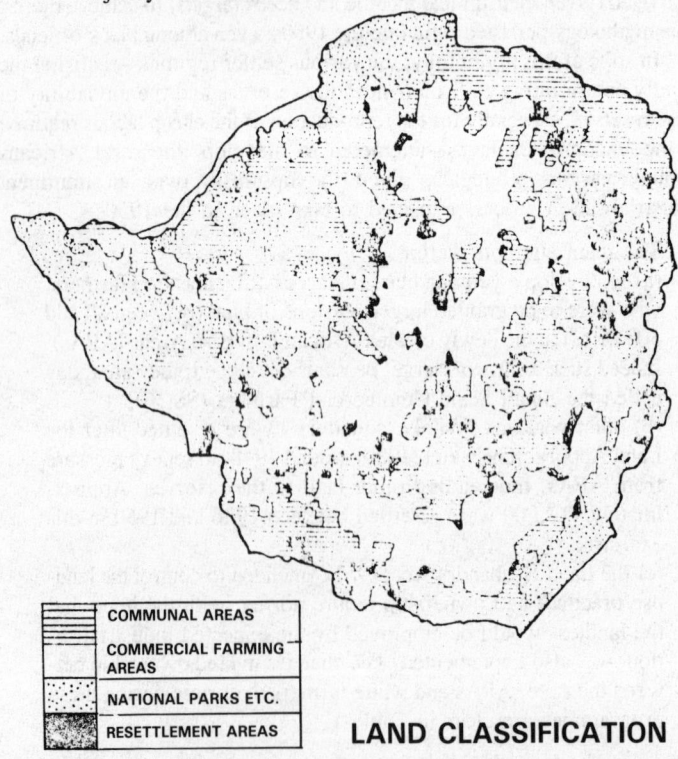

LAND CLASSIFICATION

- COMMUNAL AREAS
- COMMERCIAL FARMING AREAS
- NATIONAL PARKS ETC.
- RESETTLEMENT AREAS

The critically important role of reduced livestock in the production system in the communal areas persisted, even after independence. According to Shumba, communal farming was increasingly characterised by late planting, affecting yields, due to this problem and furthermore:

> Reduced tillage techniques in the communal areas by 1980 had led to serious problems for the production of maize; early weed infestation, incorporation of manure, pests and diseases. Under such conditions, the struggle by many communal area cultivators not only to realise sales for a commodity whose market value had by 1979 plummeted, but also to produce for their own consumption, was indeed desperate.[7]

As a result, according to Shopo, food supplies in some communal lands had decreased drastically, threatening famine conditions as a long-term trend, while cash sales from these areas had remained static in value from 1957 to 1972. Where increases in production occurred this came about through the cultivation of grazing and marginal lands.[8]

Inevitably this growing problem of land hunger and the land alienation designs of the Land Husbandry Act led to an increased broadening of the nationalist movement, which before the 1950s had been more organised through trade unions in urban areas and towards more forceful demands on the 'land question'. It was also essentially around this question that the armed liberation struggle mobilised the peasantry to support the guerrilla warfare that led to Lancaster House.

It was, however, before the Lancaster House Conference, around 1977 and during the transition to the Muzorewa government's brief puppet-show, that a serious and concerted debate on the 'land question' emerged. Some of the issues raised then were clearly reflected in the agreement at Lancaster House and have remained as central issues up until today. It is instructive therefore briefly to review the essence of these debates.

The Land Question : the Debates and the Roles of the Peasantry
It is interesting to note that, since 1978, Zimbabwe's 'land question' increasingly drew the interest of foreign organisations, which funded related 'technical' reports; for instance USAID (United States Agency for International Development),[9] the World Bank,[10] Overseas Development Institute,[11] FAO (Food and Agricultural Organisation) [12] and 'Think-Tank' of multifarious foreign origin, the Whitsun Foundation.[13] Other such foreign consultancies entered the 'land question' debate around 1982 and 1983, for example, the EEC and OECD through background country studies for foreign-aid agreements for agriculture in Zimbabwe.[14] A significant foreign-dominated participant in the debates, since independence, has been the Faculty of Land Management at the University of Zimbabwe, which has a large number of expatriate (mainly American) experts and large USAID funding, through American universities.

This widespread and concerted international interest and 'expertise' cannot be underestimated. For, indeed, most of the ensuing writings on the land question tended to react or defend position in relation to such 'technical' reports.

What, however, has been the essence of the debates? In basic terms, the 'land question'—when viewed from the point of view of the peasantry—is based on the demand for the redistribution of arable land (and land with reliable rainfall due to the agro-ecology of Zimbabwe). Now, the debates from the late 1970s up until today essentially have centred around the merits and demerits of the distribution of land: not that 'some' land should not be redistributed, but how much and which land and, most importantly, how much redistribution would cost the nation (as an aggregate unit) in terms of levels of output, foreign exchange earnings, land productivity, agricultural employment and the loss of agricultural expertise (and white farmers). The debates, however, have not focused on the demerits of not redistributing land (for example, continued land hunger, food shortages, etc.) but more on demerits related to losses of national output and financial flows. They have also not concentrated on the costs of maintaining 4,500 farmers' productivity, in real terms of income distribution. In essence, the 'land question' has been popularised within the 'growth-with-equity' parameters set out by the major government policy documents, which significantly accept some amount of land redistribution.

So, the 'land question' essentially contains on its agenda the redistribution of land, but only land which is acquired on a 'willing seller-willing buyer' basis. This in turn sets limits to the quantity, quality and location of land to be redistributed. This particular land 'free market' feature was deeply entrenched in the Lancaster House Agreement. The pace and form of redistribution, however, have largely been determined by the 'technical merits and demerits' mentioned before.

This, however, is not all; for the 'land question' is increasingly surrounded by *counter-solutions* to the land-hunger problem: that is, solutions that do not require land redistribution but instead promote rural development of the communal lands *in situ*. This type of counter-solution brings to the fore a wide range of very specific technical questions of a 'multi-disciplinary', positivistic scientific nature, far removed from the initial political issues around the 'land question', as it was fought for, during the liberation struggle.

The types of questions which have occupied the energies of many government ministries and foreign consultants, and which were openly surmised in the *Communal Lands Development Plan*[15] include:

(a) Whether urban blacks should continue to own land in Communal Areas (CAs)?
(b) Whether only those without formal employment should own land in CAs and Resettlement Areas (RAs)?
(c) Who should be responsible for 'conserving' the communal area land? (Collective responsibility?)
(d) What type of tenure should prevail? Communal, state leasing

or local government administration leases?
(e) What type of communal area political structures should take various decisions? (Village development committees or who?)
(f) What should be done about grazing land, given unequal ownership of cattle and 'excessive' stocking rates?
(g) What should be done about animal draught power, given its importance in peasant farming and unavailability? (Should tractor tillage be emphasised?).
(h) What land-use patterns should be promoted?
(i) What should happen to the next generations of the Communal Areas, given high projected population growth rates and clearly limited possiblities of increased non-farm and urban employment?
(j) Overall, what model of 'integrated rural development' (including physical planning) is appropriate to the Communal Areas?

These 'technical' questions have, in turn, brought into play a wide range of different rural development experiments (local level projects) in the various provinces, which are intended to find the appropriate model for Communal Lands development. It is also in this realm that various agricultural policies on pricing, credit, research, marketing etc., have evolved with the explicit aim of increasing support for peasant production and rural incomes within the CAs.

Conceptually, we thus find that the 'land question' has been disaggregated *topically* (e.g. land tenure, grazing schemes, population control etc.) and *spatially* (different experiments in different regions) resulting in a rather diffuse problematic.

In essence, therefore, the major issue becomes merely to 'integrate CAs into the national agricultural sectors' mainstream'.

Counter-solutions aside, the singularly most popular and dominant issue on the 'land question' concerns the differences in land use between the Large-Scale Commercial Farmers (LSCF) and the peasantry. This issue is typically viewed in two respects; one is the question of *full or underutilisation* of arable land and the other is their productivity capabilities. Regarding land utilisation land reform proponents usually suggest that the white farmers underutilise the 'prime' arable land, while the antagonists refute this: the counter-claims on this issue are enormous.

Those who claim optimal land utilisation by the LSCF have given various estimates ranging from 75% land utilisation[16] to 90% utilisation,[17] while others claim that only 15% utilisation occurs. Our own work[19] establishes the fact that only an average of 34% of the prime arable land centred around the three Mashonaland Provinces is utilised by the white large-scale farmers. This is important because it is these percentages which have been used since 1976 to estimate how much land should be transferred for resettlement.

This play on figures, therefore, requires careful analysis. For this reason it is probably worthwhile to assess some of the details of land

TABLE 3
MASHONALAND CROPPING INTENSITY FOR LARGE-SCALE COMMERCIAL FARM SECTOR
1981-1982 CROP SEASON

Province/District	A Total area (ha)	B Area Under Crops*	C % Total	D Total Arable Land	E % Cropped	F Net Arable Area	G % Cropped	H Non-Cropped Net Arable Lant
MASHONALAND WEST								
Lomagundi D.	943,911	120,123	12.7	452,133	26.6	307,450	39.1	187,327
Hartley D.	494,286	53,479	10.8	263,949	20.3	179,485	29.8	126,006
Hurungwe D.	359,779	31,787	8.8	120,166	26.5	81,713	38.9	49,926
Kadoma D.	454,991	18,768	4.1	72,344	25.9	49,194	38.2	30,426
Total:	2,252,967	224,157	9.9	908,592	24.7	617,842	36.3	393,685
MASHONALAND CENTRAL								
Bindura D.	153,170	23,706	15.5	63,106	37.6	49,912	55.2	19,206
Mazowe D.	403,698	67,644	16.8	192,564	35.1	130,944	51.7	63,300
Mt. Darwin D.	63,676	5,112	8.0	17,861	28.6	12,146	42.1	7,034
Centenary D.	121,655	10,589	8.7	35,986	29.4	24,470	43.3	13,881
Shamva D.	103,810	11,240	10.8	45,303	24.8	30,806	36.5	19,556
Total:	846,009	118,291	14.0	354,820	33.3	241,278	49.0	122,987
MASHONALAND EAST								
Marondera D.	456,718	23,866	5.2	240,599	9.9	163,607	14.6	139,741
Goromonzi D.	179,771	25,927	14.4	111,710	23.2	75,963	34.1	50,036
Harare D.	386,446	40,492	10.5	250,069	16.2	170,047	23.8	129,555
Mrewa D.	114,905	6,147	5.3	38,114	16.1	25,918	23.7	19,771
Mtoko D.	68,545	1,367	2.0	17,136	8.0	11,653	11.7	10,286
Total:	1,206,385	97,99	8.1	657,628	14.9	477,138	21.9	349,389
MASHONALAND TOTAL	4,305,361	440,247	10.2	1,921,040	22.9	1,306,308	33.7	866,061**

Sources: Columns A and B, 1982 ICA Schedule, CSO Harare; Columns D and F, Ministry of Agriculture Farm Plans, MOA Files, Harare
*Double-cropped hectares are counted as one
** 866,061 ha minus 240,000 ha in fallow = 626,061ha non-cropped net arable area.

utilisation in the LSCF focusing on Zimbabwe's prime land in the Mashonaland Provinces. Table 3 presents land use data for the 1981/82 season in order to demonstrate the intensity of land-use in the LSCF areas. The total area in these provinces amounts to 4.3 million hectares, which constitute 32% of the overall land owned by the LSCF. The data shows that only 10% of this prime land is actually cropped, and this represents 75% of the total area cropped by the LSCF in the country as a whole.

When allowance is made, however, for land which is not productively arable and inaccessible land in a farming system based on mechanisation, the net arable land in the Mashonaland provinces LSCF is greatly reduced to 1.3 million hectares.[20]

In spite of such generous allowances we still find that only 33.7% of the net arable land was cropped by the LSCF during that season.

Even if further allowance was made for the fallowing of land, we would remain with around half a million hectares of prime land under-utilised in this area. Table 3 also reveals the sharp differences in land utilisation among districts (from merely 12% to 55% cropped).

This demonstrates in itself local level productive land availability for resettlement of peasant households. Furthermore, much of the land which is inaccessible under mechanised farming would be readily accessible in peasant farming systems.

Our data, therefore, destroys the myth of the efficiency of land utilisation in the LSCF area and furthermore demonstrates that there is a significant amount of such prime land which could be transferred to the peasantry without affecting overall aggregate production. Instead, it appears that much of this underutilised prime land is increasingly being extensively used to build up beef stocks in anticipation of the EEC beef export arrangements. Although this may be justified in terms of foreign exchange earnings, it certainly does not meet rational or efficient land-use principles; for this land is best suited for crop production. On the other hand, this extensive land-use is part of a further mystification phase in the debates on the land question.

The main point here, however, is that the land question debate has been circumscribed by tedious 'scientific' analyses of relatively obvious patterns of unjust land distribution and utilisation, which fuels the pragmatists in implementing land redistribution, under the guise of accuracy over the actual amount of land which should be transferred to the peasantry.

Regarding the question of productivity, various studies have gone to lengths to show the low productivity levels of the peasantry,[21] while a few have taken pains to demonstrate that peasant productivity, especially in the wetter regions, can be comparable to the white farmers, given the correct inputs.[22]

It is therefore worthwhile to assess the peasant production/productivity issue in order to lay to rest the mythology concerning 'African land husbandry'.

Our data (see Tables 4, 5, 6 and 7) clearly shows the large leap in peasant output performance since independence, a trend towards their

TABLE 4
COMPARATIVE CONTRIBUTION OF COTTON DELIVERIES (IN TONS) ZIMBABWE'S THREE AGRICULTURAL SUBSECTORS (1982-1984)

YEAR/SECTOR	LSCF	SSCF	CFA	ARDA	TOTAL INTAKE
1982*	105,275	49,207			154,482
1983*	111,740	56,720			168,461
1984	138,728	7,768	80,776	22,972	250,244
TOTAL	355,743	113,695	80,776	22,972	573,187

Source: Cotton Marketing Board, Harare, 1985 (mid-year)
* In 1982 and 1983, LSCF included ARDA while SSCF included C.F.A.

TABLE 5
COMPARATIVE CONTRIBUTION OF MAIZE DELIVERIES (IN TONS) AMONG ZIMBABWE'S THREE MAIN AGRICULTURAL SUBSECTORS (1979-1985)

SECTOR	1979/80	1980/81	1981/82	1982/83	1983/84	1984/85
Peasant Communal Farmers	18,260 (3,6%)	41,380 (5,2%)	183,358 (9,7%)	229,472 (17,8%)	144,302 (23,4%)	341,673 (36,5%)
Small Scale Commercial Farmers	13,454 (2,7%)	17,964 (2,3%)	58,735 (3,1%)	40,836 (3,2%)	15,171 (2,6%)	54,421 (5,8%)
Commercial Large Scale Farmers	473,727 (93,7%)	725,297 (92,5)	1,650,483 (87,2%)	1,022,248 (79,0%)	457,486 (74,1%)	540,895 (57,7%)
GRAND TOTALS	505,441	784,641	1,892,576	1,292,556	616,959	936,989

Source: GMB Registry, Harare, 1985 (mid-year)

TABLE 6
COMPARATIVE CONTRIBUTION OF GROUNDNUTS DELIVERIES AMONG ZIMBABWE'S THREE MAIN AGRICULTURAL SUBSECTORS

SECTOR	1979/80 Shelled	1979/80 Unshelled	1980/81 Shelled	1980/81 Unshelled	1981/82 Shelled	1981/82 Unshelled	1982/83* Shelled	1982/83* Unshelled	1983/84* Shelled	1983/84* Unshelled	1985/86
Peasant Sector	122	933	231	1,387	146	1,725					55,500
Small scale Sector	175	165	262	185	129	284					
Largescale Sector	105	6,476	69	9,883	71	15,163					6,700

Source: G.M.B. Registry, Harare, 1985 (mid-year)
*Data not available.

TABLE 7
URLEY TOBACCO DELIVERIES BY SUBSECTOR

1979/80	No. of Growers	Total ha.	Mass sold	% Mass
Commercial	120	1,381	2,256,079	91.48
Small Commercial	46	27	17,089	0.69
Communal	584	235	193,204	7.83
Totals	750	1,643	2,466,372	100.00

Source: *Zanu PF (1985) p. 38*

increased dominance of staple food production (maize and groundnuts), as well as their significant contributions to cotton (an export crop) and a steadily increasing production of newer crops, such as soya beans and sunflower seeds (Table 12). Moreover production of drought-resistant crops (sorghum, millets, etc.) is reportedly increasing, in those Communal Areas with poor agro-ecological potential.

What is most significant here is that, even though the white LSCF dominate most of the export crops and fruits, wheat and beef for local consumption, the peasants, within five years, *have begun actually to play a major role in providing the major foods required and affordable by the poor.*

This is significant also for national food security; for only the peasants and the state farming sector can really be relied upon to produce for food security purposes. The evidence so far, although scanty, shows that in recent years LSCF farmers can hold the nation to ransom, since given their resources they can easily effect crop shifts following pre-planting price setting, which the Commercial Farmers' Union (CFU) is there precisely to lobby for while also informing its members systematically about the cost-price fluctuations.

On one hand this means that the LSCF farmers are in comprehensive control of land utilisation (in terms of cropping patterns and intensity of land-use) as well as in terms of *determining the option for export-led or food security-led land-use*. It is interesting on the other hand to note that peasants are increasingly entering the export production sector.

With regard to tobacco for example (Table 7), available statistics show that the number of peasant growers of burley tobacco has increased by 400% since independence while the mass sold by them increased by 567%. In the higher quality tobacco (Virginia tobacco) the growth has been insignificant, due of course to the high infrastructural development costs required for that crop. As it is however, the necessary long-term loans received by peasants from the Agricultural Finance Corporation (AFC) have been meagre (see chapter seven) and this sets constraints on peasant production of most export crops!

What this means, therefore, is that in the long run, with proper state support and well-coordinated and developed national planning (in terms of food export crops and domestic raw materials crops), the peasantry could play an increasingly dominant role. Having dismissed the peasant productivity myth so far, we need also to contextualise the issue in terms of access to water-controlled irrigation; because most of the peasants reside in the poorest agro-ecological regions.

The evidence on productivity in relation to the use of irrigation (Table 8) shows clearly the basis of the so-called high productivity of the LSCF.

The difference in yields per hectare from dry land and irrigated farming is vast, and it is this which partly accounts for the 'Rhodesian' productivity myth: that is omission of the real causes of increased productivity! The point is that most peasants rely on dry land farming, hence their *demands* for better land and access to productivity-increasing

TABLE 8
CROPPED AREA AND YIELDS OF MAJOR CROPS IN COMMERCIAL AREAS FOR YEAR ENDING SEPTEMBER 1980

Crops	Un-irrigated Area 000'ha	Yields %	Area t/ha	Irrigated Yields 000'h	Area %	Yields t/ha	Total 000'ha	%	t/ha
Tobacco	55.3	13.2	1.85	8.4	5.4	2.12	63.7	11.1	1.88
Maize	212.7	50.6	3.93	15.0	9.7	5.00	227.7	39.6	4.00
Wheat	-	-	-	32.6	21.1	4.75	32.6	5.7	4.75
Coffee	1.4	0.3	1.16	2.7	1.7	2.35	4.1	0.7	1.29
Tea	2.1	0.5	2.07	2.0	1.3	2.59	4.1	0.7	2.33
Cotton	47.2	11.2	1.70	27.7	17.9	2.35	74.9	13.0	1.94
Soyabeans	27.4	6.5	2.14	13.4	8.7	2.31	40.8	7.1	2.19
Sugarcane	0.3	0.1	54.59	30.2	19.5	103.43	30.5	5.3	103.00
Fruits	0.3	0.1	n.a	3.3	2.1	n.a.	3.7	0.7	n.a.
Other crops & planted pastures	73.3	17.5	n.a.	19.5	12.6	n.a.	92.7	16.1	n.a.
Total	420.0	100.0		154.8	100.0		574.8	100.0	
%	73.1			26.9			100.0		

Source: Date used by Whitsun Foundation (1981) from *ICA Supplement Crop production of Large-Scale Commercial Agricultural Units 1980 Central Statistics Office, September 1981.*

capital investments (through either loans or straight state subsidies).

The more fundamental question which is being illustrated here is the importance of viewing the land question comprehensively; including the quantity of land, the natural quality of land, access to water for irrigation and attendant legal water rights. During the colonial period access to the best land and water and related legal rights were highly concentrated and privatised on racial grounds.

TABLE 9
DISTRIBUTION OF IRRIGATION-BASED FARMING BY AGRICULTURAL SUBSECTOR IN 1981

Agricultural Subsector	Area in hectares	Percentage
Large Company Estates	30,400	23.4
Commercial Settler Farms	10,500	8.1
Commercial Farm Units	80,000	61.5
ARDA (Tilcor) Estates and Settlers	5,900	4.5
Small-scale Irrigation in Communal Areas	2,800	2.2
Small Community Irrigation Schemes	400	0.3
Total	130,000	100.0

Source: Whitsun Foundation, 1981

Regarding controlled irrigated farming, therefore, Table 9 readily reveals the uneven access in the various subsectors in 1980. The peasantry only had access to 2.5% of the controlled irrigation infrastructure.

The 'land question', therefore, also requires changing the historical policy orientation of the settler regimes, of subsidised water access to the LSCF. This is more critical also because a large proportion (23%) of controlled irrigation is owned by transnational corporations ('Large Company Estates'). This process, which began before independence and continues today with slight modifications, reflects the prevalence of the Lancaster House Agreement, and the extent to which the land question has not been resolved.

In conclusion to this section, therefore, the myth of poor peasant production and productivity is simply an ideological campaign to maintain the highly inequitable ownership of land and unequal access to financial resources and services, as well as to discourage the resettlement programmes on unscientific grounds. The point however, is that *much energy has been expended on this technicality of productivity leaving the central political demand for land aside*, because of fears that Zimbabwe would lose its aggregate agricultural output if much of the scarce prime land was resettled.[23]

The irony of the effort to establish the significance of peasant productivity, the state support for the same and the demonstrated performances of the peasantry is that the other more crucial question of the transformation of the social relations and mode of production has been subsumed. For it is not, to our mind, merely for philanthropic reasons that foreign capital—through its various lending and donor agencies—has supported the *peasant road* of transformation through credit (World Bank loan), marketing depots (USAID grants) and various research activities.[24] It is conceivable that such foreign support is meant:

a) to diffuse the 'land question' proper by demonstrating peasant productivity and hence increased incomes;
(b) to further the interests of foreign capital, as peasant use of inputs benefits the transnational agribusiness corporations engaged in agro-chemicals supplies (e.g. Ciba-Geigy and Windmill Fertilizer);
c) to demonstrate that *ipso facto* the *peasant road*, being competitive with large-scale capitalist farming, is the second best option compared to other forms of organisation or production.

In this respect, the question of promoting cooperative or state farm agricultural production is seen as counter-productive. Indeed some of the agrarian debates so far show clear biases against cooperativisation. The anti-cooperative arguments, for instance, range from banal assertions that, due to local traditions, the peasant prefers to farm individually and at best to cooperate with direct extended family members, and can only cooperate on a broader basis in primary cooperative organisations (that is marketing or labour-sharing) but not as producer collectives.[25] Others have been rather fatalistic in their analyses of cooperativisation, focusing mainly on the constraints and shortcomings of existing producer collectives (e.g. lack of management skills, finance, markets, etc.), without any positive prescriptions nor any contextualisation of the problem of cooperative development under capitalism and transitionaly development policies.[26]

Overall, therefore, the 'land question' has graduated from the peasant inefficiency mythology, which in turn has led to anti-cooperativisation, reflected in the dominant agrarian programmes. In reality, the basis of evaluating cooperative viability is itself questionable.[27] At present, therefore, the balance of forces has tilted to a reduction of the 'land question' to some form of a *peasant road* resolution.

In the following section, therefore, through a discussion of Zimbabwe's agrarian structure, the manner in which the 'land question' has been concretely dealt with so far is presented and assessed.

The Agrarian Structure, Land Potential and Land Redistribution

First an attempt is made to contextualise the 'land question' in terms of the quantity and quality of Zimbabwe's land resources and the distribution of the same among the various distinctive agricultural subsectors, which constitute the agrarian structure (see Table 10). The quality of Zimbabwe's land resources has been classified into five 'natural regions' which represent land-use potential derived from average rainfall quantities and its variability. This land classification also provides generally recommended cropping and livestock production patterns (see Map 2).

It is important to understand the interrelatedness of land-use potential and the land-ownership patterns, as they relate to existing farming practices in the various 'natural regions' by the different agricultural subsectors' farmers. This also makes it easier to appreciate the qualitative land hunger and deprivation among communal land households. The aim here is to treat the 'land question' in both quantitative terms (dealing with the numbers of hectares required for resettlement) and qualitative terms (dealing with the quality of redistributed land). An understanding of the qualitative distribution of land amongst subsectors also immediately suggests the nature and levels of productive capital investment necessary in various 'natural regions', given a strategy of minimalist land redistribution. This is important in determining, for instance, the extent of water resources development in the Communal Areas, where land hunger is not alleviated.

TABLE 10
LAND AREAS BY NATURAL REGION

Natural Region*	Suitable Intensity of Land-Use	Land Area (1,000 ha)	Percent of Total
I	Specialized and Diversified Crops	0,705	1.8
II	Intensive	5,857	15.0
III	Semi-Intensive	7,290	18.7
IV	Semi-Extensive	14,770	37.8
V	Extensive	10,450	26.7
TOTAL		39,072	100.00

Source: Cole, R., 1981.
*Note: Natural regions I and II are the best in terms of agro-ecological potential, where the majority of high value crops are grown, while regions IV and V have the most unreliable rainfall are best suited for extensive ranching.

Table 10 clearly shows that only 16.8% of the total area falls into zones where there is the potential for intensive crop and livestock production, while over half the country is best suited mainly for livestock rearing. It is for this reason that the actual land-use patterns in Natural Region II, located in the three Mashonaland provinces, were closely scrutinised earlier in order to determine the amount of high quality land available for resettlement and *to assess the congruity of current land-use with national food and raw material needs vis-à-vis* land hunger and food security needs in the Communal Areas.

Having clarified Zimbabwe's land qualitative features, we may now turn to a discussion of Zimbabwe's existing agrarian structure and land tenure in relation to the existing land-use potential.

Zimbabwe has basically six agricultural subsectors.

These are:

(1) Communal Areas (CAs)
(2) Large Scale Commercial Farm Areas (LSCF)

(3) Resettlement Model A schemes
(4) Resettlement Model B (Cooperative) schemes
(5) Small Scale Commercial Farms (SSCF)
(6) State Farms

The subsectors are distinguishable in terms of forms of land tenure, production organisation, capital and technology investment levels and, management practices, and coincide with the racial boundaries of the land ownership structure. The LSCF include within it notably large private estates owned by transnational corporations (TNCs). Although in number these do not exceed twenty estates, the land owned by such TNCs is significantly large and has the highest level of capitalisation and irrigation (per unit of labour), and dominates agro-processing.

Table 11 shows the relative distribution of land available in each of these six subsectors, with just over half the land under the CA sector, followed closely by the LSCF sector. Although the Resettlement Model A scheme of individual settler plots is relatively new—having been created since 1980—it is the third largest sector, with over 1.6 million hectares followed by the SSCF. State farmland and cooperative resettlement schemes own relatively equal land areas.

In terms of land-use potential (Table 11), in absolute terms, the LSCF occupy most of the highest quality land (Regions I and II) while the majority of poorest land (Regions IV and V) is within the Communal Areas. On the other hand over half of the cooperative land is of higher quality while most of the state land is in the poorer natural regions. This reflects the concentration of Zimbabwe's prime land in private hands, *and this is the land that is most protected by the Lancaster House Agreement.*

It is also this land which has undergone drastic purchase value increases and fluctuations, has cost the government heavily in its land acquisition programme since 1980, and has had numerous legal problems attendant on such purchases.

Tables 2, 11a and 11b[29] demonstrate vividly the general trend of land transfers since independence. First, national non-farming, game reserves and parks land has apparently increased since 1969, rather than declined for redistribution to peasants. This apparently reflects the increasing importance that some of Zimbabwe's land for wild-life conservation, and tourist land resource utilisation, has been gaining recently, given the much-vaunted foreign-exchange earnings that tourism contributes to Zimbabwe's development. It is quite interesting that this land category occupies more high quality land (Region I) than the communal lands.

By far the biggest transfer of land occurred in the resettlement sectors, which began with zero land, and now occupy a substantial 4.5% of the nation's land! As can be seen, however, most of the resettlement land is of middle to low quality. The major land transfer has obviously been from the LSCF (8%) but close scrutiny shows that this was mainly from the poorest land regions.

In absolute terms, however, the amount of land transferred from

TABLE 11(a)
DISTRIBUTION OF AGRICULTURAL LAND IN HECTARS BY NATURAL REGION AND AGRICULTURAL SUBSECTOR

Natural Region	Communal(1)	%	LSCF*(1)	%	Resettlement Model (A) (2)	%	Resettlement Model B (2)	%	SSCF***(a)	%	State(3)	%
I	119,882	0.7	418,900	3.0	6,783	0.4	14,471	21.7	7,300	0.5	6,457	8.2
II	1,427,739	8.7	3,982,397	28.6	308,840	18.5	32,663	48.9	252,100	17.8	1,042	1.3
III	2,798,955	17.1	2,438,772	17.5	782,187	46.9	19,641	29.4	536,100	37.9	14,614	18.6
IV	1,780,382	47.6	3,519,098	25.2	506,702	30.9	-	-	523,000	36.9	22,609	28.7
V	4,228,622	25.9	3,583,679	25.7	64,721	3.8	-	-	97,600	6.9	33,980	43.2
TOTAL	16,355,580		13,943,446		1,669,233		66,775		1,416,100		78,702	

Sources: Compiled by Neiner et. al. (1984) from:
(1) Agritex Planning Branch, Ministry of Agriculture. LSCF figures adjusted for resettlement for period up to August 1983.
(2) Ministry of Lands, Resettlement and Rural Development (MLRRD). For period up to August 1983.
(3) Agricultural and Rural Development Authority (ARDA). For period up to July 1984.

TABLE 11(b)
LAND DISTRIBUTION BY SUB-SECTORS, ACCORDING TO THEIR AGRO-ECOLOGY IN 1969 AND PERCENTAGE LAND REDISTRIBUTION BY 1984

	1969	1984	I	II	III	IV	V
				(Percentages)			
National & Unreserved Land (forests, Parks & other non-farming land)	14.4%	17.2%	0.3	0.9	2.1	6.5	6.0	1.4
Communal Lands (CLs)	41.5%	42.7%	0.2	3.1	7.0	18.1	12.8	1.5
Small-scale Commercial Farms (SSCF)	3.8%	3.5%	-	0.6	0.7	1.5	0.5	0.2
Large-scale Commercial Farms (SSCF)	40.0%	32.1%	1.2	9.8	5.6	9.7	5.7	0.1
Resettlement Areas	0.0%	4.5%	0.1	0.4	2.4	0.5	1.1	-
TOTAL			1.8	14.8	17.8	36.3	26.1	3.1

(Natural Regions)

Source: Ministry of Lands, Agriculture and Resettlement, Land Reform Policy Workshop, September, 1985.

various sectors for resettlement has not been substantial. By mid-1984, the government had acquired approximately 2.5 million hectares of land at a total cost of Z$52 million,[30] and most of the land acquisition took place in the 1981/82 and 1982/83 seasons (Table 12).

Land acquisitions fell drastically in the 1983/84 period partially due to the effects of the three-year drought, the international economic recession affecting the economy and escalating land prices. More importantly, however, the decline in purchases can be reasonably associated with the economic 'structural adjustments' that occurred in 1983, decreasing the budgetary outlays to resettlement. (The reader may look at chapter three for details on the economic developments and to chapter seven on agricultural policy and rural allocations.)

It is also interesting, however, that there has been a regional and provincial differentiation in land acquisition as shown in Table 13, which generally conforms to patterns of land quality distribution as can be discerned in Map 2 and in the political boundary map in chapter one.

TABLE 12
LAND ACQUISITION AND COST PATTERNS (1979/84)

Year	Area (ha)	Cost (Z$)
1979/80	116,003	202,500
1980/81	223,202	3,357,238
1981/82	957,772	19,308,987
1982/83	1,005,922	21,029,579
1983/84	220,700	6,867,978

Source: ZANU (PF), 1985, p. 2

TABLE 13
PROVINCIAL DISTRIBUTION OF RESETTLEMENT LAND PURCHASE (1979 to June 1984)

Province	Area (Ha)	Cost (Z$)	Number of families settled
Manicaland	539,538	14,104,890	10,728
Masvingo	366,467	7,205,561	3,578
Mashonaland Cent.	124,774	3,408,201	2,138
Midlands	406,515	6,989,285	4,524
Mashonaland East	208,954	5,878,190	4,426
Mashonaland West	282,350	4,580,090	3,036
Matabeleland South	458,042	8,423,932	948
Matabeleland North	136,959	2,258,033	833

Source: ZANU (PF), 1985, p. 3.

The most evident trend is that Manicaland Province had by far the highest land purchases and numbers of settlers, supposedly because most of the farms abandoned by white farmers by 1979 were in this area, due to the intensity of war there. It has also been suggested that this had to be so, due to the fact that most of such land was already occupied by squatters, so that it was a matter of officialising land occupation, through the 'accelerated resettlement schemes', by the land-starved populace there. It is, however, interesting to note that even up to today, some two or more years after land acquisition rates plummeted, the major squatting problems and land disputes in general between resettled peoples and locals still has its highest manifestation in Manicaland Province. This observation is based on field studies by this author. Indeed, this is not surprising given the high localised population densities in that province in relatively poor arable land, although this is not uncommon elsewhere. The obvious demand and pressure for land in this province has to be related, however, to the underutilisation of prime land in the Mashonaland provinces discussed earlier, in order for the 'land question' to be understood in its proper national perspective. As will be seen in Table 13, the levels of land acquisition in the same Mashonaland provinces were very low, as were the numbers of families settled there, and yet land prices there appear to be comparatively higher per unit.

In general, therefore, the pattern of land transfer to the peasantry, in quantity and quality, as well as *the survival of an essentially unchanged agrarian structure five years after independence*, suggest that the 'land question' as it was posed during the struggle has drastically changed its configuration in 1986 and has not substantively fulfilled the land hunger, self-evident in squatter problems and the drought-relief programmes under way today.

It would thus appear that the more substantive agrarian changes since independence have been those related to counter-solutions that would at least increase or 'improve' the productive capabilities of certain segments of the peasantry.

The Agrarian Reforms and their Impact

Our discussion of agrarian reform will treat each subsector separately and merely highlight critical issues, beginning with the communal lands.

Communal Areas Reforms

The majority (57%) of Zimbabwe's population live in the Communal Areas which are located mainly in Natural Regions IV and V (see Map 2 and Table 11). Approximately 2.65 million people (60% of the Communal Area population and 35% of the national population) live in these marginal zones. Due to the migrant labour system's requirements the CAs' demography reflects sex-age imbalances with close to half the households headed by females,[31] and high dependency ratios (children and geriatrics to active population).

Land degradation and an overall lack of access to annual production inputs, and diminished means of production (especially draught power) are the major constraints in CAs. The relative frequency of the occurrence of drought and decreasing commercial farm and urban employment in the last decade have created a survival crisis, and the long-term viability of the CAs is in serious doubt. These objective conditions underlie Zimbabwe's 'land question', and specific demands for agricultural services and water development

There is, on the other hand, a small proportion of CA households residing in more favourable 'natural regions', which have become highly productive as a result of the introduction of non-discriminatory pricing, marketing and credit policies (see the following chapter). The evidence on surplus crop production among such households glaringly reveals the importance of land quality as a major factor in the peasantry's ability to take advantage of state support services. The emerging pattern is that the majority of the peasant-marketed output emanates from Natural Regions II and III and mainly from the three provinces (see Table 14).

Furthermore, the imbalance in gains from agrarian reform (due to ecological factors and attendant support) is amply reflected in provincial figures of peasant-marketed output (Table 15). In this respect, the Mashonaland and Midlands (officially Gokwe) provinces were the main beneficiaries of agrarian reforms.

Moreover, only CAs in the poorer agro-ecological regions—which have geographic locations in proximity to the Harare-Gweru and Mutare transportation axis, where agricultural services and infrastructure were located during the colonial period for the benefit of LSCF—have increased their marketed outputs.

The patterns of increased marketed grains by Communal Farmers in Zimbabwe, therefore, has a clear *regional differentiation* that demonstrates the constrained impact of some of the major agrarian reforms. Furthermore, the 'bumper harvest' essentially represents increased peasant production on *prime land*, but *in situ*: that is, without significant land redistribution.

Relatedly, although the tables show that over 60% of peasant deliveries are made by the individual cultivators to Grain Marketing Board collection points, and not the overly-praised marketing and supply cooperatives, the role of 'middlemen', some of which are 'approved buyers', has been steadily rising.

Peasants are receiving farm-gate prices below 66% (based on field survey estimates by this author)[32] of the government-set producer prices, due to the takings of such middlemen in the name of handling and transport costs. This means the actual gains from increased production/productivity are steadily eroded, even among the 'better-off' peasants.

There is thus, at the most, 20% of the peasantry gaining from the reforms and less than this in real terms so that there is an emergence of *regional and social differentiation in the communal lands*. Our analysis leads us to the conclusion that there is the emergence of 'kulakisation' in a few regions of Zimbabwe, suggesting further polarisation of the existing agrarian structure, with the 'land question' contradictions sharpening as a result of the 'minimalist' reform strategies.

This pattern of differentiation is not limited to maize production alone; it includes production of sorghum and sunflower seeds (Tables 16 and 17).

Furthermore, these patterns of regional and social differentiation have persisted over the five-year period since independence (see Table 15). Although this data relates mainly to maize, this trend introduces a further socio-political dimension, *the regional (provincial) resolution of the land hunger and food security problem* into the 'land question'. This needs state policy-making consideration, in this phase of national democratisation and unity.

The Large Scale Commercial Farm Sector (LSCF)
In the LSCF approximately 4,400 whites own farms on a freehold title basis. During the last six years it is estimated that approximately 300 black Zimbabweans have joined their ranks and are members of the highly organised Commercial Farmers' Union (CFU), an apex body of numerous farm produce sub-unions. The CFU has mobilised resources and developed a sound lobby which is influential, especially on pricing, foreign-exchange allocations and other aspects of government policy-making. This organisational feature, together with its black representation, seems incresingly to be the focus of agrarian reform

TABLE 14
MARKETED MAIZE DELIVERIES TO G.M.B. FROM COMMUNAL AREAS
BY NATURAL REGION AND MANNER OF CONVEYANCE (in Kgs) IN 1984 (1983-84 season)

	NATURAL REGION I & II	NATURAL REGION III	NATURAL REGION IV	TOTALS OF KNOW DELIVERIES
1. Producer Deliveries	133,804,944 53.3%	37,465,470 17.7%	40,137,520 19.0%	211,407,934
2. Coop Deliveries	33,934,925 67.7%	9,981,143 19.9%	6,223,058 12.4%	50,139,126
3. Approved Buyer Deliveries	19,448,065 55.3%	10,695,690 30.4%	5,002,624 14.2%	35,146,379
4. TOTALS	187,187,934 Kgs (87,189 tons) 63.1%	58,142,303, Kgs (58,142 tons) 19.6%	51,363,202 Kgs (51,363 tons) 17.3%	296,693,439 (296,693 tons)

Source: GMB Registry, 1985

Table 15
PROVINCIAL MARKETED MAIZE OUTPUT (1979/80–1984/85): PEASANT SECTOR

PROVINCES	1979/80 ton	%	1980/81 tons	%	1981/82 tons	%	1982/83 tons	%	1983/84 tons	%	1984/85 tons	%
Mashonaland East	3,590	19.69	8,903	21.56	36,125	19.78	77,804	34.00	26,843	18.73	79,980	23.40
Mashonaland West	10,963	60.14	16,542	40.06	65,260	35.75	79,858	34.90	88,356	61.65	141,018	41.27
Mashonaland Central	2,157	11.83	5,658	13.70	23,416	12.82	36,772	16.07	22,214	15.50	52,309	15.30
Midlands	218	1.19	6,301	15.26	34,296	18.78	15,738	6.87	1,530	1.06	32,533	9.52
Manicaland	334	1.83	2,070	5.01	7,414	4.06	10,193	4.45	2,637	1.84	17,748	5.19
Masvingo	182	0.99	1,185	2.87	11,782	6.45	5,351	2.33	16	0.01	3,771	1.10
Matabeleland North	Nil	-	180	0.43	306	0.16	1,122	0.49	856	0.59	12,648	3.70
Matabeleland South	783	4.29	446	1.08	3,943	2.16	2,346	1.02	851	0.59	1,667	0.48
TOTALS	18,227	99.96	41,285	99.97	182,545	99.96	228,818	100.13	143,303	99.97	341,674	100.05

Source: *Grain Marketing Board Registry, 1985 (mid-year)*

TABLE 16
SORGHUM DELIVERIES FROM COMMUNAL (1983/84 SEASON)

Province	Kgs Delivered	Percentage of Total
1. Manicaland	521,382	22.1
2. Mashonaland West	217,617	9.2
3. Mashonaland East	243,666	10.3
4. Mashonaland Central	141,661	6.0
5. Midlands	675,931	28.7
6. Masvingo	548,699	23.3
7. Matabeleland North	4,324	0.2
8. Matabeleland South	1,112	0.0
TOTALS	2,354,392	99.8

Source: GMB Registry, 1985

TABLE 17
SUNFLOWER SEED DELIVERIES FROM COMMUNAL LANDS BY PROVINCE (1983/84 season)

Province	Kgs Delivered	Percentage of Total
1. Manicaland	217,041	3.4
2. Mashonaland West	2,100,471	33.2
3. Mashonaland East	687,220	10.9
4. Mashonaland Central	320,884	5.1
5. Midlands	2,778,389	44.0
6. Masvingo	37,945	0.6
7. Matabeleland North	162,267	2.7
8. Matabele and South	6,798	0.1
TOTALS	6,311,015	99.9

Source: GMB Registry, 1985

counter-solutions.

The LSCF's predominance of Zimbabwe's agrarian structure is demonstrable beyond doubt. In 1984 it produced 75% of the total agricultural output, and 90% of the marketed output. In that year out of Z$398 million realised from agricultural exports, 56% came from LSCF tobacco sales, 15% from their cotton, 13.8% from sugar and 8.8% from maize. In broad terms the 1981 agricultural export earnings contributed 46% of the total domestic export value, a level not previously achieved since 1975.[33] The role of the LSCF in foreign exchange earnings and as a major employer of permanent labourers (165,000 persons) and seasonal labourers (56,000)[34] and the strong linkages with the service and industrial sectors of the economy cannot be overstated.

These facts, however, reveal the apparent 'benefits' from the LSCF (which are orchestrated by antagonists of land reform), yet there is little revelation of the 'costs' of maintaining the LSCF. Firstly, the sector has always been dependent upon an abundant and cheap labour force, until minimum-wage regulations since 1980, to which the LSCF has reacted by labour substitution through increased mechanisation, especially of harvesting activities, and labour casualisation. Even then, the current minimum wage of Z$85 per month is approximately below 50% of various estimates of the poverty datum income level. Furthermore, such farm labourers' families are the most undernourished in Zimbabwe, compared to other communities.[35] Outside the effects of resettlement, therefore, there has been a general reduction in LSCF employment with 51,000 permanent jobs lost between 1980 and 1982 and a further 2.8% decrease in 1983 resulting in a decline in the ratio of workers to cropped hectares from 0.47 to 0.37.[36]

Secondly, although much has been said about the foreign exchange earnings role of the LSCF and its productivity there is scarcely any analysis of the import costs in foreign exchange for inputs required to achieve LSCF output. We have thus no existing balanced cost-benefit assessment of LSCF maintenance at the macro-economic level to go by in this debate. Tobacco, for example, consumes much foreign exchange to procure the large inputs of liquid and solid fuels as well as agrochemicals needed to produce it, and in turn is exported largely in unprocessed form at auctions, with an unclear analysis of value added. A final aspect is the nature of land utilisation of prime land by the LSCF: is this for overall national benefit or for individual farmer benefits? For example, in the 1981/1982 crop year, there were 2,626 large-scale commercial farms in Mashonaland. The average farm size was 1,640 hectares, although the average area under crops was only 168 hectares per farm.[37] Also, in that cropping year, 468 farms, or 17.8% of all the farms in Mashonaland, did not grow any crops at all.

Resettlement Sector
The resettlement subsector emerged in 1980, to redistribute land to the poorest peasant households, the landless and the urban unemployed. One major feature of the resettlement programme is that most of the land redistributed is qualitatively the poorest. A second feature is the incomplete state support provided on many schemes and a rather slow pace of resettlement. These features result from constraints enshrined in the Lancaster House Agreement, namely that the government can only purchase land on a 'willing seller-willing buyer basis.' Although this provision can conceivably be circumvented in a number of ways, the attendant reconciliation policy of 1980 and the short-term need to prevent a white farmer exodus appear to have placed constraints on the level of access the peasantry has had to Zimbabwe's prime land. This state of affairs was worsened by financial constraints generally faced by the government during the period under study.

Other important aspects of the programme are that the land is owned by the state and tenure has yet to be decided upon, labour migrancy among settlers is not permitted and there is a close scrutiny of land-use practices on individual settler schemes. Most of these aspects indicate the state's attempt to ensure certain production levels and land conservation and to create incomes for the poorest sections of the society.

It is important also to note that foreign aid funds for resettlement have not been readily available (especially British and American pledges) and that escalating land prices have dampened the form and pace of the resettlement programme especially with regard to the cooperative model of resettlement.

The evidence (Table 11 on resettlement) indicates that the majority of resettlement schemes were on an individual household basis, and were located mainly in Natural Regions III and IV, with a few schemes in Natural Region II.[38] The number of individual settlers by 1984 was approximately 31,000 families, on 2.2 million hectares, representing the movement of over 250,000 people. This, however, was below one-third of the initial target for resettlement. Slightly over 60% of those resettled were from communal lands, the rest being refugees, the landless and unemployed persons.

By 1984, about 41 collective producer cooperatives, occupying approximately 35,000 hectares, were established on whole farms bought from LSCF farmers. Settlers range in number from thirty to over one hundred per farm and some of these have been provided with an establishment grant. Apparently most cooperatives have not received such grants and they now tend to rely on Non-Governmental Organisation funding. Most of the collectives, however, have been established on qualitatively good land.

On the whole, therefore, the resettlement exercise has mainly resettled individual families and is thus essentially reproducing social relations of production similar to those in the Communal Areas.

Small Scale Commercial Farm Sector
The Small Scale Commercial Farm (SSCF) sector consists of approximately 8,500 farmers who hold land on a freehold basis, ranging in size from 50 to 200 hectares, mainly located in the poorer natural regions, with low contributions to national marketed surplus. Created by the colonial regime to develop an elite African farming class, it has failed to emerge as a significant sector, having been peasantised by accommodating extended family members from Communal Areas,[39] and due to the continued existence of unequal access to state support services.

Although farmers in this sector are relatively better off than those in Communal Areas, and are fairly well organised under their Zimbabwe National Farmers' Union (ZNFU), which seems to be engaged in policy bargaining with state organs, their power base and resources are by far below the CFU, whose interests dominate such policy 'negotiations'. It is, however, interesting to note that quite a number of Zimbabwe's black petit bourgeoisie emerged from households in this sector, and this class

State Farm Sector

The State Farm Sector began in the 1960s with state-controlled estates, intended for privatisation in the long-term, which were merged after independence into the Agriculture and Rural Development Authority (ARDA). ARDA operates eighteen large-scale estates, which are heavily mechanised and irrigated, and are located in marginal areas, and thus productively use large tracts of previously idle land. ARDA produces mainly cotton, wheat and tea, although individual estates have substantial crop diversity (see Table 18).[41] That ARDA has a fair degree of export orientation is self-evident, although its import-substitution thrust (wheat and rice) and its efforts to produce seeds for further multiplication and distribution are notable, and in line with stated government policies.

At independence, state-owned estates were conceived as one way of effecting the transformation to socialism through the following objectives:[40]

(a) to plan, coordinate, implement, promote and assist agricultural and rural development in Zimbabwe;
(b) to prepare and, with the agreement of the minister, to implement schemes for the betterment of agriculture or for rural development in any part of Zimbabwe;
(c) to plan, promote, coordinate and carry out schemes for the devlepoment, exploitation, utilisation, settlement or disposition of state land specified in the Third Schedule;
(d) any other functions and duties which may be imposed upon the Authority by any enactment.

ARDA's generalised mandate is to pursue any undertaking engaged in the development of any area and through its activities *benefiting the inhabitants of that area* including any mining, industrial, commercial, agricultural or forestry undertaking.

Some of the main transformation instruments of ARDA include:

(a) increasing national agricultural production and productivity through *state farming* and *the associated tenant farming* on each scheme;
(b) forging backward and forward linkages between production, processing and marketing of agricultural products wherever possible;
(c) engaging in the production of strategic agricultural commodities on a commercial basis. The three areas are food crops, seeds and breeding stock of all classes of livestock;
(d) acting as a stimulant to production and productivity to riparian farmers through provision of machinery and equipment renting services.

The programmes implied by some of these instruments include:

TABLE 18
ARDA ESTATES CROPS/PRODUCE DATA (1981-1985)

Crops/Produce	1981/82 Weight Sold (Tonnes)	1981/82 Income Received ($000's)	1982/83 Weight Sold (Tonnes)	1982/83 Income Received ($000's)	1983/84 Weight Sold (Tonnes)	1983/84 Income Received ($000's)	1984/85 Weight Sold (Tonnes)	1984/85 Income Received ($000's)
Barley	1,342	241	1,113	218	-	-	-	-
Burley Tobacco	2	4	3	4	5	6	-	-
Cotton	14,595	6,460	15,314	7,500	22,881	12,301	23,735	11,862
Green Coffee	51	81	78	146	584	1,143	515	2,130
Green Mealies	-	18	*	97	-	68	*	129
Groundnuts	475	122	753	200	862	262	309	183
Made Tea	471	529	594	1,091	787	2,941	830	2,341
Maize	9,530	819	3,555	425	4,110	528	3,872	750
Rice	1,280	317	746	**	708	423	802	114
Millet	-	-	55	10	-	-	-	-
Milk	-	-	1,429	446	3,905	1,352	4,217	1,657
Seed Beans	53	21	-	-	-	-	-	-
Sorghum	59	6	11	2	180	24	172	25
Michigan Pea Bean	-	-	-	-	-	-	20	26
Soya Beans	176	32	848	213	453	129	402	124
Sunflower	-	-	95	24	1	-	-	-
Sugar Beans	319	182	170	233	201	211	211	349
Virginia Tobacco	60	106	75	123	163	308	137	329
Vegetables	-	-	-	563	2,537	1,015	2,788	1,142
Wheat	20,768	3,821	11,312	2,489	13,243	3,241	15,475	4,289
TOTAL	49,171	12,759	34,922***	12,775	50,620	24,027	53,485	25,450

Source: 1. *ARDA Annual Report and Accounts: 1982/83*, p. 6
2. *ARDA Annual Report and Accounts: 1984/85*, p. 6

(a) *Pure state farms* which engage in the production of 'strategic commodities' such as breeding stock, seed and selected food crops;
(b) *Nucleus estates*, which primarily encourage individual tenant farmers to engage in technically sound production;
(c) *Agro-Industrial estates*, which integrate commodity production with processing.

One contradictory aspect of ARDA's estate operations in respect of long-term goals of socialising the economy is the nature and pattern of its labour utilisation. Table 19 shows that its overall permanent labour force has grown slightly from 1981 to 1985.

The growth, however, of casual labour on the estates has been fairly high, and the ratio of permanent to casual labour shows a high degree of casualised labour on the estates. This of course is related to cotton-, tea- and tobacco-packing and reflects the effects of the export-oriented production of ARDA. Indeed these labour processes on estates located in marginal natural regions, in proximity to numerous drought-stricken peasant households, appear to be like a new labour reserve phase in Zimbabwe.

Close analysis of the ARDA programmes[42] indicates a clear interest to maintain estates which are individually economically viable and competitive. Thus, although ARDA appears on the surface to be a major area of agrarian reform since independence, its required viability in capitalistic business terms places serious doubts on its relevance as a means of agrarian transformation. In fact, it would appear that some of ARDA's activities are contradictory to the short- and long-term transformational objectives.

One issue of relevance in this context is the nature of social relations of production that ARDA fosters and is reproducing. It appears that the state farms are managed and run in similar terms of labour utilisation and profitability as the white-owned farms. This 'good management' and 'profit-making' on individual estates is based on capitalistic social relations of production, albeit that profits are used for the development of other national projects. Furthermore, there are reports[43] that the social conditions[44] of workers (housing, health, etc.) on ARDA farms are in some cases worse than those in the LSCF sector.

To wit: ARDA was among the agro-industrial estates which apparently 'resisted' paying the new minimum wages of Z$143.00 per month in 1985, and as a result some of their estates were ridden with worker strikes.[45]

In the case of nucleus estates also, ARDA is promoting outgrower and tenant farming, which are specific forms of capitalist integration of the rural peasantry. This not only creates dependency and control relationships with peasants but also engenders 'kulakisation' through restricted tenant farmer selection. This merely consolidates the process of rural class differentiation which began in the colonial period, while estate farm development essentially augments the 'labour reserve' process.

TABLE 19
ARDA EMPLOYMENT PATTERNS (1981-1985)

Region	1981/82 P	1981/82 S	1982/83 P	1982/83 S	1983/84 P	1983/84 S	1984/85 P	1984/85 S
Lowveld	1,800	10,700	1,800	11,100	2,110	13,200	2,100	8,787
Manicaland	359	400	654	306	750	350	935	2,283
Mashonaland	602	1,600	1,008	1,288	1,010	1,516	895	1,741
Matabeleland	480	1,200	588	1,287	587	1,345	643	1,335
TOTALS	3,241	13,900	4,060	13,981	4,457	16,411	4,573	14,146

Source: 1. ARDA Annual Reports and Accounts: 1982/83, p. 7
Source: 2. ARDA Annual Reports and Accounts: 1984/85, p. 7
Key: P—Permanent employees
S—Seasonal employees

Regarding the predominant types of crops ARDA produces—mainly cotton, tea and other export crops—there seems to be a consolidation of macro economic 'export-led growth' policies (preferred by the IMF), which contradicts overall government policy to promote agro-industrialisation and integrated rural and national economic development.

In short, the role of ARDA as a vehicle for resolving the land question and spearheading agrarian transformation is clearly in doubt.

Concluding Remarks

This paper has shown the emergence of six agrarian subsectors as a result of the redistribution of largely poor land. The process has essentially left the LSCF in control of most of Zimbabwe's 'prime land'.

In the main, capital socialist relations of production in state farms, the Communal Areas and Individual Resettlement Schemes have been reinforced, while the process of social differentiation in the agricultural sector as a whole is increasing. That is: the agrarian structure and land control have altered slightly, but the process of uneven agrarian capitalist development, which began eighty years ago, has tended to be reinforced in the last six years.

Quite evidently—in spite of increased and equitable state support services to the blacks, land redistribution, the emergence of blacks in the LSCF and open unionisation of African farmers—the 'land question' *per se* remains unresolved.

Apart from continued 'squatter' settlements on state and private land, as well as the evident promotion of regional development associations' activities (such as the Manicaland Development Association) [46] the momentum and pressure for land redistribution has waned for now. Even the 1986-90 Five Year Development Plan[47] has very modest stated objectives and targets for land redistribution. Specifically, it is planned to resettle only 15,000 families annually, amounting to a total of 75,000 families.[48] This number of families, together with the approximately 36,000 already settled, would bring the total resettled in 10 years (if the plan's targets were achieved) to approximately 111,000 families. Interestingly, this figure would not meet the planned targets of 162,000 families, set in 1982 for a three-year period, by over 50,000 families.

It may well be that, for the time being, in spite of evident food shortages and increased unemployment among sections of the population, the social forces that initially fuelled the overt struggle around the 'land question' are themselves temporarily dissipated, given the 1986-90 plan's objective to continue to support expanded production in a variety of crops among Zimbabwe's peasantry. Whether projected growth rates of over 6% per year in the peasant subsector will be sustained may well determine the configuration of the 'land question' in the coming years.

Obviously the new class relations emerging, within a context of renewed confidence by local and foreign capital in Zimbabwe's investment climate, will continue to be the focus of contradictions between stated long-term agrarian policy objectives and the further entrenchment of capitalism.

Furthermore, since wage incomes are in general currently well below the average poverty datum line in Zimbabwe,[49] and while prospects for growth in agricultural employment are bleak, employment having in fact declined,[50] the increased demand for land seems to be the only logical alternative for the majority of the poor. In spite of this clear coincidence of economic hardships in both the rural and urban environments, there is no visual development of a (concretely programmed) worker-peasant alliance in terms of political organisation. However, the continued existence of 'worker-peasants' (engaged in rural contract/seasonal work and those in urban temporary work situations), as well as the continued reliance of rural households on remittances from urban incomes, which have gradually been eroded by inflation, and the reduction of food subsidies, may bring to the forefront the 'land question' again in its proper national and regional context.

REFERENCES

1. Government of Zimbabwe, *Growth with Equity: An Economic Policy Statement*, Government of Zimbabwe, February 1981.
2. Government of Zimbabwe.
(a) *Transitional National Development Plan. 1982/83-1984/85*, Vol. 1, Government of Zimbabwe, November 1982.
(b) *Transitional National Development Plan. 1982/83-1984/85*, Vol. 2, Government of Zimbabwe, May 1983.
3. *New York Guardian*, February 1985.
4. *Ibid.*
5. Shopo, T., *Political Economy of Hunger*, ZIDS Working Paper, p. 42.
6. *Ibid.*, p. 60.
7. Shumba, E., Application of the Farming Systems Research Approach in Mangwende Communal Area in the Murewa District, *Zimbabwe Agricultural Journal*, Vol. 82, No. 42, 1985.
8. Shopo, T., *op. cit.*
9. Harbeson, J.W., *Land and Rural Development in Independent Zimbabwe: A Preliminary Assessment*, USAID, Job 81, 1981.
10. (a) IBRD, *Zimbabwe: Land Sector Study*, draft, World Bank Report No. 5878—ZIM, 1985.
(b) World Bank, Zimbabwe Agricultural Sector Study, Report No. 4401—Zimbabwe, 1983.
(c) World Bank, 1982.
11. (a) Kinsey, B.H., Forever Gained: Resettlement and Land Policy in the context of National Development of Zimbabwe, *Africa*, Vol. 25, No. 3, 1982.
(b) Kinsey, B.H., Emerging Policy Issues in Zimbabwe's Land Resettlement Programmes, *Development Policy Review*, Vol. 1, No. 2, November 1983.
12. The Food and Agricultural Organisation of the United Nations.

13. (a) Whitsun Foundation, *Land Reform in Zimbabwe, Harare.*
(b) Whitsun Foundation, *A Strategy for Rural Development and Data Bank, No. 2: The Peasant Sector,* Harare, 1978.
14. EEC and OECD. Various country studies by the OECD and EEC have been done as background documents for aid agreements.
15. MLRRD, *Communal Lands Development Plan: A 15 Year Development Strategy* (1st Draft), Harare, Ministry of Lands Resettlement and Rural Development, 1985.
16. Hawkins Associates, *Investigation into the Intensity of Land Utilisation in Selected Farming Areas of Zimbabwe,* Washington, D.C., 1982.
17. Whitsun Foundation, *Land Reform in Zimbabwe, op. cit.*
18. Riddell, R.C., *The Land Problem in Rhodesia: Alternatives for the future,* Mambo Press, Harare, 1978.
19. (a) Moyo, S. and Weiner, D., *Land Use and Productivity: Myth or reality,* A ZIDS Work-in-Progress Paper (Mimeo), 1984.
(b) *Ibid.*
20. Weiner et al, Land Use and Agricultural Productivity in Zimbabwe, *Journal of Modern African Studies,* Vol. 23, No. 2, pp. 252-285.
21. (a) Kinsey, B.H., *Emerging Policy Issues in Zimbabwe Land Resettlement Programmes, op. cit.*
(b) Whitsun Foundation, *Land Reform in Zimbabwe, op. cit.*
22. Moyo, S. and Weiner, D., *op. cit.*
23. (a) Whitsun Foundation, *Land Reform in Zimbabwe, op. cit.*
(b) *Economist,* London, 21 April 1984.
24. (a) World Bank, *The Small Farm Credit Scheme,* Staff appraisal report, 1982.
(b) Moyo, S., *The Effects of Foreign Aid on Zimbabwe's Agriculture* , A proposal submitted to CODESRIA to be published soon.
25. Bratton, M., *Draft Power, Draft Exchange and Farmer Organisations,* Department of Land Management, University of Zimbabwe, Working Paper No. 9/84, 1984.
26. Mbengegwi, C., *Some aspects of Zimbabwe's Post Independence agricultural producer coops: a Profile and Preliminary Assessment,* Harare, University of Zimbabwe, 1984.
27. Moyo, S., *A Critical Evaluation of Methodologies Used to Study Producer Cooperatives,* A ZIDS work-in-progress paper on a study of Markoni OCCZIM district Union, 1986.
28. Cole, R.S., The Land Situation in Zimbabwe, *Report of Proceedings of Commonwealth Association of Surveying and Land Economy Seminar* held in Malawi, 3 April 1981 (London 1981).
29. Ministry of Lands, Agriculture and Resettlement, *Land Reform Policy Workshop,* September 1985.
30. ZANU (PF), *Zimbabwe: At 5 Years of Independence; Achievements, Problems and Prospects,* ZANU (PF) Department of the Commissariat and Culture, Harare, 1985, p. 2.
31. CSO, *Zimbabwe 1982 Population Census, Main Demographic Features of the Population of Zimbabwe: an Advance Report based on a Ten Percent Sample,* Central Statistical Office, Harare, 1985.

32. These estimates of percentage returns to the peasant households from crop sales have been estimated from field studies in Mashonaland provinces by this author over the last eighteen months. Estimates are based on prices paid by middlemen.
33. Mumbengegwi, C., *Some Observations on the Problems and Prospects of Socialist Transformation in Zimbabwe*, 20th International Summer Seminar on Planning for Development and Social Progress in Socialist and Developing Countries, University of Economic Science, Bruno Leischner, GDR, Berlin, June 1983.
34. CSO, *ICA Crop Production Statistics—1981/1982 Crop Season* Harare, 1983, and *Crop Production of Commercial Farms, 1982*, Harare, 1983.
35. Chikanza et al, The Health Status of Farm Worker Communities in Zimbabwe' *Central African Journal of Medicine*, Vol. 27, No. 5, 1981.
36. CSO *ICA Crop Production Statistics—1981/82, op. cit.*
37. Moyo, S. and Weiner, D., *op. cit.*
38. Weiner et al, *op. cit.*
39. Cheater, A.P., *Idioms of Accumulation: Rural Development and Class Formation Among Freeholders in Zimbabwe*, Mambo Press, Harare, 1983.
40. ARDA, *Arda Functions, Policies, Strategies and Projects*, Agricultural and Rural Development Authority, Harare, 1983.
41. ARDA, *Arda Annual Report and Accounts: 1984/85*, 1986.
42. ARDA, *ARDA Functions, Policies, Strategies and Projects, op. cit.*
43. See various issues of *The Herald*, 1983 to 1984. Personal visits in 1983 to some estates confirm this although current ARDA social service expenditures (see *ARDA, Annual Report and Accounts: 1984-85*) conceivably could have improved these conditions.
44. Comparisons may be made with the findings of Sachikonye et al., *Conditions of Work and Life of Women in the Food Processing Industries in Zimbabwe*, ZIDS Working Paper (Mimeo) 1984.
45.(a) *The Financial Gazette*, 9 August 1985, p. 13.
(b) *The Financial Gazette*, 27 September 1985, p. 25.
46. The Manicaland Development Association was formed by top officials in government and other organisations and businessmen to facilitate development programmes within that province. This in itself is not a harmful activity (in fact it may be quite useful), but there is a tendency for it to engender regional political strife through provincial biddings for resources allocation. Although this has not specifically emerged in Zimbabwe, the experiences of such associations in other African countries (particularly in West Africa) has shown numerous cases of internal strife resulting from such associations.
47. Government of Zimbabwe, *1986-1990 Five Year Development Plan Vol. 1, 1986, April 1,* Government Printers, Harare, 1986.
48. *Ibid.*, p. 28,.
49. Mutandare, J.I., *The Herald,* 1 May 1985.
50. Shopo, T. and Moyo, S., *The Valuable Labour Segments of Zimbabwe*, a consultancy report to the ILO.

7. CONTINUITY AND CHANGE IN AGRICULTURAL POLICY
Clever Mumbengegwi

Introduction

A number of writers have convincingly argued that Zimbabwe's early agricultural history is an account of the triumph of white agriculture over the indigenous African farmers. This was achieved through purposive and systematic measures designed to serve minority settler class interests. The key actor in this triumphant story was the state, over which the white farmers had the dominant influence. The range of policy instruments utilised by the settler regime to achieve its objectives included physical and political coercion of African peasants, legislative discrimination and a host of direct economic measures designed to disadvantage the indigenous farmers *vis-à-vis* the white settlers. The pursuit of such discriminatory policies was given internal momentum initially by the British South African Company's failure to find a 'Second Rand', then by the devastating economic effects of the Great Depression of the 1930s and by the settler elite's vision of white supremacy for all time.

By the time the Rhodesia Front party declared independence unilaterally in November 1965, the agricultural sector had developed into a distinctively dualistic structure made up of what is now called the Large Scale Commercial Farming sector (formerly white areas) and the Communal Areas (previously called Tribal Trust Lands). Thus, the thrust of agricultural policy during the UDI period was aimed at maintaining the dominance of white agriculture and perpetuating the lopsided pattern of development that had already evolved over preceding decades.

Independence (18 April 1980), ushered in a new political reality, necessitating the dismantling of this lopsided pattern of development. Despite this, agricultural policy over the first five years of independence (1980-85) displays the absence of any sharp discontinuity with that of the UDI period (1965-79). In some circles, this has been hailed as the key to Zimbabwe's post-independence agricultural 'success story'. Yet there has been some change in emphasis, if not in direction, that may have contributed to that apparent success. What were the policies pursued both before and after independence? What post-independence policy changes can be identified and wherein lie the elements of continuity? What are the implications of this continuity and change on Zimbabwe's desired transition to socialist agriculture? How real is Zimbabwe's image as an agricultural success story? These are some of the questions and issues this chapter addresses.

The chapter is divided into four sections. The first gives a brief outline and assessment of agricultural policy during the UDI period. This background is necessary to understand the current conjuncture and the problems of transforming the structure of the agricultural sector. The second deals with the theme of 'continuity and change' and examines the policy changes that occurred after independence, highlighting the transitional problematic facing Zimbabwean policy-makers. The third draws on the implications of this 'continuity and change' on Zimbabwe's long-term prospects for socialist agricultural transformation. The fourth is a summary of both the main issues and the conclusions.

Agricultural Policy During UDI (1965-79)

The act of UDI, and the subsequent imposition of economic sanctions, to a large extent determined the policy objectives of the period. Sanctions meant increasing difficulty in the procurement of imported inputs and consumer items, loss of easy access to foreign markets, and increasing political and economic isolation from the rest of the world. This necessitated inward-looking policies. This import substitution meant minimum importation of agricultural commodities that could be produced locally and curtailment of production of those that could not be exported with ease. Thus, four major objectives were pursued during the UDI period, namely:

(a) stimulation of growth in aggregate agricultural output;
(b) attainment of self-sufficiency especially in food production and raw materials;
(c) diversification in the structure and output composition of the sector;
(d) maximisation of foreign exchange earnings.

The policy instruments chosen were intended to guarantee that the commercial farmers played the pivotal role in the pursuit of the regime's objectives. Increased state intervention in directing and allocating resources became a necessity to ensure Rhodesia's survival in a hostile world. These can be categorised into two groups. There were the broad instruments designed to provide aggregate incentives to commercial farmers to stay on the land and were non-discriminatory across crops or lines of production. The second group were specifically targeted instruments designed to promote each objective and hence could be discriminatory across lines of production. Among the first group of instruments were political and legislative discrimination, pricing, marketing, credit, taxes and subsidies, and low agricultural wages.

More than other instruments, political and legislative discrimination was meant to instil white farmers' confidence in the regime. The Land Tenure Act of 1969, which adjusted the 1930 Land Apportionment Act guiding the racial division of land, and the continued forced movement of peasants out of 'white areas' are examples of such instruments. The removal of Chief Rekai Tangwena and his people from Gaeresi Ranch is a good example of these punitive measures. Pricing instruments played a pivotal role in maintaining the economic viability of the commercial farm sector. During the first decade of UDI, post-planting producer price determination was the usual practice but due to the economy-wide boom that prevailed, producer prices were very favourable. However, from 1974 onwards, the economy as a whole experienced a steady downturn due to both domestic and international factors. The system of post-planting producer pricing began to falter and there was loss of confidence and uncertainty among farmers. Thus, in 1975, the regime introduced the system of pre-planting producer prices for all 'controlled crops' to stave off the effects of this uncertainty. These are minimum guaranteed prices announced in advance of the planting season so that farmers can plan the output mix that maximises their returns to factors. This proved a powerful policy instrument to the government since producer prices can be manipulated in such a way that farmers, through their individualistic pursuit of self-interest, can respond in a manner consistent with the national objectives. The other advantage of pre-planting prices is that they reduced, for farmers, the price uncertainties associated with primary product markets.

Pricing in Zimbabwe has always been closely linked with marketing, especially for controlled crops that are marketed through statutory authorities. State intervention in both pricing and marketing began with the Maize Control Acts of 1931 and 1934, which logically led to the establishment of the Grain Marketing Board and the Cold Storage Commission in 1937. This system of elaborate statutory control over marketing was reinforced during the UDI period. The Agricultural Marketing Authority (AMA) was set up in 1967 to assume responsibility for all statutory boards and an advisory role to the Ministry of Agriculture on pricing and marketing policy matters. This was followed in 1969 by the establishment of the Cotton Marketing Board (CMB). More crops were added to the list of controlled products. A unique feature of marketing in Zimbabwe, even up to today, is that the boards absorb all the losses on the trading account and do not appropriate any surplus that may arise therefrom. This is achieved through the system of 'supplementary payments' where the board makes an interim payment to the farmer on the sale of his product. At the end of the marketing year, if a surplus has been made on any individual crop's trading account, the board distributes this to the producers but if a deficit is made, it is absorbed and financed by the exchequer as a direct subsidy to producers and/or consumers. Thus the marketing boards, unlike in most developing countries, were and still are used as instruments to support farmers rather than extracting a surplus or a tax from them. Jansen[2] has established that only groundnut producers were implicitly taxed while all other crops were subsidised.

The tax laws made it very difficult to estimate commercial farmers' taxable income. This, combined with generally low rates of taxation and the various credits and grants, made for added incentives to commercial production. Riddell estimates that in 1977, only 1,419 of the estimated

6,000 commercial farmers paid any tax[3] while a Rhodesia National Farmers' Union (RNFU) report said that in 1978, 40% of white farmers were technically insolvent but continued operations through massive state subsidies and grants.[4] Subsidies operated both in the input and output markets, with the result that some producers were kept in production at the price of increasing inefficiency. Credit was another vital instrument when discrimination in favour of commercial farmers was practised. Virtually all the credit and financial institutions were geared to assisting the commercial farmers to the total exclusion of the peasants. It was not until 1978 that a small farm credit scheme to which peasants could have access was established.

In addition to all the above instruments, a deliberate policy of low wages for agricultural workers to keep costs of production down and to increase profitability was systematically pursued. Although agriculture was the biggest employer of labour, accounting for 33% of formal wage employment in the economy, its wage bill was only 6% of the national total, whereas agricultural earnings were 25% of the national earnings. These broad instruments worked to instil confidence as well as provide incentives for production and growth to commercial farmers. Due to the institutional bottlenecks imposed by the regime their incentive effects on peasant producers was negligible.

As noted earlier, some policy instruments were targeted to the achievement of a specific objective. Diversification was one such objective which assumed an important position in agricultural policy. This arose largely from the production structure of the sector at UDI. In 1965, flue-cured tobacco dominated the sector. It was the biggest contributor to gross value of agricultural output, foreign exchange earnings and wage employment. It was the single crop hardest hit by economic sanctions, as this meant loss of lucrative overseas markets and increasingly difficult export channels. Thus, this objective aimed at diversification out of tobacco into the production of other crops, particularly food grains. The instruments used combined incentives to other crops and disincentives to tobacco-growing. Generous loans and cheap credit were advanced to those farmers who responded to the government's objective. Stoneman notes that in 1975 Z$111 million in cheap credit was extended to some 6,200 commercial farmers;[5] a figure which had mounted to Z$153 million by 1980. Riddell also estimates that subsidies to tobacco farmers in the late 1960s were in the order of Z$88 million.[6] Incentive prices were also instituted for alternative crops, especially maize, wheat, cotton, soya beans and coffee, to encourage movement out of tobacco farming. Since tobacco has always been marketed freely on the auction floors, price policy was not a significant instrument open to government. The disincentive instruments applied were quantitative restrictions on area planted and marketing quotas to keep production and marketing low. Sometimes the government bought the quotas from farmers to regulate the quantity coming on to the auction floors. At one time there were no less than two or three quota brokers in Salisbury. The Tobacco Cooperative was established in 1966 for the sole purpose of buying excess tobacco from farmers, arranging storage and eventual disposal on international markets. As a result of these measures, the share of tobacco in gross value of output declined from 80% in 1965 to 28% in 1969.

Food self-sufficiency as an explicit objective dates back to the 1940s when promotion of maize production was pursued through guaranteed prices based on sample surveys of production costs.[7] By 1955, the country had become self-sufficient in the major staple grain, maize. After UDI, the increased procurement difficulties and foreign exchange constraints gave food security and self-sufficiency added importance. All the nation's wheat requirements were previously satisfied from imports. A vigorous import substitution programme under winter irrigation was initiated. Promotion of maize, wheat, sorghum, oilseeds and other small grains became the central focus of this policy objective. The main policy instruments used were:

(a) incentive producer prices which were fixed above import or export parity;
(b) assured and efficient marketing through statutory boards;
(c) budgetary subsidies where necessary;
(d) irrigation support in the case of wheat.

These instruments, added to the disincentives attendant to tobacco, enabled the country to achieve the objective within a relatively short period of time.

The policy objectives of growth, diversification and food self-sufficiency constituted an important substituting strategy whose other purpose was to conserve the already dwindling foreign currency reserves. There was also need to promote industrial raw material crops, notably cotton, to complement the country's import substitution industrial policy. It was noted earlier that tobacco was the major foreign exchange earner the international marketing of which had become both costly and demanding in sanctions-busting expertise. The policy instruments used with respect to agriculture's role in conserving foreign exchange involved elaborate planning, machinations and imaginative pieces of ad-hockery to produce domestically what was previously imported, curtail production of those crops that could not easily be exported and to made sanctions by exporting at deflated prices through third parties, notably South Africa.

All the above policies and instruments were adopted by the UDI regime to cope with the economic realities of the time and to pursue its vision of the future. How effective were the instruments used in the achievement of the objectives? To answer this question is no easy task, for three reasons. Firstly, it should be clear that agricultural performance cannot be wholly explained in terms of the purely economistic policy instruments outlined previously. However, it cannot be denied that theirs was the dominant influence especially in the first ten years of UDI (1965-75). Secondly, the dualistic structure of the agricultural sector poses serious difficulties for standard performance evaluation given the structural interdependency and exploitative relationship between the commercial and communal subsectors. Stoneman has noted that:

the two sectors, although totally different in character and separated from each other geographically, institutionally and in most other ways, have been, and to a large extent still are, closely related through their competition with each other for land, labour, capital and markets.[8]

The difficulty arises from the discriminatory application of the described policy instruments. To evaluate agricultural policy during UDI is in fact to discuss the fortunes of white commercial agriculture and the continued underdevelopment and impoverishment of the communal sector. While theoretically, pricing and marketing policy instruments were not discriminatory, the institutional framework within which they operated for the communal farmers rendered them just as blatantly discriminatory as the instruments relating to land alienation, credit provision, subsidies, taxation, extension and general infrastructural provision.

Thirdly, data for the communal sector for this period is either generally poor or unavailable for a more disaggregative performance evaluation exercise. However, within the limitations of this data, we indicate to the extent possible the performance of the two sectors, and their respective roles in achieving the government's four-pronged policy objectives.

In aggregate terms, the growth performance of agriculture was impressive during the first decade of UDI (1965-74). Real value of aggregate output grew at 7.8% p.a., 1% above the economy-wide growth rate. A characteristic of this growth in both sectors is that it was derived from expansion in area cultivated rather than intensive utilisation of existing land. In the communal sector, area under cultivation increased by 26% while crop production rose by 32% over the same period. Thus 81% of growth in crop production was due to land expansion, and this means that factor productivity growth has been an insignificant factor in the growth of peasant production. In fact, some studies have painted a more pessimistic picture than this. The same pattern is repeated in the commercial sector but on a somewhat reduced scale. While the greater part of growth was due to factor productivity increases (56%), land expansion accounted for a significant 41%. A growth pattern based on the extension of a finite resource could not be sustained as the basis of development indefinitely. It was a matter of time before the growth bubble burst, as land, especially in the communal areas, became the critical constraint. The artificial restrictions imposed by the Land Tenure Act coupled with the growing rural population meant extension of cultivation into marginal areas, more often than not at the expense of grazing land. Given that the communal farming system was dependent on animal traction power, de-stocking was no viable option either. The outcome was overpopulation of the communal areas. It is worth emphasising that these effects were no new creations of the UDI regime, but were the deliberate policies of all preceding colonial regimes.

For the same period, marketed output from both sectors increased considerably and employment creation was second to the manufacturing sector. Job creation in commercial agriculture was, on average, expanding at the rate of 6,800 per year. The data on farmers' net incomes is not readily available, although the estimates indicate a corresponding improvement in commercial farm incomes.

From 1974 onwards, with the intensification of the liberation war, world recession, oil price increases, foreign exchange shortages, military call-ups and greater government expenditure on defence, there was an economy-wide economic downturn. Agriculture was more severely affected by these factors, which rendered the policy instruments for the achievement of this objective ineffective. Between 1975 and 1979 real output decreased by 8% such that by the end of UDI per capita agricultural output stood below the 1965 level. The decline was more severe in the communal areas, where discriminatory policies combined with the domestic and international recession had added negative effects. Factor productivities showed a continuous downward trend up to 1979. Thus, the last five years of UDI saw an erosion of the gains that had been made in the initial decade. Overall the growth performance of agriculture was characterised by an initial upswing and then a steady decline leading up to independence. Since there was no change in the kit of policy instruments for promoting growth, it is a reasonable inference that the relative decline in performance in the twilight of UDI was due to factors exogenous to the instruments. However, with respect to the intensification of the war it could be seriously argued that the demise of UDI was accelerated by the discriminatory application of these very same instruments.

In the context of growing food deficits in most of sub-Saharan Africa over the last two decades, Zimbabwe has been hailed as a success story in that it is one of the few exceptional countries that have been able to achieve and maintain a reasonable degree of self-sufficiency in food production. Starting from a position of importing all its wheat requirements in 1965, it became self-sufficient in wheat by 1972 and by 1979 it was 39% above domestic requirements. However, these global statistics conceal the intra-sectoral syndrome of chronic food deficits in the communal areas. Several studies have suggested that the growth of cotton and other cash crops in the communal areas was at the expense of food production. This, coupled with the increasing rural population, meant that by the mid-1970s communal areas were net importers of food from the commercial sector. Thus, food self-sufficiency was achieved only in global terms such that over the entire UDI period, food imports were necessary only during drought years.

Diversification was the most impressive dimension of performance achieved. As noted earlier, in 1965, tobacco accounted for 80% of the value of agricultural output. Through the policy instruments outlined, the sector expanded production of maize, wheat, and cotton which could easily be substituted for tobacco. Tobacco's share in output declined threefold while cotton increased from a 3% share in 1965 to an average share of 22% for the 1970-4 period. The corresponding figures for wheat and maize are 0%:8% and 14%:28% respectively. Other crops such as soya beans, sorghum, coffee and groundnuts also emerged during this period. By the end of UDI, the crop mix of the sector had become more balanced than at the beginning. Livestock production was also another crucial line of the diversification process. Beef herds in the commercial sector almost doubled between 1965 and 1977 as a result of increased mixed farming in the tobacco-growing areas.

Continuity and Change: Agricultural Policy and Performance Since Independence (1980-85)

It has been suggested in the foregoing that agricultural policies and instruments during the UDI period were fairly consistent with the achievement of the regime's objectives, especially over the initial decade. Thus, at independence (1980), the new government inherited not only a lopsided dualistic agricultural sector but also a pampered, powerful and yet hostile white agrarian bourgeoisie which had to be handled with extreme caution lest it frustrate the government's policies and programmes of transforming and restructuring the agricultural sector. Policy towards agriculture had of necessity to be cautious and pragmatic, not just because of the manner with which independence was achieved but, more so, because of the structural dependency of the economy on the commercial farmers for the satisfaction of some of the new government's objectives. In 1980, the commercial sector accounted for 75% of gross output, 95% of marketed surplus, nearly 100% of agricultural export earnings and 33% of the national formal wage employment. In terms of factor productivities, land and labour were, respectively, six and seven times greater than in the communal areas.

These statistics, notwithstanding recent attempts to argue the contrary,[9] provided powerful ammunition for the commercial farmers' lobby, the Commercial Farmers, Union (CFU), to portray the commercial sector as containing the success rather than the failure elements for Zimbabwe's future agricultural development.[10]

Thus they sought to preserve the inherited structure of agriculture, with minor adjustments to the racial division of land. On the other hand, the peasants saw the essence of political independence as the satisfaction of their land hunger and the reversal of the discriminatory elements of colonial agricultural policies. Therefore, the real problematic for the state was how to effect peasant-biased transformation without offending the 'efficiency' and 'productivity' counter-arguments posed by the commercial farmers. This problematic is clearly reflected in the adoption of the reassuring catch-phrase *Growth with Equity*[11] as the government's first economic policy statement. However, it is conventionally well-known that, where equity issues are pitted against efficiency arguments, it is the former that usually suffer; and this is what appears to have happened, with the result that policies pursued during the first five years of independence reflect greater continuity than radical departure from those of the UDI period.

The policy objectives in agriculture were outlined in the policy statement *Growth with Equity* and elaborated upon in the *Transitional National*

Development Plan.[12] Agriculture and rural development were singled out as top priority in the government's development plans. Socialist transformation was the broad framework within which policies were to be formulated. Both documents list ten objectives which vividly illustrate the nature of the transitional policy problematic and the conflicting interests of the commercial and communal (peasant) farmers. These objectives can be divided into those oriented towards maintaining the *status quo* and thus reassuring the commercial farmers of their traditional role and contribution to the economy; and those that can be termed 'restructuring transformationist' objectives. The former included growth in aggregate output, domestic food self-sufficiency, regional food security within the context of SADCC and the extension of the role of agriculture as a foreign exchange earner. What is of significance is the omission of diversification as an explicit objective, implying that the sector's output mix had reached a more or less optimal combination.

This set of objectives is identical with those for the UDI period, and were pursued through the same policy instruments as before. Hence we shall not discuss them any further, except to note that it is in these that the elements of continuity in policy are located. The latter group of objectives are the most important and politically difficult to implement. They were designed to redress the imbalance between the two subsectors and transform the structure and character of agriculture in Zimbabwe.

It is in this set of objectives that the elements of change can be found. Specifically, they aimed at achieving an acceptable and fair distribution of land ownership, elimination of discriminatory practices in output pricing, input provision, marketing, credit, extension, infrastructure and the provision of other back-up services; and raising peasant incomes through productivity-raising measures.

The same transitional policy problematic noted for objectives is reflected in the articulation of the government's strategy. The TNDP stipulates socialist agrarian transformation, involving the 'integration of commercial and peasant sectors into a national agricultural system' as its long-term goal. However, in the short term, it advocates 'the establishment of a number of production systems'. This short-term strategy in agriculture was discussed elsewhere[13] as involving (a) the development of the peasant sector on communal tenure basis by use of productivity-raising inputs, (b) retention of the commercial sector to ensure short-run stability in food supplies, employment and foreign exchange earnings and (c) gradual establishment of a socialised sector through the introduction of producer co-operatives and state farms. But on how this short-term tactic translates into the long-term strategy for socialist integration of the two sectors, the TNDP is silent.

The policy instruments for the achievement of the 'restructuring transformationist' objectives included land redistribution, which is discussed in greater detail in chapter six of this volume. However, to the extent that land policy and its distribution constitute the central issue in Zimbabwe's agricultural *conundrum*, it merits brief treatment in the context of this chapter. Neither the Zimbabwean government nor the peasantry are particularly happy about the manner in which the constitution curtails the state's ability effectively to implement a comprehensive land reform programme. Expropriation or nationalisation of land for purposes of redistribution are deemed unconstitutional. Compensation for all land compulsorily purchased (not expropriated) has to be paid in foreign currency. Thus the sole instrument by which land can be redistributed to the peasants is through acquisition at full market price on a 'willing seller-willing buyer' basis. The financial resources required to implement this are of such a magnitude as would seriously impinge on other development activities. This constitutional constraint has had a debilitating effect on policy formulation to an extent where, five years after independence, Zimbabwe has not been able to come up with a comprehensive policy on land distribution, tenure or the whole vexed question of agrarian reform. The Land Acquisition Act recently passed by parliament is an attempt to shatter the shackles imposed by the constitution.

Despite these legal constraints, some progress has been made in land redistribution. Between 1980 and 1985, 2.5 million hectares were acquired for redistribution to some 35,000 peasant families at a cost of Z$53.6 million. This however falls far short of the government's target of 162,000 families in three years, which some estimate requires nine million hectares or 60% of the commercial land as at 1980.[14] As has been outlined in chapter six, several features characterise the land redistribution exercise. Initially, abandoned or underutilised land was the prime acquisition target and hence land resettlement proceeded much faster without serious opposition from commercial farmers.

However, after the first three years, 'willing seller-willing buyer' land tended to dry up and prices rose significantly, due to a combination of better agro-ecological conditions and unavailability of willing sellers. As a result, land purchase prices rose by 48% between 1980 and 1985. The redistribution exercise did not so much lead to relief of population pressure among existing peasant farmers but provided livelihood to the landless, the urban unemployed and those with insufficient land. This took place as a resettlement programme under technocratic methods of implementation rather than through popular participation and mass mobilisation. The models of resettlement are described in greater detail in chapter six of this volume.

Although it has been argued that the magnitude of the resettlement exercise—notwithstanding its failure to achieve the targets—is unparalleled in the history of land resettlement in Africa,[15] questions still remain as to the effectiveness of the exercise and its potential in redressing the imbalance in the distribution of land. So far the impact of the programme has only been marginal, benefiting less than 5% of the estimated 800,000 peasant families in the communal areas and taking up 16% of the commercial farm land. The communal area population increase alone over the same period far outstrips the resettled numbers. The logical conclusion seems to be that, no matter how impressive or extensive the programme in the future, resettlement alone can never be a lasting solution to the land question. Perhaps the answer lies not so much in the exercise itself as in a combination of this and other policy instruments to remove the discriminatory aspects of colonial policies, especially in areas of output pricing, credit provision, marketing and expansion of back-up facilities.

Regarding post-independence producer pricing policies, there was no fundamental shift in the mechanism of fixing producer prices. However, there was a move towards improvement of the peasants' institutional framework such that the pricing policy changes that took place were more implicit than explicit. Over the years, producer price fixing has been a matter of great complexity, involving prolonged negotiations between producers' associations and government. Although pricing decisions were, and sometimes still are, made on an *ad hoc* basis in response to seasonal crises, there have always been, since the UDI period, some basic long-term pricing principles involved.

While for any one season it may be difficult to identify the dominating factor in arriving at the particular set of prices, the following were, and still are, the main principles guiding the long term trends in agricultural producer prices.

(a) Market realities expected during the marketing year.
(b) Market realisations from both domestic and international disposals.
(c) Production costs.
(d) Impact of any proposed set of prices on the marketing boards' trading accounts and any consequent budgetary implications on the treasury.
(e) Resource allocation efficiency.
(f) Implications of any proposed set of prices on domestic wage goods.
(g) International price competitiveness in the case of exportable commodities.

Towards the final stages of UDI, there was a gradual shift towards laying greater emphasis on costs of production when fixing producer prices in order to guarantee a reasonable return to the farmer. However, the costs taken into account were consciously those of the commercial farmers. The rationale is given in the following quotation (from a policy statement by the Ministry of Agriculture, December 1978):

> It may be objected that the producer prices are determined in the interest of commercial agriculture and do not recognise the contribution of small-scale and peasant production. Such production, however, is generally at a much lower cost of production and producer prices set with the commercial sector in mind should therefore provide a handsome return to these farmers in respect of their disposable surplus. Data collection for the small-scale farmer is improving and their economics of production can be monitored. If it becomes evident that producer prices are inadequate to meet the production costs of small-scale farmers,

this would be sufficient cause for revision of these prices. *In short, we can expect the producer prices set for commercial agriculture to provide a price umbrella for all stages of agriculture* (our emphasis).

Whether or not the above argument holds is an empirical and interesting question for further research. However, apart from the racial and ideological bias in the quotation, there are a number of factors that immediately suggest that peasant costs of production may be higher or at least not much lower than those of the commercial farmers.

Peasant farmers are generally in the poorer agro-ecological regions, and hence require more input application to achieve comparable yields per unit area or, conversely, realise lower yields for the same input application.

Furthermore, the communal areas are poorly served with roads, transport and marketing infrastructure such that they have higher unit costs for input and greater unit costs on delivering output to Marketing Board depots. Also, the small-scale nature of operations means that they cannot realise the pecuniary economies from high-volume input purchases and output deliveries. All these factors suggest that peasants may well have higher costs of production than those considered when fixing producer prices. After independence, there has been explicit theoretical recognition of these factors, but in practice, pricing policy decisions continue to be made on the basis of commercial farm costs due to continuing paucity of data. The net effect is inadvertently to continue with the past discriminatory elements in producer price fixing.

However, whether or not pricing is an effective instrument of policy is a subject of much debate in the literature. One is, however, persuaded by the argument that pricing policy can only be relevant as a fine tuning instrument in an environment with a well-developed infrastructure and a high degree of market participation or orientation among farmers. Producer price manipulation is irrelevant to the farmer if he/she has no easy physical access to markets or the marketing costs are so high as completely to erode the incentive element in the price.

Temu has correctly pointed to the common misconception in procucer price analysis that regards the government-announced price as the producer price.[16] In fact, the real producer price is what the farmer actually receives after meeting all the transport and other marketing deductions. The more isolated the farmer is from marketing and infrastructural facilities, the lower is the producer price. Given the inherited unevenness in the provision of these facilities, it stands to reason that communal farmers in Zimbabwe generally face lower real prices for their products.

In recognition of the above difficulties, improvement in marketing facilities became the focus of communal area development. The effect of improving marketing facilities has been to reduce farmers' costs and increase the real price for output delivered to the marketing boards. Organisationally, there have been few changes in the marketing system.

The most significant change has been the quantitative expansion in marketing depots in the communal areas and the inclusion into the category of controlled crops of the minor grains, *munga* and *rapoko*, which are largely grown by communal farmers. The government planning policy documents aim at each farmer being no further than 40 kilometres from a Grain Marketing Board (GMB) depot. However, this target has not as yet been achieved due to financial constraints. To alleviate the situation, the GMB has operated a system of seasonal collection points depending on the forecast crop yield for the season in a particular area. While this represents a significant improvement, high transport costs and long distances to the nearest depots remain the biggest marketing constraints to communal farmers.

Even in this system of collection points are embedded some disadvantages, as the communal farmer has to bear not only the full cost of transport from his/her farm to the nearest collection point but also that from the collection point to the nearest GMB depot at the rate of $1.00 per bag or $10.00 per tonne, whereas the commercial farmer who is nearer, and delivers directly to the depot, does not have to bear similar costs. While there has been an increase in direct deliveries by peasants registered as producers with the GMB, a significant proportion of communal farmers still market their output through approved buyers or co-operative associations with no guarantee that they receive the full price for crops delivered. Although no systematic study of the farmers' net producer price has been undertaken, it is generally accepted that approved buyers pay a lower than prescribed price, either by undergrading the crops delivered or overpricing goods sold to the farmer tied to the purchase of grain. In most cases, approved buyers are rural traders and shop owners.

Up to 1978/9, credit to the communal sector was virtually non-existent. Thus, the major element of change in credit policy in agriculture was not the reduction of credit to commercial farmers but its expansion to communal areas. The state-owned Agricultural Finance Corporation (AFC) (formed in 1971) is the major source of communal area credit. It operates three lending programmes.

(a) Short-Term Loans: these are loans to finance seasonal inputs like seeds, fertilisers, agricultural chemicals and hired labour. They are repayable within twenty-four months.
(b) Medium-Term Loans: these loans are granted for the purchase of capital equipment and major farm implements and are repayable within a period of two to five years.
(c) Long-Term Loans: this type of loan is for long-term capital development such as land purchase and construction of irrigation facilities. It is repayable within a period of up to twenty years.

Although theoretically these programmes are open to both peasant and commercial farmers, in practice, communal farmers have access only to seasonal loans. The major constraint is the small-scale nature of

TABLE 1
AGRICULTURAL FINANCE CORPORATION LENDING BY CATEGORY OF FARMERS 1978-85

Year	Communal Farmers No. of Loans in 000's	Communal Farmers Amount Z$m	Resettlement Farmers No. of Loans in 000's	Resettlement Farmers Amount Z$m	Small Scale Commercial Farmers No. of Loans in 000's	Small Scale Commercial Farmers Amount Z$m	Large Scale Commercial Farmers No. of Loan in 000's	Large Scale Commercial Farmers Amount Z$m
1978/9	-	-	-	-	1.3	1.1	2.7	69.0
1979/80	2.5	0.6	-	-	1.9	1.0	2.2	75.6
1980/1	18.0	4.8	-	-	3.3	3.1	2.5	87.5
1981/2	30.2	10.1	0.9	0.4	3.5	4.5	2.1	88.8
1982/3	38.9	13.2	4.2	1.5	2.9	4.5	1.7	88.7
1983/4	50.0	23.4	18.3	8.3	2.5	5.9	1.3	96.2
1984/5	68.6	24.7	22.6	12.2	2.0	8.6	1.5	110.7

Source: AFC Annual Reports

communal production, which results in low incomes and repayment difficulties. The absence of acceptable collateral conflicts with the AFC's requirement for its own financial prudence. Generally, the communal farmer fails to satisfy the loan conditions which are required for access to the medium- and long-term loans. Table 1 shows the extent of AFC lending to communal and commercial farmers for the period 1978/79 to 1984/85.

The data confirms a significant expansion in communal farmer credit since independence. Over the five-year period, the numbers of successful loan applicants increased by 96% while the volume of loans increased by 98%. This phenomenal expansion, covering 68,600 successful applicants in 1984/85, represents only 8% of communal farmers, while the $24.7 million is only 16% of total AFC lending to the agricultural sector. Although in comparison with the narrow base year average figures, this is quite impressive, credit provision still excludes the majority of communal farmers. In per capita terms, commercial farmers receive 205 times the average loan to communal farmers. A further aspect of communal area credit provision is that loans are tied to the purchase of specific inputs and delivery of output to the marketing boards via a system of stop orders. This is done in the interest of easier loan recovery by the AFC. Thus, the farmer is the residual recipient of any proceeds from sale of his crops. This situation therefore tends to work better for and favours those farmers whose scale of operations results in marketed surpluses and who hence have greater chances of receiving AFC loans. Small and poor peasants, whose output in most years is only sufficient for their own consumption and who would not normally deliver output to marketing boards, are excluded. The implication is that the expansion in communal area credit has been directed more towards the larger and richer peasant, thus raising the possibility of intensified rural stratification. This is a point also raised by Sam Moyo in the previous chapter.

In terms of reducing the differentials between the commercial and communal areas, the post-independence policy on credit expansion has thus succeeded in narrowing the relative rather than the absolute gap, and a lot more still needs to be done to expand credit to the poorer peasants who either are going without it or rely on informal sources or remittances from urban areas. Credit expansion is imperative, since it plays an important role in small farmer growth in production, productivity and incomes. Without finance, the farmer can neither adopt new high productivity technology and inputs nor market his output through official channels, since to do so he has to be a registered producer with the Grain Marketing Board. Despite the three years of drought 1981-1982 to 1983-1984, there was real growth in aggregate output of 16% over the entire period.

With the exception of the 1982-83 season, which recorded a -6%, growth in all other years was positive in real terms. However, the most significant feature of performance relevant to the post-independence policies is the structural change in the composition of output between the two subsectors. While the commercial sector has continued to grow in absolute terms, its relative share in aggregate output and marketed surplus has been declining. The corollary to this development is the gradual emergence of the communal sector from the pre-independence stagnation. A most notable feature is the increase in the peasants' degree of market participation as shown from two indicators. In 1980, the peasants' share of crop sales to/through marketing boards was 6%. By 1984, this had increased more than twofold to 15%. Maize deliveries, which make up the bulk of peasants' marketed output, rose from 11% to 41%, indicating that communal farmers may soon play a leading role in the production of the nation's staple food-crop. Furthermore, on the assumption that all output not delivered to marketing boards is retained for own consumption, there was a decrease in production for own consumption from 80% in 1980 to 59% in 1984, thus indicating that subsistence production is no longer the only motivating factor for communal farming. From the above it may be clear why Zimbabwe has been labelled the new 'success story' in agriculture. On one hand, the policies have been sufficiently supportive of the commercial sector to permit continued growth and its traditional role as contributor to national food supplies, foreign exchange earner and employer of wage labour. On the other hand, the changes implemented, despite some limitations, have given the communal sector a real boost both in the motivation of peasant farmers and the role they have begun to play in national production. If the trend in the last five years continues, the communal sector will soon be a serious challenge to the commercial sector in many dimensions of performance.

Implications for Socialist Agrarian Transformation

The strategy of preserving the commercial farming sector while instituting measures to improve production in the communal areas has its own internal attractiveness. To some, this represents a prudent appreciation of objective realities to avert the now common post-independence agrarian crisis characteristic of most sub-Saharan African countries. It is precisely this approach to agrarian transformation that has contributed to the common perception of Zimbabwe as the new success story in African agricultural experience.[17] To some extent this view is not baseless, as can be seen from the performance of the communal farmers who now are serious competitors with the commercial sector especially in the production of maize, cotton and other less technologically demanding crops. However, our concern here is to evaluate the implications of the policies and strategy for the achievement of the long-term goal of socialist transformation in agriculture. But first, the implications have to be understood in the context of the political and economic realities determining the evolution of these policies and strategy.

As has been discussed in chapter one, the apparent cautiousness in agricultural policy has a lot to do with the manner in which Zimbabwe attained independence. During the war of national liberation, the most contested issue was the land question. It is precisely over this that the majority of the peasantry joined the war. This factor, combined with the ruling party's Marxist-Leninist ideological leaning, had given reasonable expectations of radical policy changes in agriculture. That these radical changes did not materialise in the aftermath of independence is now a mote point. What is now clear is that the forces of imperialism, through the constitutional agreement hammered out at Lancaster House, manoeuvred the final stages of the independence struggle in a direction designed to guarantee continuity and protection of the commercial farmers from any radical reforms. This agreement so compromised the character of the new Zimbabwean state that it was constrained from acting decisively in the interests of the peasants, especially over the land issue, but to some extent also on the objectives and instruments of policy. Whereas during UDI the state had used the armoury of legislative, political and economic instruments to act decisively in the interests of the national and international agrarian bourgeoisie (the commercial farmers) to the detriment of the peasants, the post-independence state found itself reduced to the role of mediator between the conflicting interests of the two agrarian classes. The commercial farmers demanded continuity while the peasants expected change. This configuration of class forces is one of the determinants of the policies, the problematic and the contradictions inherent in government policy documents.

In outlining the policy objectives, the TNDP failed to give recognition to the contradiction between the two sets of objectives discussed in section two of this chapter. It appears the plan's implicit assumption was that the two can be achieved simultaneously without any trade-offs. The same observations can also be made about the plan's strategy. Even if one were to rationalise the strategy along the lines that socialist integration of the two sectors is the long-term goal, while the establishment of a number of production systems is merely a short-term tactic, this would still leave many questions to answer as to how this tactic translates into a long-term integrated socialist sector. On this issue, the TNDP is silent. The recently published Five Year National Development Plan (1986-1990) is even less concerned with this issue.

Despite these problems, significant attempts have been made towards ameliorating the position of the peasantry by removal of discriminatory aspects of past policies. However, such measures as have been implemented in the communal areas act like a double-edged sword. While improvements in output prices, marketing, credit and extension facilities form the interlocking spurs in the landscape of a small farmer improvement programme, they may also act to diffuse the pressure for real reform. Often, such measures are implemented when comprehensive agrarian reform is not a real political option for governments. The logic of this approach is that if output, incomes and productivity can be increased through intensification or use of high productivity inputs, the pressure for land reforms and structural transformation will be automatically eased. In most LDCs agricultural policy instruments, as the soft option, become the *de facto* substitute for comprehensive agrarian reforms. Zimbabwe has not escaped this problematic, which explains why policy emphasis is on 'resettlement' rather than 'agrarian reform', since the latter carries connotations of radical changes not only in land distribution but also in the nature and ownership of property.

The basis for socialist agrarian transformation lies in major restructuring of the pattern of ownership and distribution of the means of production along social lines. That improvement in the economic status of the peasant farmers has had a solid beginning in itself carries little significance for the government's desire for socialist transformation. What is needed is the transformation of property relations and the relations of production from private to social ownership and production. The two inherited modes of ownership in the commercial and communal areas pose a challenging agenda for the transition to socialism. Private ownership in the commercial sector is clearly inconsistent with the desired ends, while communal tenure which gives rights to land-use and usufructuary rights for peasants in a defined community, without individual titles, superficially appears to be not inconsistent with socialist goals. However, since production is carried out on a family basis, in some cases using wage labour, therein lies the potential for kulakisation and the development of a peasant capitalist class. Thus, both sectors require different but appropriate strategies for the transformation of property relations to make them consistent with the socialist mode of production. Such strategies have as yet not been devised. The producer cooperative development programme (Model B schemes) is still limited to the resettlement areas without any indications as to when and whether it will be extended to both the commercial and communal areas.

Transition to socialism is a long process, involving decades of ideological struggle to resolve the class character of the state in favour of the peasants and workers. To think that the long-term implications of Zimbabwe's policies and strategy can be drawn on the basis of five years of independence would be rather presumptuous and premature. We need to await the next few years, when a lot of the constitutional constraints will fall away, before any definitive statement of the implications can be made. At this stage, it could be easily argued that current policy and strategy form a solid base from which to launch socialist reforms from a position of strength. If the peasants' role in agriculture can be raised to a level where dependence on the commercial farmers becomes an unimportant issue, then the government could be rid of one of the albatrosses around its neck. But who knows what new albatross the peasants may become? There is no guarantee that the peasants would be any more willing to move on the socialist road, especially in their newly-acquired prosperity from government measures discussed earlier.

The final point we raise is the usual dilemma in the economics and politics of transition: that of 'speed' versus 'direction', or left-wing adventurism versus right-wing revisionism. This is a very relevant issue for debate in Zimbabwe's contemporary development strategies. Did the circumstances surrounding policy-makers during the first five years of independence genuinely inhibit a speedier transition to socialism or did the policy-makers use those circumstances as a pretext for not laying a solid foundation for future socialist transformation? While it is accepted that both the speed and direction are important ingredients of any process of transition, it is not universally accepted that they have to follow any predetermined sequential pattern. The Zimbabwean experience in both speed and direction does not unambiguously point towards the road to socialism.

Summary and Conclusions

The chapter has dealt with some of the intricate policy issues in Zimbabwe's agricultural sector. The following are its major conclusions:

(a) The policies of UDI managed to achieve the regime's internal objectives, but to the economic detriment of the peasants.

(b) Agricultural policy formulation after independence was significantly determined by the legacy of UDI to an extent where even the government's determination to transform the sector along socialist lines sometimes seems overshadowed. As a result, policy is characterised by greater continuity than radical change.

(c) Significant improvements have been made in the provision of credit, marketing facilities and output pricing to communal farmers, leading to improved performance, even though these may have become *de facto* substitutes for fundamental reforms.

(d) The implications of the post-independence policies for the transition to socialism are ambivalent. They may strengthen the government's future ability to effect substantive socialist reforms, or may assist in entrenching vested interests both in the commercial and peasant sectors to an extent where future efforts of socialist transformation become so difficult as to nullify the revolutionary momentum that had gathered during the liberation war.

(e) The aggregate statistics indicating Zimbabwe's image as the new 'success story' in agriculture may have some justification, even though this may be at the expense of the much-needed structural reforms for the achievement of government's socialist objectives.

REFERENCES

1. For example, Arrighi, G., Labour Supplies in Historical Perspective: A Study of the Proletarianisation of the African Peasantry in Rhodesia, *Journal of Development Studies*, Vol. 6, No. 3, 1970; pp. 197-234, and Palmer, R., The Agricultural History of Rhodesia, in Palmer, R. and Parsons, N. (eds), *The Roots of Rural Poverty in Central and Southern Africa*, Heinemann, London, 1977.
2. Jansen, D., *Agricultural Prices and Subsidies in Zimbabwe*, mimeo Harare, May 1982.
3. Riddell, R., Skill Needs in the Agricultural Sector, *IUEF*, Vol. 3, No. 11, 1980.
4. As quoted in Stoneman, C. (ed), *Zimbabwe's Inheritance*, Macmillan, London, 1981, p. 139.
5. *Ibid*.
6. Riddell, R., *op. cit*.

7. Jansen, D., *op. cit.*, p. 12.
8. Jansen, D., *op. cit.*, p. 127.
9. Shopo, T.D., *The Political Economy of Hunger*, ZIDS Working Paper, No.2, Harare, 1985.
10. This point is elaborated upon in Mumbengegwi, C., Agricultural Producer Cooperatives and Agrarian Transformation in Zimbabwe: Policy, Strategy and Implementation, *Zimbabwe Journal of Economics*, Vol. 1, No. 1, 1984.
11. See *GROWTH with EQUITY: A Policy Statement*, Govt Printers, Harare, 1981.
12. Republic of Zimbabwe, *Transitional National Development Plan*, Vol. 1, November 1982.
13. Mumbengegwi, C., *op. cit.*
14. Kinsey, B.H., Some Emerging Policy Issues in Zimbabwe's Land Resettlement Programmes, *Development Policy Review*, Vol. 11, No. 2, November 1983.
15. *Ibid.*
16. Temu, P.E., *Marketing Board Pricing and Storage Policy with Particular Reference to Maize in Tanzania*, Vantage Press, New York, 1984.
17. Republic of Zimbabwe, *Commission of Inquiry into the Agricultural Industry*, 1982.

8. THE POLITICAL ECONOMY OF HUNGER
Thomas D. Shopo

The intimate connection between the pangs of hunger suffered by the most industrious layers of the working class, and the extravagant consumption, coarse or refined, of the rich, for which capitalist accumulation is the basis, is only uncovered when the economic laws are known. (p. 811)

The insufficiency of food among the agricultural labourers fell as a rule chiefly on the women and children, for the man must eat to do his work. (p. 809)

Long before insufficiency of diet is a matter of hygienic concern, long before the physiologist would think of counting the grains of nitrogen and carbon which intervene between life and starvation, the household will have been utterly destitute of material comfort; clothing and fuel will have been even scantier than food. (p. 811)

Karl Marx, *The General Laws of Capitalist Accumulation* in *Capital*, Vol. I

Introduction

We have in Zimbabwe in 1986 a number of *ad hoc* programmes in the field of child health and nutrition being carried out sporadically in mission hospitals or selected plantations, or as isolated departmental activities. This patchwork of disjointed, pluralistic and liberal efforts will not lead to a solution, in the absence of a well-conceived, comprehensive national food policy for the eradication of this colonial inheritance of widespread under-nutrition amongst the 'bornfree'. We have sometimes allowed ourselves to be swayed by passing winds and fashions, and imported leads such as the 'child survival revolution', the protein fiasco and the nutrition educators' attempts to short-circuit 'the ignorant mother' through the promotion of direct or on-the-spot feeding.

The magnitude of the problem requires a very careful understanding of the operation of the general laws of capitalist accumulation in the concrete historical circumstances of Zimbabwe. It is some of the clauses of these general laws of capitalist accumulation that need serious questioning, rather than the weighty tomes called the *Statute Law of Rhodesia*. Already concerned international lawyers have launched a movement that calls for the legal recognition of food as a human right, and it won't be too long before this wind of fashion blows into our borders. Even if that were to happen and our Bill of Rights were amended to that effect, the hunger problem would not have been solved. For, it is not the written laws in the Statute Book that constitute our colonial inheritance but rather some of the unwritten social and economic laws of capitalist accumulation.

In our attempt to uncover these social and economic laws, the question of their relative 'efficiency' does not merit serious concern. And cleverness in bourgeois economic science, no matter what form it takes, will not unequivocally state the basic truth that the logic underlying capitalist development in Zimbabwe cannot be grasped in terms of a market-based explanatory frame. A market-based approach fails to shed light on the historical transformation of structures because it treats economic rationality as being invariant under qualitatively different relations of production. The issue then, if we root ourselves in the problematic of the transition in Zimbabwe, is not the *pragmatic* acceptance of the inherited market forces but whether their advance in commodifying our collective social product should be arrested.

The historical analysis of the modern problem of hunger in Zimbabwe will have the 1940s as the chronological assemblage point, purely for heuristic purposes in that it was around that period that colonial policy-makers first realised that the swollen tummies of the 'picannins' were not a sign that 'natives' of Southern Rhodesia were wallowing in luxury under the yoke of imperialism.

Following a brief descriptive essay on some of the social manifestations of hunger since 1945, our historical narrative will attempt to uncover the underlying causes, and then the basic economic causes. Finally, there will be a brief statement on issues that have to be addressed in order to secure the removal of impediments to the achievement of adequate nutritional food in Zimbabwe for the working population.

The Modern Dawn of The Problem

> Persons as well-informed as Native Commissioners are liable to be led astray. One Native Commissioner confessed that for many years he had regarded the swollen stomach of the native 'piccannin' as a sure indication that malnutrition was absent.

Southern Rhodesia Government, *Report on Social Security Part II*, The Government Printers, Salisbury, 1944, p. 2.

Thus proceed the occasional flashes of brilliance in providing accurate materialistic diagnoses of why the 'natives' in Bulawayo and Salisbury were to be so restless in April 1948.

While the learned Commissioner cited above had seen the problem as being one of mere ignorance by those who should have been concerned, some perceptive members of the settler colonial law-enforcement agency clearly saw the post-1945 period as a watershed in the life of settler colonialism.

The shoots were cut back this time easily and without any real trouble and difficulty and as no doubt they can be cut back again. But underground the seeds will take root and the day can conceivably dawn when like a noxious weed revolt will spring up across the land beyond our immediate power to stamp it out.[1]

The dimensions of the modern problem of hunger were first recognised in Southern Rhodesia during the 1940s. During the 1940s the export sector of the colonial economy—which had long been primed to provide the luxury consumption of workers in the metropolitan heartland—the United Kingdom—took off. As Ian Phimister has observed:

> During this period the movement towards tobacco cultivation was so pronounced and the expansion of the domestic economy so rapid that the Colony lost its previous self-sufficiency in basic foodstuffs. Faced with its commitment to feed Empire forces and Italian prisoners of war, as well as with difficulties of trading in war-time, the Southern Rhodesian government began to convert existing control boards into marketing boards to oversee the supply and distribution of agricultural produce.[2]

The basic foodstuff in Southern Rhodesia for workers and peasants had, by the 1940s, become maize meal. But the adoption of maize on the part of working households had not been a matter of free choice in the global world supermarket, i.e. the adoption of maize was not a sign of the working out of the subjective preference theory of economic choice that had been so assiduously described by Adam Smith in the *Wealth of Nations* in the eighteenth century. The adoption of this deficient diet based on maize was not a question of a natural transition from discretionary consumption to necessary consumption, as Arrighi has attempted to characterise changing consumption patterns. Arrighi saw the labour flow from the reserves as having become a self-generative process as 'people (got) used to what they consumed'.[3] To this he added that items not essential to satisfying subsistence requirements could 'with the mere passage of time, become necessities, whose consumption (was) indispensable'.[4] His attempt to delineate 'necessary' from 'discretionary' consumption however does not tell us why maize, which had not been the staple diet of the African people, became their basic foodstuff. In the formalist and Neo-Smithian way Arrighi posed the problem, 'choice' is made the essence of the economic laws of society, and the concrete culture becomes a mere fetish of the economy and its 'market' form is made a universal constant—the self-generative process. The distinction between production and consumption is purely a marketing definition—with consumption being seen as the sole end purpose, so that productive activities are perceived as merely those concerned with earning a wage or income, and consumption the spending of that income.[5]

It is therefore totally unnecessary for us to be working out the comparative advantage of the colonial Zimbabwe peasant household in growing maize. The adoption of maize as the staple diet was forced on the people of this country through the state of absolute impoverishment imposed on their lives by the progressive needs of British monopoly capital. The reliance on maize as a staple diet has long been recognised as a symptom of poverty in Europe and there is really no reason why its surplus production in Zimbabwe should now be seen as the final 'arrival' of indigenous *homo oeconomicus*:

> Maize spread widely as a crop through Spain and from there to other parts of Europe—to Italy, Hungary, Yugoslavia and France. It was easy to grow, filling as a food, and cheap. Rulers, princes and landlords encouraged its production, thereby boosting their tax, tithe and income yields, and at the same time providing cheap food for the poor. But where landlessness increased (and hence rural poverty as in Italy and France in the eighteenth and nineteenth centuries) various kinds of tenant farming and share-cropping also spread. *Under these conditions where people did not own or control their land, they were not free to grow what they wanted, and hence were not able to obtain a balanced diet.* Nor could they keep animals and poultry to provide themselves with meat and dairy produce. Many were compelled to grow maize for the landlord. General conditions of rural poverty hence increased the reliance on maize as the staple. This was especially true when people were encouraged or compelled to grow cash-crops, or were landless or sharecroppers, or were drawn into rural wage labour. This has happened also in Southern United States and Egypt, at the end of the nineteenth century, and in large areas of Southern Africa and India in the present century, where it continues today.[6]

So why indeed should bumper maize harvests in post-colonial Zimbabwe be seen as a sure sign of success? As we shall suggest later when dealing with the basic causes of hunger, the ready reason that comes to mind is the persuasive power of multinational agribusiness and its international fertiliser salesmen. For in the final analysis, even if all the landless were to be resettled, the land would still not be theirs, given the addiction of our soil to fossil-based fertilisers.

The post-1945 period, which as we have noted above was marked by a tobacco export-led growth, fuelled by the luxury consumption of the British working class, can thus not be seen as a 'golden age' of liberalism, but rather as a period marking the deepening of the imperialist clutch over the lives of the working population. Between 1945 and 1947, an estimated £7 m was invested in tobacco growing. And over the same period the black labour force employed in tobacco plantations was augmented by about 25,000 additional souls. Most of this expansion represented a shift of resources to tobacco from lower value crops that did not constitute the luxury consumption of the British proletariat.[7]

In a classic move of passing on the buck, the pressing needs of the British state to provide for the luxury consumption of its starving bands of ragged-trousered philanthropists were passed to the Zimbabwean working population. The fact that the British state had been forced to do this by circumstances created by the whole proud history of the Pax Brittanica missed the petit bourgeois bureaucrats of Southern Rhodesia, and the most visible signs of some disorder and confusion were only apparent to those economic commentators who wanted an ordered analytical framework. Thus Ian Phimister has written on the state of the settler Rhodesian economy in the halcyon days of the tobacco export boom:

> Such pronounced imbalance between agricultural sectors greatly aggravated Southern Rhodesia's shortfall in maize and beef cattle production. While the Government maintained that increased tobacco output and expanded food production were perfectly compatible, citing as evidence for this tobacco's preference for sandy soils considered marginal for other crops, larger and more efficient tobacco planters generally outbid medium and small-sized cattle ranchers and maize growers for capital and labour. For example, when tractors and artificial fertilisers were at a premium immediately after the war, tobacco growers were usually the only farmers who could afford them. Similarly, inflated land prices due to the tobacco boom deterred many potential (ranchers) from entering the cattle industry. Even those who could afford the initial capital outlay found it difficult to absorb the effect of the annual capital charges on the cost of production. For their part, maize farmers who resisted the temptation of joining the tobacco rush, were subsequently stymied in many instances by lack of labour. Unable to match the higher wages paid by planters, some farmers grew smaller acreages. Others cut back on labour-intensive and time-consuming good husbandry practices.[8]

In the rush to provide for the luxury needs of the British proletariat, the production of basic marketed foodstuffs fell further and further behind the demand of employers of black labour and cattle-ranchers. One clement season aside, marketed maize output declined in absolute volume as well as relative terms between 1945 and 1949. By the end of the decade of the 1940s, the colony was spending £750,000 per annum on imported maize. The beef cattle industry, as a result of the increased cost of feedstuffs, was faring no better. Although the number of white-owned cattle increased every year after 1938, as a result of the enforced destocking of African reserves, the rate of expansion failed to keep up with the protein needs of the British fighting forces at home and abroad. During the war and immediately afterwards, Phimister tells us the difference between demand and supply was satisfied at the expense of the export trade and by slaughtering younger cattle each year.

> Between 1937 and 1946 the number of slaughterings for local consumption for Empire forces and Italian prisoners of war increased by 107% and for export decreased by 56%, while the average weight of all cattle slaughtered in the Colony ... (dropped by) about 60-70 lbs per beast.[8] But when cattle herds were

decimated by drought in 1947, there was indiscriminate culling of immature animals and of animals suitable for breeding.[9]

The fact that the supply of both maize and meat had to be rationed during 1947-8 caused the settler administration to modify the laissez-faire policy to white agriculture that it had adopted in the wake of the flood of manufacturing capital after the war. The settler administration decided to step in and subsidise the labour costs of the white farmers. The Rhodesian Native Labour Supply Commission, which had been established as a parastatal, was directed to give preference to food producers.

The Rhodesian Native Labour Supply Commission owed its origin to the consumer cooperative that had been set up in the early years of the twentieth century, when settler farmers and miners had joined hands to establish a collective recruiting agency for the importation of extra-territorial black labour through the Rhodesia Native Labour Bureau. The upgrading of the bureau into a parastatal commission institutionalised state subsidisation of white commercial agriculture. And from all available signs the RALSC was a highly efficient parastatal. Whilst colonial Zimbabwe as a whole had built up a high level of dependence on extra-territorial labour, throughout the 1900-40 period, commercial agriculture as a low-wage sector was even more dependent on state subsidisation in the allocation of this labour. Under the contract system the RALSC imported the equivalent of 338,204 souls working one year, or an average inflow of 13,628 from 1946-71.[10]

From 1947 onwards white commercial farmers were able to recruit thousands of foreign workers from Nyasaland and Mozambique not only because of the 'cushion from capitalist market forces' but because of the drought and famine raging throughout Southern Africa.

Asking whether this drought was an act of God or man will unnecessarily obfuscate the question and can only deepen the whole poverty of Western academic philosophy. And the facts point more to the hand of British colonial man. For instance in one of the major labour reservoirs for white commercial agriculture, the Southern Province of Nyasaland, Megan Vaughan tells us that in the course of the famine of 1949 many people died not only through shortages of food:

> When prayers of all types failed, some people looked round at their neighbours to see who might be 'holding the rain' for their own ends. The usual suspects were old men with grey hair or bald heads, but people who were making bricks were also in line for accusation—after all they would be the first to suffer if the rain fell. One man working in Blantyre at the time heard stories of such accusations being made in his home village. The people accused there were those who had long been labelled as 'lazy' and who, even in favourable conditions, never had enough to feed themselves. The accused were made to drink water and hot pepper, and if they were men (as they generally were) they had chilli powder rubbed into their testicles...
>
> Quite quickly the consensus seems to have emerged that this

drought, unlike less severe ones, was the work of God and could not be attributed either to human action or to the anger of ancestors.[11]

Of course in the whole drama the European god of acquisition and its market forces were not perceived as the witch.

In the midst of such tribulations, and given the restless nature of the native population of Southern Rhodesia, the refugees from the famine in the imperial backwater of Nyasaland were indeed heaven-sent for the Commissioners of the RALSC. For the female refugees from the famine, the so-called 'free-flow migrants' who were just following the dictates of 'nature', the capital of Southern Rhodesia indeed appeared as a land of milk and honey. Some of these women are reported to have sung:

Ndigopita Limbe
Ndikakwere bus
Makwacha ndine ndemwe

Lilongwe Makonyora
Limbe Makonyora
Blantyre Makonyora
Salisbury Makonyora[12]

Within the settler territory of Southern Rhodesia, the growth of the economically viable export agriculture since World War II had had the effect of maintaining employment in agriculture very much higher than could be met by the country's food supplies, and it had been able to attract indigenous labour only because of the recurrent droughts to 1951.

Pressures were also applied on peasant households to produce the cheap food required by the state, through a combination of marketing and pricing incentives, land conservation measures and the land reform that constituted a 'Five-Year Plan' for agriculture—the Land Husbandry Act.

But the paradox—amidst shortages of marketed foodstuffs—was that, while food shortages were being reported in the south and the south-east of the country, in some areas 1948 was considered a record year for crop production; and in some areas the surplus of small grains which were also being imported was so abundant that the crop had to be left on the fields.[13]

As further inducement, and a form of giving the horse of racial partnership the carrot rather than the stick to produce cheap food, a system of subsidies for black farmers was devised from 1948 to 1956. The susbsidy was required to absorb the high cost of imported maize, and was really a consumer subsidy. The producer price was set very little under the local selling price—and very little benefit accrued to African producers whom it was meant to benefit. When maize had to be imported, the subsidy kept the urban cost of living down through price control on maize meal, but in years of exportable surplus, the urban cost of living became excessively high![14]

The war years had contributed to spiralling inflation, which had hit the African labour force of colonial Zimbabwe hard. And in addition to the inflation, the years from 1942 right up to 1951 were marked by intermittent droughts. The 1942 season had been the worst in over a decade. Maize rations were reduced by 25% in early 1942 and the country's industrial scene was marked by intermittent bursts of worker unrest culminating in the General Strike of 1948.

Even in the eyes of many a sanguine observer, something was amiss. A survey carried out under the auspices of the Reverend Percy Ibbotson's Native Welfare Society, and published in 1939, based on a sample of 6,000, showed that average wages were £1/11/1 per month. The reasonable minimum budget for a man and wife and two small children was calculated at £2/16/6 which did not allow for hut tax, recreation, school fees, tobacco or luxury items.[15] In 1943 Reverend Ibbotson published a report on *A Survey of Urban African Conditions in Southern Rhodesia*. Of 27,000 urban Africans sampled in seven urban areas, Ibbotson found that 66% of the employed Africans received payment in combined form of cash, accommodation and food, generally of insufficient quantity and inferior quality. Of those receiving their wages only in cash, 52% of these wages went to food and a further 29% to rent, light and fuel. Many urban workers were living in squalor. Ibbotson found cases of three or more married couples sharing a single room.[16]

How then did the workers manage to survive in such conditions and not die off in the long run to 1980? Explanation has been sought in the dynamics of the so-called 'straddling' phenomenon—that is household production and consumption being located in both the rural areas and the urban areas. But as we have observed above with the de-stocking campaign and poor rains, there was not much that could have been expected in the form of intra-household subsidies during these years. The understanding of the survival strategies of the labouring classes has been obfuscated by the tendencies to see them constituting a kind of subsidisation between spatial categories, i.e. rural areas subsidising urban areas, or as subsidisation between sectoral categories, i.e. communal agriculture subsidising the reproduction costs of modern industry.

Going Beyond the Physical Manifestations of Hunger in Zimbabwe
Boris Gussmann, who had carried out extensive research during the 1940s in colonial Zimbabwe's areas as a Beit Research Fellow, reported thus on these survival strategies:

> Little starvation is found at present because of the vast amount of food sent into town by rural Kinsmen—most of which are illegal or immoral—to which many townsfolk resort from sheer necessity.[17]

'Illegality' or 'immorality' are however very vague concepts in a world ruled by the dictates of capital, and enforced by the powers of coercion of a petit bourgeois municipality of the British Empire—the government of Southern Rhodesia. Further, such notions, when applied as economic laws when faced with the problem of the starvation of the most hardworking sectors of the population, mystify the basic processes at work by resorting to the coincidence in a bourgeois biological and economic science—between the 'genetic potential model' and the subjective preference theory. The genetic potential model conceives of the human body as a system which is not only self-regulating, but also self-optimising, so that for each individual worker there is postulated to exist a preferred state characterised by a unique set of values of the variables which describe the system's (the human body) components (weight, height, blood levels, etc.). The preferred states are optimal for that individual with respect to all aspects of function. If there are no constraints on diet, or continued environmental influences, an individual will always tend to seek out and return to the preferred state. And indeed if he is fully endowed with all the five senses, and if given the opportunities in a 'free market' environment, if he fails to attain the optimal state alloted to him by the circumstances of his birth, then that individual alone is to blame. This ideological 'genetic potential model' has found its corollary in certain general laws of economic equilibrium long pondered on by bourgeois political economy, in its attempts to rationalise the social costs of production of capitalist robbery and exploitation. This general economic law has been described as the 'subjective preference theory', which takes the world as a global 'Alice in Wonderland' type of supermarket. Consumers enter this supermarket, having an 'inborn tendency' to express a consistent set of preferences as between the various food items they want to buy. From such intellectual premises social biologists, social planners armed with good balance sheets and ISIC codes have descended from the Food and Agricultural Organisation (FAO) and International Labour Organisation (ILO) to measure and predict for post-colonial Zimbabwe how consumption would be distributed within a society 'where a free market operates', and for how many people food consumption would fall below biological needs. As part of their contribution to fighting the hunger problem, for instance, the FAO in 1985 organised a cooking competition, with the best prize going to the woman who cooked a meal whose nutrient components had the international stamp of approval!

The other variation or progression on the subjective preference theory to develop in the modern cognition of the problem of hunger has been that touted by United Nations agencies to the left of the World Bank, and International Monetary Fund—i.e. the 'social cost perspective' which attempts to select 'target groups' for international action. This 'social cost perspective' or 'target group' mentality has involved the identification of the actual classes or social groups experiencing actual physiological damage or who have adapted to the fullest possible extent to low good intakes. In Zimbabwe today this target group would be constituted by the following vulnerable segments of humanity:

(a) The children of commercial farm workers who in the very productive agricultural hinterland of Mashonaland Central Province, amongst whom two researchers have demonstrated that, though less than 4% of their sample had second or third degree malnutrition in the first six months of life, this rose to 33% for children in the 6-23 months are range after which it dropped to 21%.[18]

(b) The 7% of children below one year and the 16% of children in the 1-4 year group who were undernourished as per survey during the joint United Nations Children's Fund (UNICEF) and World Health Organisation (WHO) immunisation programme.

(c) That group that can be demographically located in the country's medico-statistical profile by singling out for study those women in the childbearing age of 14-45 who have suffered infertility as a result of the ailment called amenorrhoea. Megan Vaughan, in one of her footnotes to the study of the 1949 Nyasaland famine cited above—the impact of which on the Zimbabwean labour market was well evident—writes:

> The role of amenorrhoea in bringing about a fall in the rate of conception during famines is now well documented for Europe in the twentieth century, and there is evidence to show that it was also a factor in seventeenth century famines: E. Le Roy Ladurie, 'Amenorrhea in Time of Famine, Seventeenth to Twentieth Century', in E. Le Roy Ladurie (ed), *The Territory of the Historian*, trans. Ben and Sian Reynolds (Hassocks, 1979), pp. 255-73. A decline in libido and a higher incidence of miscarriage are other factors which commonly lower the birth rate during famine: Jeliffe, 'Effects of Starvation', p. 57.

If in all the social targeting that is carried out on the basis of the contemporary conjuncture of world capitalist market forces, and their reflections in the crystal balls of the travelling Gypsy caravans of the European and North American petit bourgeoisie, the minimum effort were made to understand group (c) listed above, some progress would be made in understanding the underlying causes of hunger in Zimbabwe, and not just their very obvious and self-evident manifestations, e.g. the loss of libido as a result of permanent and structural undernourishment.

And even if the last socio-biological group enumerated above, based on consideration of the rate of infertility, were a bit too indiscreet for academic attention, even a consideration of groups (a) and (b) would be an important break with the reactionary modernism that currently infects collaborative research on the subject by Zimbabwean researchers and international non-government researchers.[19]

A discreet look even at the condition of the living potential labour for enhancing the maximum national productive capacities of worker and peasant households would transcend this 'reactionary modernism' and bring about a strategic intervention by the country's physical, natural and social scientists into the whole problem of uniting the nation's collective production and consumption faculties. There already exists widespread consensus in the strategic field of devising child survival and development strategies that low birth weight reflects the poor nutritional state of the mother, since *birth weight* distribution in any society from the North Pole to the South Pole, and from the Equator to the Amazon, reflects the impact of environmental and social conditions surrounding intra-uterine growth. Further, the mean birth weight is increasingly being recognised as a sensitive indicator of socio-economic development.[20]

In order to bring out this very sensitive indicator of economic development statistical and cliometrical exercises, no matter how rigorous, will not provide useful data about the living nature of the problem, but rather a very denatured comparative stasis rooted in a form of intellectual *rigor mortis*. More useful data on which to base *concerned* action would emerge from a disaggregation of morbidity and mortality statistics. As far as infant mortality is concerned disaggregation according to the age of the child is the most important one. This is because the specific *immediate* causes of deaths of children older than one month are most frequently related to the environment, as the causes of high peri-natal and 'neo-natal' mortality rates are primarily the result of the poor health and nutritional status of the mother.

In Zimbabwe those studies credited with statistical rigour and with being situation-specific in the last ten years have shown wide regional and contextual variations.[21] A World Bank Report two years ago stated that Zimbabwe's Infant Mortality Rate (IMR) compares favourably with other countries, but that it showed up badly on malnutrition by comparison with other countries on the continent. The discrepancy between the IMR and malnutrition, in the opinion of World Bank socio-medical demographers, was attributable to the relatively infection-free natural environment of Zimbabwe.[22]

Despite talk of this 'naturally infection-free' environment, less rigorous, albeit dynamic, research by public researchers in urban hospitals shows some of the dimensions of the problem. A Ministry of Health Report (1980) gives the following statistics in respect of the registered causes of peri-natal deaths. The report shows that the total for such deaths, i.e. peri-natal, for the year ended 31 December 1980, was 2,287 out of a total of 5,069 infant deaths registered by principal factors. This means that over half of child deaths were due to conditions associated with intra-uterine growth and the poor nutritional status of the mother. Further disaggregation of these peri-natal deaths showed that 731 deaths, i.e. just about a third, were caused by slow foetal growth, foetal malnutrition and immaturity. And 754, i.e. about a third, were caused by hypozia, birth asphyxia and other respiratory conditions.[23]

These statistics were collated from mainly urban environments with a relatively infection-free environment and with access to clean, piped water, and other modern social facilities.

The causal factors for infant mortality, according to hospital and clinic records of 1979, were pneumonia, gastroenteritis/diarrhoea, measles, tetanus, birth injury and difficult labour, congenital abnormalities and malnutrition. Contributing to the high incidence of these diseases were low birth weight/malnutrition and inadequate nutrition.

Though the study of the socio-physical manifestation of the problem of hunger in Zimbabwe—and UNICEF's present emphasis is on descriptive studies by their field officers of situation analyses of women and children—is well-intentioned, innocent and even harmless, there is need to sound a mild caveat. There is a danger of straying away from the problem in streams of scholastic consciousness and literary philistinism that do not reflect the concrete problems faced by the working populace in Zimbabwe in its daily struggle for its daily bread.

For, it must never be forgotten that child malnutrition is not the only problem that Zimbabwe's transitional politics have to deal with.

Child malnutrition is not the only problem, but the most visible even on photographs—and it is also the most easily demonstrated and measured symptom of the nutritional deprivation of the family of a particular class of families. We therefore have to be very careful in adopting the most 'vulnerable segment' approach, i.e. farm workers, women, squatters, prostitutes, contract workers, etc. Such a strategy, if it leaves out significant categories of people, is likely to be self-defeating and even counter-productive. If under-nourishment is basically a problem of pervasive poverty, exclusion of certain categories of persons on the basis of sex and age from the poverty-stricken will also not be of any use. Taking the case of such clinical manifestations of hunger as amenorrhoea and the social manifestations of unorganised prostitution and squatting in a country like Zimbabwe, it is quite clear that market-based simultaneous equations will never be quite able to bring about any sensible and coherent correlation. For even in the Amazonian ranks of Western academic economistic feminism, the shortage or presence of libido has never been attributed to either the lack or absence of money.

What are the Basic Institutional Causes of Hunger in Zimbabwe?

As we have detailed above there is a very real danger, in our search for the basic causes of hunger, of getting lost in unstructured flights of fancy. While there is a general consensus among left-wing, right-wing and populist scholars in Zimbabwe that poverty in Zimbabwe is closely related to the inherited patterns of agricultural development—not only because the agriculture industry is the source of livelihood of more than 80% of the population but because of the patterning of social relations along lines that maximised the consumption of white commercial farmers in the past—we still seem to be shying away from the fundamental problem about hunger. While glib statements now abound about the 'agrarian question', there is still a crippling inability to examine the 'agrarian' question in a co-ordinated fashion around the whole problem of labour value. The payment for this failure has been manifested in our failure effectively to communicate or articulate, in the various academic styles we have employed, the laws governing the accumulation of luxury goods based on agricultural produce—i.e. the export sector of agriculture which ranges from sugar to tobacco to spring water to the tourist trade.

We therefore need to make an unequivocal departure from circular market-based explanatory frameworks for our political, economic and social problems. Market-based explanatory frameworks based on the most excellent of metaphors conjured up by Western bourgeois 'crisis political economy', e.g. 'in the long run we shall all be dead', has failed to come up with explanations that can be aligned with the working population's own abstract understanding of how it produces and expends its labour power in order to maximise its collective production and consumption. It is of course too late at this stage for us to be wallowing like hippopotami in the mud of racist myths that African labour has never been capable of abstract thought.

Market-based explanations of social reality have also done a disservice, insofar as they have complicated our understanding of the problem of hunger by concentrating on price factors, and as a result have wasted intellectual labour power in complicated statistical abstractions whose end point is nothing but the ancient propaganda of British political economy about the sacred nature of market forces.

The whole myth about price preceding value leads to an overconcentration on paper wars about the manifestations and underlying causes compatible with the cost of production perspectives of monopoly capitalism that are usually put forward as labour codes etc. amongst official labour analysts.

Amongst agricultural scientists, this myth—coupled with a blind faith in the saving grace of modern technology—has induced a form of soporific amnesia that the historical progress made in improving scientific techniques for getting the best from a given input of soil, through the application of modern scientific inputs and techniques of human management, has caused widespread malnutrition. Without putting too fine a point on it, our 'pure' scientific intelligentsia, in both private and public sectors, for reasons known only to themselves, seem to be intent on mystifying an age-old truth that many of our ailments in the transition from post-white settler colonial Zimbabwe have their roots in the way our society was reorganised after colonisation i.e. the institutional framework created for the accumulation of capital and for the extraction of primary agricultural produce.

Our legal scientists have, for their part, forgotten that it was not only the institutional arrangements as codified in various marketing legislation or the due historical processes of law involved in changing 'tribal reserve' to 'communal lands' or 'European Area' to 'Large Scale Farming Commercial Sector' (LSCF), but also the very *positive* developments in the lives of the cultivators and wage earners e.g. literacy in the *English language*. These positive achievements in the face of perpetual adversity need no longer be celebrated as the African intiative. We need to examine the social differentiation they produced, insofar as the organic link between production and consumption in the family (nuclear or extended) was severed by the commodification of the social products of our culture.

Our professional historians, who perhaps should have led in the search for strategic solutions of mass poverty of which household food insecurity is but a manifestation, have wasted much energy debating when exactly price became more important than value amongst the indigenous population. The search thus far seems to have been fruitless, as the following bemused reaction by a research student working on a dissertation paper on 'The Development and Diversification in the Lowveld of Zimbabwe: The Case of the Big Company Estates (Triangle and Hippo Valley)', shows:

> The industry is now not merely farming, but is producing cardboard boxes and cans to put its products. Thus the industry controls production, manufacturing and distribution (Field, Factory and Shop). Indeed an offcical of one of them said, 'It is a sad fact that most nutritional food products marketed by commercial firms are aimed at the segment of society least in need of them.'

Our perceptive student, however, cannot understand such naked obscenity, as he goes on to write:

> *What is even more embarrassing is the fact that the better-off consumers—those able to pay the higher prices—set the market conditions, leaving many of the former (farm) labourers at a disadvantage in getting the very products they are producing. This is indeed the nature of agrarian capitalism.*[24]

Our list of the state of the arts and sciences in Zimbabwe could be endless. Let us therefore reiterate that, even more important than the understanding of the physical and social institutions constructed by monopoly capitalism in Zimbabwe, we need to extend the whole definition of institutions by a radical inquiry into those harmless and informal institutions usually called habits of mind that were nurtured in the grey womb of settler colonialism.

A breakthrough can be made in this respect if we can begin to divest all talk of 'market forces', 'technology' etc. of the aura of natural mysticism that presently affects it. Having been immersed in capitalist culture for only eight decades this should prove an easier task than detailing the transition from feudalism to capitalism in Europe or from merchant capital to international finance capital in the United States of America. In the metropolitan countries, given the deadweight of a history of plunder and exploitation of the working household going back four hundred years, this had admittedly been a very difficult task. Michael Taussig has graphically described some of the difficulties in attaining the social cognition that market forces are not a product of nature:

> In capitalist culture this blindness to the social basis of essential categories makes a social reading of supposedly natural things perplexing. This is due to the peculiar character of the abstractions associated with the market organisation of human affairs: essential qualities of human beings and their products are converted into commodities, into things for buying and selling on the market. Take the example of labour and labour time. For

our system of industrial production to operate people's productive capacities and nature's resources have to be organised into markets and rationalised in accord with cost accounting: the unity of production and human life is broken into smaller and smaller quantifiable components. Labour, an activity of life itself, thus becomes something set apart from life and abstracted into the commodity of labour time, which can be bought and sold on the labour market. This commodity appears to be substantial and real. No longer an abstraction it appears to be something natural and immutable, even though it is nothing more than a convention or a social construction emerging from a specific way of organising persons relative to one another and to nature.[25]

Failure to disengage from the scientific petit bourgeois worldview will indeed mean that the state-projected transition to socialism will be a messy abortion. For, if the economic laws of world class economists in the International Monetary Fund, World Bank, ILO and FAO triumph instead of a transition to socialism, the nation's professional men of science will lead the nation back into the world British settler colonialism created in Zimbabwe, where the economic laws written into marketing and pricing legislation will predominate. No matter how the end purpose of these is examined, their purposeful logic was—and still is—to ensure the luxury consumption of the international robber barons in London and Washington, whose vision of a free Zimbabwe is one wherein their economic laws triumph over our ethical ones: a Zimbabwe in which production, not man, is the aim of the economy, and commodities rule their creators.

Conclusion: The Monumental Project of Recomposing the Value of Labour Power

The struggle against hunger in Zimbabwe's transition to socialism is by necessity a multi-faceted one, involving the reorganisation of the nation's material and non-material culture in order to restore the organic composition of labour—not so much by a return to pre-colonial dietary habits, but through a total and uncompromising assault on the cultural paradigm imposed by British capitalist culture.

The solution of the problem is long-term but that does not have to block the autonomous generation of strategic ideas. A beginning could be made with the constituting of a National Nutrition Board which would be charged with the formulation of a National Nutrition Policy, and on which would be represented all relevant departments of government dealing with science and technology, agriculture, health, education, labour, and mass communications to ensure a consistent and co-ordinated policy consistent with our overall national objectives to reduce poverty, increase employment or cut underemployment, and to increase food and industrial production; all this activity should be co-ordinated with related programmes of health, child and maternity health.

In the final analysis, if social science is to make an appreciable impact on the science of government, it is no longer useful for social scientists blindly to follow the flares of the romantic anti-capitalists and contracted airborne professorial Narodniks of the international civil service. A historical perspective even on how the daily comforts of the *povo* in colonial Zimbabwe were regulated would be of immense value. Following the attainment of independence in 1980, there is no longer a scholarly or other excuse for social scientists to remain silent concerning the working of those minute causes by which the many are affected, whilst magnifying the more obvious and self-evident facts by which the destinies of rulers have been swayed. In following this course, convenience has of course been an important factor, since it is easy to record the more notorious facts; while it must generally be a more arduous task to analyse questions such as the pangs of hunger which are influenced by a succession of minute causes, and exposed to the constant action of disturbing influences.

In the words of an essayist in the 1834 edition of the *British Almanac and Companion*, writing on 'Wages and prices' during the British industrial revolution:

> There can be no doubt, however, concerning the comparative usefulness of such historical writers, and the labours of the more humble annalist, who enables succeeding inquirers to determine the rate and amount of progress made by a nation in the march of social improvement.[26]

There is, however, a need, in the division of labour and specialisation entailed in the radical understanding of these 'minute' moments in the social life of the people, to avoid becoming the powder-monkeys, spanner boys and grease-monkeys of the gargantuan machinery of Western monopoly capitalism. Such fragmentation will not bring about a full realisation that the political economy of hunger in Zimbabwe involves the multiple dimensions of mental domination, colonial exploitation and marginalisation in their interrelated manifestations, and the relationship of the petit-bourgeois settler state bureaucracy and the masses, not just as a relationship between classes but also as one between the principal carriers of the virus of modern capitalism—market forces—and their interface with social order. In the absence of a thoroughgoing critique of the pseudo-scientific tenets of Western modernisation theory, the analyst becomes a problem, rather than an agent for change. And specifically on the burning academic question of food, it is important to bear in mind that production in colonial Zimbabwe was not instructed by national food needs, i.e. that it was not based on the consumption needs of the African working population, but by the luxury consumption of the British working class both in the imperial heartland and in the colonies and Her Majesty's dominions.[27]

The agricultural sector of the Zimbabwean post-colonial economy still bears the brunt of the efforts by international monopoly capital to restucture and deepen the alignment of national productive and consumptive capacities with its own anarchical demand structures. In the long run, the solution to the hunger problem is therefore intricately bound up in the new state's efforts effectively to upgrade the value of labour power across all sectors, by the elimination of the inbuilt depressors of that value, primarily manifested by the so-called 'agrarian question'. For the very modalities by which national agricultural production was structured by the settler colonial bureaucracy still act as an institutional depressor of the value of labour power of the black labouring population in the foreign-owned agro-plantation sector, communal lands and urban factories. The first six years of independence, from all available statistical indices, have not seen a drastic reversal of the pre-independence undervaluation of labour power, despite greater access to the market by the peasantry and the passing of minimum wage legislation and other administrative reforms. The national undervaluation of labour continues to be sealed, as the more advanced industrial and agrarian production sectors each still seeks to minimise the social costs of labour reproduction. In many instances, as a result of the competition for labour between the two sectors, consultations with the state as 'referee' for mutual benefits have been reached, e.g. the gradation of agro-industrial workers, who form a vital linkage between the agricultural and industrial sectors. As the president of the General Agriculture and Plantation Workers' Union was recently moved to comment on some of these 'irrational' categories which have ensured the national undervaluation of labour power:

> A person who picks oranges at Mazowe Citrus Estates is an agro-industrial worker while a combine harvester driver or a person who picks cotton is not.[28]

We have sought to demonstrate in this chapter that the political economy of hunger has not been primarily the existence of low wages, high malnutrition rates, etc., which have been but the manifestations of a deeper rooted problem—the institutional and structural depression of labour value.

REFERENCES

1. National Archives of Zimbabwe, File ZBZ 1/2/1.
2. Phimister, Ian, Discourse and the Discipline of Historical Context: Conservationism and Ideas about Development in Southern Rhodesia 1930-50, *Journal of Southern African Studies*, Vol. 12, No. 2, April 1986, p. 263.
3. See Arrighi, G., Labour Supplies in Historical Perspective: A Study of the Proletarianisation of the African Peasantry in Rhodesia, in Arrighi, G. and Saul, J.S. (eds), *Essays on the Political Economy of Rhodesia*, Monthly Review Press, New York and London, 1983, pp. 180-234.
4. *Ibid*, p. 198.
5. See Shopo, T.D., *The Political Economy of Hunger in Zimbabwe*, ZIDS Working Paper No. 2, February 1985, The Government Printer, Harare.
6. Leftwich, Adrian, *Redefining Politics: People' Resources and Power*,

Methuen & Co. Ltd., London, 1983, pp. 108-109.
7. Phimister, Ian, *op. cit.*
8. *Ibid.*
9. *Ibid.*, pp. 268-269.
10. Clarke, D.G., Black Contract Labour and Farm Wage Rates in Rhodesia, Labour Research Seminar No. 2, Department of Economics, University of Rhodesia, 1973, mimeographed paper.
11. Vaughan, Megan, Famine Analysis and Family Relations: 1949 in Nyasaland, *Past and Present*, No. 108, 1985, p. 182.
12. Translated by Vaughan, Megan in *ibid.*
 'I must go to Limbe
 and Board a bus
 My body will pay the fare
 It will do, it will do.

 In Lilongwe, my body will do
 In Lilongwe, my body will do
 In Blantyre it will do
 And in Salisbury, it will produce money'.
13. See Shopo, T.D., *op. cit.*, p. 41.
14. *Ibid.*, p. 42.
15. National Archives of Zimbabwe, File SR/9/1/5/11.
16. Ibbotson, P., Urbanisation in Southern Rhodesia, *Africa*, Vol. 16, 1946, p. 78.
17. Gussman, Boris, Industrial Efficiency and the Urban African—A Study of Conditions in Southern Rhodesia, *Africa*, Vol. 23, 1953, p. 38.
18. Loewenson, R., The Bindura Farm Health Worker Scheme unpublished mimeographed paper, April 1983.
19. For an inventory of some of the problems that have emerged as a result of the 'unholy alliance' between European and North American petit-bourgeois academics and the African executive petit-bourgeois bureaucracy see Shopo, T.D., *The Fundamental Problems of Science and Technology in Zimbabwe's Transition to Socialism,* ZIDS Occasional Staff Paper No. 1.
20. See Ljungqvist, Bjorn G., Maletnlema, T.N., Kavishe, Festo P., Ballart, Angelina, Medhin, Mehari Gebre et al, *Determinants of Reproductive Performance and Child Survival in An African Rural Community,* TNFC Report No. 927, TNFC Project 246, May 1985, Dar es Salaam.
21. Brydone, Determination of the Neo-Natal and Infant Mortality Rate in Mufakose, Salisbury, Rhodesia, *Central African Journal of Medicine*, Vol. 21, No. 6, June 1975.
R. T. Mossop, Are We Winning? *Central African Journal of Medicine*, Vol. 28, No. 5, May 1982.
22. World Bank, Zimbabwe, *Population, Health and Nutrition Sector Review*, Vol. 1, June 1983.
23. Government of Zimbabwe, *Report of the Secretary for Health For the Year ended 31st December, 1980,* Cmd R.Z. 6 - 1982).

24. Makani, Dzingai, Development and Diversification in the Lowveld of Zimbabwe: The Case of the Big Company Estates (Triangle and Hippo Valley), B.A. Honours Economic History III Dissertation Paper: July 1986, mimeographed paper. Dept of History, University of Zimbabwe, p. 6.
25. Taussig, M., *The Devil and Commodity Fetishism in South America* The University of North Carolina Press, 1980, p. 4.
26. Archives, Standards of Living of the Working Classes during the Industrial Revolution, *Population and Development Review*, 11, No. 4, December 1985, pp. 737-755.
27. Personal communication, Mkhalelwa Mazibuko, 14 July 1986.
28. *The Herald*, 21 July 1986.

9. STATE, CAPITAL AND TRADE UNIONS
Lloyd Sachikonye

Introduction

The substantive character of the industrial relations of any society reveals the salient aspect of the dominant social and political relations which underpin its development. Such relations determine and underlie the 'capitalist', 'social democratic' or 'socialist' character and directions of that society. Thus, state, capital and trade unions play significant roles in varying degrees in the determination and modification of industrial relations and ultimately the social and political relations in society. This chapter is a tentative exercise in the analysis of industrial relations in Zimbabwe since independence in 1980; its tentativeness arises from the fact that the process of evolution in these relations is still in a state of flux and presumably only their broader and more striking aspects may be identified and assessed at this juncture.

The first section of the chapter consists of a general theoretical discussion of the historical and contemporary forms of relations between capital, unions and state in capitalist society. The discussion forms the basis of a condensed review of the evolution of trade unionism in Zimbabwe: the basis of an analysis of the labour militancy which underlay the nation-wide strikes of 1980 and 1981 which are discussed at some length in the second part of the chapter. In the following sections, the different roles and responses of state, capital and unions to the 'industrial relations crisis' are assessed. The awesome adminstration and image problems of the Zimbabwe Congress of Trade Unions (ZCTU) in its first four years of existence are then examined, as well as the possibilities and problems relating to state intervention in the restructuring of trade unionism and industrial relations. Furthermore, the immediate tasks and challenges facing the labour movement as a whole are identified.

Capital, State and Unions

The theoretical issues pertaining to the relationships among state, capital and unions are discussed in very general terms but, in the latter parts of the chapter, illustrated with specific references to the Zimbabwean experience in industrial relations historically but mainly since the attainment of independence in 1980. Some of the most important of our theoretical considerations relate to the relationship between capital and labour; the emergence and character of trade unions; the nature of the relationship of state to capital in general and their strategies of restructuring industrial relations in particular.

Both the working class and its trade unions emerged from the womb of capitalism: to be precise, from its mode of production. They are a vibrant expression of the underpinning social relations of exploitation. As Engels and Marx remarked, the development of the proletariat as a class of labourers 'who live so long as they find work and who find work only as their capital increases capital' depended proportionately on the development of capital itself.[1]

Indeed, the genesis of the working class created conditions for struggles with the bourgeoisie over working conditions generally and the terms of the price of the labour-power of workers. If at first the contest was carried on by individual labourers or by the work-people of a factory, these coalesced into one trade union that directed its attacks not against the bourgeois conditions of production but against the instruments of production themselves:

> at this stage the labourers still form an inchoate mass, broken by mutual competition. If anywhere they invite to form more compact bodies, this is not yet the consequence of their own union but of the union of the bourgeoisie.[2]

Initially, therefore, the nature of the relationship between capital and labour under capitalism tends to reflect the material and ideological dominance of the former and the reactive response of the latter. Thus, although trade unions may represent tenacious resistance against the encroachments of capital, they seem to limit themselves 'to a guerrilla war against the effects of the system instead of simultaneously trying to change it by using their organized forces as a lever for the emancipation struggle from capital'.[3]

In most instances, however, the short-term strategic material interests of unions centre around the quest for wage increments. It is a quest which is neither an objective nor tactical imperative which addresses itself fully to the long-term priority of the abolition of capitalist exploitation. Indeed, while some individual workers or unions may acquire a perception of the politico-economic dimension of their struggle, most unions seem generally unable to break out of the ideological straitjacket of economism. The implications of this prompted Marx to note that trade union struggles to secure wage increments did not fundamentally disturb the whole wage system because, in 99 cases out of 100, their efforts at securing better wages were only efforts at maintaining the given value of labour; that the necessity of debating their price was inherent to their condition of having to sell themselves as commodities; and that therefore by cowardly giving way in their everyday conflicts they would certainly disqualify themselves from the initiation of any larger movement.[4] As institutions, therefore, trade unions:

> do not challenge the existence of classes but merely express it: thus trade unions can never be vehicles of advance towards

socialism in themselves (because) by their nature they are tied to capitalism. They can bargain with society, but not transform it.[5]

These observations, based on analytical studies of trade unions organised in capitalist Europe, could equally be drawn from studies on trade unions in the peripheral capitalist societies of Africa, Latin America and Asia. The level of capitalist development in the latter varies regionally and it certainly has not yet attained the scales of intensity in the north. This notwithstanding, there can still be identified certain other broad characteristics of trade unionism with which progressive theoreticians and practitioners need to be acquainted. Such acquaintance restrains too hasty dismissals of possibilities of progressive trade unionism; and an excessive preoccupation with the limitations of its economism. Lenin cautioned that the central importance of the economic struggle of the proletariat and the necessity of such a struggle had been recognised by Marxism from the very start. As eary as the 1840s, Marx and Engels had conducted a polemic against 'utopian socialists' who denied the importance of this struggle.[6] As he observed:

> The resolution adopted at the 1866 workers' congress in Geneva spoke explicitly of the importance of the economic struggle and warned the socialists and the workers, on the one hand, against exaggerating its importance (which the English workers were inclined to do at the time) and on the other, against underestimating its importance (which the French and Germans, particularly the Lassalleans did...). The resolution declared that the trade unions must not devote attention exclusively to the 'immediate struggle against capital', must not remain aloof from the general political and social movement of the working class; and that they must not pursue 'narrow aims' but must strive for the general emancipation of the millions of oppressed workers.[7]

But it is not only their tendency to embrace economism which the trade unions need to transcend: the bourgeois stratagems to emasculate them are legion. Lenin explained the apparent quiescence of the British unions during the imperial scramble for colonies in terms of the strategic predilection of capitalists to:

> devote a part of their super-profits to bribe their own workers to order to create something like an alliance (recall the celebrated alliances described by the Webbs of English unions and employers) between the workers and capitalists of the given nation against other countries.[8]

The imperial bourgeoisie could economically bribe the upper stratum of 'its' workers by spending on this 'investment' a hundred million or so francs a year. For, its super-profits amounted to thousands of millions. And:

> how this little sop is divided among the labour ministers, 'labour

representatives', labour members of war industries committees, labour officials, workers belonging to narrow craft unions etc. is a secondary question.[9]

Yet the 'economic bribery' of workers by the bourgeoisie is only one among its various methodologies in its emasculation of the labour movement. Selective bribery tends to abet divisions in the ranks of workers and between unions; and the resultant labour disunity on the whole benefits the bourgeoisie. But what are the other strategies used to impede or accommodate trade unions? First is the ideological hegemony of the bourgeoisie. Given that capitalism represents a complex of work relations and social relations of production, of which 'industrial relations' form one aspect, the basic character of capitalism exerts a pervasive influence on the nature of industrial relations, most crucially through the manner in which it shapes the structure, actions and objectives of trade unionism.[10] Under normal conditions, as Hyman observed:

> trade union action has two fundamental features which are mutually reinforcing: it tends to react rather than initiate and it is oriented less towards workers' general predicament than to their particular and sectional grievances.[11]

Second, public discussion of industrial relations is shot through with evaluative and ideological terminology, which reflects the general orientation of the dominant social ideas whose impact is overwhelmingly supportive of capital. The principal elements of such a discussion include a notion of 'national interest' which is closely bound up with the interests of the bourgeoisie; and the conception of labour organisation, objectives and activities as necessarily sectional, and probably selfish, irresponsible, disruptive and subversive. And since class bias was built into everyday thought and languages:

> worker self-conception in essentially sectional terms is encouraged: the notion of a working class as a group with common interests opposed to those of employers as a class is excluded from everyday language. Fragmented in their presentation, the interests of the majority can thus paradoxically be construed as minority interests, to be pursued defensively and apologetically.[12]

The calculated assaults on trade unions by the bourgeoisie are facilitated by the capitalist state. The bourgeoisie could not succeed for so long in its encapsulation of labour were it not for the regulatory role of the state. Some aspects of such a regulatory or cooptive role include, of course, certain institutional infrastructure of a legal variety—industrial relations codes, industrial boards or tribunals, etc.—and those of a more repressive nature (industrial courts, state security apparatus and the propensity of the state to deploy the police) to quell strikes or harass ringleaders. The shape of the state apparatus itself, and its supportive measures to sustain the necessary conditions for capitalist development or growth, reflect its bourgeois character and propensities.

Of particular significance to socialist theoreticians and activists, then, is the methodology whereby the capitalist state organises capitalist structures in such a manner as to reproduce them while guaranteeing the continued existence of conditions of capitalist accumulation. This project of ensuring the stability and security of accumulation both nationally and internationally necessarily involves the maintenance of conditions and relations of exploitation which, in essence, define the relations between capital and labour. As discussed in chapter one of this volume, in this contemporary era of imperialism, states in peripheral capitalism perform this indispensable function in varying degrees which range from those with fascist and militarist tendencies (Chile, South Africa, etc.) to those with social-democratic and 'progressive' tendencies (Tanzania, Algeria, etc.). The bulk of the developing states in peripheral capitalism would seem to be caught up between these two tendencies. For the ravages of the international recession, growing protectionism and monetarist policies of certain powers and financial institutions have enforced on them increased dependence on foreign assistance and investment with required 'attractive labour conditions', a euphemism for a docile labour force. It is therefore in this context that the role of the state in the restructuring of both capital and industrial relations to suit the former's requirements may be discussed.

To assert that the capitalist state regulates the relations between capital and workers is not tantamount to postulating that it is a disinterested institution. Its basic function is to protect and partake in the reproduction of the bourgeoisie and the bourgeois social and political relations of production. It is not an anti-bourgeois state in spite of some of its regulatory policies which may seem to annoy the bourgeoisie: policies on taxation which provide the financing of requisite social services; labour laws which guarantee minimum wages and acceptable working conditions; and welfare policies which ensure the basic, minimum needs for the unemployed, old, infirm and young. The net impact of these cushioning measures is to defuse and deflect the potentially revolutionary thrust which labour militacy might assume and develop. The capacity of the state to accommodate such a possible thrust is enhanced in the long-term interest of capital. But in what specific ways has the state attempted to restructure the industrial relations and capital to suit the long-term goals of the latter?

In peripheral capitalism, the process of restructuring industrial relations in order to stabilise the conditions of accumulation commenced during colonialism. With the exception of a few settler colonies, it was recognised quite early that there was a necessity for the creation of some framework of industrial relations which incorporated trade unions. Such unions were expected to be the representative channels of workers as well as instruments of control over them. As Damachi *et al* have observed:

> the concern of colonial powers was to develop a system of industrial relations that suited their own administrative

convenience, and in that system unions were to take a central place. Hence governments actively supported the formation and growth of unions...What was being introduced via government support was a kind of 'guided democracy' which has continued to exist until now.[13]

It is, of course, true that during the independence struggle the trade unions were often in the thick of the fight against colonialism: in many colonies, trade unions constituted the industrial wing of the nationalist movement. On that crest of patriotic nationalism fused with unionism such leaders as Sekou Touré, Tom Mboya, Siaka Stevens and Modibo Keita were swept into power. But the state apparatus inherited by these eminent 'freedom fighters' proved very adept at maintaining the stranglehold of capital on labour. Even in such potentially radical states such as Tanzania and Zambia, an element of continuity existed in policies on industrial relations.

In addition to harnessing the restraining and productionist capacities of trade unions in order to maintain favourable investment conditions which thrive on cheap, docile labour, states have played an interventionist role in the restructuring of trade unionism itself. The ostensible reason for the restructuring of unions has been the search for an elusive labour unity frustrated by the proliferation of splinter unions. It is not uncommon to find a multiplicity of such splinter organisations in a single industry with all the attendant dangers of competitive cut-throat struggles to outdo each other in their vying for membership and fomenting of industrial disputes. The rationale for the restructuring of unions into industrial unions is therefore posited as the enhancing of cohesiveness in the labour movement as well as providing one of the preconditions for stable industrial relations. It is not unusual for the project of industrial unionism to win the simultaneous endorsement of capital, state and trade unions.

Studies on the reorganisation of unions in such diverse countries as Ghana, Nigeria, Kenya, Tanzania and Zambia seem to have a common thread running through their analyses: and it is that state intervention in those reorganisation exercises was a key element in the restructuring of industrial relations, which had the effect of stabilising these as much as possible after the labour upheavals of the colonial era. It would therefore appear that the role of the state in industrial relations in peripheral capitalism has not been unproblematic. While there may have been the motivation to heal splits in and between trade unions, there has also existed a thirsty (even though veiled) desire to exert control over unions to achieve the various tasks of 'national economic development'. Such exertion of control has been possible via legislative fiat and sometimes through such repressive measures as the detention of unionists and often by the incorporation of the unions into the state or party apparatus. The effects of such incorporation and repression do not generally threaten the conditions of accumulation. For the immediate purposes of this paper, however, it is the significance for political economy of the relations between state, capital and trade unions that we wish to assess.

The Labour Movement Prior to 1980

Comprehensive studies on the evolution of trade unionism in Zimbabwe are conspicuous by their paucity. Yet a proper understanding of the character of post-independence trade unionism is possible only if its historical dimensions are taken into consideration. In this respect, it is necessary to allude to the impact of capitalist penetration on the various strategies of labour extraction and the response of that labour. In Southern Rhodesia, as colonial Zimbabwe than was called, the earliest endeavours to establish and regulate a labour market were:

(a) the founding of the provincial labour bureaux in 1895;
(b) the establishment of the Labour Board of Southern Rhodesia in 1899; and
(c) the Rhodesia Native Labour Bureau (RNLB).

The labour procurement institutions had their role facilitated by such labour legislation as:

(a) the Master and Servant Act of 1901;
(b) the Pass Law of 1902;
(c) the Private Locations Ordinance of 1910;
(d) the Industrial Conciliation Act of 1934;
(e) the Native Registration Act (1936);
(f) the Sedition Act (1936);
(g) the Compulsory Native Labour Act (1943).

The overall object of this paraphernalia of legislation was, of course, to control the flow or labour and impede unionisation and political activity among black workers. State laws and the related institutions must be construed as responses to the imperatives of capital to broaden its production capacity and scope to reproduce itself. They were therefore necessary conditions for its accumulation and reproduction.

The colonial state was an organ of capital: it gradually developed into an apparatus that was essentially repressive with regard to the agrarian and labour questions, which were interpreted as constituting formidable obstacles to capitalist penetration and accumulation. The state therefore consistently provided capital with the necessary infrastructural support, subsidies and other necessary services in addition to its 'normal' police functions with regard to the labour question. Whatever obstacles to accumulation existed at the levels of production and exchange were 'progressively' eliminated by the state. Firstly, the ownership of land, the crucial basis of capitalist agriculture, was resolved with the enforced expropriation of that land from peasant producers and their resettlement in labour reserves. Secondly, the self-sufficiency and resiliency of productivity of the peasant producers was broken via the manipulation of exchange relations between the producers and merchant capital. Thirdly, the labour question was tackled through the taxation of the producers and the compulsory insistence that labour was a form of taxation preferable to payment in cash or kind.

The harsh and dismal working conditions which existed under the regime of mining companies, transport services and plantations provoked open hostility and organised strikes even as early as 1895 and through the 1920s at mines such as Shamva and Wankie among others: and more covert responses in the form of desertions from centres of employment. In the 1920s and 1930s the Industrial and Commercial Workers' Union (ICU) played a leading role in the mobilisation of workers against the suppressive and exploitative working conditions. Indeed, according to Mapuranga, the dominant labour leader spanning the period from the 1920s to the 1950s, Charles Mzingeli, was the champion of the African working class in the mines, plantations and in the towns. Mapuranga also observed that:

(a) grievances of both the rural and urban proletariat and peasantry were exploited to radicalise them against the settler colonial state and its capitalist ruling class;
(b) the ICU represented the first formalised 'union-type' opposition of workers *qua* organised workers outside the more elitist African organisations;
(c) the ICU's leadership and support were founded on an indigenous and foreign migrant proletarian class which had rejected the dominant, elitist African organisations;
(d) Mzingeli and the ICU leadership were systematically constrained in their operation — by deportations, banning of meetings, withholding of official recognition, harassment by civil authorities, imprisonment and exclusion from mining compounds.[14]

Specifically, the introduction of the Industrial Conciliation Act (ICA) in 1934 and its amended version in 1959 were pledged to emasculate black trade unionism. The Act was the first comprehensive piece of labour legislation in terms of its regulatory scope; and the strictures on those unionists who contested for executive posts in the trade unions were a deterrent. Barred from office for five years were any unionists previously convicted of any offence involving fraud or dishonesty; and banned for ten years any person who had been sentenced for a term of three months or more on conviction of any offence under the Law and Order (Maintenance) Act (Chapter 65) or the Unlawful Organizations Act (Chapter 91). More explicitly, suppressive clauses prohibited the use of funds and facilities by trade unions for political purposes. Trade unions were denied rights:

(a) to affiliate with any political party or political organisation;
(b) to use any of their monies or funds for the furthering of interests of any political party or political organisation;
(c) to (by any provision in their constitution) require or permit any member thereof to subscribe to the funds of any political party or organisation;

(d) to use or permit use of any of their services, equipment or facilities for the purpose of furthering the interests of any political party or political organisation;

(e) to accept any monies or services from any organisation which is permitted by their constitution or otherwise to use their monies or funds for furthering the interests of any political party or political organisation.

The detailed references to the possibilities of linkages between trade unions and nationalist parties reflect the apprehension of the white minority regime at the prospect of the actual fusion of the trade union and nationalist struggles during the 1950s and 1960s. It has never quite been possible to separate economic struggles from political struggles; and under colonialism the convergence between the two was quicker than under normal conditions of capitalism or post-colonial struggles.

It is scarcely surprising that in the 1960s and 1970s a dark cloud hovered over trade unionism in Zimbabwe. A decimation of the leadership of unions through its incarceration in detention or exile, the onerous labour laws, in addition to the dubious role of international labour institutions such as the Brussels-based International Confederation of Free Trade Unions (ICFTU)—all had a generally weakening impact on the unions. In summary, the impediments to a vigorous unionism during this period have been summarised as follows:

(a) police harassment (there were 68 unionists in detention in 1973);

(b) absence of continuity in leadership due to harassment;

(c) the privileged but divisive status of the white labour aristocracy;

(d) role of international labour interests;

(e) the creation and presence of an industrial reserve army to pull down wage costs;

(f) internal power struggles in unions;

(g) financial problems due to an erratic and optional check-off system.

It was therefore not accidental nor particularly flabbergasting that, come independence in 1980, the Zimbabwe labour movement was in a weakened state due to internal fractions and external harassment. Nevertheless the cumulative effects of the struggles in the 1940s through to the 1970s were not negative to trade unionism as a whole. Their collectivisation of pan-ethnic interests *qua* workers, Clarke observed, had created new bases for further organisation:

a slow process that had required sustained worker pressure to force employers to yield and give concessions as Strike Inquiry Commissions transformed into Labour Boards and eventually, for some workers, into fully-fledged (but still circumscribed) bargaining instruments under the ICA. A foothold in the political arena has also been acquired in various forms. The institutionalisation of wage-setting machinery has meant the breaking in part of the employer monopoly on wage determination, even though this process is far from complete. The exercise of labour's power has established the basis for intervention in the system and resulted in the development of additional threats to employer interests. The institutionalization of unionism has permitted the entrenchment of a protective instrument of working-class welfare, this being not an insignificant achievement in the climate of repression during the period under review.[15]

The impressionistic image of trade unionism at independence as one of chronic debility and torpor is therefore an over-simplification of the true state of affairs. The thrust towards the democratisation of the labour movement would, however, require to overcome the structural impediments and ideological lapses that had been built into their *modus operandi* under the last decades of quasi-fascist white settler minority rule.

The Labour Unrest of 1980
Zimbabwe at independence was confronted with one of most severe industrial relations crises in its history. The collapse of the white minority regime which had relentlessly pursued repressive labour and social policies seemed to have opened up a pandora's box of militant labour protest and industrial action. It would be short-sighted and naive though to assume that the widespread nationwide uprising of the workers was an automatic gesture of defiance against capital. Political conditions of suppression and the economic framework of exploitation had created the basis of a smouldering cauldron of labour restiveness which was bound to explode sooner or later. A series of such explosions had already occurred, if intermittently, in 1948, 1964 and 1979. The explosions left labour casualties in their wake: miners shot dead, industrial workers detained and masses of workers intimidated. The advent of independence, therefore, assumed added significance to the workers: the introduction of such political freedoms as the vote, of association and of expression — all of which were fruits of the armed liberation struggle — removed the more draconian aspects of state and capital repression of the working class (see Table 1).

There was, however, a gaping vacuum in the unity of the labour movement owing to the proliferation of several vying labour centres when the first spate of strikes erupted in March 1980. Most of the strikes in March, April and May of that year tended to be both contagious and spontaneous. But they were all mostly unanimous on the objectives of increased pay, better working conditions, dismissal of abusive managers and supervisors, the reinstatement of dismissed militant workers and clarification on the question of pension schemes. The strikes demonstrated their wide-embracing nature nationally and industrially: agricultural, agro-industrial, mine, municipal, transport and public service workers participated in one way or the other in those strikes. As we pointed out, there was deep and widespread dissatisfaction with the wage structure, general working conditions and cumbersome industrial conciliation procedures. There existed revulsion against most aspects of legislation on industrial relations: such legal pieces as the *Master and Servant Act*, the *Industrial Conciliation Act*, the *African Juvenile Employment Act*, the *African Labour Regulation Act* and the *Foreign Migratory Act* were viewed as an affront to the dignity and interests of workers. Even weeks before the formal transfer of power to the new government in April 1980, the country shook from massive withdrawals of labour. As R.M. Gwavava of the Zimbabwe Congress of Trade Unions (ZCTU) described the unfolding situation:

> strikes were spontaneous actions arising from the fundamental problem of the Zimbabwe workers' inability to live on the current level of wages. The settlement of wage claims required Government's immediate attention to find common ground between workers and management.[15]

At the same time, the upsurge in strikes revealed the obsoleteness of the capitalist machinery of the conciliation of labour disputes. In the analysis of Phineas Sithole of the African Trade Union Congress (ATUC), the strikes represented an attempt to bypass the industrial conciliation procedures and appeal directly to the government for higher wages:

> the process of industrial negotiation is slow and they want immediate action... I do sympathise to some extent with the strikers as their aspirations have not been met.[17]

The structure of industrial relations, with a few exceptions, prior to independence revealed their infiltration by tendencies of a suppressive and racist nature. Workers were treated as sub-human tools of production who were denied consultation and participation at the workplace. The new Minister of Labour, Mr. Kangai, candidly admitted that he had, in his role as a trouble-shooter, been surprised during the course of his discussions with management and workers at the dearth of communication between them. In his view 'some employers either ignored, or were completely unaware of the legitimate grievances of their workers, some of which had existed for a long time'.[18]

If, initially, it was the disregard of the need for communication with workers in order to ascertain their views on wages, working conditions and social aspirations which accounted for the contagious rash of strikes which took the country by storm, the fundamental basis of the strikes was nevertheless the deep-rooted antagonism between capital and labour. Although workers could not articulate cogently the essence of the character of this antagonism, they focussed on wage conditions, racism and managerial dictatorship at the work-place. Independence presented a unique opportunity to strike some blows at capital, no matter how uncoordinated and spontaneous these might have been. An official of the Zimbabwe Federation of Labour remarked that it was natural for the workers to behave as they had because of high expectations about improvements which the new government had pledged to undertake. In its own comments *The Herald* observed that the major reason for:

> the sudden industrial unrest was the 'crisis of expectation' coming after the general election but other factors ranging from possible agitation to pure misunderstanding also contributed to what had happened.[19]

It added that:

> some of the workers did not seem to know why they were striking; some were acting on incorrect information; and no doubt to others it was the expectation of large pay packets from the word go.[20]

Notwithstanding the bourgeois cynicism and misrepresentation which informed this view, these were perceptive observations on the disorganised character of the strikes. Although they underlined the antagonistic character of the capital-labour relations, they did not constitute a coherent programme of assault on capital: the political content of the strikes never really became progressively explicit. Their spontaneity and contagious adventurism were not transformed into a broad social and political anti-capitalist movement. Improved wages, better working conditions, the establishment of communication channels with management and freedom of association or organisation could be resisted by capital but these certainly were not incompatible with its stability.

No sooner therefore had the spate of strikes gripped the country, engulfing such transnational enterprises as the Hippo Valley and Triangle Estates, Rio Tinto Zinc and Wankie Colliery, Steward and Lloyds and David Whitehead Textiles, and so forth (see Table 1) than a co-ordinated response by capital, in conjunction with the state apparatus, defused and eventually dissipated the strikes and other forms of labour militancy. The ideological hegemony of capital had ably succeeded in portraying the strikes as irresponsible, disorganised, unpatriotic and subversive social elements bent on economic sabotage. It could be demonstrated fairly easily that the labour force in this country was none of these. But this did not restrain *The Herald* from editorialising that workers who refused to use the recognised channels:

> who resorted to strike action not in the end but at the start of bargaining process (and even before it starts) must be told firmly that this is no way to achieve their ends. Action of this kind amounts to sabotage of the country's economy and in the circumstances in which the young nation of Zimbabwe finds itself, it is totally unacceptable.[21]

Some months later, the paper would truthfully note that the economy was so 'fragilely balanced that the effect of the April strikes was to wipe out the trade surplus for May while exports were down almost 10% at a time when the costs of imports is rising.'[22] Quite clearly, 'industrial unrest over even a short period has an immediate effect on our foreign currency earnings'.[23] If the bourgeoisie had immediate worries at that juncture, these were profits and foreign exchange earnings: never mind the inhuman working and wage conditions which workers experienced!

Nevertheless there was no doubt that the strikes (on the unprecedented scale on which they occurred) left a permanent dent on the smug complacency of the bourgeoisie. They were now more clearly aware of the capacity of labour to upset conditions of production, profitability and accumulation. The President of the Association of Rhodesian Industries (ARNI), Mr. Hillis, remarked that his Hillis association was gravely concerned over the 'sudden rash of illegal strikes throughout the industry' and that he intended to draw the attention of 'all concerned to the proper machinery for settling industrial disputes which is so ably regulated by the Industrial Conciliation Act.'[24] It was however precisely this legislative machinery of regulating industrial conflict which had hopelessly failed to arrest the deterioration in industrial relations. The obsoleteness of the machinery—especially in the post-independence era—rendered capital vulnerable to intermittent blows from labour in the form of massive, if short-lived, withdrawals of labour. It also made it an object of inarticulate demands for the redress of wage and social grievances. In the confrontation, capital naturally sought the assistance of the state and its massive apparatus for the resolution of the one of the worst crises in industrial relations which the country had ever experienced. The Minister of Labour, government industrial relations officers and party officials all played a mediatory role in the defusing of the crisis.

The Responses of State, Capital and Unions

Some brief references have already been made concerning the character of the response of the state and capital to the labour upheavals. But as a necessary preamble to an assessment of this response, it is not unreasonable to review briefly the status of trade unionism at independence. The remark has been made above that there was a gaping vacuum in organised trade unionism at independence. When the strikes erupted in 1980, it had immediately become apparent that trade unions could not be counted upon to articulate workers' demands or restrain their members from spontaneous industrial action. They were neither radical enough to articulate in a cogent and progressive manner the unanimous platform of the workers on wages and working conditions nor strong enough to rein in the militants who pushed for strikes. Both from the radical and bourgeois perspectives, therefore, the existing trade unions were ineffective, disorganised and almost moribund institutions. The spotlight was turned on them and the bourgeoisie and state did not like what they saw!

It was, however, one of the veteran trade unionists, Mr. Bloomfield, President of the Associated Mineworkers' Union for 37 years, who highlighted the general concern with the fissiparous tendencies in trade unionism. The wave of strikes, in his opinion, had demonstrated the need for an expansion and professionalisation of trade unionism in Zimbabwe:

> a good, developed union run by professional, educated men, which are very necessary these days in unions, can help rather

than hinder the economic development of industries. Unions are a braking mechanism, as opposed to the damaging wildcat strikes that we are seeing now. They can stop the trouble before it gets out of hand. They can render assistance both to employers and employees.[25]

The significant observation in these remarks was that trade unions possessed the capacity to play a restraining role in the circumstances of radicalised labour action such as strikes. To that extent, capital valued highly such a moderating and mediatory role of organised unionism. It was therefore greatly disappointing to capital and the state that unions at independence had very little muscle to show, hence the rapid proliferation of strikes throughout the country.

The then Minister of Labour observed that, from his own investigation since his assumption of office, the current wave of strikes could have been averted if there had been grassroots liaison between unions and workers:

Trade unions should be the first to know of any dissatisfaction which exists among workers who they are supposed to represent. But most union officials were out of touch with workers and guilty of taking workers' dues by misrepresentation. The only contact these unions have with the workers has been by telephone. It is not enough.[26]

The loss of contact between unions and their rank-and-file members was an eloquent commentary on the chronic weakness of unionism generally: the colonial state itself had assiduously blocked the development of a more vigorous variety! But if divided and weak unionism was a boon to the colonial regime and capital, it was a serious liability at independence. The media joined in the lambasting of the 'irresponsible, inefficient and effete unionists.'

The National Observer reiterated the general concern that:

One major discovery has come in the wake of the strikes—trade unions are not as efficient as they should be...Collecting dues and making phone calls are not enough. They should take the lead from the nation's top trade unionist, Howard Bloomfield, and get out there among the people they represent.[27]

It was in an attempt to fill the conspicuous vacuum in labour organisation that steps were taken to create a single labour centre. In the preliminary steps towards its creation, the government was closely involved in discussions with both the United Trade Unions of Zimbabwe (UTUZ), which was later ignored and allowed to dissolve, and the Zimbabwe Congress of Trade Unions (ZCTU), which was later acknowledged as the sole national labour centre. That the party and government were represented in the initial discussions to found the ZCTU testifies to the deep interest and significance which they attached to the establishment of a cohesive labour organisation which would not only represent the generality of workers but also participate actively in the maintenance of stable industrial relations. The interim co-ordinating committee consisted of Messrs. Makwarimba, Sithole, Nyashanu, Mugabe, Mawere, Gwekwerere, Ndawana, Soko and Chamunogwa. Most of these figures would later become quite prominent in Zimbabwe labour politics; some as controversial divisionists; others as centres of allegations of maladministration and corruption; while others resigned in due course. But right from its inception in July 1980, the ZCTU was embroiled in problematic controverises.

The focus on the quest for a cohesive labour organisation precisely because none existed at independence should not deflect our attention from the quest for another institutional mechanism to moderate industrial conflicts. There was a poor state of communication between management and workers in most firms; the strikes had thrown into broad relief the yawning gap in communication flows while management was particularly worried by the militancy displayed by workers in conflicts on the shop-floor. As *The Herald* editorialised:

> in each of the stoppages, one of the main reasons seems to be lack of communication between management and workers... There are faults on both sides, but many companies are beginning to learn that they stand to gain more by fostering active, responsible worker-employer relationships than they do by wielding the big stick.[28]

The state saw a solution to the communication gap or blockage in the establishment of 'liaison committees' which later became known as 'workers' committees'. The Minister of Labour urged workers to channel their grievances to management through committees elected by workers themselves. Negotiations with management would be conducted by those workers' committees on matters pertaining to conditions on the shop-floor. Thus the establishment of workers' committees in the various enterprises may be viewed as an additional response to the industrial conflagration experienced at independence. But it was an industrial relations expert, Mr. Nehwati, who frankly discussed the dimensions of the crisis and the efficacy of workers' committees. Urging employers to devise a new strategy to pre-empt strikes in the country, he observed that the wave of labour unrest had been replaced by a 'shop-floor revolt' which was a by-product of the new social order in Zimbabwe:

> it is true that the workers feel that the political change at the national level must be reflected at their work-place. Because of this, management is now under very close scrutiny for anything that they consider to be a perpetuation of the former racial system...Workers' committees are very essential and employers must recognise them. The solution lay in management motivating the workers to feel that they were also part of the company and could participate in decisions through the workers' committees.[29]

Essentially, workers' committees could operate to the advantage of companies in vetting grievances, discussing them with management and defusing 'shop-floor' crises whenever they occurred.

Perhaps the most significant response of the state to the spate of industrial action in 1980 was the legislation on minimum wage scales in that same year. This represented a historical departure from the wage policy of the colonial regime: never before had the bulk of the workforce been affected by, and directly benefited from, legislation which decreed minimum scales. The Minister of Labour remarked that, in order to counter the 'crisis of expectation' among workers, wages needed to be increased with immediate effect. With the advent of independence, workers had fallen victim to 'a crisis of expectation' which resulted in a wave of industrial strikes, the minister observed. He added that it was therefore logical that the government must of necessity enable every citizen to have access to a job that would enable him 'to feed, clothe and house his family'. From the 1 July 1980 a minimum wage of 30 dollars a month for domestic and agricultural workers was introduced; and all workers in urban centres and those covered by industrial agreements and industrial regulations, with the exception of those in agriculture and mining, were to receive 70 dollars a month, which was to be further raised to 85 dollars per month in January 1981. The Minister of Labour said:

> The primary consideration had been to take steps which would bring immediate benefit to the most lowly paid workers without causing redundancies or endangering the economic expansion which will take place as a result of Zimbabwe assuming her rightful place amongst the trading nations of the world.[30]

There was widespread support for the introduction of minimum wages which were seen as a direct tangible benefit that had been fought for in the industrial struggles of that year. It was, however, pointed out that, although union leaders had generally welcomed the introduction of the minimum wages for workers in the various industries, they felt that the minister had not gone far enough.[31] Trade union leaders noted that workers earning more than 70 dollars a month had been disappointed 'as they had expected something more from the new government'. They felt that if the government had involved them in consultations leading to the minimum wage legislation, they would have suggested a wage more related to that recommended in a poverty datum line survey, which was about 120 dollars a month. In a critical editorial, *The Sunday Mail* was quite blunt:

> the minimum wages introduced are far less than expected by employers. They are not high enough: they do not meet the level of the poverty datum line and do not offer a reasonable living standard. Think about it dispassionately. How well off is a worker with $70 in his pocket and a wife and family to feed?[32]

The minimum wage legislation, in spite of its limitations, was a significant landmark in the field of industrial relations, especially in that it set an important precedent in Government intervention in wage-setting for the lower-income categories of workers. There was therefore widespread resistance to the new legislation by the bourgeoisie, particularly at the implementation stage. The bourgeois response was the retrenchment of workers just before the bill of minimum wages became law in July 1980. It even became necessary for the Minister of Labour to appeal to employers to desist from dismissing workers; and when the appeal fell on deaf ears, he had to warn them to expect 'the severest penalties' which amounted to a maximum of $1,000 plus 3 months labour. He also spoke against certain 'unscrupulous employers' who had reduced wages from a figure well in excess of the required minimum to the minimum level. Retrenchment and reduction of wages to the minimum scales were tactics of the bourgeoisie to minimise the impact of the new scales on the profitability of their firms. There were the inevitable cut-downs of labour in various sectors including domestic service and capitalist agriculture. What the introduction of minimum wages demonstrated was the capacity of the state to intervene actively in industrial relations on the side of the workers.

Wage increases had been long overdue. The resistance of the bourgeoisie to the new scales was not only predictable but also underscored their capacity to cut their possible losses in surpluses by quickly adjusting to the new labour and income measures. The minimum wage scales were not universally acclaimed; they would be adjusted from time to time but, more importantly, they would not seriously undermine the general prevailing conditions of capitalist production, reproduction and accumulation.

The Labour Relations Act (1985)

One of the most significant pieces of social and political legislation which the Zimbabwe Parliament debated and approved during the first five years of independence was the Labour Relations Bill of 1985. It was a comprehensive code of regulations relating to employment, remuneration, collective bargaining, the settlement of disputes, the registration and certification of trade unions and employers' organisations. The Labour Relations Bill, however, incorporated some of the provisions of the Industrial Conciliation Act (which was accordingly repealed) and most aspects of post-independence ligislation relating to minimum wages, conditions of employment, procedures of dismissal and redundancies.

The objectives of the Labour Relations Act (LRA) were quite wide-ranging. They were specified in the preamble as the declaration and definition of the fundamental rights of workers; the definition of unfair labour practices; the regulation of conditions of employment and other related matters; provision for the appointment and functions of workers' committees; to provide for the formation, registration, certification and functions of trade unions, employment councils and employment boards; to regulate the negotiation, scope and functions of the Labour Relations Board and the Labour Relations Tribunal; to regulate and control employment agencies; to repeal the Industrial Conciliation Act; and finally to provide for matters connected with or incidental to the foregoing.[33]

Significantly, the new elements among others in the LRA relate to the definition of fundamental rights of workers and unfair labour practices; the legalisation on the appointment and spelling out of the functions of workers' committees; the regulations of the negotiation, scope and enforcement of collective bargaining agreements; the regulation and control of employment agencies.

Quite clearly, the definition of the fundamental rights of workers represented a departure from previous legislation, which had excluded some categories of workers on racial grounds from the jurisdiction of the law (the Industrial Conciliation Act of 1934) and excluded farm and domestic workers from its protective provisions (the Industrial Conciliation Act of 1960). Whatever references to workers' rights had existed were in a generally watered-down form and even then the machinery for their enforcement was often obsolete. As a corrective the scope of the fundamental rights of workers in the LRA ranges from entitlement to membership of trade unions and workers' committees without fear of reprisals or victimisation from management; the protection of workers against discrimination in recruitment, advertisement of employment; in the determination of remuneration and benefits; and in the creation, classification or abolition of jobs. Discrimination on the basis of race, tribe, place of origin, political opinion, colour, creed or sex in relation to the foregoing has been outlawed and made punishable by a considerable fine or imprisonment.[34]

In addition to these rights, there are clauses to safeguard workers' rights to fair labour standards which relate to minimum wages, maximum amount of hours of work per day, occupational health and safety. The rights of the worker to seek access to 'any lawful proceeding that may be available to enable him lawfully to advance or protect his interest as an employee' is guaranteed. The contravention of fair labour standards is an offence subject to penalty. Furthermore, the protection of workers' rights to democracy in the workplace is also guaranteed. For that purpose, every employer is required to allow a labour relations officer or representative of the appropriate trade union or employment board to have reasonable access to his employees at their workplace during working hours for the purpose of advising workers in the law relating to their employment; advising and assisting workers with regard to the formation or conducting of workers' committees and trade unions; and ensuring that the rights and interests of workers are protected and advanced. In addition, the employer was expected to provide these officials with reasonable facilities for the exercise of such functions.

Probably the most controversial sections of the LRA relate to the specification of the circumstances and sectors in which industrial action could be resorted to and the extensive scope for ministerial intervention in industrial relations. The right to industrial action was generally accepted to be a fundamental right of workers; any encroachment on it was regarded as a potentially disruptive operation conducive to economic and political chaos. Governments, by their very nature, would favour as many safeguards and restrictions as possible on strikes. The lengthier the procedures that need to be followed before it was 'lawful' to strike, the less inconvenient. Hence the ideological and legal paraphernalia which portrays strike activity as essentially 'anti-social', 'disruptive' and 'irresponsible'. And the more workers were induced to perceive strike activity as not only the last resort but also 'a privilege', the less workers would perceive industrial action to be their inherent right.

Under the LRA, the sectors in which strikes were prohibited constitute a vast portion of the economy. These sectors, euphemistically termed 'essential services' include the following: any service relating to the generation, supply or distribution of electricity; any fire-brigade or fire service; any sewerage, rubbish disposal or other sanitation service; any health, hospital and ambulance service; any service relating to the production, supply, delivery or distribution of food or fuel; any service relating to the supply or distribution of water; mining, including any service required for the working of a mine; any communications service; any transport service and any service relating to the repair and maintenance, or to the driving, loading and unloading of a vehicle for use in any transport service; any service relating to any road, railway, bridge, ferry, pontoon or airfield; and any other service or occupation which the ministers may, after consultation with the appropriate trade union and employers' organisation, declare by notice in the Gazette to be an essential service.[35]

The very broad scope of the 'essential services' sector underscored the deterrent aspect of LRA with regard to industrial action. Even in those sectors outside its ambit, the procedures that had to be followed before such an action becomes 'legal' are constrictive enough. No industrial action could be countenanced unless redress in respect of the dispute concerned has been sought in terms of (Part XIII) or in respect of any matter that has been determined or disposed of in terms of (Part XIII); or in contravention of a 'show cause order' or 'disposal order'. That is also the case if the matter in dispute is governed by existing regulations or collective bargaining agreements or by any workers' committee if there is in existence a certified trade union which represents the unions concerned and has not authorised the strike; by any trade union unless it is certified; or by any workers' committee if there is in existence a union agreement which provides for the matter in dispute.

There was, however, a new departure in the LRA in that strikes could take place where occupational safety and health conditions of work constitute a risk to workers. They could also occur where the existence of a trade union or workers' committee is in jeopardy. Nevertheless, the anxiety concerning the undermining of the negotiating strength of unions due to the proliferation of essential services seems real enough. The possibility that unscrupulous employers could take advantage of this aspect of the legislation does exist. Given the contradictions in the state, it is also extremely possible that the pressures of structural constraints, lobbying of elements within the government and the lack of comprehensive alternative policies could lead the state to enforce its anti-strike legislation in increasingly authoritarian ways. This would be done in the 'national interest' especially given both the production/investment crisis in the economy and the promise of regional destabilisation. The lack of hegemonic alternatives on the part of the state would, however, make this 'national interest' argument increasingly problematic, but would retain a given level of credibility as long as the perspectives of the labour movement remain as confused as they are at present.

The practical implementation of the legislation would have to depend on the pivotal role of the Minister of Labour, who wields extensive powers under the LRA. The diffus nature of his authority underlay the whole Act and resulted in the diminution of power which, ultimately, is a reflection of state power. In this instance its concentration in the hands of the minister signified consciously increased state intervention in industrial relations. Such expanded intervention is virtually guaranteed under the LRA. Thus the minister might intervene if he/she wishes in the investigation and administration of trade unions; in their registration and certification; in the control and constraining of strikes; in the fixting of minimum and maximum wages; and 'where the national interest so demands' in the supervision of elections of registered or certified trade unions. The minister had also been invested with powers to annul collective bargaining agreements between workers and management if he deemed that they are not in the interest of consumers or the economy in general.

Why was it judged necessary for the state to possess such extensive powers in industrial relations? One of the possible factors to explain the paternalism that permeated the bureaucratic (industrial relations) apparatus of the state was what was perceived to be a fraction-ridden labour movement that had undergone crisis after crisis during the first four years of independence. Whether that paternalism was justified or the wisest response to the problem of a fractured labour movement, developments in labour relations in the next few years should provide an answer.

The extensive state intervention in industrial relations must be assessed in relation to three factors:

(i) The strikes of 1980/83 demonstrated the potential for conflict between labour and the state, during a period in which the labour movement's own objectives were diffuse and unclear. In addition, the immediate post-independence years represented a period of consolidation of state power during which an unclearly defined relationship with labour activity had proved to be extremely problematic.

(ii) The fractures and disorganisation of the central labour organisations provided no clear focal point through which labour could channel its struggles, nor with which the state could formulate a joint policy.

(iii) The problematic relationship between nationalism and the labour movement, especially after the 1950s meant that, while the nationalists articulated certain broad multi-class aspirations, the specific weight of the labour movement's input into the definition of those national interests decreased. As has been outlined in chapter one, the wage-earning class was only one factor—and not the dominant and leading one—in the struggle for national liberation. This aspect, combined with the increasing difficulty of labour organisation during the UDI period, and the changed nature of the struggle during the 1970s, helps to explain some of the current problems between the state and labour in the period since 1980.

At a fundamental level, however, the passage of the LRA represented a major advance for the working class to the degree that its fundamental rights have been formally specified and guaranteed; and to the extent that its previous gains accumulated since independence were consolidated. It was the realisation of the progressive character of these measures that led the representatives of the bourgeoisie—the minority party representatives in the Zimbabwe Parliament, the financial press and elsewhere—bitterly to attack its introduction.[36] There was also an element of posturing in the attitude of employers to the LRA. A representative from the Employers Confederation of Zimbabwe (EMCOZ) clearly stated that much of the new legislation was standard in most countries. Moreover, he noted that the anti-strike legislation clearly favoured employers, since the strike was labour's fundamental weapon. At the same time, the long gestation period of the legislation constituted a testimony to the complexity of the issues covered and the cumbersomeness of the processes of consultation in its drafting. The haggling that accompainied the deliberation of the legal draftsmen and the interminable meetings with employers' organisations underlined the sort of semantic and ideological struggles which characterise duels between the intellectual representatives of the bourgeoisie, state apparatus and trade unions. In that respect, the LRA therefore reflects the social reality that in contemporary Zimbabwe the balance of class power is still heavily weighted in favour of the bourgeoisie.

Labour Problems in Agro-Industry 1985

The conflict between the state and agro-industrial enterprises and spontaneous industrial action by workers in the enterprises during the last quarter of 1985 revealed the brittleness of industrial peace in the country. More fundamentally, it exposed the festering sore that had characterised labour relations and working conditions in agriculture and the agro-based processing industry for many years. The inhospitable working conditions and wage structure within the industry during colonialism were notorious. At independence, as a consequence of pent-up bitterness, some of the most prolonged strikes were organised on such agro-industrial estates as Hippo Valley and Triangle which specialise in sugar; at Mazoe, the hub of fruit production, and in the Eastern Highlands, where tea and coffee production is specialised. These enterprises were not only characterised by their transnational ownership and control (concentrated mainly in Anglo-American and Lonrho) but also by a tradition of labour militancy repeatedly subjected to repression before independence. The roots of this militacy may be traced to the collective response of workers against harsh conditions on the enterprises and to the favourable advantage for mobilisation of greater concentrations of workers engaged in related labour processes. The concentration of hundreds and often thousands of workers on plantations and in the adjacent processing factories which utilise raw materials from the plantations spawns a common workers' identity, culture and radical response to capitalist exploitation.

The strikes which were organised on tea and coffee plantations in the Eastern Highlands—and elsewhere, including the Arbor Acres poultry estate—had their immediate cause in the refusal of employers to pay new minimum wages. In the July 1985 wage guidelines, workers in agro-industry were entitled to a new minimum wage of Z$143 per month. Workers engaged in purely agricultural tasks interpreted the new guidelines as concerning them as well. It was, therefore, when employers insisted that the new minimum wages were payable only to workers engaged in the various aspects of processing that agricultural workers felt piqued by the discriminatory scales. Quite spontaneously, the workers who were paid less than the stipulated minimum participated in work stoppages. State-owned agro-indistrial enterprises were also affected by these stoppages in September and October 1985. For their part, agro-industrial companies pleaded their inability to award the minimum wage: imminent bankruptcy was cited by the transnationals, individual farmers and state-owned enterprises.

It was not until November of the same year that some kind of compromise was hammered out among the state, agro-industry and trade unions. The major bone of contention between them had reportedly been the incapacity of the companies to pay the new minimum. In post-independence labour legislation there had always been allowance for exemptions to pay the minimum wage if a particular enterprise could not economically afford to do so. In this particular instance, the companies clamoured more or less for mass exemption. The resolution of the dispute therefore centred on the offsetting of the new minimum. After extensive consultations in Manicaland and Chiredzi, state officials reached the conclusion that purely agricultural enterprises which were not engaged in processing could not afford to pay the monthly Z$143.75.[37] Lower minimum wages were then stipulated for 355 small-scale, commercial, parastatal and transnational enterprises which had submitted applications for exemptions. Agricultural workers would then be paid a new minimum wage of Z$85 per month; and those in agro-industry Z$110. It was reported that the cabinet had assessed the various aspects of the enterprises which had applied for exemption: those aspects included the economic viability of each enterprise in relation to the employer's ability to pay the new minimum as well as the 'strategic importance' of the commodity that was being produced.[38]

The stoppages in agro-industry and the resultant compromise were reflective of the social contradictions of capitalism in contemporary Zimbabwe. In the last analysis, it had been the collective force and reaction of capital which had forced the re-interpretation and modification of the social legislation on minimum wages and working conditions. Elements of capital proved to be not averse to holding the government and masses to ransom when they perceived a mortal threat to the conditions of their accumulation and reproduction. The revision of wage-scales in agro-industry clearly demonstrated the limits of state intervention in the redistribution of social wealth. It also generally reflected the limited efficacy of progressive labour legislation under capitalism. The incidence of work stoppages on state agro-industrial enterprises and state-sponsored joint ventures underscored the persistence of social contradictions in publicly-owned enterprises.

The Labour Movement: Problems and Future Prospects
During the period 1981 to 1985, the ZCTU underwent a debilitating crisis in its leadership and in its relationships with some of its affiliated unions. The crisis arose from problems relating to its vulnerably total dependence on external sources of material support, which provided opportunities for corruption, embezzlement, maladministration, nepotism and authoritarianism. The combination of financial irregularities and the suspected embezzlement of donated funds by some of the leading brass in the ZCTU resulted in a backlash from both within the organisation and other quarters. From within the Congress emerged recriminations against some of the leaders: one clique was identified as making the sole decisions on monies from outside the country, on how to handle and share it amongst themselves. There were allegations from within the Congress that, in fact, one of its leaders had managed to purchase a house in the posh suburb of Gunhill in Harare; that another owned the Headlands Hotel; and that another had also bought a house, a bottle store and grinding mill in Seke on the outskirts; and that yet another played a dual role as an employers' representative in the Industrial Boards and as an employees' representative in the National Industrial Council (NIC). The political affiliations of members of the Congress leadership were discussed in the context of those recriminations; some were alleged to have supported Muzorewa's and Chikerema's parties, others, ZANU (Mwenje) of Sithole. By mid-1984, the atmosphere of corruption, graft and conspiracy seemed to have clouded activities and simultaneously provoked adverse publicity in the media and public discussion. Somehow, the belief was general and articulated that if the Congress had failed to put its house in order, the state should step in on its behalf. Hence state intervention at the beginning of 1985, when senior industrial relations officers were seconded to the ZCTU to sort out its parlous financial affairs and prepare for its Second Congress.

The altruistic intentions of state intervention were vindicated in the total eclipse of the executive of the ZCTU at the July 1985 elections and the election of a more dynamic and articulate executive drawn from some of the best organised trade unions in the country. Clearly, the democratic spirit which permeated the various unions and structure in the labour movement prevailed during the Second Congress of the ZCTU in July

1985. A comprehensive social and economic programme embracing social welfare, workers' education, research, wages, prices and investment was unveiled, demonstrating a much clearer grasp of the immediate tasks which the labour movement identified as its major priorities.

The Zimbabwe state is of course deeply interested in the direction in which trade unionism is moving. Indeed state intervention in the restructuring of industrial relations and of trade unionism cannot be assumed naively as disinterested because such intervention is imbued with some class character of some sort. In the project of socialist transition, the political and ideological complexion of unionism becomes of utmost significance to the state. Nevertheless the class character of the state would be an important determining element in the thrust of its intervention. A bourgeois state and its apparatus cannot, without upheavals of some kind, implement socialist labour policies and industrial relations.

It is in this respect that, in Zimbabwe, the decisive factor in the formation and consolidation of trade unionism supportive of socialist objectives and ethics may not so much emerge from state intervention as from the role of the political organisations which have a strong representation of the working class. The exertion of its hegemony in the organisations or party could transform the character of trade unionism and inevitably that of the organisations or party as well. Such transformation would necessarily have to involve mass political and ideological mobilisation of workers. Such a transformation would also require the encouragement of democratic forces and processes in trade unionism as legalistic forms of state intervention by an untransformed state apparatus would have a limited, if not mixed, impact on restructuring unionism and industrial relations. As a leading poliburo member of ZANU (PF) observed:

> the point cannot be over-emphasised that a weak working class yields a weak congress of trade unions and that [such] a weak congress cannot hope to spearhead the working class struggle against the international bourgeoisie.[39]

It might have been added that the struggle inevitably would also be against the local bourgeoisie which services its international mentors! In a succinct analysis of this sort, the problems the ZCTU experienced—of theft, forgery and the existence of splinter unions—could therefore be explained in terms of low class-consciousness. How to raise and generalise that consciousness should therefore be the priority not only of the trade unions and political organisations but also of progressive theoreticians and researchers.

Conclusion

In this paper we have attempted to assess the pertinent issues that arise from the substance of the contemporary forms of industrial relations in Zimbabwe. It was suggested at the beginning of the paper that industrial relations reveal the substantial character of the social and political relations of any given society; and that state, capital and trade unions in varying degrees play significant roles in the determination and modification of industrial relations and ultimately class and political relationships. The theoretical discussion of the character of capital, state and unions, their supportive and divergent relationships underlined a number of probematics which have historically bogged down those relationships:

(a) the economism of trade unionism;
(b) the economic and ideological hegemony of capital;
(c) the political expression and consolidation of that hegemony in the state;
(d) the tendency towards the ideological subordination of trade unionism to that of capital and state.

These various aspects of relationships which express and condition class struggle raise very fundamental issues with regard to strategies and tactics for working-class struggles to usher in socialism. The absence of such strategies and alliances with progressive forces at independence created a vacuum into which the capitalist state—never mind how peripheral or welfarist stepped—to create centralised union federations or coopt into its apparatus the existent labour movement. The objective and result of such intervention or cooption invariably tended to be *not* the transition to *nor* the construction of socialism but the consolidation of capitalism by a careful regulation of the requisite labour conditions for capitalism. Yet it would be mistaken from strategic and tactical points of view to dismiss trade unionism. Scientific analyses of concrete conditions and conjunctures rather than dogmatic formulations of the problematics would be the prerequisite to the adoption of appropriate strategies and techniques of the struggle.

It was demonstrated cogently how the upsurge in labour militancy which was channelled in the widespread, and in some instances prolonged, strikes of 1980 and 1981 underscored the repressive character of the relationship between labour and capital. The eventual concessions which the bourgeoisie made to the workers were not inconsiderable, but these were at the behest of a popularly elected government. Nevertheless, both the concessions by the bourgeoisie (in the form of payment of minimum wages, reinstatement of dismissed workers, and the phasing out of racial and sex discrimination) and the positive intervention on behalf of workers by the state did not affect the overall framework and conditions of capitalist production and social relations very substantially. It was as if the project to encircle capitalism while building up workers' power at the site of production and within the party was left to hang in the balance. Six years after independence, the resolution of this problem lies at the heart of Zimbabwe's future: the postponement of its resolution would buy more time for the bourgeoisie to continue regrouping and entrenching itself!

TABLE I

THE 1980 AND 1981 STRIKES: THE AFFECTED ENTERPRISES AND THE GRIEVANCES

March 1980

1.	Fashions Enterprises (Private)	Protest against contributions to a pension scheme involving the company and the union.
2.	Cone Textiles (Private) Ltd	Protest against the abuse of a worker by the production manager.
3.	Tube and Pipes Ltd	Demand that the minimum factory wage be increased from 30 cents to $1 and hour.
4.	Concorde Clothing (Private) Ltd	Demand for dismissal of a floor manager and two supervisors.
5.	Rhodesia Weaving Mills Ltd	Dispute on working hours.
6.	W.S. Craster (Private) Ltd	Protest against pay conditions and inadequate protective clothing.
7.	Bata Shoe Company	Demand for more pay.
8.	Grain Marketing Board	Demand for more pay.
9.	Roberts Construction Co.	Pay conditions.
10.	W R S Cabinet Factory	Pay conditions.
11.	Sparrow Garment Factory (Umtali)	Pay conditions.
12.	Consolidated Textile (Bulawayo)	Pay conditions.
13.	Dalny Gold Mine	Pension payments.
14.	Bowline Furniture Co.Ltd (Salisbury)	Higher wages.
15.	R.K. Footwear Ltd Salisbury	Increased wages.
16.	National Foods Ltd Salisbury	Increased wages.
17.	Quadcon (Private) Ltd Salisbury	Increased wages.
18.	John Sisk Ltd Salisbury	Increased wages.
19.	Kariba Batteries (Gwelo)	Increased wages.
20.	Cold Storage Commission (Gatooma)	Higher wages.
21.	David Whitehead Ltd	Higher wages.
22.	Gatooma Municipality	Higher wages.
23.	Lobels Bakery	Unspecified.
24.	London Bakery	Unspecified.
25.	North-West Bakery	Unspecified.
26.	Arbor Acres	Unspecified
27.	Venice Mine	Unspecified.
28.	David Whitehead (Gatooma)	Unspecified.
29.	Zona Tea Estates (Chipinga)	Wage dispute.
30.	Rhodesia Omnibus Co.	Unspecified.

April 1980

31.	Rodia Chemical Industries	Overtime pay.
32.	Borrowdale Park Race Course Grooms	Higher wages.
33.	British Leyland (Umtali)	Wage dispute and demand for

		dismissal of a factory manager.
34.	United Touring Co. Drivers	Wage dispute.
35.	Supersonic Radio Manufacturing Co. (Bulawayo)	Higher wages.
36.	Footwear and Rubber Industries	Unspecified.
37.	York and Skyline Taxi Services	Wage dispute.
38.	Wankie Colliery	Wage dispute.
39.	Hippo Valley Estates	Working conditions and pay.
40.	Regent Mine (Mtoroshanga)	Unspecified.
41.	Enterprises	Unspecified.
42.	Triangle Sugar Estates	Wage dispute.
43.	Grain Marketing Board (Bulawayo)	Unspecified.
44.	Chibuku Breweries (Seke)	Wage dispute.
45.	Boart Drilling (Wankie)	Unspecified.
46.	Empress Nickel Mine	Unspecified.
47.	Arcturus Mine	Reinstatement of dismissed workers.
48.	Chisumbanje	Unspecified.
49.	Kapotas Bakery (Chiredzi)	Unspecified.
50.	Chiredzi Motors	Unspecified.
51.	Cementation (Shabanie Mine)	Unspecified.
52.	Machado Building Contractors (Seke)	Unspecified.
53.	Globe and Phoenix Mine	Pay conditions.
54.	Nandi Estates (Chiredzi)	Pay conditions.
55.	Umtali Board and Paper Mills	Unspecified.
56.	Hippo Valley Estates	Pay dispute.
57.	RISCO	Pay dispute.
58.	Redcliff Muncipality	Unspecified.
59.	Redcliff Engineering (Private) Ltd	Unspecified
60.	Shackleton Mine (Chiredzi)	Pay dispute.
61.	Rhomet Smelting Plant (Que Que)	Unspecified.
62.	Dairy Marketing Board (Salisbury)	Pay dispute.
63.	Swift Transport Service (Salisbury)	Demand for the dismissal of a senior white official.
64.	Bentwood Cabinets (Private) Ltd Bulawayo	Wage dispute
65.	Lancashire Steel	Wage and working conditions.
66.	Sable Chemicals	Wage and working conditions.
67.	Steward and Lloyds	Wage and working conditions.
68.	Lyons Maid Ltd	Wage and working conditions.
69.	Knowle Enterprises (Private) Ltd	Unspecified.
70.	Cold Storage Commission Ltd	Unspecified.
71.	Karina Textiles(Norton)	Unspecified.

June 1980

72.	Ministry of Roads Works (Inyanga)	Pay and working conditions.
73.	Footwear and Rubber Industries (Private) Ltd	Pay and working conditions.
74.	Dunsinane Estate (Penhalonga)	Sacking of workers.
75.	Ceasar Mine (Mtorashanga)	Dismissal of a worker.
76.	Troutbeck Inn	Unspecified.
77.	Textile Mills Holdings Ltd	Unspecified.
78.	Air Zimbabwe	Pay dispute.

270 *Zimbabwe*

79.	Umtali Municipal Workers	Pay dispute.
80.	Kamative Mine	Unspecified.
81.	Zimbabwe Omnibus Company	Assaults and harassment.
82.	Cold Storage Commission (Fort Victoria)	Dismissal of fellow workers.
83.	How Mine (Bulawayo)	Pay dispute.
84.	Artcraft Manufacturers (Bulawayo)	Unspecified.
85.	Lyons Maid (Bulawayo)	Pay dispute.
86.	Gwindingwe Estate (Melsetter)	Labour regulations.
87.	Umtali Council Employees	Unspecified.
88.	Boarder Timbers (Melsetter)	Unspecified
89.	Old West Mine (Penhalonga)	Demand for the dismissal of a Mine Captain.
90.	British Leyland (Umtali)	Temporary stoppage.
91.	Erin Forest (Inyanga)	Wage dispute.
92.	Monomotapa Hotel Workers	Unspecified.

October 1980

93.	Hartley Municipal Workers	Unspecified.
94.	Associated Textiles (Gatooma)	Pay dispute.
95.	Rixi, Creamline, A1 and Avondale Taxi Drivers	Pay dispute.
96.	Ratelshoek Tea Estate	Unspecified.
97.	Southdown Estate (Chipinga)	Unspecified.
98.	Golden Shaft Mine (Mazoe)	Unspecified.
99.	Zimbabwe Omnibus Company	Wage structure.
100.	Chrome Mines (Selukwe)	Wage dispute.
101.	Haggie Wire and Rope Ltd (Que Que)	Wage dispute.
102.	Budget Hotel Group Workers	Unspecified.
103.	Salisbury Municipality Ambulance Drivers & Firemen	Pay differentials.
104.	Wankie Colliery	Temporary stoppage.
105.	David Whitehead Ltd	Racial discrimination.
106.	Bulawayo Municipal Firemen	Wage dispute.
107.	Andrew Fleming Hospital general workers	Racial discrimination and ill-treatment.
108.	Salisbury Magistrate Court Recorders	Wage dispute.
109.	Gwelo Municipal Firemen	Wage dispute.
110.	Grey's Inn (Bulawayo)	Dismissal of a worker.
111.	Bulawayo Magistrate Court Recorders	Wage dispute.
112.	Zimbabwe National Soccer Team	Allowances and Insurance coverage.
113.	Air Zimbabwe	Wage dispute
114.	MacDonald Brothers (Private) Ltd (Bulawayo)	Reinstatement of dismissed workers.
115.	Hippo Valley Estates	Demand for the sacking of a Personnel Official.
116.	Bulawayo Black Firemen	Unspecified.
117.	F. Issels and Son Ltd (Bulawayo)	Unspecified.
118.	Schwepps (Salisbury)	Demand for reinstatement of a dismissed worker.

November and December 1980

119. Colcom Central Co-operative Ltd	Demand for dismissal of two white employees.
120. Bulawayo Muncipal Medical Assistant.	Unspecified
121. National Foods (Bulawayo)	Unspecified.
122. Spring and Forging	Wage dispute.
123. Consolidated textiles	Unspecified.
124. Wankie Colliery	Pension fund deductions.
125. Lyons Brooke Bond	Wage dispute.
126. Trojan nickel mine workers	Unspecified.
127. Tabex Tobacco Factory (Salisbury)	Unspecified.
128. Gladstone Gold Mine (near Salisbury)	Demand for dismissal of a mine manager.
129. Piggot, Maskew (Private) Ltd (Bulawayo)	Demand for the reinstatement of a workers' committee member.
130. R S R Sugar Refinery (Bulawayo)	Temporary stoppage.
131. A1 Taxi Drivers	Dismissal of workers' committee members.

January—June 1981.

132. Buchwa Iron Mining Company	Dismissal of an African boiler-maker.
133. Makasa Sun Hotel	Pay dispute.
134. National Railways of Zimbabwe	Wage dispute.
135. Sparrow Garment Manufactures	Retrenchment.
136. Nazareth House for the Aged	Wage dispute.
137. Baobab Hotel	Dismissal of a worker.
138. Umvuma Council Employees	Pay conditions.
139. David Whitehead (Hartley)	Dispute over representation.
140. Salisbury Municipal Ambulance Drivers	Pay differentials.
141. Rhodall (Gwelo)	Pay structure.
142. Shushine Bus Company	Dismissal of workers and wage conditions.
143. University of Zimbabwe workers and students	Wage conditions and demand for the dismissal of a catering/accommodation officer.
144. Churchill and Roosevelt Schools	Dismissal of a worker.
145. Selous Hotel	Redundancy of staff.
146. Zimbabwe Express Motorways	Threats of dismissal of workers.
147. Ascot Racecourse Grooms	Wage conditions and dismissal of a worker.
148. Ambassador Hotel	Retrenchment of workers.
149. Lange Menswear factory	Dismissal of a worker.

July—December 1981

150. Tyre Threads (Bulawayo)	Dismissal of a worker.
151. Spilhous Family Planning Centre	Dismissal of senior nurse.
152. Mazowe Mine	Demand for the dismissal of a senior mine official.
153. University of Zimbabwe workers	Court appearance of the SRC President, Mashiri.
154. Garden Room Restaurant	Unspecified.

155.	Selukwe Peak Mine	Dismissal of a worker; and rents.
156.	Athol Evans Hospital	Pay conditions.
157.	Victoria Falls Town Council	Pay conditions and bad treatment.
158.	Supersonic Factories	Pay conditions and poor treatment.
159.	Z S R Sugar Refiners (Bulawayo)	Sacking of a worker.
160.	Wankie Colliery	Various grievances of contract workers.
161.	Boart Drilling and Construction Ltd	Retrenchment.
162.	Marandellas Municipal workers	Sacking of a worker.
163.	Salisbury Municipal workers	Working conditions and inadequate protective clothing.
164.	Meikles Hotel	Dismissal of a worker.
165.	Salary Service Bureau (SSB)	Attitude of director to black advancement.
166.	Cutty Sark Hotel	Sacking of three workers.
167.	Lebena Biscuits (Salisbury)	Sacking of workers' committee members.
168.	Rhodian Clothing Factory	Pay conditions.
169.	Athol Evans Hospital	Dismissal of a worker.
170.	Lobels (Bulawayo)	Pay conditions.
171.	Irvines Day Old Chicks	Pay conditions and accommodation.
172.	Air Zimbabwe	Pay and working conditions.
173.	Shangani Mine	Abusive language.
174.	National Railways of Zimbabwe (Bulawayo)	Pay and working conditions.
175.	Teachers	Pay differentials.
176.	Berkfield Consolidated (Private)	Arrest of workers.
177.	Irvine's Day Old Chicks	Demand for the release of the chairman and secretary of the workers' committee.
178.	National Railways of Zimbabwe	Pay dispute.

Sources:

The Herald
The National Observer
The Sunday Main

REFERENCES

1. Engels, F. and Marx, K., The Manifesto of the Communist Party, *Four Classical Texts on the Principles of Socialism* , London, Unwin, 1960, p. 21.
2. *Ibid.*, P. 22.
3. Marx, K., Value, Price and Profit, *Four Classical Texts on the Principles of Socialism op. cit.*, p. 101.
4. *Ibid.*, p. 100
5. Anderson, P., The Limits and Possibilities of Trade Union Action, in Clarke, T. and Clements, L. (eds), *Trade Unions under Capitalism*, Brighton, Harvester Press, 1980, p. 334.
6. Lenin, V.I., *On Trade Unions*, Progress Publishers, Moscow, 1970, p. 55.
7. *Ibid.*

8. *Ibid.*, p. 288.
9. *Ibid.*, p. 289.
10. Hyman, R., *Industrial Relations, a Marxist Introduction*, MacMillan, 1975, p. 91.
11. *Ibid.*
12. *Ibid.*
13. Damachi, U.G., Seibel, H.D. and Tratchtman, L. (eds), pp. 146-47, *Industrial Relations in Africa*, Macmillan, 1979, pp. 6-7.
14. Mapuranga, T. Machiwenyika, *L.C. Mzingeli: His Role in and Contribution to, the Awakening of Action Trade Union and Political Consciousness in Rhodesia*, Sept. 1971, National Archives of Zimbabwe pp. 1-21. Quoted in Clarke, D., The Underdevelopment of African Trade Unions in Rhodesia, Mimeo, 1974, pp. 1-2.
15. *Ibid.*, p. 39
16. *The Herald*, 21 March 1980.
17. *The Herald*, 20 March 1980.
18. *The Herald*, 29 March 1980.
19. *The Herald*, 23 March 1980.
20. *Ibid.*
21. *The Herald*, 14 May 1980.
22. *The Herald*, June 1980.
23. *Ibid.*
24. *The Herald*, 21 March 1980.
25. *The National Observer*, 21 March 1980.
26. *The Herald*, 22 May 1980.
27. *The National Observer*, 30 May 1980.
28. *The Herald*, 17 October 1980.
29. *The Herald*, 7 August 1980.
30. *The Herald*, 29 May 1980.
31. *The Herald*, 30 May 1980.
32. *The Herald*, 1 June 1980.
33. The Labour Relations Bill 1985, (Preamble).
34. The penalty is a fine of not more than Z$2,000.00 or imprisonment not exceeding two years or both such fine and such imprisonment.
35. Labour Relations Bill, pp. 65-66.
36. See Parliamentary Debate on the Labour Relations Bill, 1985, Vols. 9-11.
37. *The Herald*, 27 November 1985.
38. *Ibid.*
39. *The Herald*, 17 July 1984.

10. HUMAN RESOURCES DEVELOPMENT AND THE PROBLEM OF LABOUR UTILISATION

Brian Raftopoulos

Historical Background

The origins of the current problems of labour utilisation and development must be sought in the nature of imperialist expansion in Zimbabwe and the forms of exploitative labour practices that emerged within a capitalist economy dominated by settler colonial rule. Zimbabwe came under colonial rule as part of the expansion of imperialist interests in Southern Africa. Cecil John Rhodes, through the British South Africa Company (BSAC), crossed the Limpopo in search of a 'Second Rand'. When this quest for gold turned out to be substantially less lucrative than expected, the BSAC sought to recoup its losses by encouraging the immigration of white settlers to enter into various economic fields, particularly farming. Thus the violent military defeat of the Chimurenga uprisings in the 1890s was followed by a rapid increase of white settlement and the establishment of the initial state structures of settler colonial rule. The first settlers were composed of a variety of employment categories ranging from administrators, soldiers and policemen to farmers, artisans, semi-skilled workers and clerks. Between 1901 and 1911 the white population expanded from 11,000 to 23,000.[1] As Mandaza noted, there therefore developed:

> not only a greater white settlement element than the average colony in Africa was to experience, but also a class structure within that white population that would, by virtue of its consciousness of its economic privileges and political ambitions, be equally more formidable in its resistance to African aspirations.[2]

A crucial feature of this expansion of white immigrants was that, as Arrighi has pointed out, the settlement of white workers was a 'consequence of, and did not precede, capitalist development in the country'.[3] A major consequence of this feature was not only the absence of 'poor-white-ism', as in South Africa before the rise of Afrikanerdom, but the effects that development was to have on labour utilisation and development in the colony. First, the economy was to rely, for the most part, on white immigrants for formally skilled labour. A direct result of such a policy was seriously to limit the development of vocational/technical training in the country. The Salisbury and Bulawayo technical colleges were characterised by low, mainly white, enrolment, and were in no sense intended to provide the institutional technical training to service the economy in any comprehensive manner. The first government training institutions established at Domboshawa and Tjolotjo in the 1920s were established at a time when the view of the 'Native Affairs Department' on 'native policy' was to ensure:

> the development of the native in such a way that he will come as little as possible into conflict or competition wth the white man, socially, economically or politically.[4]

Thus, by the 1930s, education for Africans was seen by the government as being closely related to the broader issues of so-called 'community' development. In the conditions of a growing capitalist economy this 'community development' meant the subjugation of the peasant to the demands of developing capitalist relations of production. In accordance with this, the education system being advocated by the whites amounted to an attempt to restrict African education to the narrow demands of the economy. In educational terms, this meant an emphasis on 'practical subjects' which, as part of the 'community development', the settlers purported, would equip Africans to cope with the economic 'realities' of the time.[5]

The settlers' attempt to limit the availability to 'natives' of formal academic education was witnessed by the fact that by 1958 there were only three government secondary schools for Africans. Chapter ten elaborates on these and other issues about the nature of colonial education.

In the Apprenticeship Training System, introduced in 1934, the state demonstrated the secondary role it attached to the development of a local technical training infrastructure, and the emphasis is placed on immigration for the provision of formally skilled labour. Table I shows both the limited number of apprentices enrolled between 1974 and 1980, and the racial bias of enrolment. Moreover, even among the whites, the apprenticeship option was 'very much concerned with enabling the not-so-intelligent white youth to survive in Rhodesian society'.[6] In white schools as well, technical subjects were usually given low priority. As Challiss noted:

> Generally the emphasis in European schools was on what can be conveniently called an academic education, to the neglect of technical training and the acquisition of manual skills.[7]

This emphasis on academic education was also the result of the lack of clarity on the part of settlers as to what constituted a sound technical education. This confusion was particularly apparent in the settler policy towards education for blacks, where, despite some attempts to introduce a 'practical' education for people considered suitable only for manual work, much of the education veered towards an academic ethos. This was the result both of African resistance to attempts to have second-rate practical education foisted on them, in an economy in which academic education was clearly more prestigious, and because the settler association of manual work with 'native labour' engendered confused notions

TABLE 1
INTAKE OF APPRENTICE ACCORDING TO INDUSTRY AND RACE 1974-1980

Industry	Year	Intake No.	Whites No.	Whites %	'Coloureds' No.	'Coloureds' %	Africans No.	Africans %	Others No.	Others %
Aircraft										
	1974	23	23	100	-	-	-	-	-	-
	1975	65	62	95	2	3	-	-	1	1
	1976	134	134	100	-	-	-	-	-	-
	1977	113	106	94	1	1	6	5	-	-
	1978	109	102	94	2	2	5	5	-	-
	1979	79	73	94	1	1	5	6	-	-
	1980	65	58	89	1	2	6	9	-	-
Building										
	1974	125	39	31	33	26	48	38	5	4
	1975	83	20	24	19	23	44	53	-	-
	1976	39	15	39	6	15	17	44	1	2
	1977	41	15	37	2	5	23	56	1	2
	1978	29	17	59	1	3	10	35	1	3
	1979	48	15	31	7	15	24	50	2	4
	1980	89	15	17	14	16	60	68	-	-
Electrical										
	1974	150	130	87	6	4	12	8	2	1
	1975	203	166	82	8	4	29	15	-	-
	1976	183	147	81	9	5	25	14	2	1
	1977	149	110	74	3	2	35	24	1	1
	1978	164	124	76	6	4	30	19	4	2
	1979	213	156	75	15	7	37	17	2	1
	1980	310	260	84	8	3	38	12	4	1
Mechanical										
	1974	308	245	80	33	11	25	8	5	2
	1975	451	305	68	52	12	88	20	6	1
	1976	413	301	73	31	8	72	17	9	2
	1977	367	239	65	30	8	93	25	5	1
	1978	375	266	71	21	6	79	21	9	2
	1979	425	259	61	66	16	96	23	4	1
	1980	511	345	68	41	8	117	23	8	2
Motor Trades										
	1974	191	165	86	12	6	13	7	1	1
	1975	258	181	70	32	12	39	15	6	2
	1976	236	150	64	28	12	47	20	11	5
	1977	204	140	69	13	6	49	24	2	1
	1978	243	177	73	17	7	43	18	6	2
	1979	248	169	68	29	12	48	19	2	1
	1980	328	227	69	26	8	68	21	7	2
Printing										
	1974	51	48	94	3	6	-	-	-	-
	1975	80	49	61	7	9	18	23	6	8
	1976	61	40	66	9	15	10	16	2	3
	1977	64	35	55	6	9	16	25	7	11
	1978	67	42	63	5	8	17	25	3	4
	1979	89	42	47	8	9	34	38	5	6
	1980	90	50	56	8	9	28	31	4	4
Hairdressing										
	1974	32	29	91	3	9	-	-	-	-
	1975	42	35	83	5	12	1	2	1	2
	1976	32	24	75	2	7	6	19	-	-
	1977	45	31	69	8	17	6	13	-	-
	1978	33	29	88	3	9	1	3	-	-
	1979	38	29	76	4	11	5	13	-	-
	1980	38	33	87	1	3	4	10	-	-

Note: Because of rounding not all of the above percentages add to one hundred percent.
Source: National Manpower Survey 1981, Vol.1, p.61.

about the role of vocational/technical education.

Second, this reliance on immigration encouraged the belief that the latter was 'a low-cost source of supply of skilled manpower',[8] and an indispensable source of skilled labour and future development. The belief in the indispensability of white skills was encouraged by the protective practices surrounding the employment of the white labour aristocracy. During the colonial period skilled unions were for the most part dominated by whites who had brought their union-organising abilities with them to the colony. These unions were organisationally strong, enjoyed active support and had regular contact with state and political officials and regularly participated in negotiations with employers in the National Industrial Councils, according to the guidelines set down by the Industrial Conciliation Act (1934). The latter Act excluded 'natives' from the definition of employee, and in so doing formally barred them from formal union activities, and also formal skill training. It was largely through pressure from white workers to protect themselves from competition in the labour market that the Act was introduced. As a leading black trade unionist has noted:

> What brought white workers together was probably fear of black competition; they were, after all, a part of a white minority that constituted a ruling class... They could have hardly looked upon themselves as a part of the exploited labouring poor.[9]

Using their privileged legal and organisational status, white unions negotiated rapid advances in the wages of skilled workers:

> not by negotiated wage minima, but by the creation of a shortage of supply of skilled workers relative to the demands of industry. The workers achieve this by the dual expedient of influencing the rate at which additional workers gain the necessary skills and of preserving categories of work for such skilled workers. They are able to exploit the strategic alliance between white capital and white labour that both these groups perceive to be in their long-term interests, but are weakened by the short-term cost advantages that white employers are able to reap from a short-term alliance with black labour.[10]

In addition to limiting the number of skilled workers on the market, employers and white skilled unions also generated the practice of undercategorising the level of skills amongst blacks. Thus, many black workers who acquired knowledge of skilled trades on the job were nevertheless, for the most part, neither classified as 'formally' skilled nor given the opportunity to acquire such categorisation through formal training. In effect, such workers were categorised as 'semi-skilled', a nomenclature that, in the settler colonial economy, often disguised the real level of skill attainment. For employers, the undercategorisation of skill levels had an obvious advantage in terms of the exploitation of skilled labour well below the remuneration due to such labour. For white workers, the confinement of blacks to 'semi-skilled' status reduced the number of formally skilled workers on the market, and so reduced the level of job competition.[11]

Employers did make various attempts to overcome the artificial shortage of skilled labour created by white skilled unions, by attempting to engage in job fragmentation. However, the settler state in the early 1970s made its position reasonably clear on this issue. Thus the Minister of Labour and Social Welfare in 1971 noted:

> Any erosion of the rate for the job, for example, by massive fragmentation negotiated for reasons of expediency at the industrial council table, will inevitably mean a lowering of standards, a situation which Government cannot accept if it is to protect the interests of the country as a whole.[12]

Job reservation was yet another means of both 'protecting' white skills and creating artificial shortages. Such job reservation took place in such occupational categories as management, executive and professional posts. Table 2 shows the occupational distribution by race soon after independence. The figures illustrate the disparity of occupational distribution, with whites representing 44% of the Professional, Technical and Related group, and 74% of the Administrative and Managerial Group. This occupational disequilibrium is further manifested in the major inequality of income distribution. Thus Table 3 shows that Europeans, who represented 5% of the labour force for non-educational establishments covered by the 1981 National Manpower Survey (NMS), accounted for 37% of the estimated total salary/wage bill; the figure for Africans, who represented 90% of the labour force, was 60%.

As a result of such job reservation, and heavy reliance on immigration, there was a serious under-utilisation of African professional and skilled labour. African graduates, because of limited job openings, were for the most part forced to enter such professions as teaching, where, the state reasoned, they could serve their own people. There were many such cases of under-employment or unemployment of African graduates. A Commonwealth Secretariat study carried out in 1979 estimated that the participation rate for educated Africans in the labour force in 1969 was less than 50%.[13]

In the public service, the exclusion of blacks from top administrative and professional/technical posts was also the order of the day. In 1931 the Public Service Act was passed, which for the first time in the history of the colonial public service legally excluded Africans and people of mixed race from entering established posts in the civil service. Africans and 'coloureds' could, however, continue to be employed in the low grade, non-established posts.[14]

The 1931 Act must be seen within the context of the pressures for protection of white labour that found its apotheosis in the 1934 Industrial Conciliation Act. Whatever miniscule changes took place during the Federation period did nothing to change the pattern of racial discrimination that generally characterised the federal public service.[15] During the UDI period, the illegal regime made its position on public servants very clear. Not only were blacks largely excluded from the established posts in government, but even for whites it was stated by the Minister of the Public Services in 1973:

> the mere possession of an academic qualification is not in itself a criterion for appointment to any job... We have to consider the suitability of the candidates bearing in mind certain factors. Perhaps the most important single factor so far as the public service is concerned is loyalty to the State... Secondly, the national security.[16]

In summary, several features characterised the pattern of labour utilisation and development during the colonial period.

First, the existence of a large settler community in which white workers were largely an imported phenomenon. As a consequence of this, it was in the interests of white workers to prevent the development both of a reserve army of labour and of a stable, educated and skilled urban African population that would provide competition in the employment market. Such objectives were attained by strengthening the bargaining strength of white skilled workers through the discriminatory Industrial Conciliation Act of 1934. Skilled unions thus limited the numbers of formally skilled labour on the market, while the development of a comprehensive local technical training infrastructure to develop indigenous skills was undermined by a predominant reliance on immigrant skills. The general lack of vocational/technical training in the colony must however be seen as fundamentally related to the essentially supervisory role of white skilled workers. Because of the largely operational role of the under-categorised, semi-skilled black workers, and their exploited position in relation to both capital and white workers, the latter represented a small elite of protected, highly paid supervisors of black labour. This set of labour relations therefore undermined efforts at developing a large-scale technical training infrastructure, since skilled labour was a category applied to a small percentage of the labour force (12% according to the NMS: See Table 4); and it was, therefore, seen to be more economically viable to import a relatively small group of skilled supervisors.

White workers formed part of an alliance that also included the agrarian bourgeoisie, the petit bourgeoisie and international capital. Whatever contradictions existed among them (e.g. between international capital and agrarian bourgeoisie/white worker interests), such differences were in the final analysis subordinated to their common pursuit of exploiting black labour. The fact that white settler ideology was able to mobilise the various classes amongst the white population was because the latter ideology incorporated, in varying degrees, the interests of these classes. Farmers feared competition on the land, while both white workers and the petit bourgeoisie were strongly averse to competition from black labour, thus favouring the existence of an unstable black workforce with low skills. Such an unstable migrant workforce was also in the interests

TABLE 2
ALL SECTORS SKILL AND RACIAL DISTRIBUTION BY OCCUPATION

Major Occupation Group		Professional Afr.	Professional Eur.	Professional AS/Col	Skilled Afr.	Skilled Eur.	Skilled AS/Col	Semi-skilled Afr.	Semi-skilled Eur.	Semi-skilled AS/Col	Totals Afr.	Totals Eur.	Totals AS/Col	Grand Total
Professional, Technical and Related	No	9,184	9,479	532	2,432	1,993	116	2,940	313	42	14,556	11,785	690	27,031
	%	34	35	2	9	7	-	11	1	-	54	44	3	100
Administrative and Managerial	No	2,151	7,929	563	159	181	11	26	62	2	2,336	8,172	576	11,084
	%	19	72	5	1	2	-	-	1	-	21	74	5	100
Clerical and Related	No	1,935	1,897	116	8,848	8,101	1,180	23,339	8,521	2,109	34,122	18,519	3,405	56,046
	%	4	3	-	16	14	2	42	15	4	61	33	6	100
Sales	No	492	1195	317	2,749	3,304	648	5,768	1,463	448	9,009	5,962	1,413	16,384
	%	3	7	2	17	20	4	35	9	3	55	36	9	100
Service	No	416	141	5	4351	1,114	138	16,178	453	235	20,945	1,708	378	23,031
	%	2	1	-	19	5	1	70	2	1	91	7	2	100
Agricultural, Animal Husbandry and Forestry Workers, Fishermen & Hunters	No	18	71	-	5,057	5,949	70	31,831	140	35	36,906	6,160	105	43,171
	%	-	-	-	12	14	-	74	-	-	86	14	-	100
Production and Related Workers, Transport Equipment Operators	No	101	67	14	29,003	9,348	1,495	72,573	3,973	1,149	101,677	13,388	2,658	117,723
	%	-	-	-	25	8	1	62	3	1	86	11	2	100
Occupations Inadequately Described	No	104	155	16	897	297	68	2,254	78	52	3,255	530	136	3,921
	%	3	4	-	23	7	2	58	2	1	83	13	4	100
TOTAL	No	14,401	20,934	1,563	53,496	30,287	3,726	154,909	15,003	4,072	222,806	66,224	9,361	298,391
	%	5	7	1	18	10	1	52	5	1	75	22	3	100

Employees of education and training institutions are excluded from this table.
Source: *National Manpower Survey 1981, p. 74*

TABLE 3
NON-EDUCATIONAL ESTABLISHMENTS:
PAYROLL DISTRIBUTION BY RACIAL GROUP, JULY 1981

Race	Persons No.	%	Estimated Total Salaries/Wages $'000	%
Africans	723 356	90	89 830	60
Europeans	70 769	9	54 766	37
Coloured	8 321	1	3 189	2
Asians	3 593	-	1 957	1
Total	806 039	100	149 742	100

Note: Data are based on wage and salary level statistics provided by employers.
Source: *National Manpower Survey 1981 p. 51*

TABLE 4
SKILL CATEGORY OF EMPLOYED PERSONS REPORTED IN THE NATIONAL MANPOWER SURVEY

Category	Persons Reported By Educational Establishments No	%	Persons Reported By Non-Educational Establishments No	%	Total No	%
Professional	29 928	53	36 898	5	66 826	8
Skilled	18 236	33	87 509	11	105 745	12
Semi-Skilled	2 017	4	173 984	22	176 001	20
Unskilled	5 795	10	507 647	63	513 442	60
Total	55 976	100	806 038	100	862 014	100

Source: *National Manpower Survey 1981, Vol.1, p.73*

of white farmers, who relied heavily on a cheap labour force whose reproductive requirements were to a significant extent borne by the former Tribal Trust Lands. Industrial capital, whose requirements pointed to a more stable, educated and skilled workforce, was nevertheless dependent on the rest of the settler alliance for a political base.[17]

The ability of white skilled workers and the settler state to carry out such measures also reflected the weakness of African trade unionism, as Sachikonye has outlined in chapter nine. The African trade unions were weak because of a number of reasons that included the following: the migrant nature of the workforce which affected both the organisational and ideological development of unions; the repressive labour legislation and administrative practice of the state apparatus; and opposition not only from organised skilled unions but also from highly centralised and organised employers' associations with ready access to state representatives.

Second, in order to 'protect' white skills and engender the impression of a shortage of skills (and with this the indispensability of white skills) the colonial economy generated practices such as undercategorisation of skills, job reservation, and under-utilisation of black skills. The result of such practices was also to create serious wage/salary differentials.

Third, the reliance on immigration seriously undermined the comprehensive development of apprenticeship training and technical colleges and the production of high level manpower at the local university. Thus, apart from the immigration factor, apprenticeship training was weak because of its total reliance on employers, with the apprenticeship authority having no power to compel employers to take on apprentices; and because of the employers' desire for greater job fragmentation.[18] In the colleges enrolment was low, particularly in the areas of technical colleges. Thus, of the total 6,870 students registered in the technical colleges soon after independence in May 1982, 478 (7%) were registered in mining engineering, 569 (8%) in mechanical and automotive engineering, 363 (5%) for electrical engineering and 532 (8%) for mathematics and science technology. This gave a total of 1,942 (28%) in technical areas.[19] At the university, in the same year, of the total 558 graduating students, 31 graduated in agriculture, 9 in engineering, 65 in the field of medicine and 39 in general science: in all, a total of 144, or 26% of the graduating total.[20]

Thus not only was there a low enrolment at tertiary level but also those enrolled in the technical/scientific fields represented a low percentage of total output. During the colonial period, because of the difficulties of enrolment for Africans at the university, many blacks left the country to find places at universities and technical colleges in other countries. It has been estimated that by 1980 there were between six and eight thousand Zimbabweans in such institutions.[21] There were thousands of African secondary school leavers either entering the job market or seeking places at tertiary institutions. Much of this secondary school expansion accompanied the growth of industrialisation in the 1950s, and the demand for education persisted despite the frustrating employment market awaiting most school leavers. For the reality of the colonial political economy heightened the status of academic education, even while the state was trying to squeeze blacks into more 'practical-oriented' training, such as was being offered in F2 schools.

The National Manpower Survey (1981)

As has been outlined in chapter one, independence brought with it the 'warning' that had been repeated at every attempt to resolve the 'Rhodesian question', namely that any settlement had to consider the interests of whites and white confidence. The assumption was always that because whites dominated the professional, managerial and formally skilled positions in the economy, any precipitant exodus of such skills would be disastrous and so prove deleterious to the majority rule project. The 'warning' had an important bolstering effect on the ideology of settler colonialism, in that it fed on a long-held settler belief in the indispensability of their skills, and the assumption that any meaningful development was coterminous with the white presence. In terms of international capital, the threats about the effects of the rapid loss of skills served as an important argument in cautioning the new Zimbabwe government about the dangers of a too rapid implementation of radical programmes. The 'indispensability' of white farmers has been a favourite example of this argument. The Lancaster House constitution therefore represented not only the perceived short-term protection of white political interests, but also a certain perception about the indispensability of minority skills. As Shopo has written, the constitution:

> insidiously represented a view long held about our society vis-à-vis the rest of the continent—that the white man here was *homo technologicus* par excellence... The continued white presence in Zimbabwe has, in short, in many a prognosis of our future become the most important technical condition of production.[22]

The first major government response to such 'warnings' and threats was to embark on a National Manpower Survey in 1981. The overall objective of the survey was to assess the size, characteristics and shortage areas of the labour force, and to formulate both short- and long-term training policies for its development. Because the survey took place in the immediate post-independence period, after a lengthy period of repressive labour legislation, and soon after the 1980/81 wave of labour unrest in which approximately two hundred strikes broke out across the country, the level of mistrust and conflict between labour and capital and between the latter and the state was at a peak. Employers were initially reluctant to participate in the survey as they saw it as a first step towards undermining the security of whites in the economy. Questions on the racial distribution of skills and salary differentials were often treated with extreme hostility, as they sought to delve into the extreme inequalities in these areas. White employers and employees feared retribution on publication of the survey results'.[23]

With the publication of the survey results in 1983 the business press, after an initial cautious statement on the 'complicated document',[24] as they referred to it, responded in a most vehement manner. *The Financial Gazette* labelled the NMS the 'product of pseudo experts'. Further vilification was concerned with its being 'somewhat schizophrenic in nature'. The schizophrenia, it appeared, was the result of the following:

> The basic underlying theme is correct. Black Zimbabweans have been denied access to skills on a consistent basis, dictated by the unacceptable racial attitude of past governments. But the manner in which these facts and the recommendations are presented indicates a desire to maintain, or even heighten, a

conflict with the alternative to Marxism.[25]

The criticisms of *The Financial Gazette* thus related to the political position taken in the Director's 'Introduction' to the NMS, entitled 'The National Manpower Survey in the Context of the Political Economy of Zimbabwe'. The introduction sought to provide the following.

(a) An analysis clarifying the conditions that characterised colonial capitalist penetration in Zimbabwe, and the ways in which such penetration determined the utilisation of labour in the economy. In this way, the forms of labour categorisation which were, and indeed continue to be, utilised could be better understood within the context of the social relations in which they emerged.
(b) To outline the obstacles to manpower development imposed by such forms of labour utilisation.
(c) To formulate alternative strategies based on clear conceptions of the problem of labour utilisation in a society dominated by capital, the forces in society that generate those problems, and the organisational and training structures required to overcome such problems.

That the NMS inspired such a vitriolic attack from the business press must therefore be seen within the context of its exposure of some of the myths of the indispensability of white skills. The survey acknowledged and quantified the existence of shortage areas in the fields of:

- *Administration and Management*
- Accountants,
- Financial and project analysts,
- Stenographers, senior typists, shorthand typists and bilingual secretaries.

- *Agriculture*
- Veterinarians and related workers,
- Extension and land-use planning specialists,
- Agricultural engineers,
- Lecturers for agricultural colleges.

- *Engineering*
- Civil,
- Mechanical,
- Electrical,
- Mining,
- Structural,
- Draughting,
- Computer.

- *Medicine*
- Physicians,
- Dentists,

- Pathologists,
- Psychiatrists,
- Pharmacists,
- Occupational therapists,
- Opticians,
- Medical technologists.

- *Education*
- Instructors in technical colleges,
- Lecturers in instructor-training colleges,
- Teachers in secondary schools especially for mathematics and science subjects,
- Lecturers at the University of Zimbabwe.[26]

In the field of artisans, the occupational groups in which vacancies were hardest to fill were: machine fitters, machine assemblers and precision instrument makers and electrical fitters and related electrical and electronics workers. The above shortage areas were confirmed in the Annual Occupational Survey of Employees carried out in 1984.[27]

However, beyond pointing to existing shortage areas, the NMS outlined the reasons underlying the shortages, namely the neglect of technical training infrastructure and reliance on immigration. Equally important, the survey highlighted the importance of the 'semi-skilled' as an important reservoir of under-categorised skilled labour, and therefore an important immediate resource for countering the threat of the loss of skilled labour. It is nevertheless true that the then Ministry of Manpower Planning and Development sometimes underestimated the problems of upgrading the semi-skilled in the midst of the battle to counter the warnings of the 'loss of skills' brigade. (The problems of policy implementation are dealt with below.)

The NMS should therefore be viewed not only as an attempt to provide a statistical base for manpower planning in the country but also, of equal importance, as a political intervention against certain stereotypes relating to labour utilisation and development, and as a contribution towards the debate for socialism in Zimbabwe. Indeed in replying to the histrionics of the business press, the Director of the NMS made precisely this point, writing:

> What disturbs us most is that there should be in Zimbabwe such an arrogant and orchestrated anti-leftist lobby, bent on discrediting both progressive ideas and persons who dare utter such ideas.[28]

Having produced an analysis and quantitative statement of human resource development in the country, the state still had to tackle the following problems. First, there was a need to expand the limited technical and high-level manpower training capacity to cope with the perceived future requirements of the economy, and the massive expansion of school leavers. Second, the racial imbalance in the Apprenticeship Training System had to be redressed, and steps taken to stop the flow of skills from Zimbabwe to other countries. Third, the settler policy of immigration promotion had to be reversed and a more stringent control of foreign recruitment introduced. Fourth, the serious drift of critical skills from the public to the private sector had to be addressed. We will now turn to an analysis of the measures taken to address each of these problems.

Expansion of Technical and High-Level Human Resource Training Capacity

For developing countries, the area in which they are most able to intervene and effect change in the immediate post-independence period is the field of social services, especially education and training facilities. This has been the case particularly in Africa where, between 1960 and 1980, enrolment grew at a faster rate than in the other major 'developing' regions of Latin America and South Asia, at both primary level (with a mean annual growth rate of 10.7%) and secondary level (11.3%).[29] It was only at the level of higher education that the eightfold increase in enrolment in Africa was surpassed by the ninefold increase in Latin America. In addition, by 1978 expenditure on education in Africa represented 4.8% of GNP.[30] In terms of technical/scientific training, even while there was an expansion of such training on the continent in the 1970s, graduates in the scientific/technical field (natural science, engineering, medical science and agricultural science) represented less than half of the total number of graduates on the African continent (i.e. between 20 and 40%).[31]

This tendency for states in the developing world to intervene in the democratisation of the social services is a result of the greater control of these states of the supply side of the training equation, rather than any effective authority over the means of production. More fundamentally, the expansion of education and training has been the result of social and political pressures for such an expansion. As Carnoy has written:

> The unceasing and probably increasing demand for education in developing countries is a fact of political life in such societies. Education has become a form of social right for populations whose material standard of living increased slowly in the 1970's. As unemployment has risen in the 1970's and 1980's the demand for education has increased, because unemployment is generally higher for those with less schooling, particularly in urban areas. Thus more than the rate-of-return or equity arguments put forth as educational spending rationales by international agencies, political reality dictates educational expansion in response to education as a public right.[32]

As the next chapter on education in Zimbabwe indicates, the democratisation of education has taken place primarily as a result of the demands of popular participation during the liberation struggle, and the new government's commitment to the right of every child to a certain minimum level of education.

The massive expansion of primary education in Zimbabwe (from

819,128 in 1979 to 2,147,898 in 1984) also coincided with changes in the international approach to investment in education. By the early 1980s, the consensus on investment had moved towards an expansion of basic primary education which, it was argued, could be justified not only as a basic need in itself but also in terms of improved health and reduced mortality and fertility rates.[33] This approach was a move away from the view of the early 1960s that an important obstacle to economic growth in the developing countries was the absence of middle- and high-level human resources. However, the increasing problem of economic development in the Third World brought with it the reality of the over-production and unemployment of secondary school leavers and university graduates.[34]

However, the 1980s also brought a renewed interest in science and technology. *The Lagos Plan of Action for the Economic Development of Africa 1980* stressed the importance of developing an indigenous technological capability and set out a series of human resource policies related to this objective. This view (about the need for indigenous technological capability) differed from the 'mood of naive optimism' that characterised the conceptualisation of the role of science and technology in the 1960s. Cooper has described this 'naive optimism':

> Not only did it seem easy to introduce science and technology in the underdeveloped countries, but it was also obvious, or seemed so at the time, that a bit more science and technology would open a wide perspective of new productive possibilities. It might even solve the problems of underdevelopment.[35]

This view was part of the modernisation theory that dominated social sciences at the time and stressed a form of unilinear pattern of growth for all countries.

The critique of modernisation theory by the dependency theorists was an important corrective to such unilear conceptions of economic growth; and the critique also involved a more critical analysis of the role of science and technology in the 'periphery'. Greater attention was given to analysing the concentration and control of scientific and technological capabilities in the developed countries, as well as the mechanisms of technological transfer and the politico-economic effects of particular technological choices.[36] The concept of indigenous technological capability in the Lagos Plan of Action has benefited from this critique of earlier naive conceptions of the role of science and technology.

In Zimbabwe, the role of science and technology has been accorded an important place, at least in the pronouncements of the state. A Scientific Council of Zimbabwe had been established and is responsible to the Prime Minister's office; and the post of Scientific Council Liaison Officer has also been established in the Cabinet Office. The Scientific Council has already produced a report, based on a consultative meeting of Zimbabwean scientists. The report's major objective was to develop ways of making science and technology a more effective instrument of development policy in the country. A study of the manufacturing sector in

Zimbabwe was commissioned by the Ministry of Industry and Technology and has been published. Its recommendations include mechanisms for improving local technological capacity.[37]

There have been problems in terms of linking this commitment to local scientific/technological development to high-level human resource development. The enrolment at the University of Zimbabwe has greatly expanded from 1,481 students in 1979 to 4,482 in 1985, a 200% increase. However, the enrolment of science/technical graduates (agriculture, engineering, medicine, science, veterinary science) remains relatively low, standing at 33% of total enrolment in 1980, 34% in 1981, 32% in 1982, 29% in 1983, 30% in 1984 and 32% in 1985. This represents an average of 31% of total enrolment over the last six years (see Table 5). Similarly, in the technical colleges, enrolment has expanded from 4,434 in 1980 to 13,776 in 1985 (see Table 6). However, there has been a relatively smaller percentage of enrolment in the technical/science field. An examination of the enrolment figures in technical college departments reveals the following. Of the total 5,732 students enrolled in 1981, 1,775 (30%) were in the technical/science fields; the figures for 1982 and 1983 were 2,195 (31%) and 2,386 (30%) respectively (see Table 7). In colleges that were either donated (Kwekwe College from Union Carbide) or newly established by the government (Gweru, Mutare and Masvingo), much of the training has been in the business and commercial field. However, it is planned that the college at Gweru will eventually become a Technical Teacher Training Centre, while the centre at Masvingo will lean towards sugar technology.[38]

TABLE 5
STUDENT ENROLMENTS AT THE U.Z. ACCORDING TO FACULTY AND YEAR

Faculty	1980	1981	1982	1983	1984	1985
Agriculture	96	108	128	151	178	225
Arts	274	343	394	478	605	590
Commerce & Law	443	577	699	871	950	1 010
Education	275	172	294	566	645	700
Engineering	117	140	181	232	269	280
Medicine	292	362	366	419	460	520
Science	167	194	238	250	290	340
Social Studies	360	424	540	627	690	745
Veterinary Science	-	-	18	26	44	72
TOTAL	2 024	2 320	2 858	3 620	4 131	4 482

Source: University of Zimbabwe

TABLE 6
STUDENT ENROLMENT IN TECHNICAL COLLEGES FROM 1980 TO 1985

Year and Student Number					
1980	1981	1982	1983	1984	1985
4 434	6 713	7 280	12 232	13 483	13 776

*Source: Department of Rersearch and Planning
(Ministry of Labour, Manpower Planning and Social Welfare).*

TABLE 7
STUDENT ENROLMENT IN TECHNICAL COLLEGE DEPARTMENTS

Division/Department	1983	1982	1981
Technical			
Automotive Engineering	402	324	211
Civil Eng. & Building	371	362	265
Electrical Engineering	635	516	327
Mechanical & Prod. Eng.	436	360	443
Printing & Graphic Arts	205	244	280
Science Technology	337	289	249
Sub-Total (Technical)	2386	2195	1775
Business Education			
Business Studies (day)	449	2292	1758
Business Education (evening)	1853	-	-
Secretarial Studies	1269	1276	915
Hairdressing	36	67	73
Sub-Total (Business Eduucation)	3589	3635	2746
Adult Education	1792	1094	1211
Mass Communication	32	-	-
TOTAL (all courses)	7799	6924	5732

Source: Compiled from MLMPSW Statistics. (Produced in Manpower Development Project draft. Vol.1, 1985. Government of Zimbabwe. p.68)

The government has also established two Vocational Training Centres (VTC) for the purpose of upgrading 'semi-skilled' workers. Of the two centres, one has been established in Bulawayo and is funded by the French government, and the other in Harare and is funded by the West German government. The idea of the VTCs is to upgrade 'semi-skilled' workers, mostly in the automotive and mechanical trade areas, through a combined system of modular and in-service training. Table 8 shows the numbers that have been upgraded at the Vocational Training Centres in 1983/84. Another aspect of training related to the 'semi-skilled' worker

TABLE 8
NUMBERS ENROLLED IN UP-GRADING TRAINING AT THE VOCATIONAL TRAINING CENTRES

MASASA V.T.C. TRAINEES (Harare)

Trades/industry Courses	Motor Mechanics 1983	Motor Mechanics 1984	Auto Electricians 1983	Auto Electricians 1984	Fitters 1983/84	Automotive 1984	Mechanical 1984	Total
Class I								
Part I	-	12	-	-	-	12	-	12
Part II	-	-	-	-	-	-	-	-
Class I								
Part I	14	58	-	12	-	-84	-	84
Part II	-	43	-	6	-	49	-	49
Class 3								
Part I	12	-	-	34	-	46	-	46
Part II	-	10	-	6	-	16	-	16
Class 4								
Part I	-	23	-	-	64	23	64	87
Part II	-	-	-	-	-	-	-	-
TOTALS	26	146	-	58	64	230	64	294

WESTGATE V.T.C. TRAINEES (Bulawayo)

Class 3								
Part I	-	36	-	-	-	-	-	36
Part II	-	-	-	-	-	36	-	-
Class 4								
Part I	12	-	-	-	-	12	-	12
TOTALS	-	48	-	-	-	48	-	48
GRAND TOTAL	26	194	-	58	-	64	278	64
								342

Source: Division of Vocational and Technical Training, Ministry of Labour, Manpower Planning and Social Welfare. (In Annual Review of Manpower 1984) p.61

is the system of trade-testing introduced by the government. Through this system trade tests are administered to under categorised 'semi-skilled' workers in order to give them an opportunity to be regraded into one of four skill categories. Table 9 illustrates the number of workers who have been upgraded either by trade-testing or through on-site assessments. The latter measure has had to be utilised because of both the large backlog of workers awaiting regrading (presently assessed at 140,000) and the shortage of trainers and facilities to carry out the trade tests.

TABLE 9
NUMBERS OF WORKERS TRADE TESTED (1982-84)

	Assessment		Test		Total
	No	%	No	%	
Grade I	2 222	68	1 035	32	3 257
Grade II	943	48	1 046	52	1 979
Grade III	827	50	814	50	1 641
Grade IV	584	51	561	49	1 145
Ungraded	97	54	82	46	179
Total	4 673	57	3 528	43	8 207

Source: Division of Research and Planning, MIMPSW

The upgrading and trade testing operations since independence have been an important breakthrough for the working class in Zimbabwe. Based as this policy was on the recognition of under categorisation of 'semi-skilled' workers in Zimbabwe, the upgrading exercise was a challenge to a basic assumption of the colonial capitalist categorisation and utilisation of labour. The policy has highlighted the operational role of the 'semi-skilled' and their right to a more equitable categorisation and remuneration. In so doing, the policy has also stressed the importance of localised training and questioned the expatriate syndrome of the colonial period.

The upgrading programme has not been without opposition, precisely because it has questioned certain basic employer assumptions and raised the prospect of an increased wage bill. Thus a top official of the General Engineering and Metal Workers Union made the following criticism of the attitude of certain employers to the upgrading programme:

> I think many people are scared to go for trade tests because they are afraid of losing their jobs. We have tried to confront the Ministry of Labour, Manpower Planning and Social Welfare on this but we have not got far. The Government should come up with a strict move to stop this practice. If some employers are allowed to get away with this there won't be much progress in the industry.[39]

Methods of victimisation used included retrenching general workers with the new journeymen so that the act would not be seen as victimisation, and reassigning the journeymen to sweeping jobs.[40] The Employers Confederation of Zimbabwe also expressed reservations about the upgrading of workers, with its accompanying wage increases, unless the exercise was undertaken within the economic restraints that the economy can afford, without an over-emphasis of the faults, real or imagined, of the previous wage structure.[41]

Expansion of training has also taken place through the Scholarship System co-ordinated through the Ministry of Labour, Manpower Planning and Social Welfare. Through this system, scholarships are for the most part awarded in areas of study that are considered critical shortage areas. The figures in Table 10 illustrate that 55% of the scholarships awarded have been in the science/technical field.

In terms of legislation, the Manpower Planning and Development Act, 1984, has given the state the power to control the expansion and development of training in accordance with national objectives. For example, employers contribute a levy (1% of their bill) to the Zimbabwe Development Fund, the money from which is then directed into areas of training that are considered national priorities.

Problems Related to the Expansion and Democratisation of Education and Training

Thus far, we have addressed some of the problems that have accompanied the expanded training programme. However, there are some general problems relating to the expansion that need to be discussed. One of the major constraints on the expansion of technical programmes has been the shortage of staff in technical areas. Much of the expansion that has taken place in training has been carried out within existing salary structures. Given the larger numbers that entered the colleges and the shortage of trainers, the result was a movement of these trainers to the more lucrative private and parastatal sectors. Table 11 gives a breakdown of total vacancies in the three main colleges in the country in 1985. As the figures show, 123 (72%) of the vacancies were in the science/technical field. At the university, there were 270 staff resignations from the academic professional categories between 1980 and 1984. A large part of these resignations was in the technical staff category, and the most affected categories were Medicine, Science and Agriculture (see Table 12). The issues raised by the internal manpower drift are discussed below.[42] These vacancies are relatively high if one considers, for example, that the vacancies at the three largest colleges represented about 30% of the staff complement in 1984. In order to provide a short-term 'solution' to the problem in the colleges, the government has utilised bilateral agreements with countries such as Canada, UK and the US. Accordingly, expatriates are sent from these countries to fill the vacancies for a short-term period. In addition, trainees have been sent to such countries to become trainers. An important development at the University of Zimbabwe has been the increasing influence of Western aid in its programmes. This is reflected, for example, in the staff development programmes. As

TABLE 10
EXPECTED YEAR OF RETURN OF PERSONS AWARDED SCHOLARSHIPS FOR STUDY OUTSIDE ZIMBABWE BY MAJOR FIELD OF STUDY

Field of Study	1981	1982	1983	1984	1985	1986	1987	1988	1989	1990	Year Unknown	Total
Social Science and other Humanities	6	14	22	33	13	13	13	9	2	0	29	143
Agriculture & Related Fields	1	10	10	15	32	6	13	17	2	0	32	138
Engineering & Related Fields	10	98	73	74	51	38	40	41	10	3	80	518
Medicine & Medical Fields	4	6	17	20	15	22	27	22	24	4	28	189
Aircraft & Related Fields	3	10	10	6	0	5	0	4	0	0	11	49
Mining & Related Fields	0	3	6	12	8	1	9	11	3	0	6	59
Natural Science	6	20	13	10	9	10	7	4	4	0	14	27
Accountants, Law & Commerce	5	19	19	15	12	15	3	1	5	0	16	110
Unspecified	3	25	6	23	44	19	12	14	10	0	317	473
TOTAL	38	205	176	208	184	129	120	116	60	7	533	1776

Source: Scholarship Division, Ministry of Labour, Manpower Planning and Social Welfare. (Annual Review of Manpower 1984) p. 73.

TABLE 11
LIST OF VACANT POSTS OF LECTURERS BY DIVISION/DEPARTMENTS

Division/Department	Harare Polytechnic Established	Vacant	Bulawayo Training College Established	Vacant	Kweke Training College Established	Vacant	Total Vacant
Business Manangement	-	-	19	3	-	-	3
Business Studies	30	12	-	-	18	4	16
Secr. Clerical	29	5	22	2	-	-	7
Computer Studies	7	1	-	-	-	-	1
Mech. Eng.	30	20	53	21	12	4	25
AVTD Eng.	38	20	-	-	7	3	23
Civil/Building	32	10	10	6	-	-	16
Mining	-	-	8	3	-	-	3
Building Craft/Fabrication	-	11	25	10	-	-	10
Elec. Eng.	33	-	35	18	9	3	32
Science/Health	-	-	21	8	-	-	8
Arts	-	-	7	1	-	-	1
Hotel School	-	-	8	1	-	-	1
Science Tech.	14	14	-	-	-	-	14
Mass Communications	9	1	-	-	-	-	1
Adult Education	3	-	-	-	-	-	-
Printing & Graphic Arts	24	8	-	-	-	-	8
Total	247	82	208	73	46	14	170

Source: Manpower Development Project Vol.1, 1985, P. 113.

at 31 December 1985, of the 55 Fellows on staff development programmes 21 (31.8%) were in the United States and 25 (37.8%) were in the United Kingdom. The distribution of these programmes covers the arts, social science and physical science categories.

TABLE 12
UNIVERSITY OF ZIMBABWE
STAFF RESIGNATIONS—1980-1984

Category	1980	1981	1982	1983	1984	TOTAL
Professor	0	0	4	3	3	10
Associate Prof.	1	1	1	0	1	4
Senior Lecturer	4	8	4	7	5	28
Lecturer	15	15	14	16	11	71
Research Fellow/Ass.	0	3	3	5	2	13
Teaching Assistant	3	4	4	2	0	13
Technical Staff	18	30	27	21	11	107
Other (i)	6	5	4	7	4	26
TOTAL	47	66	61	61	37	272

Source: University of Zimbabwe

A more general problem of high-level human resource expansion, and one that was alluded to earlier, is the relationship between the supply of and demand for manpower. There is at present in Zimbabwe only a very general relationship between critical shortage areas, as defined initially in the National Manpower Survey 1981, and the output of middle and high-level human resources. The scholarship system has, for example, sent many Zimbabweans abroad to study in general shortage areas. Yet there remain problems as to the number that will be utilised on their return, given the minimal control of the state over the means of production in the country. Thus, the utilisation of the trainees sponsored by the government will, in cases where they cannot be utilised by the state, depend on the vagaries (and discretion) of capital. Moreover, some of the training that has been carried out abroad has been inappropriate for local conditions. There is the case of the training, carried out in West Germany under the auspices of the Otto Benecke Foundation, about which a seminar was arranged to discuss the problems of the training given. At the seminar one employer commented, describing the response of his foremen to a few of the trainees:

> Both foremen stated that they found standards of skill well below that of an assistant artisan, the procedure applying skills, nil perception and diagnostic skills badly lacking.[43]

There have been other cases in which the training given to Zimbabweans has been below local requirements. At one level this problem has arisen because, given the lack of high level training that has characterised the colonial period, and given the poor planning structures that understandably existed in the first five years of independence, the government sometimes responded to scholarship offers that were not always suitable for our economy. On the other hand, certain developed countries also made their own assumptions about the training needs of Zimbabwe. As one commentator noted at the seminar mentioned above, there is often the assumption in both developed and developing countries that the technological requirements of the latter are inferior to those of the former, and the training provided is 'often coloured by this assumption'.[44]

At the university, as we have already noted, the enrolment in the critical technical areas is still relatively low, and about on average with other developing countries. Amongst reasons for this are: on the one hand, the shortage of technical scientific staff coupled with the relatively lower number of 'A' level science graduates who enter the courses at the university, and on the other, the more fundamental reason, namely that of relating high-level manpower supply, especially in the technical areas, to the demand structure. The means of production in Zimbabwe are still controlled by international capital, whose production and human resource imperatives are locked into an international rationale of accumulation. Thus, the demand for defined human resources is still very much dependent on the vagaries of capital accumulation in the country, and this poses serious problems for meaningful human resource planning. The development of a technical and scientific culture is also hampered by the transnational domination of these areas. For example, a good deal of technological capacity in the Zimbabwean economy is based on the use of acquired technology from the developed countries. As a result, engineers whose work is geared to research and development (R & D) have a limited function in a situation where R & D is carried out at a minimal level, and most of the work is geared to operations and maintenance.[45]

The problems of the use of high-level scientific/technical capability in developing countries have been aptly described by Cooper in the following terms:

> ...scientific institutions are alienated from production activities or 'marginalised' because there is no demand for locally developed technologies from the productive sectors. Consequently science in underdeveloped countries is largely a consumption item, whereas in industrialised countries it is an investment item. Furthermore, the lack of pressures on science from the local economy means that the main determinants of research orientation are the individual decisions of research workers, and these research workers take their lead from the international orientation of research.[46]

When, therefore, the state has been asked to engage in manpower forecasting such are the problems it has to face. According to the usual methods of projecting manpower, projections are first made of the output of a given sector, and then a manpower coefficient is applied to an absolute production increase. A forecast of extra labour requirements is then arrived at and such requirements are fed into the educational system.[47] In developing countries such projects often become mere academic exercises in the face of the serious external constraints on economic development.

There is one final aspect of the expansion of technical training that needs to be discussed and this relates to what has become known as the 'school-leaver problem'. The highly commendable democratisation of education that has taken place since 1980 has done so within an economy that has been unable to expand sufficiently to cope with numbers of school-leavers. Thus, for example, in 1982 while there were 80,000 school-leavers, only about 10,500 jobs were created.

In addition, there has been a decline in employment between 1981 and 1984; thus total employment declined by 0.8% from 1,060,000 in 1981/82 to 1,034,600 in 1983/84, representing 8% less than the planned employment figures in the Transitional National Development Plan (TNDP). In the material production sector, employment dropped by 2.8%, from 732,000 in 1981/82 to 680,000 in 1983/84. The sectors in which the decline was most apparent were agriculture (-2.0%), manufacturing (-6.8%), mining (-5.1%) and construction (-2.0%). Increases in employment took place in the non-material production sector, from 328,000 in 1981/82 to 354,000 in 1983/84.[48] This inability to cope with large numbers of school-leavers is, moreover, not a novel feature of this economy. It was quite characteristic of the colonial period. The problem has been highlighted partly because of the much larger numbers that are leaving school (estimated at 2,322,518 between 1983 and 1994 (see Table 13); and also because once the popular demand for education had made the democratisation of education a fundamental right in the country, the requirements of the school-leavers for employment had thrown up new demands.

However, unlike the expansion of education in which the state could and did make a decisive intervention, the question of employment has raised much more fundamental issues about the control and direction of the production structure. In the event it has been much too difficult to tackle the issues of production and thereby provide alternative economic policies to restructure the distortions of the current economy. A symptom of the difficulties associated with this problem is the fact that the responsibility for employment creation has been placed on one small department, the Department of Employment and Employment Development, in the Ministry of Labour, Manpower Planning and Social Welfare. Of necessity, the task has proved too formidable for one department, and more recently an inter-ministerial Employment Advisory Committee has been formed, a step which has at least led to a greater realisation of the central nature of the problem.

Recently, the Ministry of Youth, Sport and Culture and UNICEF sponsored a *Report on the Needs of Rural Youth and Prospects of Their Integration into the Zimbabwean Economy*. The report concluded that:

TABLE 13
SECONDARY SCHOOL LEAVERS BY LEVEL AND SEX 1983-1984

Year	Form IV	Form V	Form VIU	Total	Form IV Male	Form IV Female	Form V Male	Form V Female	Form VIU Male	Form VIU Female
1983	24509	2189	2890	29588	14078	10431	1283	906	1954	936
1984	71014	3112	2911	77037	44085	26929	1738	1374	2142	769
1985	91763	3246	3200	98209	53837	36926	1858	1388	2259	941
1986	93092	-	4000	97092	55632	37460	-	-	2824	1176
1987	141593	-	4200	145793	84616	56977	-	-	2965	1235
1988	152122	-	4500	156622	90908	61214	-	-	3177	1323
1989	180047	-	4800	184847	107396	72451	-	-	3389	1411
1990	267677	-	5100	272777	159963	107714	-	-	3600	1500
1991	325448	-	5400	330848	194487	130961	-	-	3812	1588
1992	306714	-	5800	312514	183291	183423	-	-	4095	1705
1993	301165	-	6200	307365	179975	121190	-	-	4377	1823
1994	303626	-	6200	309826	181446	122180	-	-	4377	1823
TOTAL	2258700	8547	55201	2322518	1350913	907857	4879	3668	38971	16230

Source: Statistics Unit, Ministry of Education

> Current prospects for integrating youths in the form of regular wage employment in the economy are apparently very limited.[49]

The basic reason for this pessimistic conclusion is that:

> the bulk of the economy and particularly its private owners see the *raison d'être* of their role in the economy as the earning of high returns on their investments, not only now but for the forseeable future. However, this is not currently seen as guaranteed and even likely in the future. Indeed the question of youth unemployment itself is most likely to be used by private investors in gaining further concessions from Government as regards this very issue of investment.[50]

The report also observes that thus so far the government has invested a 'small and comparatively insignificant' amount of money to generate youth employment.[51]

One of the major effects of the school-leaver debate is that, unlike the *Report on the Needs of Rural Youth* discussed above, it has increasingly concentrated not on the problems of restructuring the economy but on the nature of the education system, and its relevance to the current constraints in the economy. In other words the focus has been increasingly placed not on the crisis of production and investment, but on the qualities and relevance of educational expansion. Increasingly, there is a tendency to take for granted the current distorted demands of the economy and to seek to adjust the supply of labour accordingly. An example of this trend was an announcement in September 1985, later corrected by the Prime Minister, that children entering secondary school from the beginning of 1986 were to be screened. Before the announcement was corrected by the Prime Minister, a leading Sunday paper made the following *Comment*:

> Given the oft-repeated pupils' indiscipline in schools and the disturbingly high failure rate, Cde. Mutumbuka's decision represents the triumph of enlightened pragmatism over dogmatic inflexibility. While government policy firmly states that education is a right for all our children, it does not say public funds should be wasted forcing education into an unable and unwilling head.[52]

The solution put forward is that the more 'academically dull' pupils, assumed to be 'talented in practical fields', should be placed in technical schools, and that, therefore, there should be a deliberate bias towards the establishment of more agricultural training institutions.[53] This *Comment* by *The Sunday Mail* was fittingly entitled 'Right Policy'.

This tendency to resort to explanations of failure that increasingly centre the blame on the child results from a failure to analyse the problems of teachers and facilities that have accompanied expanded enrolment as well as a failure to recognise the persistent social and economic problems that affect the educability of children. It is part of the flight from the need to confront the production structures in our economy. As the problems of budgetary constraints have increased, the argument for the right to education has been more frequently confronted by a questioning of the functional relation of this education to the demands of the existing economy. This has also been accompanied by the argument for vocationalisation of education, either in a rural-oriented manner, or for self-employment. There are serious dangers in this argument. First, there is the danger of creating a dual educational structure in which vocational training will be regarded as being of a lower status than the academic field; and therefore suitable for the 'less able'. The latter will almost be synonymous with the children of the poorer classes, simply because of the harsh conditions in which many continue to live and learn. Moreover, the effect of downgrading the importance of technical education, as being for the less able, will undermine any attempt to create an all-round polytechnic education for all children.

Second, the assumption that a ruralisation of vocational education will somehow increase the opportunities for employment is based on a misunderstanding of the structural linkages between industry and agriculture; and of the manner in which the mechanisms of accumulation in one sector has affected the other. It is no accident that those ruralisation vocational programmes in Africa that have attempted to keep youths in the rural areas have failed to keep these youths from seeking employment and a type of education suited to the formal sector. The study of youth in Zimbabwe already discussed provides further evidence of this. The structural roots of poverty cannot be abstracted from the relations in the economy as a whole. Moreover, changes that have taken place on the land and continue to take place indicate increasing class divisions and the creation of more landless labourers. In such conditions where are youths, given ruralised vocational education, supposed to find employment?

There is more than a little truth in Clive Thomas's critical observation that the:

> tendency among urban planners... and some elements of the petty-bourgeoisie to romanticize the virtues of poverty and/or overestimate the qualities of rural life as it stands has been of inestimable significance. These are not sufficiently seen and understood as malformations of human existence—the very factors which call forth socialism in theory and practice in the first place.[54]

In sum, there is a tendency to relate the solution of school-leaver unemployment increasingly to training of a particular orientation without, however, looking at the structures of production. The sometimes hurried attempts to set up courses for school-leavers is a symptom of this approach.[55] It must also be stated, however, that the future direction of education and training is still being hotly debated, and the contradictory statements over the selection of secondary school students is a reflection of this debate.[56] A fundamental issue in the debate relates to the crisis of state legitimacy that would be likely to arise in the face of any serious threat to the democratisation of education that has been set in motion over the last five years.

Other Measures Taken Towards Overcoming Colonial Manpower Legacy

(a) *Apprenticeship Training*

As an attempt to stop the flow of skills out of the country, and in so doing help to stabilise the pool of skills for all sectors within the country, the government introduced Bonding Regulations for apprentices in 1982. The loss of skills and the potential for loss, given the racial breakdown of apprenticeship intake in 1980, was cause for serious concern soon after independence.

In February 1981, out of a total of 5,103 apprentices in Zimbabwe, 3,316 or 56% were Europeans, 1,330 or 26% Africans, 374 or 7% 'Coloured' (i.e. mixed race) and 83 or 1% Asians. In addition, Europeans dominated apprenticeship in the technically critical trades: aircraft (89%), electricity (84%) and mechanical engineering (68%).[57]

As far as journeymen were concerned, while in December 1976, the number stood at 13,663 by December 1978 and 1980, it stood at 11,955 and 9,024 respectively.[58]

As a further illustration of the problem, Table 14 compares the loss of journeymen through emigration in 1981 with the number of apprentices who completed their course in the same year. The figures show a net loss of 72 journeymen in that year.

TABLE 14
LOSS OF JOURNEYMEN THROUGH EMIGRATION COMPARED WITH APPRENTICES WHO COMPLETED IN 1981

Industry	Immigrants	Emigrants	Net Emigrants	App. Contracts	Gain or Loss
Aircraft	14	50	36	78	+42
Building	42	120	78	25	-53
Electrical Eng.	116	211	95	139	+53
Hairdressing	1	40	39	35	-4
Mechanical Eng.	155	470	315	276	-39
Motor	62	211	149	72	-77
Printing	24	49	25	40	+15
TOTAL	414	1151	737	665	-72

Source: Annual Report of the Apprenticeship Training for the Year Ended 31st December 1981.

Clearly, critical skills in such vital areas as mechanical engineering and the motor industry were being lost to other countries such as South Africa. In response to this trend the government introduced the Bonding Regulations under Emergency Powers Regulations. The major objectives of the bonding were:

— to stop the emigration of the apprentices who were in training and had no intention of serving the country on completion of their training;
— to deter prospective apprentices intent on using the limited technical facilities in the country only to leave on completion of the training;
— to ensure that the apprentice who subsequently breaks his contract, or chooses to emigrate after completion, pays for the investment made in him; and
— to discourage employers from recruiting apprentices who are likely to emigrate.

The reaction to the bonding by many white apprentices and employers was one of extreme anger. A meeting addressed by the Secretary of the Ministry of Manpower Planning and Development:

was marred by very bad behaviour on the part of the many white apprentices present, who jeered and catcalled...[59]

The business press warned that many employers had indicated that there was likely to be 'mass apprenticeship resignations in all industrial fields'[60] as a result of the bonding regulations.

The terms of the bonding required that, once qualified, journeymen would have to work in the country for the period of time spent training. Alternatively, they could pay back the government the amount spent on their training.

As a result of the bonding, 791 apprentices cancelled their contracts, representing approximately 13% of registered apprentices and 22% of white apprentices.[61] Table 15 gives a breakdown of these 791 apprentices by trade.

TABLE 15
CANCELLED APPRENTICESHIPS BY TRADE—JULY 1982

TRADE	Harare	NUMBER Bulawayo	Gweru	Total
Mechanical Eng.	139	125	28	292
Electrical	77	99	36	212
Motor	81	40	21	142
Printing	42	26	1	69
Building	2	5	1	8
Hairdressing	20	1	0	21
Aircraft	47	0	0	47
TOTAL	408	296	87	791

Source: Apprenticeship Authority.

TABLE 16
APPRENTICESHIP INTAKE 1984/85 BY RACE

INDUSTRY	European	African	Coloured	Other	Total
Aircraft	7	43	-	-	50
Building	4	51	2	3	60
Electrical	29	217	6	2	254
Mechanical	77	333	22	4	436
Automotive	47	85	10	1	143
Printing	10	26	1	1	38
Hairdressing	7	9	1	1	18
TOTAL	181	764	42	12	999

Source: Apprenticeship Authority.

How effective was the bonding? First, it did not produce the 'mass' resignations predicted in certain quarters, as the 13% figure demonstrates. Second, by making employers more aware of the need to indenture young men who are likely to remain in the country, it has helped to correct the racial imbalance in apprenticeship intake (see Table 16).

In addition to the bonding measures, the state has also begun the process of centralising the recruitment of apprentices. Through this process it is intended, first, to remove the racist practice of apprentice selection practiced by many employers; and second, to initiate a mechanism that will inject a more planned element into the recruitment and distribution of apprentices. However, the output of journeymen is still dependent on employers, and this is reflected in the fluctuation of apprenticeship intake. Thus the apprentice intake dropped from 2,044 in 1981 to 792 in 1982, and then rose to 1,250 in 1983. At various points in the history of the colonial economy, this fluctuation of training, in which intakes were reduced during slump periods, led to shortages subsequently when the economy picked up again. The lack of institutional training for apprentices makes this fluctuation a continued probability.

(b) *Foreign Recruitment*

As we have already observed, foreign recruitment during the colonial period was an integral part of the formally skilled input into the labour force. Immigration promotion, however, was also an important part of the strategy to 'keep Rhodesia white', and it was for this reason that immigration/emigration statistics became a significant barometer of the level of white 'confidence' in the settler colonial structure.

It was therefore important for the new government both to break the expatriate syndrome in terms of the perceived need for imported skills and to discourage the forms of racist immigration patterns that had characterised the colonial period.

The National Manpower Survey revealed that while Zimbabweans accounted for 84% of all employed persons, dual citizenship holders and non-Zimbabweans accounted for 2% and 14% respectively of the labour

TABLE 17
ALL SECTORS (a)
SKILL AND NATIONALITY BY OCCUPATION

Major Occupation Group		Professional			Skilled			Semi-skilled			Totals			Grand Total
		Zim	Dual	N/Zim	Zim	Dual	N/Zim	Zim	Dual	N/Zim	Zim	Dual	N/Zim	
Professional, Technical & Related	No. %	14392 53	905 3	3898 14	3572 13	171 1	798 2	3008 11	38 -	249 -	20972 78	1114 4	4945 18	27031 100
Administrative & Managerial	No %	6912 62	770 7	2961 27	251 2	19 -	81 1	36 -	3 -	51 -	7199 65	792 7	3093 28	11084 100
Clerical & Related	No %	2919 5	342 1	14092 1	823 25	3214 1	29657 6	653 53	3659 1	46668 7	1818 83	7560 3	56046 14	65424 100
Sales	No %	1431 9	162 -	411 3	5042 31	578 4	1081 7	6642 41	75 -	962 6	13115 80	815 5	2454 15	16384 100
Service	No %	522 2	3 -	37 -	4481 19	92 -	1030 5	15612 68	124 1	1130 5	20615 90	219 0	2197 10	23031 100
Agricultural, Animal Husbandry & Forestry Workers, Fishermen & Hunters	No %	82 -	2 -	5 -	9243 21	333 1	1500 3	25877 60	185 -	5944 14	35202 82	520 1	7449 17	43171 100
Production and Related Workers, Transport Equipment Operators	No %	141 -	12 -	29 -	33309 28	572 -	5965 5	70844 60	376 -	6475 6	104294 89	960 -	12469 11	117723 100
Occupation Inadequately Described	No %	203 5	16 -	56 1	1063 27	11 -	188 5	2073 53	1 -	310 8	33389 85	28 1	554 14	3921 100
TOTAL	No %	26602 8	2212 1	8084 3	71053 24	2599 1	13857 5	153749 51	1455 -	18780 6	251404 84	6266 2	40721 14	298391 100

*Employees of education and training institutions are excluded from this table

Source: NMS 1981 Vol. 1, p.74.

TABLE 18
APPROVED EXPATRIATE PERSONNEL BY MAJOR OCCUPATIONS GROUP (1982/1984)

Occupation Groups	1982	1983	1984
Professional, Technical and Related Workers			
Civil Engineers	27	28	26
Electrical and Electronics Engineers	3	15	7
Mechanical Engineers	7	11	13
Mining Engineers	2	2	10
Other Engineers	53	99	130
Chemists, Pharmacists, Biologists & Other Life Scientists	10	10	10
Other Physical Scientists	2	3	5
Geologists/Surveyors	25	13	19
Draughtsmen/Architects	29	8	-
Electrical & Electronics Technicians	52	74	76
Other Technicians	39	108	124
Aircraft Officers	8	5	10
Medical Doctors	78	67	88
Dental Surgeons	2	8	7
Professional Nurses	25	23	37
Medical Technicians	14	13	25
Veterinarians	10	-	2
Accountants, Financial Controllers, etc	38	53	27
University Lecturers	17	37	33
Secondary School Teachers	396	447	248
Technical Instructors	15	52	32
Other Professional, Technical and Related	64	150	203
TOTAL PROFESSIONAL TECHNICAL AND RELATED	**916**	**1226**	**1132**
Administrative and Managerial			
General Managers/Directors	74	36	22
Production Managers	10	8	18
Other Managers	45	44	66
TOTAL ADMINISTRATIVE AND MANAGERIAL	**129**	**88**	**106**
TOTAL CLERICAL AND RELATED	**36**	**45**	**16**
TOTAL SALE WORKERS	**3**	**13**	**7**
TOTAL SERVICE WORKERS	**52**	**32**	**31**
TOTAL AGRICULTURE AND ANIMAL HUSBANDRY Workers, etc.	**22**	**21**	**30**
Production and Related Workers			
Production Supervisors and General Foremen	34	5	18
Blacksmith, Toolmakers, Machine Assembler	12	16	4
Electrical Fitters	12	1	6
Diesel Fitter/Mechanic	24	69	12
Other Fitters and Turner	49	113	43
Printers and Related Workers	14	5	1
Machinery Fitter/Assembler	58	17	14
Computer Programmer/Systems Analysis	17	14	14
Other Production Workers	118	115	61
TOTAL PRODUCTION AND RELATED WORKERS	**338**	**395**	**179**
GRAND TOTALS	**1494**	**1820**	**1496**

Source: Annual Review of Manpower 1984. p.49

TABLE 19
ECONOMICALLY ACTIVE IMMIGRANTS AND EMIGRANTS 1982 TO 1984

OCCUPATIONS	IMMIGRANTS 1982 Male	1982 Female	1983 Male	1983 Female	1984 Male	1984 Female	EMIGRANTS 1982 Male	1982 Female	1983 Male	1983 Female	1984 Male	1984 Female
PROFESSIONAL, TECHNICAL AND RELATED WORKERS												
Physical Scientists & Related Techn.	27	-	31	-	16	-	-	35	34	-	32	-
Architects Eng. & Related Techn.	-	-	436	-	468	-	-	-	509	-	512	-
Life Scientists & Related Techn.	-	-	13	-	24	-	-	-	48	-	27	-
Medical, Dentistry, Veterinary & Related Workers	-	-	77	124	91	99	-	-	126	267	119	241
Accountants	79	-	46	22	38	7	142	178	40	40	145	40
Teachers	373	167	385	138	261	159	117	453	204	215	215	214
Others	609	226	161	89	234	76	784	41	204	146	250	141
Administration & Managerial Workers	170	16	158	22	134	9	525	1082	464	45	438	38
Clerical & Related Workers	145	175	114	136	68	90	379	78	299	939	301	755
Sales Workers	45	9	43	12	30	7	195	83	174	50	176	41
Service Workers	24	28	27	19	27	17	223	7	189	62	150	57
Agriculture & Related Workers	72	3	67	2	33	4	188		315	11	274	9
PRODUCTION & RELATED WORKERS												
Production Supervisor & Gen.Foremen	-	-	64	-	74	-	-	-	135	-	131	-
Miners, quarrymen, Welldrillers & Related Workers	-	-	8	-	6	-	-	-	188	-	184	-
Machinery fitters, Assemblers & related Workers	-	-	129	-	107	-	-	-	368	-	384	-
Electrical fitters, Electronics workers & Related workers	-	-	80	-	97	-	-	-	177	-	172	-
Printers & related Workers	-	-	17	-	4	-	-	-	34	-	33	-
Bricklayers, carpenters, Other construction & Related workers	-	-	28	-	9	-	-	-	69	-	47	-
Labourers	-	-	12	-	5	-	-	-	690	-	626	-
Others	575	9	153	14	91	13	1866	17	316	23	244	22
Workers inadequately Described	134	39	113	20	21	11	353	94	293	90	314	87
Uniformed persons	-	-	15	-	14	1	-	-	39	-	48	1
TOTAL	2334	672	2177	598	1852	493	4807	2033	5017	1894	4786	1646

Source: Central Statistical Office.

force (see Table 17). However, non-Zimbabweans and dual citizenship holders made up an important segment of critical occupational categories, representing 22% of the professional, technical and related group, and 35% of the administrative and managerial group.

After independence, the state introduced a Manpower Planning Committee on Foreign Recruitment whose objective was to restrict expatriate recruitment to areas of critical shortage, for a limited period of time (two years), and with the provision that the recruiting employer undertake to provide a local understudy for that foreign recruit. Table 18 shows that the figure for approved expatriate personnel moved from 1,494 in 1982 to 1,820 in 1983, and back to 1,496 in 1984. However, the table also shows that, while there has been an increase in the figures in the 'professional, technical and related' occupational categories, those for the 'administrative and managerial' and 'production and related' categories have declined.

The immediate reason for the continued need for foreign recruitment can be seen from the continued short-term emigration of people in the critical 'professional' 'technical and related', and 'production and related' workers categories. Thus, Table 19 on immigrants and emigrants shows a net loss, between 1982 and 1984, in such shortage area skills as architects, engineers, and related technicians; medical, dental, veterinary and related workers; accountants, teachers, managers, production supervisors, electrical fitters and machine fitters.

The system of foreign recruitment control is still encountering certain problems. Among these are the fact that the system of monitoring is still inadequate and therefore it is difficult to assess the effectiveness of the understudy scheme. In addition, certain international agreements have included skill input arrangements, resulting in the import of skills that are locally available. Foreign recruitment is likely to be an important part of the Zimbabwean labour market for the foreseeable future.

Internal Drift of Manpower and Africanisation

The existence of certain skill shortages in Zimbabwe has resulted in a disturbing loss of certain key skills from the public sector. Tables 20 and 21 illustrate the number of officers and employees by ministry who resigned from the public service in 1983. As the tables show, there were 993 employee and 759 officer resignations from the public service in 1983. The resignations from the officer grade are more significant as they relate to critical skill areas. Thus from Table 21 it can be seen that 78% of the total resignations were from the technical/professional group. The magnitude of this drain is considerable given that only 10.5% of workers in this occupational category were in the public sector in 1981.[62]

Parastatal organisations also experienced a large loss of skills. Thus between January and December 1983, parastatals experienced a drift of 2,332 people from their structure. Table 22 gives a more detailed breakdown of this number. As the table shows, the resignations from the production and related, and professional, technical and related workers categories represented 32% of the resignations.

TABLE 20
EMPLOYEE RESIGNATIONS BY MINISTRY AFFECTED—1983

Ministry	No. of Resignation	Percent of Total Resignations
Home Affairs	165	17
Finance, Economic Planning and Development	129	13
Agriculture	90	9
Roads and Road Traffic	60	6
Health	84	8.4
Public Service	58	5.8
Justice	54	5.4
Manpower, Planning and Development	49	5.0
Lands, Resettlement and Rural Development	38	3.8
Labour and Social Services	33	3.3
Local Government and Town Planning	37	3.7
Defence	23	2.3
Transport	21	2.1
Water Resources and Development	25	2.5
Others*	127	13
TOTAL	993	100

* Others are all those Ministries that had less than 20 resignations or less than 2 per cent of the total resignations.
Note: The employee category includes such workers as clerks, drivers, typists, receptionists, registry clerks and supervisors, dip attendants, etc.

Source: Annual Review of Manpower 1983, p. 29 Ministry of Labour Manpower Planning and Social Welfare.

TABLE 21
RESIGNATIONS BY CATEGORY OF OFFICER: 1983

Group	No. of Resignations	Percent of total
Deputy Secretaries	7	1
Under-Secretaries	7	1
Assistant Secretaries	7	1
Officers (Administration etc.)	145	19
Technical and Related Staff	593	78
TOTAL	759	100

Source: Annual Review of Manpower 1983, p. 30

TABLE 22
RESIGNATIONS FROM PARASTATALS BY OCCUPATIONAL GROUP

	Number	Per Cent
Clerical and Related	1,194	51
Production and Related Workers	391	17
Professional, Technical and Related	349	15
Sales Workers	102	4
Administrative and Managerial	68	3
Service Workers	27	1
Agriculture, Animal and Related	17	1
Occupations Inadequately Described	184	8
TOTALS	2,332	100*

*Percentage figures are rounded up.
Source: *Annual Review of Manpower, 1983*

The Public Service Incentive Scheme provided an important mechanism for manpower drift in the immediate post-independence period. The Incentive Scheme was introduced in 1979 by the 'Internal Settlement' regime, its aim being to guard the interests of white civil servants in the event of a majority rule government. The Incentive Scheme became part of the Lancaster House Agreement and amongst its most important conditions are the following:

> (a) any officer or employee appointed before 1 October 1978 who was a contributor to the pension scheme, and who was replaced or suffered loss of office as a result of being replaced by a black officer, could retire with full benefits before pensionable age;
> (b) the scheme was based on a scale of increasing benefits designed to induce officers to remain in service;
> (c) the scheme guaranteed remittability of certain benefits to any person who is 'ordinarily resident outside Zimbabwe-Rhodesia'.[63]

An analysis of 696 retirements from the public service in 1983 reveals that 567 (81%) of the people retired under the Incentive Scheme.[64] A further breakdown of the retirements reveals that approximately 90% of these took place among people of non-pensionable age, thus resulting in a premature manpower drift from the public service. One writer has estimated that between 1979 and 1985 almost 5,000 officers left the public service as a result of the Incentive Scheme.[65]

Whites also flowed into the private sector because of their antagonism to the policies of the new government, and once there, have endeavoured to form a new 'white laager'. At one point, the Minister of Labour even 'threatened to prohibit' the employment, by the private sector, of former civil servants who had retired under the scheme.[66]

Another immediate reason for the manpower drift from the public to the private sector had been the problem of wage/salary differentials between the sectors. The Minister of Labour, Manpower Planning and Social Welfare, having seen his ministry lose 48 Industrial Relations Officers (including four Chief Industrial Relations Officers) to the private sector, remarked in November 1984:

> It would appear that most officers join the department mainly and almost solely as a station for passage to the more lucrative private sector.[67]

However, it is important to note that the wage factor must be seen within the context of the technical training deficiencies of the service during the colonial period, and the resulting shortages in crucial technical areas.

The importance of the 'internal brain drain' can be more comprehensively understood as a factor of transnational penetration of the Zimbabwean economy. As a recent critique has noted

> ...foreign capital employs a remarkable share of the locally available but scarce resources of highly skilled manpower. This manpower is not only no longer available to the other socio-economic sectors of the economy, but often drained off by the TNCS from these sectors' especially the public sector.
>
> The movement of skills between sectors within a single country does not involve an aggregate loss of skills from that country. However within the context of given class relations at a given stage of a society's development, the unequal control over utilisation and development of limited skilled and professional labour power by economically dominant foreign capital, can and does affect the scope and successes of transformative policies embarked on by a young progressive government.[68]

The dislocation caused by the large movement of whites from the public service has been to a significant degree offset by the accelerated advancement of Africans into top posts of the civil service. At independence, of the total 10,570 established officers in the public service, 3,368 (31%) were black, with the grade of Senior Administrative Officer being the highest rank held by an African.[69]

Table 23 gives a breakdown of the effects of the Presidential Directive. For example, while in 1981 there were 13 non-white Permanent Secretaries, by 1984 there were 24.

This process of Africanisation has been a major achievement in terms of changing the orientation of the public service and in producing a civil service more amenable to the new policies of the government. This process has not, however, been without its problems and there have been some very serious incidents of corruption, incompetence and inefficiency. Such problems, however, need to be analysed within the context of a vastly expanded public service, dealing with the needs of an expanded population, and in the process attempting to develop the skills, structures and experience necessary to cope with the new demands.

Prior to 1980 the civil service was small and designed to serve settler

TABLE 23
CHANGES AS A RESULT OF THE PRESIDENTIAL DIRECTIVE 1981-84

	1981 TOTAL	%	1984 TOTAL	%
(a) Permanent Secretaries				
White	17	57	4	14
Non-White	13	43	24	86
(b) Senior Management Under-Secretary & above				
White	1143	53	60	22
Non-White	129	47	209	78
(c) Professionals (Established Officers)				
White	669	56	409	28
Non-White	524	44	1,057	72
(d) Technical				
White	419	41	181	13
Non-White	611	59	1,181	87
(e) Established Officers				
White	5,207	37	3,047	12
Non-White	8,711	63	22,814	82

Source: Annual Review of Manpower 1984, p.36

colonial interests. The need to initiate the democratisation of the civil service, consolidate state power 'and ensure that there would be as wide a power base and framework of government as would as far as possible reflect and attend to the aspirations of the mass of the people'[70] necessitated an expansion of the civil service. Thus the public service expanded from 68,495 in 1979 to 92,129 in 1986.[71]

The problems of developing a progressive ideological orientation in the public service have been formidable. Several blacks in top civil service positions have gone into the private sector. Once in the private sector, some have gone into lengthy diatribes about the inefficiencies in government in a manner not very different to the ahistorical criticisms of many voices in the private sector.[72] There have been other cases where public servants have used their positions in the public sector to prepare for greener pastures in the private sector. In this context, it is important to note the allegations that were levelled against certain Industrial Relations Officers in the Ministry of Labour, Manpower Planning and Social Welfare. These included:

— officers deliberately misrepresenting regulations to the workers thereby causing confusion;
— officers investigating grievances through management rather than offering workers an opportunity to air their grievances freely;
— some officers leaking confidential information to

management, thus preparing management to the disadvantage of both the government and the workers.[73]

Because the petit bourgeoisie in the state has, for the most part, no effective control or foothold in material production in the economy, the state has been used as either a means of accumulation, through corruption, or as a stepping stone to the more lucrative private sector. This is a feature to be encountered in developing countries, though not to the total exclusion of the developed countries. In addition, because in the past blacks were denied access to the senior and more lucrative positions in the private sector, many blacks responded eagerly to the opportunity to enter some of the formerly proscribed areas in the private sector. However, it is also interesting to note that, in the important managerial and administrative group in the private sector, there has been little meaningful Africanisation. Thus, in 1984, whites still comprised the majority (53%)[74] of the latter occupational category. Blacks have for the most part been appointed to personnel and industrial relations positions, where they are seen to represent a more presentable front both to workers on the shop floor and to the state.

Finally one last point needs to be made about Africanisation. Where it has taken place in the public sector it has been within the class relations of the post-colonial state. As a recent government report noted:

> It is not, however, sufficient that we should judge the success of manpower development in the public sector, only by changes in the complexion of that sector. This is important in terms of the public service presenting a more national image. However, while the social basis of such changes continues to be generated by capitalist social relations, then even the Africanisation that has hitherto taken place, will have been achieved within the context of salary differentials and an ideological ethos strongly permeated by the imperatives of capital.[75]

Conclusion

The human resource legacy inherited by the Zimbabwean government has, as in other fields, presented formidable problems to the new state. From the expansion of technical training capacity to the process of Africanisation, it has had to grapple with the constraints and contradictions of the class/race dialectic in an economy dominated by international capital.

There have been important successes in the democratisation of vocational/technical training, and the increasingly national and anti-racist thrust of the apprenticeship programme. Moreover, the policy of upgrading 'semi-skilled' workers represented an important challenge to the colonial capitalist categorisation of a certain level of workers in Zimbabwe.

Nevertheless, serious problems remain. The continuing constraints on the availability of technical labour power and the accompanying shortage of technical instructors is likely to result both in the delay of development of local vocational/technical infrastructure, and in the continued reliance on expatriate labour. This, in turn, will impede the conditions necessary for the greater technical education of workers, and in so doing hinder the technical process necessary for workers to increase their self-confidence in their crucial role in the political process. In an economy dominated by foreign capital, the continued reliance on expatriate labour can be, and has been, used to maintain control of certain skill areas, and so perpetuate foreign dependence.

Moreover, in its effort to equip workers with a greater technical base, the state is likely to face opposition from the private sector because a more skilled working class has serious implications in terms of both wages and union organisation. In both areas, there is a potential challenge not only to capital but also to the state if its policies do not seek to break the power of capital.

Finally, the still dominant ideological ethos of capitalism in the country and the lack of a clear conception by many civil servants of the problems of transition to socialism will continue to create obstacles to the progressive development of the state. In such conditions the power of international capital to influence the policies of the state could increase. This could manifest itself both in the influencing of senior officials in the state and through a continued pull on high-level human resources which, in the absence of a more systematic allocation of such resources, could prove disruptive. The utilisation and development of human resources in Zimbabwe is likely to be an important arena of class struggle for the foreseeable future.

REFERENCES

1. Arrighi, Giovanni, The Political Economy of Rhodesia in Arrighi, G., and Saul, J. (eds), *Essay in the Political Economy of Africa*, Monthly Review Press, London, 1973, p. 337.
2. Mandaza, Ibbo, The National Manpower Survey in the Context of the Political Economy of Zimbabwe, *National Manpower Survey*, 1981, Vol. 1, Ministry of Manpower Planning and Development, p. 24.
3. Arrighi, G., *op. cit.*, p. 338.
4. Quoted in Riddell, Roger, *Education for Employment*, Mambo Press, 1980, p. 9.
5. Raftopoulos, Brian, Academic and Vocational/Technical Education Towards a New Strategy in *Report on the Workshop on Educational Reforms, The Zimbabwe Case*, University of Zimbabwe, Harare, 6-12 December 1982 (eds. Chivanda, G.C. and Mudzi, T.C.).
6. Mothobi, B., *Training for Development*, The Association of Round Tables in Central Africa, Salisbury, 1978, p. 60.
7. Challis, P.J., The European Educational System in Southern Rhodesia—1890-1930, supplement to *Zambezia*, 1982, p. 96.
8. Harris, Peter, Industrial Relations in Rhodesia, *The South African Journal of Economics*, 42, 1, 1974, p. 74
9. Chigwendere, I., Trade Unions in Zimbabwe, unpublished mimeo, 1978.
10. Harris, P., *op.cit.*, p. 68.

11. For a fuller discussion on this issue, see Mandaza, Ibbo, *op. cit.*
12. *Government's Policy on Labour,* Ministry of Labour and Social Welfare, 30 April 1971, quoted in P. Harris, *op.cit.*, p. 73.
13. *The Immediate Manpower and Training Needs of an Independent Zimbabwe,* Commonwealth Secretariat, June 1979.
14. See, for example, Murapa, Rukudzo, Race and the Public Service in Zimbabwe 1980-1983, in Schatzberg, Michael G. (ed), *The Political Economy of Zimbabwe,* Praeger, New York, 1984, p. 58.
15. *Ibid.*, p. 60.
16. *Zimbabwe: Notes and Comments on the Rhodesia Question,* Centre of African Studies, Eduardo Mondlane University, Maputo, 1977, p. 34. Cited in NMS, 1981, *op. cit.*, p. 27.
17. See Arrighi G., *op. cit.*, for a more comprehensive analysis of this settler alliance.
18. Mothobi, B., *op. cit.*, p. 27.
19. Ministry of Manpower Planning and Developmen, *Three Year Transitional Plan.*
20. Raftopoulos, B., 1982, *op. cit.*
21. Mandaza, Ibbo, *op. cit.*, p. 26.
22. Shopo, Thomas D., *Rethinking Parliament's Role in Zimbabwean Society,* Zimbabwean Institute of Development Studies Working Paper No. 3, Harare, August 1985, p. 23.
23. *National Manpower Survey 1981,* Vol. II, Ministry of Manpower Planning and Development, p. 111.
24. *Comment, Financial Gazette,* August, 1983.
25. *Ibid.*
26. NMS, 1981, Vol. 1, *op. cit.*, pp. 54-55.
27. See *Annual Review of Manpower 1984,* Department of Research and Planning, Ministry of Labour, Manpower Planning and Social Welfare.
28. Mandaza, I., Comments on (Negative) Criticisms of the NMS Report, *Manpower Information Services (MISS),* Vol. 3, No. 2, 1983, p. 27.
29. *Education and Endogenous Development in Africa: Trend, Problems and Prospects,* UNESCO ED/82/MINEDAF 13, p. 18.
30. *Development of Education in Africa: A Statistical Review,* UNESCO, 1982.
31. *Education and Endogenous Development in Africa, op. cit.*, p. 28.
32. Carnoy Martin, The Political Economy of Africa, *International Social Science Journal,* Vol. XXXVII, No. 2, No. 104, UNESCO, 1985, p. 170.
33. King, Kenneth, Science, Technology and Education in the Development of Indigenous Technological Capability, in Fransman, Martin and King, Kenneth (ed), *Technological Capability in the Third World,* Macmillan, London, 1984, p. 32.
34. *Ibid.* See also Carnoy, Martin, *Education and Employment : A Critical Appraisal,* Paris, 1977.
35. Cooper, C., Introduction, in Cooper, C. (ed), *The Political Economy of Technical Advance in Underdeveloped Countries,* Frank Cass, London, 1973, p. 2.
36. *Ibid.* See also Seers, D. (ed), *Dependency Theory: A Critical Re-*

Assessment, Frances Pinter, London 1981.
37. *Study of the Manufacturing Centre in Zimbabwe*, DP/ZIM/84/018 Zimbabwe, UNIDO. 3 volumes.
38. See the paper presented by Muringi, R., Deputy Secretary, Vocational and Technical Training, Ministry of Labour, Manpower Planning and Social Welfare, at the Vocational and Technical Training Seminar held 26-30 August 1985, at Holiday Inn, Harare.
39. *The Herald*, 28 Febrauary 1984.
40. *Ibid.*
41. Makings, G., *Contributions to the NMS, Evaluation Seminar*—MISS. Vol. 3, No. 2, Nov, 1983. p. 3.
42. For a fuller discussion of the problems of internal manpower drift see, Raftopoulos, B., Wittich, G., Nldela, D., *The Internal Brain Drain, its Effects on Government Development Policy and Possible Alternatives—the Case of Zimbabwe*, forthcoming.
43. Ministry of Manpower Planning and Development, Zimbabwe: Report of the Otto Benecke Stiftung, Seminar, Harare, 24-28 October, 1985. p. 116.
44. *Ibid.*, p. 165.
45. Nldela, D.B., Kaliati, J., Mutungwazi, D. and Zwizwai, B., *A Study of the Transfer of Technology in Zimbabwe's Metals and Metal Goods Sector*, forthcoming.
46. Cooper, C., *op. cit.*, p. 6.
47. For a critique of this method see Psacharopoulos, G., Assessing Training Priorities in Developing Countries: Current Practices and Possible Alternatives, *International Labour Review*, Vol. 123, No. 5, September/October 1984.
48. *Annual Review of Manpower 1984, op. cit.*
49. Harare, 1985. The author and co-ordinator of the Report was Fanuel Nangati.
50. *Ibid.*
51. *Ibid.* See also the discussion (in *The Herald*, 12 December 1985) on 'Study Questions Lack of Job Creation Policy'.
52. *The Sunday Mail*, 15 September 1985.
53. *Ibid.*
54. Thomas, Clive, *Dependence and Transformation*, Monthly Review Press, New York, 1974, p. 173.
55. See the criticism of the problems relating to the new B. Tech. course established at the Harare Polytechnic in *The Financial Gazette*, 11 October 1985.
56. The comments by a Public Service Commissioner, Dr. Ibbo Mandaza, at the graduating ceremony at Belvedere Teachers College in December 1985, against the functional arguments being used against the expansion of education, should be viewed as an intervention in this debate. *The Herald*, 9 December 1985.
57. NMS, 1981, Vol. I, *op.cit.*, p. 60.
58. *Ibid.*
59. White Apprentices Disrupt Meeting to Explain New Bonding Regula-

tions, *Financial Gazette,* 18 June 1982.
60. Exodus of Apprentices Expected, *Financial Gazette,* 18 June 1982.
61. Only 13% of Apprentices Have Quit, *The Herald,* 15 July 1982.
62. See *Annual Review of Manpower 1983* for a more detailed analysis of this internal drift.
63. How Smith Took The Bishop For A Ride, by 'The Scrutator', *The Herald,* 26 January 1985.
64. *Annual Review of Manpower* 1983, p. 37.
65. How Smith Took The Bishop For A Ride', *op. cit.*
66. Shava Threat on Retired Civil Servants, *The Herald,* 5 November 1984.
67. Exodus of Officials to Private Firms Riles Shava, *The Herald,* 5 November 1984.
68. Raftopoulos, B., Wittich G. and Ndlela D.B., *op.cit.*
69. Mandaza, I., 'The Zimbabwe Public Service', paper presented at the United Nations Inter-Regional Seminar on Reforming Civil Service Systems for Development, Beijing, China, 12 August 1985.
70. *Ibid.*
71. *Ibid.*
72. See the critique of T. Mswaka, former Permanent Secretary in the Ministry of Finance, Economic Planning and Development, by 'The Scrutator', *The Herald,* 14 September 1985.
73. Exodus of Officials to Private Firms Riles Shava, *op. cit.*
74. *Annual Review of Manpower 1984*, Appendix III, p. 78.
75. *Ibid.*, p. 1.

11. EDUCATION AND THE CHALLENGE OF INDEPENDENCE
Rungano J. Zvobgo

The Colonial Education System

Education has always been in the forefront of politics in Zimbabwe both before and after independence. During the years of colonial rule, it was used as an instrument for sustaining white power and consolidating white control of the key positions in the socio-economic and political spheres.

The educational policies of successive colonial governments from the BSA Company to the Rhodesia Front era, and the pattern of educational development, conformed to the racist nature of colonial administrative policies and systems. The evolution of a dual system of education, one for Africans and the other for whites, was intended, first and foremost, to support the policy of separate racial development and to ensure that there was no competition between blacks and whites. Thus racism was the cornerstone of colonial policy in education as it provided the ideological framework for economic and social policies. As has been outlined in chapter one, colonialism played a crucial role in the 'rooting' of capitalism; and education was in itself a major agency in this process.

Racism, as a concept, was used by the white ruling class in an attempt to internalise in Africans the real or imaginary differences between the racist coloniser and the colonised. Through this process, whites hoped to assign certain values to these differences to their advantage and to the detriment of blacks. Also, they tried to make these valued differences absolute in space and in time by generalising from them and claiming that they were final determinants of socio-economic and political status. Thus, racism was used to guarantee the enclave character of colonial capitalism and its attendant privileges while ethnicity was used to rationalise the wholesale confinement of blacks to reserves (Tribal Trust Lands) as a strategy to maintain an impoverished mass as cheap labour. This aspect was more evident in the sphere of education, where racism became the cornerstone of not just uneven educational provision, but uneven development between blacks and whites. Within the framework of the colonial racist ideology, colonial education assumed definite characteristics. First, educational policy conformed to the general racist policy of separate development to the extent that a dual system of education was established, one for blacks and the other for whites. Second, the structure and organisation of curricula also sought to conforme to that pattern. Consequently, institutions and systems of education tended to resemble either overtly or explicitly the racist nature of colonial society. Third, colonial educational policy and ideology emphasised the training of colonial subjects for roles in the colonial capitalist division of labour.

Thus, one of the main aims of colonial educational policy was to perpetuate the existence of a divided colonial society. Poor and limited educational opportunities for blacks were intended specifically to consolidate the pre-capitalist base of African society as a guarantee for the continuation of a reservoir of cheap labour. Moreover, poor education sought to ensure a blockage of mobility (i.e. socio-economic and political) and thereby ensure the dominance of the settler regime in colonial Zimbabwean society. Inferior educational facilities were provided for blacks in keeping with the colonial concept of black inferiority. This racist notion served to consolidate white security and hoped Africans to internalise in the idea that they were indeed inferior. Whites would therefore be guaranteed a secure political future and dominance in the socio-economic shperes. It was within the context of white racist idology that colonial education developed in colonial Zimbabwe, and all aspects of education during the ninety years of white rule were intended to conform to that ideology. But, as other writers have illustrated, there developed in time a disparity between this colonial conception of society and the unfolding reality of the colonial situation.[1]

In April 1899, Cecil John Rhodes, the founder of the colony, advised a committee which was deliberating on the first education ordinance on the structure of the country's education system. A racially segregated system was evolved and a disproportionate emphasis was laid by the colonial government on the development of European education, while African education was left exclusively in the hands of white Christian missionaries. For decades to come, white administrators focused their efforts and resources on promoting European education to the complete neglect of African education. No government participation was forthcoming until the late 1940s. Missionaries bore the greater responsibility for African education throughout the colonial era. The only assistance from government was in the form of grants-in-aid instituted in 1899 to help missionaries expand their Christian work.

This facility was extended only to those mission schools which agreed to operate on policy lines laid down by the BSA Company. The policy requirement was that a school devote half its daily working hours to non-academic (manual) work. From the very beginnings of mission education, the BSA Company wanted to ensure that African education developed along lines different from those of European education, hence the policy of emphasising industrial rather than academic education. This was part of the overall white policy to ensure that Africans were not given an education which would bring them into competition with whites.

Several constraints were placed on those mission churches which failed to operate within the framework of government policy. Power was given to the Chief Native Commissioner (CNC) to keep mission school activities within acceptable limits and stern measures were taken where it was felt that such activities undermined white rule and interests. For example, the CNC and NCs were empowered to withdraw the leases of those schools which were suspected of promoting 'feelings of ill will or hostility against the State'.[2] In a number of ways, mission educational activities tended to conflict with government interests, particularly as they attracted a great deal of the potential labour force required to work for the white economic system. Moreover, graduates of the mission schools were generally regarded as an expensive labour force and a source of trouble and labour unrest at work places. It was also the opinion of most white settlers that mission education made:

> the native unfit for the work they were required to perform. They [would] refuse to work preferring to loaf about as learned vagabonds rather then stoop down to what they regarded as below their literary knowledge.[3]

Thus, the segregated system of education in colonial Zimbabwe was designed to keep Africans under subjugation. It was intended to provide for non-whites limited means of social mobility while affording whites the best possible opportunity for rapid advancement. One minister in the former Rhodesia Front government categorically stated that the priority of all previous governments in education had always been to provide a system of education for Europeans, Asian and Coloureds which was as good or better than could be obtained anywhere.[4]

African education was bedevilled by several problems—financial, material and administrative. Of these, the most serious was the government's negative policy which placed many constraints in the way of its development. From the time of the enactment of the First Education Ordinance, it was clear that the BSA Company envisaged the creation of a system of education structured along racial lines and conforming to the superstructure. But this was not all. Matters of policy and administration of African education were at the forefront of government considerations. What were to be the curricula in African education? What would be its purpose? How was the African system to be financed and organised? All these were questions of great importance to the administration, as indeed they were to the various missionary organisations involved in African education. What emerged clearly from the company administration's thinking was that definite differentials had to be maintained between European and African education, in terms of both curricula and content. The administration's thinking was that African education should not be purely academic but should contain a fair degree of elements of vocational education. It was to be the kind of education which would guarantee the existence of a large pool of cheap, unskilled, uneducated black labour. Education was not to be allowed to arm Africans with the kind of knowledge or skills which would make them despise manual work or bring them into competition with whites in all spheres of life. There was, therefore, a deliberate attempt by the company administration, from the very early stages of African education, to control missionary educational work and influence policy away from academic work.

The administration justified its decision on the grounds that formal academic education was least relevant to the needs of African development in the rural areas and that financial constraints simply did not make it possible for the company administration to provide adequate facilities for a large African population. This of course was not true, given the fact that the Africans contributed significantly towards national coffers through the various taxes paid. For example, in 1904/5, African contribution to public revenue amounted to 41.4% of all government revenue. By 1918, Africans were still contributing over one-third of the total revenue of the country[5] from funds earned through forced labour and also due to the increasing articulation and systematic destruction of the pre-colonial mode of production by colonial capitalism which had the effect of forcing Africans into the European system.

The government did, however, make financial contribution to African education although this fell far short of its requirements. The reasons for the lack of adequate aid to African education were political and economic rather then financial. Pressure on the administration, from the white population, for protection against African competition was an important reason. Many of the white settlers were hardly educated and feared that rapid expansion of African education would obliterate them. A rapid rise in the social mobility of Africans, it was feared, would also threaten white superiority.

State grants to African schools were made under regulations contained in a very important and long-standing government Statute Order 'D'. This statute prescribed, from time to time, conditions under which schools qualified for state aid. The conditions included minimum school enrolment and attendance per year as well as curricula. For example, at least 40 pupils were required to attend school on 150 days of four hours during each year. In addition, the school had to offer a systematic programme of industrial education and teach pupils to speak and understand the English language.[6] The Order was therefore a prescriptive document requiring mission African schools to adhere to specific government regulations. Thus the government had devised a mechanism for exercising some degree of administrative control over missionary activities and in particular curricula.

Under the 1912 Ordinance, powers were given to the administration to ensure that missionary tendencies to push African education in the direction of scholastic achievement rather than educative agencies of an industrial nature were controlled.[7] Most colonial administrators, particularly Chief Native Commissioners, while approving of the endeavours by missionaries to educate Africans, held the view that Africans stood to benefit more from industrial than academic learning.[8] The objective was to create functionaries rather than competitors within the colonial system. As one CNC advised in 1918:

> The native should be trained not so much as a competitor with the white man in the business of life but as a useful auxiliary to help in the progress of the country.[9]

The impression amongst most colonial officials about Africans was quite clear. As far as they were concerned, there was ample proof to show that:

> it is not the nature of the native to spontaneously improve himself on legitimate lines.[10]

As such, he had to be carefully guided to acquire habits of industry, not through academic learning but through a programme of industrial education. He had to be taught to become useful to himself and his employer and to work with contentment.[11]

The industrial education idea was taken up enthusiastically by H. S. Keigwin, one of the Native Commissioners in the Department of Native Affairs, and led to the introduction of an industrial education experiment at two notable institutions of Domboshawa and Tjolotjo in 1921 and 1922 respectively.

The government's intention was to provide an education which would enable Africans to operate and survive within the confines of their TTLs. Keigwin had no intention of offering such training as would bring Africans into competition with whites. The plan was designed to

> stimulate effort amongst the people, to put purpose into their lives and to develop such skills in industries that [did] not offer direct competition to Europeans.[12]

For that reason he emphasised that he had

> deliberately sought out those industries that lend themselves to primitive hand methods rather than to progressive and highly productive machinery. One [had] to remember that what [was] wanted amongst backward natives [was] something of this old-fashioned craftsmanship of 50 or 100 years ago.[13]

So, from the very beginning, Keigwin's programme had a heavy racial bias characteristic of colonial systems and the attitudes of colonialists towards the development of the colonised. The courses he envisaged at the two schools were those outside the European occupational structure. These were Hides and Skins, Food Production, Rope and Mat Making, Basket and Chair Making, Pottery and Tibs, Carpentry and Building. By their very nature, the courses were intended to produce an African artisan living in the TTLs and one who would develop without offering competition to Europeans.

In the sphere of African academic education financial contraints also created problems which hindered rapid expansion, In 1901 only three out of the numerous mission village schools in operation qualified for government aid. The amount was only £133 for 265 pupils. This amounted to only £0.50 per pupil. By 1910 only 115 schools were registered and shared £2,780 made available by the government. Enrolment had risen to 9,873, which meant that each child got a grant of £0.25 per year. A sharp rise in the number of registered schools was noted in 1920. Some

750 mission schools were recognised by the government. Enrolment had reached a 43,094 mark and government grants totalled £3,467, which meant that each child got £0.22 per year.[14] So, while enrolment and the number of schools increased, government aid decreased, thus undermining the development of education.

As if oblivious of the problems in African education, further cuts in government aid to mission schools were made between 1929 and 1932. The reclassification of schools in 1929 rendered many village schools ineligible for government grants. At least 9,000 pupils were affected by this action.[15] After the cuts in government aid in the 1932-33 financial year, government aid to African education fell by 25% from what it was in 1926, leaving a sum which accounted for only 10% of the full cost of running African schools.[16] Missionaries had to supplement costs with funds from overseas to sustain education. By 1923, when responsible government was attained, African education was not compulsory and the Director of the Department of Native Development thought that the idea was inconceivable. The majority of African children had to walk long distances to school; educational facilities were, in many parts of the country, inadequate. Under the circumstances, it was thought impossible to ensure that all African children received education. However, the government took no steps to ensure that adequate facilities were made available for African children. It was that attitude which accounted for lack of provision and the slow development of African education.

Meanwhile in 1930, under the Compulsory Act, education for Europeans became compulsory for all children between the ages of seven and fifteeen. Government also provided scholarships at both the primary and secondary level while all African children were required to pay for their education.[17] Disparities like these were part of the cause of racial conflict because they reflected the racialism inherent in colonial educational policy. The government's concern was primarily with European education. African education was left to missionaries.

However, the enlistment of as many as 8,448 whites in the Second World War, out of a total white population of 176,300, created shortages of skilled personnel and led to improvements being made to boost African education.[18] Government grants were raised in 1944 and the state undertook to participate in the provision of secondary education for Africans. But the government was missing the fundamental point, which was the African desire to see disparities between educational provisions for whites and blacks removed. Provisions made by the government during the war period were seen largely as an attempt to lure African support for the war, given the widespread pro-Hitler spirit in South Africa. Indeed, after the war ended, radical changes in government policies were observable. The 1945-48 railway strikes which nearly paralysed the nation were an expression of African opposition to the repressive policies of Huggins' government. The policy of reserving most professional jobs for Europeans and wage differentials for blacks and whites angered educated Africans and trade unionists.

Education began to assume an even much more important position in the policies of colonial Zimbabwe with the institution of the Federation of Southern Rhodesia, Northern Rhodesia and Nyasaland in 1953. Although state policy since 1890 had been designed to protect white interests, development in education after federation came into effect indicated a deliberate attempt by the colonial regime firmly to entrench white political power.

Proponents of federation, in particular white politicians in the three territories and the British government, campaigned for federation on the grounds that it would bring about multiracial partnership and a nation unconscious of the colour or race of its people. However, Africans saw this as an attempt by whites to consolidate white control of the economy and political state apparatus in the whole region. They could not trust whites to agree to share political, economic and social equality with them.

Their fears and concerns were vindicated by clear-cut statements by the first federal premier, Godfrey Huggins, who said that the only partnership he could perceive between blacks and whites was that of a horse and the rider.[19] None of the multiracialism which had characterised the debate for federation was evident. On the contrary, the sharing of responsibilities between federal and territorial governments brought out clearly the racialism of the federal government. All affairs relating to European development and administration were taken over by the federal government while matters concerning African affairs were made the responsibility of each territorial government. This arrangement confirmed the continuation of a racist policy on development and education. The consequences of this were inequalities in educational provisions for whites and blacks and wide disparities in the allocation of funds for the education of these two main races. For example, between 1951 and 1955, federal government expenditure on European education rose by £3,096,175[20] compared with a rise of only £2,209,389 for African education in the three territories. To cite another example, between 1955 and 1956, the difference in expenditure on African and non-African education was as in Table 1:

TABLE 1

	African	Non African
Southern Rhodesia	£1,544,211	Federalised
Northern Rhodesia	£1,711,741	Federalised
Nyasaland	£329,965	Federalised
Total	£3,585,917	£ 5,252,802

These inequalities are more powerfully brought out when one realises that in 1955-56 there were only 50,000 Europeans and 6,000 Asian and Coloured children in federal schools being educated at a cost of £126 per pupil, while 800,000 African children in aided schools in all the three territories were being educated at £6 per head.[21] Thus European education benefited considerably.

The struggle for the control of education by whites also arose from the central role it occupied in the federal franchise system, which was based on education, property and income. An applicant to the electoral register had to satisfy these qualifications in order to qualify for a vote.

There were two rolls on which federal citizens could register for a vote and therefore for participation in the politics of the state. The general roll under which Africans were expected to qualify presented requirements well beyond the reach of the majority of blacks. These were:-

General Roll
(a) income of £720 p.a. or ownership of immovable property valued at £1,500 or
(b) income of £400 p.a. or ownership of immovable property valued at £500 plus completion of primary education (for Africans standard six) or
(c) income of £300 p.a. or ownership of property valued at £500 plus completion of four years of secondary education or
(d) being a minister of religion who has undergone a certain stipulated course of training and period of service in the ministry and who follows no other profession, trade or gainful occupation or
(e) being a Chief recognised as such by the respective governments and capable of satisfying the literacy qualifications.

Virtually no African had an income or property of the value stipulated in either (a), (b) or (c). Only a few black ministers of religion and chiefs qualified under (d) and (e) but their numbers were insignificant. A most interesting aspect of the requirements was that relating to education. The combination of income, property and educational attainment disqualified a large number of potential African voters who had a standard six or four years of secondary education but who lacked the other qualifications.[22]

Most important, however, was the central role which education assumed in federal politics. This requirement was evidently intended to exclude the majority of blacks from exercising political influence and thus protect white colonialism and power. Because of its role in politics, the struggle for the control of educational policy and the acquisition of education was brought to the forefront. This explains, in part, the reasons for the federal government's decision to take direct control of European education. The second special roll had no particular educational requirements and was intended to give an opportunity to those who failed to qualify for the general roll. But even though the requirements were said to be less stringent than those in the general roll, the property, income and implied literacy still rendered many blacks ineligible to vote. These were as follows.

Special Roll
  (a) income of £150 p.a. or ownership of immovable property valued at £500 or
  (b) citizenship of Rhodesia and Nyasaland or status of British protected person by virtue of connection with Northern Rhodesia or Nyasaland or
  (c) willingness to make a solemn declaration of allegiance to the crown or
  (d) two years residence in the Federation and three months in the Constituency or
  (e) ability to speak, read and write in and understand English and complete the prescribed voting form unassisted.

A wife shall be deemed to have the 'means' qualifications of her husband but in the case of a polygamous marriage, this privilege will apply to the first wife only. Wives must have educational qualifications in their own right.[23] Conditions laid down in (a) and (b) virtually excluded all Africans and although conditions (c) and (d) were fairly permissive, item (d) disqualified the majority of the black masses.

The 1953 territorial elections conducted on the basis of this franchise revealed that the electorate in all the three territories was predominantly European and, as a result, the Federal Assembly was dominated by Europeans as shown in Table 2.

TABLE 2
MEMBERS ELECTED BY TERRITORIAL ELECTORATE ROLLS (Race Not Specified)

S. Rhodesia	N. Rhodesia	Nyasaland	Total
14	8	4	26
Electorate	Electorate	No African	
99% European	99% European	on rolls	
African Members			
2	2	2	6
Electorate	Elected by an	Elected by African	
as above	African	Protectorate	
	Representative	Council	
	Council		
European Members Representing African Interests			
1	1	1	3
As Above			
Appointed by Governors			
17	11	7	35

The table clearly shows the extent to which the federal constitution strengthened white political power and seriously weakened African political influence. The whole mechanics of government administration was designed to achieve exactly this objective, hence the assertion that federation was a grand design to strengthen white hegemony in Central Africa. None of its instruments of governance and systems reflected in spirit or form the multiracialism which proponents of federation had used to advocate it.

Although great strides were made in Southern Rhodesia to improve African education during Garfield Todd's years as Premier (1954-58), the racial structure of education remained intact, Also, not many Africans were educated because of limited opportunities. For example, in 1956, of all the African schools in the country, only 597 offered an education up to standard 3, while only 22 offered up to standard 4. Because of shortage of provisions at upper primary level, enrolment fell from 14,194 in standard 3 to 3,544 in the next grade. In the same year almost half of the African children were enrolled in schools which terminated with only standard 1. Also, with the exception of 4% pupils attending government schools had access to free education.[25] Table 3 shows the plight of African children in school.

WASTAGE IN AFRICAN EDUCATION
Southern Rhodesia

Intake Year	Sub A	1947	81,821
Standard	II	1950	23,366
Standard	VI	1954	4,429
Form	II	1956	1,888
Form	IV	1958	379
Form	VI	1960	15

This 'low triangle' policy, broad-based but coming to a point almost at once, meant that 85% intake of African children swiftly fell to 1% in the 10th year of schooling. On the whole, 80% of African children in Southern Rhodesia, got schooling up to Standard 2, 36% of 80% went up to Standard 4 and 18% of 36% were able to get full primary education. Of these, only 4% got to Form 4 while only 1% of 2% got to Form 6 (full six years of secondary education). This means that the number of African pupils was drastically reduced at every stage of the school system. This situation prevailed throughout the period of colonial rule under what came to be referred to as the bottleneck system.

Educational Policy and Practice under the Rhodesia Front Party Rule: 1965-79
The most serious conditions were created during the years when Ian Smith's Rhodesia Front Party was in power. The party was formed in 1960 by right-wing whites as a front against African nationalism and the reformist tendencies of Todd and Whitehead. It was an organisation fully committed to the consolidation of white hegemony and was determined

to intensify the system of separate racial development. In accordance with that philosophy, it spelt out clearly in its constitution the commitment of the government to provide separate facilities for development for blacks and whites in every sphere of life.[28]

In pursuit of this policy, central government took over all responsibility for all aspects of European administration and development while African district councils became responsible for all African affairs. The objective of this arrangement was to ensure that Europeans were afforded the best facilities for development from the richer central government budget.

The same principle applied in the sphere of education. Education for Europeans was taken care of by the central government while African education became the responsibility of district councils and private bodies.

Soon after coming to power, the Rhodesia Front (RF) government introduced a system of Community Development (CD) under which the government proposed the complete transference of the development and administration of primary education from missionary churches to African local councils. The objective was to make Africans responsible for their own education and development in line with the RF government's policy of separate racial development.

To a party committed to racialism, the Community Development idea was only a means of achieving that objective. Local Councils, though in existence since the 1940s, had never borne such responsibilities and had neither the experience nor the resources with which to administer and develop so complex and expensive a system as education. Councils were required to raise most of the funds needed to run primary education from their own sources, supplemented by grants from the central government.

The first step towards implementing the policy of separate racial development under the community development programme was to order churches to hand over their schools to the local district councils. Under the role changes, after 1967 no mission church could establish new primary schools in rural areas. Only local councils could do so. However, the autonomy of local councils was severely limited in the sense that they could not determine educational policy and programmes, neither could they implement new plans without the written permission of the Provincial Officer. The Provincial Education Officer was the symbol of the strength of central government control over the way local councils conducted their affairs, and his overriding authority revealed the constraint on local councils in the overall administration and organisation of education. This negated the very concept of the decentralisation policy, as Africans were overtly given responsibility to determine their own educational affairs as they saw fit, but were in fact without power and the necessary resources to enable them actually to determine policy and implement it.

Another aspect of the RF's educational policy became evident in 1966 when the so-called New Education Plan was announced. The plan introduced radical policy changes with regard to the selection process for pupil entry into secondary education. Under the new policy, in future, only 12½% of all African children completing their primary education each year would be allowed to proceed to academic secondary education (F1).[29] Thirty seven and a half percent were to be admitted to the F2 vocational secondary education.[30] The remaining 50% were left with no provision whatsoever for any form of secondary education within the formal school system,[31] contrary to previous practice, when it was possible for those who failed to gain entry into secondary school in one year to reapply the following year. The only alternative left for this majority was to undertake studies.[32]

Equally drastic was the change in the government's financial policy towards overall African education, which reduced government expenditure on African education from 8.6% of the Gross National Product (GNP) in 1965 to 2% in 1967.[33] The cuts were severely felt in primary education, which had previously enjoyed 70% of the total education sum but lost much of this on transfer to African local councils. While African education was being subjected to all these policy changes, European education remained unaffected.

F2 secondary education has a stigma placed on it right from the time of its introduction. The implicit suggestion was made by the 1962 Judges Commission that the scheme would be for the less able, that is, those children who were considered by the selection process to be unfit or unable to cope with the rigours of academic work.[34] As a result, teachers, parents, pupils resented it, particularly as they knew that a certificate in non-academic courses such as agriculture, carpentry or building offered less employment prospects than one in academic subjects.

Despite all attempts by the government to promote the Keigwin approach to African education through the provision of large loans to responsible authorities interested in this experiment,[35] little progress was made because of public resentment. Between 1966 and 1971, out of the projected 300 F2 schools 21 were operative[36] and only 3,807 students had enrolled.[37]

Vocational secondary education really failed to capture public favour because of the racist philosophy behind its introduction. It was seen as part of the RF's policy of separate racial development and an attempt by the government to provide Africans with inferior education.

The 1966 plan was severely criticised by black nationalists and most churches. The thrust of the opposition was towards government attempts to clamp down on any further expansion of the (F1) academic secondary school system. Indeed between 1966 and 1971 the effects of that clampdown became evident.

Whereas between 1962 and 1966 the number of government schools doubled from 8 to 16, only 1 government school was established between 1966 and 1971. Similarly on the missionary side, between 1962 and 1966 the number of secondary schools rose from 33 to 71. But between 1966 and 1971 the overall increase was only 14.[38] In fact, after 1970, no mission secondary school was established. The effects of limited opportunities for secondary education became apparent in the small number of students who succeeded in obtaining either Form 4 or Form 6 education. For example, the 1966 Form 1 enrolment of 6,137 fell to 6,021 at Form 2 level but at Form 3 it fell drastically to 2,062 in 1968; 1,967 of that figure proceeded to Form 4 in 1969 but only 187 of these proceeded to Lower 6 (Form 6). 183 reached Upper 6 in 1971.[39]

As Murphree also showed in his study, of the 127,790 pupils who enrolled in Grade 1 in 1971, only 10,360 of them got to Form 1. Of the 10,360 a mere 1,525 got to Form 4 and 183 succeeded in reaching Form 6.[40] Such was the extent of RF policy on African education. Advancing the educational ladder became a privilege for only a small proportion of the African children. The situation was different in European education, where provisions were more than adequate. Between 1961 and 1969, for example, some 39,224 white children obtained four years of secondary education compared to only 7,676 blacks. Similarly, between 1970 and 1977, 43,059 white children obtained three to four years of secondary education compared to 32,298 black children.[41] Clearly the situation in African education during RF rule was depressing. One missionary summed up the feelings of many churches.

> The education system for Africans in Southern Rhodesia under the new policy had become such a depressing example of separate and unequal facilities between the races that it is no longer possible for missionaries to remain silent.[42]

The extent of racialism was evident in the role of the government in European and African education. In 1976, there were 168 European, Asian and Coloured primary schools. Of these, the government administered 150 (89%) with an average of 226 pupils per school. In contrast, of the 3,498 African schools the government ran only 95 (3%) with an average of 932 pupils per school.[43] In the same year, the government was directly responsible for 37 out of the 43 European, Asian and Coloured secondary schools (86%). In contrast, the government administered only 27 out of 152 African secondary schools (18%), 17% of the F1 schools and 19% of the F2 schools.[44]

The overall effects of the RF's politics of racialism and discrimination in every socio-economic and political sphere, and at every level of education, produced racial conflict of an unforeseen magnitude which engulfed this country in the form of a protracted war of independence by Africans from the late 1960s until the achievement of black majority rule in April of 1980.

Attempts by whites to maintain racial privilege were evident in the passing of the 1979 Education Act. After the signing of the internal settlement in 1978, and the introduction of cosmetic political and social reforms, the white-controlled black government passed an Act designed to exclude the majority of African children from entering Group A schools (formerly all-white schools).[45] The zoning system legally barred children whose parents did not reside in the former European surburbs from enrolling in white schools. The Secretary for Education was given wide-ranging powers to restrict the majority of African children to schools within the

African townships.[46] Thus, the Act was designed to protect white control of the privileged schools by limiting African enrolment to the minimum. Only children from African families which had acquired property and resided in the European suburbs were allowed into the schools. Thus, the plentiful facilities in these schools continued to be made use of largely by Europeans. This just proved that Europeans were not, in any way, prepared to abandon racism because it was the basis of their privileged higher status in Rhodesia colonial society.

Developments which are taking place in education since independence are an attempt to transform the system in order to make it service the new political order and the majority of the people. Educational reform since 1980 is a response to the challenge of independence.

The Transformation of Education since Independence: The Rationale of Educational Reform

The transformation of colonial education began with independence in 1980. The first black majority government declared its total abhorrence of the education system Zimbabwe inherited from colonial Rhodesia and committed itself to implement sweeping reforms in state policy and the organisation and administration of education.

The direction of educational reform and the government's commitment to decolonise education were reflected in the 1980 election manifesto of the ruling party, ZANU (PF). Item L of the Manifesto declared the Party's intention, once in government, to:

> (a) abolish racial education and utilise the education system to develop in the younger generation a non-racial attitude and a common loyalty to the state;
> (b) establish a system of free and compulsory primary and secondary education;
> (c) abolish sex discrimination in the education system;
> (d) orient the education system to national goals;
> (e) give every adult who had no or little educational opportunity the right to literacy and adult education;
> (f) make education play an important role in transforming society;
> (g) place education in the category of basic human rights and strive to ensure that every child had an educational opportunity to develop his mental, physical and emotional faculties.[47]

The objectives enunciated in this manifesto, particularly the democratisation of education, reflected the party's democratic principles and desire to end the iniquitous system of colonial education. The intention was to bring education to the doorstep of every home so that every citizen would be able to develop himself to the full. Millions of blacks who, for nearly nine decades, had suffered at the hands of various colonial governments aspired to acquire education. Moreover, the end of the war and the return of thousands of refugees from neighbouring states created new demands for education to which the new government had to respond urgently.

The declarations of the 1980 election manifesto constituted the basis for government policy. These declarations were consistent with the government's declared philosophy of scientific socialism based on Marxist-Leninist principles which the Prime Minister Robert Mugabe described as the basis of socialist revolution and the advancement of social equality.[48]

In education, the primary objective of the government was to provide equality of educational opportunity in order to facilitate rapid transformation of society and the economy. However, the ambition to provide free and compulsory primary and secondary education implied a heavy financial, material and human resource burden on the state. While the democratisation of education at primary level is a sound democratic ideal, a commitment to do the same at the secondary level, at the very early stages of independence, was both impractical and unrealistic. The resources needed to implement that declaration were beyond the reach of the government. At independence, the government was not looking at the transformation of education only; it was involved in a massive network of other development programmes such as the resettlement of persons displaced by the war, Agriculture, Health, Defence, Telecommunications etc. It was a campaign to achieve broad-based development. The government emphasised, in 1981, its commitment to achieve this objective.

> The Government of the Republic of Zimbabwe, conscious of the basic characteristics of the past and indeed still prevailing socio-economic order of this country, is determined to undertake a vigorous programme for the development of the country, within it, to pursue and implement policies based on socialist, egalitarian and democratic principles in conditions of rapid economic growth, full employment, price stability, dynamic efficiency in resource allocation...[49]

It appeared, therefore, from the government's declarations on education that the massive resources needed to achieve the anticipated degree of expansion would produce lopsided development by denying other national programmes adequate financial support. For the government to consider making both primary and secondary education free was inconceivably ambitious and an over-commitment.

What was important, however, was the awareness, on the part of government, that education was at the centre of national development and, therefore, had to be extended to every citizen. It was this awareness which led to the implementation of an educational system which was both revolutionary and ambitious. The government was convinced that nothing short of an educational revolution would produce the kind of changes necessary for effecting a social and economic revolution. The task of transforming an essentially capitalist economic system would not be achieved except through a socialist education and through socialism itself. Educational reform was seen as part of the struggle against capitalism, and socialism as the effective weapon for a dismantling it, as the Prime

Minister explained in 1982.

> Capitalism cannot annihilate capitalism... It is the antithesis to capitalism that can effectively overhand capitalism and institute people-oriented reforms. That antithesis is socialism...[50]

The educational revolution which the government undertook was intended to enhance the socialist struggle to dismantle colonial capitalism.

From another dimension, the wide-ranging reforms in education which the government set out to implement were a political imperative. The masses, having overthrown colonialism through armed struggle, wanted to see a definite improvement in the quality of their lives. They wanted to see definite programmes of development and a rapid expansion of educational opportunities. The government's decision to democratise education was intended to satisfy people's aspirations for development.

The government had specific objectives to achieve by democratising education. These included:—

a) the development, in the citizen, of positive attitudes towards:
   (i) the immediate community,
   (ii) the nation/state,
   (iii) all forms of work which contribute towards the development of the nation.
(b) the achievement of personal development in the service of the community/nation;
(c) having, at least, some fundamental ideas about the citizen's rights and duties and the various arms of goverment;
(d) an awareness of the key role of education in development;
(e) the promotion of traditional culture and a sense of nationhood;
(f) the achievement of basic literacy and numeracy by the majority of the people;
(g) the production of skilled manpower needed to transform the economy and achieve self-reliance;
(h) the training of political cadres with a commitment to the development of the nation, a sense of responsibility towards the people, cadres who would champion the struggle for socio-economic transformation and interpret correctly, as well as implement, government policies and programmes.[51]

Thus education was seen as a major weapon for producing a politically conscious nation; aware of and devoted to the promotion of the welfare of the state.

The general emphasis given in the foregoing aims of education to the development of the individual, the community and the state was not incidental but reflected the government's belief that the fundamental role of education in Zimbabwe's struggle to consolidate its independence was to initiate and support national development. A revolution in the attitudes of society towards the welfare of the nation and the citizen's commitment to it was considered a primary factor in the process of transforming education in order to achieve development. So, the revolution in Zimbabwe's post-colonial education is an attempt to provide the country with a socialist education; an education which, in essence, is an undertaking to transform the human into a powerful being.

One of the important innovations in educational reforms since independence has been the policy of involving the masses of the people at grassroots level in educational administration and development. Under the government's decentralisation policy, educational administration still falls under various authorities such as the state, local government operating through district councils, mission organisations and private committees. But, the main point of departure from previous colonial practice is the increased role of the community in education, particularly in areas of administration and educational development.

The purpose of decentralisation policy is to confer on the people the right and power to determine their own affairs as part of the democratic processes of self-rule. This democratic practice is effected through an important arm of central government, namely the district council.

District councils fall under the Ministry of Local Government, Urban and Rural Development. Members of the councils are democratically elected by the people and are therefore instruments of implementing the programmes and plans of the people. Councils have been granted the political power to make policies and decisions and implement educational programmes consistent with their people's priorities for development. Unlike in the past, when district councils had no real power to effect changes within their districts without central government approval, they are now in a position to plan and implement development programmes within the framework of central government's socialist policies.

It was decided to make district councils responsible for the development of the districts they administer and represent because they are better placed to identify priority areas for development and evolve effective strategies for linking their educational plans to economic development in order to produce a dynamic economy. The advantage of this is that district councils, working together with the people, are able to deal with their own problems and find solutions for them.

The education department of the district council is the policy-making body which determines the pattern of educational development, organisation and administration. This takes place under the supervision of the District Administrator appointed by the central government to monitor council affairs. He is the link between local and central government. The District Administrator, who is the district council's Chief Executive Officer, is assisted by the Council's Education Executive Officer in co-ordinating and implementing all development programmes including education.

Council operations are funded by resources from central government and those generated locally. The policy of self-reliance, in which people within each district provide labour and some financial resources in all development programmes, has helped to expand the education system rapidly. This has also enabled central government to reduce educational costs.[52]

Community participation in educational administration and development is effected through school committees. These consist of elected representatives of parents within a given community, teachers and headteachers. The functions of a school committee are to plan for the physical development of its school. Thus the committee organises parents to mould bricks and construct classrooms and teachers' houses. The central government provides roofing material only. In this way, several schools have grown rapidly to accommodate ever-increasing enrolments. The committee also proposes to the council the best ways of making education effective, for example, through efficient school administration and discipline amongst teachers and pupils.[53] School committees are so powerful in school administration that they have been known to dismiss undisciplined teachers and headmasters from their schools. Parents are now aware of their strength and the role they can play in making education an effective instrument of national development.

Other responsible authorities such as mission organisations and private committees have their own administration infrastructures and procedures. They also have their own sources of finance but, like district councils, receive aid from central government through the grants-in-aid system. Their contribution to the development of education, though no longer as dominant as during the colonial days, remains significant.[54] But even the private organisations have come to recognise the advantages of the policy of self-reliance and utilise the support of the community in advancing their educational programmes. They rely considerably on the labour input from parents in the construction of schools and expansion of facilities.

Although the most obvious feature of colonial education— namely racism, which accounted for the dual system of education—was removed at independence, the education system still remains organised and structured along colonial lines. The task of implementing radical reforms to transform colonial education has been a difficult one, with some aspects of change requiring tough and effective legislation to dismantle the various structures within the system. The Deputy Minister for Education has expressed disappointment at the government's failure to effect radical reform in this area.

> Indeed we have outlawed much of the explicit forms of racial prejudice from our society, but the subtleties of racism will linger on for a long time. Nowhere are these subtle manifestations of racism more entrenched than in education... We inherited in our education system inbuilt mechanisms of white racism like the division of schools into A and B schools. Complemented by the system of zoning and the creation of community schools, the whole system implied that the best educational opportunities became the legal preserve of the rich....[55]

For some reason, the organisation of the school system along the classifications of A, B and C laid down under the 1979 Education Act continues to exist. It is precisely this system which continues to perpetuate aspects of colonial education and promotes and sustains the colonial class structure of our society. The Group A schools continue to be elite institutions for the privileged white and black pupils from within former European surburbs while Group B (formerly African government schools) continue to cater for urban blacks and of course the Group C rural schools cater for black rural children. The removal of the racial barrier in school enrolment policy has not really changed much. The few non-white pupils who live in wealthy former European surbubs and now attend former white Group A schools feel superior and more privileged because they have been admitted into the white society. At independence, black students admitted into these schools found themselves subjected to insults from white fellow-pupils and teachers alike.[56] Although the situation has changed tremendously since independence, black children in these schools are from middle and working class families.

The zoning system continues to deny the mass of black children from high density (African) townships the legal right to admission in these schools. They are therefore restricted to Group B schools, as rural children are restricted to the Group C schools.

Recently, private schools and colleges have become a new haven for white kids whose parents cannot stand racial integration in schools. Private colleges charge exceptionally high fees which prohibit the majority of black children from gaining admission. Financial restrictions are being used to replace the blatant racial discrimination of the past but achieve the same results, that is European children are able to find places where the policy of privilege dominates. Although, government insists that 60% of enrolment in these institutions should be black, the fees are forbidding and as a result few black children are able to enter those schools.

The advantages in Group A schools are numerous. There are well-supplied with educational facilities such as textbooks, writing materials, superior library facilities and superior recreational facilities inherited from the days of colonialism. The teachers are far better trained and qualified and the pupil/teacher ratio much lower than in the group B and C schools. On the average, it is 30:1 as compared to 49:1 in group B and C schools. In many respects, group A schools are vestiges of the colonial system. It is the Group B and C schools which have taken the greatest burden of overcrowding and discomfort as they struggle to cope with high enrolments.[57] For example, whereas enrolment in Group A government primary schools rose by 178.16%, from 19,690 in 1980 to 35,081 in 1982,[58] the rise in Group C schools in the same period was 152.1%. In terms of numbers this was a far greater rise.

The decision by the government to implement the policy of free primary education for all children, in accordance with the 1980 election manifesto declaration, has had serious implication for education. The government has had to undertake a task of great magnitude to expand the system in order to accommodate unprecedented rises in enrolment. Several schools have had to be built and those closed during the war needed reopening.

Quantitative developments of a significant nature resulted from the decision to democratise education. Following the declaration seven months after independence that primary education had become free, enrolment increased by 232% between 1980 and 1982. In the secondary education sector, enrolment rose by 330% while in teacher education enrolment soared by 254% and university education by 145%.[59]

In terms of educational institutions, primary schools increased by 16%, secondary schools by 397%, teacher colleges by 175%. The number of school-teachers rose by 261% in the primary sector.[60] In the secondary sector, the number of teachers increased by 236%, including a large number of recruits from Australia and Britain brought into the country to assist in coping with enrolment, which had reached a two million mark in less than two years since independence. The expansion that has taken place in primary education since independence is shown in Table 4.

The table shows that, as a result of primary education being made free, enrolment rose by 150.89% from the 1979 figure of 819,128 to 1,235,994 in 1980. Enrolment for 1981 showed a rise of 135.93% over 1980 while the rise in 1982 intake was 115.14% over 1981. By 1983, enrolment had reached the two million mark—a 105.68% increase over 1982. The trend continued and by 1984 a 105.03% rise over the 1983 figure had been recorded, while in 1985 the enrolment figure had nearly reached the 2.25 million mark. Overall the rise in enrolment between 1979 and 1985 was a staggering 272.16%.

Such an expansion rate raises questions of costs in terms of financial, material and human resources. For a small country like Zimbabwe, the burden on the state could prove too much. More and more provisions and learning facilities have to be made available and teachers have to be found to staff huge classes of, on average, 50 children or more.

Apart from the known enrolments, projections show that the trend is not likely to change. More children will continue to enrol in primary schools, as shown in Table 5.

The table reveals that, within a decade, enrolment will rise from over 2 million to more than 3.75 million. If this trend holds true, as current patterns seem to suggest, considerable strain will be placed on resources.

The effect of the sharp rise in primary school enrolment is most evident in the strain this has put on manpower and financial resources. Most primary schools are operating on a very high teacher/pupil ratio of between 1:44 1:49. Moreover the teacher shortage crisis has led to the employment of untrained teachers. Of the 45,467 teachers in service in 1982, as many as 21,768 were untrained.[61] This situation prompted the government to undertake a gigantic and most expensive programme of in-service teacher training with the assistance of the United Nations Children's Fund (UNICEF). The Zimbabwe Integrated National Teacher Education Course, as the programme is called, was introduced to alleviate the crisis and support the conventional teacher training programme. These efforts did not prove adequate, and the government found itself compelled to recall retired teachers into service.

TABLE 4
ENROLMENT IN ALL PRIMARY SCHOOLS

Year	No. of Schools	1	2	3	4	5	6	7	Special Classes	Aided Communists Classes	Total	Inc. in % Pre. Year
1979	2401	173050	142702	125864	110753	99254	88089	77887	1476	53	819128	
1980	2905	376392	207899	170420	144746	125977	112890	97099	571		1235994	150,89
1981	3418	455536	370141	236901	182348	160447	145378	128647	745		1680143	135,93
1982	3880	410453	428976	360025	228316	187107	166805	152187	745		1934614	115,14
1983	3960	368329	374850	397734	331032	219817	183498	168769	818		2044847	105,69
1984		368329	341503	360829	372641	313987	214922	182742	1715		2147898	105,03
1985		346335	326426	331028	347265	357937	304416	214121	1868		2229396	103,79

Source: Quarterly Digest of September 1983 p.5. and September 1985 p.5.

TABLE 5
ENROLMENT PROJECTIONS 1983—1994

YEAR	\multicolumn{7}{c}{Primary School}	Total
	1	2	3	4	5	6	7	
1983	367,275	374,041	396,888	330,465	219,570	183,280	168,563	2,040,082
1984	370,275	345,239	351,599	373,075	327,160	217,374	185,113	2,169,835
1985	381,275	348,058	324,503	330,503	369,344	323,889	219,548	2,296,143
1986	390,375	357,459	327,175	305,053	327,198	365,651	327,128	2,399,939
1987	405,275	366,859	336,011	307,544	302,003	323,926	369,307	2,410,925
1988	420,275	380,959	344,847	315,850	304,469	298,983	327,165	2,392,548
1989	435,275	395,058	358,101	324,156	312,692	301,424	301,972	2,428,679
1990	445,275	409,159	371,355	336,615	320,915	309,565	304,439	2,497,323
1991	455,275	418,559	384,609	349,074	333,249	317,705	312,661	2,571,132
1992	465,275	427,959	393,445	361,532	345,583	329,916	320,883	2,444,593
1993	475,275	437,359	402,281	369,838	357,917	342,127	333,215	2,728,012
1994	485,275	446,759	411,117	378,144	366,140	354,338	345,548	2,787,321

Source: Report of Education Review Committee, 1983.

Financial and Other Implications of Government Policy
The sharp rise in enrolment has had serious financial implications for the government. In 1980, the cost of education jumped from the 1979 figure of $120,437,000 to $184,712,000, a rise of 53.36%.[63] Administrative costs soared high as the system expanded and required more manpower at all levels. Of this, primary education received $41,970,000.[64] This amount proved quite inadequate and prompted the ministry to request a further rise during the 1981-82 financial year.

The 1980-81 sum was raised by as much as $71,381,000 to $290,070,000. Of this, some $45,777,000 was allocated to primary education alone, an increase of $3,807,000 over the previous financial year.[65]

Due to the ever-increasing costs of an expanding system, this allocation proved inadequate and led to a further increase in financial allocation by the government during the 1982-83 financial year. An unprecedented $408,400,000 was allocated to education.[66] Primary education received $56,918,000 out of this: an increase of $11,141,000 over the previous year.[67] Overall, the 1982-83 education allocation represents 22% of the national budget. There is a danger that education will soon cost more than the government can afford. In fact it already is proving to be the most expensive item to the government. A situation may be reached when education will begin to depend on borrowed money. This is a problem of the Third World. A small nation, no matter how poor, will—soon after acquiring independence—embark on some of the most expensive programmes because political considerations demand that that happen. If alternative ways of funding education and cutting down costs are not found, the system may sooner or later become impossible to sustain.

While free primary education for all is a sound democratic ideal, it is not sound and practical economics, particularly for a developing country. To place those who have the means to pay for their children's education in the same category with the poor and disadvantaged is not a realistic policy because it means spending scarce resources on those who least need the help.

Those who have the means must be made to pay. If our system of education is to survive, it may be necessary for the government urgently to consider asking those who earn more than the minimum wage of $150 per month to pay for their children's primary education so that the money the government is able to save can be used to pay for the education of the less fortunate. In fact, the 1983 report of the School Fees Committee recommended wide-ranging reforms in the present school fees structure and even identified strategies for an equitable and sensible fee structure both at the primary and secondary level.[69]

Moreover, some of the money that the government would save could be injected into human resources development in teacher education colleges so that teachers can be trained for the schools by expanding existing training facilities. More staff development programmes can be organised in order to improve the professional competence of teachers, head teachers, teacher trainers, District Education Officers and other professional and administrative staff engaged in the day-to-day running of our education system.

The rise in the education cost since independence can be shown in graph form.

As is clear from Graph 1 the rise was highest between 1979 and 1982. However, economic realities have already begun to impose restrictions on further rises. The high increase in school enrolment was reflected in the high increase in administrative costs incurred in primary education since independence. During the 1980-81 financial year, the Administration and General Services vote stood at $10,024,000.[70] Each Regional Office was allocated $22,100 out of this vote and the rest was utilised by head office.[71]

Pressure from a rapidly growing administration demanded a greater increase in the Administration and General Services vote. As a consequence, 1981-82 vote for this purpose was raised to $29,491,000 an increase of $19,467,000 over 1980-81.[72] As much as $6,858,000 of this went into the payment of salaries and wages, an increase of $1,218,000 over the previous year.[73]

As enrolment continued to soar, so did the administrative infrastructures both at the head office and regional level leading to a further rise in the Administration and General Services vote for 1982-83. This was increased to $41,022,000 representing a rise of $11,531,000.[74] Salaries claimed $8,550,000 of this vote, while regional offices claimed $36,000 each.[75]

It was becoming clear that there simply was no money to meet the demands. Consequently the increase in the vote for 1983 was very small compared to previous years.

Despite attempts by the government to reduce state expenditure on education, its vote has continued to rise. In 1985, the Education vote reached a record $500 million making education the most expensive item for the state.

Secondary education has seen more expansion in the last five years than in all the years of colonial rule. Since independence, a great deal of work has been done to bring secondary education closer to every child.

As a first step towards achieving that goal, government declared at independence that every child would have the right and the opportunity to avail himself of secondary education. In other words, unlike during Smith's regime when only 12½% of all primary school graduates could proceed to Form I, the transition rate is now 100%. However, the government's wish to make secondary education free as in the primary sector proved unrealistic. The financial costs of making secondary education free were found to be exorbitant and impossible to meet. Consequently, parents have to pay fees for their children's education at that level.

Stunning evidence of the rapid expansion in secondary education can be seen when it is considered that the number of secondary schools rose from 197 in 1980 to a stagering 694 in 1981. By 1982, the figure had reached 738 and rose further to 790 in 1983. By 1985 the number had soared to over 1200 schools.[76] Most of these have been built in rural areas, the most neglected during the colonial period. Enrolment has risen in a similarly spectacular manner as can be seen in Table 6.

The Table shows that 1980 enrolment rose by 1,426 pupils from 73,540 in 1979 to 74,966 while the 1981 rise represented a 101.93% increase over 1980. By 1982 the figure had reached 224,609. Between 1982 and 1983, the rise was 140.88%. By 1985, the enrolment figure stood at 497,766. This meteoric rise in enrolment can be shown more vividly in Graph 2.

GRAPH 1: Increase in the Education Vote between 1979 and 1985

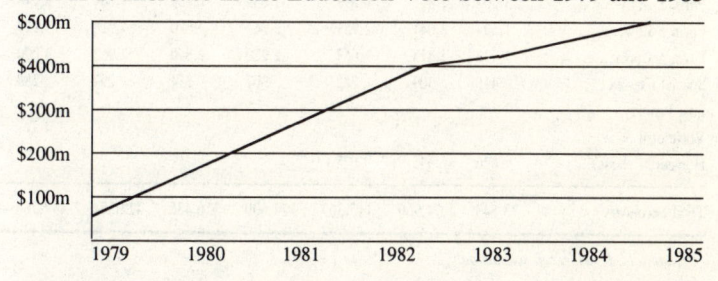

GRAPH 2: Enrolment in Secondary Education between 1979-85

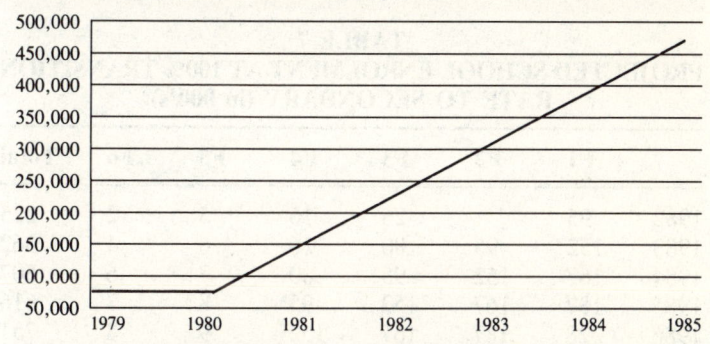

Source: Chief Education Officer (Standards Control), *Paper read at the Teacher Education workshop at Gweru Teachers' College 6th January, 1984'*.

The sharp rise in enrolment characterises government policy and is a pointer towards the magnitude of problems that are bound to arise.

Overall, since independence, considerable achievements have been made in the expansion of secondary schools. Distribution of schools to overcome rural/urban disparities in terms of facilities has improved, tremendously, the availability of opportunities for secondary education in rural areas. The greatest expansion has taken place in rural areas where, for example, between 1979 and 1982, 613 schools were built compared to 117 in urban areas. Enrolment projections indicate even greater expansion.

Projected figures for the next eight years show high increases in

TABLE 6
RISE IN ENROLMENTS IN SECONDARY SCHOOLS 1979-1985

SECONDARY	1979	1980	1981	1982	1983	1984	1985
Grade 8/Form 1...	19,962	22,201	82,262	94,841	110,725	140,045	153,439
Grade 9/Form 2....	18,094	17,251	24,855	79,465	95,539	107,052	137,943
Grade 10/Form 3....	14,720	15,891	15,478	26,572	93,232	93,232	101,970
Grade 11/Form 4....	13,294	12,926	15,547	16,416	24,509	71,632	91,723
Form 5....	3,202	1,815	1,893	1,858	2,189	3,164	3,246
Form 6 Lower....	1,594	2,641	2,751	,3,243	3,680	4,218	5,957
Form 6 Upper.......	1,432	1,413	1,667	2,220	2,890	2,962	3,200
Special Classes.......	416	309	282	307	334	297	288
Post Primary Vocational & Homecraft classes..	826	645+	628+				
Total Secondary	73,540	74,966	145,363	224,609	316,438	422,584	497,766

Private (aided) homecraft schools only.

TABLE 7
PROJECTED SCHOOL ENROLMENT AT 100% TRANSITION RATE TO SECONDARY (in 000's)

	F1	F2	F3	F4	F5	F6	Total
1982	95		26	16	5	2	225
1983	152	95	80	26	6	4	362
1984	167	152	95	80	7	6	507
1985	187	167	152	95	8	7	616
1986	228	187	167	152	9	8	751
1987	360	228	187	167	10	9	961
1988	429	360	228	187	10	10	1,224
1989	411	429	360	228	10	10	1,448
1990	400	411	429	360	10	10	1,620
1991	415	400	411	429	10	10	1,676

Source: *CEO Planning Paper, Ministry of Education 1981.*

enrolment which characterises our expansionist policy. This is evident in Table 7.

The Table reveals that between 1982 and 1991, Form 1 enrolment is expected to rise from 95,000 to 415,000, Form 2 from 80,000 to 400,000, Form 3 from 26,000 to 411,000 Form 4 from 16,000 to 429,000, Form 5 from 5,000 to 10,000 and Form 6 from 2,000 to 10,000. Overall, an increase from 225,000 to a staggering 1,676,000 is expected. Even allowing for unforeseen factors which may lead to a fall in enrolment growth, the 1991 estimation is not likely to differ substantially from the given projection, taking into consideration the current high trends in enrolments and population growth.

These figures are, from the point of view of government expansionist policy, a tremendous achievement. But this rate of expansion has several implications for education and national development. First, considerable strain has been put on financial and manpower resources to a degree not anticipated. Second, much strain has also been placed on the education system itself in terms of the size to which it has grown. Third, there is the question of the provisions that have to be made for the future employment of such large numbers of students who will leave school each year to seek jobs in an economy that it not growing at a corresponding rate. Fourth, this policy affects long-term planning for national development. Under current planning strategies in education, national human resources development targets, particularly in the technical and professional areas, are not likely to be met because there has so far been no radical transformation of the curriculum to facilitate the achievement of national objectives. Without that transformation, little national development can be expected to result from the efforts which the government is making in education. The planning does not also appear to address itself sufficiently to the growing dangers of massive school-leaver unemployment problems, which will become a thorn in the flesh of society within a few years.

The overriding objective behind current planning strategies is the provision of school facilities and opportunities to all children. This is, of course, a moral, social and political obligation which the government has to fulfil, given the fact that this is partly what the armed struggle was all about. It was a fight for equal access to education for children of all races. This objective must be carefully planned for and achieved without incurring problems for which there may eventually be no solutions.

Since independence, secondary education has claimed a substantial portion of the education vote. During the 1981-82 financial year, government Group A and B secondary schools alone received some $38,394,000, an increase of $3,230,000 over 1980-81.[79] Of that allocation, school services cost $7,440,000 and school running expenses $3,797,000, an increase of $2,320,000[80] over the previous year in the case of the former and $798,000 in the case of the latter.[81] The considerable work of expansion necessitated a significant rise in the secondary education allocation in the government sector the following year. The 1982-83 cost rose to $46,183,000, an increase of $5,789,000 over the previous year. Schools services cost an extra $1,660,000, raising the allocation to $9,100,000.[82] School running costs soared by another $1,505,000 to $5,300,000 to cover per capita grants, the cost of stationery, library books and consumable materials for science and other subjects.[83]

The private aided sector has cost the government the most. The 1981-82 allocation to this sector was $36,200,000, an increase of $16,600,000 over the 1980-81 allocation.[84] Of this, building and equipment grants cost some $5,000,000, an increase of $4,500,000 over the 1980-81 vote.[85] The following financial year, 1982-83, the sum had risen to $46,231,000, an increase of $9,593,000 over the previous year, as a consequence of increasing expansion costs.[86] Building and equipment costs rose to $9,500,000, an increase of $4,500,000 over 1981-82.[87]

Since the system is costing the government so much in financial resources, plans and strategies that are adopted should ensure positive returns for the state by generating essential manpower and promoting national development. As the system continues to expand and calls for more resources from the state, it will become even more necessary to ensure that the plans drawn up and the strategies adopted in developing secondary education produce definite results and benefits for the country.

The massive expansion programme in secondary education has also put considerable strain on human resources. A critical shortage of qualified teaching staff has developed as a result. Of the 8,386 teachers in all secondary schools throughout the country,[88] less than half are certificated teachers. In fact, the majority of teachers in Upper Tops are Form 4 graduates with only 3 or 4 passes. The pupil/teacher ratio has risen, since independence, from 24:1 to 39:1 in 1985.[89] In most schools, the ratio is in fact much higher.

As a result, considerable resources have been invested into increasing facilities in teacher training colleges. At present, a massive recruitment exercise of expatriate teachers from Australia, Britain and Mauritius is under way to reduce the staffing shortage problem. Between 1981 and December 1982, some 600 expatriate teachers were recruited from these countries.[90] Most of these teachers have been deployed in rural schools where the shortage is most acute. However, reliance upon expatriate teachers is not desirable since these are twice as expensive as Zimbabweans.[91] There is therefore a need to revamp the training of teachers locally in order to meet the serious existing shortage.

The government has considered several alternative methods of producing teachers. At the primary level, an integrated in-service type of teacher training was introduced in 1980. The Zimbabwe Integrated Teacher Education Course (ZINTEC) is a new system funded largely by UNICEF and is based on distance education. It aims at training the student teacher on the job. The advantage of this system is that it has injected large numbers of student teachers into schools to replace untrained teachers. Thus, during the four years of training, the student teachers have provided great service to the education system and the nation. Over four thousand teachers graduated through this programme between 1980 and 1985.

The conventional teacher training programme underwent unprecedented expansion between 1981 and 1983; enrolment rose from 2,108 to 4,158. [92] Also, reorganisation in training strategies has led to the change from college-based training to the in-service type in which the teacher spends two of the four years of training in the field practising teaching in a live classroom situation and thus providing a much-needed service to the nation. The other two years are spent in college learning the theory of education.

Secondary teacher education has also seen considerable expansion and reorganisation in terms of training techniques. It has embraced the four-year training pattern and facilities have been increased in response to the rising enrolment in schools. Between 1981 and 1983, enrolment in secondary teachers colleges rose from 1,005 to 3,005. Overall, enrolment in all teacher colleges, primary and secondary, rose from 2,824 in 1980 to 9,504 in 1985.[93]

Teacher requirement projections by the Planning Section of the Ministry of Education reveal that, given the current high transitional rate of pupils from grade 7 to secondary, large numbers of trained teachers will be required between 1982 and 1991 to staff secondary schools under a variety of options. The options are given in Table 8.

Basing the teacher projection requirements on the current grade 7 transitional rate to secondary of 100%, the table reveals that under option A, which proposes to reduce the pupil/qualified teacher ratio from the 1982 figure of 42:1 to the standard figure 28:1, an additional 7,579 teachers would be required in 1983. This would raise the total number of qualified teachers from the 1982 figure of 5,314 to 12,893. Quite clearly, there is no way of raising that number of trained teachers within one year, given our current teacher output rate from colleges and the university's Faculty of Education. To cope with the high enrolment increase in secondary schools, the 1983 figure would need to be raised from 17,929 in 1984 to 59,321 by 1991. This means that an additional 53,864 trained teachers would be required by that time to service the secondary school system. Under option B, which also proposes to reduce the pupil/teacher ratio to 28:1 but assumes a drop in the transitional rate from grade 7 to Form 1 to 70%, some 6,079 additional teachers would be required in 1983 to bring the total qualified staff to 11,397. A further 3,050 would be required in 1984 and by 1991 a total of 36,293 additional teachers would be needed in secondary schools. This option does not explain how the fall in transition rate to secondary would come about, given current government policy of providing secondary education for all children in primary schools. But even if that fall did come about, there simply are no adequate training provisions to generate that number of teachers by 1991.

Option C proposes an operational pupil/teacher ratio of 56:1, which would increase the strain on the teachers' performance in the classroom

TABLE 8
NUMBER OF TEACHERS REQUIRED UNDER DIFFERENT OPTIONS

Qualified Tchr./Pupil Ratio G.7 Transit. Rate	Option A 1:28 100% Add	CF	Option B 1:28 70% Add	CF	Option C 1:56 100% Add	CF	Option D 1:56 70% Add	CF	Option E 1:84 100% Add	CF	Option F 1:84 70% Add	CF
1982		5,314		5,314		5,314		5,314		5,314		5,314
1983	7,579	12,839	6,079	11,397	1,137	6,446	382	5,696	1,016	4,298	1,516	3,798
1984	5,036	17,929	3,050	14,442	2,518	8,964	1,625	7,321	662	4,960	433	4,881
1985	3,821	2,1750	1,986	16,429	1,911	10,875	893	8,214	2,290	7,250	2,111	5,476
1986	4,750	26,500	2,321	18,750	2,375	13,250	1,161	9,375	1,583	8,833	774	6,250
1987	7,429	33,929	5,071	23,821	3,714	16,964	2,356	11,911	2,477	11,310	1,691	7,941
1988	9,357	43,286	6,536	30,357	4,679	21,643	3,268	15,179	3,119	14,429	2,178	10,119
1989	7,964	51,250	5,607	35,964	3,928	25,625	283	17,982	2,654	17,083	1,869	11,988
1990	6,000	57,393	4,286	40,250	3,071	28,698	2,143	20,125	2,048	19,131	1,429	13,417
1991	1,928	59,321	1,357	41,607	965	29,661	679	20,884	643	19,774	452	13,869
	35,864		36,239		24,347		15,590		14,460		8,555	

and inevitably affect the efficiency of the system. That ratio is proposed on the basis of our present limitations or inability to produce adequate teachers. But the option takes the 100% transitional rate as a reality. Under those conditions, some 1,132 additional qualified teachers would be required in 1983 and the figure would rise to 2,518 in 1984, bringing the total number of trained teachers in secondary schools to 8,964. By 1991, a total of 24,347 additional trained teachers would be needed. Using the same operational ratio of 56:1 but a transitional rate of 70%, the number of additional trained teachers required under option D in 1983 woule be 382. That figure would rise to 1,625 in 1984, bringing the number of qualified teachers in schools to 7,321. By 1991 an additional 15,590 teachers would be required to bring the total number to 20,804.

A fifth option proposes to raise the pupil/teacher ratio from 56:1 to 84:1. The professional problems a teacher would have to contend with in handling a class of that size are simply enormous and are indicative of the magnitude of the problems involved in educational reform. The ratio is a pointer towards the kind or problems a young developing country can expect to face in its struggle to reform colonial education. Financial and human resource limitations further complicate the problems and make the task of teacher training all the more difficult.

An operational pupil/teacher ratio of 84:1 is obviously an undesirable situation. But even then, to operate at that ratio would require an additional 14,460 trained teachers by 1991 in order to meet the staffing requirements necessitated by a 100% transitional rate of pupils from primary to secondary.

Under the sixth option E, which uses the same pupil/teacher ratio but a reduced transitional rate of 70%, a total of 8,555 trained teachers would be required to sustain the secondary sector by raising the total number of qualified staff to 13,869.

Options A, B and C are not really practical because we do not have the means to produce the high numbers of additional teachers required while options D, E and F are also not practical because of the professional implications of the large teacher/pupil ratio involved in each case. Yet, some option has to be adopted in planning teacher education in relation to enrolment in schools. But even if it were theoretically possible to provide the additional qualified teachers required under those six options (between 1982 and 1991) there is one constraint which would make the achievement of that objective practically difficult. It would be very difficult for the government, currently funding several programmes of national reconstruction and development, to pay those teachers at the present rate, where the average pay is $8,200 (excluding allowances) and $9,020 (including allowances) annually.

One senior ministry official warned that a serious socio-political problem would arise as a result of thousands of qualified teachers being unemployed. The high costs involved in paying these teachers would be beyond the reach of the government. The vote for secondary school teachers, salaries and allowances for the 1981-82 financial year was only $59.5 million for the 6,112 teachers in service. For 1982-83, it increased by only $10.3 million to $69.8 million. The ministry estimated that, at our present rate of teacher production, some $418.8 million would have to be found to pay teachers between 1983 and 1991. No such money can be raised by the government. The problem is therefore quite clear. Althoug teacher requirements will continue to grow and therefore call for higher output from colleges, the government would have the problem of paying an ever-increasing teaching workforce. This would mean that some trained and badly needed teachers would simply be unemployable. Strategies will have to be found to reconcile our ever-increasing teacher requirements and the size of the purse from which the teachers would have to be paid.

Conclusion

On attaining independence, most African countries found themselves landed with an education system that needed extensive surgery in order to turn it into a tool serviceable to the needs and aspirations of the majority of the people. For most, the operation has been a traumatic one, bedevilled with sometimes conflicting demands of politics, economics and social pressure. Zimbabwe's quest to transform colonial education into an instrument of national development demonstrates the nature of the problems.

However, in spite of the financial, material and human resource problems emanating from current government policy, the task of providing every citizen, young or old, with education has been worthwhile. A developing country cannot afford the luxury of choosing between literacy and illiteracy, between development and underdevelopment. But it has the responsibility of considering the most effective methods of achieving literacy and development. It has to adopt the most appropriate ways of making the policy of free education effective in achieving national development. Sometimes the choice of strategies is a difficult one. For example, how does a poor developing country justify the choice of an expensive system of education given its poverty? Where will it obtain the resources needed to develop and sustain such a system? Even if the resources were obtainable from foreign donors, what are the implications of such aid? Could a poor country afford the repayments? Assuming, for the sake of argument, that it could repay the loans, what are the implications of that aid in terms of independence? In other words, what would be the price people would have to pay in return? It is common knowledge that foreign aid, almost always, has strings attached to it. Poor recipient countries often lose their independence by accepting foreign aid. They become aligned and subtly compelled to support policies of donor countries that undermine the freedom, of the developing world. No country can, without freedom achieve development. Mwalimu Nyerere concludes that:

> Freedom and development are as completely linked together as are chickens and eggs. Without chickens you get no eggs and without eggs you get no chickens.
> Similarly, without freedom you get no development.[95]

What alternatives are available in educational planning? Can a developing country afford a policy of ever-expanding education in view of the unavailability of resources? What would be the economic implications of such a policy on the overall development of the country? If the government cannot afford such a policy, should it shrink the state purse which finances the policy? Can it, in fact, do so without shrinking enrolment? What would be the socio-economic and political implications of such a decision? In other words, how does a country emerging out of colonialism reconcile the needs and aspirations of its people with its poverty and inability to pay for the achievement of those aspirations?

These are considerations which cannot be ignored because they are crucial in the planning of educational transformation and national development and are fundamental to the achievement of wider national goals.

Quite clearly, a more judicious approach is needed in the planning of development programmes. Serious considerations should be given to the resources available. Development programmes should always be planned with the resources available in mind. It may be necessary to defer those programme that cannot be immediately funded. In education, the concept of free education should be carefully studied with a view to assessing its financial implications. It is possible to achieve reasonable development of education without denying any child the opportunity to acquire education. It is also possible to implement urgent reforms in education without over-committing the government financially. Development achieved through borrowed money leads to underdevelopment and enslavement. It is therefore important that governments in developing countries do not lead themselves towards underdevelopment in the struggle to achieve development too quickly. This is particularly important in education, where massive school-leaver unemployment can worsen existing problems of underdevelopment. Thus educational expansion should take place in a situation of economic development. This means that educational planning should be closely related to economic planning in order to ensure that graduates from the school system will be absorbed into the economy.

REFERENCES

1. See, for example, Mandaza, Ibbo, Education in Zimbabwe: The Colonial Framework and the Response of the National Liberation Movement, in *Zimbabwe: Towards a New Order: An Economic and Social Survey*, Vol II, UNCTAD/MFD/19, UND P-PAF/78/010, Geneva, November 1980, pp. 341-400.
2. *Report of the Chief Native Commissioner for the year 1928,* p. 5.
3. *Southern Rhodesia Native Affairs Department, 1932*, No. 16, pp. 100-101.
4. Riddell, Roger, *Education and Employment in Zimbabwe*, From Rhodesia to Zimbabwe, Series 4, 1979, p. 5.
5. Loney, Martin, *Rhodesia—White Racism and Imperial Response*, Penguin Books, Harmondsworth, 1978, p. 42.
6. *Southern Rhodesia Miscellaneous Reports, 1924*, p. 39, para'. 274.

7. *Southern Rhodesia: Report by H.S. Keigwin Esquire, Native Commissioner, on the suggested Industrial Development of Natives, 1920*, p. 1.
8. *Report of the Chief Native Commissioner for Matabeleland, 1914*, p. 7.
9. *Report of the Chief Native Commissioner for Matebeleland, 1981*, p. 4.
10. *Report of the Chief Native Commissioner for Matebeleland, 1917*, p. 4.
11. *Report of the Chief Native Commissioner for Matabeleland, 1918*, p.4
12. Keigwin, H.S., An Educational Experiment, *Southern Africa Journal of Science*, Vol. XVIII, No. 1, p. 172.
13. *Southern Rhodesia: Report by H.S. Keigwin Esquire, Native Commissioner, on the suggested Industrial Development of Natives, 1920*, p. 1.
14. Franck, Thomas, *Race and Nationalism, The Struggle for Power in Southern Rhodesia*, Fordham University Press, 1960, p. 118 and *Report of the Native Education Enquiry*, 1951, p. 22.
15. Franck, *op. cit.*, p. 77.
16. *Report of the Director of Native Development for the year 1932*, p. 5.
17. Riddell, Roger, *op. cit.*, p. 5.
18. *Ibid.*
19. Franck, Thomas, *op. cit.*, p. 118.
20. *Ibid.*
21. *Ibid.*
22. Raven, Faith, *Central Africa—Background to Argument*, African Publications Trust, London, 1962, pp. 17-18.
23. *Ibid.*
24. *Ibid.*, p. 9.
25. Franklin, Harry, *Unholy Wedlock: The Failure of the Central African Federation*, George Allen and Unwin, London, 1963, p. 178.
26. Keatley, Patrick, *The Politics of Partnership: The Federation of Rhodesia and Nyasaland*, Penguin African Library, 1963, p. 372.
27. Franklin, *op. cit.*, p. 178.
28. See Rhodesia Front Party Constitution, *Rhodesia—The Background to the Present Conflict and Policy for the British Government*, A Study Group of the Billericacy Constituency of the Labour Party, 1968, V/2/2.
29. *Annual Report of the Secretary for African Education for the year 1966*, p. 3.
30. *Ibid.*
31. *Ibid.*
32. S/M/S/R/B. 1964-66, District Synod Minutes for 1966, *Comments on the Ministerial Statement on the future Policy on African Education made in the Rhodesian Parliament, 20th April, 1966*, WMMMS Archives, Box 1964-66.
33. Rich, F., The Economics of Education, *Rhodesia Journal of Economics*, Vol. 1, No.1, August 1967, p. 19.
34. *Summary of Points in the Judges' Commission Report for consideration by Matabeleland School Managers and Principals*, p. 3. File A/97, 1965, Southern Rhodesia Educational Developments, Council for World Missions Archives.
35. *Annual Report of the Secretary for African Education for the year*

1971, p. 4.
36. *Ibid.*
37. *Ibid.*
38. *Annual Reports of 31st December, 1970*, p. 28 and *1974*, p. 54.
39. O'Callaghan, *Southern Rhodesia, The Effects of a Conquest Society on Education, Culture and Information*, UNESCO, Paris, 1977, p. 65., Table 2.
40. Murphree, M.W., *Education, Race and Employment in Rhodesia*, Article Publications, London, 1975, p. 25.
41. Stoneman, Colin, *Skilled Labour and Future Needs*, Rhodesia to Zimbabwe Series, No. 4, Catholic Institute for International Relations, London, 1978, p. 5.
42. S/M/R/B. 1976, District Synod Minutes for 1986, Cap.F. WMMS Archives, Box 1967-70.
43. *Rhodesia, Census of Population*, 1969, CSO, Salisbury, 1976, Table 10 with forward projections to 1976.
44. *Ibid.*
45. *Rhodesia. The Education Act, 1979*, paras. 5-6.
46. *Ibid.*
47. *ZANU-PF 1980 Election Manifesto*, p. 12, Item L.
48. *Press Statement 922/82/DB, 8, October 1982*, Prime Minister Robert Mugabe on 'School Curricula should orient children to Zimbabwe's new order'.
49. *Press Statement 1173/81/PR/JS*, Government of Zimbabwe, 1982, p. 11.
50. Gwarinda, T.C., *Socialism and Education*, The College Press, 1985, p. 105.
51. *Ibid.*
52. Zvobgo, R.J., *Transforming Education—The Zimbabwean Experience*, College Press, 1985, pp. 38-39.
53. *Ibid.*
54. *Ibid.*
55. *Press Statement 1052/81/NM*, Deputy Minister for Education on Racism in the Education System, December 7 1981.
56. *Ibid.*
57. Zvobgo, R.J., *op. cit., p. 42.*
58. *Quarterly Digest of Statistics*, May 1980.
59. Calculated from *ibid.*
60. Gwarinda, T.C., *op. cit.*
61. *Quarterly Digest of Statistics*, May 1986.
62. *Annual Report of the Secretary for Education for the year ended 31st December, 1980*, p. 21.
63. *Ibid.*, p. 21.
64. *Ministry of Education and Culture Vote 21, Notes on the Estimates of Expenditure, 1981-82*, p. 1.
65. *Ibid.*, p. 41.
66. *Ibid.*, p. 1.
67. *Ibid.*

68. *Ibid.*, p. 2.
69. See *Report of the School Fees Committee, November, 1983*, pp. 11-14.
70. *Ministry of Education and Culture Vote 21. Notes on the Estimates of Expenditure, 1981-82*, p. 2.
71. *Ibid.*, 1982-83, p. 2.
72. *Ibid.*
73. *Ibid.*
74. *Ibid.*
75. *Ibid.*
76. *Quarterly Digest of Statistics*, May 1986, p. 5.
77. *Ibid.*
78. Gwarinda, T.C., *op. cit.*
79. *Ministry of Education and Culture Vote 21. Notes on the Estimates of Expenditure, 1981-82*, p. 37, item VI.
80. *Ibid.*, p. 39, 5 Vic. item 1.
81. *Ibid.* Vic. item 2.
82. *Ministry of Education and Culture, Notes on the Estimates of Expenditure, 1982-83*, p. 34, item VI.
83. *Ibid.*, VI (C).
84. *Ibid.*, VI (V), item 2.
85. *Ibid.*,Vote 21, 1981-82, p. 48.
86. *Ibid.*, Vote 1982-83, p. 43, VIII, 2.
87. *Ibid.*, p. 44, VIII, 2B, item 1.
88. National Consolidation figures based on Regional Summaries of Staffing and Returns for first term, 1981 and on Unified Teaching Service and Salary Service Bureau print-out for end of second term, 1982, Table VII.
89. *Ministry of Education and Culture: Strategy for Human Resource Development*, Needs, Plans and Utilisation of Resources, 1985, pp. 3, 5, and 9 (b).
90. *Ibid.*, p. 5.
91. *Ibid.*,
92. Calculated from consolidated figures for Teachers Colleges, 1981-83, Ministry of Education, 1984.
93. *Quarterly Digest of Statistics*, May 1986, p. 5, See Gwarinda, T.C. *op. cit.*, p. 109.
94. *Projection Estimates: Planning Section Paper*, Ministry of Education, 1983.
95. Nyerere, Julius, *Freedom and Development*, Oxford University Press, Dar es Salaam, 1973, p. 58.

12. PROGRESS AND PROBLEMS IN THE HEALTH CARE DELIVERY SYSTEM

Samuel Takarinda Agere

Introduction

This chapter is an attempt to provide a historical development of health services in Zimbabwe, the value assumptions on which the present health care paradigm is based and, more importantly, the social, political and economic factors that have contributed to the formulation and design of the present health care system. An analysis of the health system is made in order to understand how it has been made accessible, acceptable and equitable to the majority of the people in the country. In short, as an important aspect of social development, health care is analysed within the context of the political economy of Zimbabwe.

The emergence of medicine was based on two distinct political and ideological perspectives, contagionism and anticontagionism: first, contagionism assumed that diseases were contagious and spread by population movement. It was conceived in terms of individual biological conditions and mechanisms. It emphasised the germ as causing disease and consequently the treatment of the disease depended on curing the individual body. Implicit in this notion was the concept of health as the absence of disease. Cure of the disease was conceived through specifically designed treatment; for example, through the administration of drugs. This method ideologically reinforces the tendency to perceive health problems and their solutions as individual and not as social. Instead, everything is to be cured through increased individual consumption of drugs. The development of individualism in capitalism facilitated the dominance of curative medicine or personal health services over environmental and social conditions. Curative medicine is therefore a part of capitalism whose structural changes are difficult to implement in the post-colonial period. Curative medicine has, therefore, been responsible for the dominance of medical doctors in the medical field, for ignoring or paying little attention to social conditions or environmental factors.

On the other hand, anticontagionism postulated that diseases resulted from local sources, particularly from poor conditions, such as poverty, filth, malnutrition and oppression by capitalism.[1] The anticontagionism view placed emphasis on improving social conditions as a means of improving the health of the people. This view formulated social medicine, the core of which maintained that resistance to disease was not purely biological but depended on class or social position.

According to Berliner and Salmon,[2] prevention of disease was possible through adjustments or changes in the social structure of society. Conditions such as higher wages, full employment, public education and public power, removal of filthy conditions and literacy help to improve the health of the nation. Today these factors are important in social medicine. The development of capitalism in Europe also saw the development of raw technical instruments for viewing bacteria. The germ theory which emerged in France and Germany during the 1870s and 1880s became the means for constructing new conceptions of disease and health conceptions that are still maintained with slight alteration today under the rubric of scientific medicine.

In essence, contagionism gave rise to medicine as viewed in capitalist countries while anticontagionism gave rise to social medicine. Since Rhodesia was a British colony, the state's views on health and medicine were based on the capitalistic structure and therefore contagionism. The beginning of health services in colonial Zimbabwe should, therefore, be seen in terms of political and economic power; and consequently, in connection with class relations. The colonisation of Zimbabwe meant emphasis on contagionism, implemented through curative medicine which dominated the whole colonial health care delivery system.

The consequences of colonial health care practice extend far beyond the physiological or biological domain, and the social relations involved in medical care reflect other aspects of capitalist economic and social structures. Thus, class divisions in society are reinforced by the social organisation of medicine[3]. The colonial health care system was shaped and moulded by the particular character of the development of capitalism in colonial Zimbabwe. The present government was to inherit this structure at the attainment of independence in 1980.

The profit-seeking activities of both doctors and drug industries, the content of medical education, the admission policies of medical schools, the control exercised by doctors in the health care delivery system, and the role of medical insurance groups in the organisation of post-colonial health care—all place serious limitations on the desirable transformation of the health care delivery system. The inaccessibility of health care to the majority of people is yet another limitation on this struggle. Yet, despite these structural limitations of the inherited colonial health care, independent Zimbabwe has had some notable successes in this sector. Among these are the advances towards the equitable distribution of health resources, efforts at the redefinition of Zimbabwe's health needs, attempts to use appropriate technology and, more importantly, the quite impressive programme of involving the masses in the identification and prevention of diseases as well as in public health education.

Health Services in Colonial Zimbabwe

With the inception of colonialism in Zimbabwe, the distribution of health resources followed the pattern of white settlement. These were also the areas of concentration of capital, mainly the cities. Accordingly, the first doctors were attached to the British South Africa Company. In some cases, the doctor was also an explorer and above all an agent of colonialism. As Leeson has pointed out,[4] the company (and later colonial government) doctor had as his first concern the health of his fellow expatriates and as his second that of local employees. Public health preventive measures had to be extended to the local people around European settlements for fear of the spread of the disease to the colonial agents.

To the extent that colonial medicine was part of a colonial system that sought raw materials, it was entirely subject to the imperative of the primary accumulation of capital. As the expanded reproduction of capital and its labour force became more important when manifested as farms, mines and factories, colonial medicine also spread in these areas of exploitation.

The colonial hospital was built in the first place to meet the needs of colonial administrators and their families and other Europeans resident in the colony.[5]

Webster, a former Permanent Secretary of Health in the Rhodesian colonial regime, pointed out that whenever there was any outbreak of disease, it was the European community that received attention first. When, for example, in 1923, malaria broke out in European farms and mines, a medical officer was detached from headquarters to tour European areas to educate the farmers and miners in the prevention of malaria.[6] Gelfand points out that the colonial administration did not regard the care of the general population as its responsibility and it took little note of the mass of the African population.[7] Van Onselen has also concluded that the role of colonial medicine was aimed at protecting the colonial agents (Europeans).[8]

In addition to the health services provided by the colonial administration and mining industry, there were also those provided by the church. The missionaries were generally placed away from the cities and tended to concentrate on the rural residents. In rural areas, there is no doubt that the missionaries provided better health care than the state and industry combined. However, some missionaries were both doctors and explorers, such as Dr. David Livingstone, and their roles were inseparable from those of the colonial agent.

Missionary medical care, like religion, appears to have played an important role in pacifying the Africans. It denigrated local traditional beliefs and substituted Christian teaching and Western medical care. Medical care was provided at the mission centre, open to those who had been converted to Christianity. Traditional methods of healing, such as traditional medicine and herbal treatment, were viewed in negative terms and thus discouraged.

As stated before, Church and state values were inseparable. Van Onselen, for example, observed that many missionaries—primarily Anglicans, Methodists and Catholics—articulated an ideology compatible with that of the mining industry and state. He states that in 1901 the Jesuit priest from Chishawasha Mission wrote to the administrator approving of a system of forced labour, under police supervision.[9]

One Catholic missionary wrote:

It seems that the only way of doing anything at all with these natives is to starve them, destroy their lands and kill all that can be killed.[10]

The Church was therefore supportive of, if not part of, the colonialist state. To the extent that they discouraged traditional medicine, the missionaries also contributed to the break-down of the Africans' social organisation, particularly their ability to manipulate and relate to their environment.

In all three areas—i.e. those of administration, mines/industries and missionaries—of health provision, medicine was administered by European physicians who were trained in Europe. Determined and designed in Europe where emphasis was on the germ theory, the medical system reflected the interests of the rulers rather than the ruled.

Because the European physicians controlled the medical system in the colonies, the health care system emphasised the curative approach dominant in Europe (where they trained and practised before going to the colonies). Thus the health care delivery system was controlled by a small group of people who were also in control of wealth (income and property) and the state. This group determined the pattern of investment, production and consumption.

The health care provided to a wage-earning population was concentrated around capital, and the emphasis on cure for increased profit and productivity's sake marked the beginning of unequal distribution of health resources: between urban and rural areas; between industrial estates and villages; and between racial and socio-economic neighbourhoods within the urban areas. The central point of these inequalities and contradictions was the existence and location of capital. The present health care system is therefore built on this background. Any genuine structural and fundamental changes of the health care paradigm will have to be considered in the context of the overall transformation of the political and socio-economic structures that Zimbabwe inherited in 1980.

The class and racial structure of society was replicated in the health care delivery system which was in the main controlled by the state. During the colonial era, there were four different providers of health services; namely the central government through the Ministry of Health, voluntary associations which consisted primarily of Christian church organisations aided by the state through grants, industrial medical services and, finally, the private sector which included private practitioners.

Health services, like many other services before independence, were racially separated between European (white) and African (black). Gilmurray and colleagues showed that Europeans had access to a wider range of health facilities. They state that:

> The racial breakdown of general hospital beds gives one bed for every 219 Europeans and one bed for every 525 Africans. In general each racial group has its own hospitals and clinics although some specialist services in the central hospitals may be used by all races. With the exception of Harare and Mpilo

Hospitals (African Hospitals) it can be said that European hospitals especially since the building of Andrew Flemming Hospital (European) in Salisbury, are far better equipped with trained personnel and modern technology than African hospitals.[11]

African hospitals also tended to be more overcrowded than European hospitals. Because of better health facilities, higher standard of living and higher incomes, Europeans experienced better health than Africans. For example, the infant mortality rate for Africans in colonial Zimbabwe was thought to be between 120 and 220 per thousand, while the infant mortality rate for the European population was 17 per thousand.[12]

The comparative life expectancies of the races (1970-1975) are given in Table 1.

TABLE 1
LIFE EXPECTANCIES

African Male	49.8
European Male	66.9
African Female	53.3
European Female	74.0

Source: *United Nations Demographic Year Book 1977*, p.396 [13]

Disease patterns also differed by race. The disease patterns for Europeans reflected their high standard of living. These diseases were mainly heart and cerebrovascular diseases and various types of cancer. Table 2 indicates the pattern of disease among races.

According to this table, diarrheal diseases were the second largest killer (next to pneumonia) among Africans. Diarrheal diseases are faecally transmitted and waterborne diseases. This suggests the extent to which sanitation and clean water supply were unavailable to many Africans. Nutritional deficiency still accounted for a large number of deaths. This was likely to be worse in the rural areas, in the absence of proper records and statistics.

TABLE 2
PATTERN OF DISEASES AMONG THE RACES

	AFRICAN		EUROPEAN	
Cause of death	Male	Female	Male	Female
Pneumonia	840	662	35	30
Enteritis/Diarrheal	487	342	3	2
Malignant Neoplasm	375	116	54	51
Measles	373	329	-	-
Nutritional Deficiencies	325	265	-	-
Heart Disease	256	185	39	40
Anoxic Conditions	232	188	5	5
T.B.	226	81	-	-
Tetanus	206	150	-	-

Source: *Report of the Secretary of Health for the Year Ended 31st December, 1978, Zimbabwe-Rhodesia* Comd RZR 12-1979.[14]

The other aspect of racial discrimination in health care relates to the distribution of health resources, such as doctors, nurses and hospitals.

Pugh argued that the rural population had only one doctor for every 100,000 people (mostly African). The African doctors, who in 1979 numbered only 58, served mainly in the African hospitals in the urban areas.[15]

The racial differentiation was also found in the control of health resources and salaries within the health care delivery system. In 1979, of the 14,500 health sector employees, 10,200 (70%) were Africans and 4,300 (30%) were Europeans. Yet the African employees received only 40% of the total wage bill. Average African wages in 1977 were $99 a month, compared with $365 for Europeans.[16] This distribution of income along racial and class lines was certainly consistent with other sectors of the economy.

The Ministry of Health, like any other ministry before independence, was controlled by Europeans and by white males in particular. The white males were numerically the least in the health sector but they controlled the whole system in terms of formulating and implementing policies. The majority of employees in the health service were blacks who tended to fill the lowest-paid and least-skilled job categories. In 1969 there were 4,538 black males, 2,715 black females, 1,083 white males and 2,624 white females employed by the Ministry of Health.[17] The Europeans were therefore not only the controllers of health services but also the largest consumers of health care resources, in both the public and private sectors. The distribution and consumption of health resources reflected not only racial lines but also class differentiation, with the poorest persons and blacks consuming about 1/45 of the amount spent by Europeans and upper socio-economic classes. The ruling class was in control of the state and set up the pattern of production and consumption of health services. Its standards of health were modelled on standards existing in Europe and America. This racial segmentation overlapped with class-based distinctions, resulting in high-quality care for European settlers and officials; poor to moderate care for African urban workers; and rudimentary to non-existent care for the peasant masses in the countryside.

As stated before, the concentration of capital in one place determined differentiation in the provision of health services between cities and rural areas. This becomes clear when one examines the provision of hospitals, doctors, nurses and pharmacies. The central, general and district hospitals were usually placed in the urban areas. These hospitals were staffed with trained personnel and equipped with sophisticated Western technology. The rural areas were served by a few mission hospitals and clinics. The former Secretary for Health in Rhodesia, Mark Webster (1963-74), pointed out that at least 90% of the cost of medical services was related to the cost of running hospitals and clinics[18]. Most of these city hospitals had an emphasis on hospital-based and technologically-oriented medicine, especially industrial and acute episodic care. By contrast, the rural residents managed with very little health care.

The best-equipped hospitals were situated in Harare and Bulawayo. With a total African population of 410,000 in 1976, Bulawayo was served by one general hospital. The European population of 69,000 was served by three general hospitals.[19]

Thus, hospital distribution did not follow the needs and population distribution in these two cities. This pattern of distribution of hospitals and clinics was similar throughout the country. The largest concentration of government-employed doctors, private practitioners and specialist services was in Harare, the capital. The urban Africans were relatively better off than the rural Africans, both in the provision and consumption of health resources. According to this view, the poorest people who needed health services most were least served by the central government.

This maldistribution of resources in the health sector was largely consistent with the pattern of distribution of political and economic power in society, that is, the issue of who controls the means of production and reproduction.

In the tertiary sector, Europeans influenced the distribution of resources in the health sector by:

(a) expounding the 'market model' system of allocating resources, whereby resources were distributed according to consuming rather than producing power, i.e. urban-based consumer power;

(b) influencing the means of reproduction, that is, medical education;

(c) controlling the social content and nature of the medical profession, as a result of the unavailability and inaccessiblity of university education to the majority of the population.[20] This class which controlled resources had similar counterparts in Europe.

The health services as described above reflected a pattern in developed capitalist countries where health care is highly oriented towards:

(a) specialised hospital-based medicine as opposed to community medicine where a majority of people reside;

(b) urban, technologically intensive medicine in contrast to rural, labour-intensive medicine;

(c) curative medicine as different from preventive medicine;

(d) personal health services as opposed to environmental health services.

Health care was therefore not accessible to the majority of people, particularly those in the rural areas. No health infrastructure was created to improve the health of the rural residents. No clean water was supplied, no sanitary improvements were made and no direct communications were established with urban-based curative medicine. Further, even if roads were constructed, there was a long distance to travel to hospital, the cost of which could not be met by the poor residents. The only alternative form of medicine available to them was traditional medicine.

The major part of the curative services was concentrated in the urban areas, whose total population in 1976 was 1,264,000 or 19.4% of the total population. The urban male population was 503,112 while the urban female population amounted to 353,799.[21] To this extent, health services could be considered to be distributed in favour of the males, urban population and curative services.

Imbalances in consumption by the type of health care was also apparent in the distribution of, and expenditure on, health manpower. Physicians were distributed in favour of the hospitals, which were curative in orientation. Staff salaries accounted for 66.67% of hospital expenditure.[22] It seems that most of the salary expenditure went to physicians. The high earnings of physicians could be associated, to some degree, with the fact that they possessed skills that were marketable in the developed countries from which they were recruited and on which training was based.

In analysing the type of morbidity prevalent in the population (i.e. infections, diseases and malnutrition) and the comparative effectiveness of the different health activities in combating this morbidity, it would seem that environmental services and preventive personal health services should have been given far higher priority than curative services, particularly hospital services. Navarro warned that, despite this imbalance of health services between curative and preventive services, the production of human resources, through the medical education imported from developed societies, serves to perpetuated this hospital-oriented, curative medicine approach which only strengthens the maldistribution of health resources prevalent in developed societies.[23] Ten percent of the health budget was allocated to preventive services. In 1976-77 of the $3,122,308 allocated for preventive services, $1,374,600 was spent on salaries, wages and allowances of staff, the rest was spent on subsistence of staff, transport, equipment and grants. Field operations received only $517,231, which covered a rural population of approximately five million.[24]

The preventive health services were administratively divided into five provinces, each having its own health team headed by the Provincial Medical Officer of Health (PMOH), who was always a medical doctor. The team also included health inspectors, public health nurses and health assistants. In essence, it was staffed by a limited range of health professionals.

The main functions of PMOH were environmental health, epidemic and endemic disease control, special services such as tuberculosis and leprosy, health promotive services and school health.[25] Looking at the functioning of this small section of the Health Department, it was almost impossible for the staff to cover the whole country—especially the interior—where there was no means of communication. Because of this limited communication, the main task for preventive health services had been handed over to rural council authorities and their medical assistants manning the rural clinics.

These rural clinics were staffed inadequately. Because preventive services were administered through rural clinics, which were in essence curative, they were not directed at genuinely combating environmental health problems. The pattern of distribution of resources by type of care is well described by David Morley, who states:

> Three-quarters of our population are rural yet three-quarters of our medical resources are spent in the towns, where three-quarters of our doctors live. Three-quarters of the people died from diseases which could be prevented at low cost and yet three-quarters of medical budgets are spent on curative services.[26].

Public health was, therefore, given minimal attention and in a country with over 50% of the African population under the age of 15 years, over 20% under the age of five years, and with a type of morbidity caused by environmental and nutritional deficiencies, there was an under-supply of resources to cover this sector.

To the extent that owners and controllers of health resources did not allocate enough money to the rural areas where they did not live, and to the extent that some health problems were humanly created, public health problems were political. They were political because the people who lived in these poor areas and suffered from these diseases lacked power and control over economic, political and social institutions in the country.

The Struggle for Health in The Post-Colonial Period

On achieving independence in 1980, the new government realised that health care was not adequately and equitably distributed to all sections of the society. As the foregoing has illustrated, the problem was not only unequal access to health care and medicine but also that the poor could not afford good health and were worse off than any other social group in society. There was maldistribution of health resources and the quality of health differed according to race, region and social class. Most of the peasants in the most remote parts of the country, such as Binga, and the commercial farm workers and low-income urban workers had poor health, low life expectancy, many suffered from both malnutrition and a number of diseases that could be prevented.

> Infants born in town stand a better chance of living through childhood than rural infants. Of every 1000 babies born in Muakose high density suburb, 21 will die before they are one year old, but in remote Binga District, the infant mortality is 300 for every thousand babies born.[27]

The structure of health care was therefore biased in favour of certain groups such as Europeans who were in control of the health services.

The former Minister of Health, Dr. H. Ushewokunze, in an address to the House of Assembly on 20 October 1980, pointed out that to meet the health needs of the masses, he had to:

> ...utilise a Health structure inherited from the past and potentially hostile to change: a structure that was never designed to

meet the needs of the majority of the people whom I represent. This structure must, therefore, be changed or I will not be fulfilling my responsibilities to our people. Therefore, when I am accused of destroying the health services of this country I shall henceforth take it as a compliment, as the destruction of a discriminatory, archaic and undeniably imbalanced service would be an act of great service to the people of Zimbabwe.[28]

Based on this understanding of the nature of the problem with health services, the Ministry of Health adopted a policy of 'Equity in Health' which indicated a radical departure from the previous sytem. The Ministry decided to shift resources form urban to rural, and from curative services to preventive services. The appropriation account of the Ministry indicates such a shift.

TABLE 3
APPROPRIATION ACCOUNT

	1980-81	1981-82	1982-83
Medical Care Services	74,906,000	95,802,00	107,290,000
Preventive Services	5,598,000	8,442,000	17,337,546

Sources: Secretary for Health Report 1982, 1983, p.47 and 19[29] *Rebuilding Zimbabwe at 5 years of Independence,* p. 218[30]

As can be seen from these figures, the amount of money allocated for expenditure on preventive services doubled from 1981-82 to 1982-83 financial years, while expenditure on medical services increased by $12 million. The activities in the preventive services have been directed towards the prevention of ill health primarily in the rural areas where the health of the people has been a cause for concern. This was found necessary since 90% of the causes of diseases were preventable.

Despite this radical shift of resources into the preventive services, more money is still spent on curative services. This trend may be due to attempts to maintain existing services in the curative services. Most of the expenditure on both curative and preventive services was on salaries, wages and allowances, subsistence and transport, incidental expenses, supplies and services, grants to local authorities, payment for government responsibility patients, payments to non-government institutions, furniture and equipment, buildings and field operations.

On the curative services, a far greater amount is spent on central hospitals which serve less than 15 percent of the total population.[31] In an attempt to decentralise health services, the Ministry of Health adopted a primary health care approach which envisaged the establishment of a rural health centre no further than eight kilometres from each person. This scheme has resulted in the building of 163 new health centres. The existing 450 primary care clinics, which were essentially curative outpatient stations doing no preventive or outreach work, are being upgraded to function as health centres. The new Rural Health Centre provides basic but comprehensive preventive, promotive, curative and rehabilitative care. It concentrates on the following areas:

(a) mother and child care services including ante-natal care, delivery of uncomplicated births, family planning, child health and nutrition, routine immunisations for children and anti-tetanus immunisations for women of child-bearing age;
(b) environmental sanitation, especially in relation to small-scale water supplies and excreta disposal systems;
(c) control of communicable diseases, including malaria, bilharzia, tuberculosis, leprosy, trachoma and venereal diseases;
(d) other special problems including eye diseases, physical and mental handicap;
(e) general curative care, including basic dentistry.

Health and nutrition education form a routine part of all the above activities.[32]

The distribution of health resources has met with problems of insufficient funds and medical staff to man these centres. This has been more common in the most remote parts of the country, where nursing staff and drugs have been difficult to place and obtain.

Although the government has been successful in distributing health resources, it has experienced difficulties in the equitable distribution of medical doctors, particularly in the rural areas. One of the reasons for this difficulty has been the outflow of doctors from the public service to private practice where they earn much more money. The number of doctors employed by the Ministry of Health increased from 239 in 1980 to 371 in 1984. Medical practitioners registered by the Medical Council as at 31 December 1982 were 1,511.[33] It would therefore appear that more than three-quarters of those registered by the Council are private practitioners. These private practitioners are stationed in places where there is a high turnover of capital, particularly in the big cities.

These private practitioners and specialists are distributed in accordance with a health care that is highly oriented towards:

(a) specialised, hospital medicine as opposed to community medicine where the majority of the people live;
(b) urban, technologically-intensive medicine in contrast to rural, labour-intensive medicine;
(c) curative medicine as different from preventive medicine;
(d) personal health services as opposed to environmental health services.

The trend among the medical practitioners in post-colonial Zimbabwe is the same as that in a capitalist country, described earlier in this chapter. This indicates that the structure and basis of the present health care delivery system are still capitalist in orientation. The system still needs critical evaluation and structural change if it is to serve the needs of the majority of the people.

It should be mentioned that private practitioners are the hardest nuts to crack in the health sector when any reorganisation or restructuring is contemplated. The present Minister of Health, Dr. Sydney Sekeramayi, in an address to the annual meeting of provincial medical doctors and medical superintendents at Parirenyatwa Hospital, Harare, accused some private practitioners of overtly sabotaging government medical services and of the tendency to abuse public health facilities.[34] Private practitioners cannot be considered as allies in the restructuring of health services. They are likely to lose when such changes occur. They are likely, therefore, to frustrate or obstruct and make difficult the implementation of health policies which are designed to benefit the majority of the people.

While there is an element of efficiency among private doctors, there have been reports which indicate that private doctors do not give adequate services to their patients. This may be a small number of doctors who are involved in such a practice and blame should not be given to those who are very honest and professional. However, as Dr. Pram Manga points out from his study, there are some private general practitioners who have a large black clientele and who rather frequently either inject patients with water (sometimes dipped in methylated spirit to produce a sting) or vitamins, or prescribe drugs which a growing number of doctors sell directly to patients, or have patient referrals unnecessarily.[35]

This has two obvious economic consequences. Firstly, it entails an unnecessary transfer of income from patients to doctors; and secondly from the social point of view, it is an inefficient use of scarce resources. Further, Manga has observed that even the executive of the National Medical Aid Societies (NAMAS) admit that the fee-for-service method of payment for private doctors results in unnecessary patient revisits, hospitalisation, surgical intervention, higher lengths of stay in hospital and nursing homes, greater demand by doctors for diagnostic and laboratory procedures, and so on. Such results of fee-for-service occur not only in Zimbabwe but also in capitalist countries such as the USA.[36] Capital generates certain behaviour patterns on the part of doctors which are in conflict with their professional norms and practices. In some cases, doctors do not provide such health information and education as would cause patients to adopt a more rational and realistic expectation of the health care system.

This imbalance in the distribution of medical doctors was a great concern of the former Minister of Health, Dr. Ushewokunze. In September 1981, he stated that nearly four-fifths of these private practitioners were located in Harare and Bulawayo, thereby contributing significantly to the over-concentration of doctors in the main towns. The same principle applies to private specialists, nine percent of whom were in the two main cities, Harare and Bulawayo.[37] This pattern of distribution of medical doctors does indicate that the urban population is relatively better off than the rural peasants, in both the provision and consumption of health resources. The poorest people who need health services are still the least served. Thus the ideology and organisation of health care reinforce existing relations between classes and between urban and rural areas, thus reinforcing the capitalist system.

Medical aid societies and medical insurance constitute another form in which capital plays a role in the consumption of health services. In a majority of cases, medical insurance is bought by urban-based, middle or higher income workers. The low income workers, the unemployed and the peasants hardly enjoy such privileges while they are indeed already the worst deprived in terms of the health services. This subsector of health receives government subsidies in that the contributions to the medical aid societies are abatable under the Income Tax Act. The employer's contribution to Medical Aid Societies on behalf of employees is not subject to income tax.

The abatement or tax credit is in essence a 'tax expenditure' designed to lower the income tax liability of those who are rich enough to buy private insurance. Presently, employer contributions are a deduction against corporate earnings and as such constitute a heavy subsidy to the purchase of private insurance. What is most peculiar in Zimbabwe is that the purchase of private health insurance results in the erosion of both corporate and personal income tax. Besides, all the medical aid contributions, which are income to someone or some company, escape taxation.[38]

At present, health care expenditure on specific services in excess of $72 is subject to income tax abatement. Although there are many who would be entitled to this abatement, quite a large number of people are not aware of this and do not show proof of it by way of receipts. Many doctors do not issue receipts particularly to the illiterate and to the low income workers; and it is also a practice which allows them not to declare a very significant and growing proportion of their earnings for income tax purposes. Manga points out that there is a double inequity here, the evasion of income tax by rich doctors and the denial of abatements to their sick and most deserving patients. The government also subsidises private patients of private doctors who have to use government hospitals where sophisticated equipment is available.

While he was the Minister of Health, Dr. Ushewokunze also identified the problem of subsidising the private patients. He stated that:

> the beneficiaries of medical aid society schemes receive health care to an average annual value of $145 per head...the average annual health expenditure in our rural areas is a mere $3 per head annually. In some 13 districts that figure is less than $2 and in the least served district it is the outrageously low figure of 50 cents per head per annum. This means that the three percent of the population who participate in private medical insurance—and who already enjoy the best health in the country benefit from nearly 300 times the health expenditure of the two per cent of our people who live in that last district and who suffer grave ill-health.[39]

He also argued that private medicine is a luxury and should therefore not be tax-deductible and be subject to sales tax. All in all, a policy of treating private medical care as a luxury service, and removing all direct and indirect government subsidies, would raise nearly $17 million a year in revenue for the Treasury.[40] From the above account, it is quite clear that the private medical sector is subsidised by the government. This population which is thus subsidised is small and able to meet the full cost of health care. Subsidisation therefore is biased in favour of the urban wage-earner, rich people, the doctors and the elites. To the extent that it favours certain people in our society, it is political. It is my view that it is only political action which can remove those anomalies and the inequitable distribution of health resources. As long as there is this element of subsidisation of the well-to-do by the government, it would be difficult to talk of equity in health. Besides it is such a formidable task that it cannot be achieved by the Ministry of Health alone. It can be argued that any changes towards equity cannot occur without a challenge to the current political and economic structures that ensure control of resources by a few in society. King and Navarro showed in their studies of Cuba that an egalitarian society is required in order to achieve an equitable distribution of human health resources.[41] Horn also came to similar conclusions after his long period of work as a surgeon in China.[42] These studies have relevance to Zimbabwe, which has made tremendous effort in transforming our society. Political independence has not yet resulted in economic independence which will enable the state to direct resources where they are desirable.

Drugs form a third component of health care within the private medical sector. The nature and type of drugs, and the influence of their manufacturers, need a little examination.

Although the Ministry of Health has taken precautionary measures to ensure that only the right type of drugs appear on our shelves and are used by doctors, it is necessary to discuss briefly the politics of drug manufacturers experienced in other countries.

(a) One of the problems experienced by Third World countries is that they are often the recipients of drugs that would otherwise be rejected in the developed countries that manufacture them for export to developing countries. Such drugs have been known to have harmful effects on human beings. Currently, in Zimbabwe, the anti-depressant drug, Merital, which is registered with the Drugs Control Council, was reported[43] to have been found in other countries to cause serious adverse reactions not common with other anti-depressants. Some of the most common side-effects are fever, muscle and joint pains (a flu-like syndrome), and the reactions are not subject to dosage. Hoechst Zimbabwe is the company which manufactures the drug here and its parent company is based in Frankfurt in West Germany.

(b) To maintain and strengthen their role, the drug companies merge with other companies. This contributes to market concentration. The largest pharmaceutical firms have expanded their operations into the entire range of fields in the health care market, then into other areas such as prepared foodstuffs, animal health care, chemicals, confections, toiletries, household products and cosmetics.

(c) Drugs and mild foods are pushed through health professionals. The marketing prices are aimed at influencing individual physicians and the medical professionals to prescribe as many of the given brand-name drugs as possible, regardless of potential danger. They are therefore capable of collaborating with indigenous institutions and leading figures in society in order to get their drugs sold. Through patents, the state protects and supports monopolies of industry from which the owners benefit more than the consumers.

(d) The multinational pharmaceutical industries have a primary purpose of making a profit and do not serve the real needs of the majority of the population. It is to the advantage of drug companies if health services remain oriented toward a curative approach, and they direct their entire advertising effort to the promotion of products used for curative medicine.

Conscious of these facts, the Ministry of Health appointed at independence, an expert National Drugs and Therapeutics Policy Committee (NDTPC) which established the pharmaceutical policy of the country. The committee came up with a list they call PEDLIZ (Proposed Essential Drugs List of Zimbabwe). There is now an established Essential Drug List of Zimbabwe (EDLIZ). This list includes guidelines for treatment of medical conditions common in Zimbabwe. It also ensures quality control, efficiency and safety at all times. But close monitoring of drug companies is absolutely essential as their aim is more to make a profit than to improve the health of the people.

Strategies for a New Health Care Paradigm
On achieving independence, and having realised the inequities in the health care delivery system inherited from the colonial regime, the government sought to bring about the necessary changes which would suit the new social order.

The strategies proposed and implemented by government were based on two principles: one being that health was considered as a fundamental right; and the other that the achievement of good health care depended, amongst other things, on community involvement based on self-reliance.[44] The government also demonstrated the correlation between economic development and standards of living on the one hand, and such indices of health as life expectancy and infant mortality on the other. This grew out of the realisation that public health programmes are not only technical but, more importantly, political, and thus most of the solutions are political in that they require the mobilisation of the masses for successful implementation. The following are some of the strategies.

Preventive measures of public health
Preventive measures are based on the following assumptions:-

(a) Preventive services are redistributive in that they attempt to minimise the striking inequalities in the availability and consumption of health resources that previously existed between social classes, cities and regions. This is achieved through an increase in the use and production of paramedical and auxiliary personnel within the preventive care system and through a greater priority given to the rural and poor areas which hitherto have been neglected. Health education is redistributive in the same sense that knowledge about basic elements of good health is made available to all people and is not a monopoly of professionals.

(b) It is cheaper than hospital-based curative service, which caters only for a small minority of the total population with access to it. Because it has the potential of involving all the citizens in identifying a health problem and implementing its solution, it does not employ expensive, sophisticated technology and professionals. The provision of a clean water supply and improving sanitation, for example, can be done by local people themselves in self-reliant programmes with minimum expense for the government. To the extent that preventive measures are able to reduce the incidence of disease, thereby reducing the number of people needing treatment in a hospital, they are cheaper in the long run.

(c) Specific medical measures and the expansion of medical services have little effect on the overall health of the population.[45] There is abundant evidence from other countries that medical care has not dramatically improved the health of any population. This is especially so in diseases that have strong social and political determinants. In an endeavour to improve the health status of the population, it would therefore be important and correct to emphasise social, economic and political solutions.

(d) Finally, preventive care should be considered important for reasons of social justice: it is just and fair that all citizens receive the benefits of development and independence and the benefits be fairly distributed. Prevention is a logical consequence of the ethical goal of minimising the number of persons suffering death and disability. The only known way to minimise these adverse events is to prevent the occurrence of damaging exchanges or exposures in the first place, or seek to minimise damage when exposure cannot be controlled.[46]

The Ministry of Health is trying to implement these preventive measures through improvement in sanitation, provision of clean water supply, nutrition, eradication of poverty and control of infectious diseases; as well as in personal and cultural patterns of behaviour that might inhibit successful prevention measures.

Combining Traditional and Scientific Medicine
The second strategy adopted by the Ministry of Health is the combination

of traditional and scientific medicine. Traditional medicine refers to the indigenous system of medicine while scientific medicine refers to medicine developed within the developed countries. The need to combine both the scientific and traditional medicine emanates from two assumptions:

> (a) Some traditional medicine is effective and some is not. This is equally true of Western medicines. A combination of all the medicine that works may be a good and positive step towards formulating a new health care paradigm.
> (b) About 80% of our population still use traditional medicine outside the health sector.

The use of traditional medicine is part and parcel of their culture and the sooner those medicines that do not work are exposed, the better. In some other countries, such as China, unity of the two was implemented politically, organisationally, educationally and scientifically.

Horn states that politically, it expressed itself in a campaign to unite all medical workers in a common desire to serve the people and to contribute to China's socialist construction. Organisationally, it expressed itself in concern for the rights and status of traditional doctors. Educationally, the policy expressed itself by including courses on traditional medicine in the curriculum for medical students of the modern school, and by ensuring that their internship included practical work under experienced traditional doctors. Scientifically, the policy expressed itself in research work along two main lines. One was to analyse and test the efficiency of traditional methods, including acupuncture. The other was to conduct clinical research into methods of blending traditional and modern medicine so as to be superior to either.[47] There were determined efforts—particularly through the leadership of the first Minister of Health in independent Zimbabwe—to implement lessons from these and other progressive countries. But the problems that were subsequently to impede progress in this sector were not inherently different from those that would in general hamper the new government's ambition to transform society.

Planning for Health Care

The third strategy is to plan for health care. In order to restructure the inherited health care delivery system to suit the needs of the majority of the people, there is a need first to set priorities in terms of immediate needs and demands; second, to make maximum use of the present health resources, particularly for those in greatest need; third, to formulate future goals and strategies. Considering the type of health problems where malnutrition and infectious diseases are the main causes of mortality, the best way to combat these problems is to emphasise the health patterns that are almost opposite to those of the colonial system. Essentially, this would mean putting emphasis on rural-labour, intensive and community-oriented medicine, and giving higher priority to the preventive and environmental health services rather than to personal and curative services.

There are many techniques designed for optimum utilisation of available resources, such as rational planning, cost-benefit analysis and emphasis on primary health care. Cost-benefit analysis has been directed at selective attack on the most severe public health problems, preventing or treating those few diseases which are responsible for the greater mortality in less developed areas and for which intervention of proven efficacy exists. Diseases such as diarrhoea have been tackled through the assistance of UNICEF, through the administration of Oral Rehydration Therapy (ORT). But they have not been completely overcome. Diarrhoea is still the worst killer disease, as has been the case since before independence.

Primary Health Care

The primary health care programme was launched in 1982 and centred on the training of village health workers chosen from their respective communities. They are trained in basic preventive, promotive, curative and rehabilitative interventions targeted mostly at the rural areas. The Ministry aims to produce one village health worker for every 500 to 1,000 population. Up to 1984, only 3,800 village health workers had been trained. They are appointed from among the rural community members; and are therefore familiar with the language and customs, rendering them easily accessible to the peasants. To this extent, health services have been decentralised and democratised in quite a significant measure. Part of the role of village health workers is to encourage rural communities to be self-reliant in the construction of toilets, wells, and promotion of basic hygienic standards. Where necessary, they encourage the peasants to mould bricks and provide their own labour when a clinic is to be constructed. The majority of peasants have responded favourably, as they see they are to benefit from such a service, which was not available before independence. Since independence, and through the instrumentality of village health workers, 40,212 VIP Blair toilets have been constructed. Also, 10,370 protected wells have been constructed throughout the country. Such achievements have contributed to the fall in the infant mortality rate from 120 to 60 per thousand live births. Village health workers who promote primary health care are part-time workers paid less than the minimum wage.

In analysing this programme, there are two views which are contradictory. One is that the programme is extremely good in that it decentralises health services and is accessible and cheap to run, considering the limited resources. The other view highlights contradictions within the system. First, considering that the government had identified rural communities as the most neglected, how can these disadvantaged communities be allocated fewer resources than those allocated to the smaller and urban-based population? The staff who promote health care receive minimum training with little education and are part-time. This view questions the seriousness of the programme, considering that urban wage-earners receive better health services which are fully staffed, with qualified personnel on full-time covering a quarter of the whole population.

Second, the poorest of the poor are among the peasants in the rural areas. They have little education, poor social and economic services, high infant mortality rates, low life expectation and all that goes with poverty. How can such people be asked to contribute to the construction of toilets, clean water supplies and clinics when they are the ones who can least afford it? This is exacerbated by the fact that the urban wage-earners are subsidised by government to a large extent. They do not contribute either in cash or through their voluntary labour to build a clinic or a dam which will provide a clean water supply to urban residents. Such contradictions are not only found in health but also in many other services such as education, housing, etc. Although they are difficult to resolve at this stage, consideration and attention ought to be given to these contradictions, which will form the basis for structural change in our society.

A further concern associated with primary health care is the role played by non-government organisations. On the whole, they have done tremendous and commendable work in providing resources which the government was unable to provide. This is particularly so in their assistance in the construction of toilets, digging of boreholes and provision of grants to initiate such projects as poultry-farms, piggeries, etc., all of which improve the diet of the people and their quality of life. However, some of the non-government organisations have questionable motives. My own experience is testimony that organisations deny services to some peasants on political and social grounds. In Binga, for example, one organisation could not offer assistance to people who were not Christians.

Furthermore, certain non-government organisations operate only in chosen regions or provinces. Others decide at will, and quite independently, where to operate. As a result, one finds that there may be several non-government organisations operating in one district while there are none in the neighbouring district. Of course, leading local figures of such areas are not without blame. But all these anomalies result in an inequitable distribution of resources in society. It is not difficult to imagine how a non-government organisation might have undue influence on local leadership.

Whatever the case, there is need for constant review and observation of the intentions and performances of the non-government organisations, not only within the health care sector but in other social services as well.

Foreign aid, as is well known, is not neutral in the promotion of social services. It is therefore likely to influence national and local factors in the interesst of the donor agency and/or country offering aid.

Conclusion

We conclude, therefore, within a few recommendations which, if considered, may improve the sector and contribute towards progressive social development.

(a) The private medical sector should not receive direct or indirect subsidies from the government. This is short of abolishing private medicine.

(b) Contributions to medical aid societies by employees and corporations should not be abatable under the Income Tax Act.
(c) Savings from the above two should be directed to serve the rural areas that were neglected for a long time before independence.
(d) Urban wage earners should be made to assist more directly—contributing towards the promotion of rural development.

In essence these recommendations attempt to move away from the view that health is a commodity which is responsible for the maldistribution of health resources. If health is treated as a commodity, which is the case today, it follows the general laws of production and distribution.

The fundamental problem in health care is that it is influenced by the demands of capital. The socialist countries that have changed their health structures had to deal with this problem first. For as long as capital remains the motivating and controlling factor in the organisation of health care, it will continue to be unevenly distributed despite very genuine and meaningful reforms that may be recommended. But one cannot change the influence of capital on health without transforming the whole society. To this extent the problem of health is a manifestation of a societal problem which needs a societal solution.

REFERENCES

1. Berliner, H. and Salmon, J.W., The Holistic Alternative to Scientific Medicine: History and Analysis, *International Journal of Health Services*, Vol. 10, No. 1, 1980 pp. 136.
2. *Ibid.*, p. 136.
3. Doyal, L. and Pennell, I., *The Political Economy of Health*, Pluto Press, London, 1981, p. 293.
4. Leeson, J., Social Science and Health Policy in Pre-Industrial Society, *International Journal of Health Services*, Vol. 4, No. 3, 1974, p. 431.
5. Gish, O., The Political Economy of Primary Care and Health by the People: An Historical Exploration, *Social Science and Medicine*, Vol. 13c, 1979, p. 205.
6. Webster, M. Thither, Medicine in Rhodesia, *The Central African Journal of Medicine*, November 1973 p. 245.
7. Gelfand, M., *A Service to the Sick,* Zambeziana, Vol. 1, Mambo Press, Gweru 1976.
8. Van Onselen, C. *CHIBARO: African Mine Labour in Southern Rhodesia 1900-1933,* Pluto Press, London, 1976.
9. *Ibid.*, p. 183.
10. Callinocas, A. and Rogers, J. *Southern Africa After Soweto*, Pluto Press, London, 1978, p. 83.
11. Gilmurray, J., Riddell, R. and Sanders, D., *The Struggle for Health From Rhodesia to Zimbabwe*, Catholic Institute for International Relations, London, 1979, p. 37. See also Sachikonye, L.M., Ndovo H and Zwizwai, B., *Financing a Primary Health Care System in Zimbabwe,* paper presented to the international Workshop on Primary Health Care

in East and Southern Africa, Arusha, Tanzania, June 1984.
12. *Ibid.*
13. UN, *Demographic Year Book 1977*, p. 396.
14. *Report of the Secretary of Health for the Year Ended 31st December, 1978*, RZR 13-1979.
15. Pugh, A.O., New Patterns of African Rural Health in Rhodesia, *The Central African Journal of Medicine*, Vol. 15, No. 6, June 1969.
16. Gilmurray, et al, *op. cit.*, p. 41.
17. *Census of Population* (1969) Tables 51 and 77.
18. Webster, M., *op. cit.*, p. 50.
19. *Medicine in Society*, Vol. 18, 1978.
20. Navarro, V., *Medicine Under Capitalism*, Prodist, New York, 1977, p. 41
21. UN, *Demographic Year Book 1977*, p. 396
22. Webster, M., A Review of the Development of Health Services of Rhodesia from 1923 to Present Day, *The Central African Journal of Medicine*, Vol. 18, No. 12. 1972, p. 232.
23. Navarro, V., *op. cit.*, p. 40
24. *Report of the Secretary of Health, op. cit.*, p. 47.
25. Gilmurray et al., *op. cit.*, p. 40.
26. Morley, D., *Paediatric Priorities in the Developing World,* Butterworth, London, 1973 quoted in King M., Medicine in the Red and Blue, *Lancet* 1972, p. 679-681.
27. Sanders, D. and Waterston, T., Medical Institutions in Primary Health Care, *Social Change and Development*, No. 4, May 1983.
28. Ushewokunze, H., *An Agenda for Zimbabwe*, College Press, Harare, 1984, p. 122.
29. *Report of the Secretary for Health for the Year Ended 31st December 1982*, p. 47.
30. *Zimbabwe: At 5 Years of Independence : Achievements, Problems and Prospects*, ZANU (PF) Dept. of Commissariat and Culture, Mardon Printers, Harare, 1985, p. 218.
31. Ushewokunze, H., *op. cit.*, p. 158.
32. *Zimbabwe : At 5 Years of Independence, op. cit.*, p. 193.
33. *Report of the Secretary for Health 1982, op. cit.*, p. 42.
34. *Zimbabwe Chronicle*, Bulawayo, 13 December 1985.
35. Manga, P., *An Urgent Case for the Removal of the Tax and Price Subsidization of the Private Medical Sub-section in Zimbabwe*, 23 March 1982 p. 14. An unpublished paper presented at a Seminar at the Ministry of Finance, Economic Planning and Development.
36. Agere, S., Health Care Delivery System in the United States : Lessons for Africa, *International Social Work*, XXIII, No. 1, 1980, p. 4.
37. Ushewokunze, H., *op. cit.*, p. 156.
38. Manga, P. *op. cit.*, p. 3.
39. Ushewokunze, H., *op. cit.*, p. 155.
40. *Ibid.*, p. 159.
41. King, M., Health and the Developing World, *International Journal of Health Services* I, 4, 1971.

42. Horn, J.S., *Away with all Pests. An English Surgeon in People's China, 1954-1969*. Monthly Review Press, London, 1969, p. 77.
43. *The Sunday Mail* (Harare), 12 December 1985.
44. Speech by the Honourable Prime Minister, Cde R.G. Mugabe at the opening of the 13th Commonwealth Regional Health Ministers' Conference, Monday 11 November 1985.
45. Mckinlay, J.B., Epidemiological and Political Determinants of Social Policies Regarding the Public Health, *Social Science and Medicine*, Vol. 13A, 1979, p. 541-558.
46. Beauchamp, D., Public Health as Social Justice, *Inquiry*, Vol. XIII, March 1976.
47. Horn, J.S. *op. cit.*, p. 77.

13. THE WOMEN ISSUE
Joyce L. Kazembe

Introduction

The aim of this chapter is to give an account of the current situation of women in Zimbabwe, six years after independence. The chapter examines various aspects of their lives and by so doing tries to answer the question that has been asked so many times before: has there been any noticeable change in the status of Zimbabwean women? In most parts of the world, any positive change that has occurred in the status of women has not come about only through the goodwill of men, but has in most cases been a result of struggles by pioneering women and feminists who have fought and are still fighting to change societal attitudes. These are women who have, by fair means or foul, deemed it fit to break into fields normally seen as male preserves. Theirs is the clamour for equal rights, equal opportunities and equal responsibilites - with all that this entails.

The term 'women issue', therefore, refers briefly to the social, economic, political, cultural and legal status of women, including the problems they encounter in various spheres of life. It refers to their inferior status, real or imagined, as a result of the covert and/or overt discrimination against them, resulting in unequal opportunities for them in relation to men. The various efforts of different institutions in working towards the advancement of women is part and parcel of the 'women issue'. But unless otherwise stated, this paper deals mainly with the position of black women.

That the women issue could no longer be left to the whims of individual nations was recognised by the United Nations Organisation (UNO) which has, since its early years, passed a number of conventions specifically pertaining to women. The body realises of course that the degree of deprivation and its manifestation differs from continent to continent, from country to country, and, within a country, from one area to another. The UN efforts culminated in the body declaring 1976-85 the Decade for Women. The latest convention (1979) was the Convention on the Elimination of All Forms of Discrimination Against Women (CEDAW) which:

> reflects the depth of the exclusion and restriction practised against women, solely on the basis of their sex, by calling for equal rights for women, regardless of their marital status, in all fields - political, economic, social, cultural and civil. It calls for national legislation to ban discrimination; recommends temporary measures to speed equality in fact between men and women, and action to modify social and cultural patterns that perpetuate discrimination.[1]

Other international organisations have also come up with propositions for dealing with the problems that face women, as have various women's organisations which have throughout the decades asked themselves and society at large why women find themselves in underprivileged situtations.

Different schools of thought conceptualising on women's oppression have tried to analyse the problem by offering possible causes of this state of affairs. Some, like Mead, have argued that the whole problem lies in culture.[2] Values, norms, beliefs and practices, mostly developed and propagated by men, have discriminated against women throughout the various stages of development and evolution of the modes of production, from primitive communalism, through slavery and feudalism to capitalism. Under culture are incorporated religion and all forms of socialisation and education. Justification for the inferior status of women is often quoted from the Bible or the Koran, as if these books were dropped like manna from heaven, and are therefore not creations of man. The same can be said about educational material and other literature which have reproduced female inferior status by depicting men and women occupying certain roles that have since become stereotyped. Men are seen as the stronger outdoor type while women are portrayed as the weaker, if not delicate, species who must be protected and be left in the safe confines of the domestic environment or in occupations similar to their domestic ones.

Socialists, on the other hand, have placed all evils at the door of capitalism. Using a materialistic approach, they have argued that the oppression of women cannot be looked at as independent from the exploitative nature of the capitalist mode of production. This is just another manifestation of the confrontation between labour and capital, a ploy used by capitalists in their endeavours to control and own the means of production for the maximisation of profits. Only when the last brick of capitalism and its vestiges have been destroyed can a socialist mode of production thrive, where there is no exploitation of man by man—man being used here in the broad sense of *homo sapiens*. In short, it is argued, the oppression of women finds its demise in socialism.[3]

Radical feminists take a different stand altogether.[4] They argue that the socialist analysis ignores the fact that women, whether they are said to belong to the bourgeois, petit bourgeois, proletarian or peasant class, do not enjoy the same privileges as the men in the same class. They are discriminated against. Radical feminists contend that the patriarchal system of family organisation, which instituted and popularised the father or other male elder as the head of the family, is the root cause of female oppression. As head of the family, the man controls the economic production of the family unit, be it a nuclear or an extended one. Hence the marital power vested in the husband in most marriages and his consequent dominant role in controlling, if not owning, matrimonial property. This male control is extended to the political arena where men are the main gladiators in their endeavours to control the major means of production. Women are then left mainly in the private sphere of domestic life, while men take over the major functions of public life.

Elshtain aptly entitles her book *Public Man, Private Woman*.[5]

Whichever theoretical framework one wishes to apply to the Zimbabwean case, he/she will find enough material for the analysis. But in dealing with the problem of women's liberation in Zimbabwe, this chapter is also concerned with an assessment of the encouraging start already made in this regard by the government of Zimbabwe, in the form of new laws and the reforming of old ones with a view to changing the status of women in this country. This, of course, is generally in line with ZANU (PF)'s declared socialist policy and is also in recognition of the role played by women during the liberation struggle. But it is also a positive response to international influence on the question of women's rights and advancement.

Women in Pre-colonial and Colonial Zimbabwe

In order to appreciate any changes that have occurred since independence, it is imperative at this stage to give some background information on what the status of women was before 1980. This section, therefore, examines general aspects of pre-colonial Zimbabwe and gives details of the status of women under colonialism.

There is as yet no reliable research on the situation of women in pre-colonial Zimbabwe. Hence, it is sometimes difficult to know whether what we call customary law today is really what it was then. Any picture about the possible situation of women in pre-colonial Zimbabwe has to be drawn from the writings of foreigners, some of whom lacked insight into African traditional life, and also from unreliable oral tradition. Joan May gives a short account and analysis of the situation of women before, during and just after colonialism. This analysis more or less applies to all indigenous groups in the country, except the Tonga, in the northern part of the country, who are matrilineal.[6] The present writer has also very little information on the Tonga and so the rest of the paper will discuss the women issue as it pertains to the majority or women. This, though, does not mean that the analysis is not generally applicable to the Tonga, except, perhaps, the custom of *roora* (which is explained in the following lines).

Generally, it appears that very little value was placed on female participation outside the home in either the pre-colonial or colonial period of Zimbabwean history. Except for very few cases where women assumed influential positions, the most notable example being Nehoreka of Mtoko,[7] women were subordinate in political and social organisation. Probably the reason may be in one of the most important cornerstones of many patrilineal African societies south of the Sahara—the custom of *roora/lobola*, whose implications determined the status of both men and women, young and old, and also who should own what, when and how.

Roora was/is the transaction entered into between the members of the bride-giving family and the bride-receiving family, involving the transfer of cattle from the latter to the former, for a wife and hence establishing marriage between the spouses. Marriage became a family affair involving the elders of the two families wishing to join their children in marriage. This transaction transferred the labour services of the bride to the groom's family, who also secured her genitricial rights as well.[8] The bride became the wife of the whole lineage (husband's) because it was the responsibility of the groom's kin to supply the cattle used in the transaction. The society was an agrarian one where the addition of a woman and her progeny afforded the husband and his family a source of labour, while the wife's natal family acquired cattle which were a great measure of wealth then and could be used—were actually used—in getting a wife for the bride's brother. Because of *roora,* it was right for the husband and his family to expect total submission from the wife. The products of her labour and the children born of the union were his and his family's, as they were in the package deal of the *roora* contract.

The introduction of the cash economy as the dominant mode of production at the advent of colonialism, and its preponderance since, led to the abuse and commercialisation of the custom, which is today seen as a way of recovering costs expended on the daughters. The higher the educational qualifications of the girl, the higher the amount demanded. Early anthropologists' writings on the subject have been accused left, right and centre of distorting and misinterpreting the custom of *roora,* just as colonial white administrators in the form or 'native/district commissioners' have suffered the same fate and been accused of rigidifying what was formerly a flexible system.[9] While I do agree to a certain extent that this was the case, I nevertheless feel that there has been a lot of romanticisation about some old customs and practices that should no longer operate in present-day circumstances, however much we may wish to preserve aspects of our culture. Custom operates within a social context. What may have been an excellent custom in traditional life does not necessarily remain so in modern times.

Children, as I said before, belonged to the husband and his family. At divorce, only suckling babies were left in the custody of the mother, but only temporarily, until they could be transferred to the husband's family. During the colonial era, the custom was revised to allow children to stay with their mother until they attained the age of seven. Much later, in cases that came before higher courts, general law was applied to parties formerly married under the Marriages Act (Chapter 37), in relation to custody of children. The interests of the children became the paramount consideration. Children from unmarried mothers were also removed from the mother at seven years of age if the father had paid seduction damages and rearing fees. The mother had very little, if any, say in this. The arrangements were between the father of the child and the father (or his stand-in) of the mother, who was the guardian of both mother and child. So in both periods under discussion, women had no rights to children, nor could they assume guardianship should the husband die.

Joshua Mpofu gives two major sources of property for the Shona and Ndebele women in traditional society:

(a) the property a woman acquired as the mother of a married daughter, in the form of a cow *(mombe Umai/inkomo yohlanga)* and small livestock (goats) given when the daughter conceived for the first time; and

(b) property acquired as a result of her personal skill (pottery, mat and basket weaving, healing, midwifery, etc.), referred to as *maoko/izandla* (hands) property.[10]

This property was inherited by the women's natal family when she died. She also took it with her at divorce. Usually no one tampered with this property because of strong religious beliefs connected with it. Otherwise, every other item of matrimonial property belonged to the husband and his kin, no matter how much she had contributed towards it, just because by paying *roora* he had paid for her labour services as well. It follows that a woman with no daughter or personal skill was virtually propertyless, that is, in things that mattered—namely livestock. Moreover, the first type of property only came much later in life, when the daughter(s) were old enough to be married. This may be one reason why widows who, especially during the colonial era, did not wish to be inherited, or were rejected by the in-laws, were dispossessed of almost everything, children included (except the matri-estate).

When Zimbabwe was colonised by the British South African Company (BSAC), the charter granted to the Company by the British monarch made provision in Section 14 for the recognition of African customs and law.

> In the administration of justice to the said peoples or inhabitants, careful regard shall always be had to customs and laws of the class or tribe or nation to which the parties belong, especially with regard to the holding, possession, transfer and disposition of land and goods, testate and intestate succession thereto and marriage, divorce, legitimacy and other rights of property and personal rights, but subject to British law...[11]

As can be deduced from the above provision, property was held, disposed of, and devolved according to customary law. This provision on property appeared in Section 13 of the African Marriages Act (Chapter 238) and also applied to black parties marrying under the Marriages Act (Chapter 37), governing civil marriages.

With time, women ventured into formal and informal employment, though in smaller numbers because of various reasons, prominent among which was the bias against educating and employing women. It is interesting to note, as Childs (1976) writes, that it became acceptable as African customary law that:

> should a woman go out to work with the approval of her husband while under his marital control, any money she earned belongs to him under both Shona and Ndebele law...
> But if a Shona and Ndebele wife were allowed to keep her earnings, property acquired with her own money would be hers

and she would have control over it.[12]

One wonders whether there was any traditional basis to the first premise. Surely her earnings should fall under 'hands property', as she had used her personal skills. Strictly speaking, there would be no plausible reason why husbands should have demanded their wives' earnings. Luckily in latter years, after the Jirira v Jirira and Another, 1976 (1) RLR7, part of matrimonial property was given to the woman, especially for cases that came before the High Court. This is the first instance where the court applied what has since been referred to as the *test of life style* concept, because to apply customary law would have been repugnant to natural law, justice and morality.[13] Unfortunately, such rulings seldom applied to parties married under customary law, with or without registration under the African Marriages Act.

The question of succession was (and still remains) a thorn in the flesh to African women, long before the Africans Wills Act (Chapter 240) was passed and long afterwards. Very few Africans ever made wills (even today) and therefore many died intestate. As property devolved according to customary law, the wife normally did not inherit anything. Though the eldest son was the heir, the estate was administered by a male relative of the deceased man if the son was still a minor. This practice was probably very functional in pure traditional life, as the bereaved family was well looked after by the deceased husband's family. The wife was inherited by one of his brothers. But as happened with most customs, the practice was abused as more and more people developed greedy streaks under colonialism. It was no longer guaranteed that the family would be adequately cared for, if at all. The end result was that a good number of widows and their children were left destitute as the appointed administrators put the property to their own use, or for the benefit of their own immediate families. These widows had no option but to tend for their children, for survival. Even in cases where the husband had left a will in favour of his wife and children, there were still cases where they were dispossessed, with threats of the supernatural.

Under customary law, women had no land-use rights in their individual capacity. Land was allocated to the head (who was always a man) of the family by the chief, sub-chief or headman. He, head of the family in turn, gave portions of the land to his wife or wives for their subsistence production, while he worked (with the help of his wives) on the larger portion and claimed the produce.[14] On the death of the husband, the wife did not automatically inherit her husband's right to land-use for the same fields. The fields could be taken over by one of her male in-laws or could be reallocated by the headman in extreme cases. But generally, her access to land, should she remain with her in-laws, depended on their goodwill, which was usually the case if she towed the line. This applied to women in rural areas. The plight of women in formal employment was different.

Labour practices were governed by highly discriminatory legislation like the Industrial Conciliation Act (1934). Women faced two types

TABLE 1
FEMALE PARTICIPATION IN FORMAL SECTOR LABOUR FORCE 1975-1979 (Figures in Thousands)

	1975				1976				1977				1978				1979			
	M	F	T	F%	M	F	T	F%	M	F	T	F%	M	F	T	F%	M	F	T	F%
Agriculture	275.4	88.4	963.8	24.3	270.9	85.2	356.1	23.9	265.9	82.3	348.2	23.6	259.0	82.4	341.4	24.1	250.2	85.2	335.2	25.4
Mining	62.5	1.3	63.8	2.0	63.3	1.5	64.8	2.3	60.2	1.4	61.6	2.2	56.8	1.3	58.1	2.2	58.4	1.1	69.5	1.8
Manufacturing	144.0	12.0	156.0	7.7	142.1	11.5	153.5	7.5	133.9	11.2	145.1	7.7	128.3	11.0	139.3	7.9	133.5	11.2	144.7	7.7
Electricity	6.7	0.2	6.9	2.9	6.5	0.2	6.7	3.0	6.4	0.2	6.6	2.0	6.3	0.2	6.5	3.1	6.4	0.2	6.6	3.0
Construction	60.0	0.7	60.7	1.2	51.0	0.6	51.6	1.2	46.0	0.6	46.6	1.3	40.4	0.5	40.9	1.2	40.1	0.5	40.6	1.2
Finance	6.7	5.4	12.1	44.6	6.9	5.2	12.1	43.0	7.0	5.1	12.1	42.1	7.1	5.0	12.1	41.3	7.1	5.0	12.1	41.3
Distribution	64.0	13.3	77.3	17.2	61.7	12.9	74.6	17.3	60.0	12.5	72.5	17.2	56.9	12.2	69.1	17.7	55.6	11.9	67.5	17.6
Transport	42.5	2.8	45.3	6.2	42.7	3.1	45.8	6.8	42.3	3.2	45.5	7.0	40.9	3.1	44.0	7.0	40.3	3.1	43.4	7.1
Public Admin	44.4	4.5	48.9	9.2	48.8	5.0	53.8	9.3	55.4	5.2	60.6	8.6	62.9	5.4	68.3	7.9	68.2	5.5	73.7	7.5
Education	24.7	11.3	36.0	31.4	25.3	11.6	36.9	31.4	25.1	11.5	36.8	31.4	23.9	11.0	34.9	31.5	23.1	10.7	33.8	31.7
Health	6.2	7.3	13.5	54.1	6.1	7.5	13.6	55.1	6.3	8.2	14.5	56.6	6.3	8.4	14.7	57.1	6.4	8.4	74.8	56.8
Pvt Domestic	102.5	21.6	124.1	17.4	102.4	20.4	122.8	16.6	100.5	19.5	120.0	16.3	97.3	18.6	115.9	16.0	92.4	18.0	110.4	16.3
Other services	35.2	7.7	42.9	17.9	36.8	7.4	44.2	16.7	34.5	7.8	42.3	18.4	33.2	7.9	41.1	19.2	34.5	7.8	42.3	18.4
Total	874.8	176.5	1,051.3	16.8	864.5	172.1	1,036.6	16.6	843.5	168.7	1,012.2	16.7	819.3	167.0	986.3	16.9	816.2	168.4	984.6	17.1

Source: CSO Harare

TABLE 2
FEMALE PARTICIPATION IN FORMAL SECTOR LABOUR FORCE 1980-1983 (Figures in Thousands)

1975	1976 M	F	T	F%	1977 M	F	T	F%	1978 M	F	T	F%	1979 M	F	T	F%
Agriculture	242.0	85.0	327.0	26.0	225.3	69.2	294.3	23.5	215.8	58.5	274.3	21.3	206.0	57.5	263.5	21.8
Mining	65.0	1.2	66.2	1.8	66.9	1.3	68.2	1.9	62.2	1.3	63.5	2.0	59.1	1.3	60.4	2.2
Manufacturing	147.7	11.7	159.4	7.3	161.0	12.2	173.2	7.0	168.0	12.5	180.5	6.9	161.4	12.0	173.4	6.9
Electricity	6.5	0.2	6.7	3.0	6.9	0.2	6.5	3.1	6.3	0.2	6.5	3.1	6.7	0.2	6.9	2.9
Construction	41.6	0.6	42.2	1.4	46.6	0.6	47.2	1.3	50.4	0.6	51.0	1.2	48.7	0.2	49.4	1.4
Finance	7.5	5.0	12.5	40.0	8.5	5.3	13.8	38.4	9.2	5.4	14.6	37.0	10.0	5.8	15.8	36.7
Distribution	58.2	12.0	70.3	17.2	62.4	12.6	75.0	16.8	66.5	13.3	79.8	16.7	67.3	13.3	80.6	16.5
Transport	42.2	3.0	45.6	6.6	46.6	2.9	49.5	5.9	47.5	2.9	50.4	5.8	46.2	3.2	49.4	6.5
Public Admin	65.9	5.2	71.1	7.3	77.5	5.6	83.1	6.7	75.3	6.0	81.3	7.4	75.3	7.2	82.5	8.7
Education	27.9	14.0	41.9	33.4	38.5	20.6	59.1	34.9	45.9	25.9	71.8	36.1	49.9	28.1	78.0	36.0
Health	6.5	8.7	15.2	57.2	57.2	9.3	16.3	57.1	8.1	10.8	18.9	57.1	8.1	10.9	19.0	57.4
Pvt Domestic	91.2	16.8	108.0	15.6	86.3	18.3	104.6	17.5	83.1	18.3	101.4	18.0	80.0	19.8	99.8	19.8
Other services	35.9	7.9	15.6	18.0	39.4	7.8	47.2	16.5	43.3	8.4	51.7	16.2	45.8	8.9	54.7	16.3
Total	838.5	171.4	1,009.9	17.0	872.1	165.9	1,038.0	16.0	881.6	164.1	1,045.7	15.7	864.5	168.9	1,033.4	16.3

of discrimination—race and sex—and this was reflected in the wages they got, the number in employment and the types of jobs they did. In most concerns, juniors (male over 16 but under 19) and females of any age got three-quarters of the minimum wage given to men doing the same work. The only special provision in the Act was a 60 minute breast-feeding break, which was difficult to take as the baby would normally be far from the place of employment.

The situation was not any better in the public sector. Women, in whatever capacity, earned less than men for the same work because of the dubious 'breadwinner concept'. Should a woman fall pregnant, she had to resign and then reapply after delivery. She had no entitlements whatsoever. As a matter of fact, she had to start at the bottom of the pay-scale. As soon as she got married, she was taken as temporary staff. As if this was not enough, a married woman's earnings were heavily taxed as they were considered as additional income to/of the husband.

Most of the women in formal employment were in the teaching and nursing professions, and in agriculture as labourers. These were areas that were really an extension of their domestic duties and were therefore considered as traditionally female occupations (see Table 1). Table 2 shows hardly any changes in this pattern for the years 1980-83. A major limiting factor to the employment of women arose from unequal educational opportunities afforded girls in relation to boys. This dated back to the early missionary days, when mission schools were mainly for boys. Later, however, this discrimination arose from parental attitudes. The effects of this educational imbalance are still reflected today in the number of women in high status jobs. But this also offers a ready excuse to some employers bent on keeping women in low status jobs even though some may qualify for higher posts.

In the light of the foregoing account, it remains only to reiterate a few issues about the legal status of women. Under customary law, a woman was a minor from cradle to grave. Before marriage she was under the guardianship of her father or other male relative, and she fell under the guardianship of her husband after marriage. At divorce she reverted to her former position or could even fall under the guardianship of her adult son. A woman, therefore, had no *locus standi* before any court of law and had to be represented by her guardian, if he was willing. Neither could she enter into any contract without his consent. This included the contract of marriage. A few concessions were made during the colonial era whereby divorcees or widows, if they so chose, could become emancipated. But still, this did not make them guardians of their children when the husband or ex-husband died. Only a man could be a guardian and therefore this function was taken over by a designated male relative of the deceased man.

I have so far dwelt at length on aspects that had a more determining factor on the status of women in pre-colonial and colonial Zimbabwe namely *roora*, and its implications for property, children and land-use rights, labour practices and the legal minority of women. Because of societal attitudes and resistance to change, the majority of women today still live under the same conditions, and so in reality their lives have not changed, in spite of the many legal changes that have occurred since independence. Besides providing necessary information, therefore, the foregoing provides us with a backdrop against which to assess the post-independence era with respect to the efforts already undertaken to improve the condition of women in Zimbabwe.

Constitutional and Legal Enactments in the Period since Independence
With the coming of majority rule, everyone—men and women alike—had high expectations of enjoying the fruits of independence. For women, this meant also the hope for an improvement in their social, economic, legal and political status. The following pages seek to determine the extent to which this hope has been fulfilled in the period since the attainment of national independence.

Except for a few snippets here and there and short publications out of reach of most people, little has been documented about the role played by women in the course of the protracted struggle for independence. The fault lies at the feet of Zimbabwean women themselves. And yet the national liberation struggle marked a major breakthrough for the liberation of women in this country.

> Women fought side by side with men on an equal footing, demonstrating that they were indeed a force to reckon with, and thus destroying the age-old myth that a woman's place is in the kitchen.[15]

One cannot find better justification for demanding equality on the part of women in Zimbabwe. Added to this is the government's own commitment to equality. Hence, the government took upon itself the task of removing as many legal obstacles as possible within this short period in order to correct the many legal injustices that existed. Another objective was to bring everyone into the mainstream of development and social transformation. This would demand maximum participation on an equal footing, regardless of race, colour, creed, political affiliation or sex.

Let us examine constitutional and legal provisions that affect women. Perhaps the most logical step is to start by looking at the Zimbabwe constitution which, like all other constitutions, is the legal insturment around which all other laws, rules and regulations governing the people of Zimbabwe are drawn. Only subsections of Articles 11 and 23 of Chapter 3 will be looked at, as these appear significantly to affect women negatively.

The right to be treated equally, aptly described by Dworkin (1976) as the fundamental right of every person except where sufficient reasons demand otherwise,[16] is enshrined in the Bill of Rights (Chapter 3, 2(a), (b) and (c). Unfortunately, either intentionally or by an oversight of the draftsmen, 'sex' is not included in the same Chapter (Article 23, Subsections 1 and 2) which protects individuals against discrimination. The same Article 23 (Subsection 3 (a) and (b)) mentions that:

> nothing contained in any law shall be held to be in contravention

of subsection (1) (a) to the extent that law in question relates to any of the following matters: (a) adoption, marriage, divorce, burial, devolution of property on death or other matters of personal law; (b) the application of customary law in any case involving Africans, or an African and one or more persons who are not Africans, where such persons have consented to the application of customary law in that case.[17]

Some provisions in the Lancaster House Agreement, as the Zimbabwe constitution is sometimes called, have constituted the major stumbling-blocks in bringing about transformation. The above-mentioned Articles are such examples, as the areas covered under them are considered by women to be some of the causes/sources of female inferior status and oppression in Zimbabwe. The government, however, has used legal means through parliament to remove some of these injustices based on cultural, traditional, societal and colonial attitudes, all of which have kept women in downtrodden positions for generations.

Soon after independence, the government reformed some aspects of personal law which could no longer effectively apply in present day conditions.

Bekker and Coertze (1982) define personal law as:

The law of persons or status for the most part bound with the question of marriage and dealing with capacity, marriage, its consummation, consequences and dissolutions; children, their status, minority, tutelage and emancipations; and succession.[18]

The question of children and their welfare is inextricably linked with the rights and obligations of women as mothers. The Customary Law and Primary Courts Act (6, 1981) repealed the African Law and Tribal Courts Act (Chapter 237) and amended, *inter alia*, the Maintenance Act (Chapter 35). Primary Courts in the form of Village and Community Courts (CCs) were instituted to take over the judicial functions previously performed by chiefs, headmen and district commissioners in the administration of customary law. In response to the social and ideological demands, the government made further reforms to the Act which affected the administration of law in these courts.

An amendment to the Act was made in October 1982 (21/1982), whereby CCs were empowered to order maintenance for deserted and divorced wives and their children, whether the marriage had been registered or not, for customary unions. Not only was maintenance granted to children from broken marriages in the mother's custody, but also to children of unmarried mothers, until they (children) attained majority age (Section 12 (4) (a) and (b)). This was a major law reform in that it afforded such women added security for their children, especially if the man is in regular employment.

As is to be expected, claims so far have been more numerous in urban than in rural areas. One reason is that claims have to be lodged at a CC closest to the defendant's place of residence. Therefore, even women who normally stay in rural areas have to come to urban areas where husbands work. Another reason may simply be ignorance on the part of rural women, in which case legal education is essential. A third reason may be that some women realise the futility of the whole exercise if the man is an ordinary peasant with unstable and unreliable sources of income. Such men also have very little, if any, property like livestock to which a warrant of execution could be attached. Anyway, the amount of maintenance awarded depends on the economic status of both mother/wife and father/husband, as the case may be. A recent study by the Fundamental Rights and Personal Law Project Team at the University of Zimbabwe found out that 24.1% of all cases brought before 19 CCs under study were claims for maintenance[19] (see Table 3). I believe the percentage must be higher now since the Supreme Court ruling on the Katekwe vs. Muchabaiwa case, in which the Chief Justice ruled that there would no longer be seduction damages awards for major daughters.[20]

TABLE 3
COMMUNITY COURT LOCATIONS BY TYPES OF CASES TRIED

	TOTAL	SEDUCTION	MAINTENANCE	DIVORCE	LOBOLO	CUSTODY	DEBT AND CONTRACT	PETTY CRIMINAL	MATRIMONIAL	MATRIMONIAL PROPERTY	SLANDER	PROPERTY DAMAGE	ADULTERY
Mutare	114	14	26	12	25	12	2	6	5	6	-	4	2
Chegutu	44	17	1	7	3	5	3	1	3	2	-	1	1
Mt. Darwin	71	9	5	15	12	9	8	2	-	4	4	-	3
Geruve	20	3	-	2	2	2	4	3	3	-	1	-	-
Harare*	267	68	100	30	15	13	21	2	5	8	3	-	2
Bulawayo	200	32	119	13	4	8	17	2	2	1	1	-	1
Chiredzi	88	21	5	2	19	1	19	6	4	-	2	3	6
Shamva	90	19	3	19	16	15	5	1	-	-	2	1	9
Chivhu	97	24	15	-	23	6	3	5	5	3	6	3	4
Hwange/ Vic Fall	24	14	2	5	-	-	-	2	-	-	-	1	-
Mberengwa	59	14	13	2	10	3	8	3	3	2	-	-	2
Esigodini	42	4	2	5	5	2	9	4	2	-	2	5	2
Buhera	43	3	13	2	7	2	5	5	3	-	2	-	1
Zvishavane*	74	16	25	1	3	3	17	4	-	1	1	3	-
Mutoko*	37	13	5	6	2	2	4	1	-	3	1	-	-
Chibi*	59	13	9	5	12	1	10	3	1	1	1	-	2
Rusape*	64	19	3	4	21	1	4	2	5	1	1	2	1
Centenary*	55	10	3	2	17	6	2	3	3	2	3	3	1
TOTAL		313	349	131	196	91	141	55	45	34	30	26	37
PERCENTAGE		21.6	24.1	9	13.5	6.3	9.7	3.8	3.1	2.3	2.1	1.8	2.6

Source: (* Community Courts selected for Litigent Survey)

The fear of being separated from one's children, plus losing out on what one had contributed towards matrimonial property, were two major reasons why some women put up with deplorable marital life. Previously no woman married under customary law could lodge a divorce claim on her own because she had no *locus standi* before any courts of law. As such, she had to elicit the help of her former guardian (father or other male relative) to represent her in a divorce suit. This help was not always forthcoming because usually part of the *roora* had to be refunded, depending on the number of children born. Today, women can lodge divorce claims on their own (Legal Age of Majority Act, to be discussed later), without fear of losing their children. Section 3 (4) of the Primary Courts Act states that:

> (4) Notwithstanding anything to the contrary in this section, in any case relating to the custody of children the interests of the children concerned shall be the paramount consideration, irrespective of which law or principle is applied.[21]

Hence custody of children is no longer automatically decided by whether the man had paid *roora* or seduction damages and rearing fees, nor on whether the children are seven years old, as used to be the practice before the Act in question was passed. In most cases that come before CCs, women get custody of children, with an award of maintenance from the father of the children, until, sometimes, the children are self-supporting or have attained the majority age of 18.

Contrary to men's views, few women even today just decide to sue for divorce when the marriage turns sour. Most women try hard to save their marriages. But one can only do that when the other party is willing to cooperate. But he may himself ask for divorce, in order to marry again. Should all efforts to reconcile fail, the woman will usually leave and take her children with her. However, the question of guardianship still has to be clarified.

Before the enactment of the Matrimonial Causes Act in December 1985, the question of division of property at divorce—if there was any—was a vexing one. Admittedly, CCs could order some form of division of property at divorce. If the wife was in formal or informal employment and could prove, by way of receipts if necessary, that she had bought such and such an article, the CC normally ordered that she take it with her or be compensated for it. Even in some cases where the women were full-time housewives, they were usually allowed to take some articles besides the customary cooking sticks, pots, plates and their personal belongings. The reason behind this was that their housekeeping activities and budget management enabled the pair to accumulate property, especially if the man in his bachelor days had nothing or very little to show for his labours.

The very recent Matrimonial Causes Act decrees that, at divorce, matrimonial property shall be shared in whatever way the court decides. This Act has been welcomed by most women, but has met with angry reactions from a good number of men. An anonymous official in the Ministry of Labour, Manpower Planning and Social Welfare said:

> Any woman is entitled to the kitchen ware. If the law insists that property be shared between the two of us even if my wife was not working (sic) then they should legislate that *roora* be banished because in this case the men stand to lose more.[22]

This goes to show, despite arguments to the contrary, that *roora* is always used as a ground for the unfair treatment to which women have been subjected. In response to public criticism, the Minister of Justice, Legal and Parliamentary Affairs categorically stated that this discriminatory practice must of necessity cease. After all, women spend a good part of their lives contributing in one way or another towards matrimonial property. It is grossly unfair, therefore, to expect a woman to leave almost empty-handed just because an archaic customary law says that matrimonial property belongs to the man.

Men, however, argue that such legal enactments are eroding the 'African way of life', and that since independence, the government has been taking rights away from men and conferring them on women. As a result, they argue, all these legal changes are creating a mercenary attitude in women, who will now enter into marriage for what they can get out of it. They are no longer prepared to stick it out when the going gets tough - they have nothing to lose but a lot to gain! This argument implies that women are no longer interested in marriage *per se* and have suddenly become very calculating. While these arguments are largely unfounded, they nevertheless reflect interesting aspects of male chauvinism.

Another issue of property arises at the death of a husband. Very few women know that they can take refuge in a community court should the husband die intestate. Usually the widow is dispossessed of all property by avaricious relatives of the deceased man. What is unfortunate is that it is the female relatives of the deceased man who are usually in the forefront of dispossessing the poor widow and yet mourn and raise hell when the coin is reversed. Perhaps the solution is to educate people to make wills in the nuclear family's favour, though this does not always solve the problem—what with threats of the supernatural! Women are wary about encouraging their husbands to make wills for fear of being subsequently labelled the 'witches' who caused the death of their husbands for money. Women are looking forward to the day the proposed Succession Bill becomes law. It is scheduled to be tabled towards the end of 1986.

The Legal Age of Majority Act (LAMA), which became effective in December 1982, was probably the most revolutionary enactment concerned with the ideal of equality. Its passage was marked by jubilation and ululation by thousands of women at Mbare Stodart Hall in Harare. Little did the women, let alone the men, realise how far-reaching and revolutionary the implications of the Act were to become. The Act says:

> on and after the fixed date a person shall attain the legal age

of majority on attaining the age of 18 years. (Section 3 (1))

The Act applies to all laws, including customary law. To understand the concept, we must turn to common law as the concept is unknown in customary law. When someone attains majority age, it means that that person no longer has a guardian. In other words, it means he or she can sue and be sued in his or her own right, can own property, sell it or give it away without interference from anyone as long as that property is his/hers to give, and a major can enter into any contract without the need of a guardian. By virtue of this Act, it follows that any two people wishing to enter into a contract of marriage can do so with or without the consent of the woman's father or other male relative. Therefore, nobody can legally stop them from marrying simply because *roora* has not been paid. Another implication is that women can also become guardians of their children, irrespective of whether these children were born in or out of wedlock.

The LAMA does not only confer rights on individuals. Every right has an obligation attached to it, and therefore a major has the obligation to behave like one, or bear the consequences. One implication of the Act was clearly demonstrated in the much publicised Katekwe vs. Muchabaiwa seduction case, sponsored by the Law Department at the University of Zimbabwe and finally settled at the Supreme Court.[23] The Chief Justice Cde Dumbutshena, in passing judgement, had this to say:

> Does the father still have the right to sue for damages for the seduction of a major daughter? The answer is simple. He has not, because his daughter is a major and cannot vest her own right in her father. He has lost his right under customary law to sue for damages for seduction...The right to sue for seduction—a delict—now falls on the daughter...under the general law of Zimbabwe.[24]

The reason for this decision, the Chief Justice went on to explain, was because the 20-year-old woman was now a major who could marry without her father's consent. It was up to her to decide whether her potential husband should enter into a *roora* contract with her father. Hence her diminished value in *roora*, as was the reason for granting seduction damages in customary law, was highly speculative.

One can only imagine the general uproar that arose from this court decision. Note that 47% of cases brought before the CCs between 1981 and 1982 were claims for seduction damages, later falling to 21.6% between 1982 and 1983.[25] (See Table 2) Parents saw the LAMA ushering in all sorts of immoral behaviour on the part of their children, particularly girls, and a general erosion of parental respect. There was also the intolerable idea that daughters could marry without *roora* transactions. Having spent so much money to raise and educate a daughter, parents felt nobody should expect them to give her away *gratis*. 'Impossible! Unheard of! Never!' Some people have even gone as far as blaming the LAMA for the prevalence of baby-dumping and schoolgirl pregnancies, little realising that the causes lie elsewhere—in the socio-economic conditions of our society and the general erosion of moral values.

The only misgiving one may have about the Act is that it was not circulated when it was still in its bill form, to enable public debate on it and also let people get used to it. As it is, the Act was presented as a *fait accompli*. Nevertheless, it was an overdue legal requirement and people may as well get used to the Act.

Incidentally boys and girls, and women at that, are not simply going to get out of hand because of the LAMA. Surely, even men of thirty or older seek parental consent in order to marry, even if the consent so sought is actually parental blessing. How young people behave will basically depend on the personal relationship existing within each family. Men of fifty respect their parents and constantly seek their advice even if they have been majors for donkey's years. Family relationships in Zimbabwe are still very strong and our generation will probably die out before all African (black) couples marry without *roora* payments. Though the LAMA has been law since 1982, only 52 couples out of 906 registered their marriages without *roora* transactions of any sort, with or without consent, at Harare CC between April 1983 and March 1985 (from a Harare CC Presiding Officer).

The government's policies concerning labour changed the colonial situation drastically. The Minimum Wages Act (1982) stipulated minimum scales of remuneration for workers in the unskilled category. This piece of legislation was welcomed by women primarily because a large proportion of female labour falls into this category. From the $20.00 to $30.00 pittance that they used to get, the scale was set at $50.00 per month, later revised to about $60.00 and recently to between $75.00 and $145.00 per month. This caters for employees in the agricultural sector, in domestic employment and in the industrial sector.[26]

Unfortunately, a good number still get less than this but are too scared to protest for fear of losing their jobs. Some employers have cut down on numbers employed in some concerns in order to cut down on costs and also circumvent these provisions. Usually it is the women who are the first to get the sack. Labour officials from the Ministry of Labour, Manpower Planning and Social Welfare have intervened in a number of cases where employers were underpaying their employees, with some success. As to domestic workers, it becomes more difficult to monitor employers unless the employee goes personally with a case to the Ministry—and black employers are the worst infringers of these regulations. Another handicap is that a sizeable percentage of female labour is employed as seasonal and casual workers at various farms scattered all over the country, so making it very difficult to enforce the law.

These regulations outlawed the discriminatory practice which differentiated pay scales for the same job on the basis of race and sex. Today women and men with the same qualifications and doing the same type of job get the same pay. But some employers have tended to downgrade the work done by women and therefore pay them less than men.

The new Labour Relations Act allows expecting women 90 days paid maternity leave, worked to a certain percentage of one's salary, and also depending on whether the woman forfeits her annual leave days or not. If there are complications that demand that this leave be extended, arrangements can always be made.

Whatever the case may be, the woman should re-enter employment after her maternity break at the same scale of remuneration and into the same position that she occupied before taking her maternity leave. The employee's normal benefits and entitlements, including her right to seniority, advancement and accumulation of pension rights shall continue uninterrupted. Neither shall her period of service be considered as interrupted, reduced or broken by the exercise of her right to maternity leave. A nursing mother is allowed one hour or two half-hour periods for breastfeeding, which she may combine with other breaks.[27] A recent change is that women in the public sector will also get the same consideration, especially paid maternity leave, besides the one hour or two half-hour periods of breast-feeding time they already get.

Much as these regulations are welcomed, they are going to have adverse effects on the employment of women in general. Employers may not be too keen on employing women who will from time to time go on paid maternity leave, even if the Act provides that nobody should go on maternity leave more than once in 24 months and more than three times with the same employer. (This could be a way of effective family planning!) But at least the law protects those who are already employed. Probably the Sex Disqualification Removal Act (1983) may take care of that in some respects.

> Notwithstanding anything to the contrary in any law contained, women may hold any public or civil office or appointment subject to the same conditions on which such office may be held by men... The same qualifications that make men eligible for certain offices shall equally be required for women...[28]

Generally, this Act makes very good reading—and it is sometimes only that, if the complaints that have been raised at various women's conferences and workshops are anything to go by. There is still a lot of tacit sex discrimination in appointing, promoting and electing incumbents into high status positions. The problem is that it is very difficult to prove that one has not been appointed into a particular position because she is a woman. After all, competition is rather high for such positions.

There are a few other legal provisions dating back to the pre-independence periods which have economic implications for women as well, though their effects are limited to women whose husbands are in formal employment and those women with independent sources of income from both the formal and informal sectors.

Any woman over 16, married or single, may open a savings account without the consent of a guardian or spouse. She may execute the necessary documents, cede or borrow against and deal with her share of the deposit as she likes. But in practice, it is not as simple as that. There are still many wives who are forbidden by their husbands to open saving accounts and, attitudes being what they are, some wives obey meekly. Some husbands actually demand their wives' pay or force them to use it on everyday family needs while the husbands themselves spend a good part of their wages on dubious personal needs. Very few women can bear to see their children go hungry or uneducated just because the fathers are unwilling to use their earnings on their families.

Widowed, divorced or separated women who were dependent on their husbands or former husbands for subsistence are entitled to pension payments should the latter die. The same applies where the husband was receiving compensation for injury and subsequently dies. The Workman's Compensation Act (Chapter 269) makes provision for paying the widow, the percentage paid depending on the rank the man held prior to injury and also on the type of employment the man was in.

All the above legal provisions do not stop relatives of the deceased from demanding what is legally the widow's and the children's right. A few widows know that they can take refuge in the law by going to court, but the rest are too scared to challenge their in-laws and so end up collecting the moneys and handing them over to their in-laws. What is really needed are a few test cases to establish the fact and of course strong agencies to enforce the law. Going through the law books today, one still comes across conflicting laws that only manage to confuse issues, as they are not in consonance with recent legislation. The law therefore becomes subject to manipulation by clever legal professionals like lawyers. But women themselves must be prepared to fight some of these rampant practices despite public opinion.

Problems of Implementation
For any law to be effective, adequate administrative means must be provided to implement the law. Though CCs are fairly distributed across the country, the administration of court decisions has not always been easy, especially in maintenance cases. To start with, some CCs have too wide an area of jurisdiction and too many people falling under them. As a result, there is a huge backlog of pending cases awaiting trial. And justice delayed is justice denied. Some women may make four or more trips to the CC concerned before their cases are heard, an exercise they cannot afford. Neither are employers too keen to release their employees too often, which is reasonable. Come the collection of the maintenance awards and another problem presents itself.

This problem is common all over the world and is therefore not peculiar to Zimbabwe. It is difficult sometimes to trace the whereabouts of the man if he has changed his residence or employment and has not forwarded the new address to the CC. More cooperation on the part of the men and their employers, and other government agencies like the Police and the Social Welfare Department, would go a long way in alleviating this particular problem. In some cases, maintenance fees go missing and therefore do not get to the appropriate persons. Nobody seems to know how and to where the fees disappear. Records may even show that the fees were collected and signed for but the poor woman may not be able to prove that she did not in actual fact collect them.

A number of women complain that CCs lack enforcement powers and are therefore ineffective. Men on the other hand complain that women are abusing their rights by lodging unnecessary, if not false, claims for maintenance. While I do not deny there may be a few who do, I tend to think that in most cases it is just an excuse on the part of men who wish to shed the responsibility of maintaining their ex-wives and children, particularly if the latter were born out of wedlock.

Another point to note is the attitude of some presiding officers. If they are to be seen as agents of change and social transformation, as indeed they should be, their attitudes as a whole must be consonant with the legal reforms. As administrators of justice, they should not let their own prejudices colour their judgements but should weigh each case on its own merits and see to it that justice is done. Presiding officers should also take time to explain these legal reforms to litigants and so educate them on their rights and obligations.

What the law says is one thing; practice is another. For most women today, three years after the LAMA, the act might as well not exist. There is hardly any change at all. So set are women in their ways that they cannot contemplate that they could ever be equal to men. Their inferior status has become so internalised one has little hope of them living differently. Nor can a mother-in-law envisage a situation where her daughters-in-law can claim to be equal to her son who paid *roora* for her. So one finds women becoming adversaries of the Act instead of welcoming the legal reform. The same goes for the men too. 'Equal in what?' is the popular question. If this means equal opportunities in education, at work, equal salaries and the like, then this is fine for them. But they argue that nobody should tell them how to run their homes or how to behave towards a wife for whom large amounts of *roora* were paid.

Quite a number of women still come against a lot of overt and covert discrimination when it comes to contracts. Finance houses are not too keen on giving women, especially married women, any credit facilities. Some will demand the husband's or some other male's consent or presence, while others demands impossible assets and collateral, which in many cases are not there considering that most women never owned any property one can speak of in veritable form. Of course these financial institutions have to protect their interests, but somehow or other, the process most women go through when they apply for a loan or open accounts is different from the one men go through—everything being equal.

Over 70% of our population is rural-based, of which about 55% to 60% are women. Since the introduction of the cash economy and the resultant male labour migration urban drift, women have had to take over most of the functions previously performed by men in traditional society. Callear, in a study in the Wedza communal area, came up with the following list of tasks performed by women:

- all domestic work including care of children;
- fetching firewood and water from far and near places;

- cultivating and tending fields and gardens and processing the produce;
- taking maize and other corn to grinding mills and grinding some by hand;
- herding cattle and other livestock;
- guarding against baboons and other marauders and taking children to the clinic when the need arises.[29]

This list is by no means comprehensive as it does not take into account the time spent at social gatherings, political meetings and at various development projects and activities recently introduced at local level. All the above activities are very time-consuming, such that by the end of it all, at least 16 hours of continuous activity account for a normal working day in a rural area. A man from a club in Buhera said:

> If I don't have a wife no work is done because women do everything. They are heavy workers.[30]

A woman from the same club reiterated:

> Ploughing and digging of manure used to be done by men, but now women have to do it. What piques us most is that the men make the plan and then go away. We women then do all the work. When everything is done and the harvest is in, the men take the crops to the Grain Marketing Board and receive all the money. In the end we get very little for our efforts[31].

The latter statement echoes one of the major problem areas about which women in the rural areas bitterly complain. The men claim the produce because land-use rights are vested in them, as are most credit cards. A good example today is the Agricultural Finance Corporation credit cards. Like women in other sectors of the economy, rural women are just as disadvantaged, *vis-à-vis* credit facilities. If women had land-use rights in their individual capacity, some of these problems would not arise, especially where the house is permanently or even temporarily headed by a woman as a married, divorced, widowed or unmarried mother.

The government in all its development plans and policies has prioritised the rural areas as an area of great concern. After decades of colonial neglect, the government has set itself the task of supplying those basic services essential for any qualitative development, namely, good communication networks, accessible health facilities for primary health care, educational facilities and agricultural extension services, to mention but a few. Most of the recipients are women and children who form the majority. But it is general knowledge that, though women are more involved in agricultural work and in other activities as well, extension services are usually directed at men. Calls have gone out to extend these services to all people involved, for maximum returns. Apparently the calls have been heeded to the extent that women are now being encouraged to train as agricultural extension workers and officers as it is felt that they may have greater impact on women. This also is an indication that our society is really moving towards equality in training and educational opportunities. Today, at least 25% of the total enrolment at agricultural colleges are girls and women, who are proving to be equally good in a field traditionally seen as a male domain.

When all is said and done, there is a need for liaison among village health workers, community development workers, home economics demonstrators, extension officers (agricultural), educationists and all other servicing agents through, perhaps, village development committees, so that they all come up with a timetable that does not disrupt nor add excessively to the workload of women. This would also call for co-ordination of all NGO and government activities to avoid a lot of duplication and hence a waste of scarce resources. Someone still has to come up with labour-saving devices (appropriate technology) to cut down on the time spent on tedious pieces of work.

In a Highfield study, Olivia Muchena found that 50% of women were classified as 'housewives, unemployed', while 37% and 13% were employed in the informal and formal sectors respectively.[32] The situation is not likely to have altered much. Those in the informal sector sell such wares as vegetables, old and new clothes, knitted and crocheted articles, baskets, all kinds of things. Others are in illegal activities like running shebeens and prostitution. All these women are in one way or another trying to make ends meet, for survival, or to augment their husbands' earnings for the same purpose. For some of these operators, the constant police harassment does not help at all, however justified.

Though employment opportunities have improved for women since independence, the picture is not as rosy as it is painted. Women as employees or prospective employees have a number of factors militating against them.

To start with, women have been discriminated against in education since missionaries introduced education for blacks. Though today education is open to all and free at primary school level, the drop-out rate for girls is very high at all levels of education and training institutions due to a number of reasons, among which are lack of financial resources (the little being reserved for boys in preference to girls), parental attitudes to the education of girls and schoolgirl pregnancies. Furthermore, girls are still inclined towards those traditional female fields of nursing and teaching and therefore are not equipped to enter the challenging fields of science and technology.

Another obstacle is the usually negative attitude to employing women, let alone promoting them to positions of influence in a managerial capacity, or other high-status jobs. Let us turn to the public sector to illustrate a form of tacit discrimination. In 1980, 3,242 out of 10,470 established posts were occupied by women of all races. Three years later, after the implementation of the Presidential Directive, the numbers had shot to 10,228 out of 24,278 posts respectively, or, in percentage form, from about 30% to 44.2%. This looks like a great improvement, as indeed it is, but what must be realised is that the greatest expansions were in the Ministries of Health, Education and CDWA (discussed below) where there has always been a preponderance of female employees. Even in these areas, very few women actually fill the high-status jobs. The following figures should help to make the picture clearer. By 1984, 16,302 out of 26,065 established posts were in the Ministries of Health and Education, of which 9,619 were occupied by women, black and white. Fair and good. But as we move up the ladder, the picture changes drastically.[33]

TABLE 4
FEMALE EMPLOYMENT IN PUBLIC SECTOR

a. *Assistant Secretary/Under-Secretary*

	Total	Male	Female	% Female
Education	1,062	988	74	7
Health	376	311	65	16

b. *Deputy Secretary/Permanent Secretary Category*

	Total	Male	Female	% Female
Education	13	12	1	8
Health	112	96	4	14

Source: Female Employment in the Public Sector, by Cde S. Dangarembga, Public Service Commission.

All in all, women constitute only nine percent of the total number of public servants in the higher status categories.[34] Admittedly, this is excellent compared to other developing countries, but we should always judge a situation relative to that of men in a particular country. Therefore, it seems that the Presidential Directive had more of a racial than a sexual bias. Some have suggested an arrangement similar to the Presidential Directive to correct this anomaly, through perhaps a quota system, while others (mostly men) feel that the best candidate should be appointed. Of course, the latter position is the better and the writer has no quarrel with that. What is sugested is that where a male and female candidate hold the same qualifications and experience, preference should be given to the woman.

No figures are yet available to the writer on the position of women in the private sector, but it is suspected the situation is worse. Women have to prove themselves well beyond the normal standards before they can be considered for promotion. Consequently, it is not an easy task, especially where competition is high.

Recent reports in our newspapers seem to indicate that women are becoming more and more active in trade union activities. A few are now being elected into the executive posts of various trade unions while others were recently elected into the Zimbabwe Congress of Trade Unions. This sounds fine, but care should be taken that women do not get delegated to deal exclusively with women's problems and therefore not address those issues that concern labour in general. Since most of the meetings take place during office hours, household responsibilities are no excuse for the general apathy that women have been showing towards trade union participation.

National Machinery

In keeping with the UN Decade for Women objectives and also realising the importance of accelerating the advancement of women generally, The government instituted the Ministry of Community Development and Women's Affairs (MCDWA) in 1981, whose task was to:

> mobilise, organise, coordinate and monitor public and private non-governmental organisations (NGOs) geared towards closing disparities between men and women in Zimbabwe....[35]

To achieve the above, the MCDWA aimed at improving grassroot structures and mobilising resources for development through local participation in cooperatives, income-generating activities and other activities for social transformation. It is vital that women have economic independence to back up their demands for equality otherwise the whole exercise becomes ridiculous if one is dependent on the husband for survival.

One of the first tasks the MCDWA took upon itself was to conduct a nationwide Needs Assessment Survey, in conjunction with the United Nations Children's Fund, in order to ascertain those areas that needed to be dealt with, as prioritised by women themselves. Economic deprivation, negative legislation, illiteracy and child-care facilities were amongst the priority areas pinpointed by most women, not forgetting of course the negative societal attitudes inherent in the customary way of life. The MCDWA also presented to the Tax Commission, appointed by the government to look into the tax system, a report arising from consultations with various women's organisations.

The ministry has so far done a commendable job in highlighting the disadvantages of being unable to read and write and has therefore encouraged the setting up of literacy groups or classes all over the country, in conjunction with such NGOs as ALOZ (the Adult Literacy Organisation of Zimbabwe). A massive literacy campaign was launched in 1983 to give literacy skills to adults who had never been to school before or those who had only spent a few years in school and were usually semi-literate. To date, 35,000 adults, 75% of whom are women, are enrolled in literacy classes all over the country, in rural and urban areas alike.[36]

The ministry has been quite successful in encouraging the setting up of pre-schools, particularly in the rural areas. Ten percent of children in the 0-6 age group are enrolled in about 4,500 centres in the country, 4,000 of which are in the rural areas. In 1981, there were about 1,000 pre-schools (582 in the rural areas), a remarkable improvement indeed. Although this is a drop in the ocean, it is a start.[36]

The advantages of sending children to pre-schools are twofold. To start with, they prepare children for school in their formative years, and secondly, this enables mothers to do necessary pieces of work without worrying about these younger children. Girls can also attend school on equal terms with boys without taking time off to attend to their younger brothers and sisters.

Income-generating activities have been started all over the country with the help and encouragement of the MCDWA and other NGOs. Community development workers, who are the grassroot functionaries of the MCDWA, offer advice and guidance to people engaged in these projects. For example, in Mashonaland East alone, 755 groups with a membership of about 26,403 women and 7,413 men are involved in one activity or another.[37] However, considering the population in this province, a lot still needs to be done.

Educating women on their rights is an essential activity. The MCDWA has undertaken this task using material produced and provided by the Fundamental Rights and Personal Law Project team at the Centre for Applied Social Sciences at the University of Zimbabwe.[38] More work of this nature needs to be done as new legislation is passed.

Unfortunately, the MCDWA is limited by a number of factors which prevent effective implementation of its projects, and is therefore not achieving its goals. First and foremost, the projects undertaken by the MCDWA are seen as marginal to the development of the country as a whole and thus the ministry is not given enough financial backing in the annual allocation of financial resources for various ministries. This explains why there are so many literacy and pre-school teachers who are paid very little by their respective authorities or usually work on a voluntary basis, for nothing, hoping one day the MCDWA will be able to pay them. Because there is no official recognition by way of remuneration for these teachers, there is a high turnover which, in the final analysis, is a complete waste of resources as these teachers are sometimes trained by the MCDWA.

Lack of coordination at both the national and local level is another major problem. For an effective and comprehensive transformation exercise, it is vital that all ministerial functionaries at the local level liaise and cooperate. But this must of necessity start at ministerial level, otherwise a lot of confusion and duplication ensues. But in Zimbabwe, probably one of the biggest stumbling blocks to the advancement of women is the attitudes of society in general and men in particular. This explains why the majority of participants in income-generating activities are women. As a matter of fact, these projects are actually labelled as women projects. The general apathy shown by men towards projects started and dominated by women is a clear reflection of the negative attitudes towards any activities whose aim is to raise the status of women in any way. When all is said and done, the MCDWA is doing the best it can under the circumstances.

Women and Politics

Before I conclude this chapter, let me refer briefly to the political participation of women at both the national and local levels. Today, one wonders whether their present role in politics is commensurate with the role they played during the liberation struggle. At the local level, just about 10% of councillors in local governing bodies that range from district councils to municipalities are women.[39] Among the reasons given for this small percentage is the fact (or excuse) that women do not have the time or flexibility required for civic duties because of domestic responsibilities. Some argue that women are naturally apathetic to civic duties, while others maintain that women are incapable intellectually and physically. Whatever the case may be, women should assert themselves as competent individuals while men should be persuaded and encouraged to take over some of the domestic responsibilities that prevent capable women from participating in local politics effectively. This calls for a change in attitudes, by both sexes, so that women elect each other into these positions and stop the catty behaviour towards one another, arising from sheer spite, envy or petty jealousies.

The situation gets more tricky at the national level. Election into the national decision-making bodies is mostly determined by men. For example, there are 24 women in the Central Committee of the ruling party, out of 90 members, and one woman in the highest party organ, the Politburo, of 15 members. A look at the legislative body reveals that 11 out of 140 members are women, nine of whom are in the House of Assembly.[40] Of the latter, two are ministers (Cde Teurai Ropa Nhongo and Cde Victoria Chitepo) and one is a deputy minister (Cde Naomi Nhiwatiwa). Senator Amina Hughes is the other deputy minister. Of course, we must give credit where it is due, and this is a great show of how seriously the Prime Minister takes the question of women. This, however, is no reason for complacency. There is room for improvement; we would like to see more women in Parliament and there is no plausible reason why they cannot be elected if they are capable, and the election is truly democratic.

The idea of having a separate wing for women in political organisation is a dubious one, and sometimes is less than helpful. One wonders why there is nothing like a men's wing. The result is a continuation of the male/female dichotomy, where women's issues are referred to women's institutions, instead of being looked at as national issues that must be taken more seriously. A complete and thorough integration of women and men into the same national institutions, without creating others for women alone, would go a long way in dealing with problems more seriously. There would be less bickering and suspected manipulation of women by both men and women seeking to enhance their own positions by fair or foul means. Note the almost anarchic situation that arose immediately after the 1985 general elections, perpetrated by misguided women and youth who had nothing better to do, an indication of lack of direction and good judgement. Demonstrations should always have a positive goal. It would be more advantageous if women demonstrated in support of such legal reforms as the LAMA and the Matrimonial Causes Act and the proposed Succession Bill. But one thing is certain: the ZANU (PF) Women's League has great potential in the mobilisation of women. But this exercise should be directed towards achieving a better deal for women, whereever they may be.

Conclusion

It is a bit naive to attempt an analysis of the women issue in a single chapter because no single area can be dealt with adequately. Nonetheless, the aim was to point out the problem areas and give a tangential view of the situation for possible in-depth analysis later. As can be seen, the chapter had more or less a socio-legal orientation, because the writer feels the legal aspect is of vital importance in bringing about social change. This of course does not mean that one must ignore the other side of the coin, the social side, that incorporates societal attitudes. The need to change societal attitudes can never be over-emphasised for any meaningful change. The law can say one thing while society behaves in exactly the opposite way. But there is always recourse to law, when someone is prepared to challenge the status quo. Which is why women should be their own liberators. Only by concerted efforts and a willingness on their part to work towards equality in real life can women hope for a better life. Solidarity goes a long way.

Women are said to be the custodians of customs and culture, but they should realise that culture is not always progressive. So, any laws that are positively inclined towards women should be welcomed by women themselves, before they can hope to convert the men to their side. And charity begins at home. As long as women, as mothers, do not instill into their children the concepts of equality between the sexes, and practise it in the allocation of domestic work to both boys and girls, it will definitely be harder to convince grown up men that they must help in the home, that women deserve the same opportunities in all spheres of life and that women's rights are human rights.

Women probably bring some of the problems on themselves. Lack of self-confidence is detrimental to one's chances of getting a job, as is lack of ambition. Ambition and self-actualisation are not attributes peculiar to men only. If women are to be taken seriously, they must also take their work seriously and not expect to be given everything on a silver platter. Even if they do not have to prove anything, at least they can show they are equally good and competent in whatever undertaking.

Policy Recommendations

That all laws conflicting with the ideal of equality be repealed or amended.

That all citizens of Zimbabwe be governed by one set of laws.

That a nationwide legal education campaign be undertaken in order to change societal attitudes towards women and also educate women on their rights.

That women should have land-use rights in their individual capacity.

That women be given the same diverse and equal opportunities as men in education, training and employment.

That an Equality Board be set up to deal with cases of discrimination and sexual harassment of women in places of employment.

That women should have the same access to loan and credit facilities as men.

REFERENCES
1. *UN Convention on the Elimination of all Forms of Discrimination Against Women, 1979*, p. 1.
2. Mead, M., Sex and Temperament in Three Primative Societies in Rossi, A. (ed), *The Feminist Papers,* Columbia University Press, London, 1973, pp. 658-671.
3. Bebel, A., 'Working class Socialist' in *The Feminist Papers, op.cit.* pp. 496-505.
4. Delphy, C., *The Main Enemy: A Materialist Analysis of Women's Oppression*, WRRC, Exploration in Feminism, London, 1977.
5. Elshtain, J.B., *Public Man, Private Woman*, Martin Robertson, Oxford, 1981, pp. 201-228.
6. May, J., *Zimbabwe Women in Customary and Colonial Law*, Mambo Press, Gweru, 1983, pp. 41-42.
7. Holleman, J., *Shona Customary Law*, Oxford University Press, London, 1952.
8. May, J., *op. cit.*
9. Chigwedere, E., *Lobola: The Pros and Cons*, Books of Africa, 1982.
10. Mpofu, J.M., Some Observable Sources of Women's Oppression in Zimbabwe, unpublished, Harare, 1983.
11. May, J., *op. cit.*
12. Childs, H., *The History and Extent of Recognition of Tribal Law in Rhodesia*, Salisbury, Ministry of Internal Affairs, 1975, p. 91.
13. May, J., *op. cit.*
14. Bourdillon, M.F.C., *The Shona People*, Mambo Press, Gweru, 1982, p. 68.
15. *The Zimbabwe Report on UN Decade for Women*, Ministry of Community Development and Women's Affairs, 1985, p. 6.
16. Dworkin, R., *Taking Rights Seriously*, Duckworth, London, 1977.
17. Zimbabwe Constitution Order, S.I. 1979/1600, Chapter III, Article 23, 3 (a) and (b).
18. Bekker, J.C. and Coertze, J.J.J., *Seymour's Customary Law in Southern Africa*, 4th Ed, Juta and Company, Cape Town, 1982.
19. Fundamental Rights and Personal Law Project Paper, *State, Law and Women*, presented at Forum '85, Nairobi, by Joyce Kazembe and Marjon Mol.
20. Katekwe vs. Muchabaiwa, Judgement No. S.C. 87/84. Civil Appeal No. 99/84.
21. Primary Courts Act, (6, 1981), Section 3 (4).
22. *Herald* (Sunday Mail, 22 December 1985).
23. Katekwe vs. Muchabaiwa, *op. cit.*
24. *Ibid.*
25. Fundamental Rights and Personal Law Project Findings.
26. The Minimum Wages Act (1981) and recent amendments.
27. Labour Relations Act (1985).
28. The Sex Disqualification Removal Act (1983).
29. Callear, D., *The Social and Cultural Factors Involved in Production: Small Scale Farmers in Wedza Communal Area, Zimbabwe, of Maize*

and its Marketing, UNESCO, Division for the Study of Development, Paris, 1982, p. 22.
30. *Ibid.*
31. *Ibid.*
32. Muchena, O., *Women in Town*, Centre for Applied Social Sciences, University of Zimbabwe, 1980.
33. Dangarembga, S., *Female Employment in the Public Sector*, presented at the Colloquium on the Rights of Women in Zimbabwe, November 1984, unpublished.
34. *Ibid.*
35. *Zimbabwe Report on UN Decade for Women, op. cit.*, p.13.
36. *Ibid.*
37. Sithole, J., 'Reconstruction Programmes Undertaken in Mashonaland East' at UNESCO Seminar on Women in National Reconstruction, Harare, 19-22 November 1985.
38. See booklets by The Fundamental Rights and Personal Project Team at the University of Zimbabwe, Centre for Applied Social Sciences.
39. *Zimbabwe Report on UN Decade for Women, op. cit.*, p.19.
40. *Ibid.*

BIBLIOGRAPHY

Books and Articles

Politics

Adrian, Laftwich, *Redefining Politics: People Resources and Power*, Methuen, London, 1983.

Alavi, H., The State in Post Colonial Societies: Pakistan and Bangla desh, *New Left Review*, 1972.

Anglin, Douglas G., Zimbabwe: Retrospect and Prospect, *International Journal*, No. 35, 1980.

Arrighi, Giovanni and Saul, J., *Essays on the Political Economy of Africa*, Monthly Review, New York, 1973.

Astrow, Andre, *Zimbabwe: a Revolution that lost its way?*, Zed Press, London, 1983.

Baker, Colin, Conducting the elections in Zimbabwe 1980, *Public Administration and Development*, 2(1):45-58, 1982.

Barber, James, *Rhodesia: the Road to Rebellion*, Oxford University Press, London, 1967.

Bobo, N., The Zimbabwe Lesson, *Monthly Review*, 35:25-41, 1983.

Bowman, Larry W., *Politics in Rhodesia: White Power in an African state*, Harvard University Press, Cambridge, Mass., 1973.

Bratton, Michael, *Beyond Community Development: the Political Economy of Rural Administration in Zimbabwe*, From Rhodesia to Zimbabwe series No. 6, Mambo Press, Gweru, 1978.

Bratton, Michael, The Public Service in Zimbabwe, *Political Science Quarterly*, 95:441-64, 1980.

Bratton, Michael, Settler State, Guerrilla War and Rural Underdevelopment in Rhodesia, *Rural Africana*, No. 4/5, 1979.

Bratton, Michael, Structural Transformation in Zimbabwe: Some Comparative Notes from the Neo-Colonization in Kenya, in Wiley, David and Isaacman, Allen (ed), *Southern Africa: Society, Economy and Liberation*, East Lansing, Michigan State, 1981.

Cabral, A., *Revolution in Guinea: An African People's Struggle*.

Callinicos, Alex and Rogers, J., *Southern Africa After Soweto*, Pluto, London, 1980.

Campbell, H., Nkomo, Before and After, *Journal of African Marxists*, 1984.

Caute, David, *Under the Skin: the Death of White Rhodesia*, Penguin, Middlesex, 1983.

Cefkin, Leo J., Rhodesian University Students in National Politics, in Hanna, William J. et al (ed), *University Students and African Politics, Africana*, New York, 1975.

Centre of African Studies, *Zimbabwe: Notes and Reflections on the Rhodesian question*, Centre of African Studies, Maputo, 1979.

Clarke, Duncan G., Settler Ideology and African Underdevelopment in Postwar Rhodesia, *Rhodesian Journal of Economics*, No. 8, 1974.

Davidow, Jeffrey, *A Peace in Southern Africa: the Lancaster House Conference on Rhodesia, 1979*, Westview, London, 1984.

Davidson, B., Slovo, Joe and Wilkinson, A., *Southern Africa: the New Politics of Revolution*, Penguin Books, London, 1976.

Day, John, The Insignificance of Tribe in the African Politics of Zimbabwe Rhodesia, in Morris-Jones, W.H. (ed), *From Rhodesia to Zimbabwe*, Cass, London, 1980.

De Brunhoff, S., *The State, Capital and Economic Policy*, 1978.

Depelchin, J., From Lumumba to Mandela: People's Struggles to Own their History, in Mandaza, I. (ed), *Conflict in Southern Africa, Contemporary Marxism*, October 1986.

Dumbutshena, Enoch, Why the Nationalists Rejected the 1961 Constitution, in Rea, Fred B. (ed), *Southern Rhodesia: The Price of Freedom*, Manning, Bulawayo, 1964.

Dumbutshena, Enoch, *Zimbabwe Tragedy*, East African Publishing House, Nairobi, 1975.

Engels, F. and Marx, K., The Manifesto of the Communist Party, *Four Classical Texts on the Principles of Socialism*, Allen and Unwin, London, 1960.

Folson, Kweku G., Samir Amin as a Neo-Marxist, *Africa Development*, Vol. X, 3, 1985.

Franck, Thomas, *Race and Nationalism, the Struggle for Power in Southern Rhodesia*, Fordham University Press, 1960.

Franklin, Harry, *Unholy Wedlock: the Failure of the Central African Federation*, Allen and Unwin, London, 1963.

Frederikse, J., *None But Ourselves: Masses vs Media in the Making of Zimbabwe*, Zimbabwe Publishing House, Harare, 1983.

Gann, Lewis H. and Henriksen, Thomas, *The Struggle for Zimbabwe: the Battle in the Bush*, Praeger, New York, 1981.

Good, Robert C., *UDI: The International Politics of the Rhodesian Rebellion*, Princeton University Press, Princeton, 1973.

Gregory, Martyn, The 1980 Elections—A First-hand Account and Analysis, *World Today*, 36:180-88, 1980.

Gregory, Martyn, Zimbabwe 1980: Politicization through Armed Struggle and electoral politics, *Journal of Commonwealth and Comparative Politics*, Vol. 19 No. 1, March 1981.

Hanbota, J., *Mozambique: Revolution under Fire*, Zed, London, 1984.

Holderness, Hardwicke, *Lost Chance: Southern Rhodesia, 1945-58*, Zimbabwe

Publishing House, Harare, 1985.

International Defence and Aid Fund, *Rhodesia: The Ousting of Tangwena*, Christian Action Publications, London, 1972.

Johnson, Phyllis and Martin, D., *Destructive Engagement: Southern Africa at war*, Zimbabwe Publishing House, Harare, 1986.

Jordan, J.D., *Local government in Zimbabwe: an overview*, Mambo Occasional Papers—Socio-Economic Series No. 17, Mambo Press, Gweru, 1984.

Keatley, Patrick, *The Politics of Partnership: the Federation of Rhodesia and Nyasaland*, Penguin African Library, London, 1963.

Khapoya, Vincent B., Resistance or Accommodation: African Members of Parliament and African Actors in Post-UDI Rhodesia, *Ufahamu*, 4(2):127-44, 1973.

Kirkwood, K., Zimbabwe: the Politics of Ethnicity: review article, *Ethnic and Racial Studies*, Vol. 7 No. 3, July 1984.

Kitching, G., Politics, Method and Evidence in the 'Kenya Debate', in Bonstein, H. and Campbell, B.K. (ed), *Contradictions of Accumulation in Africa: Studies in Economy and State*, Sage, London, 1985.

Knight, Virginia C., Political consolidation in Zimbabwe, *Current History*, Vol. 83 No. 491, March 1984.

Lan, D., *Guns and Rain: Guerrillas and Spirit Mediums in Zimbabwe*, James Currey, London, 1985.

Leys, C., *European Politics in Southern Rhodesia*, Oxford University Press, London, 1969.

Linden, Ian, *The Catholic Church and the Struggle for Zimbabwe*, Longman, London, 1980.

Loney, Martin, *Rhodesia: White Racism and Imperial Response*, Penguin, Middlesex, 1978.

Magubane, I. and Mandaza, I., *Whither South Africa?*, Africa World Press, forthcoming.

Makonese, Philemon T., ZAPU and the Liberation of Zimbabwe, *Africa Quarterly*, 10:40-51, 1970.

Mandaza, Ibbo, Conflict in Southern Africa, *Eastern Africa Social Science Research Review*, June 1985.

Mandaza, Ibbo, Imperialism, the Frontline States and the Zimbabwe Problem, *Utafiti*, Journal of the Faculty of Arts and Social Sciences, University of Dar es Salaam, Vo. 5 No. 1, 1980.

Mandaza, Ibbo, Southern Africa: US Policy and the Struggle for National Independence, in Magubane, B. and Mandaza, I. (ed), *Whither South Africa?*, Africa World Press, forthcoming.

Martin, David and Johnson, Phyllis, *The Struggle for Zimbabwe: the Chimurenga war*, Zimbabwe Publishing House, Harare, 1981.

Matatu, G., Zimbabwe African National Union—Patriotic Front, Zimbabwe: Agenda for total power, *Africa*, No. 156, August 1984.

Mazoe, Bernard, How Zimbabwe's Liberation Struggle Began, *African Communist*, 69:19-34, 1977.

Meredith, Martin, *The Past is Another Country: Rhodesia, UDI to Zimbabwe*, Pan Books, London, 1980.

M'Gabe, Davis, The Beginning of Guerrilla Warfare, *Monthly Review*, 20(10),

1969; also in Cartey, W. and Kilson, M. (ed), *The Africa Reader: Independent Africa*, Vintage, New York, 1970.

Mlambo, Eshmael, *Rhodesia: The Struggle for a Birthright*, Hurst, London, 1972.

Moore, Dave, Zimbabwe: A Revolution that lost its way? (review article), *Review of African Political Economy*, No. 34, 1985.

Morris-Jones, W.H. (ed), *From Rhodesia to Zimbabwe: Behind and Beyond Lancaster House*, Cass, London, 1980.

Mpofu, J.M. et al, Nationalist Politics in Zimbabwe: The 1980 Elections and Beyond, *Review of African Political Economy*, No. 18, 1981.

Mtshali, B.V., *Rhodesia: Background to Conflict*, New York, 1967.

Mubako, Simbi V., The Rhodesian Border Blockade of 1973 and the African Liberation Struggle, *Journal of Commonwealth and Comparative Politics*, 12:297-312, 1974.

Mubako, Simbi V., The Quest for Unity in the Zimbabwe Liberation Movement, *Issue*, 5(1):5-17, 1975.

Mufuka, Kenneth N., Reflections on Southern Rhodesia: an African Viewpoint, *Africa Today*, 24(2):51-63, 1977.

Mufuka, K. Nyamayaro, Rhodesia's Internal Settlement: A Tragedy, *African Affairs*, 78:439-50.

Mugabe, Robert Gabriel, *Our War of Liberation: Speeches, Articles, Interviews, 1976-79*, Mambo Press, Gweru, 1983.

Mugabe, Robert and Nkomo, Joshua, *Zimbabwe: The Final Advance*, Liberation Support Movement, Oakland, California, 1978.

Munslow, B., Zimbabwe's Emerging African Bourgeoisie, *Review of African Political Economy*, No. 19, 1980.

Murapa, Rukudzo, Geography, Race, Class and Power in Rhodesia: 1890 to the Present, *Journal of Southern African Affairs*, 3:159-73, 1978.

Mutambirwa, James A.C., The Impact of Christianity on Nationalism in Zimbabwe: A Critique of the Sithole Thesis,, *Journal of Southern African Affairs*, 1:69-81, 1976.

Mutambirwa, James A.C., *The Rise of Settler Power in Southern Rhodesia, 1898-1923*, Fairleigh Dickinson University Press, Rutherford, N.J., 1980.

Mutasa, Didymus, *Rhodesian Black Behind Bars*, Mowbrays, London, 1974.

Mutiti, M. Aaron Benjamin, Rhodesia and Her Four Discriminatory Constitutions, *African Review*, 4:259-78, 1974.

Mutsuairo, S.M., *Mapondera: Soldier of Zimbabwe*, Three Continents Press, Washington D.C.,1978.

Mutunhu, T., Nehanda of Zimbabwe (Rhodesia): The Story of a Woman Liberation Leader and Fighter, *Ufahamu*, 7(1):59-70, 1976.

Muzorewa, A., *Rise Up and Walk: An Autobiography*, Evans Brothers, London, 1978.

Mzamane, Mbulelo, The People's Mood: The Voice of a Guerrilla Poet, *Review of African Political Economy*, 18:29-43, 1980.

Ndlangamandla, Dumisani, The National Democratic Revolution in Zimbabwe, *African Communist*, 77:86-93, 1979.

Ngwenyama, N.M., Rhodesia Approaches Collapse: A Study of Settler Resistance to African Nationalism, *Ufamahu*, 5(3):11-61, 1975.

Nyagumbo, M., *With the People*, Allison and Busby, London, 1980.

Nyangoni, Wellington T., *African Nationalism in Zimbabwe*, University Press of America, Washington D.C., 1977.

Nyangoni, Wellington W. and Nyandoro, G. (ed), *Zimbabwe Independence Movements: Select Documents*, Rex Collings, London, 1979.

Nyerere, Julius, *Freedom and Development*, OUP, Dar Es Salaam, 1973.

Nuzuwah, Mariyawanda, Conflict Resolution in Zimbabwe: Superpower Determinants to the Peace Settlement, *Journal of Southern African Affairs*, 4:389-400, 1979.

Ohrman, H. (ed), *The State in Tanzania: Who Controls it and whose interest does it serve?*, Dar Es Salaam, 1980.

Passmore, Gloria C., *The National Policy of Community Development in Rhodesia*, University of Rhodesia, Harare, 1972.

Ranger, Terence O., *Peasant Consciousness and Querrilla War in Zimbabwe*, ZPH, Harare, 1985.

Ranger, Terence O., *Revolt in Southern Rhodesia 1896-7: A Study in African Resistance*, Heinemann, London, 1967.

Ranger, Terence O., The Changing of the Old Guard: Robert Mugabe and the Revival of ZANU, *Journal of Southern African Studies*, 7:71-90, 1980.

Ranger, Terence O., The Death of Chamimuka: Spirit Mediums, Nationalism and ther Guerrilla War in Zimbabwe, *African Affairs*, Vol. 81 No. 324, 1982.

Ranger, Terence O., *The Invention of Tribalism in Zimbabwe*, Mambo Occasional Papers—Socioeconomic Series No. 19, Mambo Press, Gweru, 1985.

Raven, Faith, *Central Africa: Background to Argument*, African Publications Trust, 1962.

Rich, Tony., Zimbabwe: only teething troubles, *World Today*, No. 39, December 1983.

Rich, Tony, Legacies of the Past?: The Results of the 1980 Election in Midlands Province, Zimbabwe, *Africa*, 52:42-55, 1982.

Roeburn, Michael, *Black Fire: Accounts of the Querrilla War in Zimbabwe*, Mambo Press, Gweru, 1978.

Samkange, Stanlake and Samkange, Tommie Marie, *Hunhuism or Ubuntuism: a Zimbabwe Indigenous Political Philosophy*, Graham Publishing, Harare, 1980.

Saul, J.S. (ed), *A Difficult Road: The Transition to Socialism in Mozambique*, Monthly Review Press, New York, 1985.

Saul, J.S., Transforming the Struggle in Zimbabwe, *Southern Africa*, Vol. 10 No. 1, 1977.

Saul, J.S., Zimbabwe: The Next Round, *Monthly Review*, Vol. 32 No. 4, 1980.

Schatzberg, Michael G. (ed), *The Political Economy of Zimbabwe*, Praeger, New York, 1984.

Seidman, Robert B. and Gagne, Martin, The State, Law and Development in Zimbabwe, *Journal of Southern African Affairs*, 5:149-70, 1980.

Shamuyarira, Nathan M., *Crisis in Rhodesia*, Transatlantic Arts, New York, 1965.

Shamuyarira, Nathan M., *Essays in the Liberation of Southern Africa*, Tanzania

Publishing House, Dar Es Salaam, 1971.

Shamuyarira, Nathan M., Rhodesia After the Pearce Commission Report, 1972, *African Review*, 2:467-88, Dar Es Salaam, 1972.

Shamuyarira, Nathan M., The Nationalist Movement in Zimbabwe, *African Forum*, 2(3):34-42, 1967.

Sithole, M., Ethnicity and Factionalism in Zimbabwe Nationalist Politics 1957-79, *Ethnic and Racial Studies*, Vol. 3 No. 1, 1980.

Sithole, M., Focus on class and factionalism in the Zimbabwe Nationalist Movement, *African Studies Review*, Vol. 27 No. 1, March 1984.

Sithole, M., *Zimbabwe Struggles within the Struggle*, Rujeke, Harare, 1977.

Sithole, N., *African Nationalism*, Oxford University Press, London, 1968.

Sithole, N., *In Defence of the March 3rd Agreement*, Graham, Salisbury, 1979.

Sehmiley, Xan, Zimbabwe, Southern Africa and the Rise of Robert Mugabe, *Foreign Affairs*, 58:1060-83.

Smith, David and Simpson, Colin, *Mugabe*, Pioneer Head, Harare, 1981.

Soames, Lord, From Rhodesia to Zimbabwe, *International Affairs*, 56:1060-83, Great Britain, 1980.

Somerville, K., The USSR and Southern Africa since 1976, *Journal of Modern African Studies*, Vol. 22 No. 1, 1984.

Tandon, Y., The Post-Colonial State, *Social Change and Development*, No. 8, 1984.

Thompson, Carol B., *Challenge to Imperialism: The Frontline States in the Liberation of Zimbabwe*, Westview, Boulder and Zimbabwe Publishing House, Harare.

Todd, Judith, *An Act of Treason: Rhodesia 1965*, Longman, London, 1982.

Todd, Judith, *The Right to Say No*, Third Press, New York, 1973.

Utete, C. Munhamu, *The Road to Zimbabwe: The Political Economy of Settler Colonialism, National Liberation and Foreign Intervention*, University Press of America, Washington D.C., 1979.

Verrier, Anthony, *The Road to Zimbabwe 1890-1980*, Jonathan Cape, London, 1986.

Von Freyhold, M., The Postcolonial State and its Tanzanian Version: Contribution to a Debate, in Othman, H. (ed), *The State in Tanzania: Who controls it and whose interest does it serve*, Dar Es Salaam, 1980.

Windrich, Elaine, *Britain and the Politics of Rhodesia Independence*, Croom Helm, London, 1978.

Windrich, Elaine, *The Mass Media in the Struggle for Zimbabwe: Censorship and Propaganda under Rhodesian Front Rule*, Mambo Occasional Papers, Socio-Economic Series No. 15, Mambo Press, Gweru, 1981.

Windrich, Elaine, *The Rhodesian Problem: A Documentary Record, 1923-1973*, Routledge, London, 1975.

Yates, Peter, The prospect for socialist transition in Zimbabwe, *Review of African Political Economy*, No. 18, 1980.

Zimbabwe at 5 years of Independence: Achievement, Problems and Prospects, ZANU (PF).

Zvobgo, Chengetai J., Rhodesia's Internal Settlement 1977-79: A Record, *Journal* of *Southern African Affairs*, 5:25-38, 1980.

Zvobgo, Eddison, The Southern Rhodesian African National Congress: Patterns of Black-White Conflict (1957-59), *Zimbabwe News*, 14 April 1983.

Economy

Baylies, Carolyn, Imperialism and Settler Capital: Friends or Foes?, *Review of African Political Economy*, No. 18, 1980.

Bernstein,H. and Campbell, Bonnie (ed), *Contradictions of Accumulation in Africa*, London, 1985.

Bierman, Werner and Kossler, Reinhart, The Settler Mode of Production: The Rhodesian Case, *Review of African Poltical Economy*, No. 18, 1980.

Chanaiwa, David, *The Occupation of Southern Rhodesia: A Study of Economic Imperialism*, East Africa Publishing House, Nairobi, 1981.

Chidzero, B. and Moyana, K., The Structure of the Zimbabwean Economy and Future Manpower Implications, *Rural Africana*, 4/5:1-16, 1979.

Clarke, Duncan G., *Foreign Companies and International Investment in Zimbabwe*, Mambo Press, Gweru, 1980.

Clarke, Duncan G., *The Distribution of Income and Wealth in Rhodesia*, Mambo Occasional Papers, Socio-Economic Series No. 7, Mambo Press, Gweru, 1977.

Clarke, Duncan G., *The Unemployment Crisis*, From Rhodesia to Zimbabwe Series No. 3, Mambo Press, Gweru, 1979.

Clarke, Duncan G., *Unemployment and Economic Structure in Rhodesia*, Mambo Occasional Papers, Socio-Economic Series No. 9, Mambo Press, Gweru, 1977.

Cooper, C. (ed), *The Political Economy of Technical Advance in Underdeveloped Countries*, Cass, London, 1973.

Davies, Rob, *The Informal Sector: A Solution to Unemployment?*, From Rhodesia to Zimbabwe Series No. 5, Mambo Press, Gweru and Catholic Institute for International Relations, London, 1978.

Dobb, Maurice, *An Essay on Economic Growth and Planning*, Routledge, London, 1977.

Economist Intelligence Unit, *Zimbabwe's First Five Years: Economic Prospects Following Independence*, Special Report No. 11, EIU, London, 1981.

Gershenkron, *Economic Backwardness in Historical Perspective*, Cambridge University Press, 1966.

Girvan, N., Swallowing the IMF Medicine in the Seventies, *Development Dialogue*, No. 2, 1980.

Gussman, Boris, Industrial efficiency and the urban African: a study of conditions in Southern Rhodesia, *Africa*, Vol. 23, 1953.

Jonah, K., Imperialism, the State and the Indigenization of the Ghananian Economy 1957-84, *Africa Development*, Vol. 10, No. 3, 1985.

Kapungu, Leonard T., Economic Sanctions in the Rhodesian Context, in El-Ayouty, Yassin and Brooks, Hugh (eds), *African and International Organization*, Nijhoff, The Hague, 1974.

Kapungu, Leonard T., *The United Nations and Economic Sanctions Against Rhodesia*, Lexington, Mass., 1973.

Makgetla, Neva Seidman, Transnational Corporations in Southern Rhodesia, *Journal of Southern African Affairs*, 5:57-88.

Marron, A., The Bungled Experiment, *International Investor*, 1986.

Mkandawire, Thandika, Home-Grown(?) Austerity Measures: The Case of Zimbabwe, *Africa Development*, Vol. 10 No. 1-2, 1985.

Mkandawire, Thandika, State policy response to economic crisis in Africa, *East African Social Science Research Review*, Vol. 1 No. 2, June 1985.

Ndlela, Daniel Boda, *Dualism in the Rhodesian Colonial Economy*, Lund, Sweden, 1981.

Ndlela, Daniel Boda, Sectoral analysis of Zimbabwe economic development with implications for foreign trade and foreign exchange, *Zimbabwe Journal of Economics*, Vol. 1 No. 1, July 1984.

Renwick, Robin, *Economic Sanctions*, Center for International Affairs, Harvard University, 1981.

Riddell, Roger, *Alternatives to Poverty*, From Rhodesia to Zimbabwe Series No. 1, Mambo Press, Gweru, 1978.

Seers, D. (ed), Dependency Theory: A Critical Reassessment, Francis Pinter, London, 1981.

Simson, Howard, *Zimbabwe: A Country Study*, Scandinavian Institute of African studies, Uppsala, 1979.

Stoneman, Colin, Foreign capital and the reconstruction of Zimbabwe, *Review of African Political Economy*, No.11, 1978.

Stoneman, Colin, Industrialization and Self-Reliance in Zimbabwe, in Fransman, Martin (ed), *Industry and Accumulation in Africa*, Heinemann, London, 1982.

Stoneman, Colin, *Skilled Labour and Future needs*, From Rhodesia to Zimbabwe Series No. 4, Mambo Press, Gweru, 1978.

Stoneman, Colin (ed), *Zimbabwe's Inheritance*, Macmillan, London, 1981.

Sutcliffe, R.B., *Industry and Underdevelopment*, Development Economic Series, Addison-Wesley, London, 1971.

Taussig, M., *The Devil and Commodity Fetishism in South Africa*, University of North Carolina Press, 1980.

Thomas, C., *Dependence and Tranformation*, Monthly Review Press, New York, 1984.

United Nations, *Zimbabwe, Towards a New Economic Order: An Economic and Social Survey*, Working Papers, Vol. 1, United Nations, New York, 1980.

United Nations Industrial Development Organisation, *Study of the manufacturing sector in Zimbabwe: Technical report DP/ZIM/4/018*, Vol. 1: Summary and recommendations, Vol. 2: Main report, Vol 3: Statistical annexes, UNIDO, Vienna, 12 September 1984.

White, G., Development states and socialist industrialisation in Third World, *Journal of Development Studies*, Vol. 21 No. 1, October 1984.

World Bank, *Accelerated Development of Sub-Saharan Africa: An Agenda for Action*, World Bank, Washington D.C., 1981.

World Bank, *Sub-Saharan Africa: Progress Report on Development and Programmes*, World Bank, Washington D.C., 1983.

Zimbabwe: an African Business Survey, *African Business*, No. 81, May 1985.

Zimbabwe: the first five years, *African Economic Digest*, Special Report, April 1985.

Agrarian Question

Bratton, M., Farmer organization and food production in Zimbabwe, *World Development*, Vol. 14 No. 3, 1986.

Bulman, Mary E., *The Native Land Husbandry Act of Southern Rhodesia: A Failure in Land Reform*, Tribal Areas of Rhodesia Research Foundation, Salisbury, 1973.

Bush, Ray and Cliffe, L., Agrarian policy in migrant labour societies: reform or transformation in Zimbabwe, *Review of African Political Economy*, No. 29, 1984.

Calleur, D., *The Social and Cultural Factors Involved in Production by Small Farmers in Wedza Communal Area of Maize and its Marketing*, UNESCO, 1982.

Cheater, Angela P., Formal and Informal Rights to Land in Zimbabwe's Black Freehold Areas: a Case-Study from Msengezi, *Africa*, No.52, 1982.

Cheater, Angela P., *Idioms of Accumulation: Rural Development and Class Formation Among Freeholders in Zimbabwe*, Mambo Press, Harare, 1984.

Clarke, Duncan G., *Agricultural and plantation workers in Rhodesia: A Report on Conditions of Labour and Subsistence*, Mambo Occasional Papers, Socio-Economic Series No. 6, Gweru, Mambo Press, 1977.

Clarke, Duncan G., *Black Contract Labour and Farm Wage Rates in Rhodesia*, mimeo, Labour Research Seminar No. 2, Department of Economics, University of Rhodesia, 1973.

Duggan, W., The Native Land Husbandry act of 1951 and the Rural African Middle Class of Southern Rhodesia, *African Affairs*, No. 79, 1980.

Dunlop, Harry, Development in Rhodesian Tribal Areas, *Rhodesian Journal of Economics*, No. 8, 1974.

Dunlop, Harry, *The Development of European Agriculture in Rhodesia, 1945-1965*, Department of Economics, University of Rhodesia, Salisbury, 1971.

Gaidzanwa, Rudo B., *Promised Land: Towards a Land Policy for Zimbabwe*, Institute of Social Studies, The Hague, 1981.

Geza, Sam, The role of resettlement in social development in zimbabwe, *Journal of Social Development in Africa*, Vol. 1 No. 1, 1986.

Harbeson, John W., Land Policy and Politics in Zimbabwe, *Current History*, No. 81, 1982.

Hodder-Williams, Richard, *White Farmers in Rhodesia: a history of the Marandellas district*, Macmillan, London, 1983.

Hume, I.M., *A Preliminary Essay on Land Reform in Rhodesia/Zimbabwe*, Whitsun Foundation, Harare, 1978.

International Defence and Aid Found, *The Ousting of Tangwena*, Christian Action Publications, London, 1972.

Jacobs, Susie, Women and land resettlement in Zimbabwe, *Review of African Political Economy*, No. 27-28, 1983.

Kay, George, *Rhodesia: A Human Geography*, Africana, New York, 1970.

Keyner, C.F., *Maize Control in Southern Rhodesia 1931-41: The African Contribution to White Survival*, Historical Asociation, Salisbury, 1978.

Kinsey, B.H., Forever gained: resettlement and land policy in the context of national development of Zimbabwe, *Africa*, Vol. 1 No. 1, November 1983.

Kinsey, B.H., Some emerging policy issues in Zimbabwe's land resettlement programmes, *Development Policy Review*, Vol. 1 No. 2, November 1985.

Massell, Benton F. and Johnson, R.W.M., Economics of smallholder Farming in Rhodesia: a Cross-Section Analysis of Two Areas, *Food Research Institute Studies Supplement*, No. 8, Stanford, California, 1968.

Mosley, Paul, Agricultural Development and Government Policy in Settler Economies: The Case of Kenya and Southern Rhodesia, 1900-60, *Economic History Review*, No. 35, 1982.

Moyana, Henry V., Land and Race in Rhodesia, *African Review*, No. 5, 1975.

Moyana, Henry V., *Political Economy of Land in Zimbabwe*, Mambo Press, Gweru, 1984.

Mtetwa, R.M.G., Myth or Reality: The 'Cattle Complex' in South East Africa, with Special Reference to Rhodesia, *Zambezia*, No. 6, 1978.

Mumbengegwi, C., Agricultural producer cooperatives and agrarian transformation in Zimbabwe: policy, strategy and implementation, *Zimbabwe Journal of Economics*, Vol.1 No. 1, 1984.

Mumbengegwi, C., *Some Aspects of Zimbabwe's Post Independence Agricultural producer Co-opertives: A Profile and Preliminary Assessment*, University of Zimbabwe, Harare, 1984.

Mungazi, Dickson A., *The Underdevelopment of African Education: A Black Zimbabwean Perspective. A Study of the Problems that have Retarded the Full Development of Education in Africa during and after Colonial Period*, University Press of America, Washington D.C., 1982.

Munslow, Barry, Prospects for the socialist transition of agriculture in Zimbabwe, *World Development*, Vol. 13 No. 1, January 1955.

Palmer, R.H., War and land in Rhodesia, *Transafrican Journal of History*, Vol. 1 No. 2, 1971.

Palmer, Robin, *Land and Racial Domination in Rhodesia*, Heinemann Educational, London, 1977.

Palmer, Robin and Parsons, N. (ed), *Roots of Rural Poverty in Central and Southern Africa*, Heinemann, London, 1977.

Phimister, Ian, Discourse and the discipline of historical context: conservation and ideas about development in Southern Rhodesia: 1930-50, *Journal of Southern African Studies*, Vol. 12 No. 2, April 1986.

Phimister, Ian, Peasant Production and Underdevelopment in Southern Rhodesia, *African Affairs*, No. 13, 1975.

Pollak, O., Black Farmers and White Politics in Rhodesia, *African Affairs*, Vol. 74 No. 296, 1975.

Rennie, K., White Farmers, Black Tenants and Landlord Legislation: Southern Rhodesia 1890-1930, *Journal of Southern African Studies*, Vol. 5 No. 1. Riddell, Roger, Skill needs in the agricultural sector Exchange Fund, *International Universities*, Vol. 3 No. 11, 1980.

Riddell, Roger, *The land question*, From Rhodesia to Zimbabwe Series, No. 2, Mambo Press, Gweru, 1978.

Rifkind, M.L., Land Apportionment in Perspective, *Rhodesian History*, No. 3, 1972.

Sachikonye, L.M., Agribusiness in Africa: A Review Article, *Africa Development*, 1984.

Shumba, E., Application of the farming systems research approach in Mangwende Communal Area In the Murewa District, *Zimbabwe Agricultural Journal*, Vol. 82 No. 2, 1985.

Sibanda, Concern J., *The Tribal Trust Lands of Rhodesia: Problems of Development*, Centre for Development Studies, University of Swansea, Swansea, 1979.

Simon, David, Agrarian policy in Zimbabwe, *Review of African Political Economy*, No. 34, 1985.

Temu, P.E., *Marketing Board Pricing and Storage Policy with Particular Reference to Maize in Tanzania*, Vantage Press, New York, 1984.

Tickner, Vincent, *The Food Problem*, From Rhodesia to Zimbabwe Series, No. 4, Mambo Press, Gweru, 1979.

Vaughan, Megan, Famine analysis and family relations 1949 in Nyasaland, *Past and Present*, No. 108, August 1985.

Weiner, Dan et al, Land use and agricultural productivity in Zimbabwe, *Journal of Modern African Studies*, Vol. 23 No. 2, June 1985.

Weinmann, H., *Agricultural Research and Development in Southern Rhodesia 1924-1950*, University of Rhodesia, Harare, 1985.

Weinrich, A.K.H., *African Farmers in Rhodesia*, Oxford University Press, London, 1975.

Weinrich, A.K.H., *Black and White Elites in Rural Rhodesia*, Manchester University Press, Manchester, 1973.

Weinrich, A.K.H., Strategic Resettlement in Rhodesia, *Journal of Southern African Studies*, Vol. 3 No. 2.

Whitlow, J.R., A Scenario of Changes in Subsistence Land Use and Its Relevance to the Tribal Areas of Zimbabwe, *Zambezia*, No. 7, 1979.

Whitsun Foundation, *A Strategy for Rural Development and Data Bank No. 2: the peasant sector*, Whitsun Foundation, Harare, 1978.

Whitsun Foundation, *Land Reform in Zimbabwe*, Whitsun Foundation, Harare, 1983.

Whitsun Foundation, *Project 1.04: African Co-operative Societies in Rhodesia Undertaken from January to April 1976*, Whitsun Foundation, Harare, 1977.

Whitsun Foundation, *Project 3.04(2): Peasant Sector Credit Plan for Zimbabwe*, Vol. 1 (project summary) and Vol. 3 (organisation of statutory credit), Whitsun Foundation, Harare, 1980.

Whitsun Foundation, *Rural Service Centres Development Study*, Whitsun Foundation, Harare, 1980.

World Bank, *Zimbabwe Agricultural Sector Study: Report No. 4401-Zimbabwe*, World Bank, Washington D.C., 1983.

Yudelman, M., *Africans on the Land*, Cambridge, Massachusetts, 1964.

Labour Movement

Arrighi, G., Labour supplies in historical perspective: a study of the proletarianisation of the African peasantry in Rhodesia, *Journal of Development Studies*, Vol. 6 No. 3, 1970.

Brand, C.M., Politics and African Trade Unionism in Rhodesia Since Federation, *Rhodesian History*, No. 2, 1971.

416 Zimbabwe

Brand, C.M., Race and Politics in Rhodesian Trade Unions, *African Perspectives*, No. 1, 1976.

Brand, C.M., The Political Role of Unions in Rhodesia, *South African Labour Bulletin*, No. 1, 1975.

Chavunduka, Gordon L., Farm labourers in Rhodesia, *Rhodesian Journal of Economics*, Vol. 6 No. 4, 1972.

Clarke, Duncan G., African Mine Labourers and Conditions of Labour in the Mining Industry in Rhodesia 1940-74, *Rhodesian Journal of Economics*, No. 9, 1975.

Clarke, Duncan G., *Contract Labour from Rhodesia to the South African Gold Mines*, Southern Africa Labour and Development Research Unit, Cape Town, 1976.

Clarke, Duncan G., *Contract Workers and Underdevelopment in Rhodesia*, Mambo Press, Gweru, 1974.

Clarke, Duncan G., *Domestic Workers in Rhodesia: The Economics of Masters and Servants*, Mambo Press, Gweru, 1974.

Clarke, Duncan G., Institutional Wage-Supply Determinants of Plantation Labour in Postwar Rhodesia, *Rural Africana*, No. 24, 1974.

Clarke, Duncan G., Structural Trends Affecting Conditions of Labour for African Workers in Rhodesia, *Rhodesian Journal of Economics*, No. 10, 1976.

Clarke, Tom and Clements, Laurie (ed), *Trade Unions Under Capitalism*, Harvester Press, Sussex, 1980.

Damachi, U.G. et al (ed), *Industrial relations in Africa*, Macmillan, London, 1979.

Davies, R.J., Leadership and Unity in Rhodesian Black Trade Unions, *South African Labour Bulletin*, No. 1, 1975.

Harris, Peter S., *Black Industrial Workers in Rhodesia: The General Problems of Low Pay*, Mambo Press, Gweru, 1974.

Harris, Peter S., Government Policy and African Wages in Rhodesia,*Zambezia*, Vol. 2 No. 2, 1972.

Harris, Peter S., Incomes, Employment and Political Power in Rhodesia, *Journal of Modern African Studies*, No. 10, 1972.

Harris, Peter S., Industrial Relations in Rhodesia, *South African Journal of Economics*, Vol. 42 No. 1, 1974.

Harris, Peter S., Industrial Workers in Rhodesia 1946-72: Working Class Elites or Lumpenproletariat, *Journal of Southern African Studies*, No. 1, 1975.

Hawkins, Anthony M., African Labour Supplies in the Rhodesian Economy, *Rhodesian Journal of Economics*, No. 10, 1976.

Hyman, R., *Industrial Relations, a Marxist Introduction*, Macmillan, London, 1975.

International Labour Organization, Labour Conditions and Discrimination in Southern Rhodesia (Zimbabwe), *Objective: Justice*, No. 10, 1979.

Lenin, V.I., *On Trade Unions*, Progress Publishers, Moscow, 1970.

Mackenzie, John M., Colonial Labour Policy and Rhodesia, *Rhodesian Journal of Economics*, No. 8, 1974.

Malaba, Luke, Supply, control and organisation of African labour in Rhodesia,

Review of African Political Economy, No. 18, 1980.

Mandaza, Ibbo, Comments on Negative Criticisms of the NMS Report, *Manpower Information Services*, Vol. 3 No. 2, 1983.

May, Joan, *African Women in Urban Employment: Factors Influencing their Employment in Zimbabwe*, Mambo Occasional Papers, Socio-Economic Series No. 12, 1979.

Mswaka, T.E., African Unemployment and the Rural Areas of Rhodesia, *Rural Africana*, No. 24, 1974.

Murphree, Marshall W., *Employment Opportunity and Race in Rhodesia*, Center on International Race Relations, University of Denver, Denver, 1973.

Murphree, Marshall W. et al (ed), *Education, Race and Employment in Rhodesia*, Artca, Harare, 1975.

Phimister, Ian R., Origins and Aspects of African Worker Consciousness in Rhodesia, in Webster, Eddie (ed), *Essays in Southern African Labour History*, Ravan, Johnnesburg, 1978.

Phimister, Ian R. and Van Onselen, Charles, *Studies in the History of African Mine Labour in Colonial Zimbabwe*, Zambeziana Series, Vol. 6, Mambo Press, Gweru, 1978.

Pollak, Oliver B., The Impact of the Second World War on African Labour Organization in Rhodesia, *Rhodesian Journal of Economics*, No. 7, 1973.

Steele, M.C., White Working Class Disunity: The Southern Rhodesian Labour Party, *Rhodesian History*, No. 1, 1970.

Van Onselen, Charles, Black Workers in Central African Industry: A Critical Essay on the Historiography and Sociology of Rhodesia, *Journal of Southern African Studies*, No. 1, 1975.

Van Onselen, Charles, The Role of Collaborators in the Rhodesian Mining Industry 1900-35, *African Affairs*, No. 72, 1973.

Van Onselen, Charles, Worker consciousness in black miners: Southern Rhodesia 1900-20, *Journal of African History*, Vol. 14 No. 2.

Webster, Eddie (ed) *Essays in Southern African Labour History*, Ravan, Johannesburg, 1978.

'Why the gap has been allowed to grow. Contract workers—a story of poverty. Domestics still the urban poor. Survival drives women down south. My freedom from poverty campaign', *Moto*, No. 43, 1986.

Social Development
Agere, S., Health career delivery system in the United States: lessons for Africa, *International Social Work*, Vol. 23 No. 1, 1980.

Beach, D.N., *The Shona and Zimbabwe 900-1850: an outline of Shona history*, Heinemann, London, 1980.

Beach, D.N., *Zimbabwe before 1900*, Mambo Press, Gweru, 1984.

Beauchamp, D., Public health as social justice, *Inquiry*, Vol. 13, March 1986.

Bebel, A., Working Class Socialist, in Rossi, A. (ed), *Feminist Papers*, Columbia University Press, London, 1973.

Bekker, J.C. and Coertze, J., *Seymour's Customary Law in Southern Africa*, 4th edition, Juta, Cape Town, 1982.

Berlimer, H. and Salmon, J.W., The holistic alternative to scientific medicine:

history and analysis, *International Journal of Health Services*, Vol. 10 No. 1, 1980.

Bone, R.C., Educational Development in Rhodesia, *Rhodesian Journal of Economics*, Vol. 2 No. 4, 1968.

Bourdillon, M.F., *The Shona People*, Mambo Press, Gweru, 1984.

Brand, Veronica, Social work research in relation to social development in Zimbabwe, *Journal of Social Development in Africa*, Vol. 1 No. 1, 1986.

Brydone, Determination of the neo-natal and infant mortality rate in Mufakose, Salisbury, Rhodesia, *Central African Journal of Medicine*, Vol. 21 No. 6, June 1975.

Chadwick, Nanette and Volpe, P., *Zimbabwe Company Law*, 2nd edition, University of Zimbabwe, Department of Law, Harare, 1981.

Challiss, P.J., The European Educational System in Southern Rhodesia 1890-1930, *Supplement to Zambezia*, 1982.

Chanaiwa, David, *The Zimbabwe Controversy: A Case of Colonial Historiography*, Program of Eastern African Studies, Syracuse University, Syracuse, 1973.

Chavunduka, G.L., *A Shona Urban Court*, Mambo Occasional Papers, Socio-Economic Series No. 14, Mambo Press, Gweru, 1979.

Chigwedere, Aeneas S., *From Mutapa to Rhodes: 1000 to 1890 A.D.*, Macmillan, London, 1980.

Chigwedere, E., *Lobola: Pros and Cons*, Books of Africa, 1982.

Chikanza et al, The Health Status of Farm Worker Communities in Zimbabwe, *Central African Journal of Medicine*, No. 27, 1981.

Childs, Harold, *The History and Extent of Recognition of Tribal Law in Rhodesia*, 2nd edition, Ministry of Internal Affairs, Harare, 1976.

Chitepo, Herbert, The Passing of Tribal Man: A Rhodesian View, *Journal of Asian and African Studies*, No. 5, 1970.

Chizengeni, Siphikelelo, *Customary Law and Family Predicaments*, Center for Applied Social Sciences, University of Zimbabwe, Harare, 1980.

Chung, Fay and Ngara, E., *Socialism, Education and Development: A Challenge to Zimbabwe*, Zimbabwe Publishing House, Harare, 1985.

Cormack, I.R.N., *Towards Self-reliance: Urban Social Development in Zimbabwe*, Mambo Press, Gweru, 1983.

Davis, C.S., African Education in Rhodesia, *Native Affairs Department Annual*, Vol. 10 No. 1, 1969.

Delphy, C., The main enemy: a materialist analysis of women's oppression, WRRC, *Explorations in Feminism*, No. 3, 1977.

Doyal, Lesley and Pennell, I., *The Political Economy of Health*, Pluto Press, London, 1981.

Dworkin, R., Taking rights seriously, Duckworth, London, 1977.

Elshatain, Jean B., *Public man, Private woman: Women in Social and Political thought*, Martin Robertson, Oxford, 1981.

Gelfand, Michael, *A Non-racial Island of Learning: A History of the University College of Rhodesia from its Inception to 1966*, Zambeziana Series Vol. 4, Mambo Press, Gweru, 1978.

Gelfand, Michael, *A Service to the Sick*, Zambeziana Series Vol. 1, Mambo Press, Gweru, 1976.

Bibliography 419

Gilmurray, John et al, *The Struggle for Health*, From Rhodesia to Zimbabwe Series No. 7, Mambo Press, Gweru, 1979.

Gish, O., The political economy of primary care and health by the people: an historical explanation, *Social Science and Medicine*, Vol. 13, 1979.

Gwarinda, T.C., *Socialism and Education*, College Press, Harare, 1985.

Hampson, Joe, *Old Age: A Study of Aging in Zimbabwe*, Mambo Occasional Papers, Socio-Economic Series No. 16, Mambo Press, Gweru, 1982.

Hensman, Howard, *A history of Rhodesia: compiled from official sources*, Negro University Press, New York, 1970.

Hill, Sylvia, Facing social reconstruction in Zimbabwe, *Black Scholar*, Vol. 11 No. 5, 1980.

Holleman, J., *Shona Customary Law*, Oxford University Press, London, 1952.

Ibbotson, P., Urbanisation in Southern Rhodesia, *Africa*, Vol. 16, 1946.

Johnson, Nigel, Rural health care delivery system and social development task, *Journal of Social Development in Africa*, Vol. 1 No. 1.

Kachingwe, S.K., Zimbabwe women: a neglected factor in social development, *Journal of Social Development in Africa*, Vol. 1 No. 1, 1986.

Kay, George, Population problems and development strategy in Rhodesia, *Scottish Geographical Magazine*, No. 91, 1976.

King, M., Health and the developing world, *International Journal of Health Services*, Vol. 1 No. 4, 1971.

Leeson, J., Social science and health policy in pre-industrial society, *International Journal of Health Services*, Vol. 4 No. 3, 1974.

May, Joan, *Zimbabwean Women in Colonial and Customary Law*, Zambeziana Series Vol. 14, Mambo Press, Gweru, 1983.

May, J. and Kazembe, J.L., Beyond legislation, *Journal of Eastern African Research and Development*, Vol. 15, 1985.

Mossop, R.T., Are we winning?, *Central African Journal of Medicine*, Vol. 28, No. 5, May 1982.

Moyana, Tafirenyika, Creating an African Middle Class: The Political Economy of Education and Exploitation in Zimbabwe, *Journal of Southern African Affairs*, No. 4, 1979.

Muchena, Olivia N., The Changing Position of African Women in Rural Zimbabwe-Rhodesia, *Zimbabwe Journal of Economics*, No. 1, 1979.

Muchena, Olivia N., *Women in Town*, Centre for Applied Social Sciences, University of Zimbabwe, 1980.

Muchena, Olivia N., *Zimbabwean Women: A Socio-economic Overview*, African Training and Research Centre for Women, Addis Ababa, 1982.

Mungazi, Dickson A., *The Underdevelopment of African Education: A Black Zimbabwean Perspective*, University Press of America, Washington D.C., 1982.

Navarro, Vicente, *Medicine under Capitalism*, Prodist, New York, 1977.

O'Callaghan, Marion, *Southern Rhodesia: The Effects of a Conquest Society on Education, Culture and Information*, UNESCO, Paris, 1977.

Palley, Claire, *The Constitutional History and Law of Southern Rhodesia 1888-1985: with Special Reference to Imperial Control*, Clarendon, Oxford, 1966.

Parker, Franklin, *African Development and Education in Southern Rhodesia*, Greenwood Press, Westport, 1960.

Patel, Diana H. and Adams, R., *Chirambahuyo: A Case Study in Low-income Housing*, Zambeziana Series, Vol. 2, Mambo Press, Gweru, 1981.

Peel, J.D.Y. and T.O. Ranger (eds), *Past and Present in Zimbabwe*, Manchester University Press, Manchester, 1983.

Pugh, A.O., New patterns of African rural health in Rhodesia, *Central African Journal of Medicine*, Vol. 15 No. 6, June 1969.

Randles, W.G.L., *The Empire of Monomotapa*: from the fifteenth to the nineteenth century, Zambeziana Series Vol. 7, Mambo Press, Gweru, 1979.

Rich, F., The economics of education, *Rhodesia Journal of Economics*, Vol. 1 No. 1, August 1967.

Riddell, Roger, *Education for Employment*, From Rhodesia to Zimbabwe Series, No. 9, Mambo Press, Gweru, 1980.

Rogers, E.W., *Education for Socio-Economic Reality in Zimbabwe*, Mambo Press, Gweru, 1979.

Rossi, A. (ed), *The Feminist Papers*, Columbia University Press, London, 1973.

Samakange, Stanlake, *Origins of Rhodesia*, Heinemann, London, 1978.

Sanders, D. and Watersten, T., Medical institutions in primary health care, *Social Change and Developmemt*, No. 4, May 1983.

Seidman, R.B., How a bill became a law in Zimbabwe: on the problem of transforming the colonial state, *Africa*, Vol. 52 No. 3, 1982.

Shamuyarira, Nathan, Education and Social Transformation in Zimbabwe, *Development Dialogue*, No. 2, 1978.

Sylvester, Christine, Continuity and discontinuity in Zimbabwe's development history, *African Studies Review*, Vol. 28 No. 2, June 1985.

Ushewokunze, Herbert S., *An Agenda for Zimbabwe*, College Press, Harare, 1984.

Vambe, Lawrence, *An Ill-fated People: Zimbabwe before and after Rhodes*, Heinemann, London, 1980.

Volpe, Peter S., *Commercial Law of Zimbabwe: Purchase and Sale*, Department of Law, University of Zimbabwe, 1982.

Webster, M., A review of the development of health services of Rhodesia from 1923 to present day, *Central African Journal of Medicine*, Vol. 18 No. 12, 1972.

Webster, M., Whither medicine in Rhodesia, *Central African Journal of Medicine*, November 1973.

Weinrich, A.K.H., *The Tonga People on the Southern Shore of Lake Kariba*, Mambo Occasional Papers, Socio-Economic Series No. 8, Mambo Press, Gweru, 1977.

Whitsun Foundation, *Project 2.09, Adult Literacy Programme: An Appraisal of the Adult Literacy Organisation of Rhodesia and a Plan to mount a National Adult Literacy Training Programme*, Whitsun Foundation, Harare, 1977.

World Bank, *Social Infrastructure and Services in Zimbabwe*, World Bank Staff Working Paper No. 495, World Bank, Washington D.C., 1981.

World Bank, Zimbabwe: *Population, Health and Nutrition Sector Review*, World Bank, Washington D.C., 1983.

Zvobgo, R.J., *Transforming Education—the Zimbabwean Experience*, College Press, Harare, 1985.

Government Documents and Reports

Australian Parliamentary Observer Group Report on the Zimbabwe-Rhodesia Common Roll Elections, May 1979.

Organization of African Unity, *Lagos Plan of Action and Final Act of Lagos*, 1980.

Press Statement 1052/81/NM, Deputy Minister for Education on Racism in the Education System, 7 December 1981.

Rhodesia Government, Central Statistical Office, *Census of Population, CSO*, Salisbury, CSO, 1969.

Rhodesia Government, Ministry of Education, *The Educaiton Act 1979*. Harare, Government Printer, 1979.

UNIDO, *Study of the Manufacturing Sector in Zimbabwe Technical Report Vol.11*, September 1985.

Zimbabwe Government, University of Labour, Manpower Planning and Social Welfare, *Annual Review of Manpower*, 1984.

Zimbabwe Government. Ministry of Labour, Manpower Planning and Development, *Report of the Otto Benecke Stifting Seminar, Harare, 1985*.

Zimbabwe Government, *Minstry of Community Development and Women's Affairs, Evidence to the Tax Commission of Inquiry*, Government Printer, Harare, 1984.

Zimbabwe Government, *Press Statement 1173/81/PR/JS, 1982*.

ZANU-PF, *ZANU-PF; 1980 Election Manifesto*, Harare.

The Zimbabwe Constitution Order, 1979, No. 1600.

Zimbabwe Government, *Registrar-General's 1985 General Election Report*, 13 September 1985, Government Printer, Harare, 1985.

Zimbabwe Government, *Report of the Commission of Inquiry into the Agricultural Industry (Under the Chairmanship of Prof. C.L. Chavunduka)*. Government Printer, Harare, 1982.

Zimbabwe Government, *Report of the Comptroller and Auditor General for the financial year ended 30 June, 1983*, Government Printer, 1984.

Zimbabwe Government, Central Statistical Office, *The Census of Production 1982/83; Mining, Manufacturing, Construction, Electricity and Water Supply*, CSO, Harare, 1985.

Zimbabwe Government, Central Statistical Office, *Zimbabwe 1982 population census, main demographic features of the population of Zimbabwe; an advance report based on a ten percent sample*, CSO, Harare, 1985.

Zimbabwe Government, Ministry of Community Development and Women's Affairs, *Situation of Women in Zimbabwe Today*, Government Printer, Harare, 1984.

Zimbabwe Government, Ministry of Community Development and Women's Affairs, *The Zimbabwe Report on the United Nations Decade for Women*, July, 1985.

Zimbabwe Government, Ministry of Education and Culture, *Annual Report of the Secretary for Education for the year ended 31 December, 1980*, Government Printer, Harare.

Zimbabwe Government, Ministry of Education and Culture, *Strategy for Human Resource Development Need, Plans and Utilisation of Resources*, Government Printer, Harare, 1985.

Zimbabwe Government, Ministry of Education and Culture, *Vote 21, Note on the Estimate of Expenditure, 1981/82, 1982/83*, Government Printer, Harare.

Zimbabwe Government, Ministry of Finance, Economic Planning and Development, *First five-year National Development Plan, 1986-1990*, Vol. 1, Government Printer, Harare, April 1986.

Zimbabwe Government, Ministry of Finance, Economic Planning and Development, *Growth with Equity: An Economic Policy Statement*, Government Printer, February 1981.

Zimbabwe Government, Ministry of Finance, Economic Planning and Development, *Programme of Development in the Public Sector*, Government Printer, Harare, 1979.

Zimbabwe Government, Ministry of Finance, Economic Planning and Development, *Transitional National Development Plan, 1982/83-1984/85, Vols. 1 and 2*, Government Printer, Harare, November 1982, May 1983.

Zimbabwe Government, Ministry of Finance, Economic Planning and Development, *ZIMCORD-Let's Build Zimbabwe Together*, Report on Conference Proceedings, Zimbabwe Conference on Reconstruction and Development, Harare, 23-27 March 1981.

Zimbabwe Government, Ministry of Health, *Report of the Secretary of Health for the year ended 31st December, 1980*, Government Printer, Harare, 1982.

Zimbabwe Government, Ministry of Home Affairs, *National Archives of Zimbabwe-File ZBC 1/2/1*.

Zimbabwe Government, Ministry of Home Affairs, *National Archives of Zimbabwe-File/SR/9/1/5/11*.

Zimbabwe Government, Ministry of Lands, Resettlement and Rural Development, *Communal Lands Development Plan; a 15 year development strategy (1st draft)*, Government Printer, Harare, 1985.

Zimbabwe Government, Ministry of Lands, Resettlement and Rural Development, *Land Reform, Policy Workshop*, MLRRD, Harare, September 1985.

Zimbabwe Government, Ministry of Manpower and Development, *National Manpower Survey, 1981, Vol. 1*, Government Printer, Harare, 1981.

Zimbabwe Government, Ministry of Manpower and Development, *National Manpower Survey, 1981, Vol.11*, Government Printer, Harare, 1981.

Unpublished Papers

Bowman, Larry W., et al., *Zimbabwe and South Africa: Dependency, Destabilization and Liberation*, Paper presented at the Annual Meeting of African Studies Association, Washington, D.C., 1982.

Bratton, M., *Draft Power, Draft Exchange and Farmer Organisations*, Working Paper No. 9, Dept. of Land Management, University of Zimbabwe, 1984.

Bibliography 423

Clutten, J.M., *The Nickel Resource in Zimbabwe*, Paper presented at the Zimbabwe Economic Conference, Mining Section, September 1980, Harare.

Cole, R.S., *The Land Situation in Zimbabwe*, Report of Proceedings of Commonwealth Association of Surveying and Land Economy Seminar held in Malawi, 3 April 1981.

Jansen, D., *Agricultural Prices and Subsidies in Zimbabwe*, (Mimeo), Harare, May 1982.

Jassat, Ebrahim H., and Nangati, F., *Towards a Discussion on the Agrarian Question, Rural Class Structure and Socio-Economic Problems of Transformation*, ZIDS.

Loewenson, R., *The Bindura Farm Health Worker scheme*, Unpublished Mimeographed Paper, April 1983.

Mandaza, Ibbo, *The Zimbabwe Public Service*, Paper presented at the United Nations Inter-Regional Seminar on Reforming Civil Service Systems for Development, Beijing, China, 14-24 August 1985.

Mlotshwa, Sibongile, *The Matopos Research Station, Origins and Contributions to the Agrarian Development of Zimbabwe*, 9 July 1984.

Mosley, P., *The Settler Economies, studies in the Economic History of Kenya and Southern Rhodesia 1900-1983*, University of Cambridge, 1980 (PhD).

Moyo, Sam, et al, *Drought, Food Shortage and Women's Groups as a Development Strategy in Zimbabwe*, Paper presented to the Churches Drought Action for Africa Workshop, Arusha, Tanzania, 10-14 July 1985.

Moyo, Sam, *The Effects of Foreign Aid on Zimbabwe's Agriculture*, (a proposal submitted to CODESRIA), Harare, ZIDS.

Moyo, Sam, *An Elaboration of the Debate on the Under-Utilization of Prime Land and Patterns of Peasant Production in Zimbabwe*, ZIDS work-in-progress, July 1985.

Moyo, Sam, et al, *Evaluation of the District Development Fund, Zimbabwe Rural Water Supply Reconstruction and Development Programme, Report 285*, Ministry of Development Cooperation, Oslo, 1984.

Moyo, Sam, *Notes on Contradictions in the Agrarian Project of Zimbabwe*, Submitted to Ministry of Lands, Resettlement and Rural Development, July 1984.

Moyo, Sam, *The Socio-Economic Status and Needs of ex-Combatants; the Case of Masvingo Province*, ZIDS consultancy report prepared for the Lutheran World Federation, Harare, ZIDS, September 1985.

Moyo, Sam, et al, *The Root Causes of Hunger in Zimbabwe, an Overview of Hunger, and Strategies to Combat Hunger*, ZIDS working paper.

Moyo, Sam, and Shabalala, S., *An Evaluation of the Structures, Goals and Planning Procedures and Practices of the Organisation of Collective Co-operatives in Zimbabwe*, ZIDS consultancy paper, May 1986.

Mpofu, J.M., *The February 1980 Zimbabwe Elections, the Matebeleland North and South Provinces*, Zimbabwe Conference, Leeds University, June 1980.

Mumbengegwi, C., *Some Observations on the Problems and Prospects of Socialist Transformation in Zimbabwe*, Paper presented at the 20th International Summer Seminar on Planning for Development and Social Progress in Socialist and Developing countries, Berlin, GDR, University of Economic Science, Bruno Leischner, June 1983.

Ndlela, D.B., *Generation of Change in Zimbabwe's Mining Sector*, Paper presented at the Arne Ryde Symposium, The Primary Sector in Economic Development, 29-30 August, University of Lund, Sweden.

Rifkind, M., *The Politics of Land in Rhodesia*, University of Edinburgh, 1968 (MSc).

Sachikonye, L.M., *Capital, Proletarians and Peasants in Southern Africa Revisited, a Review Essay*, ZIDS Occasional Staff Paper, 1984.

Sachikonye, L.M., *The Protection of Security of Employment, the Zimbabwe Experience.* ZIDS. Consultancy Paper Prepared for the International Labour Organisation, Geneva, 1985.

Sachikonye, L.M., *State, Capital and Trade Unions since Independence.* ZIDS, Occasional Staff Paper, 1984.

Sachikonye, L.M., *Agribusiness in Zimbabwe, A Survey of Current Trends*, Occasional Staff Paper, 1985.

Sachikonye, L.M., Batezat, E. and A., Sibanda, The Working Conditions of Female Labour in the Food Processing industry in Zimbabwe, *ZIDS Consultancy Report Prepared for the International Labour Organisation (ILO)*.

Shack, William A., *Land Reform in Zimbabwe, Problems and Prospects*, Occasional paper no. 15, final report, Berkeley, Dept. of Anthropology, University of California, 20 Janauary, 1977.

Shopo, Thomas D., *The Agrarian Question in the Formative Stages of the National Democratic Revolution in Colonial Zimbabwe, 1945-1965, an Historiographical Essay*, ZIDS, Occasional Staff Papers, 1984.

Shopo, Thomas D., *A Note on the Political Economy of Research on Hunger in Zimbabwe*, Paper presented to the workshop organised by the Institute of Resource Assessment, University of Dar es Salaam and the International Union of Nutrituinal Science at Mukumi Wildlife Village, May 26-June 21, 1985.

Shopo, T.D., *The Fundamental Problems of Science and Technology in Zimbabwe's Transition to Socialism*, ZIDS Occasional Staff Paper, No. 1, Harare, ZIDS.

Shopo, Thomas D., *The State and Food Policy in Colonial Zimbabwe, 1965-1980*, ZIDS, Occasional Staff Paper, September 1984.

Shopo, T.D., *The Political Economy of Hunger in Zimbabwe*, ZIDS working paper No. 2, Government Printer, Harare.

Shopo, Thomas D., *Rethinking Parliament's Role in Zimbabwean Society*, ZIDS working paper, no. 3, October 1985.

Taylor J.J., *The Emergence and Development of the Native Department in Southern Rhoderia 1894-1914*, University of London, 1974 (PhD).

Tickner, V., *Class Struggles and the Food Supply Sector in Zimbabwe*, Paper presented to the conference on Zimbabwe, University of Leeds, 1980.

Wittich, G., *Why Development is Needed and a Suggestion How it could be Improved, the Case of Zimbabwe*, Conference Paper No. 30, Dept. of Economics, University of Zimbabwe, 1985.

INDEX

A
Aberfoyhe Holding 137
Adult Literacy Organisation Zimbabwe 399
African Law and Tribal Courts Act 387
Agriculture Marketing Authority 205
African sation 308-13
African Marriages Age 381
African National Congress 29, 75
Agricultural policy 16-17, 203-22
Agricultural production 107, 113 118, 142, 165-66, 190, 206-7
African Trade Union Congress 253
Agriculture Ministry of 205, 213
Agriculture and Plantation Workers' Union 239
Agro-industrial linkage 142, 145 150, 190-91, 195, 239
Amenorrhoes 232
Amin, S. 17-18
Apprenticeship training 276, 286 302-4, 313
Approved buyers 215
Arable land 175
ARDA 193-97
Armed struggle 1, 4, 6, 7, 28-33 50, 252
Asbestos 146, 147
Associated Mineworkers' Union 255
Association of Rhodesian Industries 255

B
Bank of Boston 136
Bloomfield, H. 255-56
Bourgeois 244-47, 266-67, 280
Budgets 105, 112, 111
Butler 26-27

C
Cabral, A. 1
Cairns-Dalgety Deal 129, 136
Campbell, Harare 7
Capital, foreign 61-63, 105, 123-40, 167
CEDAW 377
Central Statistical Office 142
Centre Africa Party 29
Centre Party 29
Chemicals 119, 143, 144, 152-54
Chief Native Commissioner 320-21, 322
Chipinge Constituency 89, 94
Chisumbanje sugar ethanol project 136
Ciba-Geigy 181
Citibank 136
Clinics 362-63
Coal 146, 149
Coffee 206, 209-10
Collection points 215
Columbus McKinnon 136
Commercial Farmers' Union 43, 179, 187, 210
Commodity Import Programme 132
Communal areas 165, 169, 170-71, 172-3, 182, 186-87, 208-9, 212, 214-18
Community Development and Women's Affairs, Ministry of 399-400,
Conditionalities 111-12
Constitution, 34, 39, 76-77, 81-83, 95, 108, 211-12, 219, 287, 387
Constructive engagement 65-66
Contagionism 355
Co-operatives 181
Copper 146, 147, 148-49
Council of Chiefs 77
Court, Supreme 388, 391

426 Zimbabwe

Customary Law and Primary Courts Act 387
Current Account Deficit 106, 112, 138
Curriculum 321-22
Village and Community 387, 394

D
Dandy Chewing Gum 137
Debt servicing 120-21, 139
Decolonisation 6, 8, 24
Delimitation Commission 87, 88
Democracy 18, 50, 75-76, 94, 260, 287, 313, 335
Dependency 9-10, 12, 102
Depelchin, J. 7
Diversification 105
District Councils 329, 335-36
Divorce 385, 386-87, 389-90
Doctors 355-58, 365-66
Drought 110, 166, 186, 228 ,229, 230
Drugs 355, 368-69

E
Education 22 ,132 ,133, 319-54
  European 341
  free 319-20, 325-26, 331
  private 336
Education policy, colonial 319-25
Educational Planning 341-50
Election, 1979, 76-81,
  1980, 40-41, 81-85
  1985, 16, 58-50, 86-94
Electoral Supervisory Commision 77, 79, 86, 88 ,91
Electro Technologies Corporation 137
Employers Confederation of Zimbabwe 263, 293
Employment 118, 141, 144-45, 146, 151, 153, 154, 155, 166, 190, 208-9, 212, 298, 397-98
Employment and Employment Development, Department of 298,
Engels, F. 244, 245,
Engineering 149, 150-52
Equality Board 402
Essential Drugs List of Zimbabwe 369
European Economic Community 132

F
Factionalism 23, 54-56, 61, 96, 251
Falcon Mines 126
Famine 171, 228-29
Fearless Proposals 27
Ferrochrome 146, 148
Feminism 378-79
Fertilisers 136, 153, 226
Fisons 136
Five Year Development Plan 61, 99-104
Food policy 17, 118, 207, 209
Foodstuffs 136, 143, 144, 154
Foote Minerals 125
Foreign Exchange 105, 108, 121, 130-31, 144, 175, 191
Frontline stanes 3, 27, 31, 32, 37, 64, 66, 67

G
Gaeresi Ranch 204-5
General Engineering and Metal Workers' Union 292
Genetic potential model 231
Geneva Conference 32, 35, 96
Gokwe 186
Gold 137, 146, 147, 148-49
Government of National Unity 35
Grain Marketing Board 187, 205, 215, 269
Gross Domestic Product 100, 101, 116-17, 131
Gross Fixed Capital Formation 100, 101, 116-17, 131
Groundnuts 209-10
Guerrillas 27, 29, 38-39, 78, 79, 80
Gussman, Bortis 239
Gwavavao R.M. 253

H
Hanlon, Joe 7
Harare Hospital 358-59, 360
Health 132, 191, 195, 237, 260, 261, 355-76
Health care, primary 364-65, 372-73
Healt Ministry of 360, 363-64
Health policy 356-58, 369-73
Hippo Valley Estate 236, 254, 263, 269, 270
Ho Chi Minh 31
Hospitals 358-59

House of Assembly 77, 81, 88
Huggins, Godfrey 324, 325
Hunger 171, 223-41

I
Ibbotson, P. 230
Immigration, white 275, 304-8
Imperialism 1, 3, 7-12, 17, 18, 21-28, 34, 69, 123, 219, 225-27, 237, 238, 245-46, 247-48, 280
Import substitution 105, 143, 145
Industrial and Commercial Workers' Union 250
Industrial Conciliation Act 249, 250-51, 253, 255, 259-60
Industrial Development Corporation 137, 144
Industrial relations 246, 247, 253, 256-59, 266-67
Industrial tribunals 246
Industrialisation 141-64
Informal sector 142
International Confederation of Free Trade Unions 251
International Monetary Fund 12, 62, 67; 111-15, 124, 138
Internal settlement 37
Intermediate goods 144
Iron and steel 146, 147-48
Irrigation 178-80

J
Joint venture 128, 136-37, 149-50
Justice, Legal and Parliamentary Affairs, Ministry of 390

K
Kaguvi, Sekuru 31
Kamba, Walter J. 73, 91-92
Kitching, G. 9, 18
Kulakisation 187, 195, 220

L
Labour aristocracy 278
Labour Relations Act 259-63, 392-93
Lagos Plan 102, 288
Lancaster House Agreement 2-3, 24, 28, 33-41, 43, 55, 59, 68, 172, 310, 387
Land Apportionment Act 167, 170, 204
Land, degradation of 170
Land question 16, 39, 50, 100, 118, 133, 165-201, 218, 249

Land, redistribution of 172, 183-86, 197, 211-12, 219
Land Tenure Act 125, 204
Large Company Estates 180
Large Scale Commercial Farmers 173-80, 183, 187-91
Law and Order Maintenance Act 250
Law, customary 381-82
Laws, economic 223-24, 230-31, 234-37
Legal Age of Majority Act 390-92
Liberalism 22, 58
Liebigs 125
Loans see Credit
Lobola see Roora
Lonho 126, 146, 263

M
Maintenance Act 387
Maize 176-78, 187, 190, 205, 206 207, 209, 218, 225-26, 227, 229, 230
Makoni, Simba 136
Malawi 25, 27, 119
Malnutrition 191, 224, 231-32, 233, 234, 363
Mangena, N. 32
Manicaland 89, 185, 200, 264
Manpower Planning and Development, Ministry of 286
Manuberi 137
Manufacturing sector 105, 118-119, 131, 141-64
March 3rd Agreement 76
Marketing boards 205, 214, 217, 218
Marriages Act 380
Marx, K. 223, 244, 245
Mashonaland 89, 173,-75, 182, 185-86, 191, 400
Mass media 32, 94
Masses 14-15, 17, 30, 40, 50, 53, 69
Matabeleland 85, 86, 89, 93, 95, 138
Maternity leave 392-93
Mechanisation 191
Medical insurance 367
Medical Aid societies 366
Medicine, private 365-67
traditional 361, 370-71
Minerals 11, 105, 113, 142-43, 145-49
Mpilo Hospital 358

428 Zimbabwe

Mao, Tse Tung 31
Morbidity 233, 363
Mortality 233, 363
Mountbatten, Lord 26
Mozambique 3, 5, 6, 7, 37, 45, 64, 71, 111, 119, 228
Mugabe, R. 30, 35, 39, 42, 53, 54, 58-59, 67-68, 80, 81, 92-93, 95, 127, 333-34
Multinational corporations 19, 49, 125, 127-31, 136-38, 180, 183, 226, 311
Mythology, revolutionary 4-7, 32
Mzingeli, Charles 250

N

National Industrial 265, 278
National liberation 3, 6, 12
National Manpower Survey 45, 48, 57, 144, 279, 283-87, 296
Nationalism 6, 7-12, 22-23, 28-35, 58, 251, 313
Native Affairs Department
Ndebele 31, 94, 95, 380-81
Nehanda, Mbuya 31
Neo-Colonialism 6, 7-12—see also Imperialism
NIBMAR 25, 34
Nickel 146, 147, 148-49
Nkomo, J. 28, 31, 35, 81, 92, 95
Nkrumah, K. 8
Nyerere J. 9, 11-12, 31
Norsk Hydro 136

O

One-party state 86-87
Organization of African Unity 33, 102
Otto Benecke Foundation 296
Overseas Private Investment Corporation 130

P

Patriotic Front 3, 33, 33-41, 75, 76, 80
Pearce Commission 1972
Peasants 1, 22, 50, 51, 165-81, 208, 211, 219—see also communal areas
Pensions 39, 108, 310
Pesticides 153
Petit bourgeoisie 1, 6, 8, 12, 14-15, 17, 22-23, 31, 46-47, 49, 51, 53-58, 60-61, 62-63, 69, 93, 192-193, 238, 313

Petroleum products 26, 105, 132, 144
Planning 17, 99-103, 110, 114, 155-59, 178, 371-72—see also Educational Planning
Post-white settler colonial state 2, 3, 13-15, 17, 41-51
Preferential Trade Area 119, 158
Presidential directive 82
Prices 205, 207, 213-14, 229, 235-36
Production, relations of 195, 197, 220, 224, 254
Productivity 145, 168-69, 172, 175-81, 193, 208, 210, 211, 219
Profits, repatriation of 125, 128, 130-31
Proletarianisation 22
Proposed Essential Drugs list of Zimbabwe 369
Public service 279, 308-13

R

Racism 22, 34, 46, 58, 214, 253, 276, 278, 279-80, 284, 319-23, 331-32, 336—see also Separate racial development
Reagan, R. 10
Recession, world 102-103
Regional economic integration 119-20, 158, 166, 211
Regionalism 23, 84-85, 95
Registrar-General 86, 87, 88
Registration of voters 87-88
Research 18, 157, 158, 297
Resettlement, rural 100, 118, 132, 133, 170, 183-86, 191-92, 212
Revolution 1, 4-7
Rhodes, C.J. 21
Rhodesia National Farmers' Union 206
Rhodesia Native Labour Bureau 228, 249
Rhodesian Native Labour Supply Commission 228
Rhodesian Security Forces 25-27, 43-44
Rio Tinto 126, 146
Roora 379-81, 389, 391
Rutenga 137

S

Sable Chemical Industries 136, 153, 269
Sanctions 63, 67, 105, 107, 126,

146, 156, 206, 207
Sandys, D. 25
Sanyo 137
Saul, John 5, 7
Schemes, Model A 132,
  Model B 132
  Model C 132
Schools, F1 338, 331
  F2 283, 330-31
  mission 320-22 329, 336
Scientific Council of Zimbabwe 288
Self-reliance 123
Senate 77, 83, 88
Separate racial development
  319-20, 325, 328-29, 330, 358
Sex Disqualification Act 393
hona 84, 85, 95, 380-81
Sitholes, Phineas 253
Social development 14, 16, 100, 107
Social services 132, 247
Socialism 5-7, 30, 124, 128, 137
  139, 165, 203-4, 211, 218-21
  266-67, 30, 333-34, 335, 378,
Sorghum 187, 207, 209-10
Squatters 185, 186, 197
State farms—see ARDA
Strikes 230, 250, 252-56, 260-64, 284, 324
Subsistence production 218
Sutcliffe, R.B. 141

T
Tangwena, Rekai 204-5
Taxes, 125, 144-45, 205-6, 247, 249-50, 367
Teachers 336, 346-50
Technical colleges 275-6, 283, 289, 290
Textiles 143, 144, 154-55
Tiger proposals 27
Tin 146, 147, 148
Tobacco 105, 143, 144, 178, 190, 206-7, 209
Trade unions 17, 243-73, 278, 279, 282-83, 398
Trade-testing 292-93
Training, manpower 150, 158, 293-96, 313-14
Transformation 99
Transition, political economy of 99-103
Transitional National Development Plan 61, 99-102, 110-11, 127, 131, 156, 210-11, 219, 298

Transnational corporations—see Multinational corporations
Transport 131, 133, 142, 149, 214
Treasury 105
Transport equipment 143
Triangle Estate 236, 254, 263, 269
Tribal Trust Lands 282
Turner and Newall 125, 146

U
Under-nutrition 223 232, 233
Union Carbide 125, 126, 130, 146, 289
United African National Council 36, 41, 75, 76, 79-81, 83, 84, 89, 90, 265
United Federal Party 29
United States Agency for International Development 132, 171, 181
United Trade Unions of Zimbabwe 256
Universities 73-74, 171, 289, 293-97
Unlawful Organizations Act 250
USA 3, 10-11, 24-36, 63, 64-68, 103, 130, 293
Ushewokunze, Herbert 366, 367

V
Van der Byl, P.K. 33
Vocational Training Centres 290-92

W
Wage, statutary minimum 93, 108, 137, 191, 247, 258,-59, 264, 392
Wages, agricultural 204, 206
Wheat 206, 207, 209
White settler colonialsim 3, 21-28, 126,
  167-68, 275, 319-20, 356-57
Wittich, G. 120
Women 377-404
Wood 143
Workers, skilled 278-79
  semi-skilled 278-79, 290-92
  domestic 392
  seasonal and casual 397
Working class 1, 17, 47-48, 51, 198, 244-49, 252, 266-67
Workmen's Compensation Act 394
World Bank 10, 12, 103, 120-21, 124, 131-32, 171, 181

Y

Youth, Sport and Culture, Ministry of 298-99
Youth unemployment 298, 301, 345

Z

Zambia 3, 25, 27, 37, 45, 104, 119, 141
ZANLA 29, 32, 43-44, 85
ZANU 3, 26, 27, 29, 31-33, 35, 36, 41-43, 56, 75, 83-85, 86, 89, 90, 92-94, 95-96, 265, 332, 401
ZAPU 3, 27, 29, 31, 33, 35, 36, 54, 75, 83-85, 89, 90, 95
ZCTU 253, 256, 257, 265-66, 392
Zimbabwe Engineering Company 152
Zimbabwe Fertiliser Company 136
Zimbabwe Iron and Steel Corporation 146, 148, 150
Zimbabwe Mining Development Corporation 146
ZIMCORD 99, 124, 131-33
ZINTEC 338
ZIPA 31, 32-33
ZIPRA 29, 32, 43-44, 85, 95
ZNFU 192

DA